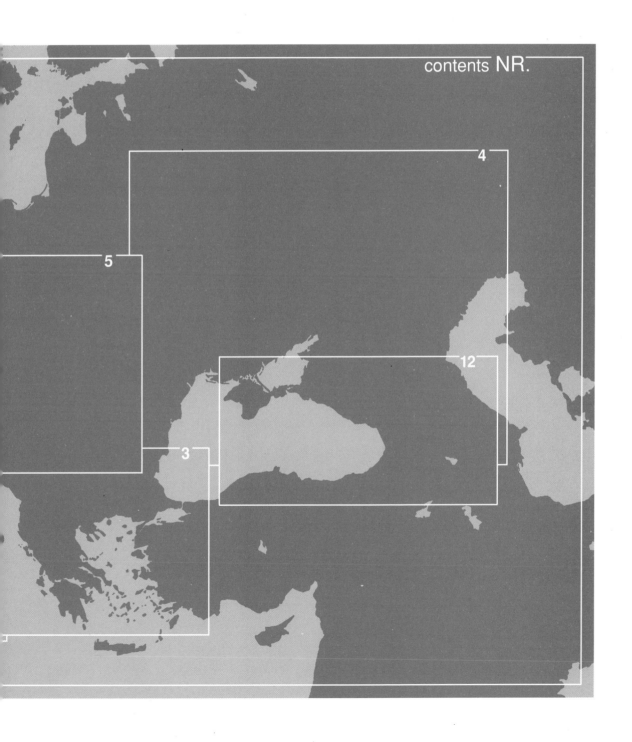

contents NR.

THE EARLIEST OCCUPATION OF EUROPE

THE
EARLIEST OCCUPATION
OF EUROPE

PROCEEDINGS OF THE EUROPEAN SCIENCE FOUNDATION
WORKSHOP AT TAUTAVEL (FRANCE), 1993

EDITED BY WIL ROEBROEKS AND THIJS VAN KOLFSCHOTEN

UNIVERSITY OF LEIDEN 1995

Published in cooperation with the European Science Foundation

ISBN 90-73368-06-5

Graphic design: H.A. de Lorm

This publication also appeared as volume 27 in the series Analecta Praehistorica Leidensia

Subscriptions to the series Analecta Praehistorica Leidensia and single volumes can be ordered exclusively at:

Institute of Prehistory
P.O. Box 9515
2300 RA Leiden
The Netherlands.

contents

acknowledgments

The production of this volume was possible through the gracious cooperation of the following people: Ms K. Fennema (Leiden), Ms C. Hardeman-Van Kolfschoten (Veenendaal), Mr H.A. de Lorm (Leiden), Ms I. Pereira (Leiden), Dr M. Street (Neuwied), Dr A. Turner (Liverpool) and especially Ms O. Yates-Wanders (Leiden). Financial support came from the European Science Foundation, The Netherlands Organization for Scientific Research (NWO-PIONIER) and the Faculty of Pre- and Protohistory of Leiden University.

Wil Roebroeks
Thijs van Kolfschoten

The Tautavel workshop: an introduction

Europe derives its name from its position relative to the rise and setting of the sun: on Assyrian monuments the contrast between *Asu*, "(the land of) the rising sun" and *ereb* or *irib*, ("the land of) darkness" or "the setting sun", is frequent, and these words are considered to have given rise to the names of Asia and Europe.[1] It was in this small and densely populated "dark" continent that the antiquity of humankind was first demonstrated, in the central decades of the nineteenth century. From the second half of that century onwards innumerable professional and amateur archaeologists screened exposures all over Europe in an extensive search for palaeolithic artefacts and fossils and so contributed to a high quality database, without parallels in other continents in terms of spatial and chronological density of sampling points. Yet despite almost one and a half century of research in Europe current evidence strongly points to Africa as the place where the human lineage originated, though the bulk of evidence there was collected in the last three decades only. Africa witnessed the "dawn" of humankind while Europe was still an 'Empty Continent' (Dennell 1983), a true land of (hominid) darkness.

The interpretation of the high quality record of the earliest occupation of this continent was at stake on November 19th and 20th, 1993, when a group of palaeolithic archaeologists and representatives of other disciplines (Fig. 1) met at the *Centre Européen de Recherches Préhistoriques* at Tautavel (France), for a workshop on the earliest occupation of Europe (Roebroeks 1994). Tautavel was chosen as the venue because of *l'homme de Tautavel*'s obvious association with the theme of the workshop, that was very kindly hosted by H. De Lumley and members of his staff.

The Tautavel meeting itself was organized by the then newly established Network on the Palaeolithic Occupation of Europe, funded by the European Science Foundation (Strasbourg)[2]. The workshop consisted of two full days of discussion on the basis of pre-circulated papers, whose updated versions constitute the bulk of this volume[3]. The aim of the Tautavel meeting was to discuss and review the evidence concerning the earliest occupation of the European regions, from Scandinavia to the Mediterranean and from the United Kingdom to the Russian Plains, and including

neighbouring areas such as the Caucasus and northern Africa. The discussion focused on four themes: chronology (chaired by Alain Tuffreau), environment (chaired by Clive Gamble), industries (chaired by Gerhard Bosinski), and subsistence (chaired by Catherine Farizy). These items were discussed *in extenso*, and some of the discussion is reflected in four synthetical contributions to this volume: Aitken's paper and Roebroeks and Van Kolfschoten deal with various aspects of chronology, the environmental backgrounds of the earliest occupation of Europe are extensively reviewed by Gamble's contribution, while one of Bosinski's contributions is a short review of European Lower Palaeolithic stone industries. Subsistence aspects proved to be a topic for a special meeting, meanwhile held at Monrepos (Neuwied, Germany) in May 1995 (Gaudzinski and Turner 1995).

Very vivid were the Tautavel discussions on the age of Europe's first occupation. Despite the large numbers of meetings devoted to Europe's first traces of settlement the dates given to the first "Europeans" vary widely (cf. Gamble, this volume; Roebroeks and Van Kolfschoten, this volume), with some proponents of a long chronology suggesting that Europe was already occupied in the earlier parts of the Early Pleistocene, whereas others opt for (significantly) later occupation. A new and very short "pan-European" chronology was advocated by our contribution to the Tautavel meeting (Roebroeks and Van Kolfschoten, this volume). A detailed reappraisal of artefactual and chronological – especially biostratigraphical – evidence for the earliest occupation of Europe led us to stress the differences between the evidence from before and after about 500 Kyr BP (Roebroeks and Van Kolfschoten, this volume: Table 1); we interpreted these differences as indicating that there is no proof of human occupation of Europe prior to about 500 Kyr BP.

Discussing the merits of the various long and short chronologies for the earliest occupation of Europe – or for that matter of any continent – is not just about getting the dates right, but more importantly, about how to translate its rich Palaeolithic record into meaningful scenarios for human behavioural evolution: if workers like Bonifay (see Bonifay and Vandermeersch 1991) and Coppens

Fig. 1. The participants of the Tautavel Workshop:
1: J.P. Raynal, 2: L. Raposo, 3: L. Larsson, 4: C. Gamble, 5: M. Roberts, 6: A. Tuffreau, 7: M. Sparreboom, 8: P. Antoine, 9: K. Valoch, 10: E. Brinch-Petersen, 11: T. van Kolfschoten, 12: A. Darlas, 13: M. Santonja, 14: M. Aitken, 15: H. De Lumley, 16: V. Ljubin, 17: M.-A. De Lumley-Woodyear, 18: J. Leopold, 19: W. Roebroeks, 20: G. Bosinski, 21: M. Mussi, 22: C. Farizy, 23: J. Combier, 24: N. Praslov.
Behind the camera: L. Magoga (invited, but unable to attend: D. Mania, C. Peretto).

(*in* Ackerman 1989) are right and Europe was first occupied at about 2 Myr ago, such scenarios could adopt more gradualistic perspectives, with hominids having plenty of time to adapt to the new environments of this continent, where the climatic oscillations of the Pleistocene were to have very profound effects. If on the other hand occupation was significantly later, for instance from the Middle Pleistocene onwards, scenarios might tend to be more punctuated, with important implications for the resultant modelling of human behaviour (Dennell 1983; Gamble, this volume; Roebroeks and Van Kolfschoten 1994, this volume). Proponents of both longer and short chronologies for Europe's earliest occupation were present at the meeting: the workshop brought together researchers with highly variant backgrounds, so that the discussions took place not between more or less like-minded scientists but within a heterogeneous, actively disagreeing multivocal group. Nevertheless, Alain Tuffreau, spoke for most participants when he concluded at the end of the Tautavel meeting that the assemblages from before about 500 to 600 Kyr BP can no longer be accepted as unambiguous proof for human occupation; their very primitive artefacts, with hardly any discernible *gestes techniques*, call for arguments other than the examination of stone implements.

Any meaningful discussion of the earliest occupation of Europe must place the evidence from this *cul de sac* of the Eurasian continent in the larger perspective of the question of the earliest dispersals of hominids out of Africa, and since the Tautavel meeting various new findings have contributed to the debate on these sorties. Some support the case for a short chronology for Europe (cf. Roberts *et al.* 1994; Gamble 1994; White 1995) but others have emphasized the necessity for building a longer Eurasian chronology for the earliest hominid immigration.

For instance, the new dates for the earliest hominids of Java (Swisher *et al.* 1994) suggest that they were already present there around 1.8 Myr BP, almost one million years earlier than most other estimates (see below). Such an early dispersal of hominids out of Africa is also supported by the dating of the Dmanisi site into the Olduvai subchron, at around 1.8 Myr BP (Ljubin and Bosinski, this volume; Dzaparidze *et al.* 1989; Gabunia and Vekua 1995) and by the new finds from the Orce basin in Andalusia (Spain), where evidence is claimed for Early Pleistocene human occupation from around 1.8 Myr BP, both in the form of hominid remains (Orce, Cueva Victoria) and as artefactual evidence, for example from Fuentenueva 3 (see Gibert 1992; Gibert *et al.* 1994; Roe 1995; Raposo and Santonja, this volume). Finally, artefacts reported from Yiron in Israel (Ronen 1991) and Riwat and the Pabbi Hills in Pakistan also nicely fit in this pattern with their estimated age (for Riwat) of around 1.9 Myr BP (Dennell 1993).

There thus is evidence to build a consistent long chronology for the initial dispersal of hominids out of Africa and into Eurasia, at a date of around 1.8 Myr BP, but it is to be stressed that none of the building blocks of such a long chronology is uncontested. De Vos and Sondaar (1994) have criticised the Swisher *et al.* (1994) dates as being far too old, for various reasons. For instance, the new 40Ar/39Ar ages are based on hornblende samples of which the geological context is not clear. Furthermore the new ages are contradicted by a wide range of established data; the discrepancy between the 40Ar/39Ar ages (1.81 and 1.66 Myr BP) and the existing magnetostratigraphy is almost one million years, while fission track ages also indicate dates all less than 1 Myr BP. De Vos and Sondaar conclude "that the 40Ar/39Ar dates of Swisher *et al.* may themselves be "technically correct", but until their geological context is established, it is premature to attach such far reaching conclusions to these new age estimates for the hominid of Java" (1994:1726).

As for Dmanisi, the find-bearing sediments themselves have not been dated yet: the 1.8 Myr BP date was obtained on basalt *below* these deposits, whose normal polarity is interpreted as correlative with the Olduvai subchron. Before the discovery of the Dmanisi mandible, the fauna of the site was thought to date from the Middle Pleistocene (Vekua 1986:87), while correlation with Near Eastern and European successions also does not give strong support to the 1.8 Myr BP age; "Estimating the age of the site within the time range of 1.5-1.0 Ma would be reasonable" (Bar-Yosef 1994:228). A recent review of the Near Eastern evidence likewise does not support "claims for occurrences around 2.0 Ma or immediately after the Olduvai subchron" (Bar-Yosef 1994:256), and the earliest sites there are also to be placed within the 1.5-1.0 Myr BP time span.

While the sample of 'hominids' coming from the Orce region is extremely controversial (e.g. Agusti and Moyá-Solá 1987 vs. Gibert 1992), a visit to the Orce Basin in April 1995 convinced us that at least one site has unambiguous stone artefacts there, Fuente Nueva 3 (see also Roe 1995).[4] If subsequent geological fieldwork would indeed corroborate the claim that this site is to be placed in the Early Pleistocene sequences exposed in the gullies near Orce, one would have to conclude that hominids trickled into the southern part of Spain hundreds of thousands of years before they left undisputable traces of their presence elsewhere in Europe. However, as long as the sedimento-logical setting of the Fuentenueva 3 site is not clear we see no compelling reasons to come to such a conclusion yet. We therefore agree completely with Roe (1994:11), who after his visit to the area concluded that it "would be most unwise at the present stage of the research to go too deeply into the potential significance of the discoveries made at

Orce. There is still some way to go before the basic facts are established beyond doubt or challenge".[5]

The recent developments summarized above clearly indicate that the question of the earliest occupation of Eurasia is far from solved and highly controversial. In our view the short chronology for Europe has not been falsified by these developments *yet*, and thus there still is the point of the gap between the earliest occupation of the "gates of Europe" – the Caucasus, northern Africa – and the first unambiguous traces within (Raynal *et al.*, [this volume] show that the gap with the Maghreb evidence, where the earliest occupation dates from just before the Brunhes-Matuyama boundary, is smaller than at the eastern "gates" of Europe, where it is minimally 500 Kyr). The Tautavel meeting saw ample discussion of the possible explanations for this chronological *décalage*, a discussion that brought together the various aspects at stake at the Tautavel meeting, such as the environmental setting of the earliest occupants, their subsistence strategies and the behavioural implications of the short and long chronologies (Gamble, this volume).

This book presents the actual data in the form of the various regional and supra-regional, synthetical contributions that formed the basis of the Tautavel discussions. The contributions are highly variable and testify to the large variety in regional research traditions within Europe. The production of this volume took almost two years, as we decided to 'wait' for most of the papers. Individual papers thus had to await publication until most of the other papers were finished and in that sense there is a striking similarity between the history of this book and Clive Gamble's (this volume) elegant explanation for the aforementioned 500 Kyr gap between the occupation of the 'land of the rising sun' and the 'land of darkness': "*any*

one region of Europe could only be colonized if it was colonized at the same time as most of the others". Palaeolithic archaeology in the spirit of a unified Europe!

notes

1 Encyclopaedia Britannica, entry on 'Europe'.

2 The European Science Foundation Network on the Palaeolithic Occupation of Europe consists of G. Bosinski (chairman - Neuwied, Germany), W. Roebroeks (scientific secretary - Leiden, The Netherlands), C. Farizy (Paris, France), C. Gamble (Southampton, United Kingdom), L. Larsson (Lund, Sweden), M. Mussi (Rome, Italy), N. Praslov (St. Peterburg, Russia), L. Raposo (Lisbon, Portugal), M. Santonja (Salamanca, Spain) and A. Tuffreau (Lille, France), with M. Sparreboom as coordinator on behalf of the European Science Foundation (Strasbourg).

3 As is often the case with such proceedings, not all attendants were able to submit their contributions on time, and we especially regret the absence of a paper dealing with the prolific archaeo-logical record of the southern part of France, a key region in the discussion on long versus short chronologies.

4 We are very grateful to Dr J. Gibert and his collaborators Dr B. Martinez, L. Gibert, Dr A. Turq and Prof. Dr M. Walker for taking the time to show us the Orce region exposures and the material from the various sites.

5 New palaeomagnetic dates for the Atapuerca-TD sequence were reported in Science (vol. 269, no. 5225, 11 August 1995) while this volume was in press. Whereas earlier estimates assigned an age of about 500 Kyr BP to the TD 6 level (cf. Roebroeks and Van Kolfschoten, this volume), the new dates suggest a late Early Pleistocene age. If future dating work corroborates the palaeo-magnetic data, one will have to conclude that the Iberian record does contain signals of earlier dispersals than the non-Iberian parts of Europe.

references

Ackerman, S.	1989	European prehistory gets even older, *Science* 246, 28-30.
Agusti, J., S. Moyá-Solá	1987	Sobre la identidad del fragmento craneal atribuido a *Homo* sp. en Venta Micena (Orce Granada), *Estudios geol.* 43, 535-538.
Bar-Yosef, O.	1994	The Lower Paleolithic of the Near East, *Journal of World Prehistory* 8, 211-266.
Bonifay, E., B. Vandermeersch (ed.)	1991	*Les Premiers Européens*. Paris: Editions du C.T.H.S.
Carbonell, E., X.P. Rodriguez	1994	Early Middle Pleistocene deposits and artefacts in the Gran Dolina site (TD4) of the 'Sierra de Atapuerca' (Burgos, Spain), *Journal of Human Evolution* 26, 291-311.
Dennell, R.W.	1983	*European Economic Prehistory. A New Approach*. London/New York: Academic Press.
	1993	Evidence on Human Origins. A Rediscovered Source in the Upper Siwaliks of Northern Pakistan, *Interdisciplinary Science Reviews* 18, 379-389.
Dzaparidze, V., G. Bosinski, T. Bugianisvili *et al.*	1989	Der altpaläolithische Fundplatz Dmanisi in Georgien (Kaukasus), *Jahrbuch des Römisch-Germanischen Zentralmuseums Mainz* 36, 67-116.
Gabunia, L., A. Vekua	1995	A Plio-Pleistocene hominid from Dmanisi, East Georgia, Caucasus, *Nature* 373, 509-512.
Gamble, C.S.	1994	Time for Boxgrove man, *Nature* 369, 275-276.
	this volume	The earliest occupation of Europe: the environmental background.
Gaudzinksi, S., E. Turner (ed.)	1995	*The role of early humans in the accumulation of European Lower and Middle Palaeolithic bone assemblages. Conference papers, Forschungsbereich Altsteinzeit des Römisch-Germanischen Zentralmuseums Mainz*. Neuwied: Schloss Monrepos.
Gibert, J. (ed.)	1992	*Proyecto Orce-Cueva Victoria (1988-1992): Presencia humana en el Pleistoceno inferior de Granada y Murcia*, Ayuntamiento de Orce (Granada): Museo de Prehistoria "J. Gibert".
Gibert, J., P. Palmquist, B. Martinez Navarro	1994	Los primeros europeos, *Investigacion y Ciencia*, Diciembre 1994, 28-29.
Ljubin, V., G. Bosinski,	this volume	The earliest occupation of the Caucasus region.
Raposo, L., M. Santonja	this volume	The earliest occupation of Europe: the Iberian peninsula.
Raynal, J.P., L. Magoga, F.-Z. Sbihi-Alaoui, D. Geraads	this volume	The earliest occupation of Atlantic Morocco: the Casablanca evidence.

Roberts, M.B.,   1994   A hominid tibia from Middle Pleistocene sediments at Boxgrove, UK, *Nature* 369,
    C.B. Stringer,   311-313.
    S.A. Parfitt

Roberts, M.B.,   this   The earliest occupation of Europe: the British Isles.
    C.S. Gamble,   volume
    D.R. Bridgland

Roe, D.A.   1995   The Orce Basin (Andalucia, Spain) and the initial Palaeolithic of Europe, *Oxford Journal
                                    of Archaeology* 14, 1-12.

Roebroeks, W.   1994   Updating the first Europeans, *Current Anthropology* 35, 301-305.

Roebroeks, W.,   1994   The earliest occupation of Europe: a short chronology, *Antiquity* 68, 489-503.
    T. van Kolfschoten

                         this   The earliest occupation of Europe: a reappraisal of artefactual and chronological
                         volume   evidence.

Ronen, A.   1991   The Yiron-Gravel lithic assemblage – artifacts older than 4.2 MY in Israel, *Archäologisches
                                    Korrespondenzblatt* 21, 159-164.

Swisher C.C.,   1994   Age of the earliest known hominids in Java, Indonesia, *Science* 263, 1118-1121.
    G.H. Curtis,
    T. Jacob,
    A.G. Getty,
    A Suprijo,
    Widiasmoro

Vekua, A.   1986   The Lower Pleistocene mammalian fauna of Achalkalaki (Southern Georgia, USSR),
                                    Palaeontographia Italica 74, 63-96.

White, C.   1995   La Grotte du Vallonet: Evidence of Early Hominid Activity or Natural Processes?
                                    Paper presented at the Palaeolithic-Mesolithic day meeting, British Museum London,
                                    March 17th 1995.

Wil Roebroeks and Thijs van Kolfschoten
Faculty of Pre- and Protohistory
Leiden University
P.O. Box 9515
2300 RA Leiden
The Netherlands

Luis Raposo
Manuel Santonja

1 The earliest occupation of Europe: the Iberian peninsula

A review of the Iberian evidence demonstrates that the oldest traces of human occupation date from the earlier part of the Middle Pleistocene. Though rare, the oldest lithic industries appear in all important river valleys of the continental interior. Larger assemblages already contain Acheulean bifaces, implying that the idea of an Iberian pre-Acheulean industrial ('pebble-culture') stage must be treated with caution.

1.   Introduction

In the last two decades, it has become common practice to postulate the existence of archaic lithic industries in the Iberian peninsula, documenting an ancient human occupation. These ideas were partially due to the conception of an original Iberian Acheulean ("meridional Acheulean", F. Bordes 1971), presumably related to the North African Acheulean, and based on the occurrence of a high percentage of cleavers (Alimen 1975) and on the abundant use of quartzite as raw material. These ideas were considerably strenghtened as a consequence of the impact caused in Iberia by Biberson's work in the 1960s in Morocco, where he claimed to have defined a "civilisation du galet aménagé" (Biberson 1961), older than the Acheulean and apparently very similar to the Pebble Industries reported in the Portuguese littoral since the 1940s (Breuil and Zbyszewski 1942-45).

The later discovery of some identical finds, i.e. pebble tools, in the higher terraces of the Guadalquivir river (Bordes and Viguier 1971) and, more importantly, the identification (Bordes and Thibault 1977) and subsequent excavation (Querol and Santonja 1983) of the site of El Aculadero in the littoral near Cadiz, contributed to the recognition (or at least to the positive expectation) of an archaic human occupation in the Iberian peninsula: an occupation dating back to the Early Pleistocene, culturally defined as pre-Acheulean. Recently, the same idea has been reinforced by the discoveries in the Guadix-Baza depression of a small fragment of an occipital bone, supposedly human (Gibert 1985; Vega Toscano 1989), as well as of some lithic artefacts (Carbonell *et al.* 1982).

Today, however, it is widely believed that none of these finds can be accepted as proof of such antiquity because of

the lack of solid dating evidence (sites in the Portuguese littoral and the Cadiz region), or because of doubts relating to the artificial character of the finds (the Guadix-Baza sites), or because the few and isolated lithic artefacts found in the interior of the Iberian peninsula will have to be disregarded (Santonja and Querol 1982) as they are insufficient evidence to support a hypothesis. In our present state of knowledge, it can be argued that the most ancient palaeolithic sites in Iberia can be dated to the beginning of the Middle Pleistocene. No sound evidence supports older dates (Santonja and Villa 1990; Aguirre 1991; Rolland 1992; Carbonell Roura 1992).

Severe limitations exist for the chronological framework of the Middle Pleistocene in Iberia, and sites are often difficult to date accurately within that period. With the exception of Atapuerca and Bolomor, these sites are all open-air localities and mostly related to fluvial sequences. Their chronological position is mainly determined by relative criteria. Absolute dating evidence for the initial Middle Pleistocene (prior to OIS 9) is only available from the site of Atapuerca (Burgos) and the Guadalquivir terraces. Two projects are presently in progress in order to obtain more absolute dates: one is concerned with such classic and important sites as Torralba and Ambrona (Soria), Bolomor (Valencia) and Cuesta de la Bajada (Teruel), the other is directed towards the open-air sites located in the Spanish sector of the Tagus basin.

Nevertheless, when the Middle Pleistocene sites of Iberia are studied in detail, they may provide evidence for placing them in a relative temporal sequence and it might thus be possible to differentiate between different major moments within that time-period. Even with these scarce data it might be possible to order the sites chronologically for the entire Middle Pleistocene, from its initial phases onwards.

2.   Towards a relative chronology

The sequences of terraces known in detail, mainly from the Iberian continental interior, give us the most complete data presently available for placing the lithic industries in a chronological order. In addition, factors such as faunal associations, pedologic characteristics of the soils and some morphostratigraphic particularities of each area, can also be used for a correlation between different fluvial valleys and/or distinct terraces levels.

Hence the knowledge of the different terrace systems constitutes one of the most important elements in the chronological order of the palaeolithic sites. In general, it can be said that the present Iberian hydrographic systems began to be formed after the deposition of the Villafranchian high detritic surfaces ("rañas"), dated to 2.5/2 Myr BP (Pérez González 1982 and 1982a; Molina 1991). Therefore, the highest river terraces in each major Iberian river can be attributed to the beginning of the Pleistocene. From that moment on a sedimentary process began, primarily controlled by tectonic factors and by the nature of the geological substratum. Climatic changes only had a secondary influence on this process. According to the number of terrace levels listed, three different terrace sequence formation models were identified in the continental Iberian interior (Pérez González et al. 1982):

1. The valleys with a large number of terrace levels (more than 20), with the highest at more than 150 m above the present river level.
2. The valleys with an intermediate number of terraces (8 to 10), and
3. Valleys with only a few terraces, with the highest at a mere 40 meters above the present river level.

This great diversity causes enormous problems, not only in the correlation between different river valleys, but also in the correlation between different geomorphological sectors within the same valley. Nonetheless, it is possible to make some general correlations and, in the case of the more developed valleys, it is even possible to isolate different series of terraces, based on the dimension of their escarpments, and to attribute them to consecutive periods within the Middle Pleistocene.

The almost complete lack of significant faunal associations in most open-air fluvial palaeolithic sites makes it very difficult to use any biostratigraphic reference tables, such as for instance the one established by E. Aguirre (1989):

EARLY PLEISTOCENE:
    faunal associations of the groups
    – "A": *Allophaiomys pliocaenicus*, together with Villafranchian carnivora like *Acinonyx, Viretailurus schaubi, Xenocyon rosi*.
    Documented in sites such as Cueva Victoria, Orce 4, Incarnal and Bagur 2 and
    – "B": *Allophaiomys pliocaenicus*, without Villafrachian carnivora, but with *Cuon priscus*, Mosbach wolf · and new Bovidae, such as *Capra* and *Soergelia*.
    Documented in sites such as Venta Micena 2, Barranco León and Orce 7.

INITIAL MIDDLE PLEISTOCENE (prior to OIS 13):
    faunal associations of the
    – "C" group: *Mimomys savini* with *Pitymys gregaloides* and *Pliomys episcopalis*, together with evolved *Mammuthus meridionalis* and, at the end of this time-period, *Mammuthus trogontherii, Dicerorhinus hemitoechus, Bison schoetensacki voigstedtensis*, different Cervidae, such as *Megaceros, Dama clactoniana* and *Cervus elaphus*.
    Documented in sites such as Atapuerca TD-3 to TD-6, Huéscar 1 and Cueva del Congosto.

LATE MIDDLE PLEISTOCENE:
    faunal associations of the groups
    – "D": *Arvicola mosbachensis* (= *A. terrestris cantiana*) instead of *Mimomys savini*, together with *Panthera (Leo) fossilis, Mammuthus trogontherii, Elephas antiquus*, some archaic horses – *Equus altidens, Equus suessenbornensis* – and *Dicerorhinus etruscus, Bison priscus*, different Cervidae, etc. Documented in such sites as Cúllar de Baza I, Pinedo, Torralba and Ambrona (lower levels) and
    – "E": similar to the preceding, without *Praemegaceros* and *Dolichodoriceros*, but with *Oryctolagus cuniculus, Equus caballus germanicus* and *Capreolus capreolus*.
    Documented in such sites as Aridos, Solana del Zamborino, Atapuerca TD-TG 10-11 and TN-2 to 6, Pinilla del Valle, Ambrona (upper levels).

INITIAL LATE PLEISTOCENE:
    faunal association of the
    – "F" group: including the last *Elephas (P.) antiquus* and *Dicerorhinus hemitoechus*, with the appearance of *Rangifer tarandus, Capra pyrenaica, Rupicapra rupicapra, Equus caballus gallicus*.
    Documented in Zafarraya, Carihuela, Cova Negra, Lezetxiki, Valdegoba, La Ermita, Abri Romani, etc.

However, the biostratigraphical limitations of these groups are stressed by Aguirre himself, either because of the uncertainty and chronological overlapping between several groups, or because of the clearly occurring different "transitional" assemblages, especially those from around the Early/Middle Pleistocene boundary. In addition, it must be emphasised that almost all the associations used to establish the oldest phases are found in purely palaeontological sites. The few Iberian open-air lower palaeolithic sites with important faunal assemblages, well-placed morphostratigraphically in the local terrace sequences and containing convincing anthropogenic evidence, are all too recent to be considered in this paper.

To summarise, it can be concluded that the discussion concerning the most ancient human occupation of Iberia is limited, primarily by the insufficiency of the chronological framework presently available. As far as the Middle Pleistocene is concerned, it is only possible to make a relative seriation between different sites, within limited zones of particular river valleys. However, this seriation does indicate in a few cases the existence of human occupation prior to OIS 9.

3.   The archaeological sites

With the chronological framework just referred to in mind, it is possible now to present the most important sites and sequences which document the first human occupation of the Iberian peninsula (Fig. 1). Emphasis will be placed only on those sites where the dates can reasonably be attributed to the initial stages of the Middle Pleistocene, presumably prior to OIS 9 (Fig. 2).

Due to the physical characteristics of the different zones of the Iberian peninsula, we will consider successively the following geographical units (according to Lautensach 1967, modified):

(1) The north of Portugal, Galicia and the littoral of Cantabria;
(2) The northern Meseta and the Iberian cordillera;
(3) The western Portuguese littoral and the lower Tagus basin;
(4) The southern Meseta, including the Spanish depressions of the Tagus and Guadiana rivers, the mountains in between (Toledo mountains) as well as the southern ones (Serra Morena), and the Portuguese western plateaus (Alentejo);
(5) The Ebro depression and the Pyrenean zone;
(6) The eastern Mediterranean littoral;
(7) The Algarve, Andalusia and the Segura basin.

3.1.   THE NORTH OF PORTUGAL, GALICIA AND THE LITTORAL OF CANTABRIA

Compared with the profusion of Middle and Upper Palaeolithic sites known in this region, the Acheulean localities draw attention due to two factors: there are only a few sites and these are all open-air (with the exceptions of the El Castillo cave, and possibly the Lezetxiki cave). Another characteristic which should also be considered is that in general they have very small lithic assemblages, often not diagnostic from a typological point of view. In fact some may not be Acheulean at all but more modern, even post-Palaeolithic (Rodriguez Asencio 1983; Cano Pan 1991; Meireles 1986). None of the sites known so far can reasonably be attributed to an early phase of the Middle Pleistocene. On the contrary, it seems that the most significant ones (such as Gelfa, Budiño, Bañugues, Llagú, Paredes and El Castillo) should be dated to a relatively late phase of that time-period.

3.2.   THE NORTHERN MESETA AND IBERIAN CORDILLERA

The northern submeseta is a region where a large number of sequences, places and lithic assemblages dating to the Middle Pleistocene can be observed and ordered into a relative chronology. Therefore, it gives us the most complete framework for a discussion of the earliest human occupation in Iberia.

In the western half of the region, west of the Trabancos-Pisuerga rivers' axis, there are relatively abundant Acheulean sites in fluvial contexts, even though they often consist of strictly superficial finds and none of them yielded significant faunal assemblages. The finds in the eastern zone are very scarce and not diagnostic, with only a few exceptions in the Douro Basin and in the Iberian cordillera. It should nevertheless be noted that it is precisely in this last sector that some of the most important and famous Middle Pleistocene Iberian sites have been found, such as Torralba, Atapuerca and Cuesta de la Bajada.

Almost all the major western river systems have lithic assemblages, manufactured mainly from locally rolled quartzite pebbles. These assemblages are in stratigraphic position within the middle terrace formations, or at the surface of the upper ones, or even sometimes at the top of the highest Neogenic surfaces. Although there may be some sampling errors due to insufficient field surveys, the existence of an extensive occupation of the territory seems clear. There is a preferential selection of locations: the confluence of rivers and the vestibular areas of secondary valleys – an observation that points to the importance of the subsidiary fluvial systems in the organisation of human movement during this period (Santonja 1992).

The sites are very diverse: some are in stratigraphic position, either with large lithic assemblages (Tera, Pisuerga and Tormes rivers) or with small lithic series (Orbigo, Agueda and Trabancos rivers). Others, very abundant, are surface sites, often numerous and dispersed over large areas (Santonja and Villa 1990; Santonja in press). In the absence of absolute dates and significant faunal associations, their chronology is based, as we mentioned earlier, on the analysis of the morphostratigraphic sequences of each fluvial valley (Pérez González 1982).

At the Pisuerga river, west of León and outside the Cantabrian cordillera, there are a total of 8 terrace levels (2-m to 125/130-m). More than twenty Acheulean sites were found there: all of them surface sites, with the exception of San Quirce which is located in the 50-m terrace level and attributed to an ancient phase of the Middle Pleistocene (Arnaíz 1990). This site originates from a very low energy environment (possibly not integrated into the original terrace formation process, a hypothesis which could perhaps contribute to the rejuvenation of the

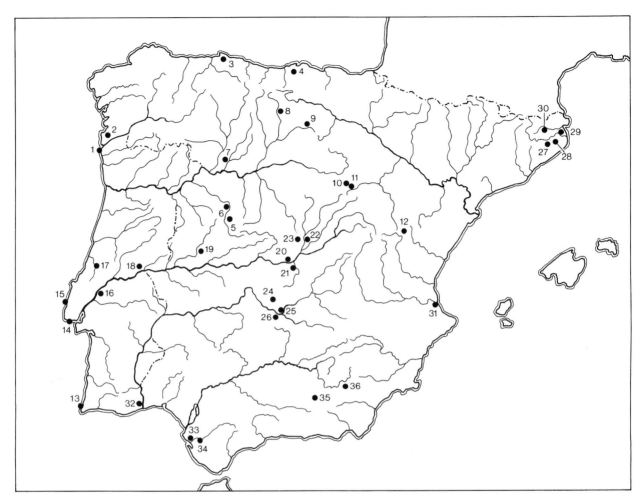

Fig. 1. Map of the Iberian peninsula, with sites mentioned in the text.

Northern Portugal, Galicia and littoral of Cantabria – 1: Gelfa; 2: Budiño; 3: Bañugues; 4: El Castillo.
Northern submeseta and Iberian cordillera – 5: La Maya; 6: Gargabete; 7: Monfarracinos; 8: San Quirce; 9: Atapuerca; 10: Ambrona;
11: Torralba; 12: Cuesta de la Bajada.
Western Portuguese littoral and lower Tagus depression – 13: Mirouço; 14: Alto Leiäo; 15: Magoito, Açafora, Aguda; 16: Vale do
Forno/Alpiarça; 17: Quinta do Cónego/Pousias.
Southern submeseta – 18: Monte do Famaco; 19: El Sartalejo; 20: Pinedo; 21: El Espinar; 22: Aridos; 23: San Isidro; 24: Porzuna;
25: Albalá; 26: El Martinete.
Ebro depression and pyrenaic zone – no sites are presented in the map.
Eastern mediterranean littoral – 27: La Selva; 28: Puig d'en Roca; 29: Cau del Duc; 30: Mollet; 31: Bolomor.
Algarve, Andalusia and Segura basin – 32: Aldeia Nova; 33: El Aculadero; 34: Laguna de Medina; 35: Solana del Zamborino; 36: Cúllar-
Baza I.

chronological attribution referred to above). An abundant lithic industry (made on local quartzite and quartz, with only some 7% of retouched tools, especially scrapers and denticulates, a few cleavers and pebble tools), has been documented, an industry apparently clustered spatially and in association with ash and a possible hearth, but without faunal remains.

The most important area with Middle Pleistocene lithic industries in the centre of the northern submeseta, with the exception of the Esla river valley and its main tributaries, is the Pisuerga river, north of Valladolid. Here are a total of 8 terrace levels, 6 of which have Acheulean-like assemblages.

In the Douro valley, the lithic assemblages are very rare. However, some of them, because of a morphostratigraphic position in the higher terrace levels (e.g. Monfarracinos and Toro, both located at the 80-m terrace level), should be considered as evidence of the most ancient human

	North of Portugal, Galicia and Cantabria	Northern Meseta and Iberian cordillera	Western littoral and lower Tagus	Southern Meseta	Eastern mediterranean littoral	Algarve, Andalusia and Segura basin
LATE PLEISTOCENE 130 Kyr	Gelfa	La Maya I	Alpiarça (upper levels)	A. Oxígeno Porzuna El Martinete		
MIDDLE PLEISTOCENE 340 Kyr	? Budiño ? El Castillo ? Bañugues	Galisancho La Maya II Cuesta de la Bajada	Mealhada Almonda (EVS) Liz (Q3) Monte Famaco Alpiarça (middle levels)	San Isidro (lower levels) Aridos Sartalejo	? Cau d'en Borrás ? Tossal de la Font Bolomor	? El Aculadero Aldeia Nova Solana del Zamborino Guadalquivir T11
		? San Quirce ? Torralba ? Ambrona (lower levels) La Maya III	Qta. Cónego ? Alpiarça (lower levels)	? Pinedo		Laguna Medina Guadalquivir T8
500 Kyr		Atapuerca TD6 Monfarracinos ? Atapuerca TD4 ?		El Espinar ? La Mesa ?		Cúllar Baza I Guadalquivir T6
730 Kyr **EARLY PLEISTOCENE**			? Magoito ? ? Mirouço ? ? Seixosa ?		? La Selva ? ? Puig d'en Roca ?	Venta Micena ?

Fig. 2. Chronological position of the most important Iberian Lower Palaeolithic sites.

Interrogation marks on the left denote serious doubts about the chronology; on the right, denote serious doubts about the anthropic evidence claimed to exist and/or the artefactual character of the assemblages. Within each space-time case sites are present without any chronological order.

occupation in the region. They date possibly to the early Middle Pleistocene or even to the end of the preceding period – if the artefactual nature of the few flaked pebbles and flakes found *in situ* in those levels is accepted.

To the east of the Trabancos river, in the southern half of the Douro basin, Lower Palaeolithic sites are almost unknown, while in the western valleys, between the Trabancos and Agueda rivers, biface and cleaver industries are frequently found. The most important sites are located in the Tormes, Huebra, Yeltes and Agueda river valleys, where in certain areas (mostly in the middle sector of each drainage system) several very complete morphostratigraphic sequences were recognised. Here, the sites are located at various geomorphological positions:

(a) on the surface of all terrace levels, assemblages have been found without any visible edge wear and varying in the number of artefacts;

(b) on the surface of the middle level terraces often large assemblages have been found, characterised by clearly worn edges;

(c) within the same terrace levels a few artefacts have been found in stratigraphic position (e.g. La Maya II and La Maya III);

(d) in the lower level terraces and other alluvial deposits, there are large assemblages with bifaces, cleavers, etc. (e.g. La Ermita, La Maya I and Villagonzalo).

In the Tormes river valley, where more research has been carried out, the Acheulean industries are all dated to the Middle Pleistocene. They have been located in the 56-m terrace level (La Maya III), the 62-m level (Gargabete), and the 8-m terrace level (La Maya I). There is no evidence of older assemblages, and those that are stratigraphically more recent than the 8-m terrace, located in the colluvial covering deposits, are clearly post-Acheulean (Santonja and González 1984).

Finally, in the eastern part of the Iberian river system region, the Acheulean sites are very rare (Santonja in press). Some of these, however, are of particular relevance due to their geological and geographical locations and to their taphonomic histories which led to the preservation of a large set of evidence (fauna, human remains, lithics, etc.). Four of the sites are worth mentioning:

(a) Atapuerca (Aguirre *et al.* 1987 and 1990; Carbonell *et al.* 1992), the importance of this site stems from the human remains found there. The existence of lithic industries is, however, also worth mentioning, including a very small number of artefacts (not entirely convincing) from a level (TD4) located "immediately" over a magnetic inversion, considered to be the Matuyama/Brunhes transition (and thus apparently dated to the initial Middle Pleistocene), and another assemblage, with bifaces, found in a level (TD6) attributed to OIS 13 on the basis of palaeontological data (it is the last level in the Atapuerca TD sequence where *Mimomys savini* is present);

(b) the classic sites of Ambrona and Torralba, located in a passage area between the Douro, Ebro and Jarama-Henares basins, and connected to the Mediterranean littoral by the Jaloca river valley (Fig. 3). The exact anthropogenic nature and chronological position of these sites within the Middle Pleistocene are still under discussion. There is no positive confirmation of dates presumably older than OIS 9. Nevertheless, these dates

are possible for the "lower complex" levels in each site (Santonja and Villa 1990);

(c) Cuesta de la Bajada, located in the upper sector of the Alfambra river valley (50/60-m terrace), in Teruel (Santonja *et al.* 1992), dating from a relatively evolved Middle Pleistocene phase, perhaps post OIS 9.

3.3.   THE WESTERN PORTUGUESE LITTORAL AND LOWER TAGUS DEPRESSION

The Iberian western littoral is the region where the first occurrence of presumably very ancient pebble-industries, has been registered (Breuil and Zbyszewski 1942-1945). Located in the Portuguese Estremadura (Magoito, Açafora, Praia da Aguda, etc.), these lithic assemblages (Fig. 4) – almost all surface finds – were collected on the top of raised beaches. Their age was calculated according to the general glacio-eustatic model (the higher finds related to the 90-m level beaches were attributed to the mediterranean Sicilian time-period). In the 1970s identical finds were published, extending the collection of original observations both in a temporal and spatial sense: older sites, on the top of still higher beaches (such as Alto Leiäo, on a beach with a height of 150-m, claimed to be dated to the Calabrian II), and new finds along the littoral in the extreme southern part of the territory (such as Mirouço which is located in the western part of the Algarve).

Doubts concerning the dates of all Portuguese lithic assemblages referred to before, have been expressed

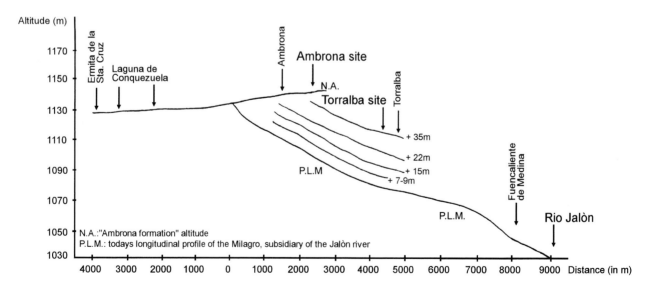

Fig. 3. Morphostratigraphic position of Ambrona and Torralba sites, within the terraces system of the Jalón river (after A. Pérez-González and M. Santonja).

repeatedly, using geological, geomorphological and typological arguments (Raposo 1985; Raposo and Carreira 1986). On the basis of present-day evidence, it must be concluded that Portuguese littoral "pebble-cultures":

(a) do not document beyond doubt any Early Pleistocene human occupation;
(b) may not constitute an independent techno-complex, either in a chronological (pre-Acheulean) or in a typological (pebble-culture) sense. In view of the limitations imposed by the small sized pebbles available in those raised beaches, they should be regarded as local variants of successive Palaeolithic techno-complexes.

A few Acheulean lithic industries have been found in some river valleys of the western Iberian littoral. The most famous site is Mealhada, in the Certima river valley, where lithic artefacts ("Upper Acheulean") have been found in association with faunal remains, reviewed by Antunes *et al.* (1988). *Oryctolagus cuniculus, Homotherium latidens, Elephas (Palaeoloxodon) antiquus, Equus caballus, Hippopotamus incognitus, Cervus elaphus*, and *Bos primigenius* are attributed to a later ("Rissian") phase of the Middle Pleistocene. The only possible evidence of an ancient Acheulean occupation comes from the surveying and excavation work recently carried out in the Lis river valley (Cunha-Ribeiro 1987, 1992). A total of 5 terrace levels were documented; two of these, the highest one, Q1a, and the penultimate one, Q3, have Acheulean assemblages, on the surface and in stratigraphic position. Although there are no absolute dates available for these two sites, the geomorphological position of the industries suggests the existence of a considerable amount of time between them, with an initial Middle Pleistocene date for the older one – a hypothesis supported by typological data coming from the site of Quinta do Cónego/Pousias (Cunha-Ribeiro 1990-91).

The last area to be focused on is the lower Tagus basin where abundant Acheulean industries are known from the surface of and in stratigraphic position within the middle terrace levels (+ 20/40-m terraces) (Breuil and Zbyszewski 1942-45; Zbyszewski 1946). The Alpiarça region is especially important due to the occurrence of successive stratigraphic Acheulean horizons. At Vale do Forno, for instance, G. Zbyszewski (1946), has described a sequence of 9 stratigraphic units, chronologically ordered from the initial Middle Pleistocene (conventional "Mindel") to the initial Late Pleistocene (early "Würm", represented by colluvial deposits). The biface industries occur in all sequences: from the basal gravels (level 2), where they were named "Clactono-abbevillian" (H. Breuil's and G. Zbyszewski's terms), to the upper silt and clay deposits. Recent TL dates for the upper levels, where "evolved"

Acheulean and "Micoquian" assemblages are present, confirmed the idea (Raposo *et al.* 1985) of its relatively recent age (final Middle Pleistocene and initial Late Pleistocene). However, the base of the sequence is dated only by classic glacio-eustatic criteria, which makes it impossible to confirm the early date proposed for the first biface industries of this region.

3.4.   THE SOUTHERN MESETA

In contrast to the northern area, the southern submeseta is a complex region from a structural point of view. Basically, it is composed of two enormous sedimentary basins – the Tagus, including the Madrid region, and the Guadiana, including La Mancha and Calatrava. These basins are separated by ancient reliefs (Toledo mountains) and limited by Central, Iberian and Penibetic systems.

In the Madrid region, the terraces of Manzanares (with lithic industries mainly made in flint) and Jarama (with assemblages mostly made in quartzite) constitute one of the most classic areas for the study of the Acheulean in the whole of Iberia (*v.* Santonja and Villa 1990). Unfortunately, almost all of these sites have been destroyed by urbanization (Santonja and Querol 1980) and none can be attributed to an initial Middle Pleistocene phase. The oldest sites in the area, San Isidro (lower level) and Aridos (particularly important because of the faunal associations and the exceptional preservational conditions observed in an elephant butchery level (Santonja and Querol 1980), probably date to a relatively late Middle Pleistocene phase. Many others, such as Arriaga and Arenero de Oxígeno belong to much more recent periods, including the initial Late Pleistocene.

From the Jarama/Tagus confluence up to the Portuguese territory, numerous sites with Acheulean lithic industries have been located along the Tagus valley and in its tributaries (mainly the Alagón-Jertes system and the Ponsul). Some are stratigraphic finds, found within the middle and upper terrace levels. The oldest assemblages, in the Tagus + 70-m terrace (El Espinar) and in the + 120-m Alagón terrace (La Mesa), have only a few uncharacteristic artefacts. The most significant lithic assemblages are found only in relation with the middle terrace levels. These assemblages correspond to two different chronological phases of the Middle Pleistocene, which are well represented by three important sites:

– Pinedo (Fig. 5) (Tagus valley, + 22-m terrace) (Querol and Santonja 1979), apparently from the older phase, even if new data on the local terrace systems would be necessary to determine the exact chronological position of this site;
– El Sartalejo (Alagón valley, + 24/26-m terrace) (Santonja 1985) and

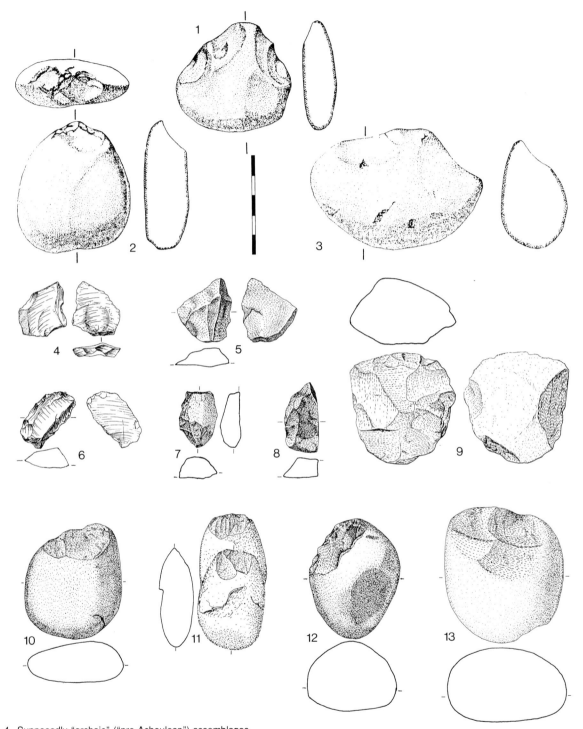

Fig. 4. Supposedly "archaic" ("pre-Acheulean") assemblages.
1, 3, 10, 12 and 13: choppers; 2, 11: chopping-tools; 4, 5: pseudo-levallois points; 6 to 8: scrapers; 9: discoid core.
All in quartzite, except 4 and 6 in flint.
Provenance – 1: Magoito; 2 and 3: Seixosa; 4 to 13: El Aculadero.
After L. Raposo 1985 (1 to 3), M.A. Querol and M. Santonja 1983 (4 to 13). Scale in cm.

– Monte do Famaco (Fig. 6) (GEPP 1977; Raposo 1987), from the younger one.

Pinedo is a site in secondary position with only a few non-diagnostic faunal remains (*Oryctolagus cuniculus, Elephas (Palaeoloxodon) antiquus, Equus, Hippopotamus amphibius, Cervus elaphus,* etc.), but it has nevertheless been possible to collect almost 6000 artefacts. This vast industry allowed the precise typological definition of what has been interpreted as an ancient stage in the evolution of the Acheulean, but where the influence of local raw materials (mainly quartzite cobbles and pebbles) could also play an important role.

El Sartalejo is a site where some 600 artefacts were collected in a systematic surface survey, allowing the establishment of an evolved typological stage within the Acheulean.

Monte do Famaco is also a surface site, where an intensive survey led to the definition of an apparently spatial patterning in the distribution of the lithic industry, which consisted of more than 1500 artefacts.

If, in addition to these sites, we take into consideration some sites located in different terraces, and if we also keep in mind all terrace sequences of adjacent valleys, it will be possible to build a chronological framework, in general identical to the one already presented for the northern Meseta (especially in the Tormes river valley): the oldest finds from the upper level terraces can be placed in the beginning of the Middle Pleistocene; Pinedo, as well as some other sites in the same geomorphological position (such as Monte do Famaco, worn series, Raposo 1987), are dated to a more recent phase of the Middle Pleistocene, but new observations on the exact position of the different terraces within each fluvial valley are necessary (in this regard, the exact datation of Pinedo, which could be more recent than previously thought, is particulary relevant); El Sartalejo and Aridos must be placed in a late Middle Pleistocene phase, but again, older than several other sites, still characterised by the presence of biface industries located in the lower terraces.

In the extreme southern part of the region, across the entire Guadiana river basin, the localities with Middle Pleistocene industries are rare. In La Mancha, for instance, there is a considerable number of surface sites, which are often very large and spatially extensive and probably represent workshop areas, dating to different periods but mainly to post-Acheulean times (Santonja 1986). At Calatrava, the Guadiana river (with 5 terraces levels) and the Jabalón river (with 8 terrace levels), both have Acheulean industries in the lower terraces (El Martinete, Alabalá, Porzuna), all of them dating to the late Middle Pleistocene or, perhaps, to the initial Late Pleistocene (Santonja 1981).

3.5.   THE EBRO DEPRESSION AND PYRENEAN AREA

Following the idea expressed earlier about the scarcity of Middle Pleistocene lithic industries in the eastern part of the northern Meseta and the Iberian cordillera, the Ebro river region and the Pyrenean zone seem to be almost deserted. Assemblages possibly dating to the final Middle Pleistocene are only reported from the Najerilla sub-basin (Utrilla 1984). They can, probably, be related to the Atapuerca sites due to the geographical connections between the two regions.

It is difficult to explain the scant evidence, which is still to be confirmed by new and more intensive field work. However, one thing is certain: it cannot be attributed to the non-preservation of sediments, since the Ebro and several other rivers in the region present well developed Middle Pleistocene deposits, occasionally formed in very low energy environments (such as the Gallego river), in which any human occupation would be preserved.

3.6.   THE EASTERN MEDITERRANEAN LITTORAL

Again in this region, there are not many Middle Pleistocene archaeological finds. In Catalonia, the existence of archaic pebble industries has been reported, dating to the beginning of the initial Middle Pleistocene or even to the final Early Pleistocene. These assemblages, in the Ter river valley (Puig d'en Roca) and in the La Selva area (Carbonell *et al.* 1978), are mainly surface finds and, consequently, impossible to date precisely. Nor can the assemblage of the Cau del Duc cave (Lumley-Woodyear 1971) be dated exactly. In this cave taphonomic processes may have mixed apparently old Acheulean tools with other, clearly more recent, ones.

The existence of an Acheulean cave occupation in this region is, however, one of its most striking aspects. In the Castellón and Valencia areas to the south of the Ebro river, the occurrence of some Middle Pleistocene human occupations in at least three caves has been reported: Cau d'en Borrás, Tossal de la Font (Carbonell *et al.* 1979; Gusi Jener *et al.* 1983; Arsuaga and Bermudéz de Castro 1984) and, more importantly, at Bolomor, presently under excavation (Fernández Peris 1990), where recent TL and amino-acid dates suggest that the basal part of the sedimentary sequence could be older than OIS 9.

Very few of these finds have been found in the remaining area of the Mediterranean littoral, up to Gibraltar. Here, the Middle Pleistocene sites are extremely scarce and only in some very restricted places, mostly in fluvial contexts (such as the upper Guadalhorce valley, near Malaga), there are a few references to small assemblages of quartzite bifaces and cleavers, without clear dates however (Barroso *et al.* 1993).

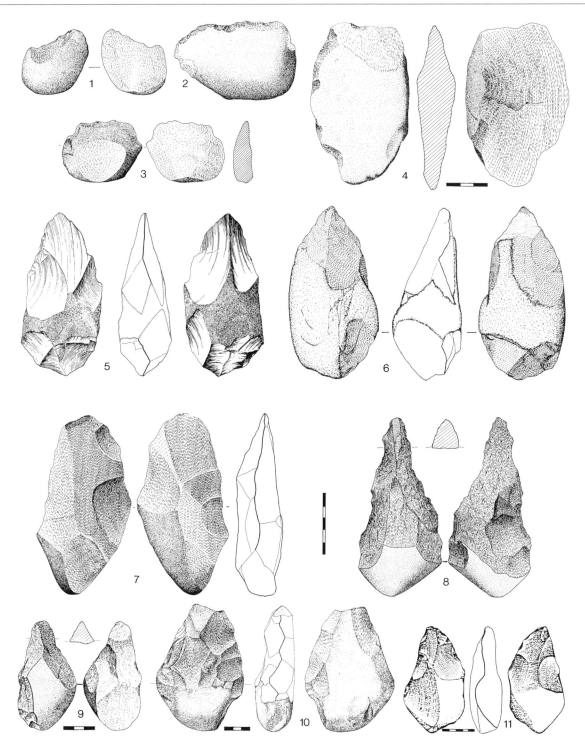

Fig. 5. Acheulean assemblages presumably older than OIS 9.
1: scraper; 2 and 3: denticulates; 4: cleaver; 5 to 7, 10 and 11: bifaces; 8 and 9: trihedrals.
All in quartzite, except 5 in flint.
Provenance – 1 to 9: Pinedo (after M.A. Querol and M. Santonja 1979); 10: La Maya III (after M. Santonja and A. Pérez-González 1984);
1: Laguna Medina (after F. Giles Pacheco *et al.* 1993). Scale in cm.

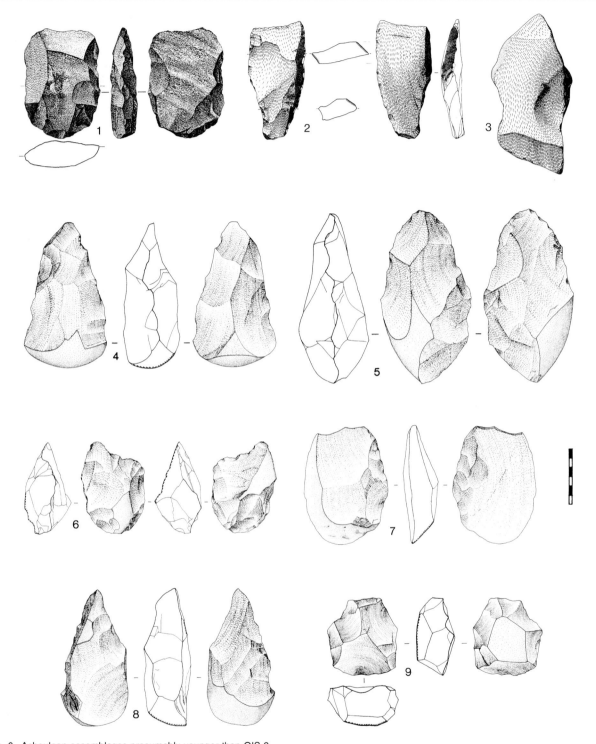

Fig. 6. Acheulean assemblages presumably younger than OIS 9.
1, 2 and 7: cleavers; 3: core used to obtain a large cleaver flake; 4 to 6: bifaces; 8: trihedral; 9: Levallois centripetal core.
All in quartzite.
Provenance – 1: La Maya II (after M. Santonja and A. Pérez-González 1984); 2 and 3: El Sartalejo (after M. Santonja in press); 4 to 9: Monte do Famaco (after L. Raposo et al. 1993a). Scale in cm.

3.7.   THE ALGARVE, ANDALUSIA AND THE SEGURA BASIN

In the south of the Iberian peninsula, the major geographical unit is the hydrographic basin of the Guadalquivir river. It is a complex zone because of its geological substratum and its morphostructural characteristics, which has a number of particularities to be treated separately from the eastern Plio-Pleistocene depressions.

The oldest human occupations claimed to be documented in this region are related to the littoral areas, especially in the Cadiz zone. The most significant site is El Aculadero (Bordes and Thibault 1977), where a vast pebble-industry found in stratigraphic order has been studied in detail (Querol and Santonja 1983) (more than 22,000 artefacts in fewer than 100 excavated sq. meters). This site was initially considered to be the equivalent of stage III of the Moroccan "civilisation du galet aménagé" (Biberson 1961). Unfortunately, it has so far not been possible to date precisely any of these supposedly ancient sites, including El Aculadero, which seems much more recent (final Middle Pleistocene or a little earlier) than was initially supposed. In consequence, like in the Portuguese western littoral, the apparent techno-typological archaism of these lithic industries, made on small sized pebbles, should rather be attributed to raw material limitations than to any particular great antiquity.

The idea of the nonexistence of an archaic Early Pleistocene occupation in this region has also been reinforced by recent work carried out near Sevilla in the Guadalquivir lower and middle course, in an area where abundant Acheulean assemblages are known. The local morphostratigraphic fluvial sequence has been described in detail by Díaz del Olmo and Vallespí (1989, 1993), allowing the identification of a total of 14 terrace levels, with a chronology supported to a certain extent by several absolute dates (U/Th and palaeomagnetism). In brief, the following sequence can be presented:

– between the T3 terrace level (+ 169-m) and the T4 level (+ 142-m) the Jaramillo event (950/890 Kyr BP) can be placed;
– the T6 level, with a normal polarity, is dated to the Brunhes epoch;
– some lacustrine deposits related to the T10 level (+ 55-m) have been dated to the Biwa phase (300 Kyr BP);
– and the Las Jarillas carbonated deposit, at the top of level T10 (+ 29-m), is dated to 80 Kyr BP (U/Th)(Diaz del Olmo et al. 1989 and 1993).

The first lithic industries found in stratigraphic position within this sequence, are related to the T6 level, dated to the initial Middle Pleistocene. Consequently, they do not confirm the supposedly earlier occupation referred to in the littoral,

nor can they be more informative about a cultural affiliation because of their scarcity. The first and rare bifaces appear in level T8, dated to the first half of the Middle Pleistocene, prior to OIS 9. However, only from level T11 onwards are the Acheulean assemblages extensively represented, with large numbers of retouched tools: bifaces, cleavers, trihedrals, clear flake-tools and, for the first time, the use of the Levallois method. In addition, it should be noted that up to level T10 quartzite is used in all industries; flint is only used in the later levels. This change is probably related to varying raw material availability as a result of changes in sedimentary fluvial processes.

Acheulean industries were also found in the Guadalete river, an ancient Guadalquivir branch, which began to form its own terrace system during the Middle Pleistocene (Zazo et al. 1985). These industries, made on compact limestone and quartzite, were located in 4 successive terrace levels (F. Giles Pacheco et al. 1992). The older one (+ 45/50-m) can, perhaps, be attributed to an earlier phase of the Middle Pleistocene and reveals the existence of Acheulean industries (such as the Laguna Medina site, Giles Pacheco et al. 1989 and 1993) equivalent to those of Pinedo.

In the Portuguese Algarve, in the western sector of the region, the only significant Acheulean industries are found in the Guadiana estuary. Some of these industries are in stratigraphic position in the 8-12-m terrace level (such as Aldeia Nova - Feio 1946). These are, however, small assemblages and not precisely dated.

Finally, the important eastern tertiary depressions must be mentioned: Granada, Guadix-Baza-Orce, Huercal-Overa and Vera. The deposits in the last two depressions originated mainly in marine environments while the others are characterised by drainage and continental deposits. The importance of these depressions derives mainly from the very complete depositional sequence they present, revealing an almost sedimentary continuum from the Late Miocene to the Late Pleistocene, including different well-dated palaeontological sites.

Nevertheless, the anthropogenic evidence is scarce (Santonja and Villa 1990). Without considering, because of their ambiguity, the supposedly human remains found at Venta Micena and dated, by biostratigraphical criteria, to more than 900 Kyr BP, the oldest site in the area is Cúllar-Baza I (Ruiz Bustos and Michaux 1976). It is dated, based on biostratigraphical arguments (faunal association including among many others *Acanthodactylus eritrurus, Eliomys quercinus, Apodemus sylvaticus, Arvicola mosbachensis (= A. terrestris cantiana), Microtus brecciensis, Canis etruscus, Mammuthus trogontherii, Equus suessenbornensis, Equus altidens, Dicerorhinus etruscus, Praemegaceros verticornis*) to the initial Middle Pleistocene, perhaps prior to Pinedo. The small lithic industry from this site (only six flakes and two choppers) does not allow a typological diagnosis (Vega-Toscano 1989), but it is nevertheless very important because it documents beyond any doubt the human occupation of this area (and, therefore, for the Iberian peninsula) in a period where it is very difficult to find well-dated sites.

Solana del Zamborino, another and from an archaeological point of view certainly the most important Middle Pleistocene site in the same depression (Botella *et al.* 1975), probably dates from a later phase. Its fauna (Aguirre's group "E") contains, among others, *Eliomys quercinus, Eliomys lusitanicus, Arvicola sapidus, Apodemus flavicollis, Panthera leo spelaea, Felis lynx pardina, Felis sylvestris, Macaca sylvanus, Elephas (Palaeoloxodon) antiquus, Equus caballus torralbae, Dicerorhinus hemitoechus, Hippopotamus* sp., *Cervus elaphus, Dama* sp., *Capreolus capreolus, Bos primigenius, Bison priscus* (Martín Penela 1987). The anthropogenic evidence, apart from an abundant lithic industry (Fig. 7) mainly on quartzite and quartz (but also on some local flint), with scrapers, denticulates and a few bifaces, includes also some habitational features: a hypothetical "trench", interpreted as a hunting trap, and an apparently convincing hearth, defined by a circle of five quartzite pebbles, with an impressive amount of charcoal and ash in the middle.

4.   Conclusions

We have reviewed the most important sites and morphostratigraphic Iberian sequences, which may indicate the possible occurrence of human occupational traces prior to OIS 9. The general conclusion is that these occurrences do exist, although they are very scarce and often dubious.

To begin with, it has been observed in several regions that no real evidence can be dated beyond any doubt to such an ancient period. This applies to northern Portugal, Galicia and Cantabria, and also to the Ebro river depression and the Pyrenean zone. In some other regions, such as the Portuguese western littoral and the Mediterranean eastern zone, there is some evidence which can be reasonably dated to the initial Middle Pleistocene, but without absolute certainty. Only in the continental interior (northern and southern Meseta) and in the Guadalquivir valley did we find proof of such an ancient occupation, although even in this case there is no clear evidence of an older human presence dating back to the Early Pleistocene.

In consequence, the oldest human traces in the Iberian peninsula must be dated to the initial Middle Pleistocene. Their exact date, however, is not well established, since most sites are dated by relative morphostratigraphical criteria. Even in the few sites from which absolute dates were obtained, not one of their archaeological horizons has been dated directly.

It is worthwhile to note, however, that these oldest lithic industries, in spite of their rarity, do appear in all the most important river valleys of the continental interior: Douro, Tagus and Alagón, Guadiana and Guadalquivir, thereby documenting an extensive human occupation. The lack of solid equivalent evidence in the whole littoral is puzzling, but this may possibly be attributed to the chronological uncertainty of the finds located in ancient raised beaches.

The oldest lithic assemblages of the Iberian peninsula are very scarce. In general, the sites placed at the top of fluvial morphostratigraphical sequences present only a few artefacts, usually fewer than ten (flakes and pebble tools). Bifaces have not yet been discovered but this may be due to the sample size. The first significant and relatively well-dated Iberian industries have already the kind of large cutting tools used to define the Acheulean (*sensu lato*). Consequently, the idea, accepted in the last two decades, of the existence of a pre-Acheulean industrial stage in Iberia, in the form of the so-called "pebble-cultures", must be treated with caution.

Contrary to what has been suggested occasionally, the biface industries in Iberia are not all relatively recent. In all major fluvial sequences reviewed, and also in some sites located in other geological environments (Atapuerca, for instance), we saw that the first large cutting tools, including bifaces, trihedrals and cleavers, appear prior to OIS 9. Again, they appear in very small numbers and the sites documenting this initial industrial bifacial phase are relatively rare – an occurrence in great contrast to the abundance and variety of Acheulean assemblages and sites dated to the second part of the Middle Pleistocene and, in some regions at least, to the initial Late Pleistocene.

The verification of such a vast chronological distribution, and the influence of some general models built elsewhere (in France, by H. Breuil and F. Bordes; in Morocco, by P. Biberson; in Algeria, by H. Alimen; etc.), led to a search for general evolutionary trends in the Iberian Acheulean. The existence of a sequence of stepped linear stages has been defended: "lower", "middle", "upper" and "final" Acheulean, some of which further divided in order to obtain greater "precision". We believe that this kind of detailed division serves no purpose, due to the nonexistence of solid and numerous absolute chronological references and to the scarcity of many assemblages. In view of the limitations imposed by the relative temporal framework currently used, in particular when inter-fluvial correlations must be made, we think that at present it is not possible to ascertain to which causes the lithic diversity and variability should be assigned: time, space, raw material availability, cultural affinities, etc. It is true that within the few fluvial morphostratigraphical sequences where different and successive chronological Acheulean stages have been

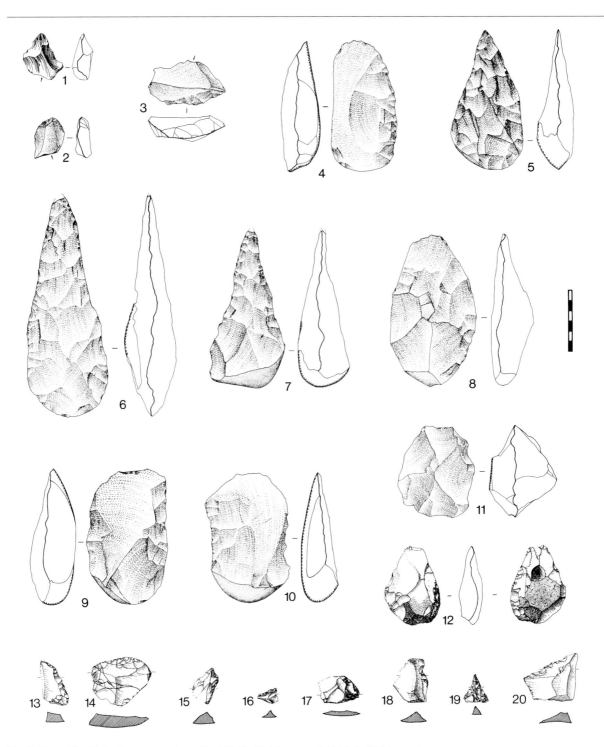

Fig. 7. Upper/Final Acheulean assemblages (final Middle Pleistocene or initial Late Pleistocene).
1: Tayac point; 2 and 17: endscrapers; 3, 4 and 14: sidescrapers; 5 to 8 and 12: lanceolate, micoquian, ovalar and cordiform bifaces; 9 and 10: cleavers; 11: bipyramidal centripetal core; 13, 16, 18, 19 and 20: denticulates and notches; 15: backed knife.
1, 12 to 20: flint; 2 to 11: quartzite.
Provenance – 1 to 11: Milharós (Alpiarça) (after L. Raposo *et al.* 1985); 12 to 20: Solana del Zamborino (after M.C. Botella *et al.* 1976).
Scale in cm.

established with some certainty, the earliest biface industries present more "primitive" technical and typological characteristics (see the summary presented in Santonja and Villa 1990:87). They are, however, not sufficient to support any generalization. With the present data-base, we believe that it is only possible to distinguish a final stage of the Acheulean in all biface industries, frequently named "Micoquian" (Manzares river, lower Tagus drainage, at Alpiarça, Guadiana, and little else), and dated, at least partially, to the initial Late Pleistocene. In relation to the Middle Pleistocene phases, the sole aspect to be retained is the scarcity of bifaces prior to OIS 9 and their abundance thereafter. This is an observation which could be subject to speculation in view of the models that suggest an intermittent initial occupation of Europe and thus question the character of the relationship (continuity/break) between the first handaxe industries (Acheulean 'Abbevillian') and the more recent Middle Pleistocene Acheulean assemblages.

The development of absolute dating programmes, either of archaeological sites or of geological formations, in fluvial contexts (as has already been initiated in the Guadalquivir river and is now being executed in the Spanish Tagus basin), clearly should be one of the first priorities of the Iberian Middle Pleistocene research. It would also be important to date some of the coastal sites, especially of the western Portuguese littoral and of the Cadiz region. With such a rigorous and detailed chronological framework, which will allow a judicious selection of particular sites and sequences, it will be useful to re-evaluate, among other questions, the existence of general evolutionary trends within the Acheulean, the functional archaeological nature of each site, the geographical distribution of different sites (within each region and all over Iberia), the relations existing between Iberia and adjacent areas, and so on. These are very important questions, particularly since, whatever model is used, it seems clear that only in southernmost Europe we can expect a continuous Middle Pleistocene archaeological record, free from significant environmental constraints. Such is the case of the Iberian subcontinent.

Final remark

Between the initial elaboration of this paper (September 1993) and its final revision (March 1995) some new observations suggested once again the possible occurrence of a scarce human occupation in Iberia, dating back to the final Early Pleistocene. Near Venta Micena, in the Guadix-Baza basin, a site containing a small, but inquestionable, lithic industry, Fuentenueva 3, has been located (Alain Turq, personal communication, to be published in the "*Compte Rendu de l'Académie des Sciences*", Paris), apparently dated to the Jamarillo event (*c.* 950/890 Kyr BP) on the basis of geomorphological, sedimentary and faunal criteria. This idea seems to be reinforced by new chronological data on the lower beds of the Atapuerca sequence (TD4 to TD6 levels) and on the middle-upper terraces of the Douro river. In this regard, the hypothesis of a final Early Pleistocene occupation in Iberia remains an open question, especially because it seems clear now that around 1 Myr ago humans were already at the southern frontiers of Europe, from the Caucasian area to the littoral of Morocco. The critical approach used in this paper plays an important role, as it became current in the last two decades to accept uncritically almost all indications of ancient human occupations in Iberia, and elsewhere. But, as W. Roebroeks already noted (1994, 302), one of the advantages of the "short chronology" scenario, favoured by ourselves and most of the participants in the "Tautavel meeting", is that "it is easy to falsify". Maybe the recent finds from Iberia, if proven to be valid in the future, can yield the evidence which is currently still missing.

references

Aguirre, E.

1989 Vertebrados del Pleistoceno continental. In: *Mapa del Cuaternario de España*, 47-69, Instituto Tecnológico Geo-Minero de España, Madrid.

1991 Les prémiers peuplements humains de la Peninsula Ibérique. In: E. Bonifay and B. Vandermeersch (eds), *Les premiers Européens*, 143-150, Paris: C.T.H.S.

1987 *El Hombre fósil de Ibeas y el Pleistoceno de la Sierra de Atapuerca*, Junta de Castilla y León, Valladolid.

1990 The Atapuerca sites and the Ibeas hominids, *Human Evolution* 5(1), 55-73, Florence.

Alimen, H.

1975 Les isthmes hispano-marocain et sicilo-tinisien aux temps acheuléens, *L'Anthropologie* 79, 399-436, Paris.

Antunes, M.T.,
J.L. Cardoso,
M. Faure

1988 Présence de *Hippopotamus incognitus* au Portugal et Remarques sur les Sites Quaternaires de Mealhada, *Comunicaçöes dos Serviços Geológicos de Portugal* 74, 165-172, Lisboa.

Arnaïz, M.A.

1990 Las ocupaciones de San Quirce del rio Pisuerga; reflexiones sobre la occupación del espacio y sus implicaciones, *Bol. Sem. de Arte y Arqueologia de la Univ. de Valladolid* LVI, 25-37.

Arsuaga, J.L.,
J.M. Bermudez De Castro

1984 Estudio de los restos humanos del yacimiento de la Cova del Tossal de la Font (Villa-famés, Casrellón), *Cuadernos de Prehist. y Arqueol. Castellonense* 10, 18-34, Diputación Provincial de Castellón.

Barroso, C.,
J.J. Durán,
F. Medina,
A. Morgado

1993 El glacis-terraza de Aljaima (Málaga) y su indústria achelense, *El Cuaternario en España y Portugal* 1, 389-397, ed. ITGM and AEQUA, Madrid.

Biberson, P.

1961 Le Paléolithique inférieur du Maroc atlantique, *Publ. des Services des Antiquités du Maroc*, fasc. 17, Rabat.

Bordes, F.

1971 Observations sur l'Acheuléen des grottes en Dordogne, *Munibe* 23, 5-23.

Bordes, F.,
Cl. Viguier

1969 Présence de galets taillés de type ancien dans la région de Carmona (Sevilla, Espagne), *Comptes r. de l'Académie des Sciences de Paris*, 269 (D), 1946-1947.

Bordes, F.,
Cl. Thibault

1977 Thoughts on the initial Adaptation of Hominids to European Glacial Climates, *Quaternary Research* 8, 115-127.

Botella, M.C.,
J.A. Vera,
J. Porta

1975 El yacimiento achelense de Solana del Zamborino, Fonelas (Granada), *Cuadernos de Prehistoria de la Universidad de Granada* 1, 1-46.

Breuil, H.,
G. Zbyszewski

1942-45 Contribution à l'étude des industries paléolithiques du Portugal et de leurs rapports avec la géologie du Quaternaire, *Comunicaçöes dos Serviços Geológicos de Portugal* 23 and 26, Lisboa.

Cano Pan, J.A.

1991 *Las industrias líticas talladas en la costa de la Guardia a Baiona*, Diputación Provincial de A Coruña.

Carbonell, E.,
J. Canal,
N. Sabchiz

1978 El Achelense superior de Puig d'Escalts, La Selva (Gerona), *Cuadernos de Prehist. y Arqueol. Castellonense* 5, 5-29.

Carbonell, E. 1979 Resultados preliminares de los trabajos efectuados en el yacimiento del Pleistoceno médio de 'Cau d'en Borrás' (Oropesa, Castellón), *Cuadernos de Prehist. y Arqueol. Castellonense* 6, 7-17, Castellón la Plana.

1982 Cueva Victoria (Murcia, España): lugar de ocupación humana más antiguo de la Península ibérica, *Endins* 8, 47-57, Palma de Mallorca.

1992 Excursion al los yacimientos mesopleistocenicos de la Sierra de Atapuerca, *1st International Meeting on Technical systems to Configure Lithic Objets of Scarce Elaboration*, 28-65, Tarragona.

Cunha-Ribeiro, J.P. 1990/91 Intervençäo arqueológica na estaçäo acheulense da Quinta do Cónego/Pousias, *Portugália*, nova série, XI-XII, 7-26, Inst. da Arqueologia, FLUP, Porto.

1992 O Paleolítico no vale do rio Lis, *Revista da Faculdade de Letras* IX(II), 401-462, Porto.

1992/93 Contribuiçäo para o estudo do Paleolítico do vale do rio Lis no seu contexto cronoestratigráfico, *Portugália*, nova série, XIII-XIV, 7-137, Inst. da Arqueologia, FLUP, Porto.

Diaz Del Olmo, F. et allia 1989 Terrazas pleistocenas del Guadalquivir occidental: geomorfología, suelos, paleosuelos y secuencia cultural. In: *El Cuaternario en Andalucía occidental*, 27-31, Sevilla: AEQUA.

1993 Cuaternário y sequencia paleolítica en las terrazas del bajo y medio Guadalquivir: aluvionamientos, coluviones, suelos y paleosuelos, *VI Jornadas de Arqueología Andaluza*, Junta de Andalucia, Huelva.

Feio, M. 1946 Os terraços do Guadiana a jusante do Ardila, *Comunicaçöes dos Serviços Geológicos de Portugal* XXVII, 3-83, Lisboa.

Fernandez Peris, J. 1990 *El Paleolítico inferior en el País Valenciano*, Univ. de Valencia (thesis).

G.E.P.P. 1977 O estudo do Paleolítico da área do Ródäo, *O Arqueólogo Português*, serie 3, 7-9, 31-47.

Gibert, J. 1985 Venta Micena: un dels jaciments humans mes antics d'Europa, *Tribuna dy arqueologia* 1983-84, 53-58, Barcelona: Direcció Gen. Patrimoni Aristic.

Giles Pacheco, F., A. Santiago, J.M. Gutiérrez, E. Mata L. Aguilera 1989 El poblamiento paleolítico en el valle del rio Guadalete, *El Cuaternário en Andalucia occidental*, 43-57, AEQUA, Sevilla.

Giles Pacheco, F., J.M. Gutiérrez López, A. Santiago Pérz, E. Mata Almonte, Aguilera Rodríguez 1992 Sequência paleolítica del valle del Guadalete: primeros resultados, *Arqueologia* 135, 16-26, Madrid.

1993 El Paleolítico Inferior de la Laguna Medina (Jerez de la Frontera, Cadiz), *El Cuaternario en España y Portugal* 1, 463-473, ed. ITGM and AEQUA, Madrid.

Gusi Jener, F., E. Carbonell Roura, J. Estevez Escalera, R. Mora, J. Maateu Bellés, R. Yll 1983 Avance preliminar sobre el yacimiento del Pleistoceno medio de la Cova del Tossal de la Font (Villafamés, Castellón), *Cuad. de Prehist. y Arqueol. Castellonense* 7 (1980), 7-29, Castellón la Plana.

Lautensach, H. 1967 *Geografía de España y Portugal*, ed. Vicens Vives, Barcelona.

Lumley-Woodyear, H. de   1971   Le Paléolithique inférieur et moyen du Midi méditerranéen dans son cadre géologique. t. II, Bas-Languedoc, Roussillon, Catalogne, *Gallia-Préhistoire* V suppl., Paris.

Martïn-Penela, A.   1987   *Paleontología de los grandes mamíferos del yacimiento achelense de la Solana del Zamborino (Fonelas, Granada)*, Granada University (thesis).

Meireles, J.   1986   Problemas e perspectivas do Quaternário do litoral minhoto a norte do rio Lima, *Cadernos de Arqueologia* II(3), 11-147.

Molina, E.   1991   *Geomorfología y geoquímica del paisaje*, Univ. de Salamanca.

Pérez Gonzalez, A.   1982   *Neógeno y Cuaternario de la Llanura manchega y sus relaciones con la cuenca del Tajo*, Univ. Complutense de Madrid (thesis).

                             1982a   El Cuaternario de la región central de la cuenca del Duero, *Actas I Reunión sobre Geología de la Cuenca del Duero* II, 717-740, Inst. Geol. y Minero, Madrid.

Pérez Gonzalez, A.,   1982   Quaternary History of Major River Valleys of the Castilian Basins - Central Spain,
    M. Santonja,   *XI INQUA Congress Abstracts* II, 243, Moscovo.
    J. Gallardo

Querol, M.A.,   1979   El yacimiento achelense de Pinedo (Toledo), *Exc. Arqueol. en España* 106, Madrid,
    M. Santonja   Ministerio de Cultura.

                             1983   El yacimiento de cantos trabajados de El Aculadero (Puerto de Santa Maria, Cádiz), *Exc. Arqueol. en España* 130, Madrid, Ministerio de Cultura.

Raposo, L.   1985   Le Paléolithique inférieur archaique au Portugal: bilan des connaisssances, *Bull. de la Société Préhistorique Française* 82 (6), 173-182.

                             1987   Os mais antigos vestígios de ocupaçäo humana paleolítica na regiäo de Ródäo, *Da Pré-História à História (volume de Homenagem a Octávio da Veiga Ferreira)*, 153-178, ed. Delta, Lisboa.

Raposo, L.,   1985   A estaçäo acheulense final de Milharós, Vale do Forno, Alpiarça, *Actas da I Reuniäo do
    J.R. Carreira,   Quaternário Ibérico* 2, 79-90.
    M. Salvador

Raposo, L.   1993   L'Acheuléen dans la vallée du Tage, au Portugal, *Publ. du CERP* 4, Univ. des Sciences et Technologies de Lille (in press).

                             1993a   O Acheulense no vale do Tejo, em território português, *Arqueologia e História* X(III), 15-41, Lisboa.

Raposo, L.,   1986   Acerca da existência de complexos industriais pré-acheulenses no território português,
    J.R. Carreira   *O Arqueólogo Português*, 4Ą(4), 7-90, Lisboa.

Rodriguez Asensio, J.A.   1983   La presencia humana más antigua en Asturias. El Paleolítico inferior y medio, *Estudios de Arqueol. Asturiana* 2, Fund. Pública de Cuevas y Yacimientos Prehistoricos de Asturias, Oviedo.

Roebroeks, W.   1994   Updating the Earliest Occupation of Europe, *Current Anthropology* 35, 301-305.

Rolland, N.   1992   The Palaeolithic colonization of Europe: An archaeological and biogeographic perspective, *Trabajos de Prehistoria* 49, 69-111.

Ruiz Bustos, A.,   1976   Le site prehistorique nouveau de Cúllar-Baza I (Grenade, Espagne), d'age Pleistocene
    J. Michaux   moyen. Étude préliminaire et analyse de la faune de Rongeurs, *Geologie Mediterrannée* III-3, 173-182.

Santonja, M.   1981   Características generales del Paleolítico inferior de la Meseta española, *Numantia* I, 9-64.

1985   El yacimiento achelense de El Sartalejo (valle del Alagón, Cáceres). Estudio preliminar, *Series de Arqueologis Extremeña* 2, 1-109, Univ. de Extremadura, Cáceres.

1992   *La adaptación al medio en el Paleolítico inferior de la Península ibérica. Elementos para una reflexión, Elefantes, ciervos y ovicaprinos*, 37-76, ed. A. Moure Romanillo, Univ. de Cantabria, Santader.

1994   El Paleolítico inferior en la Submeseta norte y en al entorno de Atapuerca. Balance de los conocimientos en 1992, *Evolución humana en Europa y los yacimientos de la Sierra de Atapuerca*, vol. 2, 421-444, Junta de Castilla y Léon.

Santonja, M.,   1980   *Las industrias achelenses en la región de Madrid, Ocupationes achelenses en el valle del*
A. Querol   *Jarama*. In: M. Santonja *et al.* (eds), Publ. de la Diputatión Provincial, Madrid.

1982   *Industrias del Paleolítico inferior arcaico en la Meseta española*, Homenage a Fernández-Chicarro, Madrid, 18-24, Ministerio de Cultura.

Santonja, M.,   1984   Las industrias paleolíticas de La Maya I en su âmbito regional, *Excav. Arqueol. en*
A. Pérez Gonzales   *España* 135, Madrid, Ministerio de Cultura.

Santonja, M.,   1990   The Lower Paleolithic of Spain and Portugal, *Journal of World Prehistory* 4 (1), 45-94.
P. Villa

Santonja, M.,   1992   Cuesta de la Bajada (Teruel). Nuevo sítio Paleolítico inferior, *Bul. del Seminario de*
E. Moissenet,   *Estudios de Arte y Arqueologia*, LVIII, 25-45, Univ. de Valladolid.
A. Perez Gonzalez

Utrilla, P.   1984   *El Paleolítico en el curso medio del rio Ebro, Calahorra y su entorno, Calahorra*, Bimilenario de su fundación, Madrid, Ministerio de Cultura.

Vega Toscano, L.-G.   1989   Ocupaciones humanas en el Pleistoceno de la Depresión Guadix-Baza: elementos de discusión. In: M.T. Alberdi and F.P. Bonadona (eds), *Geologia y Paleontologia de la Cuenca de Guadix-Baza*, Trabajos Neógeno-Cuaternario 11, 327-345, Museo de Ciências Naturales, Madrid, C.S.I.C.

Zazo, C.,   1985   Paleogeografía de la desembocadura del Guadalquivir al comienzo del Cuaternario,
J.L. Goy,   *Actas de la 1 Reunión del Cuaternario Ibérico*, vol. 1, 461-472.
C.J. Dabrio,
J. Civis,
J. Baena

Zbyszewski, G.   1946   Étude Géologique de la Région d'Alpiarça, *Comunicaçöes dos Serviços Geológicos de Portugal* XXVII, 145-267, Lisboa.

Luis Raposo
Museu Nacional de Arqueologia
Praça do Império
1400 Lisboa
Portugal

Manuel Santonja
Museo de Salamanca
Patio de Escuelas, 2
37008 Salamanca
España

Margherita Mussi

2   The earliest occupation of Europe: Italy

This paper reviews various aspects of the rich Lower Palaeolithic record of Italy, where human groups were certainly living by about 500 to 600 Kyr BP; the evidence for an earlier occupation is not compelling yet. Open and composite environments were favoured by the first inhabitants, whose artefacts are found associated with animal bones at several sites, though unambiguous evidence for human involvement with these faunas is rare. Part of the Italian "Lower Palaeolithic success" might be related to the richness and the variety of environments.

1.   Introduction

Italy is known to have a significant Lower Palaeolithic record (Fig. 1) (Mussi 1992). In this paper, we will examine the overall site preservation, and present a survey of key sites. Then controversial aspects of dating will be discussed, palaeoenvironments characterised, and the evidence related to subsistence, as well as to some aspects of lithic typology and technology, will be commented upon. Minor sites, or sites which are just poorly dated, will also be taken into account. In our conclusions, we will consider Italy in a broader perspective, and put forward some hypothesis on the causes favouring an early settlement in the area.

Not including the many uncontrolled surface collections, some 40 sites are claimed to be as early as, or earlier than, OIS 9: that is, they are approximately more than 300 Kyr old. We will not discuss here what such a "site" is: it is enough to remember that they range from Valchetta Cartoni, with two flake implements, to Venosa or Isernia, where multi-layered deposits are currently excavated over areas of hundreds of square metres.

The chronology is based on different sets of evidence, such as radiometric dates, palaeomagnetism, geo-stratigraphical correlations and evolutionary characteristics of associated faunas. In this respect, we will not take into account references to technological or typological characteristics of the industries, often leading to seriations from supposedly more archaic to more evolved industries.

Radiometric dates are available at several sites, because of the many volcanoes which have been active during the Pliocene and the Pleistocene (Fig. 2). This is in turn related to the intense tectonic activity from the late Miocene onwards, when the Apennines started to raise from the previous shallow sea (Cremaschi and Chiesa 1992). The orogenesis of the Apennines, which are the backbone of the peninsula and continue into Sicily, is also relevant to archaeology for another reason: while their eastern edge experienced compressive tectonics, resulting in an alternation of deepened basins and uplifted areas, their western edge experienced distensive tectonics, which later on led to the formation of fluvio-lacustrine basins which, as at Isernia, Venosa, Anagni, attracted herds of herbivores and their predators, and human groups as well (Fig. 3). Bone preservation is often good in such environments, which accounts for an important part of the archaeological record.

Palaeomagnetic determinations are often attempted. However, even when this method is feasible and appropriate, specific determinations are meaningful only if fitted into a complete sequence of events of known chronology (see Aitken, this volume) – which is not always the case for archaeological sites.

Geo-stratigraphic correlations must take into account the geographical peculiarities of Italy. The elongated and narrow peninsula and the islands have almost 9000 km of coasts, and fluvial systems of limited extent: the Po, which is by far the major river, is 652 km long, while there are dozens of rivers in the range of 100 km long. A large part of the geomorphological and sedimentary processes is consequently directly linked to sea level fluctuations. Correlations with isotopic stages are appropriate and more significant than in fully continental parts of Europe. However, the "marine control" of the sedimentation is a problem in itself: inland, extensive erosion surfaces develop as a consequence of falling sea-levels. Any geo-chrono-logical scheme includes a full set of erosional phases, correlated to the glacial ones, contrasting with interglacial deposition periods (see for instance Ambrosetti *et al.* 1972). It is no surprise that the archaeological record is much biased towards warm climatic phases, and odd-numbered isotopic stages, when sediments were deposited, not eroded. The gaps can be filled where natural "sedimentary traps" occur, such as caves and tectonically controlled basins.

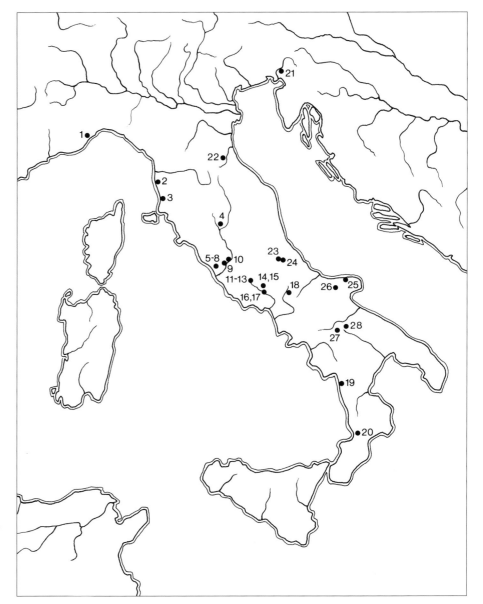

Fig. 1. Site location. 1: Gr. del Colombo; 2: Collinaia; 3: Bibbona; 4: Monte Peglia; 5: Torre in Pietra; 6: Castel di Guido; 7: La Polledrara; 8: Malagrotta; 9: Valchetta Cartoni; 10: Riano; 11: Fontana Ranuccio; 12: Colle Marino; 13: Nocicchio; 14: Arce; 15: Fontana Liri; 16: Castro dei Volsci; 17: Cava Pompi; 18: Isernia La Pineta; 19: Rosaneto; 20: Casella di Maida; 21: Visogliano; 22: Monte Poggiolo; 23: Le Svolte; 24: Valle Giumentina; 25: Foce del Torrente Romandato; 26: Grotta Paglicci (Rip. esterno); 27: Atella; 28: Venosa Loreto, Venosa Notarchirico.

As the many intra-Apennine basins have preserved an extensive array of faunal assemblages, a widely used biochronology has been worked out, which is mainly based on the larger mammals. It is also used at archaeological sites, if bones are preserved. However, large mammal evolution is rather slow, and does not allow high chronological resolution. Furthermore, it is a relative time-scale, which must be anchored to absolute chronology by dated reference assemblages. Any change in the age of the latter ones has consequences on a large number of occurrences and can lead to a re-interpretation of a whole sequence (see Roebroeks and Van Kolfschoten, this volume).

2.   Key sites

The sites which have been more accurately dated form a reference grid for many others. We will briefly describe and discuss the more relevant ones.

2.1.   MONTE POGGIOLO (ROMAGNA)

Monte Poggiolo, between Bologna and Rimini, is situated at an altitude of 200 m above sea level, some 40 km away from the modern Adriatic shores (Antoniazzi *et al.* 1984; Antoniazzi *et al.* 1988; Antoniazzi *et al.* 1993; Peretto 1992). However, it is assumed that when people settled there for the first time the coast was nearer and the Po valley still a gulf of the sea.

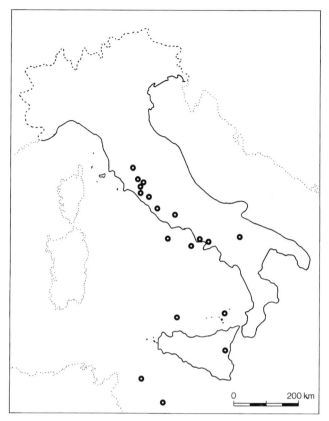

Fig. 2. The volcanoes (circles) active during the Pleistocene.

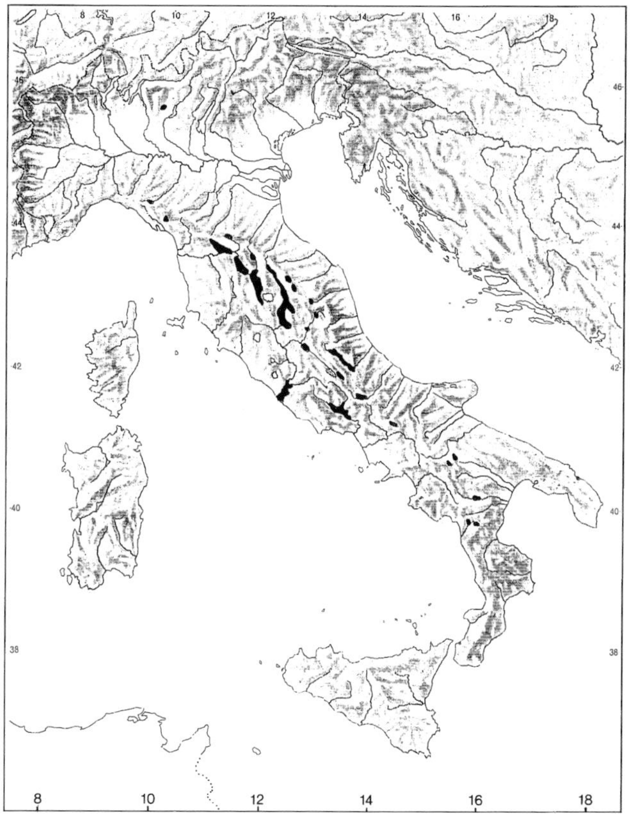

Fig. 3. Pleistocene fluvio-lacustrine basins (after Desio 1973, Fig. 176, with modifications).

At the base of the local sequence, there are marine clays, the "Argille Azzurre", 1.4-1.3 Myr old. The archaeological remains are included in the overlaying gravels of a deltaic deposit. In a single level of the latter one (lev. 107), remnants of negative palaeomagnetism were preserved. This was interpreted as meaning that the deposit is pre-Brunhes, and therefore more than 0.73 Myr old.

The deltaic gravels have been correlated with part of a sandy deposit called "Sabbie Gialle", a marker in the regional geological sequence. After the malacological assemblage found at its base, the palaeomagnetic sequence worked out in it, and two ESR dates on quartzite grains heated by exposure to sun light, an age in the range of 1 Myr has been put forward for the "Sabbie Gialle" and, consequently, for the archaeological site in the deltaic deposit.

No bones are preserved. Some 4000 lithic implements, fresh or slightly patinated, were retrieved by surface collection. They are quite small in size as flint pebbles usually less than 10 cm long were used. This assemblage includes 220 retouched flake tools – mostly notches, denticulates and side scrapers. A substantial number of core

tools is described as unifacial as well as bifacial chopping-tools. Two polyhedrons and two "protohandaxes" are also recorded. There are also hundreds of pebbles from which only a single flake was struck.

Regular excavations, down to 4 m below datum, furthermore yielded 1166 flake implements, and 153 core implements, most of them from the upper part of the stratigraphic sequence. The retouched tools are just 12: 5 scrapers and 7 denticulates, while no clear-cut distinction was possible between cores and chopping-tools. About 2/3 of the flakes are totally or partially cortical, with plain or cortical butts, and most of the cores have just one striking platform. It seems that most of the activity on this peculiar spot was related to rather expedient knapping of the locally available pebbles.

Other sites with a similar industry and in the same general setting have been found in the area, but not fully investigated.

2.2.   ISERNIA LA PINETA (MOLISE)

Isernia is located further south, more or less in the centre of the peninsula (Bahain 1993; Coltorti et al. 1982;

Cremaschi and Peretto 1988a; Giusberti and Peretto 1991; Peretto 1991; Peretto *et al.* 1983). The archaeological deposit extends with a varying density over an estimated area of more than 30,000 square metres. Three separate archaeological layers were investigated at first, which are believed to be close in time. Excavations were undertaken in two different if nearby areas, *settori* or "sectors". In *settore* I there are two archaeological layers – t.3c, the earliest, followed by t.3a. In *settore* II there is only one layer – also named t.3a – which is the most recent one of the sequence. Therefore, from the earliest to the latest, we have: Sett. I t.3c, Sett. I t.3a, Sett. II t.3a. A further archaeological horizon has recently been discovered in a stratigraphical position in between the levels already known (Anconetani *et al.* 1992). The most spectacular layer is Sett. I t.3a, which is an astonishing accumulation of faunal remains (mostly bison, rhino and elephant bones) and lithic implements. The archaeological levels are sandwiched between the final deposits of a series of lacustrine origin and fluvial deposits.

The following animal species were found, mostly in "Sett.I t.3a", but without major differences between one archaeological layer and the next, the bison being the most frequent animal: *Panthera leo fossilis* (a single tooth), *Ursus* cfr. *deningeri*, *Elephas antiquus*, *Stephanorhinus hemitoechus*, *Hippopotamus amphibius*, *Sus scrofa*, *Megaceros* sp., *Dama* sp., Cervidae, *Bison schoetensacki*, *Hemitragus* cfr. *bonali*, *Lepus* sp. Several rodent species were also recognised: *Pliomys episcopalis*, *P. lenki*, *P.* cfr. *lenki*, *Clethrionomys* sp., *Arvicola mosbachensis* (= *Arvicola terrestris cantiana*), *Microtus arvalis*/*M. agrestis*, *M. brecciensis*, *Pitymys* sp.

Well over 10,000 lithic implements have been collected during excavations. The industry is quite similar in the various layers, except for the lack of pebble tools in "Sett. II t.3a", where there is also a very limited amount of bones. The raw material was available next to the site. Flint is mostly of poor quality, and splits following natural fissures. Many of the implements are accordingly difficult to recognise, and it cannot be said if they are, or not, broken parts of once larger ones. Limestone pebbles were also easily located in the surroundings, and used for chopping-tools.

A detailed description is available for the industry of "Sett. II t.3a" where, as said, there are no pebble tools. 40% of tools are on "nucleiform" supports, i.e. exhausted cores and *plaquettes*, and fragments of them. Not considering occasional retouches, half of them are classified as borers, with many varieties, including "monolateral" ones – i.e. implements with retouches or notches adjacent to fractures, butts etc... Next come the denticulates (32.6%), and then the endscrapers (7.1%).

The absolute age of the archaeological deposit was worked out through different methods. They include K/Ar on sanidine crystals from the alluvial deposit covering "Sett. I t.3a" – and accordingly in a reworked position – which was dated to 736 ± 4 Kyr BP. Other samples, from different if correlated deposits, stratigraphically overlying the Palaeolithic level, were consistently dated to 680 ± 6 Kyr BP and 730 ± 7 Kyr BP. Higher up in the sequence the results are in the range of 500 Kyr BP.

Seven samples, i.e. elephant, rhino and bear teeth from the archaeological layer, were dated by aminoacid racemization, and found to be 550 ± 140 Kyr old, with a mean value of 545 Kyr BP. Five teeth of elephant, rhino and bison, had an ESR age in the range of 150-100 Kyr BP. Preliminary palaeomagnetic investigations point to inverted polarity. Taking into account the radiometric date of 730 Kyr BP, the site was assigned to a time close to the Matuyama-Brunhes transition.

2.3. VENOSA (BASILICATA)

Venosa is located in southern Italy, within the Apennines. After recent research, the basin of Venosa is a depositional surface of late Pliocene age, eroded during the Early Pleistocene by local streams into a long and narrow valley, 100 m deep (Lefèvre *et al.* 1993a; Soprintendenza Speciale al Museo Nazionale Preistorico Etnografico "L. Pigorini" 1991). Around the transition between the Early and the Middle Pleistocene, the effusive activity of M. Vulture, a volcano distant some 20 km, produced large amounts of sediments that the streams were unable to carry away. The hydrogeological balance was much altered. As a consequence, while the volcanic activity continued, shallow lakes and marshes developed over an area of approximately 50 by 3 km. The depression was progressively filled up by 30 to 50 m of sediments. The latter were eventually eroded after new tectonic activity during the Late Pleistocene and are now found as terraced remnants.

There are several important sites in the Venosa Basin. We will consider here the sequences found in two nearby localities, *Loreto* and *Notarchirico*. They were excavated at different times by different teams, and it is not yet possible to correlate accurately the two of them, which present quite distinct sequences.

Venosa - Loreto

A stratigraphic sequence of 30 m, including 42 levels, was described from this site (Baïssas 1980; Barral and Simone 1983). Archaeological remains were found in lev. 21 (=A), lev. 18 (=B), and lev. 3 (=C) (Fig. 4). We will not further consider level C, which is later and outside our chronological range. Most of the research concentrated on layer A, 40 to 60 cm thick, which was excavated over 25 square metres.

After Baïssas (1980), at Loreto there is an excellent and most complete palaeomagnetic sequence. The Matuyama-Brunhes boundary was located in levels 38-37, the Levantin event in levels 9-8, and the Jamaica event in levels 4-2. After sedimentological analyses, he also identified a sequence of 8 cold episodes, alternating with milder ones. He eventually correlates occupation layer A with OIS 13, and occupation layer B with OIS 11.

Faunal remains are abundant, if very fragmented. In a preliminary study of the fauna, M-F. Bonifay (1977) recognised several archaic, i.e. Villafranchian, species. A revision of the fauna, however, ruled out their presence (Alberdi *et al.* 1988; Angelelli *et al.* 1978; Caloi and Palombo 1979; Caloi and Palombo 1980). The many horse remains are now identified as belonging to *Equus* aff. *süssenbornensis* and *Equus altidens*. The bovids are *Bos primigenius* and an archaic bison, i.e. *Bison schoetensacki* cfr. *voigtstedtensis*. There is a canid with many affinities with jackal. Hippos, elephants, several rhinos, many deer and a few bears are also present.

The many flake implements are mostly of flint, often of poor quality (Crovetto 1991). Denticulates made by adjacent clactonian notches form 45% of the retouched flakes, denticulates made with continuous retouch 22%, notches 19%, scrapers 9%, piercers 6% (Fig. 5).

Unifacial chopping-tools were flaked from limestone or silicious limestone pebbles. There is a single amygdaloid handaxe, of flint, and many broken pebbles.

The revised faunal analysis underlines chronological problems. After Alberdi *et al.* (1988), the equid association is relatively archaic, and would indicate an early Middle Pleistocene age. This is in contrast with an attribution to OIS 13 or 11, and to an age in the range of 500 to 450 Kyr BP, i.e. almost identical to Fontana Ranuccio (see below), where the fauna is much more modern. Furthermore the bison is less evolved at Loreto than at Isernia, while the rhinoceros is relatively primitive (Caloi and Palombo 1980).

Venosa-Notarchirico

In this area more than 500 square metres have been excavated (Belli *et al.* 1991; Cassoli *et al.* 1993; Lefèvre *et al.* 1993b; Piperno *et al.* 1990; Soprintendenza Speciale al Museo Nazionale Preistorico Etnografico "L. Pigorini" 1991). Twelve levels were found in a stratigraphic sequence of 7 m. Each is separated from the other by 10 to 100 cm of sterile deposit. Most of the bone remains belong to *Elephas antiquus* and to Cervids (*Dama clactoniana* and *Megaceros solilhacus*), followed by *Bos* sp. and *Bison schoetensacki*.

After a preliminary analysis, lithic technology and typology are rather similar in levels A, B, C, D, F, G and H. Pebble tools, of limestone and silicious limestone, are

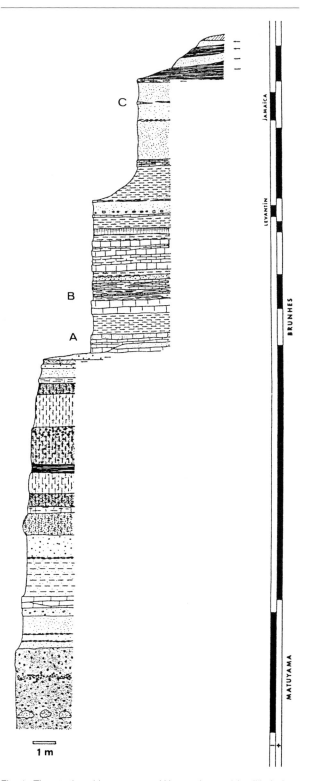

1 m

Fig. 4. The stratigraphic sequence of Venosa-Loreto (simplified after Barral and Simone 1983).

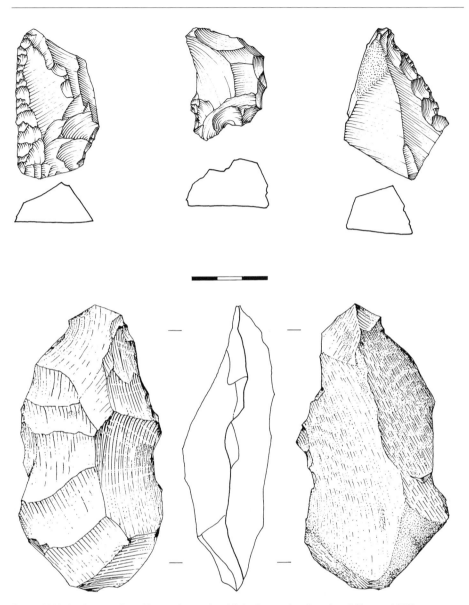

Fig. 5. Lithic implements from Venosa-Loreto level A (redrawn after Barral and Simone 1983). Scale in cm.

predominant: there are mostly chopping-tools, and some *rabots* and thick endscrapers as well. Many pebbles are just broken. There are a few flint and quartzite handaxes, rather thick and with sinuous edges. Flake tools, in a limited number, are usually quite small. Butts are plain and wide.

In levels Alfa, E and E1, on the opposite, retouched and unretouched flakes are predominant, and flint is the most frequent raw material. The associated pebble tools are of limestone. So far, handaxes have not been retrieved.

Absolute dating was attempted using several methods. A level of pyroclastic sands capping the whole archaeological sequence was dated by TL on quartz crystals to 260 ±40 Kyr BP. A human bone, found 15 cm above level Alfa was dated by U/Th, U/Pa, and Pa/Th: the average age is 359 +154/-97 Kyr. A *Bos primigenius* tooth from level Alfa was dated by isoleucine epimerization, with a resulting age of 500 Kyr ±25-30%. Another pyroclastic sand level, overlying one of the lowermost layers, i.e. level F, was dated by TL on quartz crystals to 753±60 Kyr BP.

The micromammals from level E1, however, just above this volcanic level, are indicative of a substantially later age: the assemblage of *Apodemus* sp., *Pliomys episcopalis, Arvicola terrestris, Microtus* gr. *arvalis-agrestis, Microtus nivalis, Microtus (Terricola)* sp., suggests, after Sala (1989), a climate cooler and moister than today, and an age in the middle part of the Middle Pleistocene.

2.4.   FONTANA RANUCCIO (LAZIO)

Fontana Ranuccio is another open-air site in the inner part of the peninsula, at some 60 km southeast of Rome, and excavated over about 60 square metres (Fig. 6). As the area is a volcanic one, K/Ar dating was possible (Biddittu *et al.* 1979; Biddittu and Segre 1982; Biddittu and Segre 1984; Gatti 1993; Segre and Ascenzi 1984; Segre *et al.* 1987). The only archaeological level was found to be 458 ± 5.7 Kyr old. This date is bracketed by a determination of 366 ± 4.5 Kyr BP higher up in the stratigraphic sequence, and by 487 ± 7.5 Kyr BP at a lower level. Caloi and Palombo (1986), in a thorough review of faunas from Latium, correlate the faunal assemblage, which points to a temperate and rather open environment with OIS 11.

The following species were determined in the faunal assemblage: *Cuon* cfr. *alpinus, Ursus deningeri, Panthera leo spelaea, Elephas antiquus, Equus* cfr. *mosbachensis, Stephanorhinus hemitoechus, Hippopotamus* cfr. *amphibius, Sus scrofa ferus, Megaceros* cfr. *verticornis, Dama clactoniana, Cervus elaphus, Capreolus capreolus, Bos primigenius, Bison* sp.

The lithic industry is not abundant, with scrapers, notches and denticulates on tiny flakes (Fig. 7). Flint and lava were used as raw materials. Five handaxes and a chopping tool were also found. There are also bones with reportedly retouched edges, including bone handaxes, interpreted as the result of the scarcity of good lithic raw material.

2.5.   THE SITES OF VIA AURELIA (LAZIO)

In the surroundings of Rome, a group of sites clusters along the coast in the vicinity of the Roman Via Aurelia. They are included in deposits known as the "Formazione Aurelia" or "Aurelian Formation" (Conato *et al.* 1980) (Fig. 8). The Aurelian Formation is later than the rolled fragments of volcanites included in it: the latter are the

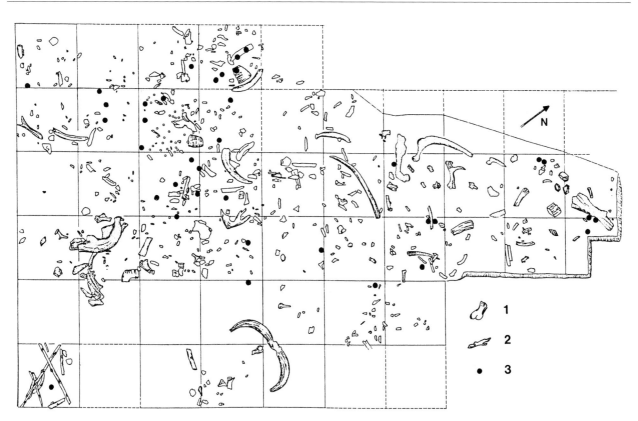

Fig. 6. The archaeological deposit at Fontana Ranuccio, grid in square metres (after Gatti 1993, with modifications). 1: bone fragment, 2: wood fragment, 3: stone artefact.

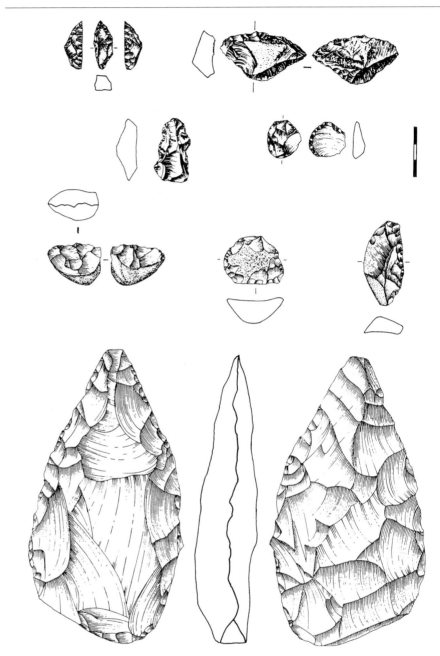

Fig. 7. Lithic industry from Fontana Ranuccio (after Biddittu and Segre 1984, and Gatti 1993). Scale in cm.

"tufo rosso a scorie nere", now dated to 442 ± 7 Kyr BP, and the "tufo litoide", with an age close to 366 ± 4.5 Kyr BP (Fornaseri 1985). The Aurelian Formation was directly dated by ESR on *Glycimeris* shells at 320-305 Kyr BP (Radtke *et al*. 1981). As a whole, it is correlated with OIS 9 (Caloi and Palombo 1986).

Torre in Pietra

Some 200 square metres have been excavated at "Torre del Pagliaccetto", in the territory of Torre in Pietra. Acheulean implements were found at the base of the series belonging to the Formazione Aurelia, and referred to as from "level m" (Malatesta 1978). This level includes

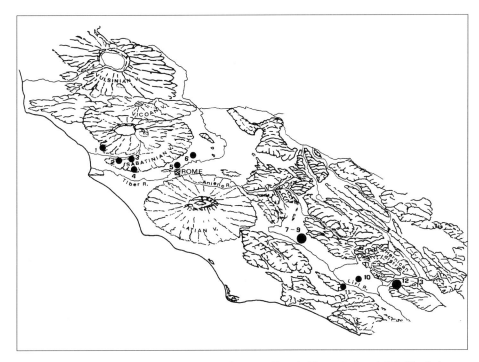

Fig. 8. The sites in the volcanic surroundings of Rome. 1: Torre in Pietra; 2: Castel di Guido; 3: La Polledrara; 4: Malagrotta; 5: Valchetta Cartoni; 6: Riano; 7: Fontana Ranuccio; 8: Colle Marino; 9: Nocicchio; 10: Cava Pompi; 11: Castro dei Volsci; 12: Arce; 13: Fontana Liri. The coast is approximately 200 km long, as the crow flies. (Modified after an original drawing by M.Parotto).

elements of a redeposited volcanic tuff known as "tufo rosso a scorie nere" (see above). It was first dated in a pioneering work by Evernden and Curtis (1965), who erroneously gave the Acheulean deposit an age close to the one of the volcanic elements: the archaeological layer is actually substantially later (see above).

The Acheulean level is not a living floor: it formed through the redeposition of eroded remnants of one or more sites. Most of the faunal assemblage consists of horse, red deer, aurochs and elephant, with some rhino bones and sporadic carnivores, including lion.

Small pebbles of limestone, silicious limestone and flint were used to make artefacts (Piperno and Biddittu 1978). Retouched tools number 173, and include 51 handaxes, 24 chopping- tools, 38 scrapers (mostly simple side scrapers), 12 notches, 10 denticulates, retouched flakes and a few borers, naturally backed knives and endscrapers.

Castel di Guido

An extensive palaeosurface with Acheulean industry has been excavated in two different if close areas, over some 350 square metres altogether (Anzidei and Sebastiani 1984; Boschian 1993; Mallegni et al. 1983; Radmilli 1984). Archaeological remains are mostly concentrated within an

erosion channel, some 20 m wide and a few m deep. They were covered by a volcanic deposit.

In the excavated material, elephants (often young or immature), horses and aurochsen are the most frequent animal species, followed by deer, while wild boars and bears are quite rare.

Approximately 300 lithic implements were found altogether during excavations. As at La Polledrara (see below), where differential preservation was suggested, they include mostly core tools: monofacial and bifacial chopping-tools, handaxes and split pebbles, all of them in limestone or silicious limestone. Then there is a restricted number of flake tools of flint, most of them being denticulates. No *débitage* was retrieved. Some flaked bones were described as intentionally modified, and include bone handaxes.

La Polledrara

The site is currently under excavation, and more than 350 square metres have been excavated so far (Anzidei *et al.* 1988; Anzidei *et al.* 1989; Anzidei and Arnoldus-Huyzendveld 1992; Anzidei *et al.* in press; Arnoldus-Huyzendveld and Anzidei 1993).

The deposit is a former paludal basin in an essentially flat landscape of lakes, moors and ephemeral streams. One such stream caused the local shallow palaeo-incision, and forming a curve gradually displaced it laterally from east to west. A concentration of large mammal bones and of lithic industry is found on this palaeosurface (Fig. 9).

The stream was too weak to move large skeletal elements, which were left undisturbed and sometimes partially articulated, but it was strong enough to concentrate smaller ones in the deeper part of the basin, or to pile them up on larger remains. Over 6000 animal bones have been discovered so far. There are a dozen or so of elephants, with mature and immature animals, and tusks up to 3.5 m long, and many *Bos primigenius* remains of great size, other species being less abundant.

Some 250 lithic implements were recovered. Small flint pebbles were mostly used, and there are a few larger silicious limestone pebbles. Raw material was possibly difficult to procure, because of the volcanic nature of the area and the consequent lack of flint.

Unretouched flakes are quite small (7-31mm) and present in a very limited amount (12%), probably due to the dynamics of the palaeoenvironment. Most of the tools, including scrapers and denticulates, are core tools, usually on pebbles. They often have more than one retouched edge and multiple tools are frequent.

Scrapers are prevalent. There are several endscrapers, many notches and denticulates, a few burins and piercers, and many chopping-tools. Some flaked bones are possible bone tools.

Dating of aurochsen teeth yielded an age of 450 ±120 Kyr BP by aminoacid racemization, and one of 186 ±45 Kyr BP by ESR. The results are blurred by the high natural radioactivity of the area.

3.   Chronology and chronological problems

A first set of problems lies with sites for which a Early to early Middle Pleistocene age has been claimed.

The earliest Italian site would be Monte Poggiolo. Dating difficulties stem from the effectiveness of the correlation between the "Sabbie Gialle" and the archaeological deposit: an age of 1 Myr and more was put forward for the "Sabbie Gialle", while the latter was not directly dated.

The evidence from Isernia is sounder. However, there are problems with the microfauna, which includes *Arvicola mosbachensis*, a junior synonym of *Arvicola terrestris cantiana*: the latter is an important biostratigraphical marker which is definitely later in age at any other European site (Roebroeks and Van Kolfschoten, this volume; Von Koenigswald and Van Kolfschoten, in press). Furthermore, the bison is more evolved towards modern forms than at Venosa-Loreto, a site supposedly 200 or 300 Kyr later than Isernia (Caloi and Palombo 1980). A later age for this superb site would better fit biostratigraphical correlations.

At Venosa-Notarchirico, an age in excess of 700 Kyr BP for the lowermost part of the sequence would also be quite early, if compared with other Acheulean industries of Europe (see Tuffreau and Antoine, this volume), and this early date still has to be confirmed by further investigations. It is also in contrast with the chronological indications given by the micromammals, which include *Arvicola terrestris*.

The chronology of other supposedly very early sites is much less well assessed. Monte Peglia, in Central Italy, yielded microfaunal assemblages dominated by *Mimomys blanci* and *Allophaiomys* sp. and referred to the Early Biharian (Van der Meulen 1973). Five lithic implements were retrieved out of stratigraphical context, and it is not even proved beyond any doubt that they were actually flaked by humans (Piperno 1972). At Arce and nearby Fontana Liri, south-east of Rome, pebble tools and flakes were picked from deposits devoid of volcanic elements, and therefore assumed to precede the local volcanic activity (Biddittu 1972; Piperno *et al.* 1984) (Fig. 8). The latter, in the so-called Hernican volcanic district, started at 700 ±20 Kyr BP (Fornaseri 1985). The assemblages from Colle Marino and Nocicchio, not far away, also assumed to be older than 700 Kyr, are dated through regional correlations which have been modified several times (Biddittu and Segre 1982; Biddittu *et al.* 1979; Segre *et al.* 1987; Gatti 1993).

Other sites are claimed to be in the range of 500 Kyr BP. At Cava Pompi, in southern Latium again, lithic implements, as well as human and animal bones, were collected and excavated. They are said to be stratigraphically overlain by a basalt flow of c. 400 Kyr BP (Piperno *et al.* 1984). This correlation was never illustrated in any detail. In a previous publication, it was underlined that it was a rather dubious one, for reasons including the distance between the outcrop and the archaeological site (Biddittu and Segre 1978). In the Atella Basin – close to Venosa – an age preceding the activity of the Vulture volcano, i.e. earlier than 500 Kyr BP, is put forward for sites with an Acheulean industry (Borzatti von Löwenstern *et al.* 1990). Unfortunately, there is no detailed geostratigraphical study of the archaeological deposits. On the coast of Tuscany, at Bibbona and Collinaia, collected lithic assemblages were dated to OIS 11, after long-distance and short-distance geostratigraphical correlations (Galiberti 1982; Malatesta and Zarlenga 1988; Sarti and Stoduti 1982). The typological characteristics of the industry, devoid of handaxes, are assumed to date the deposit, and there is no independent clue for absolute chronology.

It is not that the above-mentioned sites cannot be as old as suggested in the literature, but the point is that their chronology is not fully assessed. Many more could be mentioned, including the earliest sites of Sicily and

Fig. 9. Partial view of the excavations at La Polledrara. On the left, an area damaged by ploughing. (Courtesy of the Soprintendenza archeologica di Roma).

Sardinia: lithic series with chopping-tools and flake tools have been collected in Sicily, and assemblages with flake tools only have been excavated in Sardinia (Broglio *et al.* 1992; Martini 1992; Segre *et al.* 1982), but in neither instance is there any sound evidence for their supposed great antiquity.

An age in the range of 600 to 400 Kyr is reasonably supported by the evidence from Venosa-Loreto, part of Venosa-Notarchirico, Fontana Ranuccio, and even the minor site of Valchetta Cartoni in the surroundings of Rome: in 1936 two flakes were located by A.C. Blanc, E. Tongiorgi and H. Breuil below the "tufo rosso at scorie nere", an ignimbrite now dated at 442 ±7 Kyr BP (Blanc 1935-1937; Fornaseri 1985).

Later sites, in the range of 350-300 Kyr BP, are better exemplified by those alongside Via Aurelia, while many more of probably similar age are poorly dated. Some will be mentioned below.

### 4.	Preferred environments

There is some agreement that the many remains of herbivores at several sites must be related to a rather open environment, which provided enough pasture for the herds (Alberdi *et al.* 1988; Boschian 1993; Caloi and Palombo 1978; Sala 1983). However, shrubs and thickets were also growing, and herbivore assemblages do not point to treeless grasslands or steppes. For instance, the ubiquitous *Elephas antiquus* is assumed to have been a forest animal, based on anatomical characteristics including the very long straight tusks, not appropriate for grazing. Tusks 3 to 3.5 m long are

often mentioned, compared with those of modern African elephants which only exceptionally reach 2.5 m (Haynes 1991). It is assumed that it was basically a browser, in good accordance with mounting evidence of the nutritional importance of shrubby and arboreal forage for modern elephants (Haynes 1991).

More circumstantial evidence is available at some sites. At Monte Poggiolo, a rather limited amount of pollen from the archaeological deposit suggests a cool or even cold climate, and open vegetation (Cattani 1992): non-arboreal pollen are dominant, and include steppic elements, while *Pinus* and *Abies* are well represented amongst the trees. The gastropods – with *Cochlodina laminata*, now a mountain species – also point to a rather cold climate.

At Isernia, a sample from the palaeosurface "Sett. I t.3a" includes 80% non-arboreal pollen, Gramineae being dominant. The few arboreal pollen are from *Alnus*, *Salix* cfr. *populus*, *Platanus*, *Pinus*, *Cedrus* and oaks (Accorsi 1985).

Preliminary results are available for the upper part of the sequence of Venosa-Notarchirico, between levels C and Alfa (Soprintendenza Speciale al Museo Nazionale Preistorico Etnografico "L. Pigorini" 1991). The environment was a grassland, with a very limited amount of trees, such as fir, pine, oaks. At Venosa-Notarchirico, the malacological associations from the lowermost archaeological level (level A), are indicative of a rather humid and forested environment, but the pollen point to an arid and warm climate in association with level B, the next human occupation (Durante and Settepassi 1978). The large mammals of level A, however, include many equids, as well as other species of open environment (Alberdi *et al.* 1988): the molluscs are probably indicative of local conditions only.

Some further evidence comes from a cave site, Grotta Paglicci (Riparo esterno) in Apulia (Bartolomei 1980; Mezzena and Palma di Cesnola 1971). The micromammal assemblage, with *Oryctolagus* sp., *Eliomys* sp., *Allocricetus bursae*, *Apodemus* sp., *Microtus dentatus*, *M. brecciensis*, *M. arvalis*, and *Pitymys* sp., is indicative of an arid and steppic landscape. Unfortunately, there is no sound chronological evidence for the archaeological deposit, which yielded some fine bifaces, but an age close to the sites of the Aurelian Formation would be a good estimate. The environment, however, is completely different and possibly glacial (see Final Remarks).

Palaeobotanical investigations have not been carried out in the Acheulean levels of the sites alongside Via Aurelia, while a general reconstruction of the environment is available (Jacobacci 1978; Malatesta 1978; Conato *et al.* 1980; Anzidei *et al.* 1989; Anzidei and Arnoldus-Huyzendveld 1992; Arnoldus Huyzendveld and Anzidei 1993). During OIS 9, the rising sea-level and volcanic activity affected the landscape. The area which was already rather flat became characterised by small depressions and moors filled by the activity of ephemeral meandering streams. Muddy areas were ubiquitous, and alternated with sands and other alluvial deposits, as well as with volcanic deposits. Closer to the coast lagoons developed. The many bodies of water, from fresh to brackish and from stagnant to running, are reflected in the fauna: hippos at Castel di Guido and Malagrotta, a minor site (Cassoli *et al.* 1982) (surface collections only), beavers at Malagrotta, aquatic birds at Torre in Pietra and Malagrotta again.

This densely settled area can be compared with another one, devoid of human occupation during this same time span, i.e. the Riano lake basin, just north of Rome, which is also part of the Aurelian Formation. (Accordi and Maccagno 1962; Ambrosetti *et al.* 1972; Ambrosetti *et al.* 1980; Bonadonna 1965; Follieri 1961-1963; Leonardi and Petronio 1974; Leonardi and Petronio 1976; Maccagno 1962). Based on the count of annual levels in varved diatomites, the little lake was in existence for 15,000 to 20,000 years. It progressively shrank from a maximum initial extension of 650×250 m. Volcanic tuffs embedded in the diatomite deposit were dated to 225 ±60 Kyr BP by K/Ar, and to 280 ±30 Kyr BP by fission tracks. Animal remains were found at different levels, in the basin itself as well as in its immediate surroundings. They include well preserved and still articulated remains of a limited range of species: two almost complete skeletons and a skull of *Elephas antiquus*, fragments of *Stephanorhinus* cfr.

hemitoechus, five complete or partial skeletons of *Cervus elaphus*, a single one of *Dama clactoniana*, and isolated bones.

The flora is known both by pollen analysis, and by the study of macrobotanical remains, as leaves, fruits and seeds were extremely well preserved. It is therefore possible to cross-check the results of different lines of analyses, and to obtain a direct knowledge of the local vegetation. A very dense forest of broad-leaved trees was in existence throughout the stratigraphic sequence, while the grass cover was extremely restricted. The forest was of oceanic-temperate type below the dated tuff level, with much *Carpinus* and *Pterocarya*, and of oceanic cool type above it, with increasing percentages of beech and fir.

As mentioned above, there are so far no archaeological remains from the forests of the Riano basin: a scanty series of lithic artefacts was only collected from the earthy brown tuff which tops the lacustrine diatomitic series (Accordi and Maccagno 1962).

Evidence of settlement in forested environment is found at Visogliano, a karstic depression close to Trieste, where there are also the remains of a collapsed rockshelter. Two stratigraphic sequences (A and B) are known, but their chronological relationships have not been worked out. The age of the deposits is loosely bracketed between 700 and 300 Kyr BP (Cattani *et al.* 1991). Pollen was preserved in some levels only. A broad-leaved forest was in existence, with an association of *Carpinus*, *Fraxinus* and *Quercus* (Cattani 1992; Cattani *et al.* 1991). In the upper part of sequence A, however, which is devoid of pollen, the micromammals are typical of steppes or grasslands (Bartolomei 1980). Anyhow, the archaeological remains are extremely scarce at Visogliano, and point to discontinuous and short-lived occupation there.

As a conclusion, the available evidence suggests that open or composite environments were favoured by the first inhabitants, while densely forested ones were apparently rather avoided. Lacustrine or even marshy basins were looked for, possibly just because gregarious herbivores congregated there to water and to die. However, we must also remember that site preservation is better in such basins, as deposits accumulate rather quickly, so that we cannot rule out the possibility that they are over-represented.

5.   Scavenging and hunting

There is no question that stone tools are found associated with animal bones at several sites. Positive evidence of interaction between humans and animals, however, is rather rare.

At Isernia (Sett. I t.3a), the huge accumulation of bones mainly consists of elephant, rhino and bison remains. According to G. Giusberti *et al.* (1991), the elephant remains include many long bones and tusks, and a more limited amount of teeth, pelves, ribs and vertebrae; bison bones are mostly cranial ones – specially horns – omoplates and iliac bones; rhinos are represented by skulls, teeth and half mandibles. Their conclusions are that the bones were sorted by humans and laid on the ground on purpose. Furthermore, some remains were broken into pieces when fresh, and dislocated over a restricted area (so that refitting is possible). This, too, is said to have been the result of human activity. The general conclusions are that the remains are indicative both of a dwelling structure and of butchering activities.

Positive evidence, however, is scarce. Dwelling structures of Lower Palaeolithic age are problematic, to put it mildly (Farizy 1988-1989), and such an interpretation should be presented in considerable detail, in order to allow the reader to evaluate its merits. As far as butchering is concerned, there is no preserved cut mark (Giusberti and Peretto 1991). Most of the bone surfaces were affected by animal trampling as well as by abrasion by water and sand in a muddy deposit. Artificial breakage scars have been actually detected on a dozen of the thousands of bones of the various levels (Anconetani et al. 1992; Anconetani et al. 1993; Giusberti and Peretto 1991). The selected elements are from bison forequarters. So far, it is safer just to assume that marrow was looked for and consumed.

At Venosa-Loreto level A, bones are generally broken, most of them being herbivore remains. Broken diaphyses sometimes have cut marks and scars left by stone tools which scratched the bone surface. The site is cautiously interpreted as a possible butchering area (Barral and Simone 1983).

At Venosa-Notarchirico, the skull of a young elephant was found turned upside down, with the mandible detached and broken: after it, the area of the discovery was named "Area dell'Elefante", i.e. "Elephant Area". Further parts of the skeleton are expected to lay outside the area so far excavated. Some dozens of handaxes and choppers, and just four flake tools, were in direct contact with the carcass, clearly associated with it. The "Elephant Area" site is interpreted as a probable butchering site (Cassoli et al. 1993).

A taphonomic study of La Polledrara is under way and artificial breakage patterns have been detected (Anzidei et al. in press). As a preliminary hypothesis, it seems that at least part of the animals died a natural death in the small muddy basin and that human beings took advantage of this (Anzidei et al. 1988). Hunting activities are not ruled out: killing weak animals trapped in the mud and scavenging carcasses of dead ones were two possible options.

Some possible butchering marks have been detected on elephant bones of Castel di Guido, but only preliminary observations are available for this site (Boschian 1993).

There is therefore some evidence that, from the first presence onwards, human groups were interacting with animals, taking their share of meat and marrow.

6.   Diversity in lithic tools

We will concentrate on two aspects of lithic technology and typology: the presence or absence of handaxes, and the appearance of the Levallois flaking technique.

Handaxes so far are the only prerequisite to define an Acheulean industry as such. In Africa, industries devoid of handaxes are known to precede Acheulean industries during a period of about one million years. In Europe, as a consequence, Lower Palaeolithic industries without handaxes are usually assumed to be earlier than Acheulean industries. In Italy, the lack of handaxes at sites such as Monte Poggiolo, Isernia, Bibbona, Collinaia, Arce, Colle Marino, Fontana Liri, Casella di Maida as well as in Sicily and Sardinia, has been widely accepted as suggesting a great antiquity. Furthermore, it is often more or less implicitly assumed that handaxes are just more refined chopping-tools, related to the same or similar activities. The archaeological evidence, however, is not that clear-cut.

Monte Poggiolo is an area where raw material was easily available in the form of flint pebbles. Much primary knapping was performed, as it can be seen in the overwhelming ratio of unretouched to retouched flakes, the high amount of cortex on implements and the many cores which are difficult to discriminate from chopping-tools (Antoniazzi et al. 1993). A limited set of activities was going on, and retouched tools were scarcely needed.

At Isernia, too, flint was abundant in the immediate surroundings of the site, but of very poor quality: it is found as small blocks and plaquettes, which are much fissured and split easily, so that it is just impossible to recognise natural from man-made fractures (Ferrari et al. 1991). Limestone pebbles were used for choppers and chopping-tools. Pebble tools, however, are lacking from Sett. II t.3a, excavated over an area of 18 m × 4 m (Ferrari et al. 1991). Interestingly, animal remains, which are usually abundant, are scanty in this part of the deposit.

At Venosa-Notarchirico, industries with and without handaxes are interstratified: bifacial tools are not abundant, and are absent in level Alfa, at the top of the local sequence, and in levels E and E1, in the middle part of it. All levels have been extensively excavated. In the Elephant Area, in close association with the bones, there are many handaxes and choppers, and very few flake tools (Cassoli et al. 1993).

Amongst the sites of the Aurelian Formation, Torre in Pietra, Castel di Guido and Malagrotta yielded handaxes, while these were not found at La Polledrara. Once again, the excavations were extensive, and sampling bias is probably not involved. At La Polledrara elephant skeletons were found partially articulated (Anzidei *et al*. 1989). The bone accumulation cannot be directly compared with the ones from Torre in Pietra and Malagrotta, which are definitely disturbed and possibly redeposited, while only preliminary information is available for Castel di Guido.

The quality of raw material would account, in part or totally, for the lack of handaxes at sites such as Isernia. There is also some suggestion that pebble tools were preferred when large carcasses were available and marrow was to be extracted from heavily-built bones. However, we need further research before understanding the meaning of "handaxe sites" compared with "chopper sites" – the two being usually not exclusive of each other. The only definite evidence is that, in the Italian Lower Palaeolithic, they do not follow each other neatly in any chronological sequence.

Turning to the Levallois technique, "Protolevalloisian" industries, i.e. assemblages of flakes having dorsal scars related to some kind of core preparation, and unfacetted butts, are sometimes mentioned in the Italian literature (Radmilli 1977; Palma di Cesnola 1982). The "Protoleval-loisian" supposedly derives from the Clactonian, including choppers and flakes with large and inclinated butts. In some sites only a handful of implements are retrieved, while elsewhere larger collections are available, as at Le Svolte and Valle Giumentina in Abruzzo, and Foce del Torrente Romandato in Apulia. Such industries, however, are found in reworked conditions, and are invariably rolled. Their age is an open question.

Cremaschi and Peretto (1988b) examined "Protoleval-loisian" collections of northern Italy and presented evidence that they had been sorted by stream activity to some standard size and weight, and that handaxes were included in several such assemblages. Therefore, they are better described as Acheulean, while the flaking technique has not yet been properly described. On the basis of geo-strati-graphic correlations they date them to "an early part of the Middle Pleistocene".

As a rule, flaking is rather crude in Lower Palaeolithic assemblages. At sites such as Monte Poggiolo, Arce, Colle Marino, Venosa-Loreto only a single flake was often detached, while bipolar flaking technique was common. The latter was also in use at Isernia, and is frequent in the Acheulean assemblages collected in the basin of Atella (Borzatti von Löwenstern and Vianello 1993). There are discoidal cores at Fontana Ranuccio, but they are rarely mentioned elsewhere. The Levallois technique is not found at any site prior to OIS 9. By then, single Levallois flakes, or Levallois cores, are occasionally mentioned or just illustrated in the literature. At Grotta del Colombo in Liguria, for instance, more than 200 flake implements were found in

level 11: two are Levallois flakes, and one is an atypical Levallois blade (Tozzi 1965). After some admittedly tentative correlations with a dated stalagmite in the rear of the cave, and sedimentological and palaeontological studies, the layer was deposited during OIS 9 (Baïssas *et al*. 1986).

The only site at which the Levallois technique is fully represented and developed is Rosaneto, in Calabria. Unfortunately, the 1000 or so collected implements are only known through preliminary publications (Piperno *et al*. 1984). After Malatesta and Zarlenga (1988) the terrace of Rosaneto belongs to what they call "Second Middle Pleistocene cycle deposits", and to OIS 9. However, the industry itself is a major dating element in their reconstruction, which leads to circular arguments. The development of the Levallois technique at this site is unparalleled elsewhere at this stage and we suggest that this fact points to a later age.

7.   **Final considerations**

The age of the first human settlement of Italy has been claimed to be in the range of 1 Myr. In our opinion, it is not fully substantiated at this very early date. Human groups were certainly living in the peninsula by 600 to 500 Kyr BP, while the age of the Sicilian and Sardinian supposed Lower Palaeolithic is still an open question.

The colonization of Sicily is relevant for the first settlement of Europe, as the hypothesis of a discontinuous land bridge between Africa and Europe through Sicily has been put forward, albeit for a later phase of the Lower Palaeolithic (Alimen 1975).

We assume that natural conditions allowing the crossing of arms of the sea by archaic humans would have favoured other large mammals as well. However, the most recent immigrations of animal species from Africa happened during the Middle Pliocene, if not during the late Miocene (Palombo 1985). During the Middle Pleistocene, the Sicilian faunal assemblages are characterised by the well known dwarf pachyderms, and mostly by the little elephants, *Elephas mnaidriensis* and *Elephas falconeri*. As the second species is even more reduced than the first one, it has long been assumed that it was later, and derived from the slightly larger species. *Elephas mnaidriensis*, in turn, would had evolved from a subspecies of the European *Elephas antiquus*, i.e. *Elephas antiquus leonardii*.

The picture changed after absolute dating of several assemblages through isoleucine epimerization (Bada and Belluomini 1985; Bada *et al*. 1991): the dates cluster into two different intervals, at 455 ± 90 Kyr BP, and at 200 ± 40 Kyr BP respectively. Both the tiny *E. falconeri* and the slightly larger *E. mnaidriensis* are found in the earlier group, while only the second one is in the later one. It is now assumed that the two dwarf species are not in a phyletic relation, and that the so-called *E. mnaidriensis* of the later group is possibly a still different species, related to a new immigration of elephants. The species from which *E. falconeri* derived is consequently unknown. It cannot be ruled out that a reconsideration of the problem, as well as the study of new and unpublished faunas, could lead to a new interest in African connections (T. Kotsakis pers. com. 1994). If we accept a short chronology for the first settlement of Europe – i.e. in the range of 600 to 500 Kyr BP – an immigration of elephants from Africa around this time, admittedly so far unsubstantiated and just hypothetical, would open new and intriguing perspectives for the arrival of humans as well.

The environmental changes are recorded in a discontinuous way prior to 300 Kyr BP. However, the core extracted from Valle di Castiglione, 20 km east of Rome, goes back to c. 250 Kyr BP (Follieri *et al.* 1988). In this core, steppic assemblages are present during most of the time, interrupted by phases of forest expansion. We are inclined to believe that the situation was not that different in an earlier part of the Middle Pleistocene. The only evidence of steppic environment from archaeological sites is from the undated upper part of the sequence of Visogliano and from Grotta Paglicci. We suggest that they both formed during fully glacial periods. As said in the Introduction, because of differential preservation of sites the Italian record is much biased towards interglacials, and it is no coincidence that evidence of glacial periods is found in caves. Evidence of cold climate and of some steppic elements was also presented for Monte Poggiolo.

Even in the interglacial sites, the environment is invariably described as rather open – which is of interest, in view of the ongoing discussion on the Palaeolithic settlement of Northern Europe (Gamble 1986; Roebroeks *et al.* 1992). When comparisons are possible with densely wooded areas, as within the sites of the Aurelian Formation, the later ones are found to be devoid of human occupation.

Different environments existed even during full interglacials. This is better understood if we consider the geographical setting: Italy expands in a north-western to south-eastern direction over some 10 degrees of latitude, i.e.

from the Alps to the latitude of Northern Algeria, Tunisia and Syria. The climatological effects of this gradient are contrasted by the ranges of mountains, which follow the same direction, all the way long: during our modern interglacial winters, the mountains of Calabria and Sicily covered by snow are a common sight. At the same time, the mitigating effect of the sea means that, in northern Italy, the Riviera of Liguria nowadays enjoys warm and sunny winters, and palms are freely growing.

As a consequence, extensive ecological zonation has never been possible, and mosaic environments prevailed. This can be seen at Valle di Castiglione: the growth of plant populations was exponential when climatic conditions changed, and we assume that many refugium areas were always in existence. Even now, the vegetation of Latium is known to be both extremely rich in species and markedly heterogeneous (Caloi *et al.* 1989).

Ecologists have often linked the Pleistocene extinction of animal and plant species in Europe to the fact that seas and mountains prevented the north-south migrations and recolonizations which were possible in America or Africa. The patchy environment of Italy possibly explains the late disappearance, during the last glacial, of elephants, hippos, rhinos, as well as of plant species such as *Pterocarya* and *Zelkova*. We consider the tiny peninsula, and its major islands, as a possible refugium for many European species during the Pleistocene.

The Lower Palaeolithic record is impressive in Italy, if compared with other parts of Europe. We suggest that part of this "Lower Palaeolithic success" was linked to the richness and variety of environments over short distances, and to the fact that unspecialised hunter-gatherers were able to take advantage of this.

Acknowledgements

I am grateful to M. Parotto, Dipartimento di Scienze della Terra, Università di Roma "La Sapienza", for allowing use of an original line drawing of coastal Latium. A.P. Anzidei, Soprintendenza archeologica di Roma, kindly provided an unpublished picture of La Polledrara.

references

Accordi, B.,
A.M. Maccagno
1962   Researches in the Pleistocene of Riano (Rome), *Geologica Romana* 1, 25-32.

Accorsi, C.A.
1985   The contribution of palynology in the reconstruction of the environment. In: C. Peretto (ed.), *Homo, Journey to the Origin's of Man History*, 192-201, Venezia: Marsilio.

Aitken, M.J.,
this volume   Chronometric techniques for the Middle Pleistocene.

Alberdi, M.-T.,
L. Caloi,
M.R. Palombo
1988   The Quaternary fauna of Venosa: Equids, *Bulletin du Musée d'Anthropologie préhistorique de Monaco* 31, 5-39.

Alimen, M.H.
1975   Les "isthmes" hispano-marocain et siculo- tunisien aux temps acheuléens, *L'Anthropologie* 79, 399-436.

Ambrosetti, P.,
A. Azzaroli,
F.P. Bonadonna,
M. Follieri
1972   A scheme of Pleistocene chronology for the Tyrrhenian side of Central Italy, *Bollettino della Società Geologica Italiana* 91, 169-184.

Ambrosetti, P.,
F. Cigala Fulgosi,
C. Petronio
1980   Mammiferi del Pleistocene medio. In: *I vertebrati fossili italiani – Catalogo della Mostra*, 227-232, Verona: Museo Civico di Storia Naturale.

Anconetani, P.,
C. Crovetto,
M. Ferrari,
G. Giusberti,
L. Longo,
C. Peretto,
F. Vianello
1992   Nuove ricerche nel giacimento di Isernia La Pineta, *Rivista di Scienze Preistoriche* 44, 3-41.

Anconetani, P.,
G. Giusberti,
C. Peretto
1993   Su alcuni nuovi reperti di bisonte (*Bison schoetensacki* Freudenberg) con tracce di fratturazione intenzionale del giacimento paleolitico di Isernia La Pineta, *Atti della XXX° Riunione scientifica dell'Istituto Italiano di Preistoria e Protostoria*, 211-218.

Angelelli, F.,
L. Caloi,
A. Malatesta,
M.R. Palombo
1978   Fauna quaternaria di Venosa: cenni preliminari, *Atti della XX° Riunione scientifica dell'Istituto Italiano di Preistoria e Protostoria*, 133-140.

Antoniazzi, A.,
L. Cattani,
M. Cremaschi,
L. Fontana,
G. Giusberti,
C. Peretto,
R. Posenato,
F. Proli,
S. Ungaro
1984   Primi risultati delle ricerche nel giacimento del Paleolitico inferiore di Ca' Belvedere (Monte Poggiolo, Forlì), *Preistoria alpina* 20, 7-14.

Antoniazzi, A.,
  L. Cattani,
  M. Cremaschi,
  L. Fontana,
  C. Peretto,
  R. Posenato,
  F. Proli,
  S. Ungaro

1988   Le gisement du Paléolithique inférieur de Ca' Belvedere di Monte Poggiolo (Forlì, Italie) (Résultats préliminaires), *L'Anthropologie* 92, 629-642.

Antoniazzi, A.,
  M. Ferrari,
  C. Peretto

1993   Il giacimento di Ca' Belvedere di Monte Poggiolo del Pleistocene inferiore con industria litica (Forlì), *Bullettino di Paletnologia italiana* 84, 1-56.

Anzidei, A.P.,
  A. Angelelli,
  A. Arnoldus-Huyzendveld,
  L. Caloi,
  M.R. Palombo,
  A.G. Segre

1989   Le gisement pléistocène de La Polledrara di Cecanibbio (Rome, Italie), *L'Anthropologie* 93, 749-782.

Anzidei, A.P.,
  F. Angelelli,
  L. Caloi,
  I. Damiani,
  M. Pacciarelli,
  M.R. Palombo,
  A.C. Saltini,
  A.G. Segre

1988   Il giacimento pleistocenico de "La Polledrara" di Cecanibbio (Roma) – Relazione preliminare, *Archeologia Laziale* 9, 361-368.

Anzidei, A.P.,
  A. Arnoldus-Huyzendveld

1992   The Lower Palaeolithic site of La Polledrara di Cecanibbio (Rome, Italy). In: E. Herring, R. Whitehouse, J. Wilkins (eds), *New developments in Italian Archaeology*, Part 1, Papers of the Fourth Conference of Italian Archaeology, 141-153, London: Accordia Research Centre.

Anzidei, A.P.,
  R. Sebastiani

1984   Saggi di scavo nel deposito pleistocenico al Km. 19,300 della Via Aurelia (Castel di Guido). In: A.M. Bietti Sestieri (ed.), *Preistoria e Protostoria nel territorio di Roma*, 86-93, Roma: De Luca.

Anzidei, A.P.,
  P. Villa, P.,
  E. Cerilli

(in press)   La Polledrara di Cecanibbio (Roma). Dati preliminari sull'analisi tafonomica dei reperti faunistici. Atti del Convegno Farnese *Preistoria e Protostoria in Etruria*, Viterbo 21-23 maggio 1993.

Arnoldus-Huyzendveld, A.,
  A.P. Anzidei

1993   Ricostruzione di un ambiente fluvio-lacustre nella regione vulcanica di Roma (La Polledrara di Cecanibbio), *Atti della XXX° Riunione scientifica dell'Istituto Italiano di Preistoria e Protostoria*, 151-165.

Bada, J.L.,
  G. Belluomini

1985   Isoleucine epimerization ages of the dwarf elephants of Sicily, *Geology* 13, 451-452.

Bada, J.L.,
  G. Belluomini,
  L. Bonfiglio,
  M. Branca,
  E. Burgio,
  L. Delitata

1991   Isoleucine epimerization ages of Quaternary mammals from Sicily, *Il Quaternario* 4, 49-54.

Bahain, J.-J.   1993   *Datation par résonance de Spin électronique (ESR) du carbonates et d'émail dentaire quaternaires: potentiel et problèmes*, Thèse de Doctorat du Muséum National d'Histoire Naturelle, Paris: Institut de Paléontologie Humaine.

Baïssas, P.   1980   Données paléomagnétique et sédimentologique sur les dépôts de la coupe de Loreto, *Bulletin du Musée d'Anthropologie préhistorique de Monaco* 24, 13-56.

Baïssas, P.,
  L. Barral,
  P. Simon,
  S. Simone   1986   Le Pleistocène moyen à la grotte du Colombo (Toirano, Ligurie italienne), *Bulletin du Musée d'Anthropologie préhistorique de Monaco* 29, 5-24.

Barral, L.,
  S. Simone   1983   Le bassin fluvio-lacustre de Venosa, *Bulletin du Musée d'Anthropologie préhistorique de Monaco* 27, 5-19.

Bartolomei, G.   1980   Micromammiferi del Plio-Pleistocene. In: *I vertebrati fossili italiani*, Catalogo della Mostra, 249-258, Verona.

Belli, G.,
  G. Belluomini,
  P.F. Cassoli,
  S. Cecchi,
  M. Cucarzi,
  L. Delitala,
  G. Fornaciari,
  F. Mallegni,
  M. Piperno,
  A.G. Segre,
  E. Segre Naldini   1991   Découverte d'un fémur humain acheuléen à Notarchirico (Vénosa, Basilicate), *L'Anthropologie* 95, 47-88.

Biddittu, I.   1972   Pleistocene e industrie litiche pre-acheuleane ad Arce e Fontana Liri, *Quaternaria* XVI, 35-52.

Biddittu, I.,
  P.F. Cassoli,
  F. Radicati di Brozolo,
  A.G. Segre,
  E. Segre Naldini,
  I. Villa   1979   Anagni, a K-Ar dated Early and Middle Pleistocene Site, Central Italy: preliminary report, *Quaternaria* XXI, 53-71.

Biddittu, I.,
  A.G. Segre   1978   Paleolitico inferiore a Cava Pompi presso Pofi (Frosinone), *Quaderni del Centro Studi per l'Archeologia Etrusco-Italica* 1, 77-79.

    1982   Pleistocene medio-superiore con industria arcaica su ciottolo nel bacino di Anagni (Lazio), *Atti della XXIII° Riunione scientifica dell'Istituto Italiano di Preistoria e Protostoria*, 567-576.

    1984   Industria su scheggia e bifacciali: nuovi reperti del Paleolitico inferiore ad Anagni-Fontana Ranuccio, Frosinone, *Atti della XXIV° Riunione scientifica dell'Istituto Italiano di Preistoria e Protostoria*, 105-114.

Blanc, A.C.   1935-1937   Scheggia di tecnica clactoniana rinvenuta *in situ* nel Quaternario della Valchetta-Cartoni (Roma), *Rivista di Antropologia* XXXI, 253-266.

Bonadonna, F.P.   1965   Further information on the research in the Middle Pleistocene diatomite quarry of Valle dell'Inferno (Riano, Rome), *Quaternaria* VII, 279-299.

Bonifay, M.-F.   1977   Liste préliminaire de la grande faune du gisement préhistorique de Venosa, *Bulletin du Musée d'Anthropologie préhistorique de Monaco* 21, 115-125.

Borzatti von Löwenstern, E., M. Sozzi, S. Vannucci, F. Vianello 1990 L'Acheuleano del cimitero di Atella (PZ). Prime indagini sulla stratigrafia del sedimento e sulle industrie litiche, *Studi per l'Ecologia del Quaternario* 12, 9-29.

Borzatti von Löwenstern, E., F. Vianello 1993 Luoghi di sosta e e di insediamento lungo le rive del lago pleistocenico di Atella (Potenza), *Atti della XXX° Riunione scientifica dell'Istituto Italiano di Preistoria e Protostoria*, 139-150.

Boschian, G. 1993 Castel di Guido - Scavi 1980-1991, *Atti della XXX° Riunione scientifica dell'Istituto Italiano di Preistoria e Protostoria*, 167-178.

Broglio, A., I. Di Geronimo, E. Di Mauro, J.K. Kozlowski 1992 Nouvelles contributions à la connaissances du Paléolithique inférieur de la région de Catania dans le cadre du Paléolithique de la Sicile. In: C. Peretto (ed.), *I primi abitanti della Valle Padana: Monte Poggiolo*, 189-226, Milano: Jaca Book.

Caloi, L., G.B.L. Coccolini, M. Mussi, M.R. Palombo, S. Vitagliano, D. Zampetti 1989 Le Moustérien du Latium (Italie centrale): archéologie, milieu naturel, chronologie, *L'Anthropologie* 93, 73-98.

Caloi, L., M.R. Palombo 1978 Anfibi, rettili e mammiferi di Torre del Pagliaccetto (Torre in Pietra, Roma), *Quaternaria* XX, 315-440.

1979 La fauna quaternaria di Venosa: "Canis sp.", *Quaternaria* XXI, 115-128.

1980 La fauna quaternaria di Venosa: Bovidi, *Bollettino del Servizio geologico d'Italia* C, 101-140.

1986 Le mammalofaune plio-pleistoceniche dell'area laziale: problemi biostratigrafici ed implicazioni paleoclimatiche, *Memorie della Società geologica italiana* 35, 99-126.

Cassoli, P.F., C. De Giuli, A.M. Radmilli, A.G. Segre 1982 Giacimento del Paleolitico inferiore a Malagrotta (Roma), *Atti della XXIII° Riunione scientifica dell'Istituto Italiano di Preistoria e Protostoria*, 531-549.

Cassoli, P.F., D. Lefèvre, M. Piperno, J.-P. Raynal, A. Tagliacozzo 1993 Una paleosuperficie con resti di *Elephas (Palaeoloxodon) antiquus* e industria acheuleana nel sito di Notarchirico (Venosa, Basilicata), *Atti della XXX° Riunione scientifica dell'Istituto Italiano di Preistoria e Protostoria*, 101-116.

Cattani, L. 1992 Il ricoprimento vegetale nell'area padana durante il Pleistocene inferiore e medio. In: C. Peretto (ed.), *I primi abitanti della Valle Padana: Monte Poggiolo*, 291-302, Milano: Jaca Book.

Cattani, L., M. Cremaschi, M.R. Ferraris, F. Mallegni, F. Masini, V. Scola, C. Tozzi 1991 Le gisement du Pleistocène moyen de Visogliano (Trieste): restes humains, industries, environnement, *L'Anthropologie* 95, 9-36

Coltorti, M.,   1982   Reversed magnetic polarity at an early Lower Palaeolithic site in Central Italy, *Nature*
  M. Cremaschi,   300, 173-176.
  M.C. Delitala,
  D. Esu,
  M. Fornaseri,
  A. McPherron,
  M. Nicoletti,
  R. van Otterloo,
  C. Peretto,
  B. Sala,
  V. Schmidt,
  J. Sevink

Conato, V.,   1980   New data on the Pleistocene of Rome, *Quaternaria* XXII, 131-176.
  D. Esu,
  A. Malatesta,
  F. Zarlenga

Cremaschi, M.,   1992   Ambiente e clima. In: A. Guidi, M. Piperno (eds), *Italia preistorica*, 3-45, Roma:
  S. Chiesa   Laterza.

Cremaschi, M.,   1988a   Les sols d'habitat du site paléolithique d'Isernia La Pineta (Molise, Italie centrale),
  C. Peretto   *L'Anthropologie* 92, 1017-1040.

                        1988b   Le Paléolithique inférieur de la plaine orientale du Pô, *L'Anthropologie* 92, 643-682.

Crovetto, C.   1991   Résultats préliminaires de la comparaison des industries d'Isernia La Pineta et de
                                  Venosa-Loreto. In: C. Peretto (ed.), *Isernia La Pineta - Nuovi contributi scientifici*,
                                  79-95, Isernia: Istituto regionale per gli studi storici del Molise "V. Cuoco".

Desio, A. (ed.)   1973   *Geologia dell'Italia*, Torino: UTET.

Durante, S.,   1978   Nota sulle associazioni malacologiche del giacimento fluviolacustre di Loreto, Venosa,
  F. Settepassi   *Atti della XXIII° Riunione scientifica dell'Istituto Italiano di Preistoria e Protostoria*,
                                  141-145.

Evernden, J.F.,   1965   The potassium-argon dating of Late Cenozoic rocks in East Africa and Italy, *Current
  H. Curtis   Anthropology* 6, 343-369.

Farizy, C.   1988-   Spatial organization and Middle Palaeolithic open air sites, *Origini* 14, 39-50.
                        1989

Ferrari, M.,   1991   Aspetti tecno-tipologici e distribuzione areale dell'industria del II settore di Isernia
  C. Peretto,   La Pineta (Molise, italia). In: Peretto C. (ed.), *Isernia La Pineta, nuovi contributi
  F. Vianello   scientifici*, 49-78, Isernia: Istituto regionale per gli studi storici del Molise "V.
                                  Cuoco".

Follieri, M.   1961-   La foresta colchica fossile di Riano Romano. II. Analisi polliniche, *Annali di Botanica*,
                        1963   245-280.

Follieri, M.,   1988   250,000-year pollen record from Valle di Castiglione (Roma), *Pollen et Spores* 30, 329-
  D. Magri,   356.
  L. Sadori

Fornaseri, M.   1985   Geochronology of volcanic rocks from Latium (Italy), *Rendiconti della Società italiana
                                  di Mineralogia e Petrologia* 40, 73-106

Galiberti, A.   1982   L'industria di tipo "Pebble Culture" di Bibbona (Livorno) (Nota preliminare), *Atti della XXIII° Riunione scientifica dell'Istituto Italiano di Preistoria e Protostoria*, 463-479.

Gamble, C.   1986   *The Palaeolithic Settlement of Europe*. Cambridge: Cambridge University Press.

Gatti, S. (ed.)   1993   *Dives Anagnia - Archeologia nella valle del Sacco*. Roma: "L'Erma" di Bretschneider.

Giusberti, G.,   1991   Tipologia, frequenza e distribuzione dei reperti paleontologici e paletnologici della
M. Ferrari,   paleosuperficie T.3a del I settore di scavo di Isernia La Pineta (Isernia, Molise). In:
C. Peretto   Peretto C. (ed.), *Isernia La Pineta, nuovi contributi scientifici*, 5-42, Isernia:Istituto regionale per gli studi storici del Molise "V. Cuoco".

Giusberti, G.,   1991   Evidences de la fracturation intentionnelle d'ossements animaux avec moëlle dans le
C. Peretto   gisement de "La Pineta" de Isernia (Molise), Italie, *L'Anthropologie* 95, 765-778.

Haynes, G.   1991   *Mammoths, Mastodonts & Elephants*. Cambridge: Cambridge University Press.

Jacobacci, A.   1978   Il rilevamento geologico dei dintorni di Torre in Pietra (F 149 Cerveteri), *Quaternaria* XX, 209-224.

Koenigswald, W. von   in press   The *Mimomys-Arvicola* boundary and the enamel thickness quotient (SDQ) of *Arvicola*
T. van Kolfschoten   as stratigraphic markers in the Middle Pleistocene, *Proceedings of the SEQS Cromer Symposium, 1990*.

Lefèvre, D.,   1993a   Sedimentary dynamics and tecto-volcanism in the Venosa Basin (Basilicata). In:
J.-P. Raynal,   M. Mollieri, O. Girotti, T. Kotsakis, A. Taddeucci, C. Turner (eds), *Abstracts. Symposium*
G. Vernet   *"Quaternary stratigraphy in volcanic areas"*, 43, Rome: INQUA SEQS, CNR, Università degli Studi di Roma "La Sapienza".

Lefèvre, D.,   1993b   Contribution à la chronostratigraphie de la série de Venosa-Notarchirico (Basilicata),
J.P. Raynal,   *Atti della XXX° Riunione scientifica dell'Istituto Italiano di Preistoria e Protostoria*,
T. Pilleyre,   116-128.
G. Vernet

Leonardi, G.,   1974   I cervi pleistocenici del bacino diatomitico di Riano (Roma), *Atti della Accademia*
C. Petronio   *Nazionale dei Lincei - Memorie (Classe Sc. fis. mat. nat.)*, Serie VIII, 12, 109-208.

             1976   The Fallow Deer of European Pleistocene, *Geologica Romana* 15, 1-67.

Maccagno, A.M.   1962   Gli elefanti fossili di Riano, *Geologica Romana* 1, 33-132.

Malatesta, A.   1978   La serie di Torre in Pietra nel quadro del Pleistocene Romano, *Quaternaria* XX, 537-577.

Malatesta, A.,   1988   Evidence of Middle Pleistocene transgressions along the Mediterranean coast, *Palaeo-*
F. Zarlenga   *geography, Palaeoclimatology, Palaeoecology* 68, 311-315.

Mallegni, F.,   1983   New European fossil hominid material from an Acheulean site near Rome (Castel di
R. Mariani-Costantini,   Guido), *American Journal of Physical Anthropology* 62, 263-274.
G. Fornaciari,
E.T. Longo,
G. Giacobini,
A.M. Radmilli

Martini, F.   1992   Il più antico popolamento umano delle isole: la Sardegna. In: Peretto C. (ed.), *I primi abitanti della Valle Padana: Monte Poggiolo*, 175-187. Milano, Jaca Book.

Meulen, A.J. van der   1973   Middle Pleistocene smaller mammals from the Monte Peglia (Orvieto, Italy), with special reference to the phylogeny of *Microtus* (Arvicolidae, Rodentia), *Quaternaria* XVII, 1-144.

Mezzena, F.,   1971   Industria acheuleana nei depositi esterni della Grotta Paglicci, *Rivista di Scienze*
  A. Palma di Cesnola   *preistoriche* 26, 3-29.

Mussi, M.   1992   *Il Paleolitico e il Mesolitico in Italia*. Popoli e Civiltà dell'Italia antica vol. 10. Bologna: Stilus.

Palma di Cesnola, A.   1982   Il Paleolitico inferiore in Puglia, *Atti della XXIII° Riunione scientifica dell'Istituto Italiano di Preistoria e Protostoria*, 225-248.

Palombo, M.R.   1985   I grandi mammiferi pleistocenici delle isole del Mediterraneo: tempi e vie di migrazione, *Bullettino della Società Paleontologica Italiana* 24, 201-224.

Peretto, C. (ed.)   1991   *Isernia La Pineta, nuovi contributi scientifici*. Isernia: Istituto regionale per gli studi storici del Molise "V. Cuoco".

  1992   *I primi abitanti della Valle Padana: Monte Poggiolo*. Milano: Jaca Book.

Peretto, C.,   1983   *Isernia La Pineta, un accampamento più antico di 700.000 anni*. Bologna: Calderini.
  C. Terzani,
  M. Cremaschi (eds)

Piperno, M.   1972   The Monte Peglia lithic industry, *Quaternaria* XVI, 53-65.

Piperno, M.,   1978   Studio tipologico e interpretazione dell'industria acheuleana e pre-musteriana dei livelli
  I. Biddittu   m e d di Torre in Pietra (Roma), *Quaternaria* XX, 441-536.

Piperno, M.,   1984   *I primi abitanti d'Europa*. Roma: De Luca.
  M.G. Bulgarelli,
  F. Zevi (eds)

Piperno, M.,   1990   Découverte d'un fémur humain dans les niveaux acheuléens de Notarchirico (Venosa,
  F. Mallegni,   Basilicata, Italie), *Comptes Rendus de l'Académie des Sciences de Paris* 311 (ser. II),
  Y. Yokoyama   1097-1102.

Radmilli, A.M.   1977   *Storia dell'Abruzzo dalle origini all'età del Bronzo*. Pisa: Giardini.

  1984   Scavi nel giacimento del Paleolitico inferiore di Castel di Guido presso Roma. In: A.M. Bietti Sestieri (ed.), *Preistoria e Protostoria nel territorio di Roma*, 75-85, Roma: De Luca.

Radtke, U.,   1981   230 Th /234 U- and ESR- dating problems of fossil shells in Pleistocene marine terraces
  G.J. Hennig,   (Northern Latium, Central Italy), *Quaternaria* XXIII, 37-50.
  W. Linke,
  J. Müngersdor

Roebroeks, W.,   1992   Dense Forests, Cold Steppes, and the Palaeolithic Settlement of Northern Europe, *Current*
  N.J. Conard,   *Anthropology* 33, 551-586.
  T. van Kolfschoten

Roebroeks, W   this   The earliest occupation of Europe: A reappraisal of artefactual and chronological
  T. van Kolfschoten   volume   evidence.

Sala, B.   1983   La fauna del giacimento di Isernia La Pineta. In: C. Peretto, C. Terzani, M. Cremaschi (eds), *Isernia La Pineta, un accampamento più antico di 700.000 anni*, 71-79, Bologna: Calderini.

| | 1989 | A Preliminary Report on the Microvertebrates of Notarchirico, Venosa, *Preistoria Alpina* 25, 7-14. |

Sarti, A.
  P. Stoduti
1982
Stazione litica riferibile alla "Pebble Culture" scoperta nel Livornese, *Atti della XXIII° Riunione scientifica dell'Istituto Italiano di Preistoria e Protostoria*, 447-461.

Segre, A.
  A. Ascenzi
1984
Fontana Ranuccio: Italy's Earliest Middle Pleistocene Hominid Site, *Current Anthropology* 25, 230- 233.

Segre, A.G.
  I. Biddittu,
  F. Guadagnoli
1987
Nuovi dati sul giacimento del Paleolitico inferiore di Anagni-Fontana Ranuccio, *Archeologia Laziale* VII, 239-243.

Segre, A.G.
  I. Biddittu,
  M. Piperno
1982
Il Paleolitico inferiore nel Lazio, nella Basilicata e in Sicilia, *Atti della XXIII° Riunione scientifica dell'Istituto Italiano di Preistoria e Protostoria*, 177-206.

Soprintendenza Speciale al Museo Nazionale Preistorico Etnografico "L. Pigorini".
1991
Escursioni a Notarchirico e Isernia La Pineta, Libro Guida, XXX° Riunione scientifica dell'Istituto Italiano di Preistoria e Protostoria.

Tozzi, C.
1965
La Grotta del Colombo a Toirano, *Rivista di Studi liguri* 31, 5-43.

Tuffreau, A.
  P. Antoine
this volume
The earliest occupation of Europe: Continental Northwestern Europe.

Margherita Mussi
Dip. di Scienze Storiche, Archeologiche e
Antropologiche dell'Antichità
Università di Roma "La Sapienza"
Via Palestro 63
00185 Roma, Italy

3   The earliest occupation of Europe: the Balkans

The small number of Lower Palaeolithic sites in the Balkans, one of the most probable pathways for hominids entering Europe, is possibly the result of the limited amount of research in this area. Isolated finds and excavated sites as Yarimburgaz (Turkey), Petralona (Greece) and Gajtan (Albania) all point to human occupation from the beginning of the Middle Pleistocene onwards.

1.   Introduction

A few years ago the Balkans, and above all their southern part, represented a blank on the maps of Lower Palaeolithic Europe. Yet this region is considered to be situated on the most probable pathway that hominids took at the time of their 'conquest' of the European continent. The absence of knowledge of prehistoric man in the Balkans is actually due to the lack of prehistoric research within this area. Information on the Palaeolithic of the Balkan countries started to become available only in recent years. Data concerning the Lower Palaeolithic are very scarce and sites known from this period are not numerous (cf. Fig. 1). The only excavated sites which date to the earlier parts of the Middle Pleistocene are the caves of Yarimburgaz (Turkey), Petralona (Greece), Gajtan (Albania) and Sandalja (Croatia; see K. Valoch, this volume).

2.   Turkey

The only site in the European part of Turkey which has yielded Middle Pleistocene archaeological finds is the cave of Yarimburgaz, where archaeological research started recently. The cave of Yarimburgaz is situated 25 km to the west of Istanbul on the Marmara Sea. It has numerous halls, staggered at different levels, which contain important Quaternary deposits with numerous Middle Pleistocene occupation levels (Howell 1989). The associated fauna consists of: *Canis mosbachensis, Vulpes vulpes* ssp., *Cuon/Xenocyon* sp., *Ursus deningeri, Felis sylvestris, Felis leo, Felis gombaszoegensis, Felis (C) caracal, Equus mosbachensis, Praemegaceros* aff. *verticornis, Dama* sp., *Cervus elaphus* ssp., *Bos/Bison, Gazella* sp., *Capra* sp.

The industry comprises a number of pebble tools and a large variety of flake tools (denticulates, notches, side scrapers, composite tools). On the other hand, handaxes are absent, as well as products of the Levallois flaking technique.

3.   Greece

The only Middle Pleistocene site excavated in Greece is Petralona cave. Apart from this site, evidence for Middle Pleistocene human occupation consists of isolated finds.

3.1.   PETRALONA

Petralona cave is situated at Chalcidique (Northern Greece), approximately 35 km south-east of Thessalonique and near the village of Petralona. It is a vast cavern made up of a number of galleries more than 1500 m. in total length.

Inside the cave a remarkably well preserved anteneanderthalian skull was discovered in 1960. It was stuck, by a calcite flow, against the wall of a diverticule a few dozen cm above the surface. The skull is of a large size, while its cranial capacity is approximately 1200 cm^3. Unfortunately, the fact that the skull was not found within a stratigraphical context prevents a clear assignment to any of the levels established within the deposits in the cave. Thus the age estimates vary between 200 and 600 Kyr BP (Hennig *et al.* 1981; A. Poulianos 1982).

The quaternary deposits in some places in the cave are up to 15 m in depth (section B cf. Fig. 2) and 27 levels have been distinguished. An important stalagmitic floor seals the sediments, whilst a second one seems to be present in the middle of the deposits.

The different levels are very rich in faunal remains. The small vertebrates (all the levels combined) are represented by Pisces ind., *Bufo* sp. ind, *Pelobates fuscus, Varanus intermedius, Lacerta* sp. ind., *Lacerta* cf. *trilineata, Lacerta* aff. *viridis, Testudo graeca, Testudo* sp., *Ophidia* sp. ind., *Anser anser, Aythya ferina, Fulica atra, Buthierax pouliani, Falco tinnunculus, Alectoris graeca med., Alectoris* sp., *Perdix* cf. *jurcsaki*, Scolopacidae ind., *Larus* sp., *Columba oenas* ssp., *Columba livia* ssp., *Columba palumbus, Strix aluco, Glaucidium passerinum, Bubo* (?) sp. ind., *Corvus corax, Pyrrhocorax graculus vetus, Turdus* sp., *Lanius minor, Prunella collaria*, Passeriformes ind. I., Passeriformes ind. II., *Pachyura* cf. *etruscus* (= *Suncus*

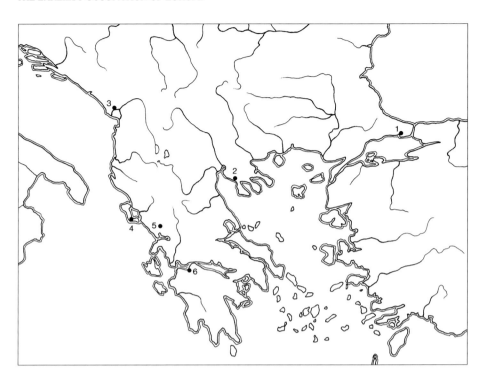

Fig. 1. Sites mentioned in the text.
1: Yarimburgaz, 2: Petralona, 3: Gajtan, 4: Korissia, 5: Kokkinopilos,
6: Vrahneïka.

etruscus), Sorex minutus, Sorex sp., *Talpa minuta,
Erinaceus europaeus praeglacialis, Rhinolophus* sp. ind.
I., *Rhinolophus* sp. ind. II., *Rhinolophus ferrumeguinum
topalensis, Myotis myotis, Myotis blythi oxygn., Myotis* sp.
ind. I., *Myotis* sp. ind. II., *Eptesicus* sp. ind., *Pipistrellus*
(?) sp. ind., *Nyctalus* cf. *noctula, Lepus* sp., *Oryctolagus*
sp., *Urocitellus primigenius dafnae, Parasmithus
brevidens, Dryominus eliomyoides arisi, Spalax chal-
kidikae, Allocricetus bursae simplex, Microtus praeguen-
theri, Apodemus* sp., *Apodemus* (*Kastormys*) *mystacinus,
Mys* (*Budamys*) *sinanthropus, Hystrix* sp. (Kretzoi and
N. Poulianos 1981). Subsequently N. Poulianos (1990)
added *Lagurus* (*Eolagurus*) *argyropuloi zazhighini,
Lagurus transiens* and *Arvicola cantiana* (= *A. terrestris
cantiana*) to this list.

The large vertebrates are represented by: *Canis lupus
mosbachensis, Vulpes* cf. *praeglacialis, Cuon priscus, Ursus
deningeri, Ursus thibetanus mediterraneus, Meles meles,
Crocuta crocuta praespelaea, Crocuta crocuta petralonae,
Hyaena perrieri, Hyaena brevirostris, Felis sylvestris
hamadryas, Panthera leo fossilis, Panthera* cf. *gombaszo-
gensis, Panthera pardus, Homotherium* sp., *Equus* cf.
mosbachensis, Asinus hydruntinus ssp., *Dicerorhinus
hemitoechus, Sus scrofa, Praemegaceros verticornis, Dama*
sp., *Cervus elaphus* ssp., *Bos primigenius, Capra ibex
macedonica* (Kurtén and A. Poulianos 1977; Kurtén and
A. Poulianos 1981; Kretzoi and N. Poulianos 1981; Kurtén
1983).

The faunal assemblage (the carnivores in particular) is
interpreted as characteristic of the first half of the Middle
Pleistocene. More precisely *H. perrieri, H. brevirostris* and
P. gombaszoegensis indicate the early Middle Pleistocene
as the minimum age, whereas *M. meles* and *P. pardus* give
the same period as the maximum age (Kurtén 1983). Thus
this fauna is characteristic of the first part of the Middle
Pleistocene and allows attribution of an age of 500 to 750
Kyr BP to the Petralona deposits. The fauna has not been
specified for each level yet, but the various authors indicate
that there are no significant changes within the total
sequence. However, three faunal sequences were distinguished on the base of the hyena material (Kurtén and
A. Poulianos 1981; Kurtén 1983): the Crenian (levels 18
to 11) characterised by an association of *Hyaena perrieri*
and *Crocuta crocuta praespelaea*, the Petralonian (levels 9
to 2) characterised by the replacement of *Hyaena perrieri*
by *Hyaena brevirostris* and the continuation of *Crocuta
crocuta praespelaea*, whereas the Thermaecian (upper
stalagmitic floor) is characterised by the presence of only
Crocuta crocuta petralonae.

Various dates have been put forward for the deposits,
ranging from 200 to 1,000 Kyr BP, but the most coherent
of these concern only the upper stalagmitic floor (Ikeya
1980; Wintle and Jacobs 1982; Shen and Yokoyama 1986).
Dating of this stalagmitic floor by the uranium disequilib-
rium method resulted in an age of more than 350 Kyr BP –
the limit of this method (Shen and Yokoyama 1986).

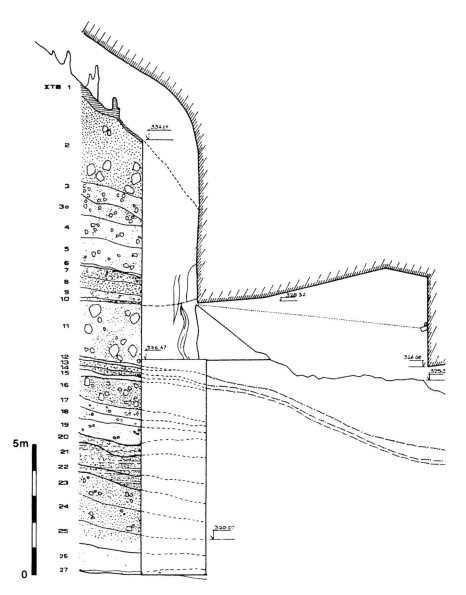

Fig. 2. Petralona: Section B stratigraphy (after A. Poulianos 1982).

As palynological and sedimentological analyses did not result in good indications on the climatic and environmental conditions during the formation of the deposits, only the faunal remains are helpful here. N. Poulianos (1990) has distinguished numerous climatic phases and has drawn up a biostratigraphic table of the deposits (Table I). The herbivores recovered in the different levels were mostly hunted by man, although some do appear to have been brought in by carnivores. The Petralona hominids mainly hunted horse (47.1% of the herbivores), cervids (21.8%)

and mountain goat (21.4%) (Kretzoi and N. Poulianos 1981).

The lithic material is abundant throughout nearly all the levels (A. Poulianos 1982). Nevertheless, as a result of a lack of detailed studies, only some scarce data and some drawings and pictures of a few artefacts are available (Fig. 3.1 and 3.2).

The industry looks rather 'archaic' and is almost always made out of quartz; occasionally unmodified bauxite fragments were used as implements. Two flint pieces were found on the surface of the deposits as well as a few within the deposits which closed the entrance to the cave. Pebble tools are rare and handaxes absent. The base of this industry is formed by small tools, made by using debris, and more rarely flakes. Side scrapers (most often formed by using a thick retouch), notches and denticulates are also frequent, while other tool types are rare.

3.2. KORRISSIA

A chopper (Fig. 3.3) was discovered *in situ* in a cutting close to the Korrissia lagoon in the south-west of the island of Corfu (North West Greece) (Kourtessi-Philippakis 1990). The artefact comes from a clay bed situated between two marine limestone horizons which rest in strong unconformity on a middle Pliocene sandy deposit. The clay bed has a normal magnetic polarity and has been attributed to the first part of the Middle Pleistocene (Jamet 1982). The chopper could, therefore, be contemporary with the Petralona industry.

3.3. KOKKINOPILOS

The open air site of Kokkinopilos lies in Epirus (North West Greece) (Bailey *et al.* 1992). A formation of Middle Pleistocene red silts, more than 40 m thick, yielded a Micoquian handaxe (Fig. 4.1), found in situ 16 m below the top of the red silts. The handaxe is, according to the researchers who found it, 250,000 to 300,000 years old (Runnels and Van Andel 1993). In any case this handaxe, with well retouched boards, would fit very well into a Middle, or indeed even Upper, Acheulean industry.

3.4. OTHER SITES

A few isolated tools collected in river terraces have been attributed to the Middle Pleistocene, e.g. finds from the middle terrace of Aliakmon (Northern Greece) and the upper terrace of Piros (Achaïa, western Greece) (Darlas 1994).

A recent discovery near the village of Vrahneïka (region of Achaïa) of two flaked pieces associated with a marine beach has been attributed to the OIS 9 transgression. A limestone slab rests unconformably on Pliocene sands at 136 m of altitude and is covered in turn by an offshore bar with coarse grained sands. The two retouched flakes were found within this offshore bar.

4. Albania

In Albania, prehistoric research started only very recently and the research is mainly limited to the region of Shkoder, in the northern part of the country. In the other regions Palaeolithic discoveries are practically non-existent. Lower Palaeolithic material is found in the cave of Gajtan and the open air site of Baran, located only 800 m from the cave of Gajtan (Fistani 1993a and b).

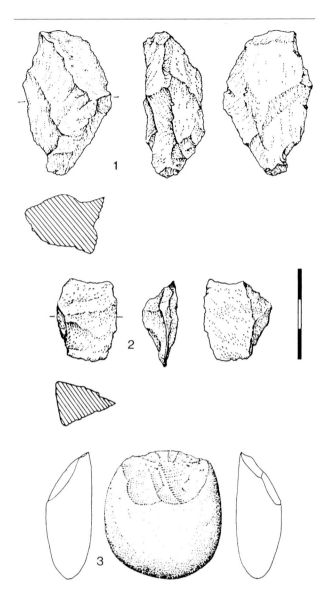

Fig. 3. 1 and 2: Petralona: quartz tools (after A. Poulianos 1978), 3: Korrissia: pebble tool (after Kourtessi-Philippakis 1990). Scale in cm.

Two fluvial terraces are exposed at the site of Baran. Only surface finds of stone artefacts, with no stratigraphic context, have been collected. A "pre-Mindel" age was attributed to the lithic material discovered on the upper terraces, because the assemblage contains archaic tools and rough handaxes, choppers, chopping-tools, and large flakes. Levallois flakes and discoïdal cores also present within the assemblage are interpreted as coming from a more evolved second industry, which represents an *in situ* evolution (*id*: 153).

Table 1: Summary of biostratigraphic and palaeoclimatic data of the Petralona Cave. The first appearance of a taxon in the Petralona Cave sediments is indicated by a dash; those taxa found only in one layer are indicated by a point; those which are observed at almost all layers are indicated by an asterisk; and, finally, those species which are found within certain layers, are indicated by a + (plus) (after N. Poulianos 1990).

Thickness (cm)	Layers	Periods	Ages (ky)	Biostratigraphy	Environment
25	1	Thermaecian	550	(top stalagmite)	Cooler
				.Cuon priscus	
255	2	Petralonian		+Crocuta c. praespelaea	
				+Dicerorhinus cf. hemitoechus	?
100	3				
				+Ursus thibetanus	
75	4				
					Savanna
90	5				
30	6			*Ursus deningeri	
				*Canis lupus mosbachensis	
30	7				
45	8				Cooler
10	9				
10(20)	10	Thracian	610	.Hyaena brevirostris	Savanna
				(travertine stalagmite)	Sub-tropic
200	11			+Crocuta c. praespelaea	
		Crenian	650	+Hyaena perrieri	Savanna/Forest
7	12			*Archanthropus europeus	
20	13			+Lagurus transiens	
15	14			-Dicerorhinus cf. hemitoechus	
22	15				
90	16			+Ursus thibetanus	
				-Equus cf. mosbachensis	
30	17			+Hyaena perrieri	Continental forest/
				.Arvicola cantiana	cold humid steppe
30	18				
				+Lagurus transiens	
60	19	Elaeochorian		-Allocricetus bursae simplex	
			700	-Apodemus sp.	Wet and warmer
30	20				
75	21				
30	22				
90	23				
				.Talpa minuta	
			730		
90	24				Cold humid steppe (±8°C)
60	25			±Lagurus transiens	
100	26	Chalkidikian			Very cold steppe (4°C)
				.L. (Eolagurus) a. zazhighini	
2	27		750		
	-28-	Aegean		(basal travertine)	
Total depth 1621					

However, the fact that these tools are surface finds, recovered outside a stratigraphical context, makes it impossible to confirm this age, whereas the presence of Levallois flakes and discoïdal cores seems to indicate a Middle Palaeolithic age. The pebble tools and the large and irregular flakes do not per se indicate a high age, as such pieces are frequent amongst industries discovered in fluvial terraces.

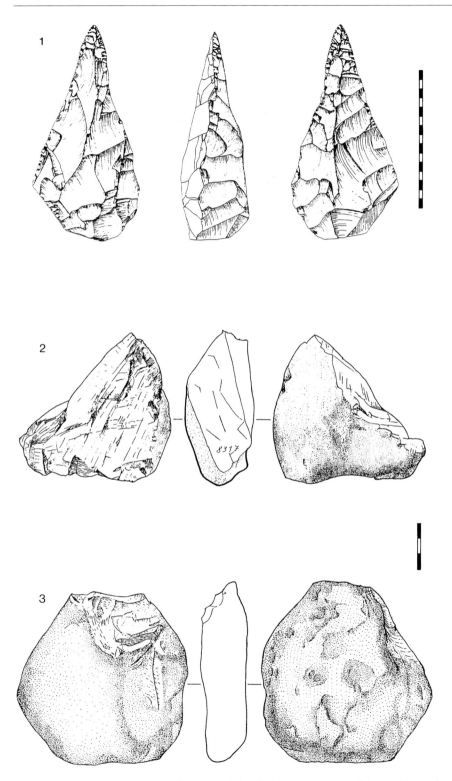

Fig. 4.1: Kokkinopilos: handaxe (after Runnels and Van Andel 1993), 2 and 3: Gajtan: pebble tools (after Fistani 1993b). Scale in cm.

4.1.   GAJTAN

The cave of Gajtan is situated to the south-east of Shkoder between the villages of Renc and Gur i zi. The cave is part of a karstic network with a number of cavities which communicate by corridors. The cave has two porches. Excavations at the first one (Gajtan I) revealed important Quaternary deposits, which can be divided into 2 assemblages: the upper assemblage contains a Mousterian industry whereas the lower has yielded a Middle Pleisto-cene fauna and a Lower Palaeolithic lithic industry. Other bone remains of the same age as those of the lower assemblage were also found in a side chamber of the cave.

The fauna of the lower assemblage contains: *Testudo* sp., *Lepus* cf. *europaeus, Hystrix* cf. *vinogradovi, Canis lupus mosbachensis, Ursus* cf. *deningeri, Ursus thibetanus, Dicerorhinus* cf. *mercki, Sus scrofa, Cervus elaphus, Capreolus capreolus, Dama dama, Bison priscus* (?), *Macaca sylvana pliocena* (Fistani 1993a, Fistani 1993b, Fistani and Crégut-Bonnoure 1993).

This Middle Pleistocene fauna is indicative of temperate climatic conditions and a mainly forested environment. The assemblage has been dated to the Holsteinian Interglacial. A large number of the bone remains show traces that are attributed to human interference, such as defleshing, intentional fragmentation and fire.

The industry discovered in this assemblage consists for the most part of quartzite. It is characterised by the rarity of small tools, absence of the Levallois technique and a high proportion (40%) of choppers and chopping-tools (Fig. 4.2 and 4.3) as well as by the presence of a few atypical handaxes or proto-handaxes.

5.   Conclusion

From the present state of Palaeolithic research in the Balkans it is only possible to say that there was human occupation from the first half of the Middle Pleistocene onwards, although the known sites are very limited and dispersed in time and space.

The only sites as yet discovered and excavated for this period are the caves of Yarimburgaz, Petralona and Gajtan. Most studies concerning these sites have been concentrated on the fauna and dating of the deposits. Apart from the faunal evidence, there is very little information about climatic and environmental conditions, and there is also practically no evidence concerning the habitat or activities of prehistoric hominids.

At other sites tools have been discovered in a strati-graphical context (Korrissia, Kokkinopilos, Vrahneïka) but too few to speak about Palaeolithic 'camp'sites. Finally there are a few small tool series, with doubtful dates, from surface sites.

In summary, two conclusions can be drawn:

1. Traces of human occupation dating from before the final phase of the Middle Pleistocene have been discovered in the southern Balkans in spite of the rarity of finds. Because of these finds this part of Europe is no longer a blank on the map of human occupation of this period.

2. The scarcity of sites is principally due to the rarity of research: traces of human occupation of Middle Pleistocene age have been discovered in nearly all regions where prehistoric research has been conducted. This leads us to infer that future research will in all probability lead to the discovery of other and eventually well-preserved sites. Such discoveries will enable us to present a more synthetic study of the first occupations of this peninsular, perhaps one of first regions of Europe to be occupied by hominids.

references

Bailey, G.,   1992   Asprochaliko and Kokkinopilos: TL Dating and Reinterpretation of Middle Palaeolithic
   V. Papaconstantinou,   Sites in Epirus, North-West Greece, *Cambridge Archaeological Journal* 2(1), 136-144.
   D. Sturdy

Darlas, A.   1994   Le Paléolithique inférieur et moyen de la Grèce, *L'Anthropologie* 98(2-3), 305-328.

Fistani, A.B.   1993a   Human Evolution in Albania for the Quaternary Period. In: Becky A. Sigmon (ed.),
                                       Before the Wall Fell: The Science of Man in Socialist Europe, 141-178, Toronto,
                                       Canadian Scholars' Press Inc.

                               1993b   Découverte d'un humerus d'ursidé à l'oléocrâne perforé dans le site de Gajtan I (Shkodër)
                                       en Albanie du Nord, *L'Anthropologie* 97(2-3), 223-238.

Fistani, A.B.   1993   Découverte d'*Ursus thibetanus (Mammalia, Carnivora, Ursidae)* dans le site pléistocène
   E. Crégut-Bonnoure   moyen de Gajtan (Shkoder, Albanie), *GEOBIOS* 26(2), 241-263.

Hennig, G.J.   1981   ESR-dating of the fossil hominid cranium from Petralona Cave, Grece, *Nature* 292,
   W. Herr,   533-536.
   E. Weber,
   N.I. Xirotiris

Howell, F.C.   1989   Yarimburgaz un nouveau site du Pléistocène moyen à occupation humaine dans l'Ouest
                                       de la Turquie (Résumé). In: E. Bonifay et B. Vandermeersch (ed), *Les Premiers
                                       Européens, Actes du 114ᵉ congrès national des sociétés savantes*, 233-234, Paris, Editions
                                       du CTHS.

Ikeya, M.   1980   ESR Dating of Carbonates at Petralona Cave, *Anthropos* 7, 143-151.

Jamet, M.   1982   *Étude neotectonique de Corfou et étude paléomagnetique de sédiments néogènes des îles
                                       de Corfou, Cephalonie et Zanthe*, Thèse de 3e cycle, Université de Paris-Sud.

Kourtessi-Philippakis, G.   1990   Les plus anciennes occupations humaines dans le territoire épirote et aux confins de
                                       l'Illyrie méridionale. In: P. Cabanes (ed): *L'Illyrie méridionale et l'Epire dans
                                       l'Antiquité-II, Actes du IIe Colloque international de Clermond-Ferrand (25-27 Octobre
                                       1990)*, 10-16, Paris, de Boccard.

Kretzoi, M.   1981   Remarks on the Middle and Lower Pleistocene Vertebrate Fauna in the Petralona Cave
   N. Poulianos   (with special reference to new Microfauna – up to 1981), *Anthropos* 8, 57-72.

Kurtén, B.   1983   Faunal sequence in Petralona Cave, *Anthropos* 10, 53-59.

Kurtén, B.   1977   New stratigraphic and faunal material from Petralona Cave, with special reference to
   A. Poulianos   carnivora, *Anthropos* 4(1-2), 47-130.

                               1981   Fossil carnivora of Petralona Cave: Status of 1980, *Anthropos* 8, 9-56.

Poulianos, A.   1982   *The Cave of the Petralonian Archanthropinae: a guide to the science behind the
                                       excavations*, Athens, Library of the Anthropological Association of Greece.

                               1990   Petralona: the Key to the Eurasian Lower-Middle Pleistocene, *Anthropos* 12, 65-89.

Runnels, C.,   1993   A Handaxe from Kokkinopilos, Epirus, and its Implications for the Paleolithic of Greece,
   H.Tj. van Andel   *Journal of Field Archaeology* 20, 191-203.

Shen G.
   Y. Yokoyama

1986   T-230/U-234 Dating of Petralona Speleothems, *Anthropos* 11, 23-32.

Valoch, K.

this volume   The earliest occupation of Europe: Eastern Central and Southeastern Europe.

Wintle, A.
   J. Jacobs

1982   A Critical Review of the Dating Evidence for Petralona Cave, *Journal of Archaeology Science* 9, 39-47.

Andreas Darlas
Université d'Aix-Marseille II
Laboratoire d'Anthropologie
Boulevard Pierre Dramard
13916 Marseille Cedex 20
France

Nikolai D. Praslov

4   The earliest occupation of the Russian Plain: a short note

The Russian Plain extends from the White Sea and Barents Sea in the north to the Caspian and Black Sea in the south. It is bordered by the Carpathian mountains in the south-west and the Ural in the east (Fig. 1). From this immense area we know only a small number of Lower Palaeolithic sites, basically for two reasons. In the first place, it used to be generally believed that the Russian Plain was not occupied by humans before the Middle Palaeolithic, and therefore no systematic survey and research took place, while the few possible Lower Palaeolithic finds were subject of heated discussions. Secondly, discovering Lower Palaeolithic sites is very difficult as a result of significant changes in landscapes since the Lower Palaeolithic. The inland glaciations covered large parts of the Russian Plain, and twice the ice went down to 50° latitude in the Don and Dnepr valleys. The enormous amount of melting water coming from the glaciers led to transgressions of the Caspian and the Black Sea. Especially large scale transgressions are represented by the Akčagyl horizon during the Late Pliocene, the Apšeron horizon during the Early Pleistocene, and the Baku horizon during the first part of the Middle Pleistocene (for the terminology see Ljubin and Bosinski, this volume). These large transgressions created a connection of the Caspian and the Black Sea through the Manyč depression, and a separation of the Caucasus region from the Russian Plain (Fig. 2). This yields the question whether the oldest occupation of the Russian Plain came from the Caucasus region or from Europe.

The Early Pleistocene sediments are mostly covered by younger deposits up to 20-40 m thick. In the middle latitudes the former presence of glaciers almost excludes the preservation of Lower Palaeolithic sites, while in the south the sites were also destroyed by the Caspian and Black Sea transgressions. Therefore there is only a narrow strip of land where Lower Palaeolithic sites may be discovered (Fig. 2). Surface finds and artefacts from uncertain stratigraphy can not prove the Lower Palaeolithic occupation of the region. Apart from contested surface finds and artefacts without a clear stratigraphical context (Boriskovskij 1953), there are only a few finds which may be considered Lower Palaeolithic, and all of them are from the southern part of the region, south of 50° latitude (Fig. 1-2).

Gerasimovka

This site is located on the shore of the Gulf of Taganrog (Mius) near the village of Gerasimovka (Praslov 1968). An old terrace 45 m above the present sea level is covered by the following deposits (from top to bottom):

– Recent Chernozem

– Loess-like loams, in the upper part a thin layer of volcanic ash.

– Last interglacial (Mikulin) soil

– Compact-reddish-brown soil as it is known all over the Russian Plain and characterizing the Lichvin Interglacial.

– 5 m of laminated loams and sands with many saltwater molluscs, predominantly Caspian types of *Didacna* (*Didacna baericrassa, D. pseudocrassa, D. miussica, D. parvula*). In addition, there are some freshwater molluscs: *Unio crassus, U. batavus pseudocrassus, Anodonta piscinalis, Sphaerium rivicola, Viviparus fasciatus.*
The saltwater molluscs date the layer to the Baku transgression of the Caspian Sea, respectively the Čauda transgression of the Black Sea.

– Sands containing freshwater molluscs and small mammals including *Mimomys, Ellobius, Microtus, Lagurus.*

– In a coarse gravel with many flint pebbles at the base of the sands remains of *Mammuthus trogontherii*. From this horizon with flint pebbles about a dozen heavily weathered and severely abraded, rolled artefacts was collected (Fig. 3). A bigger core from quartzite (Fig. 3,3) is worked on both faces and looks like a chopping tool. In addition there are three side-scrapers from flint (Fig. 3,1-2) as well as flakes. The stratigraphy of the site suggests that this small assemblage dates from the Lower to Middle Pleistocene transition.

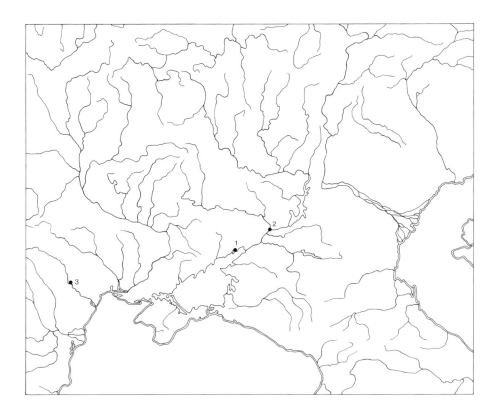

Fig. 1. Distribution of Lower Palaeolithic sites mentioned in the text. (1. Gerasimovka; 2. Chrjašči, 3. Pogreby and Dubossary).

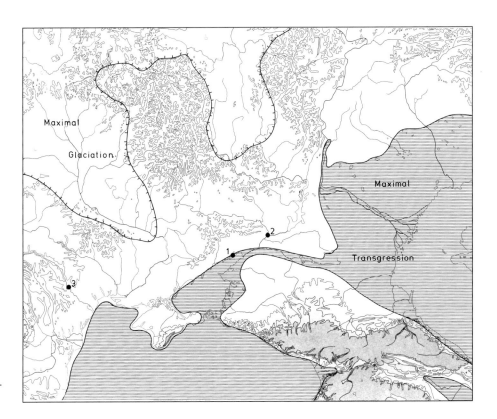

Fig. 2. Maximal glaciation and maximal transgression on the Russian Plain, and distribution of Lower Palaeolithic sites mentioned in the text (1. Gerasimovka; 2. Chrjašči, 3. Pogreby and Dubossary).

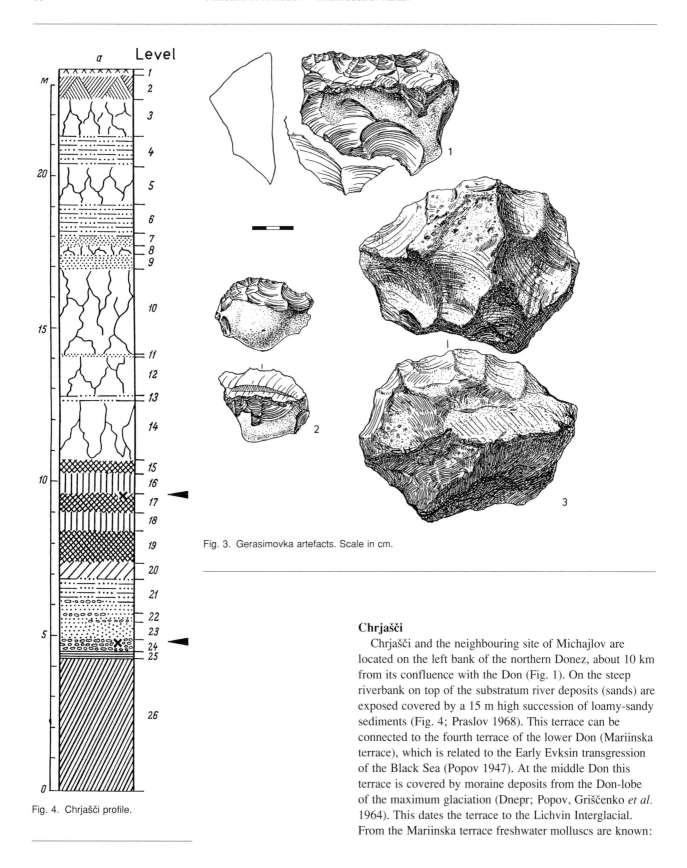

Fig. 4. Chrjašči profile.

Fig. 3. Gerasimovka artefacts. Scale in cm.

Chrjašči

Chrjašči and the neighbouring site of Michajlov are located on the left bank of the northern Donez, about 10 km from its confluence with the Don (Fig. 1). On the steep riverbank on top of the substratum river deposits (sands) are exposed covered by a 15 m high succession of loamy-sandy sediments (Fig. 4; Praslov 1968). This terrace can be connected to the fourth terrace of the lower Don (Mariinska terrace), which is related to the Early Evksin transgression of the Black Sea (Popov 1947). At the middle Don this terrace is covered by moraine deposits from the Don-lobe of the maximum glaciation (Dnepr; Popov, Griščenko et al. 1964). This dates the terrace to the Lichvin Interglacial. From the Mariinska terrace freshwater molluscs are known:

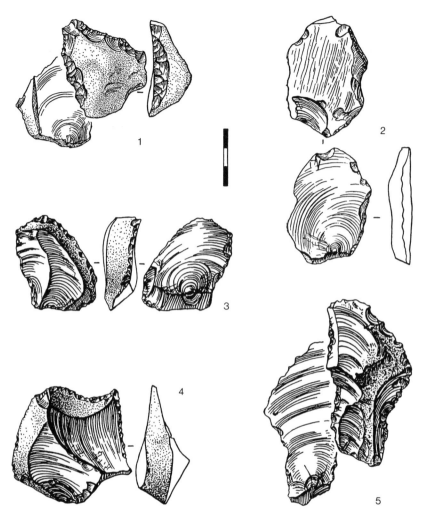

Fig. 5. Chrjašči. Artefacts from level 24. Scale in cm.

Theodoxus fluviatilis, Valvata naticina, Planorbarius corneus, Planorbis planorbis, Galba palustris, V. viviparus, V. contectus, Corbicula fluminalis, Sphaerium rivicula, Pisidium amnicum. Especially *Corbicula fluminalis, Theodoxus fluviatilis* and *Lithoglyphus naticoides* are species characteristic of Middle Pleistocene interglacials. In addition *Corbicula fluminalis* occurs in this region only in the deposits of the Mariinska terrace and the Early Evksin sediments of the Black Sea.

At Chrjašči, sands (level 24; Fig. 4) corresponding to the Mariinska terrace yielded about 60 quartzite and flint artefacts (Fig. 5-6). The finds were collected from the sections; six flakes were found during excavation in level 24. The artefacts are mostly flakes, sometimes with use

damage at their edges (Fig. 5). There are also 4 cores and 7 retouched tools including a quartzite one with a bifacially shaped working edge (Fig. 6,2). In the sediments above the terrace sands three palaeosols are present (Fig. 4). At the Michajlov find spot, 2 km from Chrjašči, Middle Palaeolithic artefacts were found in the lowermost soil (Praslov 1968). At Chrjašči itself the middle soil (level 18) contained about 20 artefacts, including 4 retouched tools (Praslov 1968).

Pogreby and Dubossary

Other possibly Lower Palaeolithic finds come from Moldavia in the southwestern corner of the Russian Plain (Fig. 1) (Anisjutkin 1987; 1989). Near the town of

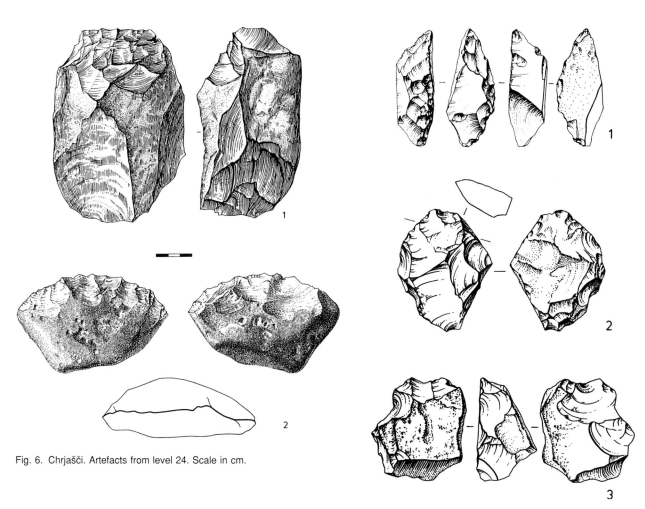

Fig. 6. Chrjašči. Artefacts from level 24. Scale in cm.

Fig. 7. Pogreby artefacts. After N. K. Anisjutkin. Scale in cm.

Dubossary artefacts were discovered in a soil of the cover sediments of the 6th Dnestr terrace. The reddish-brown soil is situated above the sand of the river terrace and covered by thick loess deposits. The soil is assigned to the Lichvin Interglacial.

At Dubossary most of the finds are from the surface. At the neighbouring site of Pogreby the artefacts (Fig. 7) come from the soil itself. Together with the lithic artefacts a tooth fragment of *Mammuthus trogontherii* was discovered (Anisjutkin 1987; 1989).

references

Anisjutkin, N.K. (Anisjutkine) 1987 De nouvelles données sur le Paléolithique ancien de la Moldavie, *L'Anthropologie* 91, 69-74.

Anisjutkin, N.K. 1989 Domust'erskoe mestonachošdenie u sela Pogrebaja na Nižnem Dnestre, i položenie ego industrij v rannem paleolite Evropejskoj časti SSSR i sopredel'nich territorij, *Četvertičnyj period. Paleontologija i archeologija*, 124-145.

Boriskovskij, P.I. 1953 *Paleolit Ukrainy*. Materialy i issledovanija po archeologii SSSR 40.

Ljubin, V.P.
 G. Bosinski this volume The earliest occupation of the Caucasus region.

Popov, G.I. 1947 Četvertičnye i kontinental'nye pliocenovye otloženija Nižnego Dona i Severo-Vostočnogo Priazov'ja, *Materialy po geologii i poleznym iskopaemym Azovo-Černomor'ja* 22.

Popov, G.I.
 M.N. Griščenko,
 Ju.F. Deev,
 N.P. Tereščenko 1964 K svodnoj stratigrafo-genetičeskoj scheme četvertičnych otloženij bassejnov r. Dona i Nižnej Volgi, *Geologija i mineral'nye resursy territorii Nižnego Dona i Nižnego Povolž'ja*.

Praslov, N.D. 1968 *Rannij paleolit Severo-Vostocnogo Priazov'ja i Nižnego Dona*. Leningrad.

 1984 Rannij paleolit Russkoj ravniny i kryma, *Paleolit SSSR. Archeologija SSSR* 1, 18-40.

Nikolai D. Praslov
Institute of Archaeology
Dvorzovaja Nab. 18
St. Petersburg 1920 41
Russia

Karel Valoch

5   The earliest occupation of Europe: Eastern Central and Southeastern Europe

Various series of primitive artefacts collected from Early Pleistocene deposits point to a high antiquity for the earliest occupation of eastern central and southeastern Europe. The earliest excavated assemblages (Přezletice and Stránska skála) date from earlier parts of the Middle Pleistocene. The number of sites increases considerably in later parts of the Middle Pleistocene.

1.   Introduction

This paper gives a short review of Lower Palaeolithic localities in eastern Central Europe, mainly from the Czech Republic but also from Poland, Hungary, Ukraine, Croatia and Romania (Fig. 1). Information about the geographical position of sites is given as well as a short characterization of the archaeological assemblages and their stratigraphical context.

2.   Czech Republic

2.1.   BEROUN, MOTORWAY CUTTING (BEROUN DISTRICT, BOHEMIA)

The site Beroun is situated between the villages of Beroun and Vráž, on the left bank of the river Berounka, about 30 km SW of Prague. The site, 70-90 m above the actual river, was located in a cutting with a length of about 500 m in which a body of sediments up to 28 m thick was exposed.

The lower part of the sequence consists of fluviatile deposits of the so called Vráž-terrace; gravel accumulation was followed by the formation of a Ferreto-soil, in its turn followed by backswamp deposits and another period of soil formation. The upper part of the sequence consists of a loessic colluvium with four intercalated brownearth palaeosols. This sequence was eroded once more by the river which formed the so-called Beroun-terrace, now covered by sandy colluvial sediments.

J. Fridrich collected three artefact assemblages from the exposures: one (A III) from the surface of the Vráž-terrace (this assemblage is probably of the same age as the Ferreto-soil), a second one (A II) from the upper part of the lowermost brownearth E and an isolated find (A I) from directly above the younger Beroun-terrace.

A total of 82 artefact-like pebbles was collected from a briefly exposed gravel surface of about 2000 m^2. The assemblage (A III) was described by Fridrich (1991a; 1991b) (Fig. 2:1-4), and the present author studied 12 pieces from this collection. Fridrich distinguished various types of choppers, protobifaces, two cleavers, cores, one pick, one polyhedron, a discoid and a subsphéroid, as well as several scrapers and 18 laterally retouched flakes. Beside pebbles some amorphic stones were used. Petrographically we are dealing with several quartzites, to a lesser degree with lydite, quartz and other silizites. All edges are more or less intensively rounded due to fluvial as well as aeolian processes. Part of the pebbles have a red-brown colour indicative of an original position within the Ferreto-soil. Most of the pebbles I studied show maximally three unifacial flake scars, three show more negatives and only one pebble was flaked on both sides.

Assemblage A II contains 9 pieces. I was able to study 7 of them and none of the specimens are figured sofar. The pebbles show the same degree of rounding as those from assemblage A III. Four pieces display probably more than three scars and one of these shows only traces of natural breakage, no conchoidal fractures. All are flaked on one side only. Assemblage A I consists of only a small chopper.

The Beroun exposure has been studied by a multidisciplinary group, who published their results in *Anthropozoikum* (Vol. 20 1991). The dating is, apart from geomorphological criteria, mainly based on the results of the investigation of the palaeosols (Smolíková 1992) and the palaeomagnetic analyses (Koči 1991). In the area of the Bohemian Massif there are no brownearth soils younger than PK VII, formed during an intra-Mindel interglacial. This soil might correspond with the uppermost brownearth A' of the Beroun sequence. The formation of Ferreto-soils ends during the late Cromerian s.l., which implies that all soils of the Beroun sequence date from the early Middle or Early Pleistocene (Smolíková 1991).

The lower and upper boundary of the Olduvai-Event has been found in the lower part of the Vráž-terrace, while the Matuyama-Brunhes boundary was identified in the deposits of the younger Beroun-terrace (Koči 1991). This implies that assemblage A III dates to the Olduvai-Event, A II to

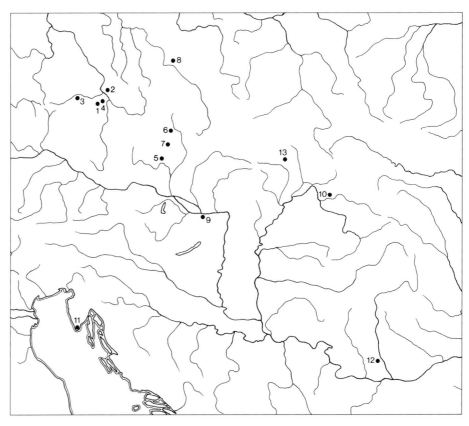

Fig. 1. Location of the sites mentioned in the text:
1. Beroun; 2. Přezletice; 3. Bečov; 4. Karlštejn; 5. Mušov, Ivaň; 6. Mladeč cave; 7. Brno: Červený
kopec, Stránská skála, Švédské šance, Černovice; 8. Trzebnica; 9. Vértesszöllös; 10. Korolevo;
11. Šandalja I; 12. Tetoiu; 13. Travertine sites in NE Slovakia.

the following part of the Matuyama-Epoch and A I to the beginning of the Brunhes-Epoch. Palaeontological remains have not been found sofar.

The lithostratigraphical as well as the chronostratigraphical position of the finds is clear. Their artefactual character is however, questionable. Assemblage A III consists of a selection from the surface of gravel deposits and it is unclear whether such fractured pebbles occur all through the gravel deposits. The assemblage A II comes from a palaeosol formed in loessic slope deposits that are said to have been devoid of other stones. Furthermore the physical appearance (patina, rounding and flaking characteristics) of the cobbles does not differ from pebble tools collected on the surface. The human intervention on these cobbles is not excluded.

2.2.   BEČOV, SITE I-B (MOST DISTRICT, BOHEMIA)

About 70 km NW of Prague, within the area of the village Bečov, lies a promontory called Písečný vrch (sandhill) where quartzite was quarried since historical times. Remains of Middle and Upper Palaeolithic

occupation were documented at several sites, while site I-B might document a Lower Palaeolithic occupation.

Three artefact bearing horizons were found in a cavity filled with Pleistocene sediments. The uppermost artefacts (I) were situated in a brownearth soil, the middle assemblage comes from the sandy lower part of the soil and the lowermost artefacts from the basal tuffit loam.

The artefacts, exclusively manufactered out of quartzite debris, have not been published yet; Fridrich (1972; 1976; 1989) mentions from layer I 107 pieces, from layer II 119 and from III 30 artefacts, mainly scraper-like forms. Choppers, polyheders and proto-bifaces are present to a lesser degree.

Based on the occurrence of a brownearth soil in the upper part of the sequence a *terminus antequem* of late Cromerian s.l. can be assumed (Fridrich and Smolíková 1976).

The artefacts from the Bečov site are unfortunately still hardly published. The good flaking properties of the quartzite would make the existence of clear traces of human flaking activities possible.

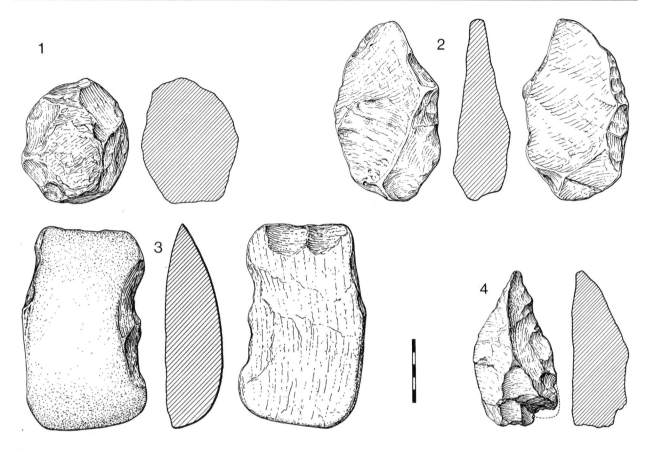

Fig. 2. Beroun, A III. 1. polyhedron; 2. proto-biface; 3. cleaver; 4. pick. Scale in cm.

2.3.   PŘEZLETICE (PRAGUE-EAST, BOHEMIA)

A small, nowadays very reduced lydite cliff (called "Zlatý kopec" = "golden mountain"), is located at the northeastern boundary of Prague, north of the village Přezletice. Pleistocene, mainly lacustrine deposits are present at the foot of the cliff.

The base of these deposits consists of eroded schist (layers 21-18), sandy and loamy deposits and silty clays (layers 17-15). On top of these is a sequence of marly loams and sandy, respectively loamy freshwater marls (layers 14-6) with irregular layers (12) and lenses (in 13) of soil sediments of the Rendzina Series and loamified quartz sands with some lydite debris. Layer 5 consists of fine lydite debris with full-red coloured soil-sediments. The sequence is covered by a fossil soil (4), reworked loess and aeolian loess (3) with a polygenetic soil of Holocene age (2-1) (Šibrava et al. 1979).

The lacustrine sediments yielded a fauna with various smaller mammals (for example *Sorex savini, Desmana magna, Trogontherium schmerlingi, Pliomys episcopalis, Mimomys savini, Microtus raticepoides, M. gregaloides* and *M. arvalidens*) as well as larger mammals (for example *Mammuthus trogontherii* and *Dicerorhinus etruscus*). Mollusc- and ostracod-associations, rich in species, as well as rather poor pollen-spectra are also recorded.

Artificially broken bones as well as bones with signs of use, a few charcoal remains, burnt bones and stones as well as a fireplace are mentioned from this site. Remains of a dwelling with outer dimensions of 4 × 3 m and inner dimensions of 3 × 1,5-2 m with in the neighbourhood a fireplace was found in level 3 (Fridrich 1989; 1991b).

Fridrich distinguished four find levels with very similar palaeolithic artefacts; level 1 with 77, level 2 with 46, level 3 with 640 and level 4 with 107 artefacts (Fridrich 1976; 1979; 1989). The raw material consists mainly of the locally available lydite, some pieces are made out of vein quartz, quartz- and quartzite pebbles from gravels in the vicinity are rare (Fig. 3).

The biostratigraphical position of the site is rather clear on the basis of the fauna, which dates to the Late Biharian Templomhegy Phase (Fejfar in: Šibrava *et al.* 1979), i.e. before Interglacial III of the Cromerian complex (Roebroeks and Van Kolfschoten, this volume). Palaeo-magnetic studies give dates of 0.59 - 0.66, 0,62 - 0.66 and 0.75 - 0.89 my to the deposits (Šibrava *et al.* 1979).

The problem of the locality lies in the artificial character of the finds (see Roebroeks and Van Kolfschoten, this volume). The available lydite has poor flaking properties: conchoidal fractures are not formed, only simple breakage patterns along the finelayered structure of the stone, and one can only recognize more or less notched edges without bulbs. It is therefore hard indeed to characterize the artefacts from a typological point of view. However, despite of this and despite of the vague traces of fire I personally do believe in the existence of worked angular debris and manuports in the locality Přezletice. However full publication as well as a detailed study of all the material is needed for a more objective assessment of the "artefact or pseudo-artefact"-problem.

2.4.   Mušov and Ivaň (Břeclav district, Moravia)

The two localities, three kilometres apart, are situated about 40 km south of Brno. Mušov I is a former gravel pit on the road to Vienna, Ivaň I a built over promontory within the village.

The geological setting of Mušov I is rather complex. The sandy gravels have a tertiary origin and were regarded as *in situ*. The discovery of artefact-like pebbles during the early 70's led to an extensive geological study which indicated that the upper and the lower part of the sequence consists of *redeposited* Neogene sediments. In between there was a few meters of fine sands of Pleistocene lacustrine/fluviatile origin. These sediments lie on top of an (early) Middle Pleistocene gravel deposit which covers the *in situ* Neogene deposits. The artefact-like finds are mainly from the lower redeposited Neogene sediments, present above the fluvial gravels.

In Ivaň I it was only possible to investigate sections in building pits, where artefact-like pebbles were found in similarly redeposited but sandy-clayey sediments with some gravels, with relics of early Middle Pleistocene fluvial deposits on top.

The assemblage from Mušov I consists of several hundred items, Ivaň I of only six. Petrographical analysis of the pebbles clearly shows their Neogene origin. The majority of the pieces has at most three unifacial scars, but there is also a number of pebbles with more unifacial negatives and also some bifacial ones (Fig. 4: 4, 5, 11), though true bifaces are absent. Besides a small number of cortical flakes with clear characteristics there is one

blade-like flake with at least three dorsal flake scars, a ventral side with a bulb and a plain striking platform. The left part of the ventral side shows four steep flake scars and a bit of cortex. The flake (Fig. 4.3) was found at the base of the sandy deposits during a joint excavation by M. Oliva.

For both localities it is only possible to put forward a minimum age, a *terminus ante quem*. Kryogenetic structures with remains of a Ferreto-palaeosol could be observed in the upper part of the lacustrine and fluvial deposits in Mušov (Valoch and Zeman 1979). In this area the formation of the Ferreto-soils took place before the end of the Cromerian complex (Smolíková and Zeman 1981; 1982), which implies a Cromerian age or older. The situation in Ivaň is similar. There the artefact-like finds were collected from sediments with kryogenetic structures and pockets filled with sands and gravels. These gravels are relics of a younger cover of sand and gravel deposited before the end of the Cromerian complex s.l. (Zeman 1974; 1981).

In sum, the complicated geological and stratigraphical position of the supposed artefacts, which originate from redeposited Miocene sediments, makes a clear judgement of the assemblages difficult. It is hardly possible that the Mušov I flake mentioned above was formed by natural processes, while a number of pebbles show negatives which *could* be the result of human activities. The Miocene sediments have not been reworked by a river, but were redeposited downslope over a short distance only. The large number of fractured pebbles cannot have been formed during this process of redeposition. There are only two possible explanations: either we are dealing with pseudo-artefacts formed in the Miocene sea or with real artefacts made when the sediments were accessible at the surface. It should be noted that the assemblage does not represent a selection from a huge number of pebbles, as we are not dealing with an actual quarry still in exploitation here: Effenberger and the present author collected the pieces by simply searching through the lower part of the deposits which were exposed in an abandoned quarry.

2.5.   Brno - Červený kopec (Red Hill)

This is the largest loess exposure in the area of Brno, and the sequence with its numerous fossil soils and terrace gravels has been described several times by G. Kukla (e.g. 1970; 1975).

During prospection of the exposures with V. Gebauer, we found a quartz pebble, totally covered with concretions, in the palaeosol PK X below the Matuyama-Brunhes boundary.

After cleaning it turned out to be a polyhedron (Fig. 4.2), flaked from various directions. Its edges are strongly rounded as a result of aeolian processes.

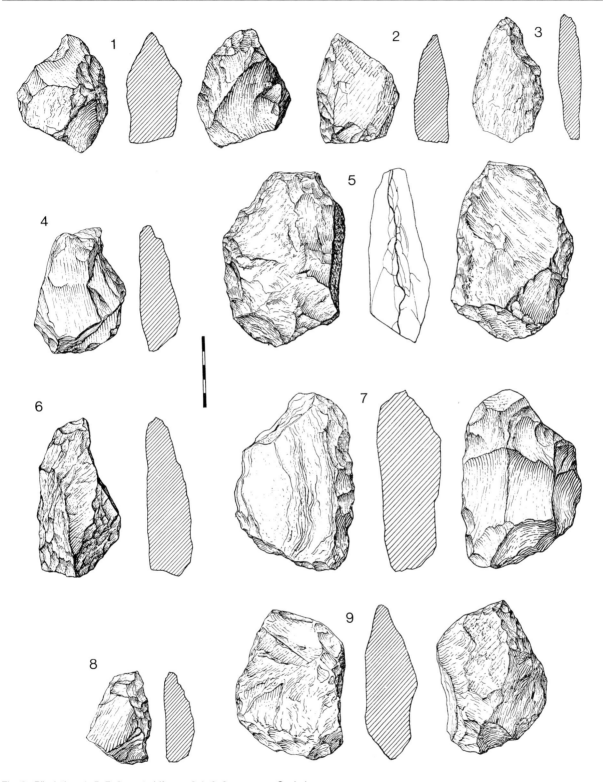

Fig. 3. Přezletice. 1, 5, 7, 9: proto-bifaces, 2-4, 6, 8: scrapers. Scale in cm.

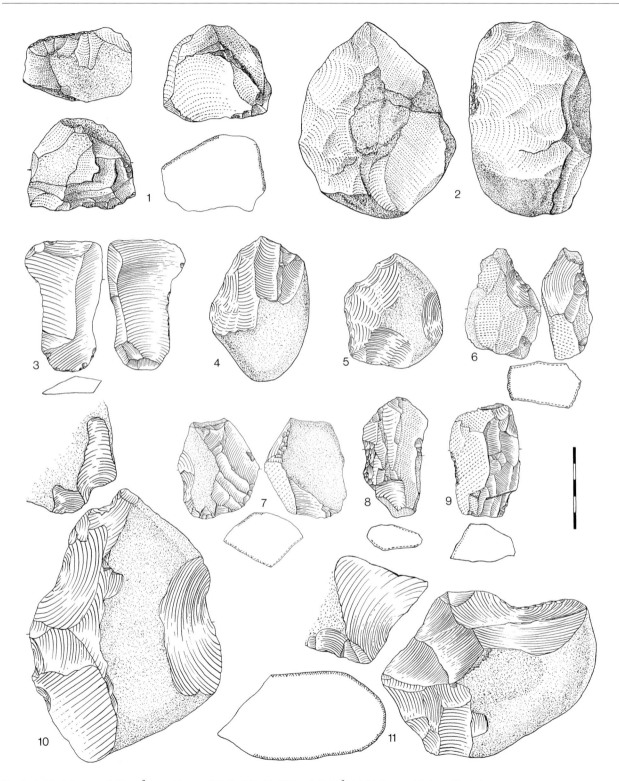

Fig. 4. 1. Mladeč cave; 2. Brno-Červený kopec (PK X); 3-5, 11. Mušov I; 6-9. Švédské šance; 10. Ivan. Scale in cm.

As the Matuyama-Brunhes boundary is located between the palaeosols PK X and PK IX the PK X has to correspond to the interglacial just before the palaeomagnetic transition.

The quartz pebble from Brno-Červený kopec was found in a soil formed in stone-free loessic sediments, with only calcite concretions. Gravel horizons from which the pebble could have tumbled down are also absent in higher parts of the sequence. In the vicinity of the find spot we also found a fragment of an antler and a piece of bone. It is almost certain that the pebble is a manuport.

2.6.   MLADEČ CAVE (LITOVEL DISTRICT, NORTHERN MORAVIA)

A cave-system (formerly Fürst-Johanns Höhle) in a limestone hill in the village of Mladeč (formerly Lautsch), yielded the famous upper palaeolithic human remains from Mladeč. During the 1959-1961 excavations here a quartz polyhedron was found in a side gallery, embedded in the calcite cover which overlies Early Pleistocene sediments.

There is no doubt about the intentional modification of the polyhedron (Fig. 4.1). Shaft III of the main cave yielded three possible artefacts; a flaked piece of chert (*Hornstein*), a large limonite flake and a small quartz pebble with one flake scar (Valoch 1993).

The age of the polyhedron is unknown; fragments of the calcite crust which covered the artefact were recently submitted for absolute dating. Judging from its faunal content, the sediment which yielded the three questionable artefacts dates to the Early Pleistocene.

While it is perhaps possible to get an indication of the absolute age of the Mladeč polyhedron, it is unfortunately impossible to accept the other three pieces as unquestionable artefacts.

2.7.   STRÁNSKÁ SKÁLA I, ŠVÉDSKÉ ŠANCE, ČERNOVICE - GRAVELPIT (BRNO DISTRICT)

These three localities are situated at the eastern boundary of the city of Brno. The most important one is a jurassic limestone cliff Stránská skála I, a second one is a much smaller limestone rock, Švédské šance, about 2,5 km south of Stránska skála I. Černovice is situated 400-500 m to the west of this former rock, on the edge of a huge sandpit which is still in exploitation.

Stránská skála (310 m above sea level) towers above a plain (240 m above sea level), which extends towards the south, and in which Švédské šance – with a height of 250 m above sea level – is hardly distinguishable. The plain is made up of a thick series of fluvial deposits (the so-called Tuřany-terrace of younger sand and gravel cover *sensu* Zeman 1974; 1981). These fluviatile deposits are exploited in the sandpit of Černovice. Augering has shown that the fluviatile deposits extend just unto the

vicinity of Švédské šance, while Miocene deposits surface in areas more to the east.

2.7.1.   *Stránská skála I*

In the northwestern slope of Stránská skála I, which is interrupted by a large former quarry, originally several passage-like caves were present, of which cave no. 4 and no. 8 are relevant in the context of this paper. Close to cave no. 8 there is a well developed body of sediments, deposited against an escarpment and containing an early Middle Pleistocene fauna (excavated by R. Musil in the period 1956-1972). Apart from remains of Würmian (=Weichselian) loess and a Holocene soil at the top (layers 17-21), there are Early and early Middle Pleistocene sediments which can be divided into four complexes. The upper one consists of a scree deposit with palaeosols and soil sediments (layers 6-16; the layers 13-15 are archaeologically important). The second complex is mainly formed by aeolian loesses (layer 5). The palaeomagnetic Matuyama-Brunhes boundary was recognized in the top of layer 5 or at the bottom of layer 6. The Jaramillo Event was found in a second scree deposit (layer 4 and 4a). The lower part of the sequence (layers 2, 3a and 3b) consists of fluviatile deposits which cover an erosional rock-terrace. Palaeontological remains are present in all the various layers.

Using this fauna, the small sections in both caves, of which the front parts were destroyed during quarrying activities, could be correlated with profiles higher up on the slope. J. Woldřich excavated cave no. 8 during the first two decades of this century (Musil in: Musil and Valoch 1968).

The layers 13 and 14 from the upper scree deposits yielded a few stone artefacts, some burnt bone-fragments and some broken bones, including a piece with several parallel striations on a concave surface. Several artefacts were found in the caves no. 4 and 8 and a burnt chert flake in cave no. 8. Here Woldřich gathered a rich macrofauna, whereas Musil could only find a small number of fossils of larger mammals. Cave no. 4 yielded microfaunal remains only. Most artefacts are made out of chert (*Hornstein*) nodules, from the locally occurring Jurassic limestone. Artefacts were only found in the layers 13 and 14 despite the fact that the scree deposits below and above the layers 13 and 14 contain limestone – as well as naturally broken chert fragments.

The sediments in cave no. 4 contain countless chert nodules and many still protrude from the wall. However, their general morphology does not correspond to the artefacts collected in this cave. Remarkable are a large core-like block and flakes from chert with limestone veins (Fig. 5.14). These flakes cannot be the result of natural rock-desintegration or frost action. These processes would follow the structure of the stone and result in a separation

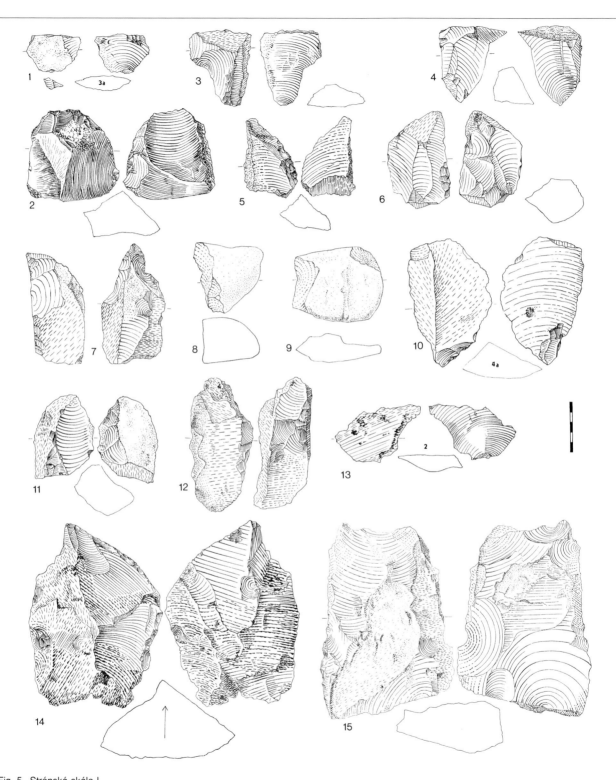

Fig. 5. Stránská skála I
1, 3, 4, 13. flakes with bulbus; 2. core-like tool with retouche; 5. scraper; 6 and 11. bifacially worked core-like tool; 7. pick; 8 and 9. choppers on pebbles; 10. limestone flake; 12. fragment with steep retouches; 14. pointed flake with bands of limestone (hatched), 15. bifacially worked core-like block. Scale in cm.

of limestone- and chert debris. As indicated by Koutek (1926) there are in Stránská skála at least three chert horizons with chert nodules of different conditions; the lowermost horizon is situated at the same level as the two caves. At least part of the artefacts seems to have been made out of chert from a higher level. Limestone flakes (Fig. 5.10) are rare.

As far as technology and typology of the assemblage is concerned, there are only a few flakes with a real bulb of percussion, a plain or cortical butt and a typically "swayed" ventral side. Concentric undulations are hardly visible (Fig. 5:1,3,4,13). Natural debris as well as corelike pieces (Fig. 5:2,6,11) were often used. We interpret the above mentioned block (Fig. 5.15) as a real core, and a split pebble as a hammerstone, both finds from cave no. 4. Two smaller pebbles – quartz and quartzite – look like choppers (Fig. 5:8-9). Regular retouch can been recognized on four artefacts (including a scraper and a pick like object (Fig. 5:5,7), partial and unregular retouch can be observed more frequently. The inferred intentionality of the parallel grooves mentioned above and of the seven striations on an elephant vertebra (excavation Woldřich) and the traces of wear of bone fragments, will be reinvestigated and evaluated by microscopic analyses in a joint project with Mrs. M. Patou-Mathis. Meanwhile, chemical analyses of some bone fragments has shown these were burnt, with temperatures of 200-500°C[1].

The artefact bearing layers 13 and 14 are situated rather high above the Matuyama-Brunhes boundary. The late Biharian fauna from Stránská skála is correlated with the Nagyhársányhegy-Phase (Horáček and Ložek, 1988) and with the period between Interglacial II and III of the Cromerian complex (Roebroeks and Van Kolfschoten, this volume). For the regional stratigraphy it should be noted that the lowermost fluviatile deposits (Layers 2 and 3) of the so-called Stránská terrace are situated one step above the accumulation of Černovice.

2.7.2.   Švédské šance

A north-south oriented trench, 8 m deep and about 200 m long, was dug at the eastern foot of the Švédské šance. The western wall of the trench showed a profile in which 15 layers could be recognized. Apart from the uppermost aeolian loess with the Holocene soil on top, there are three soil-complexes in situ, redeposited soil sediments, sandy-loamy material and a layer of debris. Kryogenetic features were visible in the layers 3-10 which cover two sandy-loamy layers (11 and 12). The lowest one contains jurassic chert-debris, isolated pebbles and some artefacts. The base of the sequence (13-15) is formed by fluvial sandy deposits. Layer 14 shows traces of soil-formation (ferritisation) (Valoch and Seitl 1994).

Four artefacts come from layer 12; three of them are fragments of jurassic chert with traces of modification and partial retouches (Fig. 4:6,8,9), comparable to those of Stránská skála. The fourth piece is a quartzite pebble, bifacially struck from various directions into a polyhedron, with a large part of the cortex preserved (Fig. 4.7). Additionally, the layers 3, 9 and 14 yielded in total four pebbles with one flake scar, but their artificial origin is not sure (Valoch and Seitl 1994).

Unfortunately we have only geomorphological observations at our disposal to date the finds from this site. The basal sandlayers (13-15) are certainly related to the Tuřany terrace and can probably be correlated to the lower part of the accumulation in the gravel-pit Černovice. The formation of the artefact bearing layer 12, as well as the overlying layer 11 with pockets of fine sands, took place directly after deposition of the basal sandy layer, probably under periodical influence of water. Within this framework it can be stated that the artefacts from Švédské šance might be of the same age as those from Stránská skála or slightly older.

2.7.3.   Černovice

A sequence of 8 to 10 m of sand and gravel is situated on top of Miocene sands and is covered by an intensive Ferreto-soil and a fairly well developed Ca-horizon with kryogenetic structures. An intercalated clay-layer yielded a rather rich mollusc (water- as well as land-molluscs) and ostracod fauna as well as remains of *Ursus deningeri*.

Last year (1993) the gravel pit here yielded a few objects which might be artefacts. They were collected by the amateur archaeologist R. Klíma, who has been inspecting the pit for several years. Three of these are undisputed, four others show less clear traces of modification. The best piece is a pointed flake made out of grey chert. It displays a pronounced bulb of percussion with a bulbar scar and a facetted striking platform, several flake scars on the dorsal side and on the left edge probably intentional retouches. All the edges and ridges are slightly rounded, and there is no cortex (Fig. 6.2). The second piece (Fig. 6.1) is a long flake, with a pronounced bulb of percussion, a bulbar scar and a cortical striking platform, made from a white patinated slightly rounded chertstone. The dorsal side of the flake shows a large flake scar and a small rest of the cortex. Both edges show natural pseudo-retouches. The third artefact is a sub-prismatic core with three parallel and one irregular flake scar made from a light grey chert pebble with intensively rounded ridges (Fig. 6.3).

The formation of the Tuřany terrace ended before the end of the Cromerian complex, as indicated by the presence of a well developed Ferreto soil on top of the terrace deposits (Zeman, 1974; 1981; Pfeifrová and Zeman 1979;

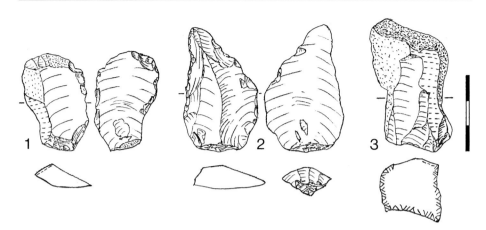

Fig. 6. Brno-Černovice, gravel-pit finds. Scale in cm.

Smolíková and Zeman 1981; 1982). According to the amateur collector, the stray finds (stones as well as faunal remains, e.g. horse and bovid molars, bone and tusk fragments) originate from the lower part of the gravel-layers, as inferred from the progression of the quarrying activities.

2.7.4. Summary

Stone artefacts, traces of fire (burnt bones and a chert flake) as well as broken bones show in my opinion unambiguously the presence of human beings in Stránská skála I. At least the quartzite polyhedron from Švédské šance and the three pieces from the gravelpit Černovice have to be regarded as artefacts. All three localities date to roughly the same period of the Cromerian complex, a period in which the river gradually deposited the sediments of the Tuřany terrace. One should remember that the fauna from Stránská skála contains a large number of water and marsh birds. The artefacts from the gravelpit are redeposited over a small distance (from Švédské šance?). The people at Stránská skála inhabited small caves. Musil suspects the former existence of a third cave above the exposed slope deposits, destroyed due to quarrying activities. The layer 13 and 14 are related to the original content of the cave. That indicates that three caves were inhabited.

2.8.   ARTEFACTS OF UNKNOWN AGE FROM BOHEMIA AND MORAVIA

In view of the large number of surface collections of pebble-tools from Bohemia (Žebera 1952), southern Moravia and recently also from Lower Austria (Zwerndorf im Marchfeld) and near Bratislava in Slovakia this problem is briefly mentioned here. Because most of these pebble-tools are collected from the surface of gravel deposits or relics of gravel-layers, there is only a *terminus post quem*, based on the position of the terrace. In southern Moravia we are mainly dealing with the younger sand and gravel sheet, rarely (e.g. Pouzdřany) with the older one. A relative dating criterion is the absence of wind polish on Late Pleistocene (Middle and Upper Palaeolithic) artefacts collected from the surface. The intensive reddish brown colour of the pale quartz pebbles – the result of impregnation of ferro-oxides – indicates the influence of chemical processes during the formation of the Ferreto-soil (Valoch *et al*, 1978).

One can therefore suspect that these pebble tools (proto-bifaces, polyhedrons, *epannelés*, chopping tools and flakes), date to the Middle Pleistocene, partially even to the early Middle Pleistocene. The finds are important because they seem to document a relatively intense occupation of the area, with numerous settlements along the banks of the river during the Middle Pleistocene.

2.9.   'HOLSTEINIAN' FINDS

Artefacts from the latest phase of the Lower Palaeolithic – the Holsteinian complex – are in the loess areas known from the soils PK VI and V. Bohemia and Moravia yielded only isolated flakes and pebble tools from that period, found during quarrying activities in those soils. Examples are the brickpits Brno-Červený kopec, Brno-Židenice I and II, Sedlešovice near Znojmo, Letky near Prague (Valoch 1977; Valoch in: Musil *et al.* 1955; Prošek 1946). Fridrich collected an assemblage of about 30 artefacts from the PK VI soil in Karlstejn near Beroun. The assemblage contains an *epannelé*, a core, scrapers and small unretouched flakes (Smolíková and Fridrich 1984). Perhaps slightly older is the assemblage from the brickpit Sedlec near Prague, collected by K. Žebera. In a charcoal layer at the base of a loess profile with intercalated paleosols, just above gravels of the 'Mindel'-terrace (Záruba 1942) he found several good choppers, chopping-tools and polyhedrons with rather sharp edges (Žebera 1969, Plate VII-XVIII). Some strongly rounded pieces (Žebera 1969, Plate III-V) are regarded as being older ("Heidelbergian"). Several 'Holsteinian' travertine deposits in Slovakia yielded artefacts at Hranovnica, Vysné Ružbachy and, possibly, the lower levels at Horka (Bárta 1974).

3.   Trzebnica (Silesia, southwest Poland)

The loam pit Trzebnica 2 is located about 15 km north of Wroclaw, in the northern part of the village Trzebnica, at the "vineyard hill" (Winna Góra).

In the southern section of the pit loamy loess-like sediments with a thickness of about 6 m (Jary *et al.* 1990) overlie a gravel deposit. In the northern profiles Tertiary clays are present beneath glacigenic deposits, which can be divided in three units: an upper till, sands and silts with layers of varve clays, sands and fluvioglacial pebble beds and a lower till (layers 3-5) (Winnicki 1990). The glacigenic part of the sequence below the loamy loess-like sediments is in the entire area a little more subdivided. The lower till covers as a moraine relict a gravel pavement (layers 1 and 2), the upper till (layer 5) is situated between fluvioglacial deposits (Burdukiewicz and Winnicki 1989).

Artefacts were found at several places in the pit. Concentration B was collected from a moraine pavement or from the sandy-loamy deposits underneath (Burdukiewicz and Winnicki 1989), concentration C above the pavement at the base of the upper till (Burdukiewicz and Winnicki 1989).

The preliminary reports (Burdukiewicz 1990; 1991; Burdukiewicz and Winnicki 1989) indicate that we are dealing with an industry with small artefacts (scrapers, notches, denticulates, atypical borers [becs]), cores and a few choppers, mainly made from flint, rarely from Devonian limestone and basalt. A small number of bone-fragments is also present, horse and rhinoceros could be identified as well as a tooth fragment of pike.

The upper till is correlated with the Drenthe ice-advance, the lower one with the southern Polish Elster ice-advance. The older assemblage therefore dates to the Ferdynandów-Interglacial (Elsterian I/II), the younger assemblage to the Holsteinian (Burdukiewicz 1990; 1991; Burdukiewicz and Winnicki 1989; Burdukiewicz and Meyer 1991). Krzyszkowski (1993) has another opinion about the age of the assemblages, as he correlates the sandy deposits with the Warthe stage and both tills with the Drenthe ice-advance.

In sum, the industry seems to be comparable with the industry from Bilzingsleben. Sofar, there is no unambiguous indication for the age of the assemblages and further investigations are necessary to clarify this problem.

4.   Vértesszöllös (northwestern Hungary)

The village of Vértesszöllös is located in the valley of the river Átalér in the shade of the Gerecse mountains about 15 km south of the river Danube. On the edge of the village is an extensive travertine limestone quarry on the 60 m river terrace. Three different sites were identified in the quarry area: the palaeolithic site (I), an exclusively palaeontological site (II) and a site where palaeolithic artefacts and footprints of animals were recovered (III). Four find horizons were distinguished at site I, three at site III. At Site I the travertine deposits reach a thickness of about 10 m and lie on top of fluviatile sediments. The find-horizons are located at a depth of 3-5 m. Layer 1 was located in between two travertine beds. Layer 2, in the middle of the upper travertine bed, is only locally present and was less rich. Cultural remains from layer 3 were scattered over this travertine bed. Above the travertine deposits was a loess layer, the upper part of it containing horizon 4 which is very poor in finds.

The rich and well-known fauna from this site includes *Macaca sylvana*, *Ursus deningeri*, Machairodontinae indet., *Stephanorhinus etruscus*, *Equus mosbachensis*, *Hippopotamus antiquus*, and some hominid remains: a human occipital bone and two dental fragments were found in layer 1 (Thoma in: Kretzoi and Dobosi 1990).

Large lithic assemblages, technologically as well as morphologically very similar, were found in all layers (I/1 3163 pieces, I/2 506, I/3 599, I/4 52, III/1 607, III/4-5 677). The industry consists of small-sized pebbles made of quartz/quartzite (50,8 %), flint (44,7 %), limestone (4,3 %) and other raw materials (0,12 %). Typologically one can recognize choppers, chopping tools, proto-handaxes, various side scrapers, borers, burins and end scrapers as well as points and some other tools (Dobosi in: Kretzoi and Dobosi 1990). L. Vértes (1965) classified the assemblage as a micro-chopper industry and called it the 'Buda industry' (see Dobosi, in: Kretzoi and Dobosi 1990 for a detailed description).

Layer I yielded several bone fragments, intentionally broken and used. Some of the fragments show cut marks (Dobosi 1983; Kretzoi and Dobosi 1990).

Traces of fire were recognized at sites I and III. I/1 yielded black spots (35 × 45 cm and 5 cm thick) with small as well as larger burnt bone fragments without charcoal (Dobosi in: Kretzoi and Dobosi 1990).

Biostratigraphical studies originally dated the site to an intra-Mindel phase (Kretzoi and Vértes 1965). Palaeomagnetic analyses showed normal polarity, supposedly the Brunhes Epoche (Latham and Schwarcz in: Kretzoi and Dobosi 1990). Radiometric dating yielded various partially contradictory results with older ages recorded above younger ones. For the travertine between the Layers I and III ages of 245 and 350 kyr BP have been obtained (in: Kretzoi and Dobosi 1990).

In sum, the Vértesszöllös sites indicate a repeated occupation of the mineral water spring during the formation of travertine deposits. Hominids brought game to the site, produced a specific miniature pebble industry with a low level of standardisation, used bone fragments as tools and were able to keep a fire going. The exact age of the occupation is unknown but is by no means younger than the Holsteinian complex.

5.   Korolevo (Transcarpatian Ukraine)

Korolevo is located in the valley of the river Tisza, in the most southwestern part of the Ukraine, hardly 10 km from the Romanian and about 20 km from the Hungarian border. Artefacts were found in several layers in profiles which were exposed in an extensive andesite quarry on the hill "Gostryj verch", on the left bank of the river.

Various sequences with up to six parautochtonic palaeosol complexes contained in total 16 palaeolithic horizons. The four lowermost horizons (Vc, VI, VII and VIII) have certainly a Lower Palaeolithic age. Vc and VI are situated within soil-deposits, VII in loamy deposits and VIII in loamy deposits with fluviatile gravels (Gladilin 1989).

The entire industry is manufactured from andesite. Complex Vc contains chips, small flakes and debris, Complex VI more than 9300 artefacts including 94 cores and 136 tools (amongst others choppers, proto-bifaces, bifaces, cleavers, scrapers, knifes and denticulates.

Complex VII consists of 1539 artefacts including 13 cores and 12 tools (6 choppers, 2 proto-bifaces and 1 biface), while Complex VIII consists of 426 artefacts including 11 cores and 12 tools (with 5 choppers and 2 proto-bifaces).

All assemblages are assigned to the Acheulean, though a small number of cores and flakes with Levallois features are present in the assemblage (Gladilin and Sitlivyj 1990).

The find bearing sediments are completely decalcified, and organic remains are hardly present, though palynological analysis yielded some results. A xerophile flora with *Zelkova*, hornbeam and *Pterocarya* is found in layer 15 (Complex Vc). The layers 16 and 17 (with Complex VI) were deposited during a cold phase, as inferred from the occurrence of *Betula verrucosa, B. pubescens, B. torbuosa, B. humilis* and *Alnus viridis*. Layer 18 dates to a warm phase during which areas with an open vegetation occurred based on the presence of Chenopodiaceae, Asteraceae and Cichoriaceae, *Fritillaria* and exotic trees such as *Zelkova*

sp. and *Pterocarya*. Layer 19 marks another cold phase; noticeable is the decrease of trees and a flora with Chenopodiaceae, sedge, Asteraceae and cereals and for example *Polemonium acubiflorum*. A short warm phase with a boreal steppe vegetation (30-45% boreal pollen) is represented in the layers 20-21, and layer 22 indicates another cold phase with birch and pine trees. Layer 23 with elm, walnut, oak, *Zalkova* and hornbeam is indicative for a warm phase. Complex VII has been collected from layer 25 with pollen from birch and pine trees and some demanding species which indicate mild cool climatic conditions. Layer 26 contained only a small amount of pollen from elm, walnut, beech, *Pterocarya* and water plants (*Azolla, Pediastrum pennales*). Artefacts of Complex VIII as well as a few pine and birch pollen are found in Layer 27, at the base of the sequence.

Thermoluminescence as well as palaeomagnetic analyses have been carried out. Layer 16 has a TL date of 360 ± 50 Kyr BP, layer 19 a date of 650 ± 90 kyr BP and layer 25 of 850 ± 100 Kyr BP. The Matuyama-Brunhes boundary is indicated between the layers 21 and 22, far above artefact Complex VII (Gladilin 1989). The lowermost series of Korolevo are without any doubt Lower Palaeolithic industries, and both stratigraphical and floral and faunal evidence suggest a rather high age. They probably belong to the Acheulean s.l. Attempts at dating the various series have not yielded unambiguous results so far.

6.   Šandalja I (near Pula, Istrie, Croatia)

Two degraded caves, located close to each other, were exposed in a quarry about 4 km NE of Pula.

The lowermost deposits in the first cave consisted of an Early Pleistocene breccia with a rich faunal association, including a left first lower incisive which was thought to be of human origin. The upper deposits contain a late Würmian/Weichselian Gravettian industry. The second cave contained only late Würmian/Weichselian deposits with human skull remains and an Aurignacian and a Gravettian industry.

A small pebble (L 64 mm, W 53 mm, Th 34 mm) made of olive-grey flint was found in the breccia. The narrow side of the pebble shows three large flaking scars which extend to halfway the dorsal side. The edge has been modified by numerous retouches. The ridges are slightly rounded, probably by aeolian activities (Fig. 7). Some bones show traces of fire while charcoal remains are also present. The dominance of immature herbivorous mammals in the fauna might indicate a selection by humans.

The fauna from Šandalja I is correlated with faunas such as St. Vallier, Perrier, Senèze, Chagny and the upper Val d'Arno fauna dating to the Middle-late Villafranchian (Malez; 1974, 1975, 1976).

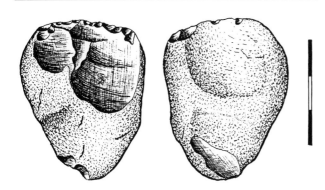

Fig. 7. Šandalja I, chopper. Scale in cm.

The chopper as well as the traces of fire point to a human presence, a statement which might find some support in the faunal evidence. In the context of the cave the chopper as well as a second pebble without clear traces of modification have to be manuports. However, the small number of finds does not allow an unambiguous interpretation of this old site and it can therefore not be accepted as unambiguous evidence for human occupation.

7.   Tetoiu (Bugiuleşti, Olténie, Romania)

Along the middle Oltet river (a tributary of the Olt) in southern Romania, well developed fluviolacustrine deposits are present between the villages Tetoiu and Irimeşti, with several layers containing rich late Pliocene faunas.

Three layers with faunal remains have been identified: the lowermost level (T-1), about 20 m thick, consists of sands and clayey sands with gravel layers. The middle level T-2 is about 40 m thick and consists of sands and lenses of gravel and pockets of clay. The uppermost level (T-3), up to 35 m thick, consists of coarse sands with numerous pockets of gravel.

A small number of flint and quartzite pebbles with possible traces of modification have been found in an exposure, Dealul Mijlociu, in a gravel- and sand layer with a thickness of 1,5 m. The layer is located in the sequence T-1, between the fossiliferous horizons La Pietris (below) and Valea Graunceanului (above).

Of the 'artefacts' found here three small chopping tools are mentioned, and two of them have been figured. Unfortunately there are no detailed descriptions yet and the pictures are not clear enough to get a good idea about the pieces. The two flint pebbles have about the same size (1: length 53 mm, width 38 mm, thickness 24 mm; 2: length 53 mm, width 39,5 mm, thickness 26,5 mm), the third one, a quartzite pebble, is slightly larger. The two artefacts which have been figured show some flake scars.

The find horizon might be correlated with the Olduvai event around 1,7 Myr BP. This is based on the presence of a middle sized *Trogontherium (T. dacicum)* in the fossiliferous horizons La Pietris below, and Valea Graunceanului *above* the findhorizon. The same species occurs in Slatina-3 (the type-locality of *Trogontherium dacicum)*. Slatina 3 has a normal polarity, assigned to the Olduvai Event (Radulescu and Samson 1991).

The artificial character of both figured pieces cannot be evaluated on the basis of the publications available. The artefacts should have an age of about 1,7 Myr BP. The authors furthermore mention finds from Dealul Viilor with a younger age of 1,2 Myr BP (Radulescu and Samson 1991).

8.   Conclusions

This paper has given a short sketch of the Lower Palaeolithic occupation of eastern Central Europe. This area has a rather large number of Lower Palaeolithic localities. Dating evidence suggests that hominids were already occupying this part of the world in the Early Pleistocene. From the earlier parts of the Middle Pleistocene onwards there are various sites with unambiguous traces of human presence, three of which – Stránská skála, Přezletice and Korolevo – have been excavated. At Stránská skála and Přezletice the artefacts were associated with a rich *Mimomys*-fauna from the second half of the Cromerian complex and the paper has explicitly dealt with the evidence for *human* occupation at the sites (*contra* Roebroeks and Van Kolfschoten, this volume and Roebroeks 1994). From this period onwards there are more Lower Palaeolithic sites in eastern Central Europe, all dating to the second half of the Middle Pleistocene.

notes

1 Since no fireplace was found in layer 13 at Stránska skála, it was necessary to analyse the black bones, believed to have been burnt. Our proof of burning is based on the assumption that bones — beside the mineral component hydroxyapatite (Posner 1985) — generally consist of organic matter also and this had to be partly removed during the stay of bones in a fireplace. According to experimental measurements, the temperatures at open fireplaces prevalently vary between 300 - 500°C. That is why we used the differential thermal analysis DTA (Mackenzie 1970) and the ROCK EVAL pyrolysis (Éspitalié et al. 1977) to prove the burning of the bones. Four sets of samples were analysed by both methods, each set from the same findspot in layer 13 and containing a bone of usual white appearance (non-burnt) and a black bone believed to have been burnt. The same quantities of both bones under the same conditions were analysed.

The results of the analyses have been very similar in all four sets. The DTA curves have shown that as a consequence of structure breaking, the burnt bones have a higher content of moisture on the one hand, on the other hand a part of organic matter is missing at temperatures between 250-450°C as compared to non-burnt (white) bones.

The results of the ROCK EVAL pyrolysis have been even more unambiguous. The amount of primary volatile organic component up to 250°C is always higher in the white bones than in the black bones). A similar picture is given by the S2 peaks: the content of non-volatile organic matter is again higher in the white bones because in the black bones it was partly cracked during their contact with fire. The index of production (IP, i.e. relative abundance of volatile compounds primarily present in the sample expressed by the ratio S1 to the sum S1+S2) of all white bones is higher than IP of corresponding black ones. The residual organic matter in the black bones therefore gives higher Tmax values than the organic matter of white (non-burnt) bones. The exception in S2 and Tmax observed in the fourth sample could be the result of a secondary (anaerobic microbial) activity, which is most remarkable in the deepest horizon.

We can conclude that the black bones from layer 13 at Stránska skála have been indeed affected by contact with fire, during which a part of organic matter was removed at temperature between 200 and 500°C.

Antonín Přichystal
Dept. of Geology and
Paleontology
Masaryk University
Kotlářská 2
611 37 Brno
Czech Republic

Mojmír Strnad
Czech Geological Survey
Brno section
Leitnerova 22
602 00 Brno
Czech Republic

references

Bárta, J.	1974	Sídliska pračloveka na Slovenských travertinoch, *Nové Obzory* 16, 133-175.
Burdukiewicz, M.	1990	Wyniki badań stanowiska dolnopaleolitycznego Trzebnica 2. *Šlăske Sprawozdania Archeologiczne* 31, 7-24.
	1991	Badanie osadnictwa dolnopaleolitycznego w Trzebnicy, *Šlăske Sprawozdania Archeologiczne* 32, 7-19.
Burdukiewicz, M., K.-D. Meyer	1991	The Analysis of Erratics from Glacial Deposits in Trzebnica (Silesia), *Šlăske Sprawozdania Archeologiczne* 32, 29-42.
Burdiekiewicz, M., J. Winnicki	1989	Nowe materialy paleolitu dolnego z Trzebnicy, woj. Wroclaw, *Silesia Antiqua* 31, 9-18.
Dobosi, V.	1983	Die Knochenartefakte von Vérteszölös, *Ethnographisch-Archäol. Zeitsch.* 24, 349-361.
Éspitalié, J., J.L. Laporte, M. Madec, F. Marquis, P. Leplat, J. Paulet	1977	Méthode rapide de caractérisation des roches mères de leur potentiel pétrolier et de leur degré d'évolution, *Rev. Inst. Franç. du Pétrol* 32(1), 23-43.
Fridrich, J.	1972	Paleolitické osídlení v Bečově, o.Most, *Archeologické rozhledy* 24, 249-259.
	1976	The first industries from Eastern and South-Eastern Central Europe. In: K. Valoch (ed.), *Les premiers industries de l'Europe*, 8-23. IX congr. UISPP, Colloque VIII: Nice.
	1979	Altpaläolithische Industrie. In: V. Šibrava *et al.*, Erforschung der Pleistozänablagerungen auf dem Hügel "Zlatý kopec" bei Přezletice (NO-Rand von Prag) I. Teil, *Anthropozoikum* 12, 117-126.
	1989	Přezletice: *A Lower Palaeolithic Site in Central Bohemia* (Excavations 1969-1985). Prague: Fontes Arch. Prag. 18, Mus. Nat. Prag.
	1991a	The Oldest Palaeolithic stone industry from the Beroun highway complex, *Anthropozoikum* 20, 111-128.
	1991b	Les premiers peuplements humaine en bohême. In: E. Bonifay, B. Vandermeersch (ed.), *Les Premiers Européens*, 195-201: Paris, C.T.H.S.
Fridrich, J., L. Smolíková	1976	Starý paleolit v profilu B, Bečov I, (Lounské Středohoří), *Archeologické rozhledy* 28, 3-17.
Gladilin, V.N.	1989	The Korolevo Palaeolithic Site: Research, methods, stratigraphy, *Anthropologie* 27(2-3), 93-103.
Gladilin, V.N., V.N. Sitlivyj	1990	*Ašel Central'noj Evropy*. Kijev: Naukova dumka.
Horáček, I., V. Ložek	1988	Palaeozoology and the Mid-European Quaternary past: scope of the approach and selected results, *Rozpravy Čsl. Akad. Věd, Řada Mat.-přír. věd*, 98 (4), Praha Academia.

Jary, Z.,
T. Chodak,
D. Krzyszkowski
1990   Utwory pyowe na stanowisku archeologicznym Trzebnica 2, *Šl. Spraw. Arch.* 31, 31-49

Koči, A.
1991   Palaeomagnetic investigation of the Beroun highwan section, *Anthropozoikum* 20, 103-109.

Koutek, J.
1926   Contribution à la connaissance des calcaires à silex du Jurassique supérieur de la Stránská skála près Brno (Moravia), *Věstník St. geol. ústavu Čsl. republiky* 2, 172-182.

Kretzoi, M.,
L. Vértes
1965   Upper Biharian (Intermindel) Pebble Industry Occupation Site in Western Hungary, *Current Anthropology* 6(1), 74-87.

Kretzoi, M.,
V. Dobosi (ed.)
1990   *Vértesszölös - Man, site and Culture*. Budapest: Akadémiai Kiadó.

Krzyszkowski, D.
1993   The Wartanian Siedlec Sandur (Zedlitzer Sandur) southwards the Trzebnica Hills, Silesian Lowland, SW-Poland: re-examination after fifty years, *Eiszeitalter und Gegenwart* 43, 53-66.

Kukla, G.J.
1970   Correlations between Loesses and deep-sea sediments, *Geol. Föreningen i Stockholm Förhandlingen* 92(2), 148-180.

Kukla, G.J.
1975   Loess Stratigraphy of Central Europe. In: K.W. Butzer, G.L. Isaac (eds), *After the Australopithecines*, 99-188, The Hague: Mouton Publishers.

Leakey, M.D.
1971   *Olduvai Gorge 3: Excavations in Beds I and II, 1960-1963*. Cambridge: Cambridge University Press.

Mackenzie, R.C.
1970   *Differential Thermal Analysis*. London and New York: Academic Press.

Malez, M.
1974   Über die Bedeutung der Entdeckung von Geröllgeräten in den Villafranchien Schichten der Šandalja I in Istrien (Kroatien), *Bull. Sci. Sect.* A, 19(3-4), 79-80.

1975   On the Significance of the Genus *Homo* discovery in the Villafrancian sediments of Šandalja I near Pula, *RAD Jugosl. akad. znan. in umetn., razred za prirodosl. znan.* 17, 181-201.

1976   Excavation of the villafranchian site Šandalja I near Pula (Jugoslavija). In: K. Valoch (ed.), *Les premiers industries de l'Europe*, 104-123, IX Congr. UISPP. Colloque VIII, Nice.

Musil, R.,
K. Valoch
1968   Stránská skála: its Meaning for Pleistocene Studies, *Current Anthropology* 9, 534-539.

Musil, R.,
K. Valoch,
V. Nečesaný
1955   Pleistocenní sedimenty okolí Brna, *Anthropozoikum* IV, (1954), 107-167.

Pfeifrová, A.
A. Zeman
1979   Černovice. In: V. Šibrava (ed.), *Quaternary Glaciations in the Northern Hemisphere*, 6th Sess. Ostrava, Guide to Exkursions, 62-64, Prague.

Posner, A.S.
1985   The Mineral of Bone, *Clinical Orthopaedics* N.200, 87-99.

Prošek, F,
1946   Nález clactonienského úštěpu v Letkách nad Vltavou, *Památky Archeologické* 42, 1939/46, 132-136.

Radulescu, C.,   1991   Traces d'activité humaine à la limite Pliocène/Pléistocène dans le Bassin Dacique
    P. Samson   (Roumamie). In: E. Bonifay, B. Vandermeersch (eds), *Les Premiers Européens, 203-207,*
    Paris: C.T.H.S.

Roebroeks, W.   1994   Updating the Earliest Occupation of Europe, *Current Anthropology* 35(3), 301-305.

Roebroeks, W.,   this   The earliest occupation of Europe: A reappraisal of artefactual and chronological
    T. van Kolfschoten,   volume   evidence.

Smolíková, L.,   1991   Lower Pleistocene Soils of the Beroun highway section. *Anthropozoikum* 20, 71-101.

Smolíková, L.,   1984   Holsteinský interglaciál na lokalitš Karlštejn v Českém Krasu: Paleopedologický vývoj
    J. Fridrich   a posice paleolitické industrie, *Archeologické rozhledy* 36, 3-19.

Smolíková, L.,   1981   The stratigraphical significance of Ferreto-type soils. In: V. Šibrava, F.W. Shotton (eds),
    A. Zeman   *Quaternary Glaciations in the Northern Hemisphere*, Sess. Ostrava 1979, Report No. 6,
    226-230.

    1982   Bedeutung der Ferreto-Böden für die Quartärstratigraphie, *Anthropozoikum* 14, 57-88.

Šibrava, V. *et al.*   1979   Erforschung der Pleistozänablagerungen auf dem Hügel "Zlatý kopec" bei Přezletice
    (NO-Rand von Prag) I. Teil, *Anthropozoikum* 12, 57-146.

Valoch, K.   1977   Neue alt- und mittelpaläolithische Funde aus der Umgebung von Brno, *Anthropozoikum*
    11, 93-113.

    1987   The Early Palaeolithic Site Stránská skála I near Brno (Czechoslovakia), *Anthropologie*
    25(2), 125-142.

    1993   Starý paleolit v Mladečských jeskyních. *Čas. Moravského musea, sc. soc.* 78, 3-9.

Valoch, K.,   1994   Staropaleolitická lokalita Švédské šance v Brně-Slatině, *Čas. Moravského musea, sc.*
    L. Seitl   *soc.* 79, 3-14.

Valoch, K.,   1978   The Middle Pleistocene Site Přibice I in South Moravia, *Anthropologie* 16(3), 229-241.
    L. Smolíková, L.,
    A. Zeman

Valoch, K.,   1979   Mušov. In: V. Šibrava (ed.), *Quaternary Glaciations in the Northern Hemisphere*,
    A. Zeman   6th Sess. Ostrava, Guide to Excursions, 62-64, Prague.

Vértes, L.   1965   Typology of the Buda-Industry, a Pebble-tool Industry from the Hungarian Lower
    Palaeolithic, *Quaternaria* 7, 185-196.

Winnicki, J.   1990   Budowa geologiczna ponocnej ściany cegielni w Trzebnicy-stanowisko Trzebnica 2,
    Śl. Spraw. Arch. 31, 25-30.

Záruba, Q.   1942   Podélný profil vltavskými terasami mezi Kamýkem a Veltrusy, *Rozpravy Čs. Akad. věd a*
    umění, mat.-přír. 52, 1-39.

Zeman, A.   1974   Quaternary of the surroundings of Stránská skála, *Anthropozoikum* 10, 41-72.

    1981   The development of the Quaternary river and lake pattern in Central and Southern
    Moravia. In: V. Šibrava, F.W. Shotton (eds), *Quaternary glaciations in the Northern*
    Hemisphere, Sess. Ostrava 1979, Report No. 6, 290-295.

Žebera, K.   1952   Les plus anciens monuments de travail humaine en Bohême, *Rozpravy Ústř. úst. geol.* 14, Praha.

                              1969   Die ältesten Zeugen der menschlichen Arbeit in Böhemen, *Rozpravy Ústř. úst. geol.* 34, Praha.

Karel Valoch
Moravské Zemske Muzeum
Zelny Trh 6
659 37 Brno
Czech Republic

Dietrich Mania

6   The earliest occupation of Europe: the Elbe-Saale region (Germany)

The oldest Palaeolithic finds from the Elbe-Saale region date to the period between the Elsterian and the Saalian Glaciations. As indicated in the sequences at Bilzingsleben and Schöningen, there are three interglacials within this period, characterised by particular small vertebrate, molluscan and floral associations. The most important site is Bilzingsleben II, with a radiometric age of 350-400 Kyr BP, where hominid remains, assigned to a late representative of Homo erectus *have been found.*

1.   Introduction

The Elbe-Saale region, the area between the northern uplands (*Mittelgebirge*: Thüringer Wald, Erzgebirge, Harz) and their northern foreland, is situated between 50 m and 1100 m above sea-level, whereas the altitude of the basins and the hilly regions ranges from 150 m to 350 m above sea level.

The Fennoscandinavian glaciers reached the northern edge of the *Mittelgebirge* several times during the Pleistocene and covered the Elbe-Saale region, the type area of the Elsterian and Saalian glaciation. The stratigraphic sequence and the chronostratigraphy of the Elbe-Saale region can be inferred from the interlacing of glacial sequences with periglacial deposits.

In 1908, E. Wüst (Wiegers 1928) drew attention to traces of human occupation in the Bilzingsleben travertine. He recognised its high age and assigned the travertine to the so-called "great interglacial" (Holsteinian Interglacial, "Holstein complex"). Woldstedt (1935), however, correlated the Bilzingsleben travertine with the last interglacial, thus establishing an incorrect idea which guided several geologists and archaeologists for a period of about 40 years (e.g. Toepfer 1960, 1970; Unger 1974). Isolated finds and small inventories of stone artefacts were still assigned to the Holsteinian Interglacial, e.g. Wangen, Wallendorf and other sites in the river gravels of the Elbe-Saale region. These finds were regarded as a strong evidence for the existence of the so-called "Clactonian" in the Elbe-Saale region (Collins 1968; Toepfer 1970). Specific conceptions of the mechanism of the climatically induced accumulation of river gravels and subsequent erosion led to the assignment of these finds to the early Saale glacial and to correlation with the Middle Acheulean

of Markkleeberg, that unambiguously belongs to the early Saalian (Baumann and Mania 1983; Grahmann 1955). Apart from the Markkleeberg inventory, these finds represented the only evidence of the earliest occupation of the middle Elbe-Saale region for a long time.

Field research carried out during the last two decades has resulted in a more detailed subdivision of the period between the Elsterian and the Saalian glaciation (Cepek 1986; Erd 1973, 1978; Mania 1973; Mania and Altermann 1970; Mania and Mai 1969; Ruske 1964, 1965), and inventories of the so-called Clactonian can now be assigned to different phases of the "Holstein complex". Furthermore, in 1969, another find horizon in the travertine of Bilzingsleben was found (Grimm *et al.* 1974; Mania 1974). As a result, a site with possible occupation structures, with artefacts and, above all, with hominid remains was then excavated and at the same time a review of its stratigraphical position undertaken. The travertine of Bilzingsleben proved to be as old as E. Wüst had already suggested in 1908 and the site has become one of the most important sites of this period in Europe (Fischer *et al.* 1991; Mai *et al.* 1983; Mania and Weber 1986; Mania *et al.* 1980).

Recently, an important site was discovered in Middle Pleistocene interglacial deposits exposed in the brown-coal mine at Schöningen, in the northern Harz foreland (Fig. 1) (Thieme *et al.* 1992, 1993). Other smaller find complexes with a Middle Pleistocene age from the Saale region can be added to this list.

A possible explanation for the absence of older artefacts in the middle Elbe-Saale region may be that until recently flint artefacts were the primary objects of interest for archaeologists. This material was first transported into our working area within the ground-moraines of the Elsterian glaciation. However, in the context of the earliest occupation-debate it needs to be stressed that objects resembling typical pebble tools may be formed in a natural way, by mechanical action on pebbles found in debris and gravels without any human interference. A lot of pseudo-artefacts were collected and described as human cultural remains in the past (e.g. Andree 1939; Adrian 1982) but also, regrettably, this is still the case today (e.g. the *Altpaläolithikum* of Widderstatt near Weimar, Schäfer 1989).

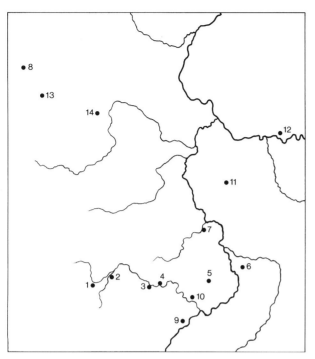

Fig. 1. The middle Elbe-Saale-Region with sites mentioned in the text.
1: Bilzingsleben, 2: Sachsenburg, 3: Memleben, 4: Wangen,
5: Neumark-Süd, 6: Wallendorf, 7: Köchstedt, 8: Schöningen,
9: Lengefeld-Bad Kösen, 10: Freyburg, 11: Edderitz bei Köthen,
12: Klieken, 13: Osterode/ Fallstein, 14: Schwanebeck/Huy.

2.   Stratigraphy and chronology

The stratigraphical subdivision of the Pleistocene
deposits in the Elbe-Saale region and its correlation to the
chronological subdivision of the Pleistocene is a hotly
debated item. There are various contradictory concepts. One
is based on the assumption that the deposits represent only
three major glaciation cycles and only two clear interglacial
phases (Eissmann and Litt 1992). In this view the Saalian
begins with the Fuhne glacial phase subdividing two Middle
Pleistocene interglacials. The archaeological horizon of
Bilzingsleben and the travertine embedding it were assigned
to the latter of these interglacials, which implies that the
entire Lower Palaeolithic of the region is correlated with
the early Saalian. Consequently, the interglacial of Bilzingsleben is regarded to be a "longer interstadial phase" within
the early Saalian. However, there is sufficient evidence of a
Mediterranean flora, of a thermophile mixed oak forest and
a fully developed *Helicigona banatica* fauna pointing to full
interglacial conditions during formation of the Bilzingsleben travertine.

This chronostratigraphical model resulted in a reduced
number of terraces (Fig. 2), by lumping terraces with little
vertical distances and assuming that very thick gravel layers

were deposited. Phases of gravel accumulation were
restricted to the three major glacial phases. The bottom of
the valley of the early Elsterian terrace is 40 to 45 m above
the present river level and the bottom of the valley of the
early Saalian terrace (*sensu stricto*) 15 to 16 m (e.g. Soergel
1924; Toepfer 1933). However, one terrace determined by
these scholars could not be argued away by the simplified
stratigraphy. The terrace is situated at 30 to 35 m above the
river level and it is generally regarded as of late Elsterian
origin. Other valley floors situated between 30 and 18 m
above the river level are disregarded in this model. In my
opinion this model is too simple. Detailed fieldwork has
resulted in a more complex stratigraphical subdivision of
the Middle Pleistocene sequence in the Elbe-Saale region
and in the Harz foreland. This subdivision is mainly based
on the stratigraphy of the terraces which will be described
in the next section. First of all I will describe the basic
cycle which can be observed in some terraces of the Saale,
Ilm and Unstrut rivers.

The basic cycle begins with several m of gravels
deposited during an early glacial phase. One or more
horizons of frost structures, predominantly from a short
pleniglacial phase, can be recognised within these gravels.
The gravels are, at some places, covered by slope debris and
loess. Erosion took place during a later phase of the glacial
cycle and the river cut into and locally completely through
the gravel deposits. Gravel deposits of low thickness, or
even limnic-telmatic sequences of the subsequent
interglacial, overlay the late glacial bottom of the valley.
These fluvial sandy gravels and gravelly sands, generally
1 to 2 m thick, interlace with stagnant water sediments such
as limnic-telmatic sequences and also with travertine
sequences, or they are affected by interglacial weathering.
Six of such terrace cycles have been observed in the lower
valley of the Wipper near Bilzingsleben (Fig. 3). The
corresponding early glacial valley floors are at 35 m, 27 m,
22 m, 18 m and 8 m above and 3 m below the present river
level. The late glacial and interglacial sequence (the fluvial
and limnic series and travertines) starts 1 to 2 m deeper. The
base of the glacial series of the Elsterian is at 45 m above
the present river level north of Bilzingsleben. Judging from
the basic cycle model, it is probable that there is another
interglacial sequence between 45 m and 35 m, a sequence
which has, however, not been identified so far.

Three Middle Pleistocene terrace-travertine cycles were
documented in the lower valley of the Wipper, below the
Elsterian terrace. They can be correlated with three interglacials (Bilzingsleben I, II and III) alternating with glacial
phases, during which sediments with indications of arctic
conditions have been deposited. The upper cycle starts at
35 to 32 m and corresponds to a terrace in the valleys of the
Saale, Ilm and Unstrut rivers, e.g. the terrace near Wangen,

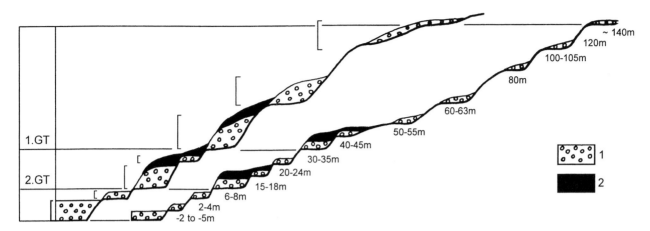

Fig. 2. Stratigraphy of the terraces in the regime of Saale river.
On the left: simplified sequence of the terraces stratigraphy, on the right: real sequence.
1. gravels; 2. glacial deposits (warved clays, groundmoraines).

with Palaeolithic artefacts. A lower terrace in the Saale-Unstrut region is called the *Corbicula* terrace because of the presence of a mollusc fauna with *Corbicula fluminalis* in the sandy-gravelly sections. These layers, at approximately 23 to 26 m above the actual river level, correspond to the middle of the three Middle Pleistocene cycles mentioned above. The so-called "Wallendorf terrace" in the Saale valley belongs to the latest of the three Middle Pleistocene cycles in the lower valley of the river Wipper near Bilzingsleben. The Wallendorf terrace is succeeded by a terrace formed during the Saale glaciation *sensu stricto*, situated at approximately 15 to 16 m above the actual river level. The glacial phase during which this latter terrace was formed was followed by an interglacial phase with which the travertine sequence of Ehringsdorf, the limnic-telmatic sequence of Neumark-Nord in the valley of the Geisel, and the Langenbogen soil complex have been correlated (Mania 1989; in press; Mania and Altermann 1970; Mania *et al.* 1990). The Warthe-Eem terrace-travertine sequence and the Palaeo-Weichselian and Holocene sequences are located below the terraces mentioned above.

3. Characteristics of the Middle Pleistocene 'Bilzingsleben' interglacials

3.1. THE EARLIEST INTERGLACIAL DEPOSITS: "BILZINGSLEBEN I"

A fluvial-limnic sequence covered by a travertine of several metres (Fig. 4) is situated on the 32 m terrace near Bilzingsleben. The sandy-gravelly sediments contain a *Theodoxus serratiliniformis* fauna. This river snail is related to *Theodoxus danubialis* found in the lower course of the

Danube. *Corbicula fluminalis* has not been observed in the fauna so far. Apart from *Helicigona banatica*, the following Mediterranean and southeast European species occur: *Aegopis verticillus*, *Discus perspectivus*, *Pseudalinda turgida*, *Iphigena tumida*, as well as the Atlantic species *Azeca menkeana*.

Larger mammals, such as the straight tusked elephant *Palaeoloxodon antiquus* and the rhinoceros *Dicerorhinus kirchbergensis*, have also been recorded from the *Theodoxus* deposits. Furthermore there are some flint flakes from the Bilzingsleben *Theodoxus* gravels. The small assemblage from Wangen probably also dates to the 'Bilzingsleben I' interglacial, as well as the finds from Memleben in the valley of the Unstrut.

A *Helicigona banatica* fauna has been collected from the overlying sandy-silty parts of the fluvial deposits. *Helicigona banatica* is typical of travertine occurrences which have yielded *Corylus* and *Quercus*. In the synchronous sandy gravels of the Wangen terrace a *Palaeoloxodon antiquus* fauna occurred, along with an aquatic molluscan fauna without *Corbicula*.

3.2. THE MIDDLE INTERGLACIAL DEPOSITS: "BILZINGSLEBEN II"

The "Bilzingsleben II" interglacial deposits consist of travertine deposits laterally interlaced with fluvial sands on top of the glacial 27 m-terrace. The sequence contains at its base the well-known Palaeolithic horizon of Bilzingsleben.

Corbicula fluminalis has not been found in the travertine of Bilzingsleben. The species, however, occurred in the synchronous river sands and gravels of the Wipper and the

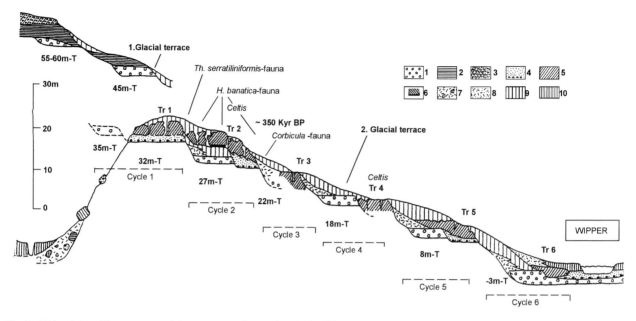

Fig. 3. Bilzingsleben. The sequence of the terraces and travertines in the Wipper valley.
1. gravels; 2. warves clay and silt ("Bänderton"); 3. boulder clay; 4. sandy gravels; 5. travertines; 6. palaeolithic horizon; 7. slope debris with material of solifluction; 8. deluvial loess and slope debris; 9. loess; 10. silts and loams.
T terrace, Tr 1-6 travertines.

Unstrut which are overlain by this travertine complex. *Theodoxus serratiliniformis* occurs occasionally in the archaeological find horizon. Species indicative of a wooded and a open environment are common in the molluscan fauna. Furthermore Mediterranean and southeast European species of the *Helicigona banatica* fauna are present, such as *Aegopis verticillus, Discus perspectivus, Iphigena tumida, I. densestriata, Truncatellina claustralis, Cepaea vindobonensis* along with Atlantic species *such as Azeca menkeana*. The smaller mammals are represented by stratigraphically important species such as the watervole *Arvicola terrestris cantiana* and the beaver *Trogontherium cuvieri. Palaeoloxodon antiquus* is well represented in the larger mammal fauna.

A study of the abundant floral remains showed the presence of a rich mixed oak-forest flora, more specifically a *Buxo-Quercetum, Buxo-Syringetum* and *Berberidion* association with many thermophile exotics such as *Buxus sempervirens, Pyracantha coccinea, Celtis australis, Syringa josikaea, Juniperus sabina, Vitis sylvestris* and other southern species. *Potentilla fructicosa*, a species with a more continental distribution, also occurs (Mai 1988).

The Bilzingsleben II travertine yielded the well known Bilzingsleben archaeological site with its numerous artefacts. Furthermore flint artefacts are known from the

Corbicula gravels near Sachsenburg in the Unstrut/Wipper valley, not far from Bilzingsleben. The *Corbicula* gravels of the Wipper, Unstrut, Ilm, Geisel, Saale and Salzke rivers correspond to this travertine sequence. There are also finds from Neumark-Süd and Neumark-Nord in the Geisel valley (from the so-called Körbisdorf gravels), and from Köchstedt in the valley of the Salzke.

The rich find complex of Wallendorf, east of Merseburg, derives from the base of gravels deposited by the Saale river, just above denudation residues of reworked Elsterian glacigenous sediments. This complex is assigned to the transition of the interglacial to the Fuhne glacial phase. One flint flake comes from the basal layers of the loess which is overlain by the main archaeological horizon correlated to the travertine of Bilzingsleben II.

3.3.   THE LATER INTERGLACIAL DEPOSITS: "BILZINGS-
         LEBEN III"

Another travertine discovered near Bilzingsleben is situated on the 22 m-level. The travertine differs distinctly from the older ones because of its lithology and its fossil content. The Bilzingsleben-III travertine contains a *Helix pomatia* mollusc fauna with exotic elements (*Aegopis verticillus, Discus perspectivus, Iphigena densestriata, Truncatellina claustralis*) along with components of a temperate

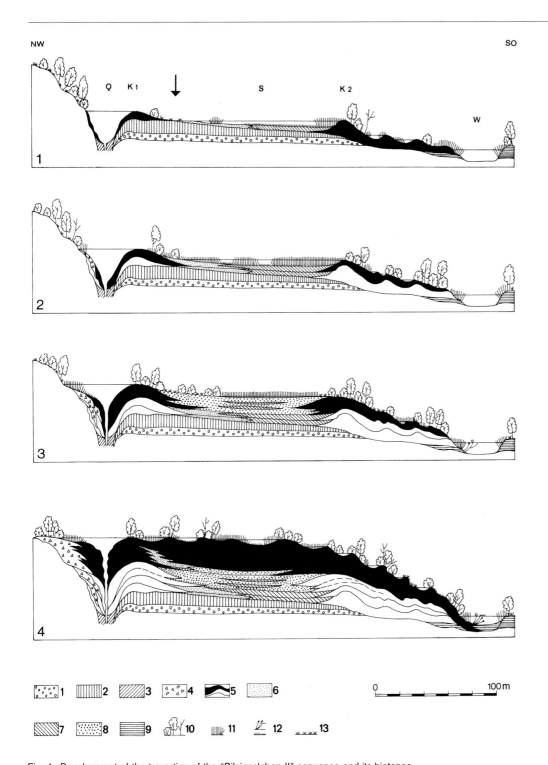

Fig. 4. Development of the travertine of the "Bilzingsleben II" sequence and its biotopes.
1. terrace gravel; 2. loess; 3. debris in the carstic spring; 4. slope debris; 5. travertine; 6. travertine sand; 7. lacustrine limestone;
8. loose travertine; 9. river sediments; 10. trees and shrubs; 11. Phragmites; 12. plants of aquatic biotops (Potamogeton, Nymphaceae, Charophytae); 13. Poaceae, Gramineae, herbs.
Q spring, K travertine cascade, S lake, W river (Wipper), the arrow refers to the position of the Palaeolithic living floor.

mixed forest (oak and hazel). Other south and southeast European representatives are: *Iphigena latestriata*, *I. tumida*, *Pagodulina pagodula*, *Valvata naticina*.

The limnic-telmatic deposits from the upper series of the Körbisdorf gravels in the Geisel valley (Mania and Mai 1969) and the slope debris soil complex of Lengefeld-Bad Kösen profile (Rudelsburg soil complex, Mania and Altermann 1970, new investigations cf. Mania 1989, 1990) are also indicative of the 'Bilzingsleben III' interglacial. A fully developed *Helicigona banatica* fauna associated with its particular *Azeca menkeana* fauna was found in the valley of the Geisel and in Lengefeld-Bad Kösen. A hornbeam-oak wood with Mediterranean and Pontic species (e.g. *Crataegus pentagyna*, *Prunus maheleb*, *Acer monspessulanum*, *Quercus pubescens*, *Azolla filiculoides*) was determined in the profile of the Geisel valley (Mania and Mai 1969). In the Rudelsburg soil-slope debris complex *Celtis* occurred.

3.4.   ASSIGNMENT

The latest Bilzingsleben interglacial (Bilzingsleben III) might correspond to the Dömnitz Interglacial (Cepek 1986; Erd 1973, 1978), which according to pollen analysis resembles the Wacken and the Schöningen Interglacial (Menke 1980; Urban *et al.* 1991). The middle Bilzingsleben interglacial (Bilzingsleben II) represents an older inter-glacial phase which does not correspond to the Holsteinian *sensu stricto* because of clear differences in the palynological record (K. Erd, pers. comm. 1993). The palynological picture shows similarities with that from the so-called Reinsdorf Interglacial deposits exposed in the browncoal-pit near Schöningen, which also contain artefacts. The pollen succession of the Reinsdorf Interglacial differs from the Holsteinian *sensu stricto* as well as from the succession of the Schöningen Interglacial because of a high amount of *Abies* pollen (Urban, in Thieme *et al.* 1993; Urban, in press).

The *Helicigona banatica - Helix pomatia - Azeca menkeana* fauna of the three Bilzingsleben interglacials represents apparently typical Middle Pleistocene features also recognised in other interglacial deposits of the "Holsteinian complex", e.g. in the travertine of Brüheim, Schwanebeck and Osterode near the "Fallstein" (cf. Mania 1973, 1983). These Middle Pleistocene faunas share the occurrence of the now extinct species *Acicula diluviana*.

A chronological indication was obtained by the ^{234}U-^{230}Th and ESR dates of the middle interglacial, the Bilzingsleben II deposits with the palaeolithic find horizon (see Schwarcz *et al.* 1988). The dates of 320 - 350 Kyr and 280 - 414 Kyr BP suggest a correlation of the Bilzingsleben II interglacial with OIS 11.

4.   The Palaeolithic finds of the Middle Pleisto-cene

4.1.   WANGEN, NEAR NEBRA

Sandy gravels from the Unstrut, situated at 30 m above the level of the actual river, yielded a small series of approximately 50 flint artefacts (Lehmann 1922; Lehmann and Lehmann 1921; Toepfer 1961, 1968, 1960). The composition of the mollusc fauna and the remains of a *Palaeoloxodon antiquus* fauna indicate that the fluvial sediments were deposited during an interglacial phase. The finds consist of relatively small flakes, cores and tools. The pieces are 30-75 mm long (average size 50 mm). Some cores display a crude platform preparation. There are simple and double scrapers, along with pointed and transversal ones, while tools with crudely denticulated and notched edges occur. The hard hammer technique is manifested by thick flakes and obtuse flaking angles with an average value of 126.

4.2.   MEMLEBEN, IN THE DISTRICT OF NEBRA

A gravel layer, approximately 1 m thick, was exposed over a length of 35 m on a plateau on the southern side of the Unstrut valley. It was overlaying Early Pleistocene quartz gravels and covered by solifluction deposits several m thick. These consisted of reworked soil material derived from a Middle Pleistocene *Parabraunerde*. Borings showed the interfingering of the gravel with gyttjas and peats from a limnic sequence containing pollen and plant remains of a mixed hornbeam-oak wood as well as fruits of *Trapa natans* and *Vitis sylvestris* (Mai 1988; Mania 1984). Shells of *Theodoxus serratiliniformis* and an interglacial mollusc fresh water fauna were found in the two types of deposits.

In total, 104 flint artefacts were recovered here by Mania and G. Cubuk in 1975. They closely resemble those from Wangen. Here, too, there are cores and flakes manufactured with a hammerstone as well as tools. The flakes are relatively thick with flaking angles between 100-145°, and an average value of 123°. The artefacts are 25 to 108 mm long, with an average size of 52 mm. All cores are exhausted, and they display crudely prepared striking platforms, while the tools display a rough retouch. There are simple and double scrapers, a transversal scraper, and some denticulates and notched pieces (cf. Weber 1977).

4.3.   BILZINGSLEBEN, DISTRICT OF ARTERN (BILZINGS-LEBEN I)

Two simple flakes, 3 to 5 cm long, as well as a simple scraper (6 cm long) come from the *Theodoxus* gravels. All pieces were made of cretaceous flint and hard hammer struck.

4.4. BILZINGSLEBEN, DISTRICT OF ARTERN (BILZINGSLEBEN II, LOESS)

The terrace travertine sequence of the middle complex displays the following succession: Wipper gravels, 1 m thick, are situated on the 27 m level. Upwards, they pass over into a gravelly solifluction layer and then into loamy solifluction debris with limestone and dolomite blocks and isolated pebbles as well as frost structures. This 30 to 40 cm thick horizon is covered by reworked loesses, covered by a primary, aeolian loess. Several ice wedge generations were observed in this loess series, which is 3 to 4 m thick. After an erosional phase the loess was bleached by a pseudogley, then dissected by a brook. The interglacial travertine precipitation had already occurred in the channels of the brook, and an up to 6 m thick travertine profile subsequently developed on top of them.

At the base of the loess sequence, close to the solifluction horizon, a 5 cm thick grey humus layer contained a patinated flint flake.

4.5. BILZINGSLEBEN, IN THE DISTRICT OF ARTERN (BILZINGSLEBEN II, TRAVERTINE)

At the base of the travertine dated to the middle Middle Pleistocene interglacial the Palaeolithic horizon is present. It rests on the loess surface, which has constituted the flat and horizontal surface of a shore terrace of a shallow lake, as well as the subsoil of the basin cut by the brook channels. Adjacent to the shore terrace, an alluvial fan composed of travertine sand was deposited from the west. The fan and the shore are the two types of facies containing the cultural remains, and are known in the literature on Bilzingsleben as the *Schwemmfächer* and the *Uferbereich* respectively.

The archaeological horizon is covered by a 60 cm thick *Chara* limestone, overlain by a complex travertine sequence several m thick.

More than 1000 m² of the main find horizon have been excavated so far. The finds seem to have been discarded at a location used as a home base by early humans, occupied for a substantial period of time during the warm-temperate maximum of the interglacial.

4.5.1. Palaeo-ecological setting

The camp site was situated on a shore terrace at the edge of a shallow lake fed by an ascending karst spring. Close to the site was the outflow of the source. To the west, behind it, the slope of the valley rose, and to the north-west, east and south-east the valley lowland spread. The prevailing vegetation of this area can be inferred from the floral remains: a light, dry oak wood, predominantly interspread by a thicket of *Buxus*. Meadows with scrubs of *Buxus sempervirens*, *Syringa josikaea*, *Pyracantha coccinea*,

Potentilla fructicosa, *Corylus avellana*, *Swida sanguinea*, *Viburnum lantana* and other species are indicated too. *Cotoneaster integerrimus* and *Juniperus sabina* shrubs grew on the slopes of the valley. Dense mixed oak forests with *Taxus baccata* occurred in the narrow valley north of the site. In the valley, thickets of willow, reeds, meadow and swampy woods prevailed.

Judging from the floral and faunal remains, the climate was warm and relatively dry. The average temperature in January was -0.5° to +3°C, in July +20° to 25°C, with a yearly average of +10° to +11°C. Seven months showed average temperatures of more than +10°C. The annual precipitation was approximately 800 mm.

4.5.2. Vegetation

The most important types of vegetation were the *Buxo-Quercetum*, *Buxo-Syringetum* and *Berberidion* (Mai 1983, 1988, 1989). They contained mediterranean and South-East European species such as *Buxus sempervirens*, *Pyracantha coccinea*, *Celtis australis*, *Syringa josikaea*, *Juniperus sabina*, *Vitis sylvestris*, associated with the subcontinental species *Potentilla fructicosa*. Furthermore, the flora consisted of the following species: *Marchantia* sp., *Thelypteris thelypteroides*, *Taxus baccata*, *Picea abies*, *Quercus robus*, *Alnus glutinosa*, *Betula pubescens*, *Populus tremula*, *Tilia platyphyllos*, *Pyrus* sp., *Prunus avium*, *Prunus padus*, *Acer campestre*, *Acer pseudoplatanus*, *Fraxinus excelsior*, *Berberis vulgaria*, *Corylus avellana*, *Salix cinerea*, *Salix purpurea*, *Rubus* sp., *Cotoneaster integerrimus*, *Crataegus* sp., *Euonymus* sp., *Cornus mas*, *Swida sanguinea*, *Hedera helix*, *Rhamnus frangula*, *Viburnum lantana*, *Philadelphus coronarius*, *Peucedanum alsaticum*, *Galeobdolon luteum*, *Phragmires communis*, Cyperaceae, Gramineae, Bryophytae, Characeae (*Charites cava*) (Nötzold 1983).

4.5.3. Molluscan fauna

The characteristic association found in the archaeological horizon and travertine is the *Helicigona banatica* fauna with in total 90 species (Mania 1983). Thirty three of these are wood species. Besides *H. banatica*, other south and southeast European species occur: *Pagodulina pagodula*, *Discus perspectivus*, *Aegopis verticillus*, *Iphigena tumida*. Species of open terrain frequently occur, indicating the occurrence of light woods, forest steppes and open regions. Apart from common open ground species (*Pupilla muscorum*, *Vertigo pygmaea*, *Truncatellina cylindrica*, *Vallonia pulchella*, *V. costata*) southern steppe forms appear (*Truncatellina claustralis*, *Cepaea vindobonensis*, *Pupilla triplicata*). Among the aquatic fauna, *Theodoxus serratiliniformis* and the snail *Belgrandia germanica* living in sources prevail. The wood fauna is associated with the Atlantic species *Azeca menkeana*.

4.5.4.   Ostracod fauna

As yet, 20 species have been determined (Diebel and Pietrzeniuk 1980). The occurrence of the semi-aquatic *Microdarwinula zimmeri*, today living in regions near the Equator, as well as a salt-water species, is noteworthy.

4.5.5.   Vertebrate fauna

The species identified are mostly from the archaeological horizon. The great number of skeletal remains can be related to the hunting activities of early hominids, while the fish remains are also considered to be food refuse left by humans.

Pisces: *Silurus glanis*, *Tinca tinca* (Hebig 1983).

Amphibia/Reptilia: *Bufo bufo*, *Natrix natrix* (Böhme 1989).

Aves: *Haliaetus albicilla* (pers.comm. K. Fischer, Berlin).

Micromammalia: *Sorex araneus*, *Talpa* sp., *Castor fiber*, *Trogontherium cuvieri*, *Glis glis*, *Apodemus* sp., *Clethrionomys glareolus*, *Microtus arvalis*/*M. agrestris*, *M. subterraneus*, *Microtus* sp., *Arvicola terrestris cantiana*, (Heinrich 1989, 1991).

Other mammals are: *Canis lupus*, *Vulpes vulpes*, *Ursus deningeri-spelaeus*, *Meles meles*, *Felis silvestris*, *Panthera (Leo) spelaea*. *Macaca sylvana*, *Palaeoloxodon antiquus*, *Equus mosbachensis-taubachensis*, *Dicerorhinus kirchbergensis*, *D. hemitoechus*, *Sus scrofa*, *Dama* sp., *Cervus elaphus*, *Capreolus capreolus*, *Bos primigenius*, *Bison priscus*. The evidence of the occurence of *Bubalus murrensis* is questionable (Fischer 1991, Guenther 1991, Musil 1991a, Musil 1991b, Toepfer 1983).

A characteristic Middle Pleistocene *Palaeoloxodon antiquus* fauna is present.

4.5.6.   The Palaeolithic finds from Bilzingsleben

Favourable conditions of preservation have preserved possible occupation structures and activity zones at the site. Awaiting the results of detailed taphonomic analyses of the site, we have already discerned several patterns within the find material, such as the foundations of three simple dwelling structures. In front of them, there were hearths and two to three workshops with anvils of stone or bone, with artefacts and fractured bones. Further away from the dwelling structures, we discern a workshop zone resembling the workshops found in front of the shelters. Within this zone, there is an oval paved area with a diameter of 9 m. It consists of pebbles and bone fragments of nut to fist-size. There were no objects found lying on top of this paved area. The distribution of specialised forms of tools, of debris related to the manufacture of the tools, as well as bone, antler, ivory and wood artefacts is an indication of the existence of other areas of specific activities. The alluvial fan stretching in from the shore-line contains the waste dump of the camp site. The camp site is assumed to have been the home base of a group of hominids for some time.

The artefacts (Fig. 5) are differentiated according to their functions. Large pebble tools were made of quartzite, limestone and crystalline rock (chopper, chopping tools, hammerstones). With small quartz hammerstones relatively small flint tools (8 to 100 mm long) were produced: knives, backed-knives ("Keilmesser"), scrapers, hand-axe shaped points, Tayac points, Quinson points, denticulates and notches. They are mainly edge retouched, but bifacial and unifacial retouches occur too. Large scrapers, backed knives, chisel-shaped tools and anvils were made of bone, while picks and club-like tools were manufactured from deer antlers. A great number of wood remains may represent artefacts: rod-like, hook- and spade-shaped forms occur. Some bone artefacts exhibit deliberately engraved sequences of lines (Mania and Mania 1988). The main source of food was constituted by large game, dominated by rhinoceros (Mania 1990; Mania and Weber 1986).

4.5.7.   The hominid remains from Bilzingsleben

The comparative study of the abundant hominid remains by E. Vlcek demonstrated that the Bilzingsleben fossils largely resemble Olduvai Hominid 9, *Pithecanthropus* VIII and *Sinanthropus* III. This is also the case with the latest finds from Bilzingsleben such as G1, A3 and B7. For this reason, Vlcek attributed these fragments to the Middle Pleistocene form of *Homo erectus bilzingslebenensis* (Mania and Vlcek 1993; Vlcek 1978, 1986, 1991). All the hominid remains from Bilzingsleben, apart from one milk-molar, can be assigned to three different individuals.

4.6.   SACHSENBURG, IN THE DISTRICT OF ARTERN

On the western edge of the Wipper-Unstrut valley gravels exposed in the seventies yielded a small series of flint artefacts. An interglacial molluscan fauna was also discovered there, with *Corbicula fluminalis* and *Theodoxus serratiliniformis*. The existence of a *Palaeoloxodon antiquus* fauna was inferred by bone remains and a tusk excavated there. Among the artefacts a polyhedric, crudely prepared core and some small flakes with obtuse flaking angles were present.

4.7.   VALLEY OF THE GEISEL, IN THE DISTRICT MERSEBURG

Only a few artefacts were discovered in the lower part of the Körbisdorf gravels (Mania and Mai 1969). They were found in the brown-coal mine of Neumark-Süd and Neumark-Nord, i.e. within the last remnants of the Körbisdorf gravels, once exposed over several square km. These gravels were divided into two sequences each consisting of interglacial sandy gravels with an overlying glacial gravel

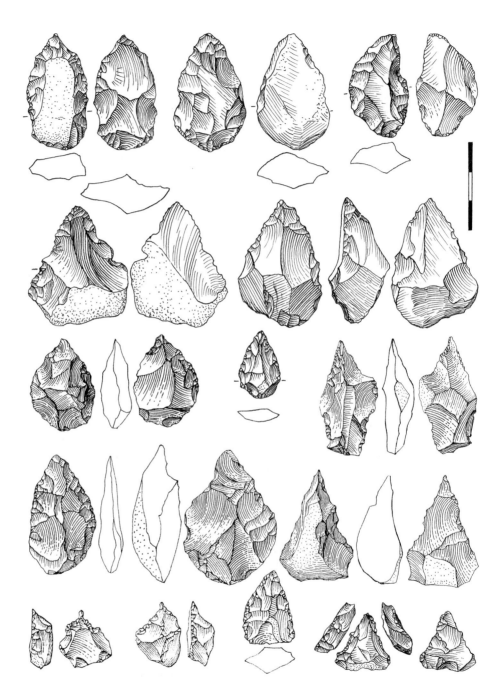

Fig. 5. Bilzingsleben: flint artefacts. Scale in cm.

cover. The sequences were separated by an erosional level area and loesses containing an arctic molluscan fauna. A molluscan fauna with an abundant occurrence of *Corbicula fluminalis* was recovered in the sandy gravels of the lower series, together with common interglacial fresh water species, some thermophile wood species and predominantly species of open terrain. Among the mammal fossils remains of *Palaeoloxodon antiquus*, *Equus* sp., *Dicerorhinus kirchbergensis*, cervids and bovids were identified. Decades ago oak trunks, pine cones and other plant remains were repeatedly observed in this horizon when the layers covering the brown-coal were removed by the mining companies. Unfortunately, these exposures were never systematically studied.

Alluvial peats and travertines were present in the interglacial fluvial sediments of the upper series, yielding a rich *Helicigona banatica* fauna, remains of a *Palaeoloxodon antiquus* fauna as well as fruits and seeds indicative of Mediterranean-subcontinental hornbeam-oakwoods as well as dry oakwoods (Mania and Mai 1969). The well-known artefacts from the *Corbicula* sands are made of flint. They consist of a small exhausted disc-shaped core and some small flakes. A chunk shows a notched edge produced by a powerful blow.

4.8.   KÖCHSTEDT, IN THE DISTRICT OF EISLEBEN

At several locations in the valley of the Salzke in the eastern Harz foreland, Middle Pleistocene gravels were exposed, mostly consisting of two fluvial series, like in the valley of the Geisel. The upper part was a gravel layer accumulated during a cold phase, generally interpreted as the early Saale glacial. It contained a *Mammuthus* fauna with *Mammuthus trogontherii/M. primigenius* and *Coelondonta antiquitatis* as well as several ice wedge generations. The lower part was a sandy gravel belonging to the *Corbicula* horizon. It was overlain by a net of ice wedges and solifluction deposits with cryoturbations, an indication of another glacial (Fuhne glacial). *Corbicula fluminalis* occurred with salt water forms such as the snail *Hydrobia stagnorum* and the salt water ostracode *Cyprideis litoralis*, *Heteocypris salinus* and *Candona angulata*. Other elements of the fauna are interglacial aquatic forms, species of bogs and of various moist biotopes, lowland wood species and some thermophile mixed wood species (species of a *Helicodonta obvoluta-Chochlodina laminata* fauna, Mania 1973). Vertebrate remains are represented by *Palaeoloxodon antiquus*, *Dicerorhinus kirchbergensis*, *Castor fiber* and *Esox lucius* (cf. Mertin 1940).

The small series of artefacts contains flint flakes, similar to those from Wangen, Memleben and Wallendorf (Toepfer 1961, 1968, 1970).

4.9.   WALLENDORF, IN THE DISTRICT OF MERSEBURG

The base of the so-called Wallendorf terrace located at the eastern edge of the Saale valley is approximately 10 m above the early Saale glacial level and is dated to the Fuhne glacial (Ruske 1964, 1965). For the greater part, the gravel cover, with a thickness of 5 m, consists of material accumulated during a cold phase, as shown by the composition of its mollusc fauna and by frost structures in its upper part. The basal layers of the gravel contain mollusc associations of a cool temperate climate, and *Palaeoloxodon* remains. This indicates that the basal sandy gravels were deposited during the transition of the late interglacial to the early glacial. Artefacts found in this part of the section were, without any exception, manufactured from baltic flint. Approximately 1000 objects are present (Mania 1984, 1988; Toepfer 1961, 1968, 1970). The denudation residue of the Elsterian glacigenous sediments at the base of the gravel seems to have been the source of the raw material, as it contains a large number of large flint nodules. The artefacts might represent the remains of workshops once situated at the bottom of the valley. Approximately 75% of the artefacts consist of flakes, 23% of cores and only 2% are tool pieces with retouche. Small preparation and retouch debris was not collected, so larger flakes dominate, with sizes between 35 and more than 100 mm, and an average value of approximately 60 to 70 mm. The cores reach sizes of more than 150 mm, but more than 80% are smaller than 85 mm, mostly exhausted exemplars. Most flakes are short and thick, irregularly shaped with their cortex often not yet removed. They have large flaking angles (95° to 150°, average value 125°) and well pronounced bulbs of percussion. Levallois cores as well as prepared cores used for the production of blades also occur, as do flakes from such cores. Only a few flake tools are present, mostly scrapers. Some flakes have notched or denticulated edges. Some crudely flaked tools resemble roughouts of handaxes.

4.10.   SCHÖNINGEN, IN THE DISTRICT OF HELMSTEDT

The locality Schöningen (Thieme *et al.* 1993) is situated in the northern region of the sub-herzynic basin north of the Harz mountains. It is located in a NW-SE channel which follows the southern edge basin of the Straßfurt-Helmstedt salt saddle. After suberosion the channel changed into a shallow swampy lake in which a sequence of 8 m sediment has been deposited. The sequence consists of five series with at the base limnic sediments which transfer into low-lying peats and swampy soils.

The interglacial deposits in which the site Schöningen 12 is located lie on top of the Elsterian glacial deposits – ground moraine and melt water sediments – and are covered by the glacial series of the Saalian glaciation *sensu stricto*.

Studies of the floral and faunal remains indicate that the lower sequence dates to a fully developed warm temperate climatic phase, the Reinsdorf Interglacial (Urban, in Thieme *et al.* 1993; Urban, in press). Two archaeological horizons were discovered in the littoral sediments of the sequence of gyttja and peats: a lower one lying in a flat alluvial fan of gyttja sands and an upper one in swampy and peat sediments 2 to 3 m higher in the sequence.

4.10.1. *Vegetation*

Pollen analyses by B. Urban yielded four vegetation phases for the lower sequence:
– phase 1a: mixed oak-pine wood period (with *Azolla filiculoides*),
– phase 1b: mixed oak-linden-pine wood period,
– phase 2: alder-hazel period,
– phase 3: hornbeam-pine-spruce-fir period (with *Pterocarya* and *Celtis*).

Archaeological find horizon 1 belongs to the transitional period of phase 2 and 3, findhorizon 2 to the final stage of phase 3.

The filling up of the lake led to the spread and abundant occurrence of the alder tree; alder bogs developed. Pine and birch trees rapidly increase in the sequences overlying the archaeological horizons. Indications of late interglacial conditions appear after a long hiatus caused by the filling up of the lake. A first early glacial interstadial is probably represented in the peat of the upper fourth sequence.

4.10.2. *Molluscan fauna*

A thermophilous fauna rich in species with Mediterranean and southeast European elements similar to the *Helicigona banatica* fauna has been recorded from the Reinsdorf (Schöningen 12) Interglacial deposits. However, *Helicigona banatica* has not yet been identified. The northwestern edge of the distribution of the species is approximately 15 to 20 km south-east of Schöningen, in the Middle Pleistocene travertines of Schwanebeck am Huy and the travertines of Osterode am Fallstein. Important exotic species in the Schöningen 12 fauna are *Aegopis verticillus*, *Pagodulina pagodula*, *Iphigena densestriata*, *Cochlodina costata* and *Vitrea subrimata*, and the meridional species *Truncatellina claustralis*. All these species characterise the climatic maximum as markedly warm temperate with Mediterranean influence. The average annual temperatures were approximately 2 to 3 degrees higher than at present. In the molluscan fauna there is a relatively high proportion of species which are indicative of open terrain – in contrast to the closed vegetation indicated by the pollen analysis. The molluscan fauna indicates a relatively dry climate and open woods in the surroundings of the site.

In the upper sequence, more warmth demanding elements are missing. In particular, associations indicative of a cool temperate phase and with a higher percentage of species which inhabit open terrain, occur. Molluscs have not yet been determined from the fourth sequence. Higher upwards arctic swampy loess and loess associations (Fuhne glacial?) already appear.

4.10.3. *Mammalian fauna*

Vertebrate remains of fish, reptiles, amphibians, birds and mammals are well represented in the interglacial deposits.

The mammal fauna identified by T. van Kolfschoten, consists of the following species: *Sorex minutus*, *Sorex* sp. (*S. araneus* group), *Desmana* sp., *Trogontherium cuvieri*, *Castor fiber*, *Lemmus lemmus*, *Clethrionomys glareolus*, *Arvicola terrestris cantiana*, *Microtus subterraneus*, *M. arvalis/M. agrestis*, *M. oeconomus*, *Apodemus* sp. The smaller mammal fauna is a typical *Arvicola terrestris cantiana-Trogotherium cuvieri* association, also described for Bilzingsleben.

A diverse larger mammal fauna with: *Ursus* sp., Mustelidae, *Elephas (Palaeoloxodon) antiquus*, *Dicerorhinus kirchbergensis*, *Equus* sp., *Sus scrofa*, *Cervus elaphus*, *Capreolus capreolus* and *Bos/Bison* has been collected as well. Remains of bovids and wild horses prevail among the fauna hunted.

4.10.4. *Culture*

The excavated artefacts have not yet been studied by H. Thieme in full detail. Artefacts (Fig. 6) manufactured of baltic flint, with a morphology resembling those from the site of Bilzingsleben, prevail. Flakes, flaking debris and a few simple cores were found. Some hammerstones of small quartz and quartzite pebbles are present. Among the tools denticulates and notches prevail. Additionally, heavy-duty small scrapers as well as flakes with convex retouched edges, Quinson and Tayac points occur. A large core was used as a chopping tool. There are some indications that wooden artefacts might be preserved at the site, while some evidence of fire is present too.

5.   Conclusion

The oldest Palaeolithic finds from the Elbe-Saale region date to the period between the Elsterian and the Saalian glaciation (Holstein complex) (Table 1). Recent investigations show that this period can be divided into three interglacials. The travertine segments connected with former valley bottoms and terraces are a strong evidence for this at Bilzingsleben. It is likely that Bilzingsleben III is identical with the Dömnitz Interglacial, the Holsteinian corresponding either to Bilzingsleben I or to Bilzingsleben II.

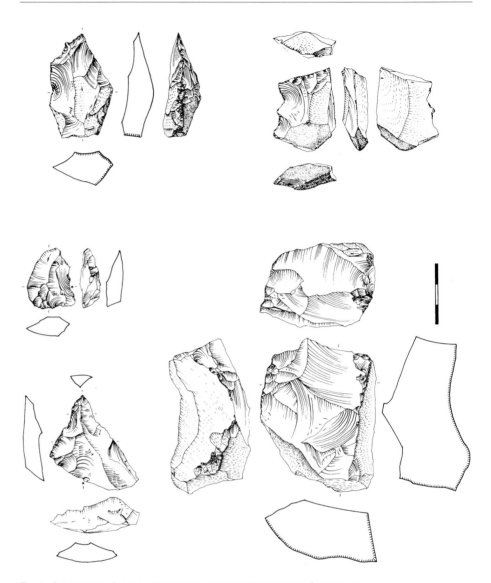

Fig. 6. Schöningen - Reinsdorf Interglacial deposits, flint artefacts. Scale in cm.

The glacials between these interglacials were characterised by arctic conditions. The glacial between Bilzingsleben II and Bilzingsleben III corresponds to the Fuhnian. All these Middle Pleistocene interglacials are characterised by particular small vertebrate, molluscan and floral associations (*Arvicola terrestris cantiana-Trogontherium cuvieri*-association, *Helicigona banatica*-association containing *Azeca menkeana*, a flora with Mediterranean and subcontinental elements: *Buxus*, *Syringra*, *Celtis* and others).

The most important archaeological find horizon is situated in the middle travertines (Bilzingsleben II) of Bilzingsleben, evidence enough to abandon its former attribution to the Dömnitz Interglacial. According to radiometric dates this travertine is 350 to 400 Kyr old. On the ground of morphological features, the hominid remains excavated there are assigned to a late representative of *Homo erectus*. The excavations brought to light a camp site with different structures and find associations (activity zones).

Table 1. Stratigraphical scheme.

	Stratigraphy of Bilzingsleben and Saale Region	Glacial deposits	Interglacial deposits	characteristics	Palaeolithic sites
Saalian Complex	Glacial (Warthian)	Loess 5-8m terrace			
	Interglacial		Bilzingsl. IV 14m level	Celtis Helix-fauna	Neumark-Nord Ehringsdorf
	Glacial (Saalian / Drenthian)	Glacial Series Loess 15-18m terrace			Markkleeberg Eythra (Leipzig)
Holsteinian Complex	Interglacial (Dömnitz-Int.)		Bilzingsl. III 20m level	Celtis Helix-fauna	
	Glacial (Fuhne-Glacial)	Loess 22m terrace			Wallendorf
	Interglacial		Bilzingsl. II 26m level 320-412 Kyr BP	Celtis Banatica-fauna Corbicula-fauna	Neumark-Süd Bilzingsleben Sachsenburg Köchstedt
	Glacial	Loess 27m terrace			
	Interglacial (Holstein-Int.)		Bilzingsl. I 32m level	Celtis Banatica-fauna Theodoxus-fauna	Wangen Memleben
Elsterian Complex	Glacial (Elster II?)	Glacial Series II ? 35m terrace			
	Interglacial ?				
	Glacial (Elster I or Elster I+II?)	Glacial Series I (+II?) 45-50m terrace			

Along with coarse pebble tools, relatively small sized specialised tools of flint appeared. Additionally, artefacts of bone, antler, ivory and wood were excavated.

A small artefact assemblage of sandy gravels from the Unstrut valley near Wangen is placed into the earlier interglacial. The inventory of Memleben seems to be of the same age. All these artefacts resemble the Bilzingsleben material. This is also true for the artefact finds from the Reinsdorf interglacial from Schöningen in the Nordharzvor-land. At Schöningen, there is apparently a similar sequence to that found in Bilzingsleben with three interglacials.

The flint artefacts coming from the Saale gravels of Wallendorf are attributed to the middle Acheulean. They derive from the transitional period of the middle interglacial to the Fuhne glacial. The large Acheulean complex of Mark-kleeberg dates from the latest part of the Middle Pleistocene interglacial sequence and belongs to the early part of the Saale glacial.

references

Adrian, W.	1982	Die Altsteinzeit in Ostwestfalen und Lippe, *Fundamenta Reihe A* 8, Köln.
Andree, J.	1939	*Der eiszeitliche Mensch in Deutschland und seine Kulturen*, Stuttgart.
Bauman, W., D. Mania	1983	Die paläolithische Neufunde von Markkleeberg bei Leipzig, *Veröff. Landesmus. Vorgesch. Dresden* 16, Berlin.
Böhme, G.	1989	Die Amphibien- und Reptilienreste der Fundstelle Bilzingsleben, *Ethnogr. Archäol. Z.* 30, 370-378.
Cepek, G.A.	1986	Quaternary Stratigraphy of the German Democratic Republic, Quaternary Glaciations in the northern Hemisphere, *Quaternary Science Reviews* 5, 359-364.
Collins, D.M.	1968	Metrischer und typologischer Beweis für die Selbständigkeit des Acheuleens und Clactoniens in England und Deutschland, *Jahresschr. mitteldeutsche Vorgesch.* 52, 27-38.
Diebel, K., E. Pietrzeniuk	1980	Pleistozäne Ostrakoden aus dem Profil des *Homo erectus* Fundortes bei Bilzingsleben, *Ethnogr. Archäol. Z.* 21, 26-35.
Eißmann, L., T. Litt	1992	The Saalian sequence in the type region (Central Germany), *SEQS Discussion Meeting 19-24.10 1992 in Halle/Saale*, Halle/Saale.
Erd, K.	1973	Pollenanalytische Gliederung des Pleistozäns der Deutschen Demokratischen Republik, *Z.f. Geol. Wiss.* 1, 1087-1103.
	1978	Pollenstratigraphie im Gebiet der skandinavischen Vereisungen, *Schr. f. Geol. Wiss.* 9, 99-119.
Fischer, K.	1991	Wildrinderreste (Bovidae, Artiodactyla, Mammalia) aus dem mittelpleistozänen Holstein-Komplex von Bilzingsleben, *Veröff. Landesmus. Vorgesch. Halle* 44, 139-147.
	1993	Vögel (Aves) und mittelgroße bis kleine Carnivoren (Mammalia) aus der Holstein-Warmzeit von Bilzingsleben (Thüringen), *Vortrag V. Bilzingsleben-Kolloquium 1-5.12.93 in Jena und Bilzingsleben*.
Fischer, K., E.W. Guenther, W.D. Heinrich, D. Mania, R. Musil, T. Nötzold	1991	Bilzingsleben IV, *Veröff. Landesmus. Vorgesch. Halle* 44, Berlin.
Grahmann, R.	1955	The lower palaeolithic site of Markkleeberg and other comparable localities near Leipzig, *Trans. Amer. phil. Soc.* N.S. 45, 509-687.
Grimm, H., D. Mania, V. Toepfer	1974	Ein neuer Hominidenfund in Europa: Nachtrag zum Vorbericht über Bilzingsleben, *Z. f. Archäol.* 8, 175-176.
Guenther, E.W.	1991	Die Gebisse der Waldelefanten von Bilzingsleben, *Veröff. Landesmus. Vorgesch. Halle* 44, 149-174.
Hebig, W.	1983	Die Fischreste von Bilzingsleben, *Ethnogr. Archäol. Z.* 24, 558-569.

Heinrich, W.D.
1989 Biometrische Untersuchungen an Fossilresten des Bibers (*Castor fiber*) aus thüringischen Travertinen, *Ethnogr. Archäol. Z.* 30, 394-403.

1991 Biometrische Untersuchungen an Fossilresten des Bibers (*Castor fiber* L.) aus der Fundstätte Bilzingsleben. Zur biostratigraphischen Einordnung der Fundstätte Bilzingsleben an Hand fossiler Kleinsäugetiere, *Veröff. Landesmus. Vorgesch. Halle* 44, 35-62, 71-79.

Lehmann, R.
1922 Das Diluvium des unteren Unstruttales von Sömmerda bis zur Mündung, *Jb. hall. Verb.* N.F. 3, 89-124.

Lehmann, H.,
R. Lehmann
1921 Die ältere Steinzeit in Mitteldeutschland, *Mannus* 13, 269-308.

Mai, D.H.
1983 Die fossile Pflanzenwelt des interglazialen Travertins von Bilzingsleben, *Veröff. Landesmus. Vorgesch. Halle* 36, 45-129.

1988 Einige exotische Gehölze in den Interglazialfloren der Mitteldeutschen Florenregion, *Feddes Repert.* 99, 419-461.

1989 Die Travertinflora von Bilzingsleben. Weitere Funde und ihre vegetationsgeschichtliche Bedeutung, *Ethnogr. Archäol. Z.* 30, 306-310, Berlin.

Mai, D.H.,
D. Mania,
T. Nötzold,
V. Toepfer,
E. Vlcek,
W.D. Heinrich
1983 Bilzingsleben II, *Veröff. Landesmus. Vorgesch. Halle* 36, Berlin.

Mania, D.
1973 Paläoökologie, Faunenentwicklung und Stratigraphie des Eiszeitalters im mittleren Elbe-Saalegebiet auf Grund von Molluskengesellschaften, *Geologie Beiheft* 78/79, Berlin.

1974 Bilzingsleben, Kr.Artern. Eine altpaläolithische Travertinfundstelle im nördlichen Mitteleuropa (Vorbericht), *Z. f. Archäol.* 8, 157-173.

1983 Die Molluskenfauna des mittelpleistozänen Travertinkomplexes bei Bilzingsleben und ihre ökologisch-stratigraphische Aussage, *Veröff. Landesmus. Vorgesch. Halle* 36, 131-155.

1984 Zur Geochronologie des Mittelpleistozäns und einiger paläolithischer Fundstellen im Saale- und mittleren Elbegebiet, *Arbeits- und Forschungsberichte zur sächs. Bodendenkmalpflege* 27/28, 13-58.

1988 Le Paleolithique ancien et moyen de la région de la Saale et l'Elbe, Allemagne de l'Est, *L'Anthropologie* 92, 1051-1092.

1989 Stratigraphie, Ökologie und Paläolithikum des Mittel- und Jungpleistozäns im Elbe-Saalegebiet, *Ethnogr. Archäol. Z.* 30, 636-663.

1990 *Auf den Spuren des Urmenschen. Die Funde auf der Steinrinne bei Bilzingsleben*, Berlin.

in press Altpaläolithikum und frühes Mittelpaläolithikum im Elbe-Saalegebiet. *Fundber. Hessens*, (ed. L.Fiedler), Marburg.

Mania, D.,
M. Altermann
1970 Zur Gliederung des Jung- und Mittelpleistozäns im mittleren Saaletal bei Bad Kösen, *Geologie* 19, 1161-1183.

Mania, D.,   1969   Warmzeitliche Mollusken und Pflanzenreste aus dem Mittelpleistozän des Geiseltals
   D.H. Mai   (südl. von Halle), *Geologie* 18, 674-690.

Mania, D.,   1988   Deliberate Engravings on Bone Artefacts of *Homo erectus*, *Rock Art Research* 5, 91-107
   U. Mania   (with comments).

Mania, D.,   1993   Latest finds of hominid remains from the Middle Pleistocene travertine of Bilzingsleben,
   E. Vlcek,   present state of research, *L'Anthropologie*, in press.
   U. Mania

Mania, D.,   1986   Bilzingsleben III, *Veröff. Landesmus. Vorgesch. Halle* 39, Berlin.
   T. Weber

Mania, D.,   1980   Bilzingsleben I, *Veröff. Landesmus. Vorgesch. Halle* 32, Berlin.
   V. Toepfer,
   E. Vlcek

Mania, D.,   1990   Neumark-Gröbern. Beiträge zur Jagd des mittelpaläolithischen Mensch, *Veröff. Landes-*
   M. Thomae,   *mus. Vorgesch. Halle* 43, Berlin.
   T. Litt,
   T. Weber

Menke, B.   1980   Wacken, Elster-Glazial, marines Holstein-Interglazial und Wacken-Warmzeit, *Quartär*
                            Exkursionen in Schleswig-Holstein 26-35, Kiel.

Mertin, H.   1940   Das erstinterglaziale Vorkommen von *Corbicula fluminalis* bei Köchstedt westl. Halle a.d.
                            Saale, *Z. f. Geschiebeforschung u. Lachlandgeologie* 16, 53-81.

Musil, R.   1991a   Die Bären von Bilzingsleben, *Veröff. Landesmus. Vorgesch. Halle* 44, 81-102.

                    1991b   Pferde aus Bilzingsleben, *Veröff. Landesmus. Vorgesch. Halle* 44, 103-130.

Nötzold, T.   1983   Charophytenfruktifikationen von Bilzingsleben, *Veröff. Landesmus. Vorgesch. Halle* 36,
                            41-44.

Ruske, R.   1964   Das Pleistozän zwischen Halle, Bernburg und Dessau, *Geologie* 13, 570-597.

                    1965   Zur Gliederung der Holstein- und Saalezeit im Östlichen Harzvorland, *Eiszeitalter und*
                            Gegenwart 16, 88-96.

Schäfer, D.   1989   Ein altpaläolithischer Oberflächenfundplatz vom Widderberge bei Weimar, *Alt Thüringen*
                            24, 7-32.

Schwarcz, H.P.,   1988   The Bilzingsleben Archaeological Site: New Dating Evidence, *Archaeometry* 30, 5-17.
   R. Grün,
   A.G. Latham,
   D. Mania,
   K. Brunnacker

Soergel, W.   1924   *Die diluvialen Terrassen der Ilm und ihre Bedeutung für die Gliederung des Eiszeitalters.* Jena.

Thieme, H.,   1992   Jagdbeutereste und Steinwerkzeuge des Urmenschen. Älteste Fundschichten Nieder-
   B. Urban,   sachsens im Tagebau Schöningen, *Mitt. Braunschweig. Kohlenbergwerke AG Helmstedt*
   D. Mania,   *u. Tochterges.* 11, 3-9, Helmstedt.
   T. van Kolfschoten

                    1993   Schöningen (Nordharzvorland). Eine altpaläolithische Fundstelle aus dem mittleren Eis-
                            zeitalter, *Archaeologisches Korrespondenzblatt* 23, 147-163.

Toepfer, V.

1933 *Die glazialen und präglazialen Schotterterrassen im mittleren Saaletal*, Naumburg.

1960 Das letztinterglaziale mikrolithische Paläolithikum von Bilzingsleben, Kr. Artern, *Ausgrabungen u. Funde* 5, 7-11.

1961 Das Altpaläolithikum im Flußgebiet der unteren Saale und der Mittelelbe, *Geologie* 10, 570-585.

1968 Das Clactonien im Saale-Mittelelbegebiet, *Jahresschr. mitteldeutsche Vorgesch.* 57, 1-26.

1970 Stratigraphie und Ökologie des Paläolithikums, *Petermanns Geograph. Mitt. Ergänzungsheft* 274, 329-422.

1983 Ein Oberkieferfragment des Löwen aus dem Travertinkomplex von Bilzingsleben, Kr. Artern, und die Fundstellen pleistozäner Löwen im Gebiet der DDR, *Veröff. Landesmus. Vorgesch. Halle* 36, 163-173.

Unger, K.P.

1974 Quartär, *Geologie von Thüringen*, 742-782.

Urban, B.,
 R. Lenhard,
 D. Mania,
 B. Albrecht

1991 Mittelpleistozän im Tagebau Schöningen, Lkr. Helmstedt, *Z. dt. geol. Ges.* 142, 351-372.

Urban, B.

in press Palynological evidence of Younger Middle Pleistocene Interglacials (Holsteinian and Reinsdorf and Schöningen) in the Schöningen open cast lignite mine (Eastern Lower Saxony/Germany), *Mededelingen Rijks Geologische Dienst* 52, 1-2.

Vlcek, E.

1978 A new discovery of *Homo erectus* in Central Europe, *Journal of Human Evolution* 7, 239-251.

1986 Les Anteneandertaliens en Europe Centrale et leur comparison avec l'Homme de Tautavel, *L'Anthropologie* 90, 503-513.

1991 L'Homme fossile en Europe Centrale, *L'Anthropologie* 95, 409-47.

Weber, T.

1977 Clactonienfunde von Memleben, kr. Nebra, *Ausgrabungen u. Funde* 22, 195-199.

Wiegers, F.

1928 *Diluviale Vorgeschichte des Menschen*, Stuttgart.

Wolstedt, P.

1935 Die Beziehungen zwischen den nordischen Vereisungen und den paläolithischen Stationen von Nord- und Mitteldeutschland, *Mannus* 27, 275-287.

Dietrich Mania
Ibrahimstrasse 29
6900 Jena
Germany

Gerhard Bosinski

7 The earliest occupation of Europe: Western Central Europe[1]

Isolated finds from the Kärlich pit indicate a late Early Pleistocene occupation. Excavated assemblages are known from the middle part of the Middle Pleistocene onwards, at Kärlich G and Miesenheim. The Mauer mandible roughly dates to that period too. Interglacial occupation is attested, while finds from Kärlich H (OIS 12) point to occupation of cold steppic environments.

1. Geographical and geological background

1.1. GEOGRAPHICAL OVERVIEW

Western Central Europe lies between the Alps and the North Sea (Fig. 1). The largest, most westerly part of the region is drained by the Rhine and its tributaries. To the southeast the region includes the upper drainage basin of the Danube, while to the northeast the Weser with its tributaries the Fulda and the Werra form the most important river system.

In the southwest of the region is the Upper Rhine graben, a region of flat land up to 50 km wide. The central part of the region – north of the rivers Main and Nahe – is formed by the Rhenish Slate Massif. The Rhine, together with its tributaries Lahn and Moselle, subdivide the massif into four regions, the Hunsrück and Taunus to the south and the Eifel and Westerwald to the north. The central Rhine region (Rhenish Shield) is undergoing a process of slow uplift, which has caused increased downcutting by rivers in relatively narrow valleys. At the centre of this region lies the Neuwied Basin, an area of lowland measuring some 20 × 30 km, which formed as a result of a lower rate of tectonic uplift at this point.

The northern part of the region is formed by the central part of the North European Plain, the flatlands of which are only interrupted by the northern upland extension of the Teutoburger Forest and the Wiehengebirge. The Plain extends southwards into the Upland Zone, in the form of the Lower Rhineland Kölner Bucht. In contrast to the Rhenish Shield, where processes of uplift operate, the Lower Rhineland is a region of tectonic subsidence. This has led to the deposition of large quantities of sediments, in particular of deep gravel beds laid down by the Rhine and the Meuse. In the northern Lower Rhineland the Pleistocene deposits reach thicknesses of as much as 1,000 m.

1.2. VOLCANISM

Tertiary volcanoes are found in the Hegau region to the west of Lake Constance, and in particular in the Hessian depression, with the large volcanic Vogelsberg massif, and in the Westerwald, where they include the Siebengebirge formation near Bonn. The Pleistocene saw the formation of the West and East Eifel volcanic fields (Frechen 1976; Schmincke, Lorenz and Seck 1983; Meyer 1986). In the West Eifel, close to Daun, are located some 200 volcanoes. The East Eifel volcanic field, between the rivers Brohl and Moselle, contains some 100 volcanoes (Schmincke 1988). Major explosive volcanic eruptions occurred in this region some 400,000 years ago (Rieden caldera), again at ca. 200,000 (Wehr caldera) and finally at 11,000 BC cal. (Laacher See caldera) (P. van den Bogaard and Schmincke 1990; Street, Baales and Weninger 1994). These explosive eruptions covered large areas of the Central Rhineland with pumice, as is particularly clear in the case of the youngest, Laacher See eruption. These volcanic deposits are of major importance to the prehistory of the region, serving both as chronological marker horizons (P. van den Bogaard and Schmincke 1988) and as cover and protection to archaeological sites. The formation of the numerous scoria cones of the West and East Eifel was a much less dramatic process and the tephra deposits of these volcanoes are normally of only local significance. Nevertheless, the lava flows and, in particular, the craters of these volcanoes and the favourable settlement locations which they offered, are also important for prehistoric research.

1.3. GLACIATION

The ice of the inland glaciation advanced at least twice across the northern Lowland Zone as far as the boundary of the Upland Zone (Fig. 1; Woldstedt 1955). The ice advance forced the Rhine into a more westerly drainage system. At the same time, the energy of the Rhine drainage system and the continual erosion of the glacier front prevented a more south-westerly ice advance (Thome 1958). The location of the different glacier fronts is particularly well preserved in the western Lower Rhineland in the form of series of moraines. In the south of the region under consideration,

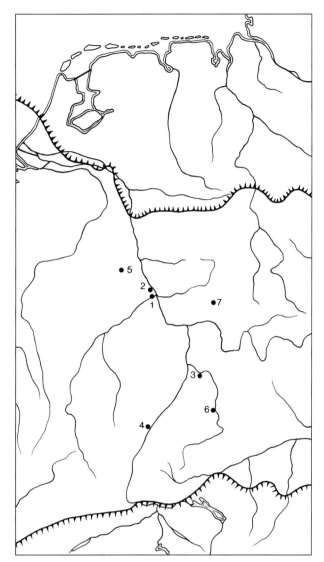

Fig. 1. Lower Palaeolithic sites in western Central Europe and extent of the Pleistocene glacial maximum.
1. Kärlich; 2. Miesenheim; 3. Mauer; 4. Achenheim; 5. Kartstein travertine; 6. Bönnigheim; 7. Münzenberg region.

the alpine glaciers also advanced far out into the foothills (Penck and Brückner 1901-09). In addition, in some colder phases, the Upland Zone above *c*. 900 m OD was also glaciated. The Black Forest and the Vosges, in particular, had an ice-cap at these periods. In glaciated regions older sites have normally been destroyed by the advance of glaciers up to several 100 m thick. It is therefore particularly important that a major part of western Central Europe lies between the alpine glaciers and the northern inland ice, and was never subject to glaciation.

1.4. RIVER TERRACES

In the present context only the river terraces of the Central and Lower Rhine are of importance. In the Rhineland, terrace formation was heavily influenced by tectonic activity. In the Central Rhineland region of tectonic uplift, the different terraces are particularly clearly defined. The High Terrace lies here at 300 m OD, 200 m above the level of the Rhine today. The Middle Terraces are also very high, between 100 m and 200 m OD, i.e. 40-140 m above the present river level (Kaiser 1961). By contrast, terrace formation in the Lower Rhineland has been influenced by tectonic subsidence so that the individual terrace formations are here stacked above each other (Brunnacker, Boenigk *et al.* 1978; Brunnacker, Farrokh and Sidiropoulas 1982; Brunnacker and Boenigk 1983; Kloster-mann 1992).

1.5. LOESS

Loess deposits, important both for Pleistocene strati-graphy and for the survival of archaeological sites, are well represented in western Central Europe and reach depths of up to 30 m. Typical loess regions are the Upper Rhine Valley, the Rhine-Hessian Plateau and the Rheingau, the Neckarland, Franconia and the Wetterau and the Hessian Depression. In the Central Rhineland, loess is found in the river valleys and in the Neuwied Basin. In the Lower Rhineland, loess characterizes the southern part of the Kölner Bucht and forms a broad belt along the northern edge of the Upland Zone.

2. Chronological framework

2.1. SUBDIVISION OF THE PLEISTOCENE

The northern and alpine moraine sequences and the Pleistocene subdivisions based upon them represent only one aspect of Pleistocene phenomena. For this reason the framework of this paper is based upon features recognized in the periglacial area, in particular the river terraces and loess deposits. Further building blocks are provided by biostratigraphy, tephra layers and absolute dating methods. In addition, deep sea isotope curves are examined for the purpose of supra-regional comparison.

Initial and Early Pleistocene deposits are particularly well represented in the Lower Rhine Basin, where they are accessible in large open cast lignite mines (Boenigk, Kowalczyk and Brunnacker 1972; Boenigk 1978). The subdivision of the Middle and Late Pleistocene is, by contrast, well preserved in the Central Rhineland volcanic region.

Only the period from the end of the Early Pleistocene until the late Middle Pleistocene is relevant for the Lower Palaeolithic of our region. This period is well represented by the superficial deposits of the Kärlich clay pit, close to

Koblenz; for this reason the stratigraphic sequence of this site will serve here as a reference section (Brunnacker, Streit and Schirmer 1969; Brunnacker, Heller and Lozek 1971; Chr. van den Bogaard, P. van den Bogaard and Schmincke 1989; Bosinski 1992).

2.2.   THE KÄRLICH PROFILE

The base of the Pleistocene sequence at Kärlich is formed by High Terrace gravels deposited by the Rhine and the Moselle (Fig. 2). The underlying Rhine facies gravels are grey, the upper, Moselle gravels are coloured red by the

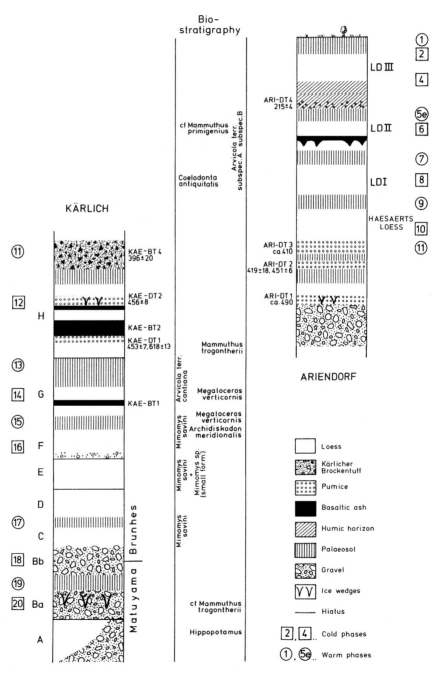

Fig. 2. Subdivision of the Pleistocene in the Central Rhineland based on the sections at Kärlich and Ariendorf.

inclusion of New Red Sandstone found in the region drained by this river. Between the two gravel facies is an illuviated sand layer. The magnetic field is reversed in this layer, but normal in layers above the overlying Moselle gravels, placing the Matuyama-Brunhes boundary in the level of the Moselle gravel facies (Boenigk, Heye *et al.* 1974; Brunnacker, Boenigk *et al.* 1976). This marks the boundary of the Early and Middle Pleistocene at 780 Kyr BP and falls within Oxygen Isotope Stage (OIS) 19. Tilted sediments (Layer A) were preserved only locally below the High Terrace sequence. They consist of normally magnetized gravel, sand and loess deposits which possibly date to the Jaramillo Event at 900 Kyr BP (OIS 23). An important piece of biostratigraphic evidence is the presence in these layers of *Hippopotamus*, which also first appears at other Central European localities dated to the Jaramillo Event (Kahlke 1985; in press).

The "mixed gravels" at the top of the Rhine gravel facies (Kärlich Ba) are affected by ice wedge pseudomorphs and cryoturbation features. This is the oldest evidence in the Central Rhineland for a pronounced cold phase with periglacial phenomena, dating to the end of the Early Pleistocene and equivalent to OIS 20. The High Terrace gravels (Kärlich B) are followed by a flood loam (Layer C) and then by loess deposits. The top of Layer C is marked by a weak soil formation. Stratigraphically important is the presence in Layer C of *Mimomys savini* (Van Kolfschoten, Roth and Turner 1990; Van Kolfschoten and Turner, in press). The overlying Loess D is poorly defined and not associated with a soil formation; faunal remains are very rare.

Above this follows a banded colluvial deposit, Layer E. Layers D and E are separated by a clear boundary, which suggests that erosional processes were active and represents a possible hiatus in the sequence. Layer E contains numerous molluscan remains characteristic of cold stage environmental conditions. The base of the stratigraphically higher Loess F shows evidence of redeposition. In particular, small, reddish-brown quartz pebbles within the layer have been derived from Tertiary "Kieseloolith" terraces. Loess F is usually pale yellow in colour and the top shows a clear soil development. Past authors have described a basaltic ash within Loess F as the oldest volcanic layer present in the Kärlich sequence, however, this tephra was not located by our recent investigations.

Loess F contains rich faunal remains (Van Kolfschoten, Roth and Turner 1990; Turner 1990, 1991; Van Kolfschoten and Turner, in press). Interesting in the macrofauna is the presence of *Megaloceros verticornis* and the identification of elephant molars as *Archidiskodon meridionalis*. The presence in the microfauna of *Mimomys savini* is important. Loess F is the youngest layer in which

Mimomys savini occurs; in layers above this, the species *Arvicola terrestris cantiana* occurs. This biostratigraphic boundary, which characterizes the end of the Biharian (Maul 1990), marks the end of the earlier part of the Middle Pleistocene (Van Kolfschoten 1990a).

A stratigraphically important change in the spectrum of heavy minerals is recognizable in Layer F. Deeper layers are dominated by the heavy minerals zircon, rutile and green hornblende, which are derived from the Rhine gravels; the overlying layer contains spectra of volcanic origin dominated by brown hornblende (Zipter 1991). Loess F is correlated with OIS 16, its soil development with OIS 15. The upper part of the following Loess G is characterized by a pronounced soil development – a major marker horizon in the Kärlich section. The lower part of the loess contains a heavily weathered basaltic tephra (Kae-BT1) originating from a volcano of unknown age and location (Chr. van den Bogaard, P. van den Bogaard and Schmincke 1989). Kärlich G contains a rich microfauna. Stratigraphically important is the presence of *Arvicola terrestris cantiana*, a species characteristic of the central part of the Middle Pleistocene. The macrofauna contains rhinoceros (*Dicerorhinus* sp.) and *Megaloceros verticornis* (Van Kolfschoten, Roth and Turner 1990).

Whereas the volcanic heavy mineral spectrum of Layer G is dominated by brown hornblende, the overlying Layer H has a spectrum of volcanic heavy minerals dominated by pyroxene (Zipter 1991). This change in the heavy mineral spectra is stratigraphically important and allows, for example, the site of Miesenheim I to be dated to between Kärlich G and H (see below). The soil development of Kärlich G is correlated with OIS 13. Loess H contains two volcanic deposits (Fig. 3). In particular, the pumice (Kae-DT1) and overlying basaltic tephra (Kae-BT2) at the base of Layer H form an important marker horizon, which is also found overlying the Miesenheim I archaeological site. Mineralogical analysis shows that the tephra Kae-DT1 originates from an eruption centre of still unknown location. Absolute dating (40Ar/39Ar single crystal laser dating) gives a *maximum* age for this tephra of 618 Kyr BP (P. van den Bogaard, Hall *et al.* 1987; Chr. van den Bogaard, P. van den Bogaard and Schmincke 1989). On the evidence of the Kärlich section and the biostratigraphic record at other sites this maximum age appears to be some 100,000 years too old and a conventional date (40Ar/39Ar step-heating) of 453 ± 7 Kyr BP appears more probable (Lippolt *et al.* 1986; Vollbrecht 1992). Slightly higher in Kärlich Layer H a pumice layer (Kae-DT2) of up to 1 m in depth lies immediately above a thin basaltic tephra. The top of the pumice layer is interrupted by ice wedge pseudomorphs. Tephra Kae-DT2 is mineralogically similar to the Kae-DT1 tephra described above and has been dated by the 40Ar/

Fig. 3. Volcanic ash in Kärlich Level H. with their *maximum* age based on 40Ar/39Ar single crystal laser dating (see text).

39Ar single crystal laser method to 456 ± 8 Kyr BP. Kärlich H is capped by a soil containing shells of temperate molluscan species (Remy 1959; Van Kolfschoten, Roth and Turner 1990; Roth, in press a) and the impressions of leaves (identified is a species of maple) and seeds of *Celtis* (Lozek 1971). The rich molluscan fauna is characteristic of an interglacial phase with slightly more continental conditions than at the present day (Roth, in press a). This soil is sealed by the "Kärlich Brockentuff" (Kae-BT4). This is a poorly sorted deposit derived from an eruption in the immediate vicinity of the site, which at this point broke through both the underlying Devonian bedrock and also Tertiary clay layers and Pleistocene Upper Terrace gravels. Blocks of all these materials form the tuff ring of the "Kärlich Brockentuff", which has been dated by the 40Ar/39Ar single crystal laser method to 396 ± 20 Kyr BP. The mineralogical composition of the tephra shows that it derives from the Rieden eruptional phase. The eruption of the Kärlich Brockentuff occurred towards the middle of an interglacial which might be equated with OIS 11. The first part of this interglacial is represented by the soil formed upon Kärlich Layer H. Deposits from the second half of this interglacial are preserved in the southeast of the Kärlich clay pit in a depression formed subsequently to (and probably as a result of) the eruption of the Brockentuff. These sediments contain the archaeological site Kärlich-Seeufer (see below). With the exception of this depression, in which younger deposits are preserved, the Brockentuff represents the summit of the sequence at Kärlich. Above the primary Brockentuff deposit are found only thin deposits of Last Glacial loess and Laacher See pumice.

2.3.   THE ARIENDORF PROFILE

Important for the younger part of the Middle Pleistocene is the site of Ariendorf (Brunnacker, Löhr *et al.* 1975; Haesaerts 1990; Bosinski 1992). At the Ariendorf gravel quarry the Devonian slate bedrock is overlain by a 30 m deposit of Rhine Middle Terrace gravels (Leubsdorf Terrace), followed by a sequence of loess deposits and palaeosols (Fig. 2). The upper part of the fluviatile sequence contains a heavily weathered and cryoturbated pumice deposit (Ari-DT1), which is dated to *c.* 490 Kyr BP and is possibly equivalent to the Kärlich pumice Kae-DT1. Higher in the sequence two further pumice layers cover a soil formation. The lower pumice deposit (Ari-DT2) has a maximum age (40Ar/39Ar single crystal laser dating) of 451 ± 6 Kyr BP. The upper tephra (Ari-DT3) is some 0.80 m thick and contains numerous impressions of leaves. It too was dated by the 40Ar/39Ar single crystal laser method to approximately 410 Kyr BP (P. van den Bogaard and Schmincke 1990) and, additionally, by conventional

40Ar/39Ar step-heating (the sample is almost certainly Ari-DT2) to 419 ± 18 Kyr BP (Lippolt *et al.* 1986).

P. van den Bogaard and Schmincke (1990) point out that both the Ariendorf tephra Ari-DT2 and Ari-DT3 and the Kärlich Brockentuff (Kae-BT4) can be assigned mineralogically and chemically to the East Eifel Rieden eruptive phase. The volcanic deposits at both Kärlich and Ariendorf were erupted during an interglacial. These arguments – same eruptive phase, similar age, interglacial context – make it plausible to regard both the Kärlich Brockentuff (Kae-BT4) and the Ariendorf tephra layers Ari-DT2 / Ari-DT3 as deposits from the same interglacial, probably OIS 11. On this basis it is possible to synthesize the sections at Kärlich and at Ariendorf (Fig. 2). The four (?) Ariendorf loess beds thus correspond to the younger part of the Middle Pleistocene and the Late Pleistocene. The deepest loess ("Haesaerts loess"; Fig. 2) could belong to OIS 10, the soil on top of it to OIS 9. From this lower part of the Ariendorf sequence there are no archaeological finds. In the western part of Central Europe only artefacts from the Kartstein travertine (see below) could date to this final stage of the Lower Palaeolitic (OIS 9). Archaeological material from the base of the third Ariendorf loess bed (OIS 8) can already be assigned to the beginning of the Middle Palaeolithic.

3.   Earliest traces of human occupation

The oldest evidence for human presence dates to the end of the Early Pleistocene and to the oldest (*Mimomys savini*-fauna) part of the Middle Pleistocene. The material consists exclusively of single, collected finds of lithic material without further contextual information.

3.1.   KÄRLICH A

K. Würges found three quartzite pebble tools in the sandy loess-loam of Kärlich Layer A (Würges 1986; Vollbrecht 1992). All three artefacts are flaked on one surface only, i.e. choppers (Fig. 4). One specimen has subsequently split along a quartz vein. A tooth fragment of *Hippopotamus* comes from the same stratigraphical unit (Turner 1990; 1991). The finds could be contemporary with the Jaramillo-Event and correlated with OIS 23.

3.2.   KÄRLICH BA

At the base of the Rhine gravel sequence of the High Terrace (Ba) K. Würges discovered an artefact manufactured of trachytic tuff (Würges 1986; Vollbrecht 1992). The piece is a core showing several flake scars and can be assigned to a late phase of the Early Pleistocene. It is older than the pronounced cold phase (equated with OIS 20) shown by periglacial activity at the summit of the Rhine Gravel facies (Ba).

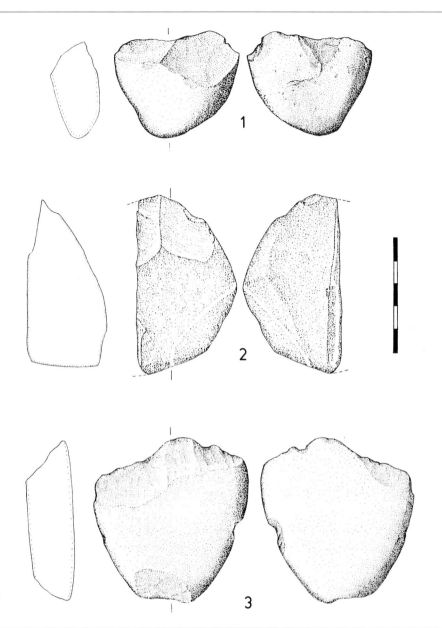

Fig. 4. Kärlich A. Pebble tools.
Scale in cm.
After Würges (1986) and Vollbrecht
(1992).

A number of stones (artefacts?) found by K. Schmude in High Terrace gravels in the Lower Rhineland possibly belong to an equivalent period (Schmude 1992).

3.3. KÄRLICH BB

K. Würges collected eight artefacts of reddish-brown quartzite from the surface of the Moselle gravel facies (Würges 1986; Bosinski 1992; Vollbrecht 1992). The artefacts are slightly rolled and are derived from a locality further upstream. There are two cores, four flakes, a "pebble-scraper" and a pick-like tool (Fig. 5). Several

bones and teeth of a deer (*Cervus* sp.) and a bovine (*Bos/Bison*) were found in a comparable stratigraphical position (Turner 1991). These finds are assigned to the initial phase of the Middle Pleistocene, soon after the Matuyama-Brunhes boundary which is located in the Moselle gravels (Bb).

Artefacts collected by L. Fiedler and A. von Berg from the surface of the High Terrace around Koblenz are possibly broadly contemporary (Berg and Fiedler 1983; 1987; Fiedler 1991). Among these quartz and quartzite artefacts are not only pebble tools, flakes and cores, but also bifaces.

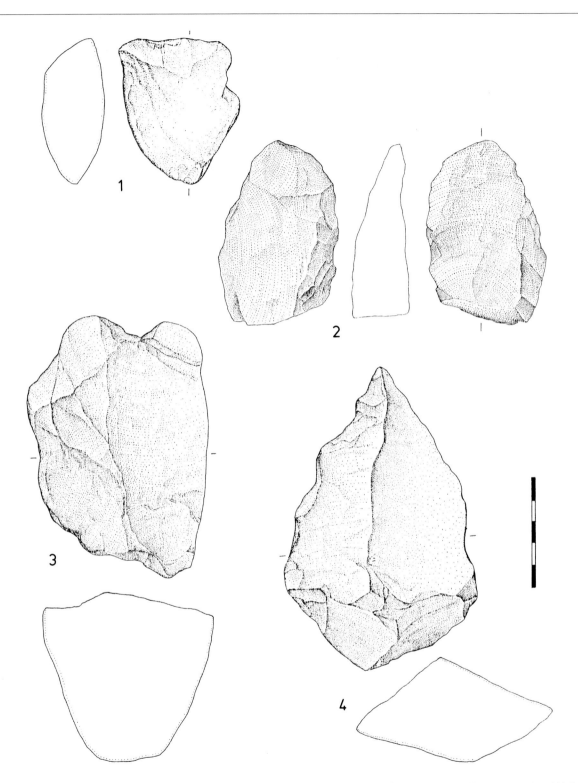

Fig. 5. Kärlich Bb. Pebble scraper (1), flake (2), core (3) and pick-like artefact of quartzite (4). Scale in cm. After Würges (1986) and Vollbrecht (1992).

4. Sites from the early Middle Pleistocene

This part of the Lower Palaeolithic is defined as comprising those finds dated to the first part of the *Arvicola terrestris cantiana* faunal stage, equivalent to OIS 14-12.

4.1. KÄRLICH G

Over a period of time 14 artefacts of quartz and quartzite have been found (mainly by K. Würges) in Kärlich layer G (Würges 1991; Vollbrecht 1992). The pieces comprise three cores, five flakes, one cleaver-like and two borer-like tools (Fig. 6). Numerous bones of large mammals were also found in layer G, including *Dicerorhinus* sp., *Equus* sp., *Alces* sp., *Dama* sp., *Megaloceros verticornis* and *Bos* or *Bison* (Turner 1991). The sediments of Layer G are correlated with OIS 14 and 13. Their heavy mineral spectrum is dominated by brown hornblende, so that artefacts from Kärlich G are older than those from Miesenheim I, where pyroxene already dominates in the profile.

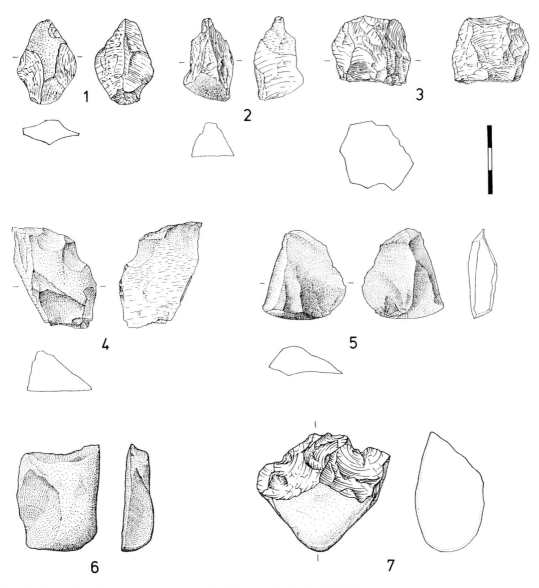

Fig. 6. Kärlich G. Quartz (1-3, 7) and quartzite artefacts. Scale in cm. After Vollbrecht (1992).

4.2.   MIESENHEIM I

Miesenheim I was investigated under the direction of E. Turner from 1982-1991. The site lies on the slope of the Nette valley, some 5 km from the Kärlich clay pit (Boscheinen, Bosinski *et al.* 1984; Bosinski, Van Kolfschoten and Turner 1988; Van Kolfschoten 1990b; Turner, in press). The site originally lay close to a shallow body of water, possibly an old meander of the Rhine. The finds are located in a dark, organic "anmoor" sediment (Layer F) and in the grey-yellow loam (Layer G) immediately underlying this (Fig. 7). Higher in the section

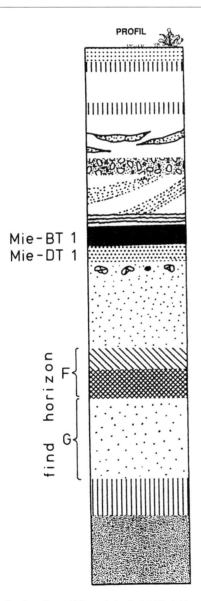

Fig. 7. Idealized section at Miesenheim I., total height approximately 5 m. After E. Turner.

are found a pumice (Mie-DT1) and a basaltic tephra (Mie-BT1) which closely resemble tephra layers in Kärlich Layer H (Kae-DT1 and Kae-BT2 respectively). The Kärlich tephra have an identical mineralogical and chemical composition to those at Miesenheim I (P. van den Bogaard and Schmincke 1990) and are dated at the former site to 618 ± 18 Kyr (*maximum* age) and 453 ± 7 Kyr BP. Since the Miesenheim I heavy mineral spectrum is dominated by pyroxene and therefore younger than Kärlich Layer G (where brown hornblende is dominant), Miesenheim I is assigned to a phase between Kärlich G and H. The site probably belongs in the same interglacial during which the thick soil formed on Kärlich Layer G and which can be correlated with OIS 13.

The rich molluscan fauna (Roth, in press b) demonstrates an interglacial climate, somewhat more continental than at the present day. In addition it shows the local presence of wetland with standing water, swamp-like banks and patches of forest. The abundant small mammal remains confirm this picture (Van Kolfschoten, in press). Beaver (*Castor fiber*) and extinct giant beaver (*Trogontherium cuvieri*) may have further contributed to the presence of wetland conditions with their dams. *Neomys* cf. *newtoni*, *Sorex savini*, *Desmana* sp. and *Arvicola terrestris cantiana* inhabited the wetter parts of the shoreline, *Sciurus* sp., *Eliomys quercinus*, *Muscardinus avellanarius*, *Clethrionomys glareolus* and *Apodemus sylvaticus* occurred in adjacent woodland.

The small mammal fauna from Miesenheim I can, in addition, be assigned to the central Middle Pleistocene *Arvicola terrestris cantiana - Sorex (Drepanosorex)* sp. Concurrent-range-subzone (Van Kolfschoten 1990; in press a).

The large mammal spectrum is characteristic for an early Middle Pleistocene interglacial. This is particularly true of the species *Canis mosbachensis*, *Equus mosbachensis* and *Ursus deningeri* (Turner, in press). At the same time, the fauna reveals details of environmental conditions close to the site. Roe deer (*Capreolus capreolus*) and red deer (*Cervus elaphus*) dominate the fauna. The presence of horse (*Equus mosbachensis*) shows that open grassland areas were also present.

Of particular interest is the taphonomic investigation of the site (Turner, in press). Roe deer is definitely represented by at least 9 individuals (3 juveniles and 6 adults), but the spatial distribution of the material suggests that at least 13 individuals might be represented. The season of death of the young animals was between August and the winter months. Possibly the bones represent the remains of a large group of animals which were killed (?) here. Red deer is represented by at least 6 individuals (2 juveniles and 4 adults). The age structure and spatial distribution of the material suggests that this may be a "harem" of females and young animals

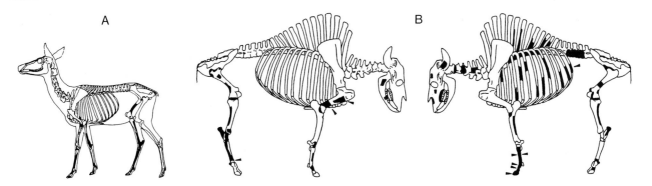

Fig. 8. Miesenheim I. A: Remains of the "partial carcass", Roe deer D as found during excavation, B: Remains of the "partial carcass" Bovid B, as found during excavation (from: Turner, *in press*).

killed (?) here in autumn or winter. Horse is represented by at least four individuals. The age structure of the material suggests that a "family group" is represented. In the case of the described species – roe deer, red deer and horse – the limb bones and skulls (with teeth) are always present, whereas elements of the rump (ribs and vertebrae) are rarely represented (Fig. 8). A similar distribution is often present on Middle and Upper Palaeolithic sites in the Central Rhineland and probably reflects a selection for meat-bearing parts by humans. A bovine carcass at Miesenheim I shows a completely different distribution pattern (Fig. 8): almost all parts of the skeleton are present in the case of

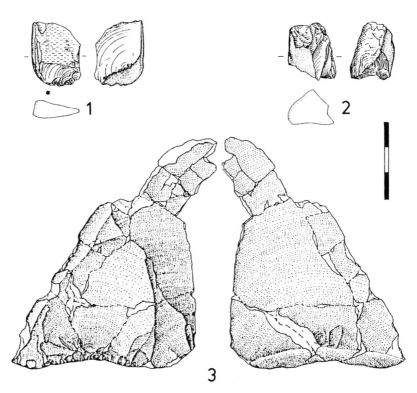

Fig. 9. Miesenheim I. Artefacts of lydite (1), quartz (2) and quartzite (3). Scale in cm. After E. Turner.

this old individual, which may plausibly have died naturally in the swampy waterside situation.

Due to fine-stratigraphical analysis it appears that the overgrown banks of the Pleistocene Rhine were repeatedly the scene of human hunting episodes. During one such episode a family group of four horses was killed; subsequently a group of 13 roe deer and a herd of six red deer were also successfully hunted. In addition, it is possible to demonstrate the presence at the site of animals which died naturally (shown particularly clearly in the case of a bovine) and were then scavenged by carnivores. The lithic assemblage is manufactured from materials which can be found in the area, such as quartz, quartzite and lydite. The presence of cores and refitted artefacts shows that most artefacts were produced at the site (Fig. 9). A flake of lydite and a large flake of fine-grained Tertiary quartzite appear, however, to have been brought to the site in their present form. The latter piece (Fig. 9.3) is retouched at the dorsal border of the striking platform and is the only modified artefact in the small assemblage. The artefacts have a similar spatial distribution to that of the faunal remains. The conjoin patterns of artefacts and of faunal remains both demonstrate relationships between different parts of the site. The artefacts probably demonstrate, similarly to the faunal remains, different episodes of activity at the waterside. At the east of the excavated area an accumulation of pebbles covering some 5 m² was uncovered. The presence of bones and artefacts next to and within this concentration links it to the human use of the site. It is improbable that this spatially defined, single layer of fist-sized pebbles is a natural accumulation. Possibly the stones were deposited here deliberately by man in order to create a drier and more stable area in the marshy sediment of the bank.

4.3. MAUER NEAR HEIDELBERG

The famous site of Mauer is located in an ancient meander of the Neckar river 10 km southeast of Heidelberg. The site was originally an aggrading river bank upon which animal bones and the human jaw were washed together. The human mandible was discovered by Daniel Hartmann on October 21, 1907 and published by O. Schoetensack in a classic monograph the following year (Schoetensack 1908).

In the section of the sandpit the Neckar sands are overlain by several loess beds and soil developments, which, on the evidence of new investigations by Bibus (1992a), represent at least the last three cold stages and interglacials respectively.

The microfauna from the Mauer sands contains the species *Talpa minor*, *Talpa europea*, both *Castor fiber* and *Trogontherium cuvieri*, *Pliomys episcopalis*, *Arvicola*

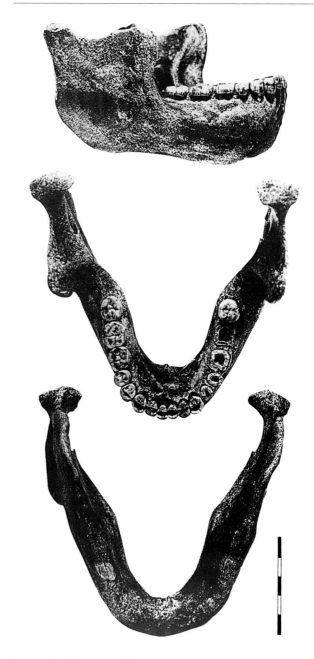

Fig. 10. The Mauer mandible. After O. Schoetensack.

terrestris cantiana, *Microtus arvalis/M. agrestis*, and *Apodemus* sp. (Von Koenigswald 1992). The large mammal fauna consists of *Canis lupus mosbachensis*, *Ursus stehlini*, *Ursus deningeri*, *Hyaena arvernensis*, *Panthera pardus sickenbergi*, *Panthera leo fossilis*, *Felis (Lynx) issidorensis*, *Felis* cf. *silvestris*, *Homotherium* sp., *Elephas (Palaeoloxodon) antiquus*, *Equus mosbachensis*, *Stephanorhinus hundsheimensis*, *Sus scrofa priscus*, *Hippopotamus amphibius antiquus*, *Alces latifrons*, *Cervus elaphus acoronatus*, *Capreolus süssenbornensis* and *Bison schoetensacki* (Von Koenigswald 1992).

This is an interglacial fauna; the presence of *Hippopotamus* shows an Atlantic climate with mild winters and a forested landscape. Biostratigraphically the microfauna is very similar to that of Kärlich G and, in particular, that of Miesenheim I. W. von Koenigswald (1992) specifically points to the occurrence of both *Arvicola terrestris cantiana* and *Pliomys episcopalis*, which dates these sites – Kärlich G, Miesenheim I and Mauer – to the central part of the Middle Pleistocene. It is probable that the "Mauerer Waldzeit" (Müller-Beck 1964) is equivalent to the interglacial represented by the Kärlich G soil formation and at Miesenheim I, and that this can be correlated with OIS 13.

The mandible of *Homo heidelbergensis* (Fig. 10) is large and massive, the teeth by contrast, relatively small. A protuberance of the chin is totally absent. The specimen corresponds best to those from Ternifine and Montmaurin, although there is also a strong resemblance to the *Sinanthropus* mandibles from Choukoutien (Howell 1960; Gabunia 1992). All these finds are assigned to late forms of *Homo erectus*, which is in good correspondence with the chronological position of the Mauer site.

During the 1950's A. Rust conducted investigations at the site. He believed that he could recognize flat pebbles of New Red Sandstone with "struck" edges and "prepared" notches and "noses" as artefacts (Rust 1956 a-b; 1957; 1965; 1971). The artificial nature of these pieces has not been generally accepted and the creation of an eponymous "Heidelberger culture", containing numerous clearly pseudo-artefacts of diverse origin, further discredited them. Recently, small chert pieces collected by K.F. Hormuth from the Mauer sands before the Second World War, have been relocated (Beinhauer, Fiedler and Wegner 1992). It is not proved that these pieces were worked by humans and unlikely that they were related to the Mauer jaw bone.

4.4.   ACHENHEIM LAYER 30

At the base of the major loess section at Achenheim near Strasbourg, bones of *Castor* sp., *Ursus deningeri*, *Dicerorhinus etruscus*, *Equus mosbachensis*, *Hippopotamus*, *Cervus* and *Alces* have been found in the Rhine sands below the loess (Wernert 1957; Heim, Lautridou *et al.* 1982; Junkmanns 1991). This fauna can be compared to those of Mauer, Kärlich G and Miesenheim I and may possibly represent the same Middle Pleistocene interglacial. In the same layer was found a cobble showing a single flake removal possibly worked by man (Wernert, Millot and Van Eller 1962).

4.5.   KÄRLICH, LOWER LAYER H

Whereas the finds described so far from the middle phase of the Lower Palaeolithic can all be assigned to interglacial conditions with a moist-temperate climate, the finds from the base of Kärlich Loess H were deposited during a period of steppe conditions with a prevailing dry continental climate. Human presence during such a climatic phase is new to this period of the Lower Palaeolithic of western Central Europe. Kärlich Layer H is younger than both Layer G at the same site and the site of Miesenheim I and is correlated with OIS 12.

In 1983 K. Würges investigated a site which lay at the edge of a channel filled with pumice (Kae-DT1) and basaltic tephra (Kae-BT2). Although the site had already been largely destroyed by quarrying machinery (Würges 1984), it was possible to recover a tusk and a thigh bone of a steppe elephant together with 60 quartz and quartzite artefacts (Fig. 11). The majority of the finds consists of flakes, a number of which are produced in bipolar technique. In addition, five cores, four struck cobbles and an intensively battered quartz hammerstone were also found. Among the modified forms are two scrapers and two "points", together with a number of partially edge-retouched artefacts. Apart from this largely destroyed situation, a number (68) of collected artefacts is known from the same stratigraphical position in various parts of the clay pit (Vollbrecht 1992). Besides quartz and quartzite artefacts, this number includes a lydite core. The majority of the pieces are "chunks" and flakes, but six cores and a small number of retouched forms are also present. Finally, J. Vollbrecht discovered and investigated a further, still unpublished, site (Kärlich III/"Uhu-site") at the base of Layer H in the northwest quarry face of the pit.

5.   Late Lower Palaeolithic sites

The late Lower Palaeolithic sites are from the period ca. 400-300 Kyr BP (OIS 11-9). The Middle Palaeolithic begins in our region at the base of the ante-penultimate loess bed (OIS 8).

5.1.   KÄRLICH SEEUFER

In the southeast of the Kärlich clay pit a topographical depression formed subsequently to the deposition of the Brockentuff. The feature seems a result of the eruption and is possibly a crater. The depression became partly filled with redeposited Brockentuff; subsequently water was able to collect and a small lake was formed. Peat deposits formed during the infilling of this lake represent, on the evidence of their contained pollen and macroscopic remains, the second half of the same interglacial in which the tuff ring was erupted (Bittmann, in press). The first phase present is a mixed-oak-forest, in which oak

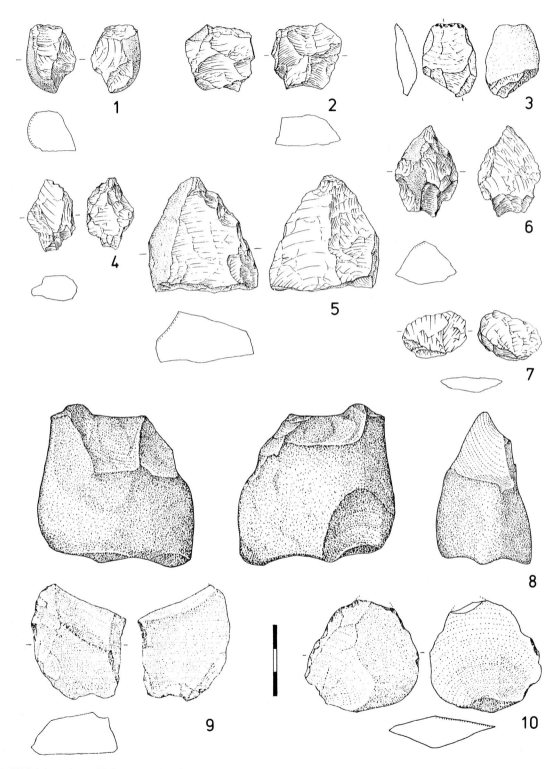

Fig. 11. Kärlich lower Layer H. Quartz (1-7) and quartzite (8-10) artefacts. Scale in cm. After K. Würges and J. Vollbrecht.

dominates over elm and lime. This is succeeded first by a phase in which hazel is the dominant species and then by a phase dominated by hornbeam. The presence of wingnut (*Pterocarya*) and nettle tree (*Celtis*) during the latter period shows that temperatures were warmer than at the present day. The pollen diagram shows a subsequent rise of fir. Finally, the values of both the hornbeam and the fir decrease and an increase in the presence of spruce and pine marks the end of the interglacial.

The palynological interpretation of the vegetational development can be complemented by a large range of plant macro-remains, including wood remains up to the size of tree trunks (Bittmann, in press).

The "Kärlich interglacial" differs from the Holstein Interglacial through e.g. the presence of *Celtis* and *Azolla filiculoides*, but also in its high values for hornbeam and low values for alder, and must represent an older interglacial phase. The best parallel is Bilshausen near Göttingen, which is assigned to the Cromer Complex (Bittmann 1990; in press). Bittmann proposes to equate the Kärlich interglacial with a "Cromer V" interglacial correlated with OIS 11. During the hornbeam phase of this interglacial, there is evidence for the presence of a group of hominids on a small "peninsula" formed in the northeast part of the lake by sandy material and Brockentuff eroding from an upslope position (Bosinski, Brunnacker *et al.* 1980; Kröger, P. van den Bogaard *et al.* 1988).

The lithic artefacts are made from materials present in the neighbouring terrace gravels, in particular from quartz and quartzite. A problem concerning the artefacts is that the eruption of the Brockentuff tuff ring not only broke through Devonian slate and Tertiary clay, but also through the High Terrace gravels, so that the Brockentuff contains numerous naturally fractured pebbles. Many of these are "cores" and "flakes". Several attempts have been made to establish criteria for distinguishing such tephrofacts derived from the Brockentuff from true artefacts (see also Raynal *et al.*, this volume). In view of the unsophisticated technology in use during the Lower Palaeolithic this is not possible for many finds, so that a large "grey area" remains of pieces which might equally have been fractured by man or by the eruption. Despite these problems it is possible to identify some 150 certain artefacts from the Kärlich-Seeufer site. Flaking technology and flake forms are generally simple (Fig. 12), but there are two cores which foreshadow the Levallois technique. Some flakes are partially edge-retouched. A fragment of wood attached by a concretion to one of these pieces may represent remains of hafting. Only a small number of flakes have regularly retouched scraper-edges. In addition, cleavers of different sizes (Fig. 13) and bifaces are also present. The two most regular bifaces (Figs 14-15) are made of reddish-brown quartzite and are

similarly proportioned and flaked. The lower surface of one piece is largely natural cortex, that of the second piece is formed by a natural cleavage plane. A further class of artefact comprises pebble tools of different types and sizes. The Kärlich-Seeufer artefacts were found in a fan of sediments originating from repeated hill wash and extending into the depression. Most of the artefacts are fresh, with sharp edges, and have certainly not been transported over a long distance. Hammerstones and conjoined artefacts are evidence for the production of artefacts at the site.

Animal bones were discovered in the same area as the stone artefacts. The most common category is formed by bones and teeth of the straight-tusked elephant, which is represented at the site by at least 8 individuals (Kröger, P. van den Bogaard *et al.* 1988). The age structure of the elephants includes juveniles, prime adults and old individuals. The most frequent body part is the head, including the molars and tusks, whereas parts of the rump are rarely represented. Besides the dominant straight-tusked elephant, bones and teeth of red deer (*Cervus elaphus*), a bovine (*Bos* or *Bison*), horse (*Equus* sp.), pig (*Sus* sp.), reindeer (*Rangifer tarandus*) and a felid were also found. Recent analysis by S. Gaudzinski (in press) indicates that the bones and stones were reworked from various directions during various periods, thus denying a primary context character for the site.

The situation excavated at Kärlich-Seeufer has parallels at Lower Palaeolithic sites in Italy (Fontana Ranuccio, La Polledrara) and Spain (Torralba, Ambrona, Aridos). At all these sites there has been a long discussion of the role of humans in the accumulation of the recovered assemblages and, in particular, about the question of active elephant hunting. Without entering into this particular discussion, which can be decided only with difficulty on the basis of the archaeological assemblage, it would be carrying things too far not to accept the shells of hazel nuts found with the lithic assemblage and the animal bones as the food remains of hominids.

5.2.   KARTSTEIN TRAVERTINE

The Kartstein travertine in the North Eifel consists of several units formed during different interglacials. The main travertine massif recently was dated about 300 Kyr BP by N. Frank (see Vollbrecht, in press) and probably belongs to OIS 9. During the investigation of younger archaeological horizons in caves and abris which had subsequently formed at the base of the massif, H. Löhr discovered pebble tools and animal bones embedded in the travertine (Brunnacker, Hennig *et al.* 1982). The context of the pieces, which are cemented into the travertine matrix, precludes a meaningful investigation of the site.

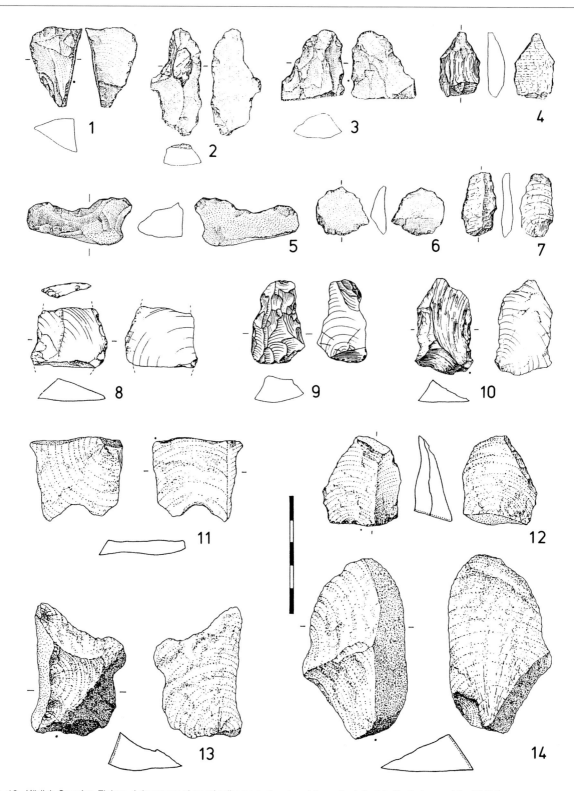

Fig. 12. Kärlich-Seeufer. Flakes. A fragment of wood adheres to the dorsal face of artefact 2. Scale in cm. After K. Kröger.

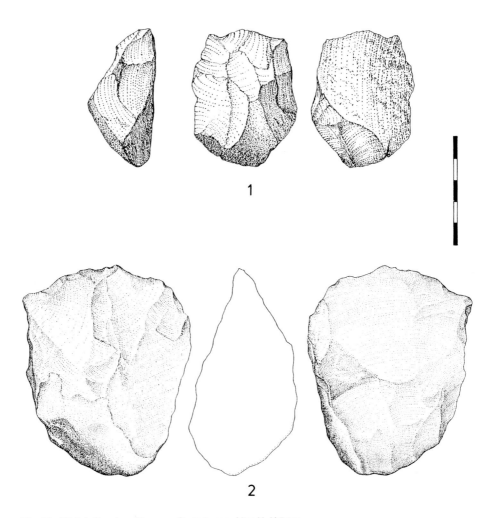

Fig. 13. Kärlich-Seeufer. Cleavers. Scale in cm. After K. Kröger.

6.   Lower Palaeolithic finds of uncertain age

6.1.   MÜNZENBERG REGION

Finds of pebble tools, flakes and bifaces collected from the surface of ancient terraces close to Münzenberg in Upper Hessia have been published in several articles by H. Krüger since the 1950's (Kröger 1959; 1975; 1977/78; 1987; 1989; 1994; Fiedler 1983; 1994; Moncel 1989). The majority of this material can, very probably, be assigned to the Lower Palaeolithic and it has also been possible to trace the find-bearing horizon below a loess section containing the two most recent loess beds (Bibus 1976). Nevertheless, this only provides a *terminus ante quem*; the true age of the material is still unknown and the investigation of a stratified site in this region remains a priority.

6.2.   BÖNNIGHEIM

Animal bones and stone tools were discovered below a stratified loess section in a pit at Bönnigheim near Ludwigsburg (Wagner 1990; 1991). The stratigraphy of the site shows that the finds are older than the ante-penultimate cold stage (OIS 8) (Bibus 1992b). The bones are identified as the remains of the skeletons and teeth of a temperate fauna, including straight-tusked elephant, rhinoceros, bison, pig and red deer (Wagner 1991). Associated with the bones was a pebble tool made of exotic tabular chert.

6.3.   STEINHEIM

The Steinheim skull (Berckhemer 1933; Adam 1988) and the finds from the travertine localities Lauster, Haas and

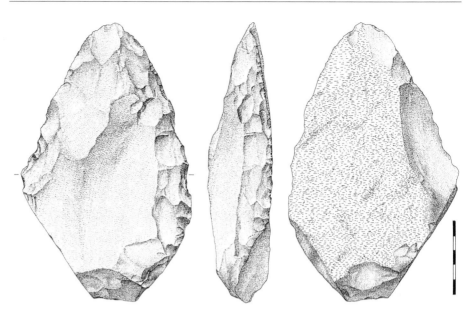

Fig. 14. Kärlich-Seeufer. Biface. Scale in cm.

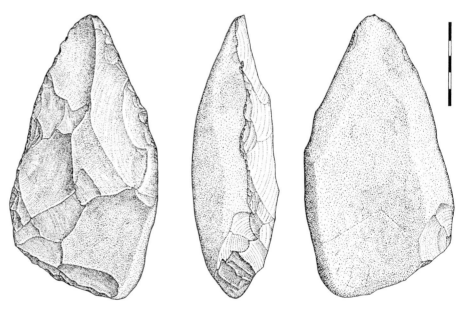

Fig. 15. Kärlich-Seeufer. Biface. Scale in cm.

"Bunker" in Bad Cannstatt (Wagner 1980; 1984; 1987; 1992; Adam, Reiff and Wagner 1986) probably derive from the interglacial dated to about 220 Kyr BP (OIS 7) and are thus rather early Middle Palaeolithic in context. At Steinheim this is rendered likely by the stratigraphic dating of the "*antiquus* layers", in which the skull was found, to before the penultimate cold stage (Adam 1988).

In the case of the Bad Cannstatt travertine, dating evidence is provided by the geographical distribution of the various travertine stages within the valley of the Neckar (Adam, Reiff and Wagner 1986), the U-series dating of the travertines to 170-295 (Haas quarry) and 145-260 Kyr BP (Lauster quarry) (Grün, Brunnacker and Henning 1982), an ESR date for an elephant tooth from the Lauster quarry of 237 ± 26 Kyr BP (Grün and Brunnacker 1986) and by the character of the lithic assemblage. The "Bunker" site, for example, besides numerous pebble tools, yielded small numbers of chert Levallois flakes (chapeau de gendarme) which could be partly refitted and were probably struck from one core (Wagner 1987, 18).

7. Conclusions

The earliest hints regarding the occupation of Western Central Europe date to the end of the Lower Pleistocene. Isolated finds (esp. Kärlich A) with only limited information probably date from around the time of the Jaramillo Event.

The occupation of our working area is better documented for the early Middle Pleistocene period. From Kärlich G there are quartz and quartzite artefacts as well as fauna including *Megaloceros verticornis* and *Arvicola cantiana terrestris*. The Middle Pleistocene interglacial at Miesenheim I is younger than Kärlich G and may correlate to OIS 13. The large mammals include *Capreolus capreolus, Cervus elaphus, Equus mosbachensis,* and *Bos/Bison.* The finds of Achenheim layer 30 and the biostratigraphically

similar material from Mauer, including the famous lower jaw of *Homo heidelbergensis* probably belong to the same Middle Pleistocene interglacial as Miesenheim I. While all the sites mentioned above date to interglacials, the site Kärlich H *unten*, below the tuff Kae-DT1 which has been dated to about 450 Kyr BP, can be situated in a glacial steppe landscape.

The approximately 400 Kyr old site Kärlich-Seeufer is an example of a late Lower Palaeolithic shore and bank site with many elephant bones as well as bifaces and cleavers. This site raises problems of interpretation comparable to those at similar sites in other parts of Europe. The finds from the Kartstein travertine date to about 300 Kyr BP and belong to the end of the Lower Palaeolithic in Western Central Europe.

note

1 Translated by Martin Street

references

Adam, K.D.   1988   Der Urmensch von Steinheim an der Murr und seine Umwelt. Ein Lebensbild aus der Zeit vor einer Viertel Million Jahren, *Jahrbuch des Römisch-Germanischen Zentralmuseums Mainz* 35, 3-23.

Adam, K.D.,   1986   Zeugnisse des Urmenschen aus den Cannstatter Sauerwasserkalken, *Fundberichte aus*
W. Reiff,   *Baden-Württemberg* 11, 1-100.
E. Wagner

Beinhauer, K.W.,   1992   Hornstein-Artefakte von der Fundstelle des *Homo erectus heidelbergensis* aus Mauer. In:
L. Fiedler,   K.W. Beinhauer and G.A. Wagner (ed.), *Schichten von Mauer. 85 Jahre Homo erectus*
D. Wegner   *heidelbergensis*, 46-73, Mannheim: Edition Braus.

Berckhemer, F.   1933   Ein Menschenschädel aus den diluvialen Schottern von Steinheim an der Murr, *Anthropologischer Anzeiger* 10, 318-321.

Berg, A. von,   1983   Altpaläolithische Funde von Winningen und Koblenz-Bisholder an der Unteren Mosel,
L. Fiedler   *Archäologisches Korrespondenzblatt* 13, 291-298.

                              1987   Faustkeilfunde des älteren Acheuléen von Winningen/Mosel, Kreis Mayen-Koblenz, *Berichte zur Archäologie an Mittelrhein und Mosel 1 (Trierer Zeitschrift, Beiheft 9)*, 73-84.

Bibus, E.   1976   Zur geomorphologischen Fundsituation und Altersstellung der oberhessischen Geröllgeräte vom Münzenberger Typ., *Rhein-Mainische Forschungen* 82, 179-203.

                              1992a   Die Löß-Deckschichten im Bereich der Fundstelle des *Homo erectus heidelbergensis* bei Mauer. In: K.W. Beinhauer and G.A. Wagner (ed.), *Schichten von Mauer. 85 Jahre Homo erectus heidelbergensis*, 151-157, Mannheim: Edition Braus.

                              1992b   Die Sedimentfolge in der Ziegelei Schmid in Bönnigheim und das mögliche Alter der Fossilfunde in den Basisschichten. Hanerbenblätter, *Historische Gesellschaft Bönnigheim* 15, 26-29.

Bittmann, F.   1990   Neue biostratigraphische Korrelierung des Kärlicher Interglazials (Neuwieder Becken/ Mittelrhein). In: W. Schirmer (ed.), *Rheingeschichte zwischen Mosel und Maas*, 67-70, Hannover: Deutsche Quartärvereinigung.

                              in press   Vegetationsgeschichtliche Untersuchungen an mittel- und jungpleistozänen Ablagerungen des Neuwieder Beckens (Mittelrhein), *Jahrbuch des Römisch-Germanischen Zentralmuseums Mainz* 38.

Boenigk, W.   1978   Die Gliederung der altquartären Ablagerungen in der linksrheinischen Niederrheinischen Bucht, *Fortschritte Geol. Rheinland und Westfalen* 28, 135-212.

Boenigk, W.,   1972   Zur Geologie des Ältestpleistozäns der Niederrheinischen Bucht, *Zeitschrift der Deutschen*
G. Kowalczyk,   *Geologischen Gesellschaft* 123, 119-161.
K. Brunnacker

Boenigk, W.,   1974   Paläomagnetische Messungen an vielgliedrigen Quartärprofilen (Kärlich/Mittelrhein und
W. Heye,   Bad Soden im Taunus), *Mainzer Naturwissenschaftliches Archiv* 12, 159-169.
W. Schirmer,
K. Brunnacker

Bogaard, Chr. van den,
    P. van den Bogaard,
    H.-U. Schmincke
1989   Quartärgeologisch-tephrostratigraphische Neuaufnahme und Interpretation des Pleistozän-profils Kärlich, *Eiszeitalter und Gegenwart* 39, 62-86.

Bogaard, P. van den,
    Chr.M. Hall,
    H.-U. Schmincke,
    D. York
1987   40AR/39AR Laser Dating of single grains: Ages of Quaternary Tephra from the East Eifel Volcanic Field, *F.R.G. Geophysical Research Letters* 14, 1211-1214.

Bogaard, P. van den,
    H.-U. Schmincke
1988   Aschenlagen als quartäre Zeitmarken in Mitteleuropa, *Die Geowissenschaften* 3, 75-84.

1990   Die Entwicklungsgeschichte des Mittelrheinraumes und die Eruptionsgeschichte des Osteifel-Vulkanfeldes. In: W. Schirmer (ed.), *Rheingeschichte zwischen Mosel und Maas*, 166-190, Hannover: Deutsche Quartärvereinigung.

Boscheinen, J.,
    G. Bosinski,
    K. Brunnacker,
    U. Koch,
    T. van Kolfschoten,
    E. Turner,
    B. Urban
1984   Ein altpaläolithischer Fundplatz bei Miesenheim, Kreis Mayen-Koblenz/Neuwieder Becken, *Archäologisches Korrespondenzblatt* 14, 1-16.

Bosinski, G.
1992   *Eiszeitjäger im Neuwieder Becken. Archäologie des Eiszeitalters am Mittelrhein. (Archäologie an Mittelrhein und Mosel* 1), Koblenz: Archäol. Denkmalpflege.

Bosinski, G.,
    K. Brunnacker,
    K.P. Lanser,
    S. Stephan,
    B. Urban,
    K. Würges
1980   Altpaläolithische Funde von Kärlich, Kreis Mayen-Koblenz (Neuwieder Becken), *Archäologisches Korrespondenzblatt* 10, 295-314.

Bosinski, G.,
    T. van Kolfschoten,
    E. Turner
1988   *Miesenheim I. Die Zeit des Homo erectus*. Andernacher Beiträge 2, Andernach.

Brunnacker, K.,
    R. Streit,
    W. Schirmer
1969   Der Aufbau des Quartär-Profils von Kärlich/Neuwieder Becken (Mittelrhein), *Mainzer Naturwisschaftliches Archiv* 8, 102-133.

Brunnacker, K.,
    Fl. Heller,
    V. Lozek
1971   Beiträge zur Stratigraphie des Quartär-Profils von Kärlich am Mittelrhein, *Mainzer Naturwissenschaftliches Archiv* 10, 77-100.

Brunnacker, K.,
    H. Löhr,
    W. Boenigk,
    J.J. Puissegur,
    F. Poplin
1975   Quartär-Aufschlüsse bei Ariendorf am unteren Mittelrhein, *Mainzer Naturwissenschaftliches Archiv* 14, 93-141.

Brunnacker, K.,
    W. Boenigk,
    A. Koci,
    W. Tillmanns
1976   Die MATUYAMA/BRUNHES-Grenze am Rhein und an der Donau, *Neues Jahrbuch Geologie Paläontologie, Abhandlung* 151, 358-378.

Brunnacker, K.,   1978   Die Mittelterrassen am Niederrhein zwischen Köln und Mönchengladbach, *Fortschritte*
  W. Boenigk,   *Geologie Rheinland und Westfalen* 28, 277-324.
  B. Dolezalek,
  K.E. Kempf,
  A. Koci,
  H. Mentzen,
  M. Razi Rad,
  K.-P. Winter

Brunnacker, K.,   1982   Die altquartären Terrassen rechts des Niederrheins, *Zeitschrift für Geomorphologie, N. F.*
  F. Farrokh,   *Suppl.* 42, 215-226.
  D. Sidiropoulos

Brunnacker, K.,   1982   Der Kartstein-Travertin in der nördlichen Westeifel, *Decheniana* 135, 179-204.
  G.J. Hennig,
  E. Juvigné,
  H. Löhr,
  B. Urban,
  R. Zeese

Brunnacker, K.,   1983   The Rhine Valley between the Neuwied Basin and the Lower Rhenish Embayment. In:
  W. Boenigk   K. Fuchs *et al.* (ed.), *Plateau Uplift, The Rhenish Shield – A Case History*, 62-72, Berlin:
                                            Springer-Verlag.

Fiedler, L.   1983   *Jäger und Sammler der Frühzeit. Alt- und Mittelsteinzeit in Nordhessen. Vor- und Früh-*
                                            geschichte im Hessischen Landesmuseum Kassel, Kassel.

                                1991   Paläolithische Funde auf Terrassen im Rhein-Mosel-Raum, *Berichte zur Archäologie an*
                                            Mittelrhein und Mosel 2, 9-19.

                                1994   *Alt- und mittelsteinzeitliche Funde in Hessen.* Führer zur hessischen Vor- und Früh-
                                            geschichte 2, Kassel.

Frechen, J.   1976   *Siebengebirge am Rhein - Laacher Vulkangebiet - Maargebiet der Westeifel. Vulkanologisch-*
                                            petrographische Exkursionen, Sammlung geologischer Führer 56, 3 ed. Berlin,
                                            Stuttgart.

Gabunia, L.   1992   Der menschliche Unterkiefer von Dmanisi (Georgien, Kaukasus), *Jahrbuch des Römisch-*
                                            Germanisches Zentralmuseums Mainz 39, 185-208.

Gaudzinski, S.,   in press   Kärlich-Seeufer. Untersuchungen zu einer altpaläolithischen Fundstelle im Neuwieder
                                            Becken (Rheinland/Deutschland). Monog. RGZM, Mainz.

Grün, R.,   1982   230Th/234U-Daten mittel- und jungpleistozÄner Travertine im Raum Stuttgart, *Jahres-*
  K. Brunnacker,   *berichte und Mitteilungen des Oberrheinischen geologischen Vereins N. F.* 64, 201-211.
  G.J. Hennig

Grün, R.,   1986   Elektronen-Spin-Resonanz (ESR)- Datierung eines Elefantenzahnes aus dem Travertin-
  K. Brunnacker   bruch "Lauster", Stuttgart-Bad Cannstatt, *Jahreshefte des geologischen Landesamtes*
                                            Baden-Württemberg 28, 43-47.

Haesaerts, P.   1990   Stratigraphical approach to the Pleistocene deposits of the Schneider quarry at Ariendorf
                                            (Middle Rhine, Germany). In: W. Schirmer (ed.), *Rheingeschichte zwischen Mosel und*
                                            Maas, 112 -114, Hannover: Deutsche Quartärvereinigung.

Heim, J.,
J.P. Lautridou,
J. Maucorps,
J.J. Puissegur,
J. Sommé,
A. Thevenin
1982   Achenheim: Une sequence-type des loess du pleistocène moyen et supérieur, *Bull. A.F.E.Q.* 19, 147-159.

Howell, F. C.
1960   European and Northwest African Middle Pleistocene Hominids, *Current Anthropology* 1, 195-232.

Junkmanns, J.
1991   Die Steinartefakte aus Achenheim in der Sammlung Paul Wernert, *Archäologisches Korrespondenzblatt* 21, 1-16.

Kahlke, R.-D.
1985   Altpleistozäne Hippopotamus -Reste von Untermaßfeld bei Meiningen (Bezirk Suhl, DDR) (Vorläufige Mitteilung), *Säugetierkundliche Informationen* 2, 227-233.

in press   Die Hippopotamus-Reste aus dem Unterpleistozän von Untermaßfeld bei Meiningen (Thüringen). In: H.-D. Kahlke and R.-D. Kahlke (ed.), *Das Pleistozän von Untermaßfeld in Thüringen*, Teil I. Monogr. RGZM, Mainz.

Kaiser, K.
1961   Gliederung und Formenschatz des Pleistozäns und Quartärs am Mittel- und Niederrhein sowie in den angrenzenden Niederlanden unter besonderer Berücksichtigung der Rheinterrassen, *Festschrift zum 33. Deutschen Geographen-Tag Köln*, 236-278.

Klostermann, J.
1992   *Das Quartär der Niederrheinischen Bucht.* Krefeld.

Koenigswald, W. von
1992   Zur Ökologie und Biostratigraphie der beiden pleistozünen Faunen von Mauer bei Heidelberg. In: K.W. Beinhauer and G.A. Wagner (ed.), *Schichten von Mauer. 85 Jahre Homo erectus heidelbergensis*, 101-110, Mannheim: Edition Braus.

Kolfschoten, T. van
1990a   The Evolution of the Mammal Fauna in the Netherlands and the Middle Rhine Area (Western Germany) during the Late Middle Pleistocene, *Mededelingen Rijks Geologische Dienst* 43(3), 1-69.

1990b   Miesenheim I bei Andernach. In: W. Schirmer (ed.), *Rheingeschichte zwischen Mosel und Maas*, 81-88, Hannover: Deutsche Quartärvereinigung.

in press   MittelpleistozÄne Kleinfauna von Miesenheim I. In: E. Turner (ed.), *Miesenheim I.* Monogr. RGZM, Mainz.

Kolfschoten, T. van,
G. Roth,
E. Turner
1990   Mollusken- und Säugetierfaunen aus der Tongrube Kärlich. In: W. Schirmer (ed.), *Rheingeschichte zwischen Mosel und Maas*, 70-74, Hannover: Deutsche Quartärvereinigung.

Kolfschoten, T. van,
E. Turner
in press   Early Middle Pleistocene Mammalian Faunas from Kärlich and Miesenheim I and their Biostratigraphical Implications, *Proceedings of the Cromer-Symposium*, Norwich 1990.

Kröger, K.,
P. van den Bogaard,
F. Bittmann,
E. Turner
1988   Der Fundplatz Kärlich-Seeufer. Neue Untersuchungen zum Altpaläolithikum im Rheinland, *Jahrbuch des Römisch-Germanischen Zentralmuseums Mainz* 35, 111-135.

Kröger, H.
1959   Frühpaläolithische Geröllartefakte vom Typ "Pebble- tool" in Oberhessen? *Eiszeitalter und Gegenwart* 10, 165-198.

1975   Typologische und stratigraphische Kriterien zur prärißzeitlichen Datierung der altpaläolithischen Geröllgerät- Industrie vom Münzenberger Typ in Oberhessen, *Fundberichte aus Hessen* 13, 1-50.

1977/78   Stratigraphisch gesicherte Grabungsbefunde zur holsteinzeitlichen Datierung der ober-hessischen Geröllgerät- Industrie vom Münzenberger Typ, *Fundberichte aus Hessen* 17/18, 1-26.

1987   Zur cromerzeitlichen Datierung der Münzenberger Geröllgeräte-Gruppe, *Quartär* 37/38, 229-240.

1989   Die Cromerzeit-Datierung der Münzenberger Geröllgeräte - ein Exempel urgeschichtlichen lIrrens? *Quartär* 39/40, 215-222.

1994   *Die altpaläolithische Geröllgeräte-Industrie der Münzenberger Gruppe in Oberhessen.* (Materialien zur Vor- und Frühgeschichte von Hessen 10). Wiesbaden.

Lippolt, H.J.,   1986   40AR/39AR Age Determinations on Sanidines of the Eifel Volcanic Fields (Federal
     U. Fuhrmann,   Republic of Germany): Constraints on Age and Duration of a Middle Pleistocene cold
     H. Hradetzky   period, *Chemical Geology* 59, 187- 204.

Lozek, V.   1971   Vorläufige Kurzauswertung der Molluskenfunde. In: K. Brunnacker, Fl. Heller and V. Lozek 1971, 83-86.

Maul, L.   1990   *Biharische Kleinsäugerfunde von Untermaßfeld, Voigtstedt und Süßenborn und ihre chronologische Stellung im Rahmen der biharischen Micromammalia-Faunen Europas.* Diss. Humboldt-Universität Berlin.

Meyer, W.   1986   *Geologie der Eifel.* Stuttgart.

Moncel, M.-H.   1989   L'industrie sur galet de Münzenberg (Oberhessen, R.F.A) du Professeur H. Krüger (Giessen). Réflexions sur plus de 30 ans de prospections, fouilles et discussions sur la datation (1952-1987), *L'Anthropologie* 93, 3-14.

Müller-Beck, H.   1964   Zur stratigraphischen Stellung des Homo heidelbergensis, *Jahrbuch des Römisch-Germa-nischen Zentralmuseums Mainz* 11, 15-32.

Penck, A.,   1901-09   *Die Alpen im Eiszeitalter.* Leipzig.
     E. Brückner

Raynal, J.-P.,   this   Tephrofacts and the first human occupation of the French Massif Central.
     L. Magoga,   volume
     P. Bindon

Remy, H.   1959   Zur Gliederung des Lösses bei Kärlich und Bröl am unteren Mittelrhein mit besonderer Berücksichtigung der Faunen, *Fortschritte Geologie Rheinland und Westfalen* 4, 323-330.

Roth, G.,   in press a.   Mollusken aus dem mittelpleistozänen "Kärlicher Interglazial" der Tongrube bei Kärlich (Neuwieder Becken/Mittelrhein), *Jahrbuch des Römisch-Germanischen Zentralmuseums Mainz* 39.

in press b.   Die Mollusken der mittelpleistozänen Fundstelle Miesenheim I. In: E. Turner (ed.), *Miesenheim I,* Monograph, RGZM, Mainz.

Rust, A.   1956a   *Artefakte aus der Zeit des Homo heidelbergensis in Süd- und Norddeutschland.* Bonn.

1956b   Über neue Artefakte aus der Heidelberger Stufe, *Eiszeitalter und Gegenwart* 7, 179-192.

1957   Eine Skizze zum vermutlichen Werdegang und Ablauf der Heidelberger Kultur in Europa, *Quaternaria* 4, 1-16.

| | 1965 | *Über Waffen- und Werkzeugtechnik des Altmenschen.* Neumünster. |
| | 1971 | *Werkzeuge des Frühmenschen in Europa.* Neumünster. |

Schmincke, H.-U.   1988   *Vulkane im Laacher See-Gebiet. Ihre Entstehung und heutige Bedeutung.* Haltern.

Schmincke, H.-U.,   1983   The Quaternary Eifel Volcanic Fields. In: K. Fuchs *et al.* (ed.), *Plateau Uplift, The*
V. Lorenz,   *Rhenish Shield - A Case History*, 139-151, Berlin: Springer-Verlag.
H.A. Seck

Schmude, K.   1992   Zwei cromerzeitliche Artefakt-Fundplätze in der Jüngeren Hauptterrasse am Niederrhein,
                                 Eiszeitalter und Gegenwart 42, 1-24.

Schoetensack, O.   1908   *Der Unterkiefer des Homo Heidelbergensis aus den Sanden von Mauer bei Heidelberg.*
                                 Ein Beitrag zur Paläontologie des Menschen. Leipzig.

Street, M.,   1994   Absolute Chronologie des späten Paläolithikums und des Frühmesolithikums im
M. Baales,   nördlichen Rheinland, *Archäologisches Korrespondenzblatt* 24, 1-28.
B. Weninger

Thome, K.N.   1958   Die Begegnung des nordischen Inlandeises mit dem Rhein, *Geologisches Jahrbuch* 76,
                                 261-308.

Turner, E.   1990   Middle and Late Pleistocene Macrofaunas of the Neuwied Basin Region (Rhineland-
                                 Palatinate) of West Germany, *Jahrbuch des Römisch-Germanischen Zentralmuseums*
                                 Mainz 37, 135-396.

                      1991   Pleistocene Stratigraphy and Vertebrate Faunas from the Neuwied Basin region of
                                 Western Germany, *Cranium* 8, 21-34.

Turner, E. (ed.),   in press *Miesenheim I. Excavations at a Lower Palaeolithic Site in the Central Rhineland of*
                                 Germany. Monogr. RGZM, Mainz.

Vollbrecht, J.   1992   *Das Altpaläolithikum aus den unteren Schichten in Kärlich.* Magisterarbeit Köln.

                      in press *Untersuchungen zum Altpaläolithikum des Rheinlandes.* Dissertation Universität Köln.

Wagner, E.   1980   Ein altpaläolithischer Rastplatz im mittelpleistozänen Travertin von Stuttgart-Bad
                                 Cannstatt, *Archäologische Ausgrabungen in Baden-Württemberg* 1979, 7-14.

                      1984   Ein Jagdplatz des *Homo erectus* im mittelpleistozänen Travertin in Stuttgart-Bad Cannstatt,
                                 Germania 62, 230-267.

                      1987   Die Fundstelle "Bunker" im mittelpleistozänen Travertin von Stuttgart-Bad Cannstatt,
                                 Archäologische Ausgrabungen in Baden-Württemberg 1986, 15-18.

                      1990   Neue paläolithische Freilandfundstellen. *Archäologische Ausgrabungen in Baden-Würt-*
                                 temberg 1989, 19-21.

                      1991   *Urgeschichte im Neckarland. Führer zu archäologischen Denkmälern in Deutschland 22*
                                 (Heilbronn und das mittlere Neckarland zwischen Marbach und Gundelsheim).

                      1992   Les découvertes paléolithiques des travertins de Stuttgart-Bad Cannstatt, *L'Anthropologie*
                                 96, 71-86.

Weinert, H.   1937   Dem Unterkiefer von Mauer zur 30jährigen Wiederkehr seiner Entdeckung, *Zeitschrift für*
                                 Morphologie und Anthropologie 37, 102-113.

Wernert, P.   1957   *Stratigraphie paléontologique et préhistorique des sédiments quaternaires d'Alsace.* (Achenheim. Mém. Service carte géol. No.4). Strasbourg.

Wernert, P.,   1962   Un "pebble-tool" des alluvions rhénans de la carriëre Hurst a Achenheim, *Bull. serv. carte geol. Alsace-Lorraine* 15, 29-36.
   G. Millot,
   J.P. van Eller

Woldstedt, P.   1955²   *Norddeutschland und angrenzende Gebiete im Eiszeitalter.* Stuttgart.

Würges, K.   1984   Altpaläolithische Funde aus der Tongrube Kärlich (Schicht H, unten), Kreis Mayen-Koblenz/Neuwieder Becken, *Archäologisches Korrespondenzblatt* 14, 17-22.

                       1986   Artefakte aus den ältesten Quartär-Sedimenten (Schichten A-C) der Tongrube Kärlich, Kreis Mayen-Koblenz/Neuwieder Becken, *Archäologisches Korrespondenzblatt* 16, 1-6.

                       1991   Neue altpaläolithische Funde aus der Tongrube Kärlich, Kreis Mayen-Koblenz / Neuwieder Becken, *Archäologisches Korrespondenzblatt* 21, 449-455.

Zipter, I.   1991   *Die Geologie des Abschnitts G der Deckschichten in der Tongrube Kärlich/Mittelrhein.* Diplomarbeit Universität Köln.

Gerhard Bosinski
Forschungsbereich Altsteinzeit
Schloss Monrepos
56567 Neuwied
Germany

Jean-Paul Raynal
Lionel Magoga
Peter Bindon

8   Tephrofacts and the first human occupation of the French Massif Central

Claims for Early Pleistocene occupation of the French Massif Central are examined within the context of the geological setting of the sites. The Massif Central is an area where volcanic processes repeatedly fractured stones, thus producing forms that look like humanly modified objects: tephrofacts. The analysis of raw material diversity proves to be an important tool to discriminate between occurrences of such tephrofacts and archeological sites, the earliest of which date from the Middle Pleistocene.

1.   Introduction

The production of geofacts, objects resulting from natural fracture and imitating artefacts (Haynes 1973), is a phenomenon long recognized in many different sedimentary contexts (Pei 1937; Mortelmans 1947; Breuil 1955; Clark 1958; Bourdier 1967; Fournier 1971; Raynal and Texier 1989; Raynal *et al.* 1990). A number of works have analyzed such objects (particularly flint ones), and have tried to elaborate a method which distinguishes clearly between intentionally flaked objects and products of nature (Boule 1889; 1905; 1921; Haward 1911; Moir 1911; Warren 1914; Grayson 1986; Schnurrenberger and Alan 1985; Peacock 1991).

The Massif Central in the central mountainous region of France experienced active volcanism since the Miocene (15-20 Myr BP) and several glacial events during the Pleistocene. Because vulcanism and frost action generate rock fracturing, there is thus a high probability of the natural occurrence of pseudo-artefacts in this area. The discovery of flint pseudo-tools confused a number of archaeologists during the nineteenth century beginning with Tardy (1869), who reported the discovery of Miocene eoliths from Le Puy Courny in the Cantal. More than fifty years later Marty was still arguing for this interpretation (Capitan and Marty 1924).

The Massif Central region is well known for important excavations of Upper Palaeolithic sites and it has considerable archaeological potential for sites yielding material from the Lower and Middle Palaeolithic periods. During the last twenty years, much research has been undertaken in the region, aimed at discovering traces of the first human occupation of Europe. These investigations have been concentrated in Velay, a province to the south of Auvergne which is rich in Plio-Pleistocene faunas, occurring in between volcanic sediments which offer the possibility of obtaining a long sequence of palaeomagnetic and radiometric dates. Basse-Auvergne and Bourbonnais have yielded a number of classic Acheulean bifaces lacking stratigraphic context, and in surface complexes of the Allier tools made on quartz cobbles have been discovered.

The lithic series discovered in the Massif Central, principally in Velay, has been classified under the name "Most Ancient Palaeolithic" (Bonifay and Bonifay 1983) and has been proposed as resolving the question of the time of the initial human occupation of Europe (Bonifay, Consigny, Liabeuf 1989; Bonifay 1981; 1983; 1989a; b; c; 1991). This perspective, which is of considerable conceptual importance and thus must be founded on decisive arguments, is not accepted unanimously by the scientific community, as doubts about the artificial character of the finds have been expressed in many publications (Delson 1989; Boëda 1990; Villa 1991; Farizy *in* Diaz 1993). We here report some results of an examination of the production of geofacts by volcanism. We will refer to these as *tephrofacts*. These pseudo-artefacts are fashioned in materials other than flint which occur in the local environment of supposedly ancient archaeological sites. Our observations, begun in 1989, are founded on the examination of a number of volcanic structures and the deposits and epiclastites associated with these structures (Fig. 1). These investigations were aimed at elucidating the possible presence of hominids in the late Pliocene and Early Pleistocene of this part of France. Special attention has been given to the site of Blassac and part of the abundant series of supposed artefacts discovered in an ancient context there and also to the site of Soleilhac, yielding the strongest evidence for an early occupation of Velay.

2.   The production of tephrofacts

The production of tephrofacts is known to have occurred in pyroclastites of the Eifel in Germany (Bosinski *et al.* 1986). We collected some tephrofacts on the site of Kärlich and in strombolian lapilli of the Schweinskopf volcano in

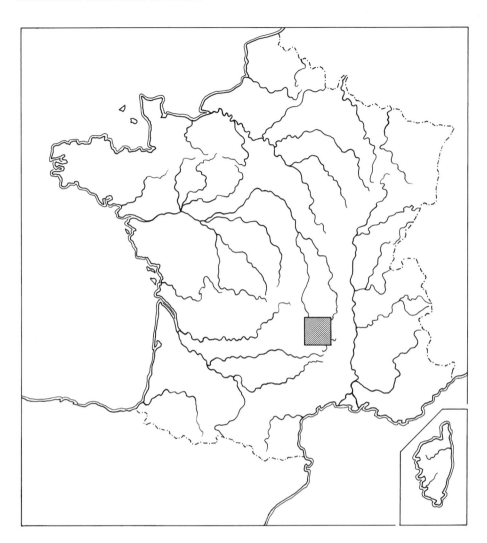

Fig. 1. Location of the study area.

the company of G. Bosinski in 1992. These tephrofacts superficially resemble artefacts and their differentiation from the latter is difficult when they are discovered outside of their primary volcanic context (Kulemeyer 1986).

In Velay, many Pleistocene maar tuff-rings (La Sauvetat, Les Farges, Saint-Eble, Soleilhac, Senèze, Blassac/Les Blanches), basanitic breccias (Sainte-Anne) and one strombolian cone have yielded tephrofacts with various petrological origins. Moreover, many other geofacts have been collected in a large number of volcanic sediments (Saint-Vidal, Vals, Brioude).

Among these are a number of flakes and some objects with multiple flake scars with a very regular pattern: none of them would be discarded out of hand if they occurred in solid archaeological contexts. *However, they are undoubtedly tephrofacts which have resulted from several mechanical and thermal actions during various different eruptive stages of volcanic events.*

3.   Petrography of the tephrofacts

The raw materials of the tephrofacts collected come from the regional basement or from the Plio-Pleistocene sedimentary formations which have been altered by the volcanic eruptions. Some of these materials still outcrop in the immediate environment of the volcanic formations investigated. The following diverse rocks have been identified: vein quartz, pegmatitic quartz, fine grained granite, oriented granite, migmatitic gneiss with sillimanite, lamprophyre and various basalts.

The Blassac-Les Blanches tuff-ring has yielded seventy-two tephrofacts. The distribution of petrographic types does not vary significantly between the chunks, flakes or pseudo-artefacts (Fig. 2a). *A strong presence of materials of mediocre flaking quality (granites and gneiss) and the absence of flint is a distinct characteristic of this series.*

4.   Natural flakes

In this paper we do not discuss the classic "pot-lid" flake form well known to occur as a result of thermally induced reduction sequences. We note however the absence in the literature of observations concerning the characteristics of these thermal fracture features when they occur adjacent to the edges of irregular chunks. The natural flakes derived from these situations exhibit a pseudo-striking platform produced when the fracture surface intersects an adjoining edge. Although these objects may be superficially identified as humanly produced flakes, this position can be readily discarded for flint when none of the other features of humanly produced flakes can be identified (point of percussion, ventral bulbar scar, radial stress marks, etc).

Fifty natural flakes were collected for study from the tuff-rings of Blassac-Les Blanches, La Sauvetat and Soleilhac (Fig. 3). Some of them were in juxtaposition with the pseudo-core. They result from repetitive uni-directional stresses, both mechanical and thermal.

Of these, fifteen (30%) exhibit cortical striking platforms. These can be subdivided into those with a total or partial cortical dorsal surface extending to the edges (11 objects) and those with non-cortical edges (4 objects). In the case of a series produced by intentional flaking, these objects would be considered of primary and secondary generation.

Flakes without cortical striking platforms represent 70% of the total (35 objects) and this group is composed of those with cortical dorsal surfaces (8 objects) and those with non- cortical edges (27 objects). In a series produced by intentional flaking, these would be considered third generation flakes.

Pseudo-retouch sometimes appearing contiguous can be seen on numerous flakes and it is comparable with the utilized or retouched edges of humanly produced artefacts (Fig. 3).

The proportion of types of naturally produced flakes in this series is very different from that obtained from our experiments with quartz pebbles. They also differ from those of the flaked quartz assemblages collected from the upper and middle terraces of the Allier in Bourbonnais: *an assemblage of tephrofacts is characterized by an over-representation of flakes with non cortical striking platforms and non cortical edges and an under-representation of flakes with cortical striking platforms and edges totally or partially cortical* (Fig. 2b).

Pseudo-flakes have a weight below 150 g in more than 96 % of the cases and rarely exceed 500 g (Fig. 2c). A few exceptions exist, represented by very large pieces which weigh over 2000 g.

The weight criterion is not a discriminating factor between tephrofacts and artefacts. The distribution of weight ratios of pseudo-flakes and flakes manufactured and recovered in primary position (whether in eruptive breccias, archaeological layers, or by experimentation) is identical. This distribution differs from those observed on collections from surface sites: for the flakes collected in Bourbonnais on the surface of the upper and middle terraces of the Allier for example, the weight ratio distribution can be explained by the removal of the smaller flakes through natural processes and selective collection (Fig. 2c).

5.   Natural objects with multiple flake scars

Events leading to the natural flaking of fragile source rocks are diverse in nature and may result in an apparently organized series of flake scars. The order in which these flakes are removed largely determines the morphology of each tephrofact. The organization of the natural flake scars on the blocks parallels the morphology of objects recognized among prehistoric archaeological assemblages.

The number of flake scars on the tephrofacts (between 1 and 22) is comparable with that observed on prehistoric objects and their random organization is comparable to the sequences observed on manufactured objects. However, contrary to what is evident on prehistoric objects, the detachment points of flakes observed on tephrofacts are very often impossible to determine and most flake scars occur in random arrangements.

On 34 faces of objects with multiple flake scars (9 unifaces and 26 bifaces) there is a linear system of "working" arranged from right to left for three flake scars in two cases and in the remaining cases the working system is non-linear with a maximum number of seven flake scars originating from one edge. In general, pseudo-working identified on the tephrofacts is mainly non-linear in arrangement.

The associations of flake scars on edges are shown in the following table:

Number of flake scars	1	2	3	4	5	6	7	Sample
Unifacially "flaked" objects	1	2	1	3	0	2	0	9 faces
Bifacially "flaked" objects*	2	3	6	5	4	3	4	27 faces

* (each face is considered separately)

Some natural objects appear similar to unifacially flaked choppers and bifacially flaked chopping tools in that they exhibit the transformation of a natural edge with at least two adjacent flakes (Fig. 4, n° 1, 2, 4, 5; Fig. 5, n° 1; Fig. 6, n° 5; Fig. 8, n° 2).

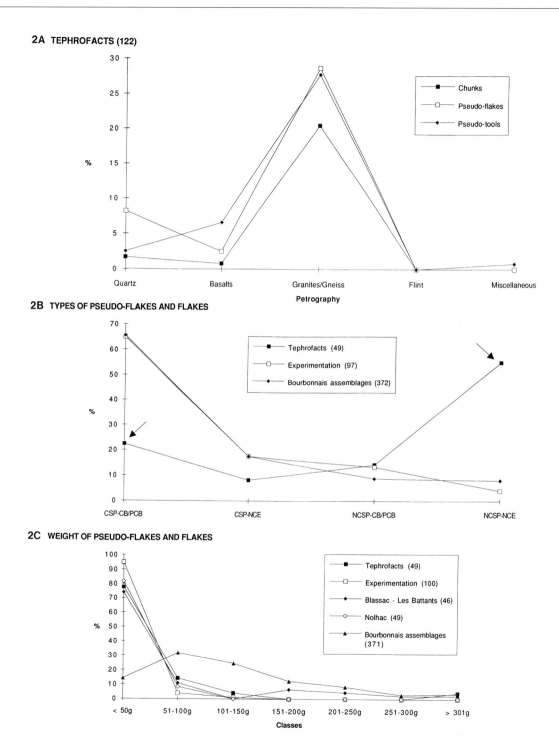

Fig. 2. 2a: Petrography of tephrofacts.
2b: Types of pseudo-flakes compared to flakes from archaeological and experimental series. CSP: cortical striking platform. CB: cortical back. PCB: partially cortical back. NCE: non-cortical edges. NCSP: non-cortical striking platform.
2c: Weight of pseudo-flakes compared to those of archaeological and experimental series.

2D COMPARISON WITH ASSEMBLAGES FROM TWO REPUTEDLY ANCIENT SITES

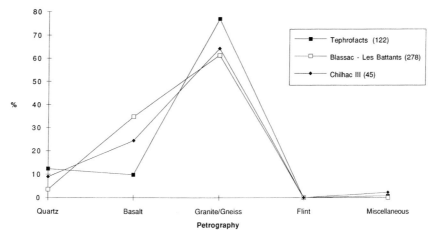

2E COMPARISON WITH THREE ARCHAEOLOGICAL ASSEMBLAGES

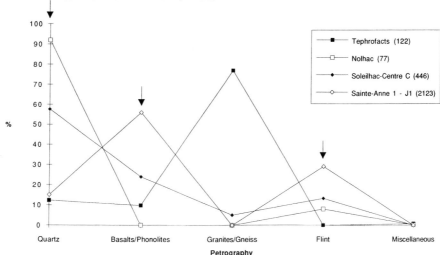

Fig. 2.   2d: Comparison of tephrofacts with lithic assemblages from two "archaeological" ancient sites.
          2e: Comparison of tephrofacts with lithic assemblages from three archaeological series.

Natural multidirectional flaking around the periphery of various chunks and pieces produces objects which are similar to invasively flaked tabular cores and discoidal cores (Fig. 5, n[os] 3; Fig. 8, n° 3; Fig. 7, n° 1, 2). Sometimes the natural morphology is similar to that seen on bifacially flaked artefacts (Fig. 4, n° 3; Fig. 6, n° 1; Fig. 7, n° 3; Fig. 8, n° 1).

Other tephrofacts look similar to flaked polyhedrons. These globular objects have a large number of scars from flakes with a high number of non-cortical striking platforms (Fig. 7, n° 2, 4; Fig. 6, n° 3, 4; Fig. 8, n° 4; Fig. 9).

As if the distinction between tephrofacts and intentionally manufactured objects is not difficult enough, the case is *further complicated by the poor raw materials in which they occur.* This observation has already been discussed in other works attempting to distinguish between geofacts and artefacts (Watson 1968), even though some progress has been made in the case of flint (Peacock 1991), a raw material for which there is today a considerable amount of information on its flaking properties.

6.   Distinguishing between tephrofacts and humanly produced objects

We have had recourse to a statistical approach to solve this problem, the details of which will be presented elsewhere. Between 24 and 62 tephrofacts, according to the

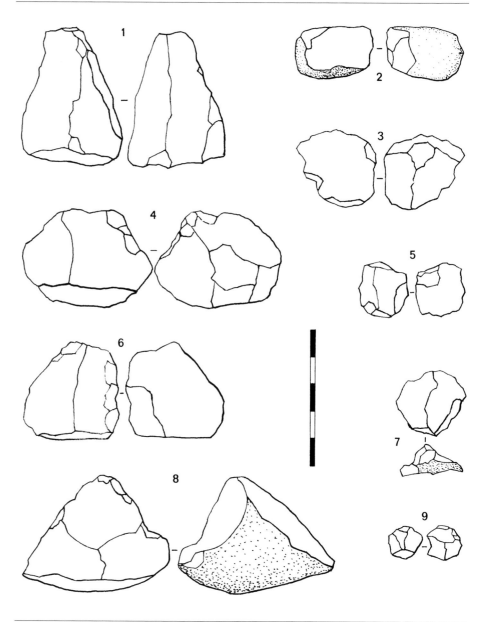

Fig. 3. Examples of tephrofacts (scale in cm) - Blassac-les Blanches Haute-Loire, pyroclastites - 1: Partially cortical backed pseudo-flake and non cortical striking platform, fine grained granite. 2: Partially cortical backed pseudo-flake and cortical striking platform, quartz. 3: Partially cortical backed pseudo-flake and non cortical striking platform, fine grained granite. 4: non-cortical backed pseudo-flake and non cortical striking platform, fine grained granite. 5: Partially cortical backed pseudo-flake and cortical striking platform, pegmatitic quartz. 6: pseudo-flake with non cortical edges and cortical striking platform, fine grained granite. 7: pseudo-flake with non cortical edges and non cortical striking platform, pegmatitic quartz. 8: Partially cortical backed pseudo-flake and cortical striking platform, fine grained granite. 9: pseudo-flake with non cortical edges and non cortical striking platform, quartz.

number in each sample, have been added to a series of humanly produced lithics. The criteria used for describing the two groups were published by J. Collina-Girard (1975; 1986). We have discarded some of those criteria, calibrated some of his non-metrical observations and added some of our own (weight and number of flake scars).

Factorial analysis of correspondences reveals that the inclusion of the tephrofacts destroys the coherence of the assemblage. The presence of two discrete and distinct groups is readily observed in each series.

In the case of a principal component analysis, taking all the characteristics except the number of flake scars into account, no true distinction can be made between tephrofacts and humanly produced objects. The natural trend in tephrofacts is towards a spherical or sub-spherical shape, which most effectively resists further natural attrition. Human intervention interrupts this trend towards a globular form. However, industries containing a preponderance of polyhedrons cannot be discarded out of hand as having a natural origin and should be studied according to the scheme suggested above.

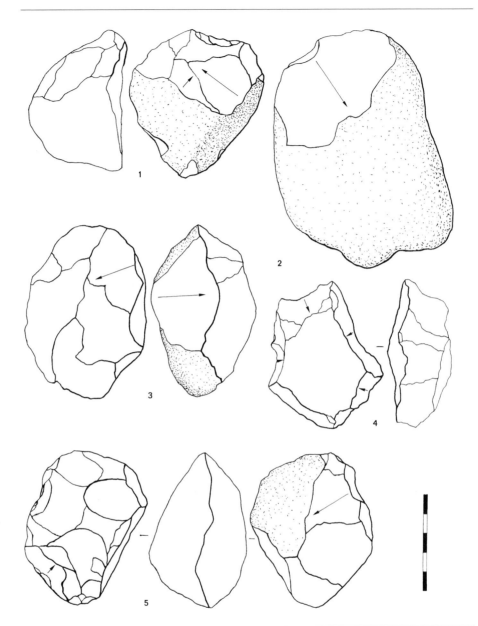

Fig. 4. Examples of tephrofacts (arrows indicate clear directions of flaking), scale in cm - Miscellaneous from Haute-Loire - 1: pseudo-chopper, basalte, Blassac-les Blanches pyroclastites. 2: pseudo-chopper, lamprophyre, Blassac. 3: pseudo-biface-like piece, basalte, Blassac-les Blanches pyroclastites. 4: pseudo-chopper, basalte, Blassac-les Blanches tuff-ring. 5: pseudo-chopping-tool, migmatitic gneiss, Senèze tuff-ring inférieur.

Parametric characteristics often used for studying a humanly produced lithic assemblage, when applied to tephrofacts, do not permit any distinction between the two. Rather than showing the differences, the results confirm the similarities between tephrofacts and manufactured objects, rendering the method useless.

7.   Remarks on two reputedly ancient sites

7.1.   Blassac-les Battants.

A series collected at Les Battants by F. Carré (1978; 1983; 1991) is dated by a number of Potassium/Argon

determinations of the basaltic lava-flow overlying the assemblage, which indicate an age around or beyond 2 Myr BP. However, the fauna of Blassac-La Girondie, in an analogous stratigraphic position, seems to be much more recent, belonging to the Peyrolles biozone and probably dating from around 1.2-1.4 Myr BP (Couthures 1982; Carré and Couthures 1982; Couthures and Pastre 1983; Fouris 1989; Bonifay 1991; Carré 1991).

A series of 278 lithic objects has been examined. This study is incomplete, however, because the matrix has been left on several objects. Observations to date are as follows:

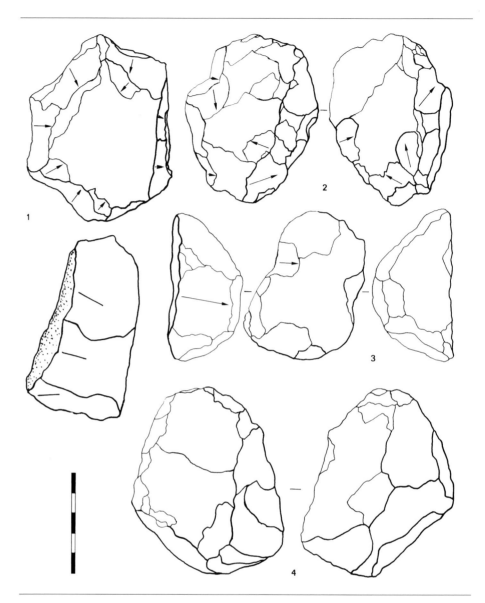

Fig. 5. Examples of tephrofacts
(arrows indicate clear directions of
flaking), scale in cm -
Miscellaneous from Haute-Loire -
1: peripherally flaked pseudo-
chopper, granite, La Sauvetat tuff-
ring. 2: pseudo-polyhedron,
pegmatitic quartz, Blassac-les
Blanches pyroclastites. 3: pseudo-
invasively flaked tabular piece,
granite, La Sauvetat tuff-ring.
4: pseudo-polyhedron, granite,
La Sauvetat tuff-ring.

– Most objects are on crystalline rocks with natural
   cleavage planes and the fractures in general follow these
   planes. This gives the pieces an appearance of being
   partly or intentionally flaked debitage. However, most of
   the flakes do not have normal feathered terminations.
– From the evidence of the flake scars, the angle of
   detachment approaches 90°, which is not usually
   encountered in intentional flaking.
– Several objects have gross crystalline irregularities which
   render them inappropriate raw materials for flaking.
– Flakes do not exhibit clear points of percussion.
– Some objects exhibit obvious thermal fractures.
– On many objects, the flake scars appear to originate from

well outside the remaining volume. Objects of similar
form, and the flakes removed from them by thermal
action, have been collected from the tuff-ring of Blassac-
Les Blanches. In several cases, these pseudo-nuclei and
their conjoining flakes were found in primary position
within the tuff with the flakes barely removed from the
parent chunk.
– Several objects of very poor flaking quality show a
   number of repetitive flake scars, which is an unlikely
   occurrence even in a primitive series of intentionally
   flaked objects. Moreover, within the same stratigraphic
   level, materials with far better flaking properties are
   present.

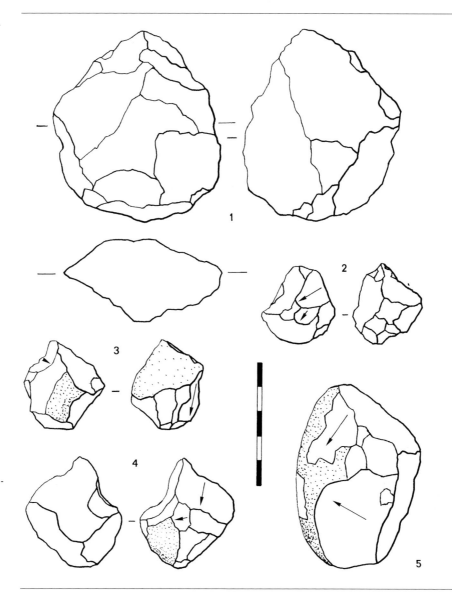

Fig. 6. Examples of tephrofacts (arrows indicate clear directions of flaking), scale in cm - Blassac-les Blanches Haute-Loire, pyroclastites - 1: pseudo-partially bifacial discoïd piece, migmatitic gneiss à sillimanite. 2: regular pseudo-polyhedron, quartz. 3: regular pseudo-polyhedron, quartz. 4: regular pseudo-polyhedron, oriented granite. 5: pseudo-chopper, fine grained granite.

– Finally, the petrographic nature of the series presents a distribution comparable to that of tephrofacts (Fig. 2d).

The geological characteristics of the site of Blassac-Les Battants deserve a full scale discussion too extensive for this paper. *We simply note here the undeniable inclusion of naturally fractured objects and the resemblance to the petrographic suite occupied by tephrofacts.*

7.2.   CHILHAC III
The fossil locality of Chilhac III is known for a rich Villafranchian fauna (Boeuf 1983) and lithic objects (Guth 1974; Guth and Boeuf 1977; Guth and Chavaillon 1985)

which occur in a level whose age is presumed to be in the vicinity of 1.8-1.9 Ma, a date arrived at through palaeontological comparisons and extrapolation from absolute dates on a lava flow close to the site.

The stratigraphic sequence exhibits deformations interpreted as resulting from solifluxion (Texier 1985) or soil slips (Chavaillon 1991). Many visits to the site during the excavations have convinced us of the existence of syn-sedimentary slumpings and removals. This clearly demonstrates dynamism of a kind known to occur on the margins of lacustrine systems and we postulate the likelihood of the existence here of an ancient phreato-magmatic structure. In this dynamic situation, the presence of relatively recent tools on quartz cobbles in adjacent localities (Le Gall and Raynal 1986) renders likely a mixture of such objects with the ancient fauna.

We have not examined closely the complete series of objects discovered in a stratigraphic context (ensembles B to K) apart from those published by Chavaillon (1991). Except for the resemblance between retouched flakes and some tephrofacts (Fig. 3), *we note that the petrographic nature of the objects offers a distribution identical to that of tephrofacts and of the series of pseudo-artefacts recovered at Blassac-Les Battants* (Fig. 2d).

A detailed examination of the site and its environment would clarify without doubt the archaeological and geological processes which resulted in the production of these objects and their association with the faunal remains.

8. Comparison of three archaeological series

We have chosen three archaeological series to illustrate the fundamental differences which exist between the petrography of tephrofacts and that of prehistoric tools from Velay. In the latter, the petrography clearly demonstrates human selection.

– At Nolhac, apart from exceptional flint objects, quartz was the principal material chosen (Rio Carra 1991; Bonifay 1991)
– In Soleilhac-Centre, quartz, basalt and flint are in that order the three dominant materials (Bracco 1991)
– In level J1 in the cave of Sainte-Anne 1 at Polignac, provisionally reported to OIS 6, basalts, phonolite, flint and quartz were in that order the materials worked.

The petrography of tools from the prehistoric sites is clearly different from that of the tephrofacts and *is characterized (outside the constant presence of flint) by a choice of materials which does not include those with poor flaking characteristics like granites and gneiss* (Fig. 2e).

9. Conclusions

9.1. TEPHROFACTS ARE WIDELY DISTRIBUTED

It is more than reasonable to assume that tephrofacts were produced in great numbers in the Massif Central during the numerous volcanic episodes which occurred since the Miocene. Without doubt, they were subsequently eroded out of their primary position and widely dispersed in the environment on numerous occasions.

The discovery in geological layers of some broken or apparently flaked pieces, flakes or objects exhibiting a more complex pattern of flake scars is therefore not considered a sufficient criterion for characterizing human activity, particularly in this region.

9.2. NECESSARY RE-EXAMINATION OF SITES

Sites considered indicative of human activity as demonstrated by the presence of a series of supposedly humanly worked pebbles and cobbles demand a close scrutiny of all the available evidence, especially in the case of Blassac and Chilhac III.

Sites which have yielded a limited number of doubtful artefacts, tephrofacts or geofacts need further detailed discussion. This is the case for Perrier-Etouaires in Puy-de-Dôme (G.U.E.R.P.A., 1984), Saint-Eble (Bonifay 1989a), le Coupet (Bonifay 1989a) and La Roche-Lambert (Bonifay 1981) in Haute-Loire.

For some sites, association of lithic objects with fragmented faunal remains is not decisive. The various models of fragmentation and preservation of the bones do not give at present sufficient evidence to identify any human involvement.

From the evidence, it must be recognized that there is considerable doubt concerning a very ancient human presence in the Massif Central.

In addition to this taphonomic approach, it is necessary to consider the following points carefully and systematically for all localities:
– Is there a possibility of pseudo-artefacts being produced?
– If so, what are the likely characteristics of these objects?
– Is there a geological explanation for the introduction of naturally flaked objects into the site?
– Are lithic objects preferentially distributed in the supposed archaeological layer? Is there a natural explanation for this?
– Do conjoinable objects exist in the site, and do they occur adjacent to each other?
– Are the flake scars observable on the objects arranged in a technologically "logical" sequence?
– Are natural objects mixed with artefacts?
– Are the faunal remains and the associated objects both in primary position?
– Does the taphonomic history of the site provide any explanation for possible association of numbers of objects of different ages, for example reflecting periglacial phenomena?

9.3. OPPORTUNISTIC EXPLOITATION?

Can we discard out of hand sites where only a few objects have been found? The utilization of materials of poor flaking quality in these sites may simply be an example of human opportunism according to the law of least effort. Additionally we have the complicating factor among ancient assemblages of the likelihood of opportunistic exploitation of naturally fractured pieces which will occur anyway as a part of the site's assemblage. *While these questions have already been discussed for several African archaeological sites, it is no doubt useful to consider the*

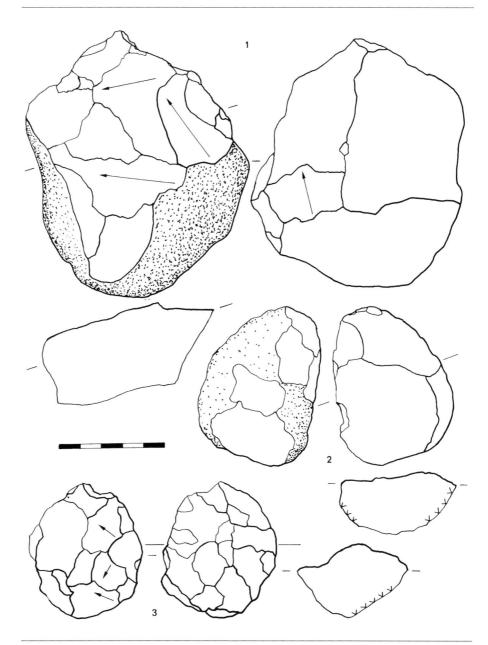

Fig. 7. Examples of tephrofacts (arrows indicate clear directions of flaking), scale in cm - Miscellaneous from Haute-Loire - 1: pseudo-invasively flaked tabular piece, granite, Blassac-les Blanches pyroclastites. 2: pseudo-invasively flaked tabular piece, basalte, Blassac-les Blanches tuff-ring. 3: pseudo-bifacially flaked discoïdal piece, basalte, Blassac-les Blanches tuff-ring.

"advantage of thinking small as archaeology explores the most ancient spans of prehistory" (G. Isaac *et al.* 1981).

9.4.   THE TIME OF FIRST HUMAN OCCUPATION

Only the sites where unquestionable archaeological elements have been discovered in a well documented long sequence should be considered to elucidate this problem. In the absence of precise dating elements for the site of Nolhac, only Soleilhac "the most recent of the very Lower Palaeolithic sites" (Bonifay 1991) remains to give an idea of the temporal remoteness of the human presence in Velay.

The age of Soleilhac has been established by biostratigraphic criteria (Bonifay and Bonifay 1981), palaeomagnetic determinations (Thouveny 1983; Thouveny and Bonifay 1984) and morphostratigraphy (Bonifay and Mergoil 1988). Soleilhac-Centre has also been studied from a sedimentological and palynological point of view (Raynal 1987 and unpublished). However, the fauna of Soleilhac belongs to the "transition fauna" which covers a broad time spectrum

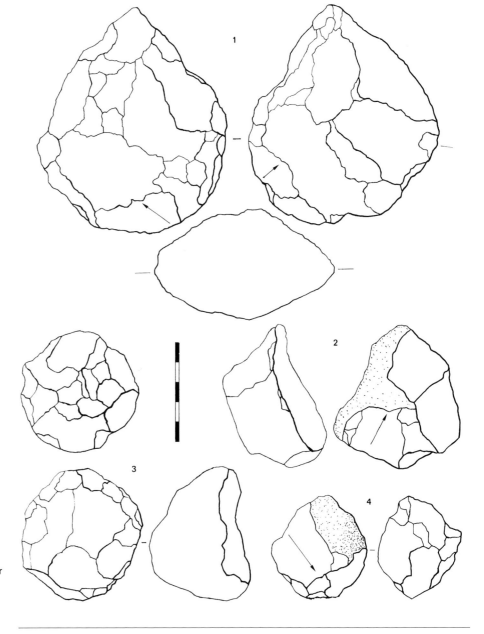

Fig. 8. Examples of tephrofacts (arrows indicate clear directions of flaking), scale in cm - Miscellaneous from Haute-Loire - 1: pseudo-biface-like piece, granite d'anatexie, La Sauvetat tuff-ring. 2: pseudo-chopper, basalte, La Sauvetat tuff-ring. 3: pseudo-invasively sub-discoïd flaked tabular piece, oriented granite, Blassac-les Blanches pyroclastites. 4: regular pseudo-polyhedron, fine grained granite, La Sauvetat tuff-ring.

(Bonifay 1987). Furthermore, the sedimentological and palynological data do not allow reliable dates to be determined and the palaeomagnetism of the complete sequence has not been studied because of the unsuitability of some layers for the application of this method (Thouveny 1983: 81). Most interest has been generated by the tephrostratigraphy reported by Teulade (1985; 1988; 1989) and determined from cores (Bonifay and Mergoil 1988).

A direct pumice ash-fall has been identified in the lake series underlying archaeological layer C. These tephra correlate with the "upper pumices of Sancy" (Cantagrel and Baubron 1983) and most particularly with the pumice of Neschers. A number of dating methods place the Neschers pumice around 0.8 Myr BP (Teulade 1989: 145). More recently, however, a ^{40}Ar/^{39}Ar age of 0,58 ± 0.02 Myr BP has been obtained (Lo Bello *et al.* 1987), which has been confirmed by a thermoluminescence date of 0,52 ± 0,04

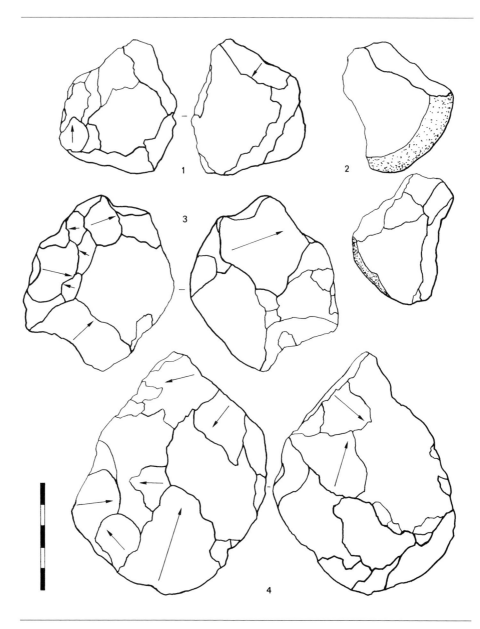

Fig. 9. Examples of tephrofacts (arrows indicate clear directions of flaking), scale in cm - Miscellaneous from Haute-Loire - 1: pseudo-polyhedron, granite, La Sauvetat tuff-ring. 2: pseudo-polyhedron, granite, Blassac-les Blanches pyroclastites. 3: pseudo-polyhedron, granite, Blassac-les Blanches tuff-ring. 4: pseudo-polyhedron, granite, La Sauvetat tuff-ring.

Myr BP obtained by the quartz red peak TL method (Pilleyre 1991). *Thus, the tephrostratigraphy contradicts the palaeomagnetic data and necessitates consideration of a date around 0.5-0.6 Myr BP for Soleilhac-Centre.* This last date is in agreement with a late Cromerian age for the fauna, as suggested by Van Kolfschoten (Roebroeks and Van Kolfschoten, this volume).

9.5.   DIRECTIONS FOR FUTURE RESEARCH

If we discard all the doubtful ancient sites occurring in the Massif Central, the earliest settlement history of the region must be rewritten. However, all is not lost yet. The evidence for the earliest occupation of Auvergne and Velay can be revisited, evaluated and carefully dissected avoiding the traps of their geological context. Paradoxically, in the final analysis it would be this last which furnishes a detailed chronology of the human presence in the region. Directions for future research are clear. Parallel to an examination of the physical and biological characteristics of the palaeoenvironment, the close study of pseudo-tools will doubtless provide much discussion and food for thought. *But clearly for each supposedly ancient site a multidiscipli-nary and broadly based study is absolutely necessary, and not only for the region discussed here.*

Acknowledgements:

The authors thank C. Guth, O. Boeuf, J. Desse and
P.J. Texier who have provided access to the excavations at
Chilhac; E. and M.F. Bonifay for permitting a number of
visits to the sites at Soleilhac, Nolhac and Ceyssaguet;
F. Carré for access to the material from Blassac and for his
hospitality and assistance during the re-examination of
Blassac - Les Battants in 1989; J. and D. Chomette,
D. Lefevre, T. Pilleyre and G. Vernet for their collaboration
in the field; J. Couthures for his unpublished information;
G. Crevola for verifying the petrographic determinations
and W. Roebroeks for reviewing the manuscript.

references

Boëda, E.   1990   Qui étaient les premiers français?, *La Recherche* 223(21), 96-968.

Boeuf, O.   1983   *Le site villafranchien de Chilhac, en Haute-Loire. Etude paléontologique et biochronologique.* Thèse de Doctorat Es-Sciences, Université Paris VII.

Bonifay, E.   1981   Les traces des premiers Hominidés en France, *La Recherche* 128(12), 1442-1444.

1983   La Préhistoire du Velay (Massif Central français) et le problème des origines de l'Homme. In: *La Recherche Archéologique en Haute-Loire*, 9-16, Annales du CRDP de Clermont-Ferrand.

1989a   Un site du Très Ancien Paléolithique de plus de 2 M.a. dans le Massif Central français: Saint-Eble - Le Coupet (Haute-Loire), *Comptes Rendus de l'Académie des Sciences de Paris* 308, série II, 1567-1570.

1989b   Les premiers signes de présence humaine. In: *Archéologie de la France: 30 ans de découvertes*, 36-37, Editions de la Réunion des Musées Nationaux, Paris.

1989c   Paléolithique inférieur et moyen: premiers témoignages humains. In: *Archéologie de la France: 30 ans de découvertes*, 32-34, Ministère de la Culture, Editions de la Réunion des Musées Nationaux, Paris.

1991   Les premières industries du Sud-est de la France et du Massif Central. In: E. Bonifay and B. Vandermeersch (eds), *Les premiers européens*, 63-80, CTHS Ed., Paris.

Bonifay, M.F.   1984   Taphonomie quaternaire: Comparaison entre sites naturels et préhistoriques du Pléistocène moyen: gisements de Soleilhac (Haute-Loire), *Journées d' étude de l'Association paléontologique française "Biocénoses et taphocénoses"*, Paris, résumé, 18.

1987   Biostratigraphie des grands mammifères d'Europe de l'Ouest, *12° Congrès international de l'INQUA*, Ottawa, Résumés, 133.

Bonifay, E., M.F. Bonifay   1981   Le gisement préhistorique de Soleilhac (Blanzac, Haute-Loire). In: *Le bassin du Puy aux temps préhistoriques. Recherches récentes*, 19-36, le Puy, Musée Crozatier.

1983   Le Paléolithique ancien en Velay et en Auvergne: civilisations préhistoriques et milieu naturel. In: *Les Inédits de la Préhistoire Auvergnate*, 90-104, Musée Bargoin Clermont-Ferrand.

Bonifay E., J. Mergoil   1988   Les maars de Soleilhac (Blanzac, Haute-Loire) et leurs séries volcano-sédimentaires, *Comptes Rendus de l'Académie des Sciences de Paris* 307, série II, 1561-1566.

Bonifay E.,   1989   Contribution du Massif Central français à la connaissance des premiers peuplements
   A. Consigny,   préhistoriques de l'Europe, *Comptes Rendus de l'Académie des Sciences de Paris* 308,
   R. Liabeuf   série II, 1491-1496.

Bosinski, G.,   1986   Altsteinzeitliche Siedlungsplätze auf den Osteifel-Vulkanen, *Jahrbuch des Römisch-*
   K. Kröger,   *Germanischen Zentral Museums* 33, 97-130.
   J. Schäfer,
   E. Turner

Boule, M.   1889   Temps quaternaires et préhistoriques du Cantal, *Revue d'Anthropologie*, 216.

                     1905   L'origine des Eolithes, *L'Anthropologie* 16, 257-267.

                     1921   *Les Hommes fossiles.* Paris: Masson Ed.

Bourdier, F.   1967   *Préhistoire de France.* Paris: Nouvelle bibliothèque scientifique Flammarion.

Bracco, J.P.   1991   Typologie, technologie et matières premières des industries du Très Ancien Paléolithique en
                                   Velay (Massif Central, France). Premiers résultats. In: E. Bonifay and B. Vandermeersch,
                                   (eds). *Les premiers européens*, 93-100, Paris: Editions du C.T.H.S.

Breuil, H.   1955   Niveaux estuariens de galets fracturés par les vagues et les plages sableuses dans la basse
                                   Somme, *Quaternaria* II, Rome, 21-29.

Bulle, T.   1987   Stat⁺, un utilitaire statistique, *Archéologues et ordinateurs* 10, CNRS, 9-12.

Cantagrel, J.M.,   1983   Chronologie des éruptions dans le massif volcanique des Monts Dore: implications
   J.C. Baubron   volcanologiques, *Geol. Fr.* (2) I, 1 (2), 123-142.

Capitan, L.,   1924   Les alluvions pontiennes des environs d'Aurillac (Cantal) et leurs silex taillés, *Revue*
   P. Marty   *anthropologique* n° 3-4, 34è année, mars-avril 1924, 1-21.

Carré, F.   1978   Eléments d'industrie lithique dans les formations sédimentaires villafranchiennes de
                                   Blassac (Haute-Loire), *Bulletin de la Société préhistorique française* 75, n° 5, 131-132.

                     1983   Le site de Blassac - Les Battants (haute-Loire). Fouilles 1971-1978. Eléments d'une
                                   stratigraphie, *Congrès Préhistorique de France, 21è session, Cahors-Montauban*, (1979),
                                   Société préhistorique française Ed. 2., 57-75.

                     1991   Les sites du Pliocène supérieur de Blassac - Haute-Loire (Massif Central, France). In:
                                   E. Bonifay and B. Vandermeersch (eds), *Les premiers européens*, 135-142, Paris: Editions
                                   du C.T.H.S.

Carré, F.,   1982   Nouveaux éléments de datation des formations volcaniques de Blassac (Haute-Loire,
   J. Couthures   France); influences sur la chronologie des faunes "villafranchiennes" du Massif central
                                   français, *9è Réunion annuelle des Sciences de la Terre*, Société géologique de France Ed.,
                                   Paris, 121.

Chavaillon, J.   1991   Les ensembles lithiques de Chilhac III (Haute-Loire): typologie, situation stratigraphique
                                   et analyse critique et comparative. In: E. Bonifay and B. Vandermeersch (eds), *Les
                                   premiers européens*, 81-91, Paris: Editions du C.T.H.S.

Clark, J.D.   1958   The natural fracture of pebbles from the Batoka Gorge, Northern Rhodesia, and its
                                   bearing on the kafuan industries of Africa, *Proceedings of the Prehistoric Society* 24,
                                   64-77.

Collina-Girard, J.   1975   *Les industries archaïques sur galets des terrasses quaternaires de la plaine du Roussillon
                                   (Pyrénnées Orientales, France).* Thèse de 3° cycle, Université de Provence.

| | 1986 | Grille descriptive et évolution typologique des industries archaïques: le modèle catalan, *Bulletin de la Société préhistorique française* 83, n° 11-12, 383-403. |

Couthures, J.   1982   *Contribution à la chronostratigraphie de formations plio-pléistocènes du Massif Central (France)*. Thèse de 3° cycle, Paris VI.

Couthures, J.,   1983   Chronostratigraphie du Plio-pléistocène d'Auvergne et du Velay: nouveaux apports des
F. Pastre   datations radiométriques et du paléomagnétisme, *Bulletin de l'Association française pour l'étude du Quaternaire* 1, 9-18.

Delson, E.   1989   Oldest Eurasian stone tools, *Nature* 340, 96.

Diaz, R.   1993   Les premiers européens venaient-ils d'Afrique?, *L'Histoire* 165, 42-45.

Fouris, M.   1989   *Sites villafranchiens du Devès et les basaltes de la vallée de l'Allier: application de la méthode Potassium-Argon*. Thèse d'Université, Clermont II.

Fournier, A.   1971   *Méthode d'étude des industries archaïques sur galet*. Diplôme d'Etudes Approfondies, Université de Provence.

Grayson, D.K.   1986   Eoliths, Archaeological Ambiguity, and the Generation of "Middle Range" Research. In: D.J. Meltzer, D.D. Fowler, J.A. Sabloff (Eds), *American Archaeology Past and Future*, 77-133, Washington: Smithsonian Institution Press.

G.U.E.R.P.A.   1984   Présence possible d'Hominidés en Auvergne au Pliocène supérieur (2,5 M.a.): l'apport des Etouaires (Issoire, Puy de Dôme), *C. R. Acad. Sci.* 299, 1091-1096, Paris.

Guth, C.   1974   Découverte dans le Villafranchien d'Auvergne de galets aménagés, *C. R. Acad. Sci.* 279, 1071-1072, Paris.

Guth, C.,   1977   Les premiers galets aménagés du Villafranchien d'Auvergne, *Le Courrier du CNRS* 25,
O. Boeuf   46-47.

Guth, C.,   1985   Découverte en 1984, de nouveaux outils paléolithiques à Chilhac III (Haute-Loire),
J. Chavaillon   *Bulletin de la Société Préhistorique Française* 82, 56-64.

Haward, F.W.   1911   The Chipping of Flint by natural Agencies, *Proceedings of the Prehistoric Society of East Anglia* 1, 185-193.

Haynes, C.V. Jr.   1973   The Calico Site: Artifacts or Geofacts?, *Science* 181, 305-310.

Isaac, G.,   1981   Small is informative: the application of the study of mini-sites and least-effort criteria in
J.W.K. Harris,   the interpretation of the Early Pleistocene archaeological record at Koobi Fora, Kenya. In:
F. Marshall   J.D. Clark and G. Isaac, *Las Industrias mas Antiguas*, X Congresso Union International de Ciencias Prehistoricas y Protohistoricas, Mexico (1981), 101-119.

Kulemeyer, J.   1986   *Die alt-und mittelpaläolithischen Funde von Kärlich*. Dissertation, Köln.

Le Gall, O.,   1986   Cerzat (Haute-Loire): Le Pié du Roy, un site préhistorique dans un volcan, *Revue Archéo-
J.P. Raynal   logique du Centre de la France* 25(1), 99-100.

Lo Bello, P.,   1987 $^{40}Ar/^{39}Ar$ step heating and laser fusion dating of a quaternary pumice from Neschers,
G. Féraud,   Massif Central, France: the defeat of xenocrystic contamination, *Chem. Geol. (Isot. geosci.*
C.M. Hall,   *Sect.)* 66, 61-71.
D. York,
P. Lavina,
M. Bernat

Moir, J.R.   1911   The Natural Fracture of Flint and its Bearing Upon Rudimentary Flint Implements, *Proceedings of the Prehistoric Society of East Anglia* 1, 171-18.

Mortelmans, G.   1947   Une cause d'erreur en préhistoire: la taille glaciaire, *Bulletin de la Société Royale Belge d'Anthropologie et Préhistoire* LVIII, 60-71.

Peacok, E.   1991   Distinguishing between Artefacts and Geofacts: A Test Case from Eastern England, *Journal of Field Archaeology* 18, 345-361.

Pei, W.C.   1937   Le rôle des phénoménes naturels dans l'éclatement et le façonnement des roches dures utilisées par l'homme préhistorique, *Revue de Géographie Physique et de géologie Dynamique* 9, 349-423.

Pilleyre, T.   1991   *Datation par thermoluminescence. Application à la chronologie des retombées volcaniques.* Thèse de l'Université de Clermont II, DU345.

Raynal, J.P.   1987   Evolution comparée de lacs de maars en Auvergne et Velay (France). Datation et contribution à la connaissance des climats pléistocènes. In: *Travaux français en Paléolimnologie*, 65-96, Documents du CERLAT, Mémoire n° 1.

Raynal, J.P.,   1989   Découverte d'Acheuléen ancien dans la carrière Thomas 1 à Casablanca et problème de
   J.P. Texier   l'ancienneté de la présence humaine au Maroc, *Comptes Rendus de l'Académie des Sciences de Paris* 308, série II, 1743-1749.

Raynal, J.P.,   1990   Un nouveau gisement paléontologique plio-pléistocène en Afrique du Nord: Ahl Al
   J.P. Texier,   Oughlam (ancienne carrière Déprez) à Casablanca (Maroc), *Comptes Rendus de l'Acadé-
   D. Geraads,   mie des Sciences de Paris* 310, série II, 315-320.
   F.Z. Alaoui

Rio Carra, M.   1991   *L'industrie sur quartz de Nolhac-Biard, un gisement du Très Ancien Paléolithique (résultats préliminaires).* DEA, Université d'Aix-Marseille.

Roebroeks, W.,   this   The earliest occupation of Europe: A reappraisal of artefactual and chronological
   T. van Kolfschoten   volume   evidence.

Schnurrenberger, D.,   1985   A Contribution to the Study of the Naturefact/Artifact Controversy. In: M.G. Plew,
   L.B. Alan   J.C. Woods, M. G. Pavesic (eds), *Stone Tool Analysis*, 133-159, Albuquerque: University of New Mexico Press.

Tardy, L.   1869   *Société d'Anthropologie de Paris*, 16 décembre 1869.

Teulade, A.   1985   *Etude téphrologique de formations lacustres de maars du Velay occidental.* DEA, Université d'Aix-Marseille II.

                                 1988   Les tephra cendro-ponceux dans les sédiments du lac de maar de Soleilhac (Haute-Loire): pétrographie et origine, *Soc. Hist. Nat. Auvergne* 53, 39-43.

                                 1989   *Téphrologie des formations cendro-ponceuses en milieux lacustres quaternaires. Méthode d'étude et application au Massif Central français (Velay) et aux Carpathes orientales roumaines (dépression de Brassov).* Thèse de l'Université d'Aix-Marseille II.

Texier, P.J.   1985   Chilhac III: un gisement paléontologique villafranchien soliflué?, *Bulletin de la Société préhistorique française* 82, 68-70.

Thouveny, N.   1983   *Etude paléomagnétique de formations du Plio-Pléistocène et de l'Holocène du Massif Central et de ses abords.* Thèse, Université d'Aix-Marseille II.

Thouveny, N.,   1984   New chronological data on European Plio-Pleistocene faunas and hominid occupation
    E. Bonifay   sites, *Nature* 308, 355-358.

Villa, P.   1991   Middle Pleistocene Prehistory in Southwestern Europe: The State of Our Knowledge and
                             Ignorance, *Journal of Anthropological Research* 47(2), 193-218.

Warren, S.H.   1914   The Experimental Investigation of Flint Fracture and its Application to Problems of
                             Human Implements, *Journal of the Royal Anthropological Institute of Great Britain and
                             Ireland* 44, 412-450.

Watson, W.   1968   *Flint Implements*. 3rd Ed. London: British Museum.

Jean-Paul Raynal
Université de Bordeaux 1
Institut du Quaternaire
UMR 9933 CNRS and GDR 1122 CNRS
Avenue des Facultés,
F-33405 Talence Cedex
France

Lionel Magoga
GDR 1122 CNRS
Résidence Raymond
48 Allée des Ailes
F-03200 Vichy
France

Peter Bindon
Department of Anthropology
Western Australian Museum
Francis Street, Perth 6000
Western Australia.

Alain Tuffreau
Pierre Antoine

9   The earliest occupation of Europe: Continental Northwestern Europe

The palaeolithic record of continental northwestern Europe is characterized by sites in a loess- and fluvial deposits context, usually preserved in the form of loess-covered river terraces. As a result relative chronologies can be established over rather large distances, allowing to infer that the earliest occupation of this region dates back to about 600 Kyr BP. This is especially well established in the Somme valley. Work in the Cagny area has placed the Acheulean occupations there in a large variety of ecological settings.

1.   Introduction

The geographical area concerned (Fig. 1) is characterised by the presence of fluvial deposits, often preserved in the form of terrace sequences, and by Middle and Late Pleistocene loessic deposits, that locally reach considerable thicknesses. Traces of former marine beaches are rather common in the Massif Armoricain, but rare in the northern part of the Channel. Karstic infillings are virtually limited to the Meuse basin. The area reviewed here is one of those European regions where Palaeolithic archaeologists have been conducting fieldwork from the very beginning of prehistoric archaeology onwards (e.g. in the Somme and Haine valleys and in the Liège region). In this paper we will give a short regional presentation of the evidence of the earliest occupation of this area, probably one of the most heavily researched regions of Europe.

2.   The Meuse basin

2.1.   LA BELLE-ROCHE (SPRIMONT)

The only site in the Meuse area that predates OIS 8 is La Belle-Roche at Sprimont, a karstic cave situated about 20 km south of Liège (Belgium) on the right bank of the Amblève river. Partially destroyed by quarrying activities, the site has been under excavation from 1980 onwards (Cordy *et al.* 1992). The finds come from a horizontal karst gallery, whose infilling consists of a basic gravel unit overlain by a series of mudstone layers containing the finds, and sealed by a calcite layer. U-series dating of the calcite covering the fossiliferous deposits yielded an age in excess of 350,000 years.

The faunal assemblage recovered from the mudstone layers contains about 50 species, among which *Canis mos-*

bachensis, Ursus deningeri, Xenocyon lycaonides, Panthera leo fossilis, Panthera gombaszoegensis, Equus mosbachensis, Dicerorhinus etruscus and *Hemitragus bonali* are present. The assemblage has been dated to OIS 13 age, i.e. at around 500 Kyr BP. The lithic industry consists of flint objects – severely weathered and in all probability in secondary position – recovered from the upper part of the fossiliferous deposits. The small assemblage contains pebbles with a few scars ("pebble-industry") and some flakes. Because of its physical condition this series is difficult to submit to a detailed analysis and some workers have even cast doubts on the artificial character of the flint objects (Roebroeks and Stapert 1986).

3.   The Haine valley

Four river terraces (Fig. 2), separated from each other by a chalk talus 10 m high, were recognised in the Haine valley (Haesaerts 1984). The oldest two (Pa d'la l'iau and Petit Spiennes) are interpreted as dating from the end of the Cromerian complex. They have been attributed to the Middle Pleistocene on the basis of correlations to the Schelde (Escaut) basin and in view of the soils present in the loessic sediments covering the two youngest terraces.

Investigations carried out by P. Haesaerts in the Somme valley have led to a correlation scheme for the fluvial deposits of the Somme and Haine basins (Haesaerts and Dupuis 1986): the Petit-Spiennes terrace can be equated with the terrace of Cagny-l'Epinette, whereas the Pa d'la l'iau would correspond with the terrace of Cagny-la Garenne. In the Haine valley only the two oldest terraces, Pa d'la l'iau and Petit-Spiennes, have yielded Acheulean industries.

3.1.   PA D'LA L'IAU (OIS 12)

A small cutting in the top of the Pa d'la l'iau plateau, where the gravels surface, yielded a few artefacts, some handaxes and two scrapers (Cahen 1984).

3.2.   PETIT-SPIENNES (OIS 10)

The Petit-Spiennes formation consists of a sequence of fluvial gravels and sands, upwards changing into greyish

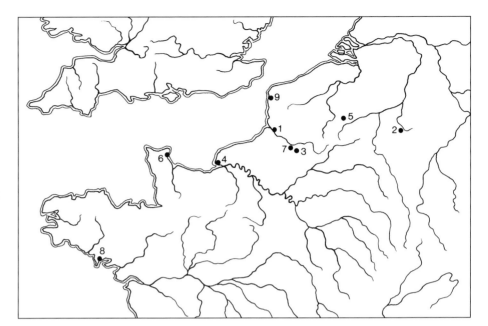

Fig. 1. Location of sites mentioned
in the text:
1. Abbeville;
2. La Belle Roche (Sprimont);
3. Cagny;
4. Le Havre;
5. Pa d'la liau/Petit Spiennes;
6. Port-Pignot (Fermanville);
7. Saint-Acheul;
8. Saint-Colomban.

sands. Most artefacts recovered from this terrace are from
surface collections, while some were uncovered in an
excavation trench. Most of them are handaxes, of various
forms: amygdaloids, ovates and *lancéolés*. Tools on flakes
are relatively few in number. The Levallois technique is
represented by cores and flakes (Cahen 1984).

4.   The Somme Basin

4.1.   CHRONOSTRATIGRAPHICAL AND PALAEOENVIRON
MENTAL CONTEXT OF THE SITES

The detailed knowledge of the geometry of the Somme
valley's terrace system allows us to position palaeolithic
sites within a series of nine terraces, regularly spaced
between 5 to 6 and 50 m above the bed-rock of the actual
river valley (Antoine 1990; 1993; Antoine and Tuffreau
1993; Haesaerts and Dupuis 1986).

Studies of the climatical and processual significance
of the various fluvial sequences have shown that each
terrace body, represented by a succession of gravels and
fine-grained fluvial deposits, forms the morphological-
sedimentary output of a glacial-interglacial cycle. In
general, primary context sites are preserved within the
fine-grained calcareous fluvial sediments, within the
'external' parts of the terraces, i.e. close to the chalk
talus. These sites belong to the end phase of the fluvial
cycle, in a mainly interglacial context (Fig. 5). In some
cases, however, Acheulean occupations from the
beginning of a climatic cycle have been documented, in a
still temperate context from the beginning of a glacial
phase (Figs 3 and 4).

A first chronostratigraphic interpretation is based on the
comparison of climatic cycles deduced from the study of
the terrace system (river terraces and its cover of loess and
palaeosols) with the oxygen isotope stratigraphy,
palaeomagnetic data (Biquant 1974; Laurent 1993) and
more recently, ESR and U-series dates (Laurent 1993).

In this interpretation, the terrace 'Formations' I to VII
date to the Middle Pleistocene Bruhnes normal epoch, while
only the present valley's gravels are attributed to the
Weichselian pleniglacial.

The oldest inferred traces of human occupation
documented in the Somme valley are the few 'artefacts'
uncovered in the river deposits from the terrace of Grâce at
Montières, dating from before the Brunhes-Matuyama
boundary (Bourdier *et al.* 1974a). However, the artificial
character of the few flakes published is not uncontested, as
the best piece is a point obtained by retouching a natural
flake. Before the Middle Pleistocene there is no solid trace
of human presence in this region, with the first industries
belonging to the Acheulean.

4.2.   THE SITES OF ABBEVILLE

4.2.1.   *Abbeville: Carpentier quarry (Formation VII,
OIS 16/15)*

The Carpentier quarry at Abbeville is located on the right
bank of the Somme, at its confluence with the Scardon, a
small tributary of the Somme. This site is well-known for
the abundant palaeontological remains uncovered from the
marne blanche (Boule, in Commont 1910; Pontier 1928).
The stratigraphy of the site, well-known since the beginning

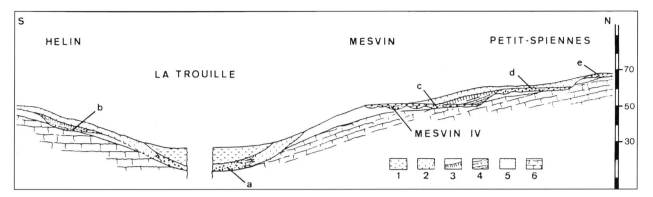

Fig. 2. Composite section through the alluvial formations in the Spiennes area (after Haesaerts and Dupuis, 1986).
a. Bottom valley gravels; b. Lower gravels of Carrière Hélin; c. Mesvin terrace aggradation; d. Petit-Spiennes terrace aggradation;
e. Pa d'la l'iau terrace aggradation.
1. Current fluvial deposits; 2. Weichselian loess; 3. Harmignies palaesoil (Eemian); 4. Saalian loess; 5. Tertiary sands (Landenian); 6. Chalk.

of this century (Commont 1906; 1910) has been integrated in various syntheses on the terraces and the palaeolithic industries of the Somme basin (Agache *et al.* 1963; Bourdier 1969a; Bourdier 1974; Bourdier *et al.* 1974a and 1974b; Tuffreau 1981; 1987).

Recently, precise measurements have situated the base of the terrace body at 40 m above the bed-rock of the present river valley. The fluvial sequence of the Carpentier quarry corresponds to the downstream extension of the seventh formation of the Somme system (Formation de Renancourt, Antoine 1990). Parallel to these studies palaeomagnetic analyses showed that the fluvial sequence belongs to the Brunhes normal epoch (Laurent 1993).

The presently visible section shows a thin fluvial sequence, from the external part of the terrace body, close to the chalk talus, covered by a thin layer of sandy-loamy deposits. The boundary between these two units is marked by an erosional level, associated with large pockets.

The fluvial sequence consists of two main units: the lower unit consists of a chalky gravel, very badly sorted in its lower parts, where it contains big blocks of chalk and flints, unrolled in a sandy-calcareous matrix. This unit contains lenses of calcareous loams that display a roughly horizontal stratification.

The upper fluvial unit corresponds to the *sables marneux verdâtres* and the *marne blanche* of V. Commont, that yielded the remains of large mammals. It consists of a succession of lenses of sandy loams and sands with calcareous oncoliths, and displays a stratification indicative of a fluvial environment of medium energy. The abundant oncoliths that characterise this deposit where formed in this environment. These ovaloid, centimetre-sized carbonated elements are the result of seasonal activities of Rodophy-cées and Cyanophysées (Adolphe 1974), algae indicative of

clear water, in a stable hydrographic setting, and pointing to temperate climatic conditions.

In general the pollen assemblages from the oncolith-deposits indicate a mosaic landscape, with forests and steppes, corresponding to a temperate continental climate (Munaut 1988 and pers. comm.). From a climatic point of view the type of sediments and the pollen indicate a clearly temperate context, an assessment confirmed by the abundant presence of oncoliths comparable to those observable in the Holocene deposits in the present-day valley.

The fauna from the Carpentier quarry contains the following species, according to Boule (*in* Commont 1910):

Lower unit: *Equus* aff. *stenonis*, *Rhinoceros* (= *Dicero-rhinus*) and *Hippopotamus*.

Upper unit: *Hyaena* cf. *crocuta*, *Homotherium latidens*, *Mammuthus meridionalis*, *M. trogontherii*, *M. primigenius* with archaic characteristics, *Elephas (Palaeoloxodon) antiquus*, *Equus stenonis*, *E. stenonis robustus* and maybe *E. hydruntinus*, *Dicerorhinus etruscus*, *D. mercki*, *D. lepto-rhinus*, *Elasmotherium*, *Sus scrofa*, *Hippopotamus*, *Cervus solilacus*, *C. (Dama) somonensis*, *C. elaphus*, *C. belgrandi*, *C. canadensis*, *Capreolus capreolus*, *Bos priscus*, and *B. elatus* or *etruscus*. A radius of a large cervid and an upper M3 of *Sus* cf. *strozzi* were found in 1989. Although it is impossible to specify the exact provenance of the large mammal remains described at the beginning of this century, the composition of the fauna ascribed to the upper unit is coherent with the type of environment mentioned above; the presence of hippopotamus in the lower unit, the gravels, seems to indicate a mixture, however.

The chronostratigraphic interpretation of the *Formation de la Carrière Carpentier* within the Somme system (OIS 16 to 15) is in agreement with the position of the Abbeville fauna in the large mammal biozonation (zone III of Cordy 1982), with palaeomagnetic evidence and with the ESR dates (600 ± 90 Kyr BP).

At the end of the last century G. d'Ault du Mesnil collected large numbers of handaxes (now at the Musée des Antiquités nationales and the Institut de Paléontologie Humaine), thought to be contemporaneous with the *Mammuthus meridionalis* fauna. According to H. Breuil and H. Kelley (1954), 'Abbevillian' handaxes, with negatives of short and thick flakes and cortex preserved at their base and edges were found. Numerous ovate handaxes and *limandes* were described by V. Commont (1910), who could not find artefacts associated with the fauna in the *marne blanche*. Breuil's work in the adjacent Léon quarry yielded only one *limande*, from above the *marne blanche*.

4.2.2.   *Abbeville: Stade and Champ de Mars (Formation VI, OIS 14 to 13)*

The sites of the Stade and the Champ de Mars are situated in the same geomorphological context as that of the Carpentier quarry. However, the relative altitude of the base of the gravels (at about +33 m) suggests a correlation to the immediately following fluvial formation, the *Formation de Fréville (VI)*. In the absence of recent observations it is impossible to give a precise description of the stratigraphical and palaeoenvironmental context of the very numerous handaxes (Fig. 3) discovered in the gravels. Most of them are ovates and limandes, though some have been classified as 'Abbevillian' by Breuil (collection of the Musée des Antiquités Nationales); Tuffreau 1987; 1992). It is therefore possible that some of the 'Abbevillian' bifaces are much more recent and that each *a posteriori* classification of artefacts without a precise stratigraphical context only yields artificial series of on the one hand rough 'Abbevillian'-type handaxes and Acheulean ones on the other. For that reason one should for once and for all abolish the term 'Abbevillian', be it in the classical "cultural" sense or, to avoid every possible confusion, in the typological sense, as still used in the typology of F. Bordes (1961).

4.3.   SITES OF THE SAINT-ACHEUL/CAGNY REGION

Fluvial terraces are particularly well-developed at Saint-Acheul, a suburb of Amiens, situated on the left bank of the Somme, at its confluence with the Avre river. The terraces belong to the Fréville formation (VI) and to the *Formation de la Garenne* (V). This last one is visible a few kilometres upstream, at Cagny-la Garenne and at Cagny-Cimetière, in the valley of the Avre, where younger river deposits are also preserved (*Formation de l'Epinette, IV*).

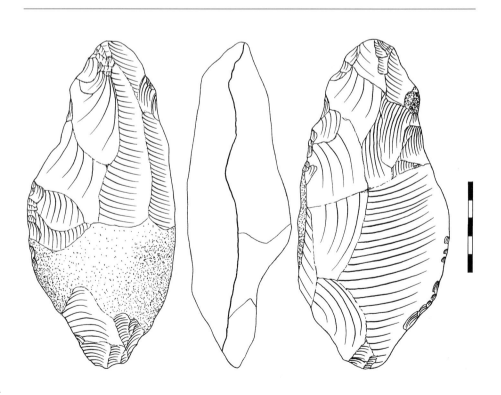

Fig. 3. Abbeville, Champ de Mars.
Handaxe. Scale in cm.

4.3.1.   Saint-Acheul, rue Marcelin Berthelot (Formation VI, OIS 14 to 13)

The sequence of the 'rue Marcelin Berthelot' at Saint-Acheul has been studied in detail in 1981 by A. Tuffreau and J.P. Fagnart during a salvage excavation. The fluvial deposits are rather thin here (about 3 m thick) and to a large extent weathered as result of their position in a more central part of the former river valley, where covering loessic layers are usually very thin. Their relative altitude allows a correlation with the Fréville formation (VI).

The numerous Acheulean artefacts collected from the gravels and the fluvial sands are usually patinated and rolled. There are various forms of handaxes (amygaloids, *limandes*) and flakes with irregular retouches. A Levallois core *à éclat préférentiel* is also present. These finds recall the artefacts mentioned by V. Commont, from de Fréville quarry (Saint-Acheul), which occupies a less 'internal' position in the same terrace body. In view of the bad conditions of preservation one cannot exclude an admixture with more recent artefacts. The importance of the site lies in its confirmation of Commont's earlier observation of the numerous presence of Acheulean artefacts within the Fréville formation (Commont 1908; 1909).

4.3.2.   Saint-Acheul, rue de Cagny (Formation V, OIS 12 to 11)

The site of the 'rue de Cagny' at Saint-Acheul is well-known because of the excavation undertaken by V. Commont (1908) during building activities in 1906. The stratigraphical sequence contains gravels and fine-grained river deposits – sands and loams – overlain by a rather thin layer of loamy deposits, the famous *sables roux*.

The gravels yielded amygdaloid handaxes with a cortical base and a few tools on flakes: scrapers, end-scrapers, notches and denticulates. The lower part of the fine-grained fluvial deposits consists of white sands. These contained a series of 220 handaxes, amydaloids and limandes, as well as tools on flakes of various types. The *sables roux* deposits, without any doubt dating from the later part of the Middle Pleistocene, (OIS 8?) yielded 300 handaxes, most (271) of them limandes, with numerous twisted edges. Just like the other series from this site the tools on flake are of various forms, and no Levallois products are present.

4.4.   THE CAGNY SITES

The sites of Gagny, 'La Garenne', 'Cimetière' and 'l'Epinette' are situated on the left bank of the Avre river, a few kilometres from its confluence with the Somme. The three sites are very close to each other, with a maximum distance of 1 km. The three sites belong to two distinct fluvial formations (Fig. 4): the *Formation de la Garenne* (terrace V, OIS 12 to 11, with an ESR age at Garenne of 400 ± 101 Kyr BP) for the first two sites and the *Formation de l'Epinette* (terrace IV, OIS 10 to 9, ESR date of 296 ± 53 Kyr BP; Laurent 1993) for the last one.

A combined study of these three sites has resulted in a model of their climatical and sedimentological evolution, in which the Acheulean occupational phases have been integrated (Antoine and Tuffreau 1993).

4.4.1.   Cagny-La Garenne (Formation V, OIS 12 to 11)

The site Cagny-La Garenne was exploited as a quarry from 1916 to 1959, when it was classified as a *Monument historique*, a few years before it was bought by the French state (1963). The site is famous for the innumerable Acheulean artefacts recovered from the Avre deposits, overlain by a thick series of loessic sediments.

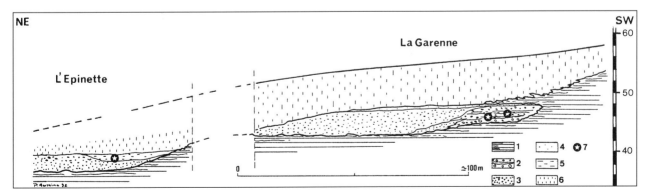

Fig. 4. General structure and relationship between Garenne and Epinette formations in the Cagny area (after Antoine and Tuffreau, 1993). 1. Chalk bedrock; 2. Slope deposit sequence with interstratified fluvial silts in the Garenne Formation; 3. Periglacial fluvial gravels of Garenne and Epinette formations; 4. Fluvial sands (Garenne Formation); 5. Fluvial calcareous silts (Epinette Formation); 6. Slope deposit sequence overlying alluvial formations (loess, slope deposits and palaeosoils); 7. Undisturbed palaeolithic settlements.

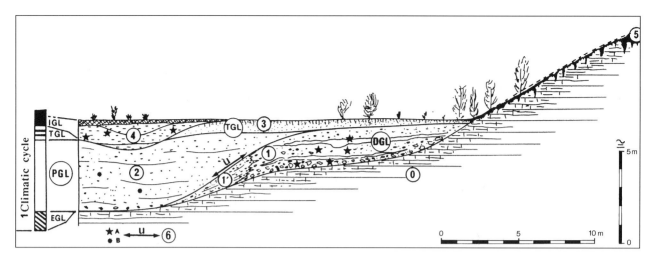

Fig. 5. Idealized section through the alluvial sequence of the Middle terrace complex in the Cagny area (after Antoine and Tuffreau, 1993). 0. Chalky bedrock; 1. Sequence of chalky slope deposits with interstratified beds of calcareous fluvial silts. The basal part of these deposits laterally pass through typically calcareous fluvial gravels (1') (1 & 1': Early glacial sedimentation); 2. Major phase of coarse sedimentation in a braided river and a periglacial environment (Fullglacial sedimentation); 3/4. Stabilisation of the floodplain: calcareous fine fluvial silts with immature soils of humid grassland (Interglacial); 5. Brown leached soil (interglacial in slope environment); 6. Unconformity between units (1-1') and (2). A. Undisturbed Palaeolithic settlements; B. Reworked Palaeolithic artefacts.

The site's stratigraphy is known through the observations of F. Bourdier (1969a), the detailed studies by P. Haesaerts (Haesaerts and Dupuis 1986) and by the data collected in 1986-1987 during an excavation in the external part of the Garenne terrace, at the foot of the large classical section (Tuffreau 1989). In 1993 new excavations started to the north of the main section, towards the Cimetière site (excavations by the universities of Lille and of Pennsylvania).

The sequence of the external part of the Garenne terrace, excavated in 1986 and 1987, is dominated by slope dynamics, with occasionally interspersed fluvial sediments. The proximity of the river course is documented throughout the sequence by overbank deposits and by a lateral shift to a typical fluvial deposit at the base of the sequence (Fig. 5, units 1 and 1').

Recent studies have shown this sequence to be older than the 'classical' river terrace described by earlier workers. This classical terrace consists of pleniglacial fluvial deposits, and a gravelly flood plain intersected by braided channels (Fig. 5, unit 3).

The first results of pollen analyses of the Cagny-la Garenne sequence (Munaut 1993) indicate for the lower part of the excavation section (Fig. 5, unit 1) a succession of continental temperate phases, corresponding to a forested-steppic landscape relatively rich in temperate taxa. After a colder period the higher levels show a change towards a boreal forest landscape, ending with a subarctic environment with *Betula*. Pollen from sand lenses in the unit 2 gravels indicate an open steppic environment, with a vegetation dominated by herbs (non-arboreal pollen 66.7 %).

This pollen-based model of the evolution of vegetation and climate confirms and details the model of climatic evolution initially proposed on the basis of stratigraphical and sedimentological observations (Antoine 1990): early glacial for the unit with the Acheulean artefacts and the large mammal fossils (*Equus caballus mosbachensis, Megaceros* sp., *Cervus elaphus* and large bovids; Moigne 1993), pleniglacial for the major coarse grained part – with reworked artefacts – of the terrace body and late glacial for the green sands covering the flood plain (Fig. 5, unit 3). The upper part of this unit displays a river valley-type pseudogley from a temperate context (Van Vliet-Lanöe, in Tuffreau 1989).

Studies of the geometry of the deposits clearly show that the first sites were on a sub-horizontal bank about 10 m wide, situated between the chalk talus along the southern bank of the river and the river itself (Fig. 5). The artefacts from the various archaeological levels (Fig. 6) are mostly products of a flint workshop exploiting the raw material present in the adjacent chalk cliff: numerous cores and handaxes, many of them discarded roughouts in various stages of production (Lamotte 1991). The presence of a very small number of Levallois cores and of Levallois flakes – often hardly distinguishable from flakes produced while making handaxes – is striking.

Various pieces show the existence of linkages between methods of handaxe production and methods of Levallois

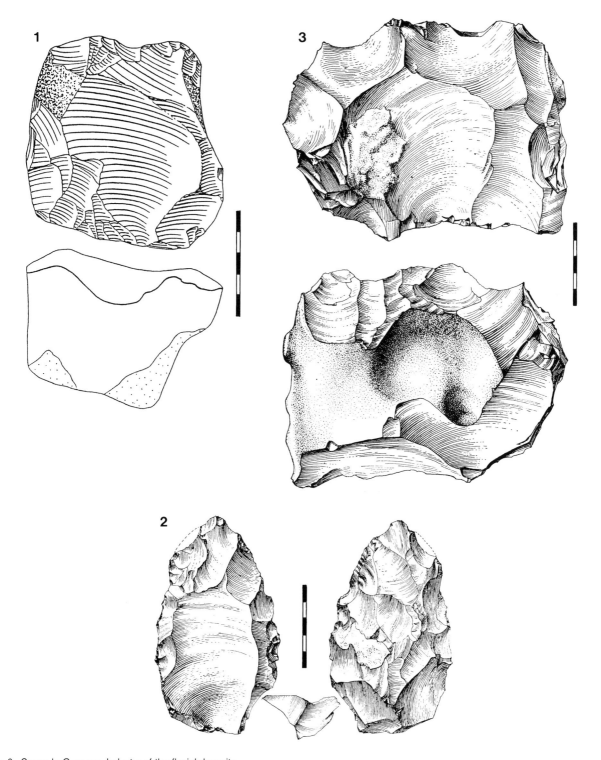

Fig. 6. Cagny-la Garenne. Industry of the fluvial deposits.
1 and 3: Levallois cores. 2: Handaxe with a negative of a removal similar to a Levallois flake. Scale in cm.

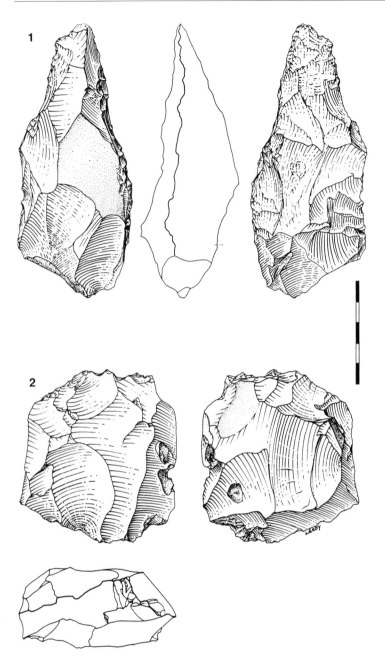

Fig. 7. Cagny-l'Epinette. Industry of
the fluvial deposits.
1. Handaxe; 2. Levallois core.
Scale in cm.

debitage. Some handaxes broken during flaking have yielded a large *éclat préférentiel*. Other handaxes, finished as shown by the presence of secondary retouch on the cutting edges, display proximally a striking platform that served for producing a large flake on the other side.

In some cases the large flake has been struck perpendicularly to the axis of the handaxe. Such examples are known both from the recent excavations as well as from old collections (Breuil and Kelley 1954). The morphology of handaxes is in a way comparable to that of Levallois cores, with two intersecting surfaces of lateral and distal convexity, one serving for the preparation of the striking platform, the other for the flaking of the *éclat préférentiel*. In view of this one could consider handaxes, discarded during production or as finished objects, as Levallois cores. The above-mentioned products obtained from them are

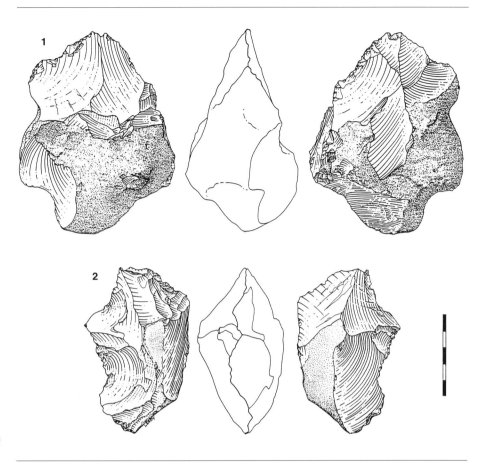

Fig. 8. Cagny-l'Epinette. Industry of the fluvial deposits. Scale in cm.

Levallois flakes. At Cagny-la Garenne there is a clear conceptual link between the production of handaxes and the presence of Levallois flaking methods.

4.4.2.   Cagny-Cimetière (Formation V, OIS 12 to 11)

The stratigraphy of the Cimetière quarry at Cagny was studied by F. Bourdier (Bourdier *et al.* 1974b) and afterwards the site was the object of excavations by A. Tuffreau (Tuffreau 1980a and 1980b; 1987; Tuffreau *et al.* 1982). Additional observations were made in 1993 during a rescue excavation at the cemetery of Cagny, adjacent to the now abandoned quarry.

The levels concerned are in the same morphological position as those from Cagny-la Garenne (relative altitude +28 m), at a distance of 200 m. The Cimetière sequence, however, was formed in a less external part of the flood plain, where the oldest sedimentary units are absent (Fig. 4).

The deposition of fine-grained fluvial sediments begins with a layer of stratified sands, deposited in channels eroding the upper part of the gravels. These sands yielded a few artefacts and contain abundant tree pollen (arboreal pollen 80 %, cf. Munaut 1974; 1988) indicating a temperate continental climate, contrasting with the conditions during formation of the gravels.

The fine-grained sedimentation continues with a large scale horizontal deposition of sands and stratified loams, subsequently affected by the formation of calcite concretions. Pollen analysis discerned three palynozones: two steppic phases separated by a more forested episode, the *interstade de Cagny* (Munaut 1974; 1988), an interpretation confirmed by the study of the small mammals (Chaline 1974).

The Acheulean sites of Cagny-Cimetière are therefore contemporaneous with several phases of silting up of the floodplain, that accompanied the establishment of temperate conditions and of a forest steppe under a continental temperate climate. Occupation continued during the interglacial and the phase of the climate deterioration marking the beginning of the next cycle.

The geometry and the stratigraphy of the units of the Garenne terrace allow us to position the industries of the fine-grained fluvial deposits of the Cimetière site – though situated in the same terrace as those of Garenne – at the end of the fluvial cycle, separated from the Garenne finds by a pleniglacial phase (the beginning of OIS 12 at Garenne, early OIS 11 at Cimetière).

The lithic industry is rather poor, comprising elongated handaxes associated with tools on flakes, mainly notches and denticulates. There are no indications to relate the lithic assemblage to the faunal remains recovered from the same deposits.

4.4.3.   Cagny-l'Epinette (Formation IV, OIS 10 and 9)

The interpretation of the Epinette sequence is based on multidisciplinary studies of the numerous sections generated during the excavations by A. Tuffreau, from 1980 onwards (Tuffreau et al. 1982; Tuffreau et al. 1986; Antoine and Tuffreau 1993. Since 1991 the site is excavated jointly by a team of the University of Lille and the University of Pennsylvania). This sequence is the stratotype of the Epinette formation (IV), with a relative altitude of 21 m above the river's maximum incision, i.e. 6 m lower than that of the Formation de la Garenne (Fig. 4).

At Cagny-l'Epinette the fluvial deposition starts with pleniglacial gravels. The top of these formed the surface during the main Acheulean occupation documented in the northern part of the excavation. Next a series of badly sorted calcareous fluvial loams was deposited. The first of these (I2) is a fine-grained calcareous loam deposited in a shallow depression in the top of the gravels. This level, probably reflecting a channel in which settling took place, could as yet only be documented over a few square metres.

The fine-grained fluvial sedimentation continues with the deposition of a calcareous loam (I1) on the external part of the terrace – loam with common rolled flints and chalk particles. In the last phase of the fluvial sedimentation a unit of homogeneous loam was deposited, again within a channel cutting through the lower levels.

The upper part of this sequence was then subjected to soil formation. The resulting loamy-humic brown-black palaeosol testifies to soil formation in a humid environment, corresponding to a stabilisation of the flood plain. Pollen analysis of the upper part of these deposits indicates an open forest of a boreal type (average of arboreal pollen: 68.4 %) and a temperate continental climatic setting. These results are in agreement with the results of the micromammal studies, which identified species characteristic of a cool-temperate climate, indicating interstadial or tardiglacial conditions (studies by J.M. Cordy and T. van Kolfschoten). The hypothesis of an interglacial pedogenesis at this level is corroborated by the abundant presence of calcite concretions in the upper part of the fine-grained deposits

and by the cementation of the gravel layer J. In fact, this 'humid environment' pedogenesis is roughly contemporaneous with the development of a brownish-red soil visible on the chalk slope, at that time the bank of the river valley (Fig. 5, unit 5).

These data indicate that the formation of the fine-grained deposits at Cagny-l'Epinette took place at the end of the climatic cycle, in an early-interglacial context, an interpretation recently confirmed by the results of the latest pollen studies. The Acheulean occupations of Cagny-l'Epinette therefore took place at the margins of the flood plain from the beginning of the climatic amelioration onwards.

In the fluvial loams the following species are present: Elephas (P.) antiquus, Equus mosbachensis, Equus hydruntinus, Equus sp., Dama dama, Cervus elaphus and Bos primigenius. Only two carnivore-remains were found yet: a fox mandible and a hyena humerus. The levels H, I and I1 differ in their faunal compositions. In H horse is well represented whereas levels I and I1 are dominated by bovids. Fragments of deer antler are common in I and I1. The presence of shed antlers and the age of the young bovids seems to indicate an occupation at the end of autumn or winter for level I1. Some bones show cut-marks.

The first human occupation took place on the top of the gravels, whereas other traces appear in the sequence of fine-grained fluvial deposits. In the fine-grained loams a clear spatial organization of finds could be discerned, with a concentration of nodules, that, judging from their morphology, might have been introduced by humans, and zones with various categories of bones (vertebrae, fragments of limb bones and antlers).

The layers covering the fluvial sequence correspond to the lower part of the covering layers at La Garenne. The industry (Figs 7-8) contains handaxes and tools on flakes, some of which were made on natural flakes, indicating a rather opportunistic attitude towards raw materials, in stark contrast to what was observed at Cagny-la Garenne (Tuffreau et al. 1995).

5.   The littoral sites of the Channel and the Atlantic Ocean

5.1.   WIMEREUX, LA POINTE-AUX-OIES

The site (Wimereux, Pas-de-Calais) is at 5 km north of Boulogne-sur-Mer, between the cliffs of la Pointe-aux-Oies and the estuary of the Slack, in a littoral cliff of Pas-de-Calais.

Above Portlandien deposits, with an upper part corresponding to an old abrasion surface, the cliff displays a sequence of gravels and brownish loams of marine origin, that have been correlated to the fluvial-marine sequence

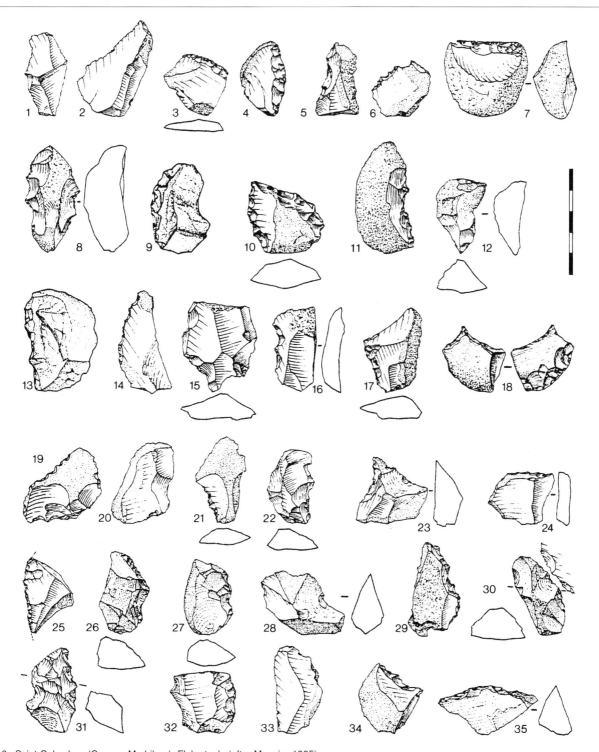

Fig. 9. Saint-Colomban (Carnac, Morbihan). Flake-tools (after Monnier 1985)
1. Flake; 2. Pseudo-Levallois point; 3 and 4. Side-scrapers; 5. Notch; 6. Denticulate; 7. Transversal side-scraper; 8. Composite flake-tool (notch and denticulate); 9. Single convex side-scraper; 10. Déjeté scraper; 11. Denticulate; 12. Bill-hook; 13. Single side-scraper; 14 to 16. Denticulates; 17. Single side-scraper; 18. Borer; 19 to 24. Denticulates and notches; 25 and 26. Single side-scrapers; 27 to 29. Denticulates and notches; 30. Scrapers; 31. Denticulate; 32. Side-scraper; 33. Naturally backed knife; 34. Denticulate; 35. Convex transverse side-scraper. Scale in cm.

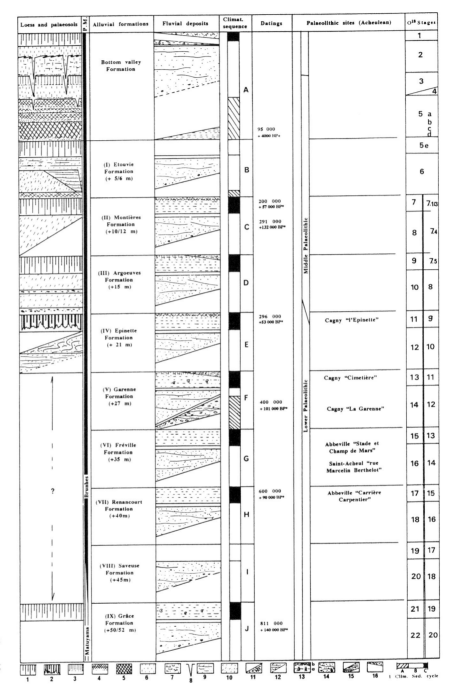

Fig. 10. Localisation of the palaeolithic sites in the sedimentary sequence of the Somme Basin, with a hypothetical correlation to the oxygen isotope stratigraphy. 1. Bt horizon of brown leached soil; 2. Bt horizon of red clayey soil; 3. Intrapleniglacial boreal leached soil; 4. Early glacial humic soil; 5. Early glacial grey forested humic soil; 6. Calcareous loess; 7. Calcareous bedded loess; 8. Ice wedges and frost cracks; 9. Sandy calcareous loess; 10. Sandy loess; 11. Rubble chalk; 12. Sandy slope colluviums; 13. Early glacial slope deposits sequence with inter-stratified calcareous silts; 14. Coarse fluvial gravels; 15. Fluvial calcareous silts; 16. Peat (modern flood plain); PS1-SR-Sol de Rocourt (Eemian). PS2, PS3, PS4-pre-Eemian palaeosols. *ESR dates on fluvial quarz. +U/Th-dates on bones. Climatic cycle: A. Interglacial; B. Early Glacial; C. Full glacial.

with *Mammuthus meridionalis* and *Hippopotamus major* of Wissant (Bourdier 1969b). The sequence furthermore consists of ancient fluvial deposits (gravels and sands) of the Slack, covered by stratified sands and the Holocene dunes. Laterally the Pleistocene deposits are overlain by a loess cover with a palaeosol of interglacial character (Sommé and Tuffreau 1976 and *in prep.*). More studies are needed

– especially palaeomagnetic ones – to specify the age of the marine deposits that bear witness to the opening of the Pas-de-Calais (Strait of Dover) from the Middle Pleistocene onwards (Colbeaux *et al.* 1980). They probably date from somewhere in the Cromer complex (OIS 13 to 21).

The lithic industry, unrolled, but with an intensive brown to yellow colour patina, was collected from the lower gravel layer (the marine deposit) that is exposed during high and strong tides on the present beach. Some more abraded artefacts have likewise surfaced from the fluvial gravels.

The assemblage mainly consists of flint nodules with a cutting edge obtained by successive or alternating bifacial flaking. A few rare handaxes with large flake-scars ('proto-bifaces') are also present. Because of the way the assemblage has been collected flakes are not numerous (Tuffreau 1971).

5.2.　　　THE SITES OF NORMANDY

The beaches of Le Havre (Seine-Maritime) have yielded many artefacts from the end of the last century onwards, for example series with many handaxes (amygdaloids and lanceolate forms) from the '*Station Romain*'. Others are characterised by the abundance of thick flakes with a wide flaking angle, that have been related to the 'Clactonian'. They also possess some handaxe roughouts, showing that in fact we are dealing with Acheulean flint knapping sites (Ohel and Lechevalier 1979; Watté 1987). Their context of discovery – the beaches – makes it difficult to establish the age of these series.

The Port-Pignot site (Fermanville, Manche) yielded a lithic industry situated on top of old marine deposits of the Cotentin peninsula, covered by Saalian slope deposits (head). In view of the regional context the old beach could be of Holsteinian or intra-Saalian age. The lithic industry, classifiable as evolved Acheulean, contains some Levallois products and a few amygdaloid handaxes. Some structures have been described from this site, amongst which four stone-lined hearths are the easiest recognizable ones (Michel 1982).

5.3.　　　SAINT-COLOMBAN

The site is situated at la Pointe de Saint-Colomban, at Carnac (Morbihan), on the southern coast of Brittany, and has been excavated from 1981 onwards (Monnier and Le Cloirec 1985; Monnier and Molines 1993). The stratigraphic sequence, visible in a cliff, consists of sands from an old marine beach covered by a head. This old beach should be older than the last interglacial, as confirmed by ESR dates (OIS 11 or 13) obtained at the Pleuvines site. The lithic assemblage (Fig. 9) from the marine sequence consists of tools on flakes (mainly notches and denticulates) and of pebble-tools, mostly choppers. "Colombanien" has been suggested as a term to indicate the specific character of this type of assemblage. An assemblage comparable to the one from Saint-Colomban has been recovered in an identical stratigraphical context at the site of Menez-Drégan 1 (Hallegouet *et al.* 1992).

6.　　　**Conclusions**

There is no trace of human occupation in northwestern France and Belgium older than OIS 15. The oldest industry comes from the Carrière Carpentier at (Fig. 10). Abbeville, and it is an Acheulean one. All lithic assemblages from or older than OIS 9 can be attributed to the Acheulean, which shows a large typological variability in the composition of handaxe forms. At Cagny-la Garenne the appearance of the Levallois debitage is situated in a context of handaxe production, indicating a conceptual link between the flaking of handaxes and the emergence of the Levallois flaking methods. The presence of sites specifically aimed at collecting meat (Cagny-l'Epinette) or lithic raw materials (Cagny-la Garenne) is also a point to emphasise. These observations show that the presence of the Acheulean is probably not the result of a local evolution, but rather an intrusive phenomenon with a large variability, that stresses the artificial character of the classical break between the Lower and the Middle Palaeolithic.

The existence of original "Colombanien" assemblages in Brittany poses the question of their individuality in the context of the Acheulean. Are we dealing with assemblages resulting from specialised activities within the Acheulean or do they reflect different traditions? The answer to this question is to a large extent dependent on the development of research in Brittany, where the Acheulean *sensu stricto* is hardly represented.

references

Adophe, J.-P.   1974   Les dragées calcaires de Montières-Grâce et de la marne blanche d'Abbeville, *Bull. Ass. Fr. Et. Quatern.* 11, 163-164.

Agache, R.,   1963   Le Quaternaire de la basse Somme: tentative de synthèse, *Bull. Soc. Géol. Fr.* (7), V,
    F. Bourdier,   422-442.
    R. Petit

Antoine, P.   1990   Chronostratigraphie et environnement du Paléolithique du Bassin de la Somme, *Publications du CERP* 2, 231 p., Univ. Sciences Techn. Lille.

                             1993   Le système de terrasses du Bassin de la Somme: modèle d'évolution morphosédimentaire cyclique et cadre paléo-environnemental pour le Paléolithique, *Quaternaire* 4 (1), 3-16.

Antoine, P.,   1993   Contexte stratigraphique, climatique et paléotopographique des occupations acheuléennes
    A. Tuffreau   de la moyenne terrasse de la Somme, *Bull. Soc. Préhist. Fr.* 90, 243-250.

Biquant, D.   1974   Position chronologique de la très haute nappe alluviale de Grâce (vallée de la Somme) par rapport α la limite paléomagnétique Bruhnes-Matuyama. *Bull. Ass. Fr. Et. Quatern.* 11, 157-159.

Bordes, F.   1961   Typologie du Paléolithique ancien et moyen, *Publ. Inst. Préhist.* Univ. Bordeaux.

Bourdier, F.   1969a   Excursion dans le bassin de Paris de l'association internationale pour l'étude du Quaternaire du 18 au 28 août 1969: étude comparée des dépôts quaternaires des bassins de la Seine et de la Somme, *Bull. inform. Géol. Bassin Paris* 21, 169-220.

                             1969b   Sur la position chronologique du Paléolithique de Sangatte, Wissant et Wimereux (Pas-de-Calais), *Bull. Soc. Préhist. Fr.* LXVI, 230-231.

                             1974   La "marne blanche" d'Abbeville, gisement type de l'Abbevillien, *Bull. Ass. Fr. Et. Quatern.* 11, 161-163.

Bourdier, F.,   1974a   La très haute nappe alluviale de la Somme, *Bull. Ass. Fr. Et. Quatern.* 11, 137-143.
    J. Chaline,
    A.V. Munaut,
    J.J. Puisségur

                             1974b   Le complexe mindelien: II- La moyenne terrasse de l'Avre, *Bull. Ass. Fr. Et. Quatern.* 11, 168-180.

Breuil, H.,   1954   Le Paléolithique ancien: Abbevillien, Clactonien, Acheuléen, Levalloisien. In: Les
    H. Kelley   grandes civilisations préhistoriques de la France, *Bull. Soc. Préhist. Fr.* LI, 9-26.

Cahen, D.   1984   Le Paléolithique inférieur et moyen en Belgique. In: D. Cahen and P. Haesaerts (ed.), *Peuples chasseurs de la Belgique dans leur cadre naturel*, 133-155, Bruxelles.

Chaline, J.   1974   Les rongeurs, l'âge et l'environnement de la très haute terrasse de Grâce α Montières (Somme), *Bull. Ass. Fr. Et. Quatern.* 11, 151-157.

Colbeaux, J.-P.,   1980   Le détroit du Pas-de-Calais: un élément dans la tectonique de blocs de l'Europe nord-
    Ch. Dupuis,   occidentale, *Bull. inform. Géol. Bassin Paris* 17 (4), 41-54.
    F. Robaszynski,
    J.P. Auffret,
    P. Haesaerts,
    J. Sommé

Commont, V.   1906   Excursion de la Société Linnéenne à Abbeville, le 25 mars 1906, *Bull. Soc. Linnéenne
       Nord de la France* 371, 110-112.

             1908   Les industries de l'ancien Saint-Acheul, *L'Anthr.* XLX, 527-572.

             1909   Saint-Acheul et Montières. Notes de géologie, de paléontologie et de préhistoire, *Mém.
       Soc. Géol. Nord* VI (III).

             1910   Excursion de la Société géologique du Nord et de la Faculté des Sciences de Lille à
       Abbeville, le 11 juin 1910. Les gisements paléolithiques d'Abbeville. Stratigraphie, faune,
       industrie humaine, *Ann. Soc. Géol. Nord* XXXIX, 249-293.

Cordy, J.M.   1982   Biozonation du Quaternaire post-villafranchien continental d'Europe occidentale à partir
       des grands mammifères, *Ann. Soc. Géol. Belgique* 205, 303-314.

Cordy, J.M.,   1992   La Belle-Roche (Sprimont, Belgium): the Oldest Site in the Benelux. A Report on a Field
    B. Bastin,   Trip. In: M. Toussaint (ed.), Cinq millions d'années, l'aventure humaine, *ERAUL* 56,
    C. Ek,   287-301, Liège.
    R. Geeraerts,
    A. Ozer,
    Y. Quinif,
    J. Thorez,
    M. Ulrix-Closset

Haesaerts, P.   1984   Aspects de l'évolution du paysage et de l'environnement en Belgique au Quaternaire. In:
       D. Cahen, P. Haesaerts (ed.), *Peuples chasseurs de la Belgique dans leur cadre naturel*,
       27-39, Bruxelles.

Haesaerts, P.,   1986   Contribution à la stratigraphie des nappes alluviales de la Somme et de l'Avre dans la
    Ch. Dupuis   région d'Amiens. In: A. Tuffreau, J. Sommé (ed.), Chronostratigraphie et faciès culturels
       du Paléolithique inférieur et moyen dans l'Europe du Nord-Ouest, *Suppl. Bull. Ass. Fr. Et.
       Quatern.* 26, 171-186.

Hallegouet, B.,   1992   Le gisement paléolithique inférieur de Ménez-Drégan 1 (Plouhinec, Finistère). Premiers
    S. Hinguant,   résultats des fouilles, *Bull. Soc. Préhist. Fr.* 89, 77-81.
    A. Gebhardt,
    J.L. Monnier

Lamotte, A.   1991   *Etude des vestiges lithiques des niveaux du gisement de Cagny-la Garenne (Somme) et de
       niveau A du gisement de Gouzeaucourt.* Mémoire de D.E.A.. Université des Sciences et
       Techniques de Lille, Lille.

Laurent, M.   1993   *Datation par résonance du Spin electronique de quartz de formation quaternaires:
       comparaison avec le paléomagnétisme*, Thèse Doctorat. Museum National d'Histoire
       Naturelle, Paris.

Michel, D.   1982   Le gisement préhistorique de Port-Pignot à Fermanville (Manche), *Gallia-Préhistoire* 25,
       1-68.

Monnier, J.L., R. Le Cloirec	1985	Le gisement paléolithique inférieur de la Pointe de Saint-Colomban à Carnac (Morbihan), *Gallia-Préhistoire*. 28, 7-36.
Monnier, J.L., N. Molines	1993	Le "Colombanien": un faciès régional du Paléolithique inférieur sur le littoral armoricano-atlantique, *Bull. Soc. Préhist. Fr.* 90, 283-294.
Munaut, A.-V.	1974	Les analyses palynologiques de la moyenne terrasse de Cagny-Cimetière (Somme), *Bull. Ass. Fr. Et. Quatern.* 11, 181-185.
	1988	L'environnement végétal de quelques dépôts quaternaires du bassin de la Somme. In: A. Tuffreau *et al.* (ed.), Cultures et industries paléolithiques en milieu loessique, Amiens, 1986, *Rev. archéol. Picardie* 1-2, 45-56.
	1989	Cagny-l'Epinette: analyses palynologiques. In: *"Livret-guide de l'excursion dans la vallée de la Somme". Colloque "L'Acheuléen dans l'Ouest de l'Europe"*, 75-79, Saint-Riquier.
	1993	Analyse palynologique des sédiments fluviatiles d'une moyenne terrasse de l'Avre à Cagny-la-Garenne (Somme) abritant divers niveaux d'occupation acheuléens. In: A. Tuffreau (ed.), L'Acheuléen dans l'Ouest de l'Europe, *Publication du CERP* 4, in press.
Ohel, M.Y., Lechevallier	1979	The "Clactonian" of Le Havre and its bearing of the English Clactonian, *Quartär*, 29-30, 85-105.
Pontier, P.	1928	Les éléphants fossiles d'Abbeville, *Ann. Soc. Géol. Nord* LIII, 20-46.
Roebroeks, W., D. Stapert	1986	On the "Lower Palaeolithic" site La Belle Roche: An Alternative Interpretation, *Current Anthropology* 27, 369-371.
Sommé, J., A. Tuffreau	1976	Les formations quaternaires et les industries de la Pointe-aux-Oies (Wimereux, Pas-de-Calais). In: Livret-guide de l'excursion A10: Nord-Ouest de la France (Bassin de la Seine, bassin de la Somme et Nord), *IXe Congr. UISPP*, 163-168, Nice.
Tuffreau, A.	1971	Quelques observations sur le Paléolithique de la Pointe-aux-Oies à Wimereux (Pas-de-Calais), *Bull. Soc. Préhist. Fr.* LXVIII, 496-504.
	1980a	Le Paléolithique inférieur de la moyenne terrasse de la Somme: Cagny-Cimétière et Cagny-l'Epinette: fouilles récents, *Bull. Soc. Préhist. franc.* 77, 197-198.
	1980b	Les fouilles paléolithiques de Cagny-Cimétière (Somme): rapport préliminaire, *Cahiers archéo. Picardie* 7, 5-17.
	1981	L'Acheuléen dans la France septentrionale, *Anthropologie* XIX/2, 171-183.
	1987	*Le Paléolithique inférieur et moyen du Nord de la France (Nord, Pas-de-Calais, Picardie dans son cadre stratigraphique*, Thèse de Doctorat d'Etat, Univ. Sciences et Techn. de Lille.
Tuffreau, A. (ed).	1989	Livret-guide de l'excursion dans la vallée de la Somme. Colloque *"l'Acheuléen dans l'Ouest de l'Europe"*, Saint-Riquier.
	1992	L'Acheuléen en Europe occidentale d'après les données du bassin de la Somme. *I primi abianti della valle padana: Monte Poggiolo*, 41-49, Milano.
Tuffreau, A., A.V. Munaut, J.J. Puisséguir, J. Sommé	1982	Stratigraphie et environnement des industries acheuléennes de la moyenne terrasse du bassin de la Somme, *Bull. Ass. Fr. Et. Quatern.* 19, 73-82.

Tuffreau, A.,   1986   Les niveaux acheuléens de la moyenne terrasse de la vallée de la Somme à Cagny-
  J.P. Bouchet,   l'Epinette (Somme), *L'Anthr.* 90, 9-27.
  A.V. Moigne,
  A.-V. Munaut

Tuffreau, A.,   1995   Le gisement acheuléen de Cagny-l'Epinette (Somme), *Bull. Soc. Préhist. Fr.* 92, 169-191.
  P. Antoine,
  Ph. Chase,
  H.L. Dibble,
  B.B. Ellwood,
  T. van Kolfschoten,
  A. Lamotte,
  Sh.P. McPherron,
  A.M. Moigne,
  A.-V. Munaut

Watté, J.-P.   1987   Gisements paléolithiques des plages du Havre (habitat acheuléen de la "station Romain")
                                 et de Sainte-Adresse (ateliers "clactoniens") (Seine-Maritime), *Annales du Muséum du
                                 Havre* 39, 1-31.

Alain Tuffreau and Pierre Antoine
ERA 37, du CRA, CNRS
Université des Sciences et Technologies de Lille
F-59655 Villeneuve d'Ascq Cedex
France

Mark B. Roberts
Clive S. Gamble
David R. Bridgland

10   The earliest occupation of Europe: the British Isles

The evidence presented here suggests that the British Isles was first colonized at the beginning of the temperate or interglacial stage that immediately pre-dates the Anglian cold Stage. Lithostratigraphic and chronostratigraphic modelling correlates the Anglian with Oxygen Isotope Stage 12, which is dated to between 478 and 423 Kyr BP. Accordingly, the earliest occupation of Britain occurred around half a million years ago. The early colonizers are assigned, from the Boxgrove specimen, to the species Homo cf heidelbergensis. *One hundred thousand years later, at Swanscombe, this group begins to exhibit some cranial skeletal characteristics usually associated with the Neanderthal lineage. Throughout the period covered by this paper there is apparent stasis in the lithic industries, which include both biface dominant assemblages and flake tool dominant assemblages. Strict division between these two types of assemblages is no longer tenable on typological or chronological grounds.*

1.   Introduction

The remit of this paper is to study the occupation of the British Isles from the first evidence of human colonization to the end of the second major temperate event after the Anglian cold Stage. Although the starting point is self explanatory, the cut-off point may seem at first to be of an arbitrary nature. However, it may be demonstrated that by this time the continent of Europe, outside the ice margins (Holm and Larsson, this volume), was colonized over a large part of its land mass and that in our geographical region of Britain and northwest Europe, the cut-off point coincides with the emergence of the Levallois technique of lithic reduction and flake production.

The sites included in this paper (Fig. 1) have either been recently or are currently being, excavated and/or studied as part of on-going research programmes. Sites that satisfy these criteria have been chosen because the research methodology utilized in their study is multidisciplinary and thus the quality of the contextual information facilitates greater accuracy in both inter-site and inter-regional correlation.

The sites have been divided into two groups, those that pre-date and those that post-date the Anglian Glaciation.

This division is not based on any shift, real or perceived, in hominid material culture nor on any concept of hominid species change; rather it reflects the large scale changes to the palaeogeography and mammalian fauna composition of Britain, that occurred as the result of physical and climatic factors relating to this glacial/cold event. The fixing in time of the Anglian Stage has not yet been unequivocally agreed upon by British Quaternary scientists but the weight of evidence suggests correlation with Oxygen Isotope Stage (OIS) 12 (see below and Table 1). The model presented here, although it fits with this hypothesis, is free-standing and allows for future fine tuning of the geochronological timescale.

On the evidence currently available to Quaternary scientists, it is thought that the first hominids arrived in Britain approximately half a million years before the present day. This view fits well with the short chronology perspective of the demographic expansion of humans through continental Europe (Roebroeks 1994; Roebroeks and Van Kolfschoten 1994, this volume) and certainly accords with the picture from northern France, Belgium, Spain and Portugal (see various contributions in this volume), where the earliest sites are dated to the end of the Cromerian Complex. There remains a problem of reconciling these dates with the much earlier dates of sites in southern France (Bonifay and Vandermeersch 1991) and central Europe (Valoch 1991 and this volume). However, many of these sites are controversial and not all of them are accepted by archaeologists as containing evidence of human occupation (Roebroeks and Van Kolfschoten 1994; Raynal *et al.*, this volume). There may however, have been sporadic colonization of the Mediterranean region for a long period of time prior to the main geographical expansion of *Homo* around 500 Kyr BP. The reasons behind this apparently sudden and dramatic movement are beyond the scope of this paper but it may be noted that solving the problem of the colonization of Europe during the Middle Pleistocene is going to be dependant on moving away from a site based approach to human ecology towards large scale regional modelling along the lines of Geographical Information Systems (GIS), to study geographic and climatic factors (Gamble 1986) that may have affected

Table 1. Revised stratigraphic correlation for part of the Middle and Late Pleistocene.
References. 1. Mitchell *et al.* 1973. 2. Roberts, this paper. 3. Adapted from Zagwijn 1992. 4. Shackleton 1987.

Conventional British stages[1]	Modified scheme[2]	Sites	Dutch/European sequence[3]	OIS[4]
OIS do not apply to this column				
Devensian	Devensian		Weichselian	5d+
Ipswichian	Ipswichian	Bobbitshole, Trafalgar Square	Eemian	5e
These stages not recognised	Cold stage		Saalian Complex	6
	Temperate/interglacial stage	Marsworth, Stanton Harcourt		7
	Cold stage			8
	Hoxnian	Hoxne?, Little Thurrock, Globe Pit, Purfleet		9
Wolstonian	Cold stage			10
Hoxnian	Temperate/interglacial stage	Swanscombe, Barnham, Beeches Pit, Clacton	Holsteinian	11
Anglian	Anglian		Elsterian	12
Cromerian	Temperate/interglacial stage	Boxgrove, High Lodge, Wivenhoe, Westbury-sub-Mendip, Kent's Cavern, Warren Hill, Waverley Wood	Cromerian IV	13
Beestonian	Cold stage		Glacial C	14

demographic expansion. Such modelling would provide a framework within which other variables such as technological capacity (Binford 1989), food availability (Roebroeks *et al.* 1992) and competition from other mammals (A. Turner 1992) could be empirically tested.

2.   Middle Pleistocene Colonization of NW Europe: Sites pre-dating the Anglian Cold Stage

2.1.   INTRODUCTION

The number of archaeological sites dated to the period of the Cromerian Complex (Zagwijn 1985; 1992) in Britain has increased dramatically in the past two decades. The sites are located within the block of time between the Cromerian *sensu stricto*, as represented in the type section at West Runton, Norfolk, and the Anglian Glaciation. There exists however a problem in fixing the position of West Runton in the Quaternary timescale; previous biostrati-graphical and lithostratigraphical work by Stuart (1975) and West (1980) postulated that the Cromerian *sensu stricto* warm stage immediately pre-dated the Anglian. This correlation was questioned by Bishop (1982) in his report on the fauna from the site at Westbury-sub-Mendip,

Somerset. Current research at Boxgrove (Roberts 1990) and on the pre-diversion course of the River Thames (Bridgland 1994), together with work in the Rhine Valley of Germany at Miesenheim I and Kärlich (Van Kolfschoten 1990; Van Kolfschoten and Turner, in press) further supports the view that there was at least one fully temperate event between the Cromerian *sensu stricto* and the Anglian/Elsterian (Table 1).

All the sites listed below are thought to occur in a temperate stage that immediately precedes the Anglian; this stage has been correlated with the interglacial Cromerian IV in the Dutch stratigraphic sequence (De Jong 1988; Zagwijn 1985; 1992). However, there exists a problem with the date assigned to this stage by the aforementioned researchers; their placement of Interglacial IV at or around 400 Kyr BP is based upon young dates for the hornblende/augite boundary from the Eifel area volcanic eruptions (Evernden *et al.* 1957; Frechen and Lippolt 1965). Current research now puts this transition earlier in the Middle Pleistocene (C. van den Bogaard *et al.* 1989; Bosinski, this volume). If the correlation of the Anglian Glaciation and cold event to OIS 12 is correct (Šibrava *et al.* 1986;

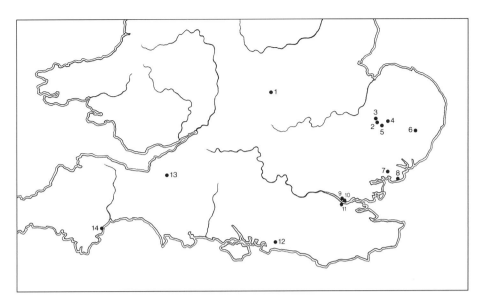

Fig. 1. Location of sites mentioned in the text:
1. Waverley Wood; 2. Warren Hill; 3. High Lodge; 4. Barnhem; 5. Beeches Pit; 6. Hoxne; 7. Wivenhoe; 8. Clacton; 9. Purfleet; 10. Little Thurrock; 11. Swanscombe; 12. Boxgrove; 13. Westbury-sub-Mendip; 14. Kents Cavern.

Shackleton 1987; Bowen 1991; Bridgland 1994), then hominids first entered the Britain in OIS 13, between 524 and 478 Kyr BP (Imbrie *et al.* 1984).

2.2.   WAVERLEY WOOD FARM PIT. SP 365 715[1]. WARWICKSHIRE

The Waverley Wood artefacts (Fig. 1) (Shotton *et al.* 1993; Wise 1993), which include three well made symmetrical andesite bifaces and a number of flakes, were recovered from the base of the Baginton-Lillington Gravel (Shotton 1953; 1968). In addition another flake was recovered from the organic deposits underlying the Baginton-Lillington Gravels (Fig. 3) (Shotton *et al.* 1993). The organic deposits at Waverley Wood Farm have been ascribed to OIS 15 by aminostratigraphic correlation (Bowen *et al.* 1989; Bowen 1991). If this date of >565 Kyr BP (Imbrie *et al.* 1984), which remains equivocal, is accepted then this occurrence of artefacts is the earliest discovered in Britain to date.

Apart from the amino acid geochronology there are other lines of evidence, essentially lithostratigraphic, that suggest the deposits are pre-Anglian (pre OIS 12). Rose (1987; 1989; 1992) proposed that the Baginton-Lillington Gravels, together with their downstream equivalents the Bytham Sands and Gravels, the Shouldham Sands and Gravels and the Ingham Sands and Gravels and their upstream correlatives at Snitterfield (Maddy and Lewis 1991) were deposited by a river (Fig. 2), in a now buried valley, that flowed west to east through the Midlands to south Lincolnshire, then southeastwards into Norfolk and Suffolk, where it was confluent with the River Thames and finally eastwards into what is now the North Sea. Rose (1989;

1992; 1994), has also suggested that this river was depositing over a substantial period of time during the Early and early Middle Pleistocene.

In East Anglia the Ingham Sands and Gravels underlies the Lowestoft Till (Anglian) and is disposed as a series of terrace aggradations (Bridgland and Lewis 1991; Lewis 1993). The oldest formation can be correlated (Lewis 1993) with the Stebbing Formation of the High-level Kesgrave Subgroup [Sudbury Formation: (Whiteman and Rose 1992)], part of the Kesgrave Group of the River Thames. The youngest formation is correlated with the entire Low-level Kesgrave Subgroup [Colchester Formation (Lewis 1993)]. Thus these gravels probably span from the Early Pleistocene to the Anglian Stage. However, these Early Pleistocene gravel aggradations in central East Anglia cannot be correlated with the Baginton Formation in the West Midlands as there are no upstream equivalents of the older terraces identified within the Ingham Formation in that area. The Baginton Formation in the West Midlands, together with the Bytham and Shouldham Formations of Lincolnshire and west Norfolk respectively, are correlated with only the lowest (and youngest) member of the Ingham Formation and probably represent a drainage pattern that existed immediately prior to the Anglian glaciation.

The organic channel fills at Waverley Wood Farm (Shotton *et al.* 1993) and Brandon (Maddy *et al.* 1994) which occur within the Baginton Formation, contain palaeoecological evidence for a warmer climatic regime. Analyses of pollen and the coleopteran assemblage (Coope, in Shotton *et al.* 1993; Gibbard and Peglar 1989; Shotton *et al.* 1993) of the lower organic deposit at Brandon and Waverley Wood suggests these channels may be of the

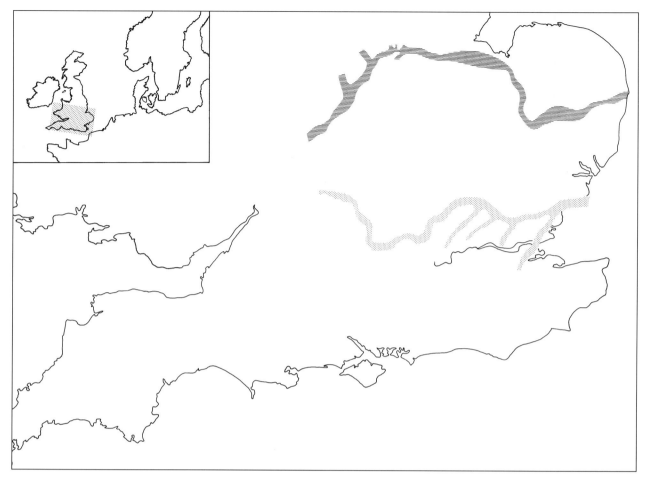

Fig. 2. Position of the Midlands/Bytham River, and the late Cromerian River Thames.

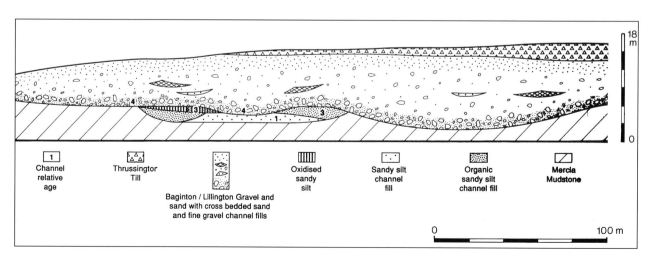

Fig. 3. Section through the stratigraphy at Waverley Wood (from Shotton *et al.* 1993).

same age in absolute terms, and probably also represent the same time span within a temperate stage or sub-stage. Maddy *et al.* (1994) suggested that the Baginton Formation may span OIS 15 to 12.

The mammalian fauna from these deposits is again equivocal as there are no truly thermophilous elements (Lister 1989), while some boreal/cold climate taxa are present. Biostratigraphically the fauna, as a group, is what would be expected from an early Anglian or early Saalian context. There are similarities with the Anglian fauna from Homersfield in Norfolk (Stuart 1981; Coxon 1979), but there are none of the classic Cromerian Complex fossils that would be expected if the sediments are as old as Rose believes. The *Sorex savini* M^1 from Waverley Wood (reported by Shotton 1989) was misidentified and therefore, as has been stated above, the mammalian assemblage contains no Cromerian Complex type fossils but only material associated in Britain and northern and central Europe with the onset of the Anglian/Elsterian cold stage or with later periods.

In conclusion the amino acid geochronological assignation of Waverley Wood to OIS 15 is seriously questioned. This site which, on the aminostratigraphic timescale, is put as older than West Runton (Bowen 1992) contains the descendant, *Arvicola terrestris cantiana*, of the West Runton form of the water vole, *Mimomys savini*. The history and nature of the change, from the rooted to the unrooted form of this rodent, is well documented (for summary see Von Koenigswald and Van Kolfschoten, in press) and accepted by all researchers into Pleistocene rodent faunas. Thus to invert the ages of these sites on the basis of amino acid ratios directly contradicts a well established and accepted biostratigraphical lineage. The evidence from Waverley Wood and its position within the Baginton/Ingham River system suggests a stratigraphic position in OIS 13 or at the beginning of OIS 12 and no older.

2.3.   HIGH LODGE, MILDENHALL. TL 739 754.
           SUFFOLK

The site at High Lodge (Fig. 1) is located at the western edge of the low Breckland Plateau and at the southeastern margin of the Fen Basin (Rose 1992; Cook *et al.* 1991; Ashton *et al.* 1992). The Pleistocene sediments are located in a channel cut into the chalk at a height range between 19-30m OD.

The archaeological material is contained within a body of silts and clays that have been transported as a wedge by the ice sheet responsible for depositing the underlying diamicton, the Lowestoft Till. These rafted, fine grained deposits are overlain and in places dissected by a series of gravelly deposits, widely interpreted as glaciofluvial outwash that contain derived archaeological material. In fact

these deposits form the highest of a series of terraces of the old Lark valley (Bridgland and Lewis 1991) and a fluviatile origin is perfectly possible. The lithic industry (Fig. 4) contained within the silts and clays may be described as a flake industry produced on the debitage from core reduction (Ashton 1992). The flakes are sometimes worked further by the flaked flake technique (Ashton *et al.* 1991), or made into classic High Lodge scrapers with semi-invasive, semi-scalar and non-stepped retouch: the mode of percussion being hard hammer. The flake industry was originally thought to be Middle Palaeolithic on the basis of the morphology of the flake tools (Anon 1968; Coulson 1990), thus post-dating the Hoxnian Interglacial. The use of typology to date the industry conflicted with views of geologists working at the site (C. Turner 1973) and led to a delay in the publication of the site report (Ashton 1992). It is now accepted on lithostratigraphical grounds that the site must pre-date the Anglian, as the only ice sheet that came as far south as High Lodge in the Middle Pleistocene formed during the Anglian (Perrin *et al.* 1979). This evidence for dating is further corroborated by the discovery in the silts and clays of a molar of *Stephanorhinus hundsheimensis*, which became extinct in northern Europe during the Anglian/Elsterian. The archaeological material in the overlying sands and gravels contains some flakes and flake tools reworked from the silts and clays below, but more importantly it is almost exclusively composed of bifaces, which given their condition are thought to derive from a nearby source and may be contemporaneous with the flake industry.

The palaeoenvironment of the High Lodge silts and clays, which contain the flake/core industry, is interpreted as a gently flowing fluvial system, forming the silts and clays as an overbank deposit, associated with a flora of spruce-pine woodland with marsh and aquatic plants. The insect fauna supports the scenario of shallow pools and swampy ground and indicates cool-temperate conditions. On the basis of the lithology (Lewis 1992), mineralogy (Rose *et al.* 1992) and the assemblage of pre-Quaternary pollen and spores (Hunt and Rose 1992), these sediments were deposited on the floodplain of a river draining source areas in the English Midlands (Fig. 2), represented by the Baginton Formation in the Midlands and by the Ingham and Shouldam Formations in East Anglia.

Thus it is likely that the High Lodge flake industry was made at the end of a temperate stage immediately pre-dating the Anglian glaciation. The age of the bifaces is problematic given their context but it is likely that they are of a similar or slightly later age of the flake industry. This industry finds parallels throughout the British Palaeolithic, for example at Clacton and Hoxne (Ashton and McNabb 1992) and is not seen to have any stratigraphic importance.

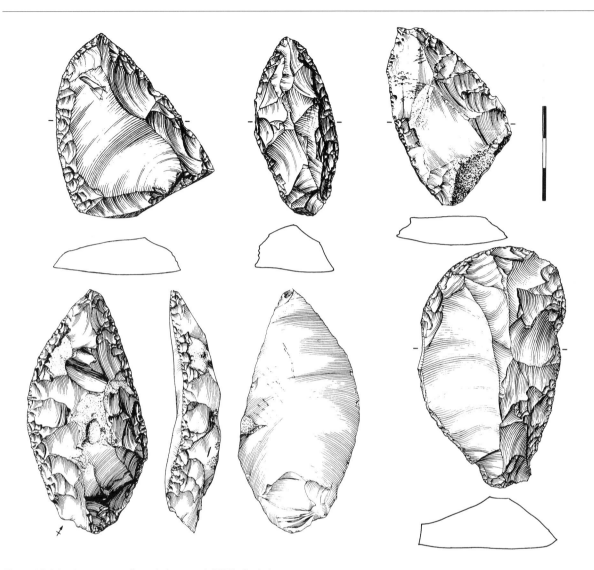

Fig. 4. High Lodge scrapers (from Ashton *et al.* 1992). Scale in cm.

2.4.   WARREN HILL. TL 744 743. SUFFOLK

This site (Fig. 1), or more accurately the deposits of this area, has produced the largest number of handaxes in Britain (Roe 1968; Wymer 1985). At Three Hills, the part of Warren Hill where gravel quarrying was undertaken, two lithologically distinct units are recognised. These are, from the base upwards, the Warren Hill Sands and Silts and the Warren Hill Sands and Gravels (Wymer *et al.* 1991). The sands and silts were deposited in a relatively low energy environment and are over 4.6 m thick, with the base of the unit extending lower than 9 m OD. The sands and gravels overlie the silts and sands, with a contact recorded at 13.6m OD. Sedimentary structures within the unit indicate that the

sands and gravels are the result of an increase in the energy of the depositing source. The unit is up to 6.5m thick with a present day surface height of 20.1m OD.

There are two current hypotheses for the source of the gravels. The first suggests that they were deposited as glacial outwash (Solomon 1933; Wymer 1985), the second, that they are fluvial in origin, deposited by a river system that flowed west-east (Bridgland and Lewis 1991; Wymer *et al.* 1991). The lithological composition of the gravel is unlike the glaciofluvial gravels in the area (Bridgland *et al.* 1995) and the high percentage of quartzite and quartz suggests that they were laid down by the same fluvial system that deposited the Ingham Sand and Gravel further to the east (Fig. 2). At this point in its development the river that deposited the Ingham Sand and Gravel was probably linked to the Baginton Formation, forming a major west-east drainage system from the Midlands into central East Anglia. There is little biostratigraphical evidence from the site, although Andrews (1930) records *Archidiskodon meridionalis*. This species is only known in Britain from the Cromerian *sensu stricto* as represented at West Runton (Stuart 1982).

The archaeological material from the sediments is mostly unprovenanced, although Wymer *et al.* (1991) record material from the lower part of the Warren Hill Sands and Gravels. The assemblage consists predominantly of bifaces with little debitage; whether this reflects sediment sorting or collection bias remains, for the present, unknown. Many of the ovate bifaces are made on flakes (Moir 1938), an uncommon phenomenon in the British Lower Palaeolithic, and are notched, although this characteristic may be the result of transportation. In addition to the ovate/cordate bifaces there are a large number of extremely battered and rolled bifaces and cores which have been interpreted as being typologically separate from the other bifaces (Solomon 1933; Roe 1981). This hypothesis needs to be re-examined taking into account the factors such as raw material availability through the development of the fluvial system and environments of deposition during the life of the river.

On the basis of the gravel lithology it is likely that the important Warren Hill lithic collections are of pre-Anglian or probably early Anglian date and fall in the other groups of pre-stage 12 sites in this paper. It also means that the latest terraces of the Ingham River and its tributaries should be investigated for evidence of early human occupation in the same manner as the post-Anglian terraces of the Thames system.

2.5.   BOXGROVE. SU 924 085. WEST SUSSEX

The Middle Pleistocene sediments at Boxgrove (Fig. 1) were deposited through a warm temperate episode into the ensuing cold event. They thus represent a wide range of modes and environments of deposition. What makes this site so important is that archaeological remains have been excavated from *in-situ* contexts, at all levels, through the stratigraphic sequence giving a continuity of occupation for this part of southern England over a 10^4 year timescale, through markedly changing climatic regimes (Roberts 1990).

The Pleistocene sediments at the site sit upon and are contained within a marine platform and chalk cliff cut into the Cretaceous Upper Chalk of the South Downs (Fig. 5). These features were formed during a Middle Pleistocene high sea-level event that entailed a marine transgression moving northwards over the deposits of the Lower Coastal Plain and cutting into the south facing dipslope of the Downs. The marine beach complex associated with this high sea-level attains a maximum elevation of 43.5m OD at the junction of the cliff and the wave cut platform; this high altitude may be the result of subsequent tectonic activity in the area (Preece *et al.* 1990). Associated with the high sea-level are a marine sand unit, the Slindon Sands which grade up into a lagoonal unit, the Slindon Silts. The known extent of these deposits is substantial: from Ports Down in the West (ApSimon *et al.* 1977; Roberts 1986) to the River Arun in the East, a distance in excess of 30 km. The Slindon Silts were formed when the direct path of the sea into a large embayment, formed by the downs, was blocked. Although the exact mechanism by which this happened is not yet known, a large salt water, tidally fed lagoon was created. At the end of the lagoonal phase a soil developed on the surface of the silts, which represents the most extensive Pleistocene landsurface at the site. Subsequent sedimentation derives from the north of the site, firstly when the soil was flooded with fresh water to create an alder/fen carr and then, secondly, as the soils covering the relict chalk cliff and the downland block, to the north of the site were stripped off, as vegetation cover declined under an increasingly severe climatic regime. Finally, under periglacial conditions large amounts of gravel from the chalk cliff and the Tertiary regolith covering the Downs moved down-slope as periglacial mass movement deposits.

The archaeology at the site (Bergman and Roberts 1988; Bergman *et al.* 1990; Wenban-Smith 1989; Roberts 1992) consists of scatters of lithic material in all the geological units, but best preserved and most extensive in the Slindon Silts and in the chalk scree material overlying the beach, from where raw material was obtained. Recently, *in situ* bifaces and refitting debitage have been found in the cold climate mass movement gravels that cap the sequence (Roberts 1992). The presence of archaeology at this level may suggest that early humans were able to survive in Britain throughout periods of extreme cold such as glacial stages. The assemblages, from the site as a whole, are mainly biface reduction scatters with some very limited core reduction. The bifaces (Fig. 6) are essentially ovates, limandes and cordate forms (Bordes 1961), although pointed forms are found when the raw material quality drops. There are few formal flake tools; two end-scrapers, a transverse scraper, a side scraper and some notched scrapers. The flaked flake technique is present but at low frequency and there is some secondary retouch on flakes for blunting and edge strengthening. Evidence of use of the lithics is apparent from butchered animal remains; these include red deer, rhinoceros and horse.

The site has been dated (Table 1) using mammalian biostratigraphy to the end of the Cromerian Complex. The marker fossils are listed below:

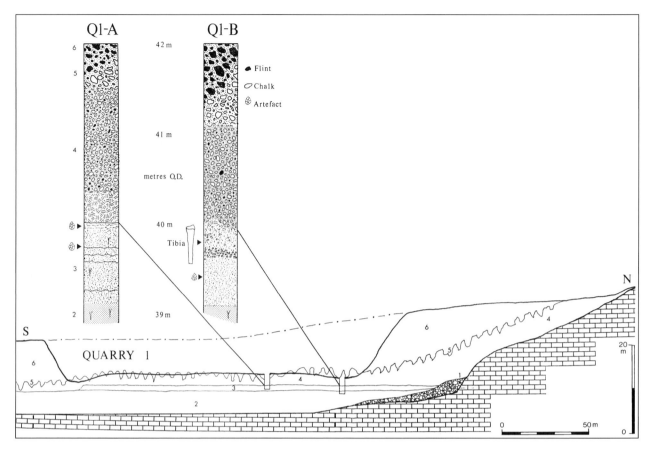

Fig. 5. Composite section through the geology in Quarry 1 at Boxgrove, including detail of deposits containing the hominid tibia. Key to the section diagram is as follows: 1. Raised beach gravels; 2. Slindon Sands; 3. Slindon Silts, with soil horizon developed in upper part at Q1-A; 4. Calcareous silts and gravels, derived from weathering of the chalk cliff; 5. Solution weathering contact; 6. Soliflucted Tertiary regolith.

Table 2. Biostratigraphically significant mammalian taxa from Boxgrove.

INSECTIVORA
   Sorex runtonensis
   Sorex savini
RODENTIA
   Pliomys episcopalis
   Arvicola terrestris cantiana
   Microtus gregalis (gregaloid morphotype)
CARNIVORA
   Canis lupus mosbachensis
   Ursus deningeri
PERISSODACTYLA
   Stephanorhinus hundsheimensis
ARTIODACTYLA
   Megaloceros dawkinsi

The biostratigraphical model contradicts the amino acid racemization ratios on marine mollusca which, using aminostratigraphy, suggest correlation with OIS 11 (Bowen 1991; Bowen and Sykes 1988). Bowen (*ibid*) correlates Boxgrove with Swanscombe, an interpretation that seems untenable given the differences in the mammalian faunas from the two sites (see below). The aminostratigraphy argument is further weakened by the fact that the ratios for Barnham (Ashton *et al*. 1994a) and Beeches Pit (R.C. Preece pers. comm.) also indicate OIS 11 and at these sites, as at Swanscombe, none of the species listed above have been found, despite an extensive sieving programme. Other methods of absolute dating, including E.S.R and T.L., have proved inconclusive thus far, or beyond the current reach of the method (Roberts 1994).

During the editing stages of this report a hominid tibia was discovered in the upper part of the Slindon Silts (Fig. 7), in a facies that is a temporal correlative of the soil horizon developed on the surface of the silts. The hominid has been assigned to *Homo* cf. *heidelbergensis* (Roberts *et al*. 1994). Further excavation of the hominid findspot is planned for 1995.

Fig. 6. Boxgrove flintwork on the surface of the marine Slindon Sands.

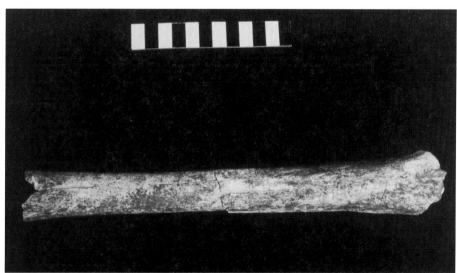

Fig. 7. The Boxgrove hominid tibia (scale in 10 mm divisions).

2.6.   WESTBURY-SUB-MENDIP. ST 506 504. SOMERSET

The Pleistocene deposits at Westbury (Fig. 1) were located in a limestone quarry situated at the southern edge of the Mendip Plateau at between 213 and 244m OD. The deposits accumulated in a cave system that formed in the Clifton Down limestone. There are two chambers which have been investigated and sampled (Bishop 1982; Andrews 1990), a main or southeastern chamber at least 70 m in length and a secondary deep, narrow side chamber, that follows a fault line to the northwest. Correlation

between the deposits in the two caves is difficult as the deposits suggest infilling from different origins. The basal member in each chamber is similar, in that this is a siliceous deposit composed of sands and gravels that were washed into the cave from outside. The fauna from this unit is sparse compared with some of the overlying units and its composition suggests that it is older and belongs to a separate Early or early Middle Pleistocene stage. Indicator species include: *Mimomys savini*, *Microtus* (*Allophaiomys*), and *Hyaena brevirostris*. Following the deposition of the siliceous sediments, both chambers experienced roof collapse episodes and subsequent deposition of angular breccias. These were succeeded by the further deposition of extensive breccia deposits, fully described by Andrews (1990). In brief it may be stated that the breccias in the main chamber, above the angular breccia, are different from those anywhere else in the cave. Their origin is from outside the cave and they were deposited as flow deposits. In the side chamber the breccias are formed from constituents within the chamber itself.

The importance of Westbury for this paper lies with the mammalian faunas recovered from the cave deposits. Firstly, from a taxonomic/biostratigraphic angle, the fauna contains those elements which are associated with a post-Cromerian *sensu stricto* and pre-Swanscombe position in the Quaternary timescale (Bishop 1982; Von Koenigswald 1973). These species include *Sorex runtonensis*, *Sorex savini*, *Arvicola terrestris cantiana*, *Microtus gregalis*, *Canis lupus mosbachensis*, *Ursus deningeri* and *Stephanorhinus hundsheimensis*. This group has very close parallels with that excavated from the open site at Boxgrove (Table 2). Secondly, taphonomic studies of the small mammal assemblages (Andrews 1990) has allowed a detailed palaeoecological reconstruction to be undertaken through the sedimentary profiles. From this reconstruction the following climatic inferences have been made. In the northwest side chamber there are two temperate episodes separated by periods of colder climate. The temperate episodes are thought to represent temperatures similar to those of today at the latitude of Westbury. For the two cold periods the first is indicative of cool dry conditions whilst the latter suggests a climatic regime considerably colder. If tentative correlation is made between the two chambers at the end of the second cold period, it may be demonstrated that this is followed by a further warm event. Andrews (*ibid*) suggests that there may therefore be more than one fully temperate or interglacial event recorded in the Westbury sequence. However in the light of the recent work on the Greenland Ice Core Project (GRIP Members 1993) it can be seen that there may be far more climatic diversity within temperate isotopic stages than previously thought. Whether the Westbury sequence contains one or more temperate stages, it is certain that the climatic complexity, extrapolated from the small mammal assemblages at the site, indicates that the *Arvicola* faunas of the Cromerian Complex (Table 1) were not developing in a pollen biozone at the end of the Cromerian *sensu stricto* (Stuart and West 1976; Stuart 1988), but belong to one or more fully interglacial stages.

Flint tools have been found at the site (Bishop 1975) but have been the subject of some controversy as to whether they were man-made or not (cf. Cook 1983). The problem

is that the flint in the Westbury sediments is chemically altered by alkaline solution (Schmalz 1960) which has made identification of the pieces difficult. The assemblage has, however, been re-examined recently by a group of experts (C. Stringer pers. comm.), who have verified its authenticity and confirmed the view of Bishop (1982), who found it difficult to explain the presence of the flint on geological grounds.

2.7.   WIVENHOE TM 005 235 ESSEX

The site at Wivenhoe is in a gravel pit located near the southern edge of the Tendring Plateau (Fig. 1), approximately two km from the River Colne. The site is now regarded as the type locality for the Wivenhoe Gravel, which is chronologically the third of the four terrace formations that constitute the Low-level Kesgrave subgroup (Fig. 8) (Bridgland 1988; 1994). This subgroup has been recently described as the Colchester Formation (Whiteman and Rose 1992), although this particular utilisation of stratigraphic nomenclature would seem superfluous given the formation status advocated for individual terrace gravels within the subgroup (Bridgland 1994). The Wivenhoe/Cooks Green Gravel terrace formation can be shown to post-date the Ardleigh/Oakley Gravel (Bridgland *et al.* 1990), which is dated to the Cromerian Complex, and pre-dates the St. Osyth/Holland Formation, which is correlated with the Anglian glaciation.

At the site, fossiliferous sediments in the form of an organic silty clay are interbedded with the Wivenhoe Gravel (Bridgland 1988). Pollen, plant macrofossils and insect remains have been recovered from the unit. The results from preliminary analyses of this material are indicative of boreal forest vegetation of a type found in many interglacial and interstadial sequences and can not be used for chronological correlation. Two small undiagnostic flint flakes were also recovered from the silty clay during sampling.

The site at Wivenhoe is unequivocally pre-Anglian as demonstrated by correlation of fluvial terraces within the Low-level Kesgrave Subgroup and by clast lithological analysis. However further work is needed at the site to ascertain whether it falls into the Boxgrove/Westbury/High Lodge group.

2.8.   KENT'S CAVERN SX 934 641 DEVON

This site is currently being re-investigated, but the information given here is mainly from earlier published work. The cave system is cut in Devonian Limestone and has a complex stratigraphy that contains archaeology from the Lower Palaeolithic to the Mediaeval Period. The Lower Palaeolithic material consists of bifacial tools including handaxes and miscellaneous flakes. The artefacts are

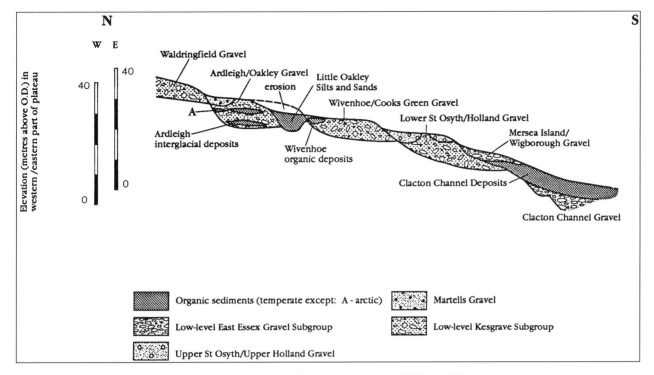

Fig. 8. Idealized section through the Pleistocene deposits of the Tendring Plateau (after Bridgland 1988).

described as archaic by Roe (1981) and typologically fall into his Fordwich/Farnham group. They occur in the breccia below the cave earth as described by Pengelly (1873a; b) and Campbell and Sampson (1971). Sediments at the site have recently been dated using the Uranium-series technique on the stalagmites but the results remain equivocal (P. Berridge pers.comm.). The most reliable age estimate for the Middle Pleistocene deposits and the archaeology is obtained by studying the composition of the mammal fauna, which includes the following species:

Table 3. Biostratigraphically significant mammalian taxa from Kent's Cavern.

Arvicola terrestris cantiana	extinct water vole
Microtus gregalis	extinct pine vole
Ursus deningeri	extinct bear
Homotherium latidens	extinct machairodont cat

Although this is a small fauna, it contains species that are biostratigraphically very important, *Microtus gregaloides* and *Ursus deningeri* have not been found in deposits post-dating the Anglian in Britain and *Homotherium latidens* became extinct throughout Europe during the OIS 12 cold event (A. Turner 1992). There does, however, exist an element of doubt surrounding the context of the remains of

the machairodont cat, as they are associated with sediments correlated with the later Pleistocene (M. Bishop and P. Berridge, pers. comm.) and there exists the possibility that they were introduced to the cave by humans, in a similar fashion to the tooth at Robin Hood's Cave (S. Parfitt, pers. comm.). The presence of *A. terrestris cantiana* is important because it demonstrates that the site is younger than the Cromerian *sensu stricto*. Accordingly the site falls in with the others in this group in terms of broad age estimates.

3.   Middle Pleistocene Occupation of the British Isles: Sites post-dating the Anglian Cold Stage

3.1.   INTRODUCTION

According to the 1973 Geological Society of London Quaternary time scale (Mitchell *et al.* 1973) there were two temperate or interglacial events after the Anglian Glaciation, the Hoxnian and the Ipswichian (Table 1). This scheme based on lithostratigraphic subdivision of the Quaternary was supported by palynological work (West 1956; 1957; 1963; C. Turner 1970; 1975; Ventris 1986) and by mammalian biostratigraphy (Stuart 1974; 1982). This sequence was first challenged by Sutcliffe (1975) and in the seminal work of Sutcliffe and Kowalski (1976), and has recently been demonstrated to be oversimplified, vindicating much of Sutcliffe's research. There are now thought to be three

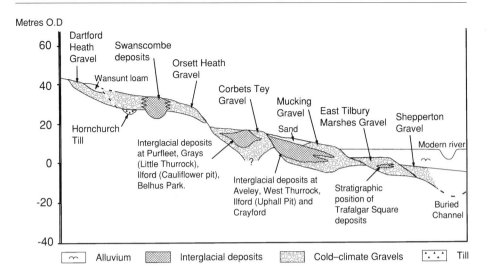

Fig. 9. Idealized transverse section through the terraces of the Lower Thames (after Bridgland 1994).

major temperate and three cold stages between the Anglian and the Ipswichian/Eemian warm stage at c. 125 Kyr BP (Bowen *et al.* 1989; Bridgland 1994). These climatic events correlate with OIS 12 to 5e (Shackleton and Opdyke 1973). The sites discussed below fall into OIS 11 and 9. The important issues that arise from studying these sites are the differences in the taxonomic composition between these faunas and those in the Boxgrove/Westbury group, with a pre-Anglian age. Of equal importance is the fact that sites that have been lumped together as belonging to the Hoxnian Interglacial may well belong to two separate temperate stages.

Later interglacial sediments, not discussed here, are represented at sites attributed to OIS 7 and Substage 5e. These have all been classified in the past as Ipswichian/ Eemian but there is now unequivocal evidence from amino acid ratios and lithostratigraphy (Bowen 1991; Bridgland 1994), which corroborate earlier ideas based on mammalian and molluscan faunas, that two separate temperate episodes are represented. The older one is equivalent to OIS 7 and the younger is the last interglacial.

3.2. SWANSCOMBE TQ 595 745 KENT

The site at Swanscombe is probably the best known of all British Palaeolithic sites. It is located in the Lower Thames Valley (Fig. 1), in the highest terrace of the post-Anglian course of the river, 5 km to the east of Gravesend. The sedimentary sequence is described in detail elsewhere (Waechter 1972; Conway and Waechter 1977; Hubbard 1982; Bridgland 1994) and will only be alluded to briefly in this paper.

The deposits at Barnfield Pit rest upon the Thanet Sand at a height of 23m OD (Fig. 9), they were laid down in a channel formed soon after the diversion of the Thames by the Anglian ice sheet (Bridgland 1988; 1994). The deposits have been divided into the following sequence:

Table 4. Archaeology and Geology at Swanscombe.

Depositional Environment	Unit	Industry
Land derived sediments	Upper Gravel	Acheulean
	Upper Loam	Acheulean
Aggrading stream deposits	Upper Middle Gravel*	Acheulean
	Lower Middle Gravel	Acheulean
Overbank deposits	Lower Loam	Clactonian
Aggrading river deposits	Lower Gravel	Clactonian
* Skull horizon.		

Previous researchers have argued for a substantial hiatus in the Swanscombe sequence at the junction of the Lower Loam and the Lower Middle Gravels. Although there is an erosional contact at this boundary, present research shows it to be the result of a change in stream dynamics rather than a long term event (Bridgland *et al.* 1985). One reason for requiring a major gap in the sedimentary record at this point had its roots in archaeological typology. The lowest two units at Swanscombe contain lithic assemblages designated as Clactonian, overlain by Acheulean artefacts. However, the site at Little Thurrock Globe Pit, in the lower terrace of

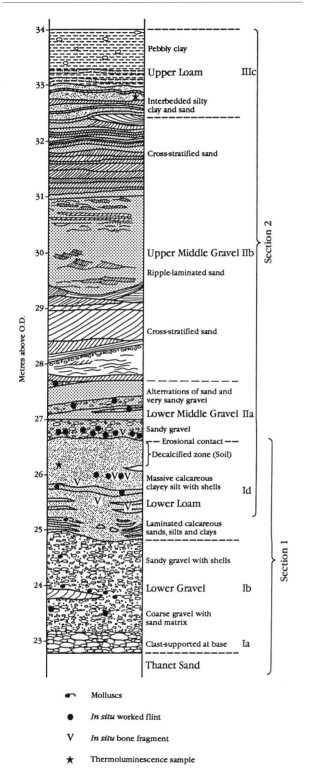

Fig. 10. The sequence at Swanscombe (after Bridgland *et al.* 1985).

the Corbets Tey Formation, also contains Clactonian artefacts. Thus it was necessary to invoke a convoluted scheme of events with the river being at one level depositing the Lower Gravels and Loams, cutting down to the Globe Pit level and then rising again to lay down the sediments containing Acheulean material at Swanscombe (King and Oakley 1936). It has been demonstrated (Bridgland *et al.* 1985) that the Swanscombe deposits represent a single gross upwards fining sedimentary fill (Fig. 10), terminating in periglacial sedimentation and involution and that the temperate sediments at the site represent the first warm event after the Anglian (Bridgland 1994). The age of the Swanscombe sequence is further supported by the clast composition of the Lower and Lower Middle Gravels (Bridgland *et al.* 1985), amino acid ratios consistent with a OIS 11 date (Bowen *et al.* 1989) and the composition of the mammalian fauna which contains none of the Cromerian Complex marker species and sees the appearance of species such as *Stephanorhinus hemitoechus*, *Stephanorhinus kirchbergensis*, *Megaloceros giganteus* and *Bos primigenius* (Stuart 1982).

The site at Swanscombe is probably best known for the refitting hominid skull fragments that were recovered from the Upper Middle Gravel. The occipital bone was discovered in 1935, followed by the left parietal in 1936 and the right parietal in 1955, the latter being poorly preserved (Stringer 1985). The skull is believed to be female with a brain size of about 1300 ml. The overall cranial shape is less angular than more archaic hominids and there are two features that have Neanderthal affinities. Firstly, there is evidence of a developed juxtamastoid eminence at the occipital margins and secondly a slight, double arched occipital torus surmounted by a central depression, a suprainiac fossa (Stringer and Gamble 1993). If the short chronology hypothesis of the occupation of Europe is accepted (Roebroeks and Van Kolfschoten, this volume), then it would mean that the Neanderthal characteristics displayed by the Swanscombe skull developed during the first 100 Kyr after colonization. If these physiognomic changes were the result of adaptation to a colder climate, then it is likely that the early population of hominids in Europe were able to operate and survive in, or close to, the climatic and hence environmental regimes associated with a major cold stage. Such a hypothesis is supported by work at Boxgrove (Roberts 1992; Roberts *et al.*, this volume), at Clacton (see below) and at Kärlich, layer H (Bosinski, this volume).

To conclude, it may be demonstrated from recent work on the Lower Thames (Bridgland 1994) that the assemblages described as Clactonian both pre-date and post-date biface industries in this region. Current re-investigation of the Swanscombe archive has revealed at least one biface from the Lower Gravel (McNabb and Ashton 1992). When this piece is considered with other evidence beginning to emerge from sites like Clacton and Barnham, it appears that the division of British Lower Palaeolithic industries into two separate, culturally distinct entities is an unsustainable concept.

3.3.   EAST FARM BARNHAM TL 875 787 SUFFOLK

The site at East Farm, Barnham (Ashton *et al.* 1994a) is located in an old brick pit 4 km south of Thetford and 24 km north of Bury St Edmunds (Fig. 1). The pit is in a dry valley that runs parallel to the present course of the Little Ouse river valley. The workings cut through temperate climate fluvial deposits which overlie the Lowestoft Till; the solid geology to the south is Cretaceous Chalk and there are also extensive spreads of glacial outwash gravel, predominantly to the north of the site. The first controlled excavations at the site were undertaken by Patterson (1937) and subsequently by Wymer (1985).

The temperate sediments at Barnham were laid down in a post-glacial river system that flowed in a channel developed in glacial outwash gravels. Prior to Ashton's work, the site was portrayed as a classic example of the British Clactonian-Acheulean succession (Wymer 1974). However, recent excavations have shown that debitage from the production of bifaces has been found in the same context, the cobble band (Wymer 1985), as that which contains the classic Clactonian Industry (Ashton *et al.* 1994b). This adds further strength to the argument proposed by Ashton and McNabb (1992), that the Clactonian cannot be viewed as a chronologically significant independent stone working tradition in the Middle Pleistocene. The silt units at the site have yielded rich ichthyofaunas, herpetofaunas and mammalian faunas (Ashton *et al.* 1994a and b). The biostratigraphical evidence from the fauna is consistent with a post-Anglian date; no Cromerian Complex indicators, such as those from the Boxgrove/Westbury group, have been recovered. The presence of *Emys orbicularis*, the European pond tortoise and *Elaphe longissima*, the Aesculapian snake indicate temperatures warmer than the present day. The herpetofauna also supports the view that this site cannot be the same age as Boxgrove, where the herpetofauna temperature signal indicates a less temperate interglacial, that is climatically similar to the current stage. These lines of evidence fit well with Shackleton's (1987) interglacial temperature histories (Table 1). Amino acid ratios from the site are consistent with a date that equates to OIS 11 (Bowen in Ashton *et al.* 1994a).

3.4.   CLACTON TM 148 128 TO TM 175 143 ESSEX

Pleistocene sediments at Clacton (Fig. 1) were first described early last century (Brown 1840), the associated

Palaeolithic archaeological material was first recognised by Kenworthy (1898), since which time the sites at Clacton have been accorded international significance for their archaeology, stratigraphy and palaeontology.

The exposures run from Lion Point in the southwest to Clacton-on-Sea in the northeast (Fig. 11). The archaeological flintwork has been collected and excavated from a series of channels that are cut through the London Clay and Middle Pleistocene gravels of the pre-diversion Thames-Medway fluvial system. The main channel of the Clacton sequence was formerly exposed in the West Cliff, Clacton-on-Sea (TM 174 143). Here the channel is over 400m wide and has a maximum depth of 15m (Bridgland *et al.* 1988). At this location the northwestern edge of the channel has been observed cutting through the Lower Holland Gravels, and at its feather edge the channel is overlain by post-diversion gravels of the Thames-Medway river. The stratigraphy of the main channel at Clacton is described by Warren (1955) (see Bridgland 1994 for a full list of references).

In brief the basal units of the channel are freshwater sediments, comprising fluviatile gravels and sands, with occasional peaty lenses. The pioneering palynological work of Pike and Godwin (1953) led to these units being assigned to biozone Ho II (Turner and Kerney 1971). Sedimentologically the freshwater series is divided into the Lower and Upper Freshwater Beds, both units contain Clactonian artefacts and the lower bed is particularly rich in faunal remains. Important faunal elements include *Trogontherium cuvieri*, *Palaeoloxodon antiquus*, *Stephanorhinus hemitoechus*, *Stephanorhinus kirchbergensis* and *Dama dama* "*clactoniana*". Overlying the Freshwater Beds lie the Estuarine Beds. These comprise loams, marls and clays with lenses of shelly sand and estuarine peat. The estuarine beds contain little mammalian fauna and artefacts are rare. Turner (Turner and Kerney 1971) places this unit in biozone Ho III. It is as well to emphasize that the main channel at Clacton is the only place where this stratigraphic succession is observed.

Two controlled excavations have been undertaken at Clacton to the east of the main Clacton Channel, the first at Jaywick Sands (Oakley and Leakey 1937) and more recently at the Golf Course site (Singer *et al.* 1973). The stratigraphy recorded at the Golf Course site (summarized in Roe 1981) is interpreted as being deposited at the end of the Anglian, as there is evidence of periglacial phenomena, and in the early part of the ensuing temperate episode. The units containing artefacts are all thought to pre-date the deposition of the main channel sediments. The lithic assemblages from Clacton are pre-dominantly composed of flaking debitage from core reduction, following a tradition (McNabb 1992) that runs through the British Lower Palaeolithic from c.500 Kyr BP to c.300 Kyr BP (Imbrie

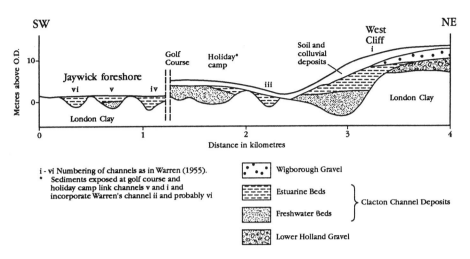

Fig. 11. Section through the Clacton area, showing the various Clacton Channel occurences (modified from Warren 1955).

et al. 1984). Keeley (1977) was able to conjoin over 20 flakes from the Golf Course Industry and found use-wear traces indicative of butchery and wood working on some of the flakes. Recently doubt has been cast on the status of the Clactonian as a separate cultural tradition (Ashton et al. 1994b) and evidence from Clacton in the form of two bifaces from Warren's collections, made at Lion Point, add support to this view (McNabb and Ashton 1992). Notes from the Warren archive also mention three bifaces from the "*Elephas*" *antiquus* bed at West Cliff, in the main channel, this bed is without doubt part of the freshwater series from the channel. Thus, although the predominant technique of lithic reduction is core based, there is also an unequivocal biface presence at the site. This revelation, occurring as it does at the Clacton type site seriously calls into doubt the validity of retaining the name Clactonian.

The sediments at Clacton were deposited from the end of the Anglian into the following interglacial (Table 1), the earliest archaeology being dated to the late Anglian. The deposits are correlated with Swanscombe on the basis of molluscan biostratigraphy (C. Turner and Kerney 1971), the mapping of long down stream profile gradients between the sites (Bridgland 1994) and on amino acid ratios (Bowen et al. 1989).

3.5.   HOXNE TM 176 769 SUFFOLK

The site at Hoxne is the type locality of the Hoxnian Interglacial Stage in Britain (Fig. 1). The site is included here as a note because there already exists a voluminous amount of literature on the site (Wymer 1983; 1985 and

Singer et al. 1993). The importance of the site to this paper is twofold. Firstly there is a growing body of opinion that believes the sediments at Hoxne to date from a separate temperate stage to Swanscombe and Barnham, based on amino acid ratios (Bowen et al. 1989; Bowen 1991) and is therefore equivalent in time to sites such as Little Thurrock, Globe Pit. There exists little evidence either to support or contradict this view. The faunas from OIS 11 and OIS 9 in terms of taxonomic composition are very similar; the archaeology found at Hoxne has been shown in this paper to be prevalent in the British Isles for over a quarter of a million years and is thus redundant as dating device. Secondly recent work on the flintwork from High Lodge and the Hoxne Upper Industry (White 1993) has shown them to have very definite technological similarities, but that these are the result of reduction strategies rather than any similarity in age (Fig. 12). The palynological work at the site (West 1956) demonstrated a continuous pollen profile from late glacial into the following temperate stage. When this evidence was considered in conjunction with the supposed mode of origin of the Hoxne deposit – in a kettle hole left by the retreating Anglian ice sheet – the case for a Stage 11 date looked quite strong, and was subsequently further strengthened by C. Turner's (1970) work on the pollen from Mark's Tey. However Bowen, arguing in favour of the amino acid ratios, suggests that the depression at Hoxne could have formed by solution of the underlying calcareous strata (Bowen 1991). Further more detailed work is required on the small mammal assemblages from the site to resolve this debate.

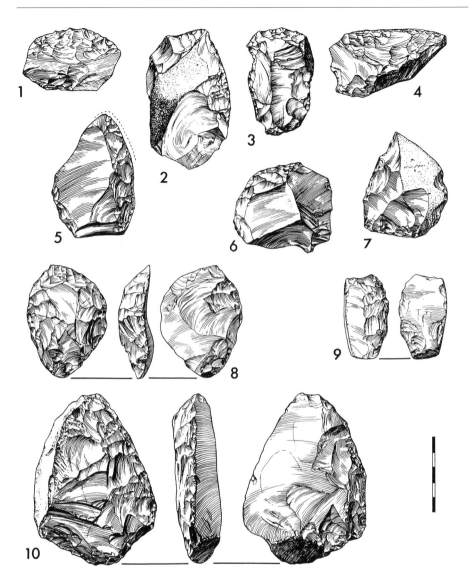

Fig. 12. Hoxne industry scrapers (from Wymer 1983). Scale in cm.

3.6.   BEECHES PIT, WEST STOW TL 798 719 SUFFOLK

The site at Beeches Pit is located 11 km to the southwest of Barnham in west Suffolk (Fig. 1). The exposures are in an old brickyard (Preece *et al.* 1991) and are currently being re-investigated by a multidisciplinary team from the Quaternary Research Association and a team of archaeologists from Liverpool University, under the direction of John Gowlett. The sedimentary sequence consists of units of clay and silty clay overlying a chalky diamicton, identified as the Lowestoft Till. In parts of the old workings a calcareous tufaceous deposit is revealed overlying the diamicton and beneath the clays. The tufa contains a rich temperate mollusc fauna that indicates formation in spring fed pools in a temperate forest (Kerney 1976, Preece *et al. ibid*). The mollusc fauna is very similar to that from Hitchin, Hertfordshire (Kerney 1956), and contains species found only at these two sites in the British Isles, although continental European correlatives are known from interglacial tufas in France (Rousseau 1987; Rousseau and Puisségur 1990). A mammalian fauna has been recovered from an organic clay band (unit 3) above the chalky diamicton and from the tufaceous deposits (Parfitt, in Preece *et al.* 1991). The fauna is indicative of a temperate woodland environment in the tufa and the lower

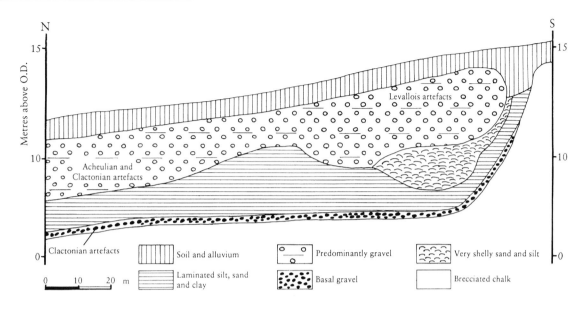

Fig. 13. Idealized section through the deposits at Purfleet (modified from Hollin 1977).

part of unit 3, while the upper part of unit 3 indicates a change to more open grassland conditions. The mammalian fauna composition is similar to that from other "Hoxnian" sites, especially that from nearby Barnham, However, there are marked differences in the tooth morphology of the water vole *Arvicola terrestris cantiana* at the two sites (S. Parfitt, pers. comm.), which given the proximity of the two samples to each other, are interpreted as indicating that the sites are of different ages.

The archaeology at the site consists of bifaces and flakes. These have mostly been collected during section cutting, but the 1993 and 1994 seasons of excavation at the site have also produced material, including refitting flakes and a refitted end shock biface (Gowlett pers. comm.).

3.7.   LITTLE THURROCK, GLOBE PIT TQ 626 783 ESSEX

The site at Globe Pit is located to the north of the River Thames in the terrace of the Lynch Hill/Corbets Tey Formation (Fig. 1). This terrace occurs below the terrace containing the Swanscombe interglacial sediments (Fig. 9). Clactonian flakes and cores have been recovered from the gravel underlying the temperate brickearths, Bridgland (1994) attributes these two units to OIS 10 and OIS 9 respectively (Bridgland and Harding 1993). Wymer (1985) suggests that the brickearths may also contain "mint" Clactonian flakes as well. The brickearth is thought to be the same unit as that found at Little Thurrock, Grays (Zeuner 1959), which contained a rich mammalian fauna

but no artefacts. However, recent re-investigation of this fauna by S.A. Parfitt (pers. comm.) has demonstrated the presence of cut marks on some of the bones. The importance of this site is that it shows that the Clactonian knapping tradition is not restricted to a single stage or interglacial and if, as some researchers believe (Wymer pers. comm.), it exists as an separate entity from the Acheulean, then it both pre- and post-dates it (Bridgland and Harding 1993).

3.8.   PURFLEET: BLUELANDS, GREENLANDS, ESSO AND BOTANY PITS, ESSEX. (FROM TQ 556-570 AND 785-786)

These pits, which are cut down to the chalk, contain Pleistocene fluvial sediments assigned to the Corbets Tey Formation (Bridgland 1994), which are in turn overlain by slope deposits (Figs 1, 9). Lithic material described as Acheulean, Clactonian (Wymer 1968; 1985) and Levallois (Palmer 1975) has been recovered from these sites. The general Purfleet sequence has Clactonian material in the basal gravel, succeeded by Clactonian and Acheulean artefacts (Fig. 13) from the gravel above the temperate sediments; higher up in this gravel unit a Levallois flake was recovered (Palmer *ibid*). At Botany Pit the basal gravel contains handaxes and may correlate with the gravel above the interglacial deposits at Bluelands and Greenlands (Bridgland 1994). The deposits range in age from OIS 10 for the basal gravel, to OIS 8 for the upper part of the gravel sequence and conform to Bridgland's (1994) model for terrace formation. The interglacial sediments are dated to OIS 9. Mention must be made here, however, of the high value amino acid ratios obtained on molluscs from the temperate sediments (Miller *et al.* 1979; Bowen *et al.* 1989). These ratios suggested a date within OIS 13 but this figure is hard to reconcile with the lithostratigraphical evidence, as the Thames was not diverted into this course until the latter part of the Anglian, which is correlated with OIS 12 (Table 1).

4.   Conclusion

The earliest evidence for the human occupation of Britain occurs around half a million years ago in an interglacial/temperate episode that immediately pre-dates the Anglian Glaciation. This stage is as yet unnamed in Britain.

The earliest occupants of Britain exploited a wide range of geographic areas and environments. There is archaeological evidence for human occupation of Britain both from cold climate deposits laid down during the Anglian and from sediments dating to the end of the Anglian. Thus hominids may have been present in Britain throughout the duration of the glacial. This point poses interesting questions about the adaptability of Middle Pleistocene hominids.

It is well known that the stratigraphic record for the British Isles between the Anglian and the Ipswichian has been oversimplified, primarily by relying too heavily on palynological work. There is now evidence that the two warm periods following the Anglian contain similar vegetational and mammalian signatures. This has led to sites of different ages being erroneously grouped together. It has been suggested recently (Bowen *et al.* 1989; Bowen 1991) that the site at Hoxne may be a whole climate cycle younger than that at Swanscombe. If this is the case then the interglacial following the Anglian will need to be renamed.

During the period that covers the initial occupation, there are both biface and flake tool industries: these industries are not mutually exclusive in the archaeological record. There is no temporal ordering between these industries, both traditions carry on throughout the rest of the Middle Pleistocene.

The so-called Clactonian Industry can be shown to pre-date and post-date biface industries after the Anglian, therefore the concept of the Acheulean succeeding the Clactonian in Britain is false. We therefore suggest that the initial Middle Pleistocene occupants of Britain utilized both biface and core reduction techniques throughout this time period. Current evidence suggests that the different techniques can be neither culturally or temporally distinguished. Thus to continue to describe these techniques in terms that imply both culture and time is misleading and accordingly, it is suggested that the terms Acheulean and Clactonian should be abandoned forthwith.

Acknowledgements

The authors are grateful to Simon Lewis (Centre for Environmental Change and Quaternary Research, Cheltenham) and Simon Parfitt (Institute of Archaeology, University College London) for critically reviewing this manuscript. We also thank John Wymer, Nick Ashton and the editors of the Journal of Quaternary Science and the Proceedings of the Geologists' Association for permission to reproduce previously published figures.

note

1 National grid reference coordinates.

references

Andrews, H.	1930	On some fossil mammals of western Suffolk, *Transactions of the Suffolk Naturalists' Society* 1, 195-199.
Andrews, P.	1990	*Owls, Caves and Fossils*. London: Natural History Museum Publications.
Anon	1968	High Lodge Palaeolithic industry, *Nature* 220, 1065-1066.
ApSimon, A.M., C.S. Gamble, M.L. Shackley	1977	Pleistocene raised beaches on Portsdown, Hampshire, *Proceedings of the Hampshire Field Club and Archaeological Society* 33, 17-32.
Ashton, N.M.	1992	The High Lodge Flint Industries. In: N.M. Ashton, J. Cook, S.G. Lewis and J. Rose (eds), *High Lodge: Excavations by G. de G. Sieveking 1962-68 and J. Cook 1988*, 124-163, London: British Museum Press.
Ashton, N.M., J. McNabb	1992	The interpretation and context of the High Lodge industries. In: N.M. Ashton, J. Cook, S.G. Lewis and J. Rose (eds), *High Lodge: Excavations by G. de G. Sieveking 1962-68 and J. Cook 1988*, 164-168, London: British Museum Press.
Ashton, N.M., P. Dean, J. McNabb	1991	Flaked flakes: what, where, when and why?, *Lithics* 12, 1-11.
Ashton, N.M., J. Cook, S.G. Lewis, J. Rose (eds)	1992	*High Lodge: Excavations by G. de G. Sieveking 1962-68 and J. Cook 1988*. London: British Museum Press.
Ashton, N.M., D.Q. Bowen, J.A. Holman, C.O. Hunt, B.G. Irving, R.A. Kemp, S.G. Lewis, J. McNabb, S.A. Parfitt, M.B. Seddon	1994a	Excavation at the Lower Palaeolithic site at East Farm Barnham, Suffolk: 1989-1992, *Journal of the Geological Society* 151, 599-605.
Ashton, N.M., J. McNabb, S.G. Lewis, S.A. Parfitt	1994b	Contemporaneity of Clactonian and Acheulian flint industries at Barnham, Suffolk, *Antiquity* 68 (260), 585-589.
Bergman, C.A., M.B. Roberts	1988	The Lower Palaeolithic site at Boxgrove, West Sussex, England, *Revue Archéologique de Picardie* 1-2 (numéro spécial), 105-114.
Bergman, C.A., M.B. Roberts, S.N. Collcutt, P. Barlow	1990	Refitting and spatial analysis of artefacts from Quarry 2 at the Middle Pleistocene Acheulian site of Boxgrove, West Sussex, England. In: E. Cziesla, S. Eickhoff, N. Arts and D. Winter (eds), *The Big Puzzle*, 265-282, Bonn: Holos.
Binford, L.R.	1989	*Debating Archaeology*. San Diego: Academic Press.

| Bishop, M.J. | 1975 | Earliest record of Man's presence in Britain, *Nature* 253, 95-97. |

| | 1982 | The mammal fauna of the early Middle Pleistocene cavern infill site of Westbury-Sub-Mendip, Somerset, *Special papers of the Palaeontological Association* 28, 1-108. |

| Bogaard van den, C., P. van den Bogaard, H.-U. Schminke | 1989 | Quartärgeologisch-tephrostratigraphische Neuaufnahme und Interpretation des Pleistozän-profils Kärlich, *Eiszeitalter und Gegenwart* 39, 62-86. |

| Bonifay, E., B. Vandermeersch (eds) | 1991 | *Les Premiers Européens*. Paris: Editions du C.T.H.S. |

| Bordes, F. | 1961 | *Typologie du Paléolithique ancien et moyen*. Mémoire 1. Université de Bordeaux. |

| Bosinski, G., | this volume | The earliest occupation of Europe: Western Central Europe. |

| Bowen, D.Q. | 1991 | Amino Acid Geochronology. In: S.G. Lewis, C.A. Whiteman and D.R. Bridgland (eds), *Central East Anglia and the Fen Basin,* Field Guide, 21-24, London: Quaternary Research Association. |

| | 1992 | Aminostratigraphy of non-marine Pleistocene mollusca in Southern Britain, *Sveriges Geologiska Undersökning* 81, 65-67. |

| Bowen, D.Q., G.A. Sykes | 1988 | Correlation of marine events and glaciations on the northeast Atlantic margin, *Philosophical Transactions of the Royal Society of London* B318, 619-635. |

| Bowen, D.Q., S. Hughes, G.A. Sykes, G.H. Miller | 1989 | Land-sea correlations in the Pleistocene based on isoleucine epimerization in non-marine molluscs, *Nature* 340, 49-51. |

| Bridgland, D.R. | 1988 | The Pleistocene fluvial stratigraphy and palaeogeography of Essex, *Proceedings of the Geologists Association* 99, 291-314. |

| | 1994 | *Quaternary of the Thames*. London: Chapman and Hall. |

| Bridgland, D.R., S.G. Lewis | 1991 | Introduction to the Pleistocene geology and drainage of the Lark Valley. In: S.G. Lewis, C.A. Whiteman and D.R. Bridgland (eds), *Central East Anglia and the Fen Basin,* Field Guide, 37-44, London: Quaternary Research Association. |

| Bridgland, D.R., P. Harding | 1993 | Middle Pleistocene Thames terrace deposits at Globe Pit, Little Thurrock, and their contained Clactonian industry, *Proceedings of the Geologists' Association* 104, 263-283. |

| Bridgland, D.R., P.L. Gibbard, P. Harding, *et al.* | 1985 | New information and results from recent excavations at Barnfield Pit, Swanscombe, *Quaternary Newsletter* 46, 25-39. |

| Bridgland, D.R., P. Allen, A.P. Currant, *et al.* | 1988 | Report of the Geologists' Association field meeting in northeast Essex, May 22nd-24th, 1987, *Proceedings of the Geologists' Association* 99, 315-333. |

| Bridgland, D.R., P.L. Gibbard, R.C. Preece | 1990 | The geology and significance of the interglacial sediments at Little Oakley, Essex, *Philosophical Transactions of the Royal Society of London* B328, 307-339. |

| Bridgland, D.R., S.G. Lewis, J.J. Wymer | 1995 | Middle Pleistocene stratigraphy and archaeology around Mildenhall and Icklingham, Suffolk: report on the Geologists' Association Field Meeting, 27th June, 1992, *Proceedings of the Geologists' Association* 106, 57-69. |

Brown, J.   1840   Notice of a fluvio-marine deposit containing mammalian-remains occurring in the parish of Little Clacton on the Essex coast, *Magazine of Natural History, Series 2* 4, 197-201.

Campbell, J.B., C.G. Sampson   1971   A new analysis of Kent's Cavern, Devonshire, England, *University of Oregon Anthropological Papers* 3.

Conway, B.W., J. d'A Waechter   1977   Lower Thames and Medway valleys - Barnfield Pit, Swanscombe, England. In: E.R. Shephard-Thorn and J.J. Wymer (eds), *South East England and the Thames Valley,* 38-44, Guide Book for Excursion A5, X Inqua Congress, Birmingham. Geoabstracts: Norwich.

Cook, J.   1983   Die Forschungsarbeit an der Fundstelle Westbury-sub-Mendip, Somerset/England, *Ethnogr.-Archäol. Zeitschrift* 24, 528-531.

Cook, J., N.M. Ashton, G.R. Coope, C.O. Hunt, S.G. Lewis, J. Rose   1991   High Lodge, Mildenhall, Suffolk (TL 739754). In: S.G. Lewis, C.A. Whiteman and D.R. Bridgland (eds), *Central East Anglia and the Fen Basin,* Field Guide, 21-24, London: Quaternary Research Association.

Coxon, P.   1979   *Pleistocene Environmental History in Central East Anglia.* Ph.D. thesis, University of Cambridge.

Coulson, S.D.   1990   *Middle Palaeolithic Industries of Great Britain, Studies in Modern Archaeology*, Vol. 4. Bonn: Holos.

Evernden, J.F., G.H. Curtis, R. Kistler   1957   Potassium argon dating of Pleistocene volcanics, *Quaternaria* 4, 1-5.

Frechen, J., H.J. Lippolt   1965   Kalium-Argon-Daten zum Alter des Laacher Vulkanismus, der Rheinterrassen und die Eiszeiten, *Eiszeitalter und Gegenwart* 16, 5-30.

Gamble, C.S.   1986   *The Palaeolithic Settlement of Europe.* Cambridge: Cambridge University Press.

Gibbard, P.L., S.M. Peglar   1989   Palynology of the fossiliferous deposits at Witham on the Hill, Lincolnshire. In: D.H. Keen (ed.), *The Pleistocene of the West Midlands,* Field Guide, 131-133, Cambridge: Quaternary Research Association.

Greenland Ice-core Project (GRIP) Members   1993   Climate instability during the last interglacial period recorded in the GRIP ice core, *Nature* 364, 203-207.

Hollin, J.T.   1977   Thames interglacial sites, Ipswichian sea levels and Antarctic ice surges, *Boreas* 6, 33-52.

Holm, J., L. Larsson   this volume   The earliest occupation of Europe: Scandinavia.

Hubbard, R.N.L.B.   1982   The environmental evidence from Swanscombe and its implications for Palaeolithic archaeology. In: P.E. Leach (ed.), *Archaeology in Kent to AD 1500,* Council for British Archaeology, Research Report 48, 3-7.

Hunt, C.O., J. Rose   1992   Recycled palynomorphs from the High Lodge clayey-silts. In: N.M. Ashton, J. Cook, S.G. Lewis and J. Rose (eds), *High Lodge: Excavations by G. de G. Sieveking 1962-68 and J. Cook 1988,* 103-108, London: British Museu Press.

Imbrie, J.,   1984   The orbital theory of Pleistocene climate: support from a revised chronology of the
  J.D. Hayes,   marine O[18] record. In: A. Berger, J. Imbrie, J.D. Haynes, G. Kukla and B. Saltzman (eds),
  D.G. Martinson,   *Milankovitch and climate* Part 1, 269-306, Dordrecht: Reidel.
  A. MacIntyre,
  A.C. Micks,
  J.J. Morley,
  N.G. Pisias,
  W.L. Prell,
  N.J. Shackleton

Jong, J. de   1988   Climatic variability during the past three million years, as indicated by vegetational
                                   evolution in northwest Europe and with emphasis on data from The Netherlands. *Phil
                                   Trans R Soc Lond* B318: 603-617.

Keeley, L.H.   1977   *An experimental study of microwear traces on selected British Palaeolithic implements.*
                                   Ph.D. thesis, University of Oxford.

Kenworthy, J.W.   1898   Note in *Essex Naturalist* 10, 406.

Kerney, M.P.   1956   An interglacial tufa near Hitchen, Hertfordshire, *Proceedings of the Geologists' Associa-
                                   tion* 70, 322-337.

                         1976   Mollusca from an interglacial tufa in East Anglia, with the description of *Lyrodiscus
                                   Pilsbry* (Gastopoda: Zonitidae), *Journal of Conchology* 29, 47-50.

King, W.B.R.,   1936   The Pleistocene succession in the lower part of the Thames valley, *Proceedings of the
  K.P. Oakley   Prehistoric Society* 1, 52-76.

Koenigswald, W. von   1973   Veränderungen in der Kleinsäuger fauna von Mitteleuropa zwischen Cromer und Eem
                                   (Pleistozän), *Eiszeitalter und Gegenwart* 23/24, 159-167.

Koenigswald, W. von,   in press The *Mimomys-Arvicola* boundary and the enamel thickness quotient (SDQ) of *Arvicola* as
  T. van Kolfschoten   stratigraphic markers in the Middle Pleistocene, *Proceedings of the 'Cromer-Symposium'*,
                                   Norwich, 1990.

Kolfschoten, T. van   1990   The evolution of the mammal fauna in the Netherlands and the Middle Rhine area (West
                                   Germany) during the late Middle Pleistocene, *Mededelingen Rijks Geologische Dienst*
                                   43(3), 1-69.

Kolfschoten, T. van,   in press Early Middle Pleistocene Mammalian Faunas from Kärlich and Miesenheim I and
  E. Turner   their biostratigraphical implications, *Proceedings of the 'Cromer-Symposium'*, Norwich
                                   1990.

Lewis, S.G.   1992   High Lodge - stratigraphy and depositional environments. In: N.M. Ashton, J. Cook,
                                   S.G. Lewis and J. Rose (eds), *High Lodge: Excavations by G. de G. Sieveking 1962-68
                                   and J. Cook 1988*, 51-85, London: British Museum Press.

                         1993   *The status of the Wolstonian glaciation in the English Midlands and East Anglia.* Ph.D.
                                   thesis, University of London.

Lister, A.M.   1989   Mammalian faunas and the Wolstonian debate. In: D.H. Keen (ed.), *The Pleistocene
                                   of the West Midlands,* Field Guide, 5-12, Cambridge: Quaternary Research
                                   Association.

Maddy, D.,   1991   The Pleistocene deposits at Snitterfield, Warwickshire, *Proceedings of the Geological
  S.G. Lewis   Association* 102(4), 289-300.

Maddy, D.,   1994   Reappraisal of Middle Pleistocene fluvial deposits near Brandon, Warwickshire and their
    G.R. Coope,   significance for the Wolston glacial sequence, *Journal of the Geological Society, London*
    P.L. Gibbard,   151, 221-233.
    C.P. Green,
    S.G. Lewis

McNabb, J.   1992   *The Clactonian: British Lower Palaeolithic technology in biface and non-biface assem-
                                                blages.* Ph.D. thesis, University of London.

McNabb, J.,   1992   The Cutting Edge, Bifaces in the Clactonian, *Lithics* 13, 4-10.
    N.M. Ashton

Miller, G.H.,   1979   Aminostratigraphy of UK Pleistocene deposits, *Nature* 281, 539-543.
    J.T. Hollin,
    J. Andrews

Mitchell, G.F.,   1973   *A correlation of Quaternary deposits in the British Isles.* London: Geological Society of
    L.F. Penny,   London Special Report Number 4.
    F.W. Shotton,
    R.G. West

Moir, J. Reid   1938   Four flint implements *Antiquaries Journal* 18, 258-261.

Oakley, K.P.,   1937   Report on excavations at Jaywick Sands, Essex (1934), with some observations on the
    M. Leakey   Clactonian Industry, and on the fauna and geological significance of the Clacton channel,
                                                Proceedings of the Prehistoric Society 3, 217-260.

Palmer, S.   1975   A Palaeolithic site at North Road, Purfleet, Essex, *Transactions of the Essex Archaeol-
                                                ogical Society* 7, 1-13.

Patterson, T.T.   1937   Studies in The Palaeolithic Succession in England: no.I., The Barnham Sequence, *Pro-
                                                ceedings of the Prehistoric Society* 3, 87-135.

Pengelly, W.   1873a   Ninth report of the Committee for exploring Kent's Cavern, Devonshire, *British Asso-
                                                ciation for the Advancement of Science: Report 1873,* 198-209.

                                    1873b   The Flint and Chert Implements found in Kent's Cavern, Torquay, Devonshire, *British
                                                Association for the Advancement of Science: Report 1873*, 209-214.

Perrin, R.M.S.,   1979   Lithology of the Chalky Boulder Clay, *Nature* 245, 101-104.
    J. Rose,
    H. Davies

Pike, K.,   1953   The interglacial at Clacton-on-Sea, Essex, *Quarterly Journal of the Geological Society*
    H. Godwin   108, 261-272.

Preece, R.C.,   1990   The Pleistocene sea-level and neotectonic history of the eastern Solent, southern England,
    J.D. Scourse,   *Philosophical Transactions of the Royal Society of London* B328, 425-477.
    S.D. Houghton,
    K.L. Knudsen,
    D.N. Penney

Preece, R.C.,   1991   Beeches Pit, West Stow, Suffolk. In: S.G. Lewis, C.A. Whiteman and D.R. Bridgland
    S.G. Lewis,   (eds), *Central East Anglia and the Fen Basin*, Field Guide, 94-104, London: Quaternary
    J.J. Wymer,   Research Association.
    D.R. Bridgland,
    S.A. Parfitt

Raynal, J.-P.,   this   Tephrofacts and the first human occupation of the French Massif Central.
   Magoga, L.,   volume
   Bindon, P.

Roberts, M.B.   1986   Excavation of a Lower Palaeolithic site at Amey's Eartham Pit, Boxgrove, West Sussex:
                                        A preliminary report, *Proceedings of the Prehistoric Society* 52, 215-245.

                           1990   Amey's Eartham Pit, Boxgrove. In: C. Turner (ed.), *The Cromer Symposium, Norwich
                                        1990*, Field excursion guide, 62-67, Cambridge.

                           1992   Boxgrove: The Lower Palaeolithic site in Amey's Eartham Pit (SU 924 085). In *The
                                        Archaeology of Chichester and District* (ed S. Woodward). Chichester: Chichester District
                                        Council. 21-24.

                           1994   How old is Boxgrove Man? Reply to Bowen and Sykes. *Nature* 371: 751

Roberts, M.B.,   1994   A hominid tibia from Middle Pleistocene sediments at Boxgrove, UK, *Nature* 369, 311-
   C.B. Stringer,   313.
   S.A. Parfitt

Roe, D.A.   1968   *A Gazeteer of British Lower and Middle Palaeolithic Sites*. Council for British Archaeol-
                                        ogy Research Report No. 8.

                           1981   *The Lower and Middle Palaeolithic Periods in Britain*. London: Routledge and Kegan Paul

Roebroeks, W.   1994   Updating the Earliest Occupation of Europe, *Current Anthropology* 35(3), 301-305.

Roebroeks, W.,   1994   The earliest occupation of Europe: a short chronology, *Antiquity* 68, 489-503.
   T. van Kolfschoten

Roebroeks, W.,   this   The earliest occupation of Europe: A reappraisal of artefactual and chronological
   T. van Kolfschoten   volume   evidence.

Roebroeks, W.,   1992   Dense forests, cold steppes, and the Palaeolithic settlement of northern Europe, *Current
   N.J. Conard,   Anthropology* 33(5), 551-586.
   T. van Kolfschoten

Rose, J.   1987   Status of the Wolstonian glaciation in the British Quaternary, *Quaternary Newsletter* 53,
                                        1-9.

                           1989   Tracing the Baginton-Lillington Sands and Gravels from the West Midlands to East
                                        Anglia. In: D.H. Keen(ed.), *The Pleistocene of the West Midlands*, Field Guide, 131-133,
                                        Cambridge: Quaternary Research Association, 102-110.

                           1992   High Lodge-regional context and geological background. In: N.M. Ashton, J. Cook,
                                        S.G. Lewis and J. Rose (eds), *High Lodge: Excavations by G. de G. Sieveking 1962-68
                                        and J. Cook 1988*, 13-24, London: British Museum Press.

                           1994   Major river systems of central and southern Britain during the Early and Middle Pleis-
                                        tocene, *Terra Nova* 6, 435-443.

Rose, J.,   1992   In: N.M. Ashton, J. Cook, S.G. Lewis and J. Rose (eds), *High Lodge: Excavations by
   H. Davies,   G. de G. Sieveking 1962-68 and J. Cook 1988*, 94-102, London: British Museum Press.
   S.G. Lewis

Rousseau, D.D.   1987   Les associations malacologique forestiere des tufs 'Holsteiniens' de la France septen-
                                        trionale. Une application du concept de biome, *Bulletin de la Centre Géomorphologique*
                                        32, 9-18, CNRS.

Rousseau, D.D., J.J. Puisségur — 1990 — Phylogenèse et biogéographie de *Retinella* (*Lyrodiscus*) Pilsbry (Gastropoda: Zonitidae), *Geobios* 23, 57-70.

Schmalz, R.F. — 1960 — Flint and patination of flint artefacts, *Proceedings of the Prehistoric Society* 26, 44-49.

Shackleton, N.J. — 1987 — Oxygen isotopes, ice volume and sea level, *Quaternary Science Reviews* 6, 183-190.

Shackleton, N.J., N.D. Opdyke — 1973 — Oxygen isotope and palaeomagnetic stratigraphy of equatorial Pacific core V28-238: Oxygen isotope temperatures and ice volumes on a 10^5 and a 10^6 year scale, *Quaternary Research* 3, 39-55.

Shotton, F.W. — 1953 — The Pleistocene deposits of the area between Coventry, Rugby and Leamington and their bearing upon the topographic development of the Midlands, *Philosophical Transactions of the Royal Society of London* B237, 209-260.

1968 — The Pleistocene succession around Brandon. *Philosophical Transactions of the Royal Society of London* B254, 387-400.

Shotton, F.W., D.H. Keen, G.R. Coope, A.P. Currant, P.L. Gibbard, M. Aalto, S.M. Peglar, J.E. Robinson — 1993 — The Middle Pleistocene deposits of Waverley Wood Pit, Warwickshire, England, *Journal of Quaternary Science* 8, 293-325.

Šibrava, V., D.Q. Bowen, G.M. Richmond (eds) — 1986 — Quaternary glaciations in the northern hemisphere, *Quaternary Science Reviews* 5.

Singer, R., J.J. Wymer, B.G. Gladfelter, R.G. Wolff — 1973 — Excavation of the Clactonian Industry at the Golf Course, Clacton-on-Sea, Essex, *Proceedings of the Prehistoric Society* 39, 6-74.

Singer, R., B.G. Gladfelter, J.J. Wymer — 1993 — *The Lower Paleolithic Site at Hoxne, England.* Chicago: The University of Chicago Press.

Solomon, J.D. — 1933 — The implementiferous gravels of Warren Hill, *Journal of the Anthropological Institute* 63, 101-110.

Stringer, C.B. — 1985 — Middle Pleistocene hominid variability and the origin of late Pleistocene humans. In: E. Delson (ed.), *Ancestors: the hard evidence*, 289-295, New York: Alan Liss.

Stringer, C.B, C.S. Gamble — 1993 — *In search of the Neanderthals.* London: Thames and Hudson.

Stuart, A.J. — 1974 — Pleistocene history of the British vertebrate fauna, *Biological Review* 49, 225-266.

1975 — The vertebrate fauna of the type Cromerian, *Boreas* 4, 63-76.

1981 — A comparison of the Middle Pleistocene mammal faunas of Voigtstedt (Thuringia, German Democratic Republic) and West Runton (Norfolk, England), *Quartärpaläontologie* 4, 155-163.

| | 1982 | *Pleistocene vertebrates in the British Isles.* London and New York: Longman. |
| | 1988 | Preglacial Pleistocene vertebrate faunas of East Anglia. In: P.L. Gibbard and J.A. Zalasiewicz (eds), *Pliocene-Middle Pleistocene of East Anglia,* Field Guide, Cambridge: Quaternary Research Association. |

Stuart, A.J.,
  R.G. West

1976   Late Cromerian fauna and flora at Ostend, Norfolk, *Geological Magazine* 113, 469-473.

Sutcliffe, A.J.

1975   A hazard in the interpretation of glacial/interglacial sequences, *Quaternary Newsletter* 17, 1-3.

Sutcliffe, A.J.,
  K. Kowalski

1976   Pleistocene rodents of the British Isles, *Bulletin of the British Museum (Natural History)* (Geology) 27(2).

Turner, A.

1992   Large carnivores and earliest European hominids: changing determinants of resource availability during the Lower and Middle Pleistocene *Journal of Human Evolution* 22, 109-126.

Turner, C.

1970   The Middle Pleistocene deposits at Marks Tey, Essex, *Philosophical Transactions of the Royal Society* B257, 373-440.

1973   High Lodge, Mildenhall. In: J. Rose and C. Turner (eds), *Quaternary Research Association Field Meeting Guide, Clacton,* 101-105, London: Birkbeck College.

1975   The correlation and duration of Middle Pleistocene interglacial periods in northwest Europe. In: K.W. Butzer and G.L. Isaac (eds), *After the Australopithicenes,* 259-308, The Hague: Mouton.

Turner, C.,
  M.P. Kerney

1971   The age of the freshwater beds of the Clacton Channel, *Journal of the Geological Society of London* 127, 87-93.

Valoch, K.

1991   Les premiers peuplements humains en Moravie (Tchécoslovaquie). In: E. Bonifay and B. Vandermeersch (eds), *Les Premiers Européens,* Paris. Editions du C.T.H.S..

this
volume   The earliest occupation of Europe: Eastern, Central and Southeastern Europe.

Ventris, P.A.

1986   The Nar Valley. In: R.G. West and C.A. Whiteman (eds), *The Nar Valley and North Norfolk,* Field Guide, 7-55, Coventry: Quaternary Research Association.

Waechter, J. d'A.

1972   Swanscombe 1971, *Proceedings of the Royal Anthropological Institute* (for 1971), 73-78.

Warren, S.H.

1955   The Clacton (Essex) channel deposits, *Quarterly Journal of the Geological Society of London* 155, 283-307.

Wenban-Smith, F.F.

1989   The use of canonical variates for determination of biface manufacturing technology at Boxgrove Lower Palaeolithic site and the behavioural implications of this technology, *Journal of Archaeological Science* 16(1), 17-26.

West, R.G.

1956   The Quaternary deposits at Hoxne, Suffolk, *Philosophical Transactions of the Royal Society of London* B239, 265-356.

1957   Interglacial deposits at Bobbitshole, Ipswich, *Philosophical Transactions of the Royal Society of London* B241, 1-31.

1963   Problems of the British Quaternary, *Proceedings of the Geologists' Association* 74, 147-186.

	1980	*The pre-glacial Pleistocene of the Norfolk and Suffolk coasts*. Cambridge: Cambridge University Press.
White, M.J.	1993	*Lower Palaeolithic Core and Flake Technology: A Comparison of Hoxne and High Lodge*. BA dissertation, University of London.
Whiteman, C.A., J. Rose	1992	Thames river sediments of the British early and Middle Pleistocene, *Quaternary Science Reviews* 11, 363-375.
Wise, P.	1993	Waverley Wood Farm Pit, *Current Archaeology* 133, 12-14.
Wymer, J.J.	1968	*Lower Paleolithic archaeology in Britain: As Represented by the Thames Valley*. London: John Baker.
	1974	Clactonian and Acheulian Industries in Britain – their chronology and significance, *Proceedings of the Geologists Association* 85, 391-421.
	1983	The Lower Palaeolithic site at Hoxne, *Proceedings of the Suffolk Institute of Archaeology and History* 35, 169-189.
	1985	*Palaeolithic Sites of East Anglia*. Norwich: Geo Books.
	1988	Palaeolithic archaeology and the British Quaternary sequence, *Quaternary Science Reviews* 7, 79-98.
Wymer, J.J., S.G. Lewis, D.R. Bridgland	1991	Warren Hill, Mildenhall, Suffolk (TL 744743). In: S.G. Lewis, C.A. Whiteman and D.R. Bridgland (eds), *Central East Anglia and the Fen Basin*, Field Guide, London: Quaternary Research Association.
Zagwijn, W.H.	1985	An outline of the Quaternary Stratigraphy of the Netherlands, *Geologie en Mijnbouw* 50, 41-58.
	1992	The beginning of the Ice Age in Europe and its major subdivisions, *Quaternary Science Reviews* 11, 583-591.
Zeuner, F.E.	1959	*The Pleistocene Period*. London: Hutchinson.

Mark B. Roberts
U.C.L. Institute of Archaeology
31-34 Gordon Square
London WC1H OPY
England

Clive S. Gamble
University of Southampton
Department of Archaeology
Southampton SO9 5NH
England

David R. Bridgland
University of Durham
Department of Geography
Durham DH1 3LE
England

Jørgen Holm
Lars Larsson

11   The earliest occupation of Europe: Scandinavia

This paper examines claims for Middle and Lower Palaeolithic finds from Scandinavia, within the context of the geological history of the area, where glaciers repeatedly modified Pleistocene landscapes. Though no unambiguous primary context traces of pre-Hamburgian occupation are known yet, a review of various localities in southern Denmark shows that this area has a great potential for such finds, to be exploited in future research.

1.   Conditions for human settlement

A study of the physical conditions for settlement is essential for an understanding of the migration of humans. Our knowledge of the Scandinavian landscape during the Pleistocene is, however, extremely fragmentary due to the fact that Scandinavia was affected by a number of glaciations. Organic sediments found intercalated in moraines throughout the whole of Scandinavia have been interpreted as pre-dating the Holsteinian Interglacial in certain cases, although their actual age is still highly uncertain. It is not until the Holsteinian Interglacial that locations of profiles investigated by pollen analyses exhibit a sufficient geographical distribution throughout the whole of Scandinavia to permit a schematic impression of the ecological conditions. The data are far too incomplete, however, to permit the relationship between land and sea, for example, to be examined with a view to identifying any physical obstacles to human expansion. During the Eemian Interglacial, the available data present an image of southern-most Scandinavia divided into a number of quite large islands similar to the present-day situation in eastern Denmark (Strand Petersen 1985; Houmark-Nielsen 1989) (Figs 1 and 2). Jutland may itself have been separated from the European mainland by a sound during certain parts of the Eemian Interglacial. This would have prevented migration during the peak of the interglacial, although hardly during its early part, when a considerable volume of water would still be trapped in the ice sheets.

Apart from the direct evidence for occupation, finds of various mammal remains can be used in the discussion on possible migration routes. Only a small number of fossils from the Cromerian and the Holsteinian have been found in lacustrine deposits in Denmark. The oldest Quaternary

bone, a piece of antler from a red deer (*Cervus elaphus*) was found in Jutland, in gyttja possibly dating from the Cromerian Interglacial (Aaris-Sørensen, 1988). An ulna of a wild horse (*Equus ferus*), was recovered from freshwater deposits, dated to the Holsteinian on the basis of pollen analysis. This find was also made in Jutland.

It is not until the Eemian Interglacial that the fossil record becomes more abundant, with beaver (*Castor fiber*), straight-tusked elephant (*Elephas namadicus* (= *Palaeoloxodon antiquus*)), Merck's rhinoceros (*Dicerorhinus kirchbergensis*), fallow deer (*Dama dama*), red deer (*Cervus elaphus*), and bison (*Bison priscus*). Some of these species were found only in secondary contexts in moraine deposits, and their specific relation to the Eemian Interglacial is based on more southern find contexts. All these finds were made in Jutland which suggests a possible migration route to that part of southern Scandinavia during certain parts of the Eemian Interglacial. Mammal finds from other parts of Scandinavia are unfortunately absent. This can be taken as an indication that larger mammals did not exist in this area. However, since the known locations of material from Eemian find spots, as those from earlier interglacials, are very few in number, the absence of finds is not a good argument for inferring that migration routes to the Scandinavian peninsula were entirely lacking.

The claim that the Eemian water basin covering parts of the present-day Baltic may also have had a connection with the Arctic Ocean via Karelia is disputed by new research. Had this been the case, there would have been a suitable migration route for terrestrial fauna including humans. Pollen analyses from northern Finland indicate deposits dated to a period before the Eemian Interglacial, presumably the Holsteinian Interglacial, with a succession of vegetation that was ecologically equivalent to that of the current interglacial (Ambrosiani 1990). This also applies to a considerable extent to the Eemian (Robertson 1991). If a land link had existed in present-day Karelia, the appropriate conditions would have existed for the migration of several species of terrestrial mammals adapted to a boreal flora.

The occurrence and the extent of the glaciations within the early Weichselian of Scandinavia remains a challenging area of research. A number of partially conflicting

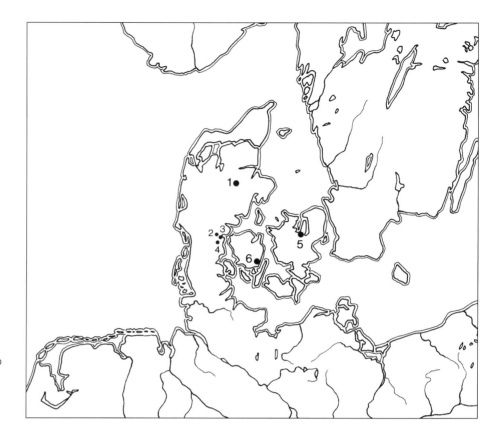

Fig. 1. Map of Southwest Scandinavia, showing the most important find locations referred to in the text.
1. Hollerup; 2. Seest; 3. Kolding Fjord; 4. Vejstrup Skov; 5. Ejby Klint; 6. Vejstrup Ådal.

proposals for further work have been submitted (Berglund and Lagerlund 1981; Strand Petersen 1985; Houmark-Nielsen 1989; Forsström and Eronen 1991; Mangerud 1991). Glaciations of varying extent have been dated to oxygen isotope stages (OIS) 5d and 5b, as well as to the transition between OIS 5 and 4. These are believed to have covered large parts of the Scandinavian peninsula, although the two oldest thawed completely during interjacent interstadials. The later glaciation, however, is understood to have varied in its extent until achieving its maximum distribution during the Late Weichselian. Of the inter-stadials, the Brørup appears from pollen analyses conducted in Denmark to have included the afforestation of the southern part of the Scandinavian peninsula.

Moraine deposits have yielded a considerable number of finds, consisting mainly of the tusks and teeth of the woolly mammoth (*Mammuthus primigenius*) in both southern and northern Scandinavia (Berglund *et al.* 1976; Aaris-Sørensen *et al.* 1990; Lepiksaar 1992). C14 dating has revealed that a number of finds give infinite values, or finite values at the range limit of the method, indicating that they belong to an early part of the Weichselian. With the exception of a couple of Late Glacial dates, the samples give values of between 32 and 22 Kyr BP. This very probably coincides

with the Hengelo and Denekamp Interstadials, for which pollen analyses indicate a sparse population of pine and birch and a predominance of Cyperaceae and Gramineae. This environment, compatible for the mammoth, existed as far as the southern parts of northern Sweden, where several woolly mammoth finds have been made.

Woolly rhinoceros (*Coelodonta antiquitatis*), giant deer (*Megaloceros giganteus*), reindeer (*Rangifer tarandus*), steppe bison (*Bison priscus*), musk ox (*Ovibos moschatus*), and saiga antelope (*Saiga tatarica*), also occur during the Middle Weichselian. The mammoth steppe, with its good grazing for both large and small herd animals, was an environment which covered considerable parts of Europe during the glacial periods and also served as suitable hunting grounds for humans. The presence of an abundant fauna suggests the existence of appropriate migration routes for hominids from both the southwest and the east.

2.   Indications of settlement during the Lower and Middle Palaeolithic

A number of uncertain Danish finds of a Lower or Middle Palaeolithic character are examined below. What is immediately clear is the fact that *all* these finds were made within the area once covered by the Weichselian ice. This

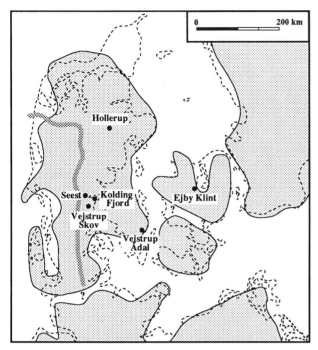

Fig. 2. Map of Southwest Scandinavia. The hatched areas indicate land during the Eemian Interglacial. The maximum extent of the land ice during the Weichselian – the Main Stationary Line is indicated.

is the area where the small number of people who have concerned themselves with the problem live, and it is only in this area that a search for early Palaeolithic artefacts has been undertaken.

2.1.   VEJSTRUP SKOV (VEJSTRUP WOOD)

Amateur archaeologists have been collecting rough flint artefacts from several localities close to the town of Christiansfeld in Southeastern Jutland since the 1960s. A feature shared by all these finds is that they derive from the bottom of V-shaped erosion gulleys up to 15 m in depth, created by the melt water from the Weichselian ice, which covered the area on a number of occasions. In 1971 a test excavation at the most promising of these localities, Vejstrup Skov, was carried out by the Institute of Prehistoric Archaeology of the University of Aarhus, under the direction of S.H. Andersen. The layer from which the finds had been washed out was successfully identified on this occasion. The layer is now the bed of the brook which flows through the valley. A small number of worked flints, similar to the finds already made in secondary contexts at the bottom of the valley, were found in a layer of rust coloured sand and gravel covered by about 8 m of moraine clay.

Larger excavation followed in 1972, this time with the involvement of quaternary geologists. A number of trenches were dug on the western slope in order to expose the

primary layers, which had been covered by recent landslips prior to the excavation. The find bearing layer was a freshwater deposit, consisting of larger stones and coarse gravel mixed with sand and overlaid by two or three Weichselian moraines, representing the same number of advances by the ice, and underlaid by the Saalian moraine. The geologists were able to establish that this was an Eemian freshwater deposit, although it is important to point out that the layer also contained many foraminifera characteristic of the Holsteinian Interglacial. This circumstance, combined with the fact that a number of the flint artefacts were rolled and thus showed signs of re-deposition, led to the assumption that the finds most probably dated from the Holsteinian. Not only Danish archaeologists, but also experts from other countries drew particular attention to the close similarity with the Clactonian industry. The find material, which does not include any handaxes, consists predominantly of rough flakes and cores, some of which may be interpreted as choppers/chopping tools, retouched flakes, end and transverse scrapers and pieces with notches and denticulates (Fig. 3).

The *Vejstrup Skov* excavation became an archaeological sensation. A degree of calm has settled on the subject since then and the finds now receive only brief mention (Andersen 1981; Becker 1977; Holm 1986). No scientific presentation has actually been made to date. This is attributed mainly to the fact that considerable uncertainty has arisen over the years about the circumstances and dating of the finds. There is a tendency to regard the find bearing deposit as a Postglacial brook layer that became covered during the Holocene by reworked moraine deposits. This view, *inter alia*, is borne out by the observation that the find bearing layer tails off rapidly within the western slope and that the layer slopes down towards the bottom of the valley. It is difficult to reconcile this view with the dating of the layer to the Holsteinian/Eemian Interglacial. Furthermore, two core samples taken in the vicinity have revealed a similar stratigraphy – an Eemian layer with redeposited or mixed Holsteinian materials.

2.2.   KOLDING FJORD

At Kolding Fjord, in Southeast Jutland, amateur archaeologists have collected a few thousand flint flakes, cores and rough implements of an early Palaeolithic character, which have been described in a brief, interim article (Stevnhoved 1992). The finds were made over a distance of 20-30 m at the foot of an approximately 30 m high coastal cliff. Immediately above this area, a recently uprooted tree exposed parts of the primary layers. These consist of a layer of brown clay – attributed to the Saalian glaciation on the basis of provisional geological analyses – visible at the very bottom, followed by a

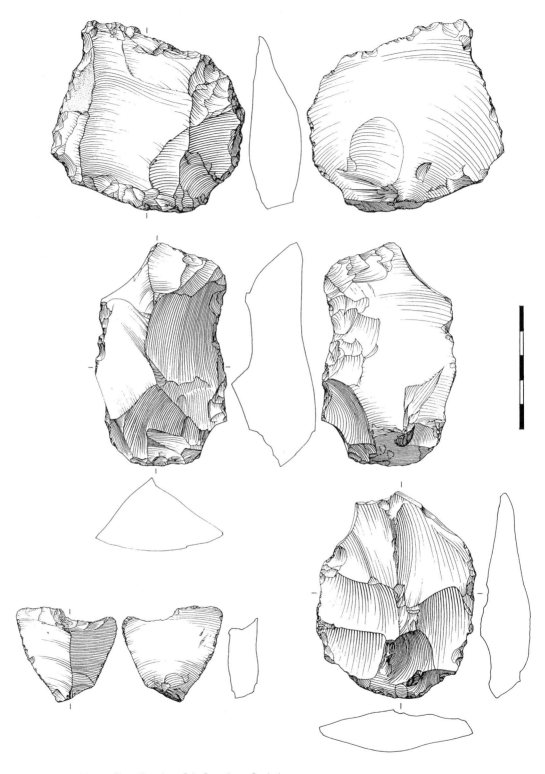

Fig. 3. Flint artefacts from Vejstrup Skov. Drawing: Orla Svendsen. Scale in cm.

50 cm layer of melt water sand, and at the top several layers of grey/greyish brown clay containing an abundance of Senon flint, presumably representing one or more Weichselian moraines. The melt water sand has been given a provisional TL-date of 170 - 210 Kyr BP. In those places where it can be observed, the foot of the cliff consists of a blackish brown solid layer of clay, probably from the Saalian.

In spite of determined efforts over many years, it has still not been possible to find any artefacts *in situ* in the cliff. A proper excavation is, in fact, ruled out by the steepness of the cliff and the frequent landslips. Stevnhoved bases her view that the artefacts must originate from a time before the most recent glaciation on two principal arguments: on the one hand the technological features and on the other hand the fact that the flint artefacts display various forms of patination which have not been observed on Danish Late Glacial and Postglacial artefacts. This includes amongst others pitted erosion surfaces, "orange-peel" (wind erosion), rounding of edges, depressions and ribs (wind erosion) and a strong, partial or full surface glaze-like polish (wind erosion). In addition, approximately 50% of the material exhibits frost fissures. These observations concur with the findings of Dutch and northern German investigations (Stapert 1976; Hartz 1986).

By far the largest proportion of the find material consists of cores and flakes. Some small cores closely resemble choppers or chopping tools. A rough, Levalloisian technique is found in conjunction with smaller cores. As a general rule, the flakes have a large striking platform, occasionally facetted, and a large (blunt) striking angle. A few irregular blade-like artifacts are present too. Only about twenty tools have been found. These are substantial flakes with high, steep edge retouche, blades with retouching on the long edge, and flakes with partial, scraper-like retouching.

Stevnhoved herself cautiously suggests a dating of the artefacts to the Eemian, or to one of the earliest Weichselian interstadials.

2.3.   EJBY KLINT (EJBY CLIFF)

An amateur archaeologist collected several thousand coarse flint flakes and cores from the beach beneath an approximately 20 m high coastal cliff at Ejby, near Isefjorden, North Zealand, including chopper-like pieces (Madsen 1963; Madsen 1968a; Madsen 1968b). In his opinion the material shows a striking similarity with the Clactonian industry (Fig. 4) (1).

Unfortunately, all these finds come from reworked deposits. In the middle of the cliff, Madsen found an Eemian marine gravel deposit, which separates an upper and a lower moraine from the Weichselian and Saalian

respectively. The flint artefacts may have been washed out from the lower moraine clay but that remains to be demonstrated.

2.4.   VEJSTRUP ÅDAL (VEJSTRUP RIVER VALLEY)

In 1978, one of the authors of this article (J.H.) found a number of flint artefacts of a Lower or Middle Palaeolithic type on the bottom of the *Vejstrup Ådal* (river valley) on Southeast Funen. Somewhat less than 1000 flint items were recovered from the bottom of the river in the course of repeated visits to the site over a number of years (Holm 1986; Holm 1987).

The valley has a NW-SE orientation, is approximately 5 km long, and reaches depths of 15-20 m. This is actually a V-shaped erosion valley, presumably formed by melt water – and perhaps even a drainage channel for the dead ice from Central Funen. The river flows into the Storebælt strait less than 4 km from the site. There is no doubt that the area was covered by ice on several occasions during both the Saalian and the Weichselian glaciations. A small number of core samples taken in a different connection in the vicinity of the site did not reveal any layers older than the Weichselian. However, a test trench dug into one slope of the valley in 1981 has revealed the presence, at a depth of about 10 m, of an approximately one metre thick series of fluviatile sands, severely displaced by the pressure of the ice, which separate an upper and a lower moraine. It must be assumed that the artefacts were washed out from deep lying layers in the slopes of the valley, although no artefacts could be found in primary contexts during the aforementioned test excavation. Another possibility is that they originate from the lower, grey, stony moraine clay that was noted during the exploratory excavation and is also encountered directly below the river bed.

The same type of worked flint can be found in the river over a distance of more than 1 km; this circumstance can be explained by the fact that the material was transported by the occasionally strongly flowing water. This means that the place of origin of the artefacts must be sought at the point at which they first occurred upstream. Artefacts are also found on the bed of a man-made canal of more recent date, which could indicate that the finds are not restricted to the river course but can occur over the entire width of the valley.

The find material consists to a great extent – more than 90% – of rough, large flakes, and a few irregular blades (Fig. 5). The flakes have large striking platforms (struck with a stonehammer – hard percussion), broad and occasionally facetted platforms, and blunt striking angles (110-120°). There are also about 25 cores, some of which are very large.

The number of actual tools is quite small, approximately 20 in number, including 2 amygdaloid handaxes (or, at any

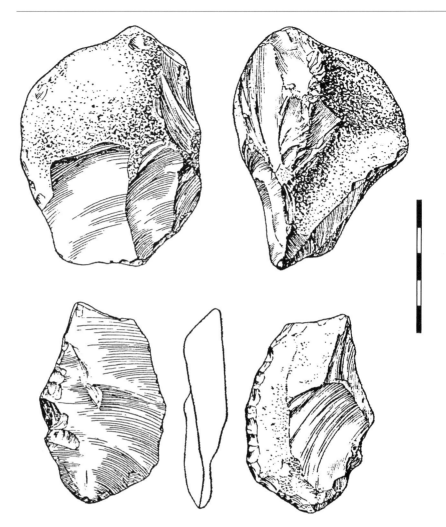

Fig. 4. Flint artefacts from Ejby Klint. Drawing: John Wymer. Scale in cm.

rate, pieces resembling handaxes), end and side scrapers, denticulates, and oblong core implements of triangular cross-section (trihedral picks). A fragment of a polished Neolithic flint axe was the only distinctly younger find.

A representative selection of the material has been shown to colleagues from other countries (2). They were unanimous in pointing out, independently from each other, the early Middle Palaeolithic (Acheulean) characteristics of the material and its close resemblance especially to the finds from Markkleeberg, near Leipzig (Baumann *et al*. 1983). Indications of a proto-Levallois technique were found in the material.

2.5.   HOLLERUP

A well-known Danish find of an early Palaeolithic character, consists of the marrow split fallow deer bones

found in Eemian freshwater deposits at Hollerup, on the northern side of the Gudenå valley to the west of the town of Langå (Central Jutland). The commercial extraction and utilization of diatom mud was conducted here from 1895 until about 1960. The geologist and botanist N. Hartz established in 1896 that the lacustrine layers extended for about 250 m, and were underlaid by layers of sand with a thickness of more than 10 m. Above this and at the deepest point is a 4 m layer of calcium rich mud, and above that in turn is a layer of about 5 m of diatom mud, the top of which has an admixture of clay and sand. Above the diatom mud lies approximately 10 m of stratified sand, and at the very top a quite thin capping of moraine gravel. The mud layers represent the whole of the Eemian Interglacial, whereas the clay bearing mud and the sand were deposited at the beginning of the Weichselian. The glaciers of the latter glacial period did not leave any traces other than the thin layer of moraine gravel.

The remains of 7 fallow deer skeletons were found in the diatom mud in the period between 1897 and 1925. In the 1950s a study was carried out on the bones from Hollerup, including one almost complete, but highly fragmented skeleton – find V from 1912 (Møhl-Hansen 1955). After refitting some of the bone fragments it was obvious that the bones not only had fresh fractures caused by being lifted, but also exhibited many old, primary fractures which have the same colour and black stains or dendrites (plant like precipitation of manganese oxide) as the rest of the bone surface (Fig. 6). In addition, the bones had been struck in pairs in the same way – the same pattern on the right and left shoulder blade and on the right and left humerus, etc.

There were distinct striking areas with shattered edges, characteristic for bones cut to remove marrow and similar to those from Mesolithic sites. It is thought provoking that the only major limb bones that are missing are the two femora. It is also noteworthy, however, that practically the entire skeleton is present. There is no sign of fire having been used, just as the presence of cut marks could not be demonstrated. One of the other skeletons from Hollerup, No. 1, shows many signs previously interpreted as results of cutting to get at the marrow.

The fallow deer bones were found in the deepest part of the diatom mud, which presumably dates from a comparatively late part of the Eemian, the hornbeam/spruce period or the spruce period, i.e. after the mixed oak forest had reached its peak.

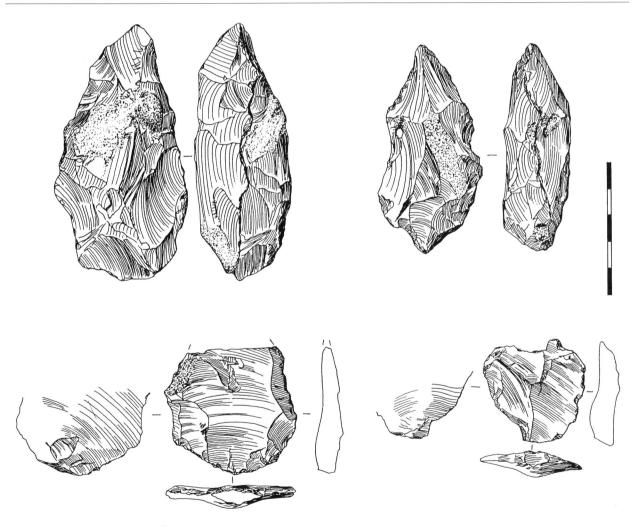

Fig. 5. Flint artefacts from Vejstrup Ådal. Drawing: Jørgen Holm. Scale in cm.

A new analysis of the bones from Hollerup is called for, with a special emphasis on discriminating between carnivore-induced and human breakage of the bones (Binford 1981).

2.6.   SEEST

Approximately 100 animal bones and a few flakes and blades, which may date from the period prior to the most recent glaciation, have been found since 1950 in a series of gravel pits at Seest, on the western outskirts of Kolding, Southeast Jutland (Westerby 1957). According to the current view held by geologists, the Seest area is part of the East Jutland young moraine landscape that was created during the Weichselian glaciation. There is broad agreement that the area was covered by ice, at least during the major advance known as the Frankfurt stage, approximately 20 Kyr BP when the ice reached the principal Main Stationary Line 10-15 km to the west of Seest, perhaps also during the latest young Baltic transgression. One problem, however, is the absence of uncontested traces of moraine deposits in the upper part of the sequences.

The finds of animal bones and flint artefacts originate from at least 7 gravel pits in the Kolding Ådal. The sediments in the gravel pits consist mainly of fluviatile sand and gravel deposits.

Unfortunately, all the remains of fauna and artefacts were found in secondary contexts, for example in the material already excavated, at the foot of slopes, and in sorted heaps of stones. The depth of the gravel pits ranges from a couple of metres down to as much as approximately 8 m.

Only part of the bone material has been identified to species level (Aaris-Sørensen 1988): *Elephas namadicus* (= *Palaeoloxodon antiquus*), *Dicerorhinus kirchbergensis*, *Megaloceros giganteus*, *Dama dama* and *Bison priscus*.

None of the bones shows traces of human involvement (such as cutting to get at the marrow and/or marks left by scraping/cutting), although it goes without saying that a location with such an abundance of bones is also a location of potential archaeological interest. The gravel pits have yielded a dozen or so unmistakable flint artefacts, including one blade about 8 cm long (Fig. 7). The piece has a yellow colour (ferric oxides) and exhibits a slight sheen in places, which may be attributed to sand polishing. The blade was found in a secondary context, but in a section of the gravel pit from which the top soil had been removed beforehand, thereby excluding the possibility of its admixture. A further consideration is the fact that sand was adhering firmly to the blade, that, according to the sedimentologists, could scarcely have come from the upper layers of the gravel pit.

The most likely explanation is that the find bearing deposits were deposited by melt water during the Late

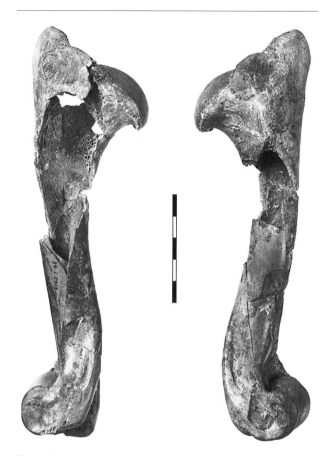

Fig. 6. Right and left humerus of fallow deer from Hollerup - split in the same way to get at the marrow. Photograph: Geert Brovad. Scale in cm.

Weichselian (glacial outwash), although the possibility cannot be excluded that these are fluvial deposits dating from the Eemian and early parts of the Weichselian glaciation. There is a good deal of evidence to suggest that the Kolding valley already existed in the Eemian Interglacial. The current view of Danish as well as Swedish geologists is that the last Ice Age did not really produce the previously assumed violent transformation on the landscape. It is possible, therefore, that the Seest finds must be explained in relation to the existence of *Kolding Ådal* (Kolding river valley) at a much earlier stage than previously assumed.

2.7.   ISOLATED FINDS; ARTEFACTS RESEMBLING HAND-
          AXES

Mention must also be made of a couple of Danish finds which bear a striking morphological and technological resemblance to Acheulean handaxes (Becker 1971). One of these is mentioned on a number of occasions in the published literature and has been endorsed as a genuine handaxe by leading experts from other countries. However, the manner in which it was obtained and its provenance pose considerable problems. The artefact is said to have been found at Villestrup, in the north of Jutland, after which it passed into the hands of a wealthy collector. This amateur archaeologist purchased archaeological specimens from an archaeological dealer, who bought specimens in France. This has given rise to so many misgivings surrounding the provenance of the artefact, that it should now definitely be disregarded. The other artefact, which has also received the endorsement of foreign experts, was found on the beach at Fænö, an island situated in the Lillebælt Strait between Funen and Jutland. It could equally be a Mesolithic flint core axe or a Neolithic artefact. The problem facing us – at least in South Scandinavia – is the difficulty, if not impossibility, of distinguishing between genuine handaxes and Late Neolithic blanks for daggers, spearheads and corn sickles. This debate has continued in Denmark for many years and cannot, in all fairness, be said to be making any progress (Glob 1972).

A fragmented and heavily rolled artefact with an altered surface, resembling a handaxe, was found at *Karskov Klint*, a coastal cliff on Langeland, an island south of Funen; details were published by a German archaeologist and a Danish geologist (Grote and Maagaard Jakobsen 1982). The impression with which one is left after reading the article is that the artefact was found *in situ* in a moraine layer, having been deposited during the most recent – Young Baltic – transgression. This is not correct, however. It was found in secondary context on the beach below the cliff (cf. E. Maagaard Jakobsen, personal communication).

3. The oldest uncontestable traces of human occupation

The remains of what is generally accepted as the earliest settlement belong to the Hamburgian Culture. The oldest sites were investigated as late as 1981-84 at Jels, in southern Jutland (Holm and Rieck 1992). Further settlement remains have been confirmed in more recent years on southern Jutland (Holm 1993), and in eastern Denmark (Vang Petersen and Johansen 1993). One site in southernmost Sweden yielded artefacts which share certain features with the earliest finds in Denmark (Larsson 1994). Radiocarbon dating of reindeer bone associated with remains from the Hamburgian Culture have produced a date of 12,520±190 BP (AAR-906) (Holm 1993). The Bromme Culture from the Allerød Interstadial enjoys a rather more widespread distribution in the Scandinavian peninsula. It is not until the early part of the Preboreal that settlements spread rapidly as far north as northernmost Norway.

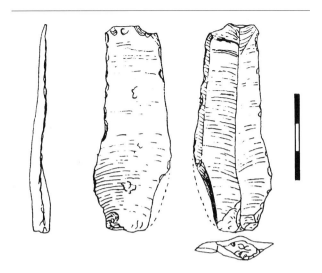

Fig. 7. Flint blade from Seest. Drawing: Erik Westerby. Scale in cm.

4. Discussion

Although a detailed knowledge of Palaeolithic settlements in South Scandinavia during the period 14 500 - 10 000 BP has gradually been built up, the study of the Lower, Middle and most of the Upper Palaeolithic is still at a controversial and pioneering stage. There is no lack of finds in Denmark which point to a fascinating technical and morphological similarity with Lower and Middle Palaeolithic types of implements in other countries. However, since most of these were found in secondary locations, detached from their original geological contexts, they are debatable. On the basis of an assessment of climatic and natural conditions, there is nothing that would have prevented humans from living in South Scandinavia, at least during interglacial periods and interstadials long before the last glaciation (Andersen 1979; Aaris-Sørensen 1988). In order to develop an idea of when the first people may have arrived here, it is obvious to take as a starting point the oldest finds in the neighbouring countries to the south. If we look at Germany and England, for example, it is clear that these sites belong to the earliest in Europe (Roebroeks *et al.* 1992).

What reasons are there that can explain why we are lagging so far behind our colleagues in countries to the south of Denmark? The most pessimistic explanation would be that we are searching for phantoms, and that, in spite of favourable climatic and natural conditions, there was quite simply no settlement so far north during the Lower and Middle Palaeolithic. However, we are more inclined to point to other reasons. First and foremost, there is no research tradition in this area, which will only be established once we have tangible, reliable finds to work with. We also lack the expertise which can only be achieved through daily contact with and firsthand study of artefact material dating from these periods.

This is a vicious circle which is made even more difficult by the fact that, for many years, the majority of Scandinavian archaeologists have refused even to discuss the possibility of such an early settlement in Scandinavia. On the whole, this topic has been taken up only by unbiased and intrepid amateur archaeologists, who do not have a career to worry about, although they are known to approach their work in a somewhat uncritical and overenthusiastic manner on occasions. It is nevertheless typical that the Late Palaeolithic finds and the more or less uncertain finds of an Lower or Middle Palaeolithic character of which we are also aware have been discovered by amateur archaeologists in the majority of cases.

The defeatist attitude to the problem amongst professional Scandinavian archaeologists is not entirely without justification, however. It is however necessary to emphasise that, apart from its marginal, northern location, Scandinavia was repeatedly covered with icecaps over the long period with which we are concerned here. This hampers the discovery of finds dating from the Lower and Middle Palaeolithic, which in most cases may be expected to be in secondary context and deeply buried. By all accounts the Saalian icecaps covered the whole of Scandinavia which reduces the chances of discovering Lower Palaeolithic finds, for example from the Holsteinian Interglacial. Chances of discovering finds from the Eemian Interglacial and later periods are better, however. There is a distinct possibility of such finds being made in the landscape created by the Saalian ice in Southwest Jutland, as this area was not crossed by the ice during the Weichselian glaciation. In other words, there should be excellent chances of discovering archaeological material here going back at least 130,00 years.

There are grounds for optimism in the fact that totally reliable finds have been made in northwest Germany, in an identical landscape (the *Altmoränen*), for instance at Schalkholz, where flint flakes were found in a peat deposit which could be dated to the Brørup Interstadial (Arnold 1978; Hartz 1986). And a fairly large number of heavily modified flint artefacts, including a hand axe of convincingly Middle Palaeolithic character, was found on the surface of a hill near Drelsdorf in the Husum area

(Kreis Nordfriesland), quite close to the German-Danish border (Hartz 1986).

The view of the authors is that the hypothesis, which maintains that all Lower and Middle Palaeolithic find occurrences in Scandinavia must be regarded as having been obliterated by subsequent ice transgressions and erosion, is too pessimistic and in fact represents the largest obstacle to a breakthrough in this area of research. One could state, with equal justification, that the very same glacial and erosional processes that are capable of destroying, are equally capable of protecting or, in favourable circumstances, of bringing originally deeply buried finds to the surface. This is supported by examples from other countries: High Lodge in England (Ashton *et al.* 1991) and finds from various gravel-pits in the Netherlands (Stapert 1981). In addition, Early Palaeolithic material in the northern parts of Scandinavia may have survived in rock fissures and caves, as were the approximately 200,000 years old finds from the Pontnewydd cave in North Wales, covered by ice on several occasions (Green 1984).

If one were to attempt a rough summary of the Danish finds referred to above, it is clear that none of these is sufficiently reliable to survive a thorough source-critical evaluation. Even if deeply buried, there are strong indications that the finds were not in primary context. One interesting consideration is that Scandinavian archaeologists have adopted a dismissive or extremely doubtful attitude to attaching a great age to the finds, whereas archaeologists from other parts of Europe with considerable expertise in Palaeolithic finds and the circumstances in which finds are made do not display the same negative attitude. Although they may not be entirely familiar with the material culture from South Scandinavia, the fact should not be overlooked that they have intimate knowledge of the problems associated with the finds. Archaeologists in other parts of Europe are also faced with the challenge of distinguishing between Neolithic and Palaeolithic artefacts collected as surface finds.

notes

1 John Wymer took part in the investigations and considers the material to possess Lower Palaeolithic characteristics.

2 The material was examined by Alain Tuffreau, who visited the locality in 1981, Gerhard Bosinski and Jan Michal Burdukiewicz.

references

Aaris-Sørensen, K.	1988	*Danmarks forhistoriske dyreverden. Fra Istid til Vikingetid.* København.
Aaris-Sørensen, K., K. Strand Petersen, H. Tauber	1990	Danish Finds of Mammoth (*Mammuthus primigenius* (Blumenbach)). Stratigraphical position, dating and evidence of Late Pleistocene environment, *Danmarks Geologiske Undersøgelse*, Serie B:14, Kobenhavn.
Ambrosiani, G.K.	1990	Pleistocene stratigraphy in Central and Northern Sweden – a reinvestigation of some classical sites, *University of Stockholm, Department of Quaternary Research Report 16.*
Andersen, S.H.	1981	*Stenalderen 1. Jægerstenalderen. Sesams Danmarkshistorie.* København.
Andersen, S.T.	1979	Istider og mellemistider. In: A. Nørrevang and T.J. Meyer (eds.), *Danmarks natur*, Bind 1, 199-250, Landskabernes opståen, København.
Arnold, V.	1978	Neue Funde aus der Steinzeit Dithmarschens, *Dithmarschen N.F. 3/4.*
Ashton, N., A. Roberts, J. Cook	1991	*High Lodge.* London: British Museum.
Baumann, W., D. Mania, V. Toepfer, L. Eissmann	1983	*Die paläolithischen Neufunde von Markkleeberg bei Leipzig.* Berlin: VEB.
Becker, C.J.	1971	Istidsmandens redskaber, *Skalk* 1971:4, 3-7.
	1977	Om istids-jægerne og deres redskaber. In: J. Brøndsted, *De ældste tider. Politikens Danmarkshistorie*, Efterskrift, 521-525.
Berglund, B., S. Håkansson, E. Lagerlund	1976	Radiocarbon-dated mammoth (*Mammuthus primigenius* Blumenbach) finds in South Sweden, *Boreas* 5, 177-191.
Berglund, B.E., E. Lagerlund	1981	Eemian and Weichselian stratigraphy in South Sweden, *Boreas* 10, 323-362.
Binford, L.	1981	*Bones. Ancient men and modern myths.* New York: Academic Press.
Forsström, L., M. Eronen	1991	New Information on the Eemian and Early Weichselian in Finland. In: B.G. Andersen and L.-K. Königsson (eds.), *Late Quaternary Stratigraphy in the Nordic Countries 150,000-15,000 B.P.* Striae 34, 31-37.
Glob, P.V.	1972	Farlig flint, *Skalk* 1972:1, 18-20.
Green, H.S. (ed.)	1984	*Pontnewydd Cave, a Lower Palaeolithic hominid site in Wales: The first report.* Cardiff: National Museum of Wales.
Grote, K., E.M. Jacobsen	1982	Der Faustkeil vom Karskov-Kliff auf Langeland (Dänemark), *Archäologisches Korrespondenzblatt* 12, 281-285.
Hartz, S.	1986	Paläolitische Funde aus dem Altmoränengebiet Nordfrieslands, *Offa*, 105-147.

Holm, J.   1986   The Quaternary and the Early/Middle Palaeolithic of Denmark. In: A. Tuffreau and S. Sommé
                                    (eds.), *Chronostratigraphie et faciès culturels du Paléolithique inférieur et moyen dans
                                    l'Europe du Nord-Ouest*, Supplément au Bulletin de l'Association Française pour l'étude
                                    du Quaternaire 26, 75-80.

                            1987   Primitiv flint i Vejstrup Ådal – de første fynboer?, *Årbog for Svendborg og Omegns
                                    Museum*, 8-16.

                            1993   Settlements of the Hamburgian and Federmesser Cultures at Slotseng, South Jutland,
                                    Journal of Danish Archaeology 10 (1991), 7-19.

Holm, J.,   1992   *Istidsjægere ved Jelssøerne. Hamburgkulturen i Danmark*, Skrifter fra museumsrådet for
   F. Rieck   Sønderjyllands amt 5. Haderslev.

Houmark-Nielsen, M.   1989   Danmark i istiden – en tegneserie. *Varv* 1989:2.

Larsson, L.   1994   The Earliest Settlement in Southern Sweden. Late Palaeolithic Settlement Remains at
                                    Finjasjön, in the North of Scania, *Current Swedish Archaeology* 2, 159-177.

Lepiksaar, J.   1992   Remarks on the Weichselian megafauna (*Mammuthus, Coelodonta* and *Bison*) of the
                                    "intraglacial" area around the Baltic, *Annual Zoologica Fennici* 28, 229-240.

Madsen, E.   1963   Primitiv flintkultur ved Isefjord, *Aarbøger for nordisk Oldkyndighed og Historie*, 79-93.

                            1968a   En arkæologisk-geologisk undersøgelse af klinten ved Ejby Bro, Isefjord, *Meddelelser fra
                                    Dansk Geologisk Forening* 18:1, 33-46.

                            1968b   Un site danois à silex préhistoriques primitifs, *Revue Anthropologique*, 14-22.

Mangerud, J.   1991   The Last Ice Age in Scandinavia. In: B.G. Andersen and L.-K. Königsson (eds.), *Late
                                    Quaternary Stratigraphy in the Nordic Countries 150,000-15,000 B.P.*, Striae 34, 15-29.

Møhl-Hansen, U.   1955   Første sikre spor af mennesker fra interglacialtid i Danmark. Marvspaltede knogler fra
                                    diatoméjorden ved Hollerup, *Aarbøger for nordisk Oldkyndighed og Historie* 1954, 101-
                                    126.

Robertsson, A.-M.   1991   The Biostratigraphy of the Late Pleistocene in Sweden 150,000-15,000 B.P. – a Survey.
                                    In: B.G. Andersen and L.-K. Königsson (eds.), *Late Quaternary Stratigraphy in the
                                    Nordic Countries 150,000-15,000 B.P.*, Striae 34, 39-46.

Roebroeks, W.,   1992   Dense Forests, Cold Steppes, and the Palaeolithic Settlement of Northern Europe, *Current
   N. Conard,   Anthropology* 33, 551-586.
   T. van Kolfschoten

Stapert, D.   1976   Some natural surface modifications on flint in The Netherlands, *Palaeohistoria* 18, 8-41.

                            1981   Archaeological Research in the Kwintelooijen Pit, Municipality of Rhenen, the Netherlands,
                                    Meded. Rijks Geol. Dienst 35, 204-222.

Stevnhoved, S.   1992   Løsfunden palæolithisk flint – en varm kartoffel i dansk arkæologi, *Arkæologi i Slesvig*
                                    1/91, 71-73.

Strand Petersen, K.   1985   The Late Quaternary History of Denmark. The Weichselian Icesheets and Land/Sea
                                    Configuration in the Late Pleistocene and Holocene, *Journal of Danish Archaeology* 4,
                                    7-22.

Vang Petersen P.,   1993   Sølbjerg – An Ahrensburgian Site on a Reindeer Migration Route through Eastern
   L. Johansen   Denmark, *Journal of Danish Archaeology* 10, 1991.

Westerby, E.   1957   Istidsmandens redskaber?, *Skalk* 2, 14-16.

Jørgen Holm
The National Museum
Dept. of Prehistory and Early History
Frederiksholms Kanal 12
DK-1220 København K.
Denmark

Lars Larsson
University of Lund
Institute of Archaeology
Sandgatan 1
S-223 50 Lund
Sweden

Vassilij P. Ljubin
Gerhard Bosinski

12　The earliest occupation of the Caucasus region

*The Caucasus area is on a main road for the dispersal of
early hominids out of Africa, as testified by the Dmanisi
site with its date of 1.8 Myr BP. The area is rich in Middle
Pleistocene sites, though dating has proved difficult due to
the endemic character of flora and fauna. Stratified open
air sites like Achalkalaki are very rare, while cave sites are
common. Acheulean industries are known from Middle
Pleistocene deposits in caves like Azych, Kudaro and
Treugol'naja.*

1.　Introduction (by V.L.)

1.1.　GEOGRAPHICAL OVERVIEW

The Caucasus – the Caucasian isthmus – forms a vast
bridge between the Pontis and the Caspian Sea and
connects the southern Russian steppe with the highlands of
the Near East. The northern part of the Caucasus is
characterized by a steppe landscape, while the central part
is dominated by the mountains of the Great Caucasus,
whose axis runs across the isthmus. The southern Caucasus
is formed by the Transcaucasian Depression (Colchis-
Lowlands and the Kura Basin) and the volcanic Transcaucasian Plateau, a northern outlier of the Armenian and
Iranian Plateau. The boundaries of the Caucasus (to the
north the Kuma-Mantysch Basin, to the south the Aras
River) are not natural barriers in a geographical sense; there
are no clear differences in the landscape in both directions,
and access to both north and south and contacts to the Near
East played a major role in the Palaeolithic settlement of
the Caucasus.

The great regional differentiation of the Caucasus
landscape is mainly the result of topography. The most
important climatic boundaries are oriented along the ridge of
the Great Caucasus and the northern slope of the Caucasus
(Suram-Chain, Stavropol Hills). The climatic boundaries
have a major influence on temperature and precipitation on
the isthmus. The Great Caucasus divides two climatic zones:
the temperate zone of the northern Caucasus and the
subtropical climate zone of the Transcaucasus. Moreover,
the topography subdivides the Caucasus region into a large
number of local climatic provinces.

The climate of the western and central part of the flat
Caucasus foreland resembles that of the southern Russian
steppe. The Black Sea region has an eastern Mediterranean
climate; the influence of the central Asian steppes is
noticeable in the Kura Basin and the eastern part of the
Caucasus foreland. The continental climate of the volcanic
Transcaucasian Highlands is dominated by aridity. Different
belts of vegetation, determined by altitude, up to the zone
of perennial snow and glaciers can be observed in the
mountains (Gvozdeckij 1963).

A particularly noticeable feature of the Caucasus
landscape is the presence of an extensive and stable refuge
of relict vegetation in the Colchis (western Georgia)
(Čočieva 1982). The core of the Colchis flora are relict
Tertiary species (Kolakovskij 1961); approximately 20% of
the species in the Caucasus are endemic and only found in
the Colchis (Pavlov 1948). More than 6,000 species of
plants are known from the Caucasus region whereas from
the vast Russian plain only some 3,500 are known. The
number of animal species is 130.

A particularly species-rich woodland is present in the
Colchis region and numerous edible wild plants can be
found there (Grossgejm 1942, 1946). The favourable
climate and the rich food sources were particularly attrac-
tive to humans, as is shown by the concentration of Palaeolithic sites in this region. The Colchis region was apparently
a particularly favourable refuge for animals, plants and
humans during the glaciations (Ljubin 1969, 1974).

Limestone formations with caves and *abris* are present in
the Great Caucasus and in the mountain chains of the
Lesser Caucasus, an eastern extension of the Transcaucasian
Highlands. A ring of karstic landscapes surrounds almost
the entire northern slope of the Caucasus and the western
part of the southern slope in the Colchis region (from
Sotschi to the Kudaro Caves in South Ossetia). In the
northern karst belt there are Palaeolithic sites in for instance
the Monaseska, Barakaevska, Mezmajska and Treugol'naja
caves. Hundreds of *abris* and caves are known from the
western part of the south slope in the Colchis, where the
mild and humid climate has led to particularly extensive
karst formation. In many of these *abris* and caves, at all
altitudes, Palaeolithic sites have been discovered and
investigated, among them the sites of Kudaro I and III, and
Cona (Fig. 1).

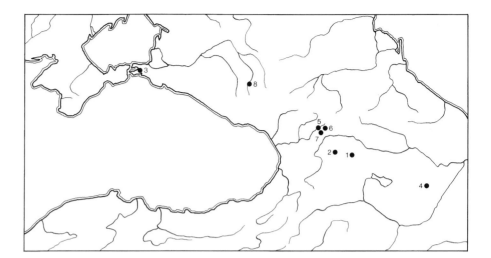

Fig. 1. Lower Palaeolithic Sites of the Caucasus Region.
1. Dmanisi; 2. Achalkalaki; 3. Taman; 4. Azych; 5. Kudaro I; 6. Kudaro III; 7. Cona; 8. Treugol'naja.

In the Lesser Caucasus karst caves are only known in the Somchetski, Sachdag and Karabach mountain ranges. In the foothills of the latter range is the multiple occupation site of Azych. Outside the karst region there are sites in caves beneath lava flows, for example in the narrow gorges of the Transcaucasian Highlands (Erevan Cave, Lusakert I and others). The volcanic region of the Transcaucasus holds a great potential for the discovery of Palaeolithic open sites; to date we only know the Lower Palaeolithic sites Dmanisi and Achalkalaki (Fig. 1).

The Caucasus region is well supplied with raw materials for the manufacture of stone tools. The range of available siliceous rocks – sedimentary and volcanic – includes almost all the lithic materials used for artefacts in the Palaeolithic; various types of flint, quartzite, sandstone, siliceous limestone, schist, obsidian, andesite, basalt etc. Volcanic raw materials (obsidian, andesite, basalt) are found in the regions of tectonic uplift in the Transcaucasus (Armenia, Džavacheti, Ossetia), whereas flint and other sedimentary rocks are dominant in the Colchis, the Black Sea area and Kuban.

1.2.   RESEARCH HISTORY

The research of the Palaeolithic of the Caucasus region started in 1898 with the discovery of the Middle Palaeolithic site of Il'skaja by the French investigator J. de Baye. The discovery of Lower Palaeolithic artefacts followed shortly after this, during the Armenian expedition of the French savant J. de Morgan. He collected obsidian artefacts from the western slopes of Mount Ararat (Morgan 1909).

After the 1917 Revolution investigations were carried out by Soviet archaeologists. Special surveys and planned investigations of Palaeolithic sites were carried out in

Abchasia and the Black Sea region of the Caucasus before the Second World War. The first Acheulean sites were discovered in the Soviet Union near Suchumi and Maikop, while the first Palaeolithic cave sites were discovered and partially excavated near Sotschi (Achstyrskaja Caves and others) (Zamjatnin 1937, 1949, 1961). The most important result in the first decade after the Second World War was the discovery of two large new find provinces with Acheulean and Middle Palaeolithic sites in Armenia (Paničkina 1950) and South Ossetia (Ljubin 1954, 1960).

The third phase of research began in 1955. The first cave sites with undisturbed Acheulean layers were discovered at Kudaro I and III (1955) and Cona (1958) in South Ossetia, and at Azych (1960) in Azerbaidschan (Ljubin 1959; Kalandadze 1965; Gusejnov 1963). At the same time hundreds of new Acheulean and Middle Palaeolithic surface sites were discovered in different regions of the Caucasus: e.g. Abadzechskoe and Chodžoch at Kuban (Autlev 1963), Bogos and other sites at the Black Sea (Ljubin and Ščelinskij 1972), Sarbebi, Čilovani and further sites in Imeretien (Tušabramišvili 1962), Džraber and Fontan in Armenia (Ljubin 1961), Ziari in Kachetia (Bugianišvili 1979), Čikiani and Persati in southern Georgia (Kikodze and Koridze 1978). Among the most important recent discoveries are the Treugol'naja Cave in the northern Caucasus (Doroničev 1992) and the open-air site Dmanisi in southern Georgia. The excavations in Dmanisi provided Lower Palaeolithic artefacts, an archaic fauna and the oldest remains of *Homo erectus* in Eurasia (Džaparidze *et al.* 1991; Gabunia 1992).

The majority of Acheulean and Middle Palaeolithic sites are located in upland situations, in the foothills and lower mountains of the western and central parts of the Caucasus isthmus. This is certainly not only a reflection of the current state of research, but far more the result of factors such as the presence of ancient routes of communication between the Caucasus and the Near East, of numerous natural rock shelters and natural resources (including lithic materials) and the particularly favourable climatic conditions especially in the Colchis refugium.

Extensive Acheulean and Middle Palaeolithic sites and ateliers have been discovered in the immediate vicinity of raw material sources. Such flint workshops are located in the Šachan Mountains of the Kuban region near Maikop (Abadzechskaja and others), in the Jaštuch Mountains of Abchasia and on the upper Imereti Plateau close to Kutaissi in southern Georgia (Sarbebi and others). Obsidian and andesite workshops are found in Armenia (Satani Dar, Erkao-blus, Atis and other sites) and in southern Georgia (Čikiani, Persati).

The lithic assemblages at the atelier sites do not represent discrete chronological units. The stratigraphical context of finds collected from river terraces, exposed hillsides, gorges and river valleys is unknown. The stratigraphic position and the age of finds from sediments overlying terrace deposits and marine sediments are also often uncertain. The age of finds from the basal alluvial facies of terraces can be established with some more certainty. Wide ranging studies of the geological-geomorphological position and age of terrace surfaces are currently in progress in the region of Sotschi and Tuapse. The subdivision of Pleistocene deposits is based here on the sequence and the geochronology of marine terraces and of the related river terraces in the Black Sea region (see Fig. 2). A number of Acheulean and Middle Palaeolithic sites have been discovered in the basal, alluvial parts of these terraces (Ščelinskij and Ostrovskij 1970; Ostrovskij et al. 1977; Izmajlov 1990).

The majority of Acheulean finds in the Caucasus comes from surface sites. Characteristic of these sites and also of the cave sites is the presence of bifaces. Acheulean with bifaces is the most important facies of the Lower Palaeolithic of the Caucasus. Bifaces are found in particularly large numbers at sites in the southern part of the Caucasus, i.e. from the Transcaucasian Highlands, which form the northern part of the extensive Near Eastern Highlands. The Acheulean in the Caucasus appears to be a northern extension of a distribution whose centre lies in the Near East. There are appreciably less bifaces on Acheulean sites north of the Transcaucasian Highlands; in Imereti, the Black Sea and the Kuban regions. The only exception to this are surface finds and sites in the west of South Ossetia (Laše-Balta, Kaleti, Cdileti and others in the foothills and Kudaro I, Kudaro III and Cona in the mountains), where numerous bifaces occur. This region is located between the Liachvi River and the Suramsk (Lichsk) mountain range

and forms a link between the Transcaucasian Highlands and the Greater Caucasus. The large proportion of bifaces from the South Ossetian sites is, most probably, related to the more southerly finds from the Transcaucasian Highlands (Džavacheti). Evidence for such a relationship might be the occurrence of bifaces at sites in South Ossetia which are made of a non locally occurring andesite (from the Džavacheti region?). The presence of cleavers in assemblages from both the Transcaucasian Highlands (Azych, Satani-Dar, Čikiani) and South Ossetia (Laše-Balta, Cona and other sites) also indicates such a relationship (Ljubin 1981a; Kikodze 1986).

Especially important and comprehensively published Acheulean sites are Satani-Dar (Paničkina 1950) and Džraber (Ljubin 1961, 1981a, 1984), both in Armenia, Laše-Balta (Ljubin 1960, 1981a) in South Ossetia, Jaštuch (Korobkov 1967, 1971) in Abchasia and Abadzechskaja in the Kuban region. Sites with Upper Acheulean artefacts (Levallois technique, small numbers of late types of bifaces) are known from the northern Caucasus. Two morphologically primitive bifaces (amygdaloid, proto-limande), cores and flakes found near Saratovsk on the Psekups River at the foot of the 35 metre terrace are the only artefacts which might be evidence of an appreciably earlier phase. Zamjatnin (1961) classified these finds as Lower Acheulean. The probable archaeological layer was geologically assigned to the early or central part of the Middle Pleistocene (Veličko et al. 1969).

1.3.   PLEISTOCENE CHRONOSTRATIGRAPHY

Different subdivisions of the Pleistocene period are used in the Caucasus region and they can only be correlated broadly in some cases (Fig. 2). The subdivision used in the eastern part of the region is based on the marine transgressions in the Caspian Sea (Fedorov 1978). In the western Caucasus transgressions of the Black Sea are the basis of classification (Fedorov 1978). In the north of the region the subdivision of terrestrial deposits, in particular moraines, established for the Russian plain is usually adopted (Nikiforova 1982). To the south, in the volcanic regions of the Transcaucasus, tephra deposits are being used increasingly for dating. Parallel to the geological zonation there exists a stratigraphical biozonation on the basis of faunal assemblages (Fig. 2).

The subdivision of the Pleistocene used in countries of the ex-Soviet Union, and therefore also in the Caucasus, differs from that in western and central Europe (Praslov 1984; Ljubin 1993a-b). The Tertiary/Quaternary boundary is located at the base of the Apšeron Layers and Gurija Layers of the Caspian and Black Seas respectively, and correlates with the Olduvai Event at 1.87-1.67 Myr BP. The Quaternary is divided into three units – Eopleistocene, Pleistocene and Holocene.

			Eastern Europe: Russian Plain, K.V. Nikiforova et al. 1980 – Sediments	Eastern Europe: Russian Plain, K.V. Nikiforova et al. 1980 – Fauna	Eastern Europe: Black Sea, P.V. Fedorov 1978, Kitovani 1976	Eastern Europe: Caspian Sea, P.V. Fedorov 1978	Central Europe	
	Holocene							
Quaternary	Pleistocene	Upper	Valdai	Mammoth Fauna: Late	New Evksin; Post-Karangat	Upper Chvalyn; Lower Chvalyn	Weichsel	Upper
Quaternary	Pleistocene	Upper	Mikulin	Mammoth Fauna	Karangat	Upper Chazar	Eem	Upper
Quaternary	Pleistocene	Middle	Moskva	Mammoth Fauna: Early	Regression	Regression	Saale: Warthe	Middle
Quaternary	Pleistocene	Middle	Roslav		Uzunlar	Lower Chazar (Kosož)	Saale: Treene	Middle
Quaternary	Pleistocene	Middle	Dnepr	Chazar	Early Evksin (upper)		Saale: Drenthe	Middle
Quaternary	Pleistocene	Middle	Lichvin	Singil'	Early Evksin (lower)	Lower Chazar (Singil')	Holstein	Middle
Quaternary	Pleistocene	Lower	Oka	Tiraspol	Regression	Regression	Elster	Middle
Quaternary	Pleistocene	Lower	Kolkotov		Upper Čauda	Urundžik (Upper Baku)	Cromer (I - V)	Middle
Quaternary	Pleistocene	Lower	Platov		Regression			
Quaternary	Pleistocene	Lower	Michajlov		Lower Čauda	Lower Baku; Tjurkjan		
Quaternary	Eopleistocene		Morozov; Nogaj	Taman	Čauda (Gurija)	Apšeron: Upper	Menap	Lower
Quaternary	Eopleistocene		Ževachov			Apšeron: Middle	Waal: C, B	Lower
Quaternary	Eopleistocene		Bošernic; Domaškin	Odessa	Gurija	Apšeron: Lower	Waal: A; Eburon	Lower
Neogene	Upper Pliocene		Ferladan; Kryžanov; Akkuleva; Čistopol	Chaprov	Kujal'nic	Akčagyl: Upper; Middle; Lower	Tegelen: C, B, A; Pretegelen	Lower
Neogene	Upper Pliocene			Moldava	Kimmerija			

Fig. 2. Pleistocene chronology in Eastern Europe (note that the stratigraphical subdivision for northern and central Europe differs from the standard division for this area; see Roebroeks and Van Kolfschoten, this volume, figure 1).

Eopleistocene

The Apšeron layers of the Caspian Sea and the Gurija layers of the Black Sea are assigned to the Eopleistocene. In the terrestrial classification system of the Russian Plain this period includes the Domaškin, Bošernic, Ževachov, Nogai and Morozov Horizons. The faunal complexes from Odessa and Taman are also assigned to the Eopleistocene.

The Eopleistocene is broadly equivalent to the Early Pleistocene of the western and central European classification and is subdivided into two further units. The Lower Eopleistocene contains the lower and lower-middle part of the Apšeron. This period is biostratigraphically characterized by the faunal assemblages from Odessa with the type species

Archidiskodon meridionalis meridionalis and is equivalent to the Late Villafranchian of western Europe.

The Upper Eopleistocene contains the upper-middle and upper units of the Apšeron and is characterized bio-stratigraphically by the fauna from Taman, with the type species *Archidiskodon meridionalis tamanensis*, a later form of the southern elephant. The equivalent stage in western Europe is the Epi-Villafranchian.

Pleistocene

The Eopleistocene/Pleistocene boundary is defined at the base of the Tjurkjan deposits of the Caspian Sea and the base of the Čauda deposits of the Black Sea. In the subdivision used in the Russian Plain region, this boundary is located at the beginning of the Michajlov horizon. The Eopleistocene/Pleistocene boundary is situated somewhat below the Matuyama-Brunhes boundary (0.78 Myr BP) which defines the beginning of the Middle Pleistocene in western and central Europe.

Lower Pleistocene

The Lower Pleistocene has two units. The older part includes in the Caspian Sea area the Tjurkjan, Baku and Urundzik layers, in the Black Sea area the Čauda layers. In the classification of the Russian Plain the equivalent units are the Michajlov, Platov and Kolkotov horizons.

The older phase of the Lower Pleistocene is defined by the fauna from Tiraspol, which includes *Archidiskodon trogontherii*, *Equus mosbachensis* and *Dicerorhinus mercki*. The younger phase of the Lower Pleistocene is represented on the Russian Plain by deposits of the Oka (= Elster) Glaciation; a period with a major marine regression of both the Caspian and the Black Sea. *Dicrostonyx* occurs in deposits of the Oka Glaciation.

The western and central European equivalent to this Lower Pleistocene is the first part of the Middle Pleistocene.

Middle Pleistocene

The Middle Pleistocene of the Caspian Sea is represented by the lower Chazar layers (Singil' and Kosož horizons), that of the Black Sea by the Evksin and Uzunlar deposits. On the Russian Plain the Middle Pleistocene contains the Lichvin, Dnepr, Roslava and Moskva horizons.

The Lichvin Interglacial is characterized by the Singil' fauna with *Palaeoloxodon antiquus*. The deposits of the Dnepr Glaciation contain a faunal complex with *Mammuthus chosaricus*, the earliest true mammoth. The Roslava and Moskva horizons are characterized by an early phase of the Late Pleistocene fauna containing *Mammuthus primigenius*.

This Middle Pleistocene can be equated with the second half of the western and central European Middle Pleistocene.

Upper Pleistocene

The Upper Pleistocene begins with the Mikulin (= Eem) Interglacial and also includes the deposits of the Valdai glaciation. The equivalent deposits in the Caspian Sea region are the upper Chazar and the Chvalyn layers, in the Black Sea area the Karangat, Post-Karangat and Novoevksin deposits. This Upper Pleistocene is the equivalent of the central and western European Late Pleistocene.

The correlation table (Fig. 2) compares the division of the Pleistocene in the Caucasus region with that of northern central Europe. The comparison should be treated with reservation and is, especially for the older part of the sequence, relatively uncertain. Correlation with the Alpine sequence seems to be quite impossible, with the exception of the Late Pleistocene. For the sake of uniformity the standard continental subdivision of the Pleistocene as used in central and western Europe will be used in the following text.

2.   The earliest occupation of the Caucasus
2.1.   EARLY PLEISTOCENE: DMANISI (BY G.B.)

The site Dmanisi lies in southeast Georgia, close to the border with Armenia, in a volcanic area which extends into Armenia and Turkey to the south (Fig. 3). Important for the area are the volcanoes of the north-south oriented Džavacheti range, to the west of Dmanisi. During the Early Pleistocene, lava from a volcano of the Džavacheti range flowed eastwards through the valley of the Mašavera river and into the lower valley of the Pinezaouri (Fig. 4). The lava is normally magnetized and has been dated to 1.8 ± 0.1 and 1.9 ± 0.2 Myr BP, suggesting it should be placed in the Olduvai Event (Majsuradze *et al.* 1991). The lava was later cut by both the Mašavera and the Pinezaouri, leaving a triangular promontory of lava, which towers 90 m above the present level of the rivers. On this promontory lay the mediaeval town of Dmanisi; the citadel in the south of the ruined town is built on Cretaceous deposits.

The Lower Palaeolithic site was discovered in the pit-cellars of mediaeval houses. Following preliminary excavations by the Archaeological Centre, Tiflis between 1983-1987 and in 1989, the site has been investigated since 1991 (Džaparidze *et al.* 1991).

Stratigraphy

In the middle of the lava flow there is a basalt ridge with accumulated sediments on both sides (Fig. 3). The base of the section, on top of the lava, is formed by black basalt sand (VI), covered by a blackish brown sandy loam (V) with numerous bones and lithic artefacts. In a concentration at the base of layer V the human mandible (see below) was found. Next, a brown sandy loam (IV) is present, which

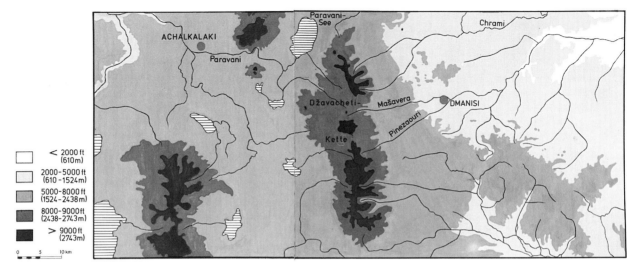

Fig. 3. Location of Dmanisi and Achalkalaki in the Dzavacheti region.

differs from the underlying layers mainly in the absence of
a component of basalt ash. Bones and artefacts are also
present in Layer IV, but less than in Layer V. A blocky
deposit, composed of mainly horizontal bands of carbonate
concretion *kerki* forms Layer III. It seems that the carbonate
concretions of the *kerki* formed as a crust developed on
the underlying sediments in warm and arid conditions.
The molluscs and seeds found in the *kerki* indicate dry
conditions. Bones and artefacts are also present in the
deposit, indicating that humans were occasionally present
during the formation of the *kerki*. Above the *kerki* follows
0.50 - 0.80 m of a yellow, weakly loamy sediment (Layer II).
In the lower part of Layer II, 0.10 - 0.20 m above the *kerki*,
there is a horizon with many stones including artefacts. The
1992-1994 excavations demonstrated that the stones of this
layer extend over a surface of at least 70 × 70 m. In order
to clarify this situation it is necessary to excavate larger
and coherent surfaces. Bones are rare in this horizon, but a
molar of *Archidiskodon meridionalis* found in 1991
indicates that Layer II is also to be dated to the Early
Pleistocene (Vekua and Gabunia 1991). The top of the
section consists of a grey sediment (Layer I), which
probably represents an alteration (soil formation) of the
underlying layer. The surface of Layer I is consolidated by
carbonate concretions. On top of layer I is a thin humus
layer with mediaeval finds and the rubble layers of the
mediaeval town.

The lower layers (VI-IV) may have been formed in a
relatively short period, by fluvial processes that decreased
through time. The layers V and IV are normally magnetized
(Majsuradze *et al.* 1991) which suggests a preliminary
correlation of these layers with the Olduvai Event. The

chronological position of the upper levels, especially of
layer II is difficult to establish. The palaeomagnetical
analysis of Sologašvili indicates that layer II is magnetically
reversed, which suggests a correlation to the Matuyama
period after the Olduvai Event.

Faunal remains

The majority of the macro faunal remains recovered to
date are from Layer V, while a number of bones belongs
to Layer IV. Layer VI directly overlies the basalt lava
and has only yielded a few bones, which, in colour and
high degree of fossilization, differ from the other bones.
The *kerki* Layer III contains only a small number of
resistant faunal remains, mainly teeth. In Layer II bones
are rare.

The fauna from Layer V is assigned biostratigraphically to
the Late Villafranchian (Vekua and Gabunia 1991, Vekua
in press).[1] The fauna is younger than the Villafranchian
complexes from Kočachuri and Čalka (Vekua *et al.* 1985),
which belong to the early Apšeronian (Gabunia and Vekua
1981, 1990; Vekua 1991a-b). Dmanisi is nevertheless, on
the evidence of the stage of development of *Archidiskodon
meridionalis*, older than ’Ubeidija (Vekua and Gabunia
1991; Gabunia and Vekua 1993; Vekua in press).

Ecologically the fauna is dominated by species typical
of warm climate, open grassland (*Struthio, Equus, Dicerorhinus etruscus, Archidiskodon meridionalis*), but species
indicative of forested conditions are also present (*Sus,
Ursus etruscus*).

The bones of Layer V lay in separate concentrations,
which repeatedly contained articulated skeletal parts
(vertebrae, foot bones). Some of the bones are fragmented.

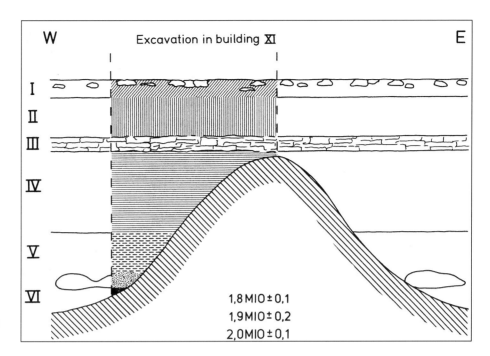

Fig. 4. Dmanisi. Schematic section
(total height approximately 4 m).

Taphonomic studies have not been carried out yet, so for the time being it is impossible to evaluate the role of humans in the accumulation of the recovered assemblage; there are bones and antlers with possible traces of modification by humans, though small mammal remains and molluscs are found mainly in the lower Layers (V, IV). The following species are identified by A. Vekua and A. Muschelišvili: *Sorex* sp., *Marmota* sp., *Apodemus* aff. *dominans*, *Allocricetus* sp., *Epimeriones* sp., *Mimomys* ex gr. *hungaricus*, *Kowalskia* sp.

Flora

Pollen is only poorly preserved in the Dmanisi section. However, in a coprolite E. Kvavadze found a spectrum containing pollen of trees (pine, spruce, beech, alder, chestnut, lime, birch, hornbeam), shrubs (rhododendron, hazel) and grass and herbs (including Polypodiaceae, Chenopodiaceae, Cyperaceae and Gramineae) (Kloptovskaja *et al.* 1991). Additionally, seeds were identified of *Buglossoides arvense, Anchusa* sp., *Staphyllea colchika, Nonea flavescens, Lycopsis orientalis* and *Celtis glabrata*.

Lithic artefacts

Lithic artefacts are particularly common in Layer II, but are also present in Layers V and IV. It is still not possible to recognize differences in the typology or technology of the various layers.

The artefacts are mainly manufactured from silicified volcanic tuffs and are occasionally of quartz (Bosinski *et al.*

1991). They are struck from cobbles which occur in the valleys of the Mašavera and Pinezaouri.

Flakes make up the majority of the artefacts (Fig. 5). A number of the smaller flakes are struck from more highly silicified flint-like tuffs, which are only rarely found in the river gravels.

The dorsal surfaces of the flakes normally have flake scars which are usually struck from the same direction as the flake itself and show serial knapping of flakes. The flake edges commonly show definite use wear (marginal retouch, splintering, small notches).

Retouched flakes (Fig. 6) are rare, but present in the form of edge retouch and stepped retouch. A multiple burin is present, manufactured on a large flake with an edge-retouched ventral face.

Cores are mainly spherical/polyhedric and struck from several directions. There are also conical cores whose striking platform is formed by one or, at most, a few blows. Pebble tools are both unifacially and bifacially worked and show a great overlap with the category of cores (Fig. 7).

The hominid mandible

The hominid mandible discovered in September 1991, in the lower part of Layer V, was found in the middle of a concentration of bones (Gabunia *et al.* 1991). Remains of *Megantereon* (cranium, atlas, epistropheus, vertebrae), *Canis* (cranium, phalanx 1, canini), *Ursus* (carpalia), *Equus* (tibia, radius, humerus, vertebrae), *Dicerorhinus* (M1-M3), *Cervus* (vertebrae), *Bos* (metacarpus, vertebrae), *Hypolagus*

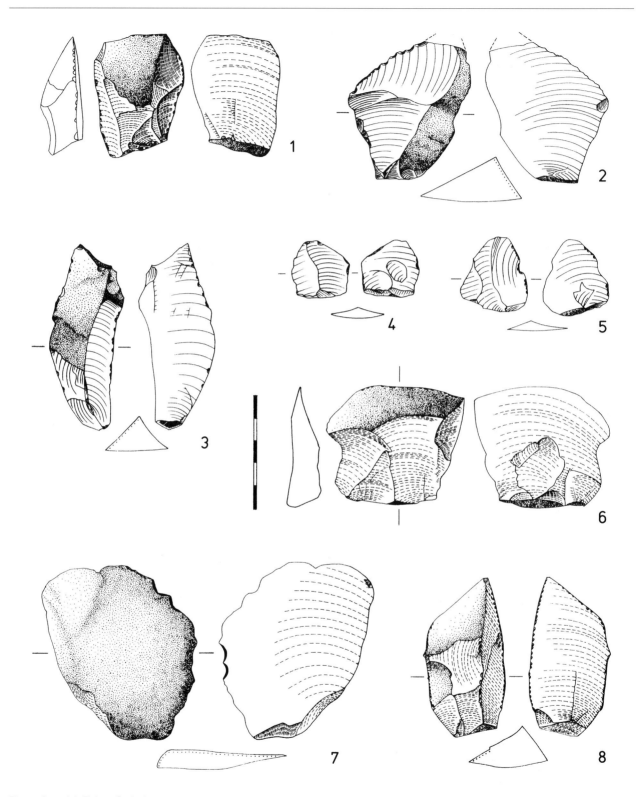

Fig. 5. Dmanisi. Flakes. Scale in cm.

(metatarsus) and Reptilia (vertebrae) could be identified. The concentration also contained artefacts and manuports. The mandible (Fig. 8) lay upside down in the middle of the concentration. The ascending ramus on both sides of the mandible has been fractured off. Otherwise the mandible is well preserved with all 16 teeth. The degree of wear on the teeth suggests an individual between 20-25 years at the time of death. The robusticity of the piece allows it to be identified as male (Gabunia 1992). The low width and the narrow alveolar arch of the medium-sized piece are notable. The region of the anterior symphysis is narrow and has a pronounced relief. The middle part of the symphysis is convex; a chin prominence is not present. The incisors project forwards and their alignment is only slightly curved. The canine is slightly pointed but does not protrude above the height of the other teeth. The premolars are relatively small. The molars have strongly folded enamel and have the *Dryopithecus* pattern and a sixth cusp (*tuberculum sextum*). The size of the molars diminishes appreciably from M_1 to M_3. According to L. Gabunia (1992) the mandible shows a range of archaic characteristics, such as the U-shaped alveolar arch, the anterior and relatively low placement of the foramen mentale, absence of the trigonum mentale, forward position of the beginning of the ascending rami and reduction of the retromolar fossa. At the same time, the mandible has certain features in common with early *Homo sapiens*, e.g. reduction in the size of the molars from M_1 to M_3, a tendency towards a vertical orientation of the planum alveolare, and only a slight recession of the anterior symphyseal surface.

The Dmanisi mandible shows similarities to certain Early Pleistocene specimens. Among African finds these are OH13 (*Homo habilis*), ER 730, ER 992 and, possibly, the admittedly very young individual WT 15000. Among the Java finds there are many similarities to Sangiran 9. L. Gabunia (1992) believes that the Dmanisi hominid and the similar *Pithecanthropus* from Sangiran represent a form derived from *Homo habilis* which already spread into Eurasia at the beginning of the Pleistocene. Derived from a hominid type which also contained the ancestors of *Homo erectus*, the representatives of this early migration of *habilis*-type hominids into Eurasia underwent their own evolution. In some features this led to parallels with the more recent *Homo erectus*, while in other ways the tempo of evolution was more rapid than for the latter species (L. Gabunia 1992).

2.2.   EARLY MIDDLE PLEISTOCENE (BY G.B.)
2.2.1.   Achalkalaki

East of the town of Achalkalaki in southern Georgia (Fig. 3) is the 1,883 m OD high volcano of Amiranis, which towers over the Džavacheti high plateau by some 150 m.

This high plateau is formed of Tertiary (Miocene-Pliocene) pyroclastic rocks and lavas and Pliocene-Early Pleistocene basalts (Maruašvili 1971; Gabunia *et al.* 1994).

In the early 1960's A. Vekua undertook palaeontological excavations on the lower slopes of Mt. Amiranis (Vekua 1962, 1987; Kahlke 1987). A rich fauna was excavated from the loamy weathered deposits, with *Ursus* sp., *Meles meles*, *Panthera* cf. *tigris*, *Mammuthus* aff. *trogontherii*, *Archidiskodon* sp., *Equus süssenbornensis*, *Equus hipparionoides*, *Dicerorhinus etruscus*, *Hippopotamus georgicus*, *Praemegaceros verticornis* and *Capra* sp. This fauna is assigned to the early Middle Pleistocene. Its composition suggests that at that time the Achalkalaki plateau and the surrounding region were covered by an open steppe vegetation. The admittedly few palaeobotanical remains support this interpretation (*Celtis, Lithospermum arvense*; Avakov 1960). It was supposed that humans were partly responsible for the accumulation of material found in Achalkalaki. For this reason M.K. Gabunia opened a test pit near the area investigated by A. Vekua. At 0.80 - 1.10 m below the recent surface he found artefacts and bones, identified as *Bison* sp., *Equus süssenbornensis*, *Equus hipparionoides, Dicerorhinus etruscus, Archidiskodon* sp., *Marmota* sp. and *Homotherium*. All these species, with the exception of *Homotherium*, were already known from this site.

Some of the limb bones were found in anatomical connection. This had also been observed during earlier investigations and suggests that the material has, at most, been only slightly reworked. An andesite flake with a broad scraper edge was associated with the bones (Fig. 9). It was thus established that Achalkalaki is also an archaeological site. Nevertheless, the precise role of humans in the accumulation of the faunal assemblage remains to be investigated.

2.2.2.   Taman, Kurgan Cimbal

A number of palaeontological sites are known from the Taman peninsula between the Sea of Asov and the Black Sea (Vereščagin 1957). Sand quarrying on the eastern shore of the Bay of Taman close to the Greek city of Kepy, has uncovered numerous animal bones. The bones were mostly bedded horizontally, both in conglomerate and in intervening sandy layers. The majority of the recovered material consists of fragments of long bones and skulls, antler and isolated teeth. Vereščagin suggests that human activity is responsible for the breakage of certain bones (Fig. 10,3-4).

"Some long bones of medium-sized animals, e.g. deer, are fractured in a manner later practised by Middle and Upper Palaeolithic people... Comparable fracture patterns are sometimes found on bones from Middle Pleistocene deposits in the Central Volga region. However, to date we know of nothing comparable

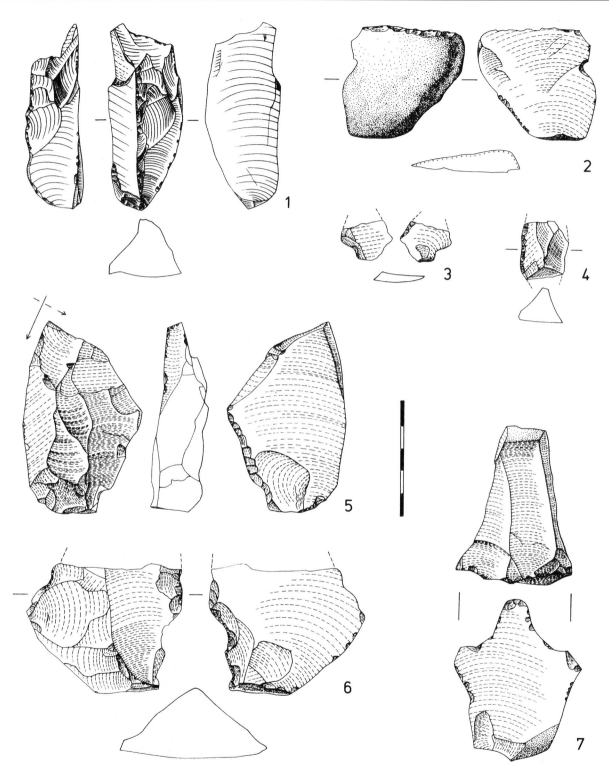

Fig. 6. Dmanisi. Retouched flakes (1-6) and core (7). Scale in cm.

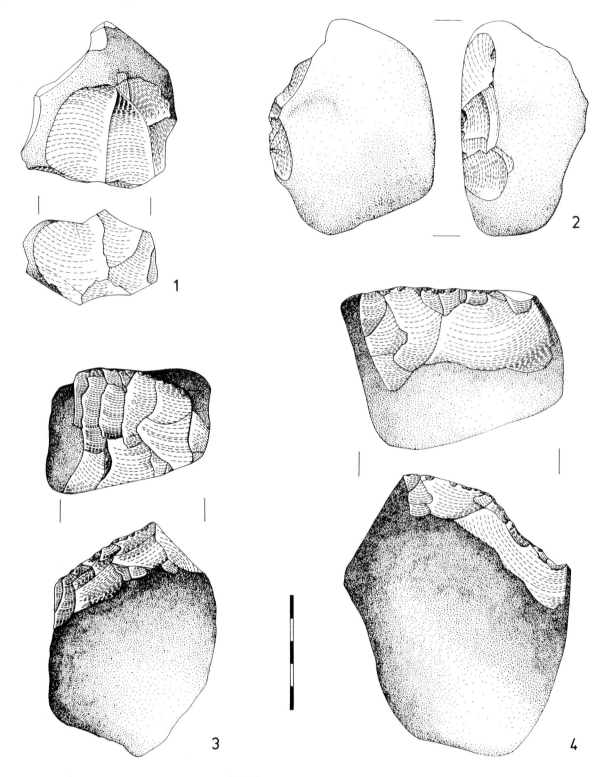

Fig. 7. Dmanisi. Core (1) and and pebble tools (2-4). Scale in cm.

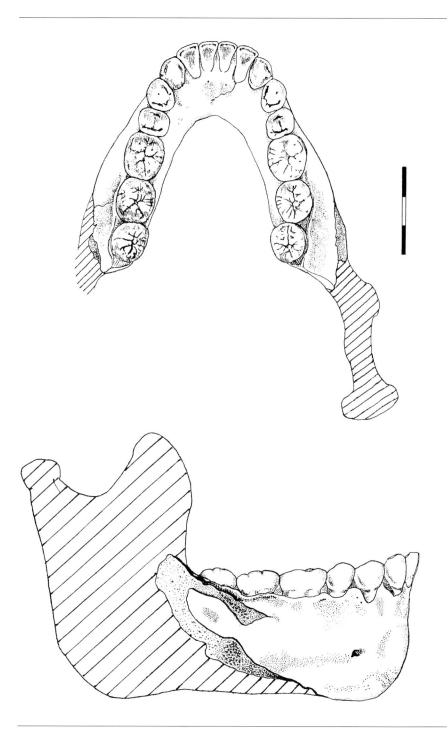

Fig. 8. Dmanisi. Human mandible.
Drawing L. Gabunia. Scale in cm.

from the well known Middle Pleistocene site at Binograd on the Apseron peninsula, where more than 35,000 different bones have already been recovered. The presence of stone artefacts at the site of Cimbal would be an important indication for a particularly early human presence in the territory of the USSR" (Vereščagin 1957a, p. 21).

Such artefacts have been found in the Cimbal pit and published (Formozov 1965). One of these is a flake with an unfacetted striking platform and a pronounced bulb of percussion, the other a disc-shaped artefact (Fig. 10,1-2; see Formozov 1965).

2.3.   MIDDLE PLEISTOCENE CAVE SITES (BY V.L.)

2.3.1.   *Azych*

This cave lies close to the village of Azych in the foothills of the Karabach Range in the southeast of the Lesser Caucasus of Azerbaidshan (Fig. 1). The cave lies at 800 m OD (200 m above the surrounding area). It forms a horizontal passage of gallery-type with a main entrance formed by five chambers and a northern and southern gallery. The total area of the cave is some 2,150 m². The site was discovered in 1960 by M.M. Gusejnov and investigated by him over a period of more than 20 years. The first test pits at the cave entrance revealed a Middle Palaeolithic horizon (Layer III), while subsequently an upper (Layer V) and a lower Acheulean horizon (Layer VI) were excavated. Even older material was discovered in 1974 (Layers VII-X) (Gusejnov 1965, 1981, 1985). The greatest depth of the deposits was 14 m, the total area excavated covered 200 m². Besides stone artefacts and faunal remains the 1968 excavation of the Acheulean layers recovered a jaw fragment of a "Pre-Neandertaler" (Gadžiev and Gusejnov 1970). In 1971 a small concentration of bear mandibles and skulls (the so-called hiding place) was discovered, while the excavation in 1972 uncovered hearths and that in 1973 a stone feature ("dwelling").

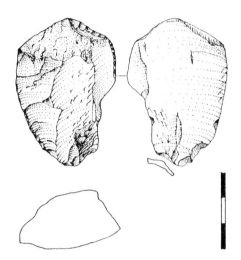

Fig. 9. Achalkalaki. Retouched flake. Scale in cm. After M. Gabunia.

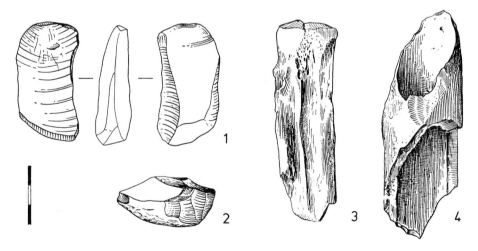

Fig. 10. Taman. Flake (1), core (2), splitted bones (3-4). Scale in cm. After A. Formozov (1-2) and N.K. Vereščagin.

Gusejnov (1974) identified 10 layers within the cave sections (I-X), but it is unfortunately not always possible to correlate these with the stratigraphy of the "main profile", sampled by Veličko, who discerned 17 horizons there. These were assigned to three units (Veličko *et al.* 1980):

Upper Unit: (Horizon 1 = Gusejnov's Layers I and II)
Middle Unit: (Horizons 2-12 = Gusejnov's Layers III-VI)
Lower Unit: (Horizons 13-17 = Gusejnov's Layers VII-X)

Fauna

Faunal remains were not recovered by lithological horizons but were assigned to the archaeological layers approximately identified by Gusejnov during excavation as "Early Acheulean" (Layer VI), "Middle Acheulean" (Layer V) etc. As a result the fauna from each of these layers is mixed due to the different conditions prevailing during the formation of the "layers". Only the small mammal remains, which were collected by Sulejmanov (1979) according to strictly defined lithological units and analysed by Markova (1982), have a good stratigraphical provenance. In the faunal list of all layers together there are 65 species, among which 11 rodents, 3 lagomorphs, 1 amphibia, 1 reptile, 4 bats and 21 birds. All 65 species are present in the deep "middle Acheulean" Layer (V). For more detailed information about the fauna the reader is refered to: Aliev 1969; Baryšnikov 1991a; Gadžiev *et al.* 1979; Guérin and Barychnikov 1987; Markova 1982 and Veličko *et al.* 1980.

Flora

The palynological investigations of Zelikson and Gubonina (1985) demonstrated repeated changes in vegetation from deciduous forest with *Pterocarya*, walnut, alder, beech, *Zelkova*, oak, chestnut and elm (Horizons 17-16, 14-13, upper part of Layer VI, lower part of Layer V), such as is found today in the lower lying uplands and valleys, to upland forest with birch, *Ostrya* and hornbeam (Horizons 15-14, 12, Layer VI, main part of Layer V). Pollen from the archaeologically sterile Layer IV shows a subalpine vegetation.

Lithic Assemblage

Stone artefacts were recovered from Layers X-VII ("Pebble Culture"), VI ("Early Acheulean"), V ("Middle Acheulean") and III ("Late Acheulean" and "Early Mousterian")

– Layers X-VII: 186 finds of among other materials quartz, silicified limestone and chalcedony were excavated from the deepest layers. The raw material consisted of cobbles from the gravels of the Kuručaj River, 53 of which were recovere,d complete, without any traces of fracture. It

is difficult to decide whether the remaining pieces are true artefacts (Fig. 11). At a conference held in Baku in 1985 some researchers believed that all pieces were artefacts, whereas others thought that all were natural, unmodified pieces. A third group (with amongst others V.P. Ljubin) thought that some of the finds might be pebble tools and flakes. The character of the finds and the provisional nature of the publications makes it impossible to come to a conclusive decision regarding the artefactual status of these finds.

– Layer VI: (after Gusejnov 1985:16-20, 33-36 and a number of drawings by the author [V. L.]) (Figs 12-13). This layer was investigated over an area of 125 m², where 1890 artefacts were recovered. Some are heavily weathered and have rounded edges. Possibly these pieces are from the base of Layer V, which was formed under wet and warm environmental conditions. The artefacts are manufactured from lydite (1084) and flint (790), a small number are made of sandstone, quartzite, basalt and aphanite). The assemblage contains cobbles (37), tools (427 = 22,6 %) and debitage. The few cores (9) have a single striking platform (2) or are discoid. The 1116 flakes include 136 blades (12,1 %). A large proportion of the flakes (40-50 %) are long (5-12 cm with a breadth of 3 cm) and thin (less than 1,5 cm). 54,5 % of the striking platforms are unfacetted, 31 % dihedral and 14 % facetted (among the latter there are 30 flakes and blades with finely facetted, arched platforms). These technological details alone make it unlikely that the industry is early Acheulean. This is confirmed by the typological composition of the assemblage. Coarse pebble tools are relatively rare. The choppers (16) and chopping tools (5) were manufactured on cobbles with one flat and one convex side, the working edge being retouched on the flat face. The 8 bifaces from this level have a variable morphology (elongate-ovates, amygdaloid, lanceolate and rounded ovate). They were manufactured on flat cobbles, whose shape was selected in order to simplify the manufacture of the desired final form. As a result, there are several bifaces which are only partially worked, shown by their large areas of cortex (Fig. 12). Three cleavers were also found. Flake tools are present in large numbers (Fig. 13). Side-scrapers are particularly common and practically all forms described by Bordes (1961) are present. Simple scrapers are dominant (97); also present are double side-scrapers (33 - in part manufactured on blades), transverse side-scrapers (21), convergent side-scrapers (13) and *déjeté* side-scrapers (20). Points are, by contrast, rare (7) and of poor quality and include 6 double points (*limaces*). The assemblage also includes 24 end-scrapers, 4 borers and a backed knife. Finally, there are 62 denticulates and 15 notched pieces.

– Layer V: This layer is subdivided into 5 horizons which yielded numerous faunal remains (65 species), but

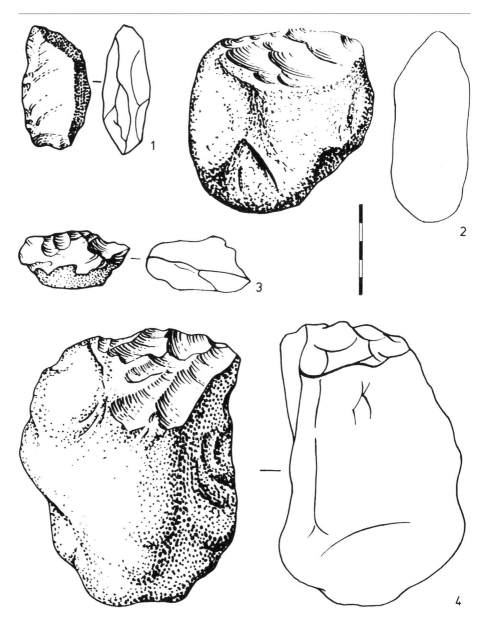

Fig. 11. Azych, levels X-VII. Artefacts (?). Scale in cm. After M.M. Gusejnov.

only relatively few stone artefacts (in 1985 Gusejnov refers to 289 pieces). The majority of the artefacts, and all the bifaces (Figs 14-15), were found in the middle part of the layer, which was described by Veličko *et al.* (1980:24) as follows: "Horizons 9 and 10 are characterized by horizontal layers of limestone slabs, lenses and concentrations of sand and charcoal and a high proportion of bone fragments. The possibility that these particular features represent a human occupation level cannot be ruled out. It should be emphasized that the hominid mandible was found in

Horizon 10". Layer V (Horizon 1) also contains a thick layer of hearth material and the remains of a stone feature (see below, "dwelling"), in which only a few stone artefacts (mainly side-scrapers) were found. The small number of stone artefacts and the high proportion of retouched forms suggest that Layer V is characterized by episodes of short term occupation. As is the case at the alpine site of Cona in South Ossetia only hunting artefacts (weapons and hide-working tools) were brought to the site. The raw material spectrum is dominated by flint (49,4%

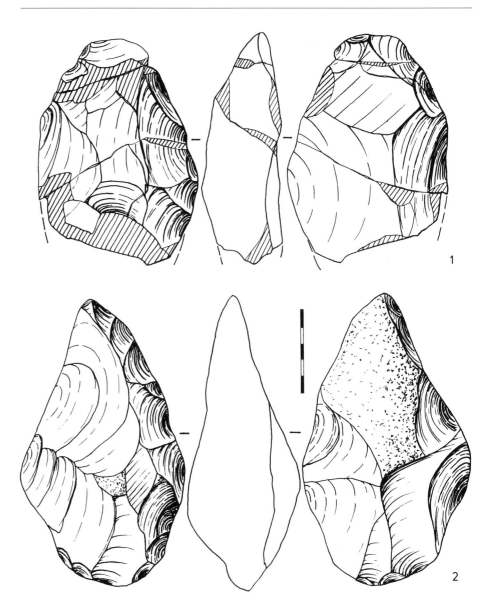

Fig. 12. Azych, level VI. Bifaces. Scale in cm. After M.M. Gusejnov.

here, 41,7% in Layer VI) and not by lydite (46,3% as compared to 57,6% in Layer VI). Artefacts are also rarely made of andesite and obsidian. Cores can have either a single striking platform (6 specimens), two or more platforms, or are of discoid form (Fig. 16,1). Flakes commonly have facetted striking platforms and a small number of Levallois flakes are present. The morphology of the choppers (6) is more uniform than in Layer VI. The 7 handaxes are manufactured from lydite, 4 of them on massive flakes. Flake tools are well represented and consist largely of side-scrapers (26), points (2), end-scrapers (4), backed knives (3) and a number of denticulates and notched pieces. An important aspect of the investigation is the analysis of use-wear on the tools of this layer by Ščelinskij (1993). Traces of wear were found on 128 tools, among which are choppers, chopping tools and handaxes. The pebble tools were used for a range of (mainly heavy-duty) functions, such as cutting wood and breaking bone. The analysis shows that handaxes were used mainly for cutting meat.

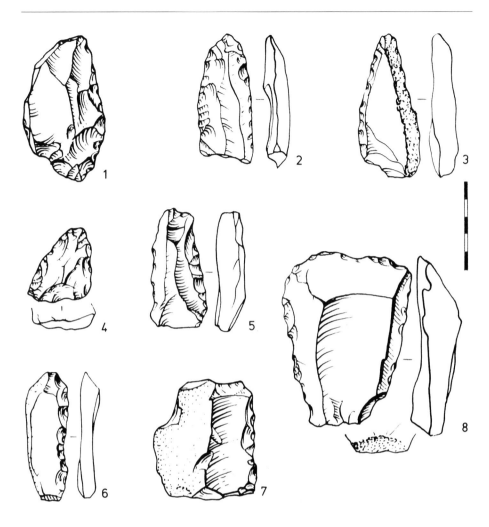

Fig. 13. Azych, level VI. Flake-tools. Scale in cm. After M.M. Gusejnov.

– Layer III: The artefacts from this layer are made of lydite (1786), flint (1293) and obsidian (14) and are probably late Middle Palaeolithic.

Settlement features

– The "Hiding place": A concentration of four bear skulls from Layer V was discovered in a vertical fissure close to the south wall of the circular chamber by Gusejnov in 1971. It has certain features in common with the "bear cult" of the "Alpine Palaeolithic". This concentration of bones probably has nothing to do with human activities.

– The "Dwelling": A circular stone feature was discovered at the base of Horizon 1 in Layer V. It was located in the northeastern part of the circular chamber close to the northern wall (Gusejnov 1974, 1975). This

"foundation" was formed of limestone slabs and, in one place, of deer antlers. The structure was preserved to a height of 20-30 cm and the inner area was 10 m². A hearth was found at the northeastern corner of the structure (Hearth 4, see below), from which a 17 cm thick layer with burnt material extended 4 m into the centre of the feature (Gusejnov 1975: 84-85). This undoubtedly interesting settlement feature is unfortunately only provisionally and inadequately documented.

– Hearths: Between 1972-1973 a total of five hearths were discovered in Layers VI, V and IV. All were found in a poorly lit part of the circular chamber, 24 to 30 m from the cave entrance (Gusejnov 1974). Hearth 1 lay 8 m below the surface in the upper part of Layer VI. The hearth was in a shallow depression and measured 20 × 30 cm, with a fill

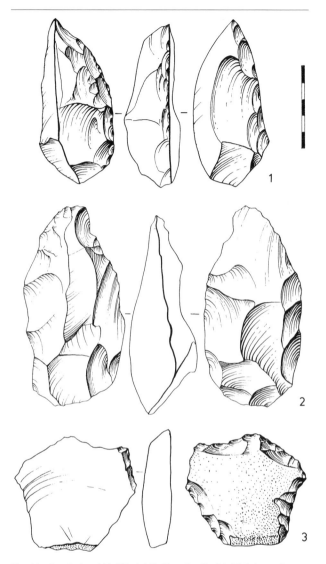

Fig. 14. Azych, level V. Bifacial (1-2) and unifacial (3) flake-tools. Scale in cm: After M.M. Gusejnov.

some 5-7 cm deep. Hearth 2 was 7 m below the surface in Layer V, horizon 4, and measured 45 × 50 cm with a 10 cm thick fill of charcoal-like material. Hearth 3 was found 5.5 m below the modern cave in Layer V, at the base of Horizon 1. This was the biggest hearth with a total surface of some 10 m², in the form of an L. Its width was 1 to 3 m. The upper part of the feature contained a layer of ash from between 7-8 to 13-17 cm thick, below which was a charred layer 6-9 cm in depth. Whereas the charred layer was of even depth, the overlying ash layer was of variable depth and in places appeared to form small piles. The 26 cm thick deposit was probably the result of the accumulation of material from several separate hearths (Gusejnov 1974).

Hearth 4 was found in the same layer as Hearth 3, but lay within the stone feature located against the northern cave wall. The hearth measured 20 × 40 cm and was dug some 15 cm deep into the floor. It was enclosed by limestone slabs and surrounded by burnt bones (Gusejnov 1974). Hearth 5, finally, was found in the Middle Palaeolithic level III, Horizon 3, 3.5 m below the surface. It was dug slightly into the floor and measured 40 x 55 cm, and its sides were lined with limestone slabs. With the exception of Hearth 4 (inside the stone feature) all hearths, irrespective of their stratigraphic position, were located at the same place within the circular chamber. This was at a point where the gallery structure of the cave caused a particularly strong draught (Gusejnov 1974).

The hominid mandible

In 1968 a fragment of hominid mandible was discovered in Layer V, Horizon 3. The posterior part of the body of the mandible and the lower part of the ascending ramus are preserved. Only the third molar is present; to judge by the fresh damage to the piece, the first two molars were probably destroyed during excavation. The crown of the second molar is missing and only parts of the roots of the first molar are preserved. A preliminary description of the find by D.V. Gadžiev emphasized the robusticity of the jaw, the small size of the teeth, the poorly developed tauro-dontism and the position of the foramen mentalis at the level of the first molar (Gadžiev and Gusejnov 1970). These and other features led to the Azych mandible being described as representing a form transitional between the late Archanthropes and the early Palaeanthropes and, in particular, to a comparison with the mandible from Mauer and finds from Arago (Charitonov 1989; Gabunia 1992).

Dating

A magnetic reversal, interpreted as the Matuyama-Brunhes boundary, was recognized in the lower part of the section in Horizon 15 (at the level of the "Pebble Culture" finds). In the layer immediately above this (Horizon 14) a tooth of *Microtus* ex gr. *arvalis socialis*, whose earliest occurrence is at the time of the Baku Transgression in the early Middle Pleistocene faunal complex from Tiraspol (Markova 1982), was found. *Bison schoetensacki* and *Equus süssenbornensis*, found in Layer VI with Acheulean finds (D.V. Gadžiev *et al.* 1979:11), also have their best parallels in the Tiraspol fauna. The finds from Layer V, including the hominid mandible fragment might more probably date to the second part of the Middle Pleistocene.

2.3.2.   KUDARO I

The Kudaro cave sites are located in the central part of the southern slope of the Greater Caucasus, in the northeastern corner of the Colchis (Fig. 1). The caves lie

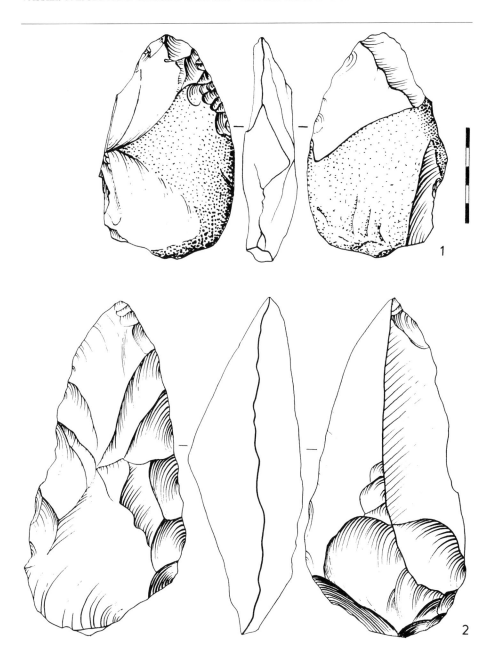

Fig. 15. Azych, level V. Bifaces. Scale in cm. After M.M. Gusejnov.

close to the tree line on the slope of the Časaval'ski mountain; Kudaro I is located at a height of 1600 m OD, 260 m above the river. The common genesis of the caves means that they are morphologically similar and, at a similar topographic position, possess similar stratigraphies. The caves, which open onto a steep slope in a bay between two ridges, consist of horizontal galleries. They face south and have an arched roof. Their entrances collapsed in

antiquity. Overall, their lithological and archaeological sequences are similar.

The Palaeolithic sites in the Kudaro caves were discovered in 1955 by the Leningrad researchers of the South-Ossetien Expedition of the Georgian Academy of Sciences under the leadership of V.P. Ljubin, who investigated the sites until 1990, with a heavy emphasis on the Kudaro I site. The results of the excavations have been presented in numerous

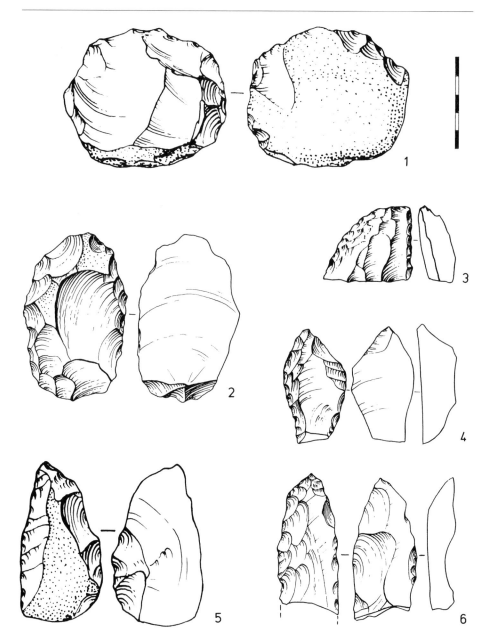

Fig. 16. Azych, level V. Core (1) and flake-tools (2-6). Scale in cm. After M.M. Gusejnov.

publications, synthetically in the book *Kudarskie peščernye paleolitičeskie stojanki v Jugo-Osetii* (Ljubin 1980a) and also in papers by Ljubin *et al.* (1978, 1985a-b); Ljubin and Baryšnikov (1985), Ljubin (1959, 1977, 1981a, 1981c, 1984, 1989, 1990, 1993a-b), Baryšnikov (1977, 1978, 1987), Baryšnikov and Dedkova (1978), Baryšnikov and Baranova (1983) and Nesmejanov (1989).

Stratigraphy

The sediments of each gallery have their own character, influenced by local fissures, erosional processes, factors of external weathering, differences in the facies of contemporary sediments and the character and degree of influence of animals and humans. This leads to special conditions in the fills of the different galleries, which can be up to 1.5-4.5 m thick, and determines the character of the lithological and archaeological horizons.

The deposits in the eastern gallery are particularly uniform and typical (Fig. 17). Six different levels could be identified: level 1 contained Eneolithic and younger finds, level 2 a few final Palaeolithic and Mesolithic finds. Levels 3 and 4 are Middle Palaeolithic, level 5 (5a, 5b and 5v) Acheulean, while level 6 was sterile. Discordances between some horizons indicate stratigraphical gaps, which are the result of erosion of sediments and possibly also of non-sedimentation during cold phases. In addition there are facies variations among synchronous sediments from the cave's entrance to the inner parts, as well as local variations in the thickness of some horizons.

In the Dark Gallery the deepest Acheulean layer (level 5v) is up to 1,0 m thick and in an undisturbed position. During the formation of level 5v and the other Acheulean horizons (5b, 5a) there was much organic material in the cave, first of all as a result of human activity, which was the source of phosphate of these levels.

Fauna

Altogether 90 species have been recorded from levels 2 to 5 (Vereščagin 1957b; Baryšnikov 1977; Vereščagin and Baryšnikov 1980a; Baryšnikov and Baranova 1982; Ljubin et al. 1985a; 1985b). The lowermost Acheulean deposits (level 5v) contained amongst others *Microtus* ex. gr. *arvalis*, *Macaca* cf. *sylvana*, *Ursus deningeri*, *Dicerorhinus etruscus brachycephalus*, *Cervus* cf. *elaphus* and *Capra* cf. *caucasia*, while the uppermost Acheulean level (5a) yielded *Arvicola terrestris*, *Ursus spelaeus*, *Alces alces* and *Rupicapra rupicapra*.

The larger mammal bones from the Acheulean horizons are typical "kitchen" waste, with small fragments of longbones. During the formation of these layers the cave was an occupation site, used for a long period of time. In the Middle Palaeolithic levels (3 and 4) there are, however, many bones of the axial skeleton and remarkably less bones from the extremities; these bones were partly deposited without human interference. The bones of the Middle Palaeolithic levels partly reflect a natural taphocoenose. Many bones from the Middle Palaeolithic levels are gnawed by large carnivores. In the Acheulean levels gnaw-marks of porcupine (*Hystrix*) occur.

Many bird remains have been collected from the Acheulean and Middle Palaeolithic layers (Burčak-Abramovič and Ljubin 1972; Burčak-Abramovič 1980; Baryšnikov and Čerepanov 1985). Furthermore these levels yielded a huge number – more than 50,000 – of fish remains. These belong without exception to the Black Sea salmon (*Salmo trutta labrax*). These salmon-fragments consist of numerous fin-radiates radalia and other parts of

the axial skeleton but also of vertebrae, hypuralia and head fragments. To judge from the better preserved vertebrae and hypuralia the size of the salmons varied between 0,5 and 1,3 m.

Pollen analysis

The pollendiagram of the cave deposits shows 14 pollen zones and a number of sub-zones, which represent part of the Pleistocene and Holocene evolution of vegetation and climate (Levkovskaja 1980; Ljubin et al. 1985a). The Acheulean levels reflect 3 warm phases (lower part of level 5v, level 5b, middle part of level 5a) and 3 cold phases (upper part of level 5v, lower part of level 5a, upper part of level 5a). The climate was especially warm and dry during the formation of the lower part of level 5v.

Lithic artefacts

The lithic artefacts are predominantly of locally occurring raw materials (quartzite, alevrite, limestone, slate, flint) which could be found either as pebbles on the bank and in the terraces of the Džodžori or as slabs at the outcrops of limestone or slate. The limestone near the cave contains layers of siliceous slate-like material, in parts transforming into alevrite and clayey limestone. Non-local raw materials are only represented by a few pale, reddish and red flints and a single obsidian artefact (a *limace* in level 5v). Most of the artefacts are made out of quartzite (sandstone), followed by flint and flint-like rocks, alevrite, slate, and limestone. There are important differences in the rock types represented in the various levels. In the deepest level (5v) more than one-third of the artefacts consist of badly sorted, local raw materials from the slate-like, clayey, silicified limestone-sediments. In the upper levels (5a, 5b) the raw material-selection was better. Local silicified rocks are present in smaller numbers and the use of alevrites, slates and flints increases. The artefacts of the Acheulean levels are characterized by a high percentage of retouched tools and artefacts with use retouch (about 50%). The following types are numerous (Figs 18-21): chopper, chopping tools, bifaces, simple and transversal side-scrapers, scraper-like tools, notched and denticulated pieces, cleaver-like artefacts, *limaces*, Quinson-points, triangular pieces with notches.

The various raw materials with their different knapping-characteristics resulted in a selection of specific rocks for specific tools. Choppers, chopping-tools, bifaces, side-scrapers, cleaver-like tools and big notched artefacts (with Clacton-notches) are mostly made out of quartzite pebbles. The artefacts from flint-like rocks are smaller (seldom longer than 5-6 cm) and more carefully worked. Some types – Quinson points, *limaces* – are only made

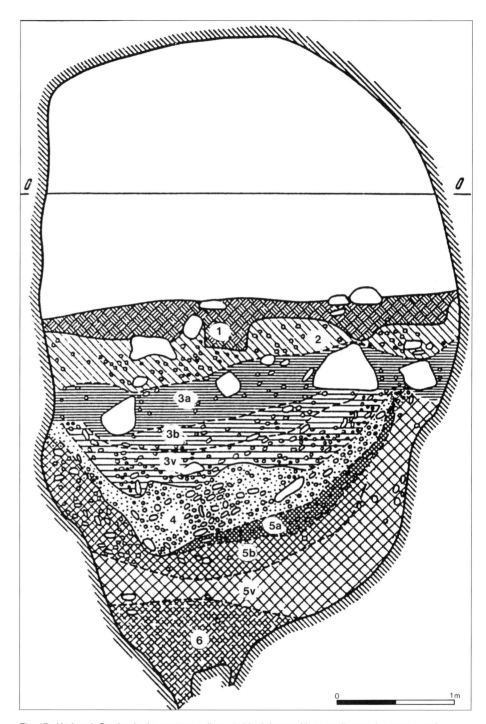

Fig. 17. Kudaro I. Section in the eastern gallery. 1: black loam with sporadic angular stones and limestone blocks; 2: yellow-grey loam with numerous sharp-edged stones and larger blocks; 3: clay-rich, porous yellow-white (Horizon 3a) and grey-brown (Horizon 3b, 3v) loam; 4: grey-white, clay-rich loam with heavy carbonate dissolutions; 5a: Compact, clay-rich yellow-grey loam with grey-green layering; 5b: clayey compact yellow loam with some rounded, not much corroded limestone debris; 5v: yellow-brownish loam, in parts stone-like by phosphatisation; 6: brownish-yellow sandy clay or clayey alverit with well developed crumby structure, the upper part phosphatized.

out of flint. Other flint tools are simple and transversal side-scrapers. Hammerstones, cores and many cortical-flakes indicate that stone knapping took place within the cave.

Altogether there are 5,000 artefacts from the Acheulean levels (5a,b,v). The cores are globular or with one striking platform as well as disc-like. The flakes have broad, plain – sometimes cortical – striking-platforms, well developed percussion cones and bulbs. Careful edge-retouch – stepped retouch, marginal retouch – is rare and occurs only on some side-scrapers, small end-scrapers, isolated *limaces* and Quinson-points of flint (Fig. 21). The edges of numerous flakes show irregular use-retouch. The more than 50 bifaces vary in form and knapping-technique (Figs 18-20). Those made from slate-like rocks have 'steps' on their surface as a result of the laminated structure of the raw-material. Some bifaces made on flat pebbles or flakes are only partly retouched. Six very 'archaic', massive slate bifaces were found at the base of level 5v. Their almost rectangular shape with a slightly rounded distal end, makes them similar to cleavers. Other bifaces also have an almost rectangular outline. Especially well worked are two lanceolate quartzite-bifaces with slightly convex edges and thin, elongated and pointed distal parts. Other bifaces are almond-shaped. The cleavers are less typical than in the Cona cave. An especially characteristic flake-cleaver was found together with 4 bifaces in front of the entrance of the Dark Gallery. The flake-cleavers also comprise some partially retouched bifacial tools which are trapezoidal at the distal end. The pebble tools found in all Acheulean levels and in all parts of the cave are mostly made from quartzite pebbles. Especially numerous are unifacially retouched pebble tools with straight or convex working edges. In addition there are side-scrapers and points as well as many notched and denticulated pieces.

Hominid remains

Three hominid teeth (two incisor fragments and one premolar) were discovered in the Acheulean levels in 1959 and 1984. The fragment of a middle lower incisor was found in level 5b in the Central Chamber (Zubov 1980). The other two finds – the fragment of a permanent incisor and the premolar – come from level 5a and 5b of the Dark Gallery (Charitonov 1989).

Palaeogeography and chronology

The palaeontological results indicate a distinct change in the amplitude of the vegetation belts. The variations in the frequencies of many larger mammals, rodents and birds in the different levels and the occurrence of some species in certain periods of the Pleistocene illustrate these changes. In the Acheulean levels, 5b and 5v, the percentage of *Cervus*

elaphus, indicative of a forested landscape, is almost twice as high as the percentage of *Capra caucasica*, a species which inhabits subalpine meadows. In layer 5a *Capra caucasica* is much more important. The importance of *Capreolus capreolus, Martes, Meles meles, Bison* etc. also increases during forested phases (Baryšnikov 1977, 1978; Vereščagin and Baryšnikov 1980a; Baryšnikov and Nikolaev 1982; Ljubin 1980b).

The variation in the Pleistocene vegetation belts is also reflected in the portion of bears which represent the main part of the faunal material. In the lower levels, where forest-steppe conditions are indicated, 75-85 % of the bones are from bears, whereas in levels from colder periods this is only 30-45% (Baryšnikov 1977; Baryšnikov and Dedkova 1978).

The composition of the fauna in the lower level 5v, with *Macaca* cf. *sylvana, Ursus* cf. *thibetanus* and *Dicerorhinus etruscus brachycephalus*, indicates a forest-steppe or a savannah-like warm climate landscape. This corresponds to the results of pollen analysis. Palynological data as well as the mammal fossils indicate cold conditions during the deposition of the upper part of level 5v and a second warm optimum in level 5b. In the upper part of level 5v animals of the mountain meadow belt occur for example the rodents: *Marmota caucasica, Prometheomys schaposh-nikove* and *Chionomys gud*. The warm climate during the formation of level 5b is underlined by the occurrence of forest dwellers (*Castor fiber, Glis glis, Capreolus capreolus*) and animals which prefer a warm climate (*Hystrix*).

Dating the climato-stratigraphical succession in the Kudaro caves is a difficult enterprise. Earlier Uranium/Thorium measurements of the Acheulean layers of Kudaro I yielded dates of 250-300 Kyr BP for level 5v and 110 ± 10 Kyr BP for the upper part of level 5a (Čerdyncev *et al.* 1959). Corresponding TL ages were recently obtained by Kulikov: level 5v in the South Gallery 360 ± 90 Kyr BP (RTL 379), level 5b 350 ± 70 Kyr BP (RTL 373) (Ljubin and Kulikov 1991). The dates of Čerdyncev and Kulikov give a first indication of the age of the Acheulean in the Caucasus region. An assessment of these dates by other methods seems very necessary, however.

Earlier a correlation of the lower Acheulean levels to the Mindel-Riss interglacial (Ljubin 1974; Levkovskaja 1980) or the Riss-Würm interglacial (Ljubin, Rengarten *et al.* 1978) was proposed. In the meantime palaeomagnetic analysis by M.A. Pevzner showed a reverse magnetisation of the basal level 6. As a result new pollenzones were established and new indicator species such as *Dicerorhinus etruscus* and *Ursus deningeri* were discovered. These new observations demand a cautious revision of the date of the lower Acheulean levels (Ljubin *et al.* 1985a). *Dicerorhinus etruscus, Ursus deningeri* and *Macaca sylvana* commonly

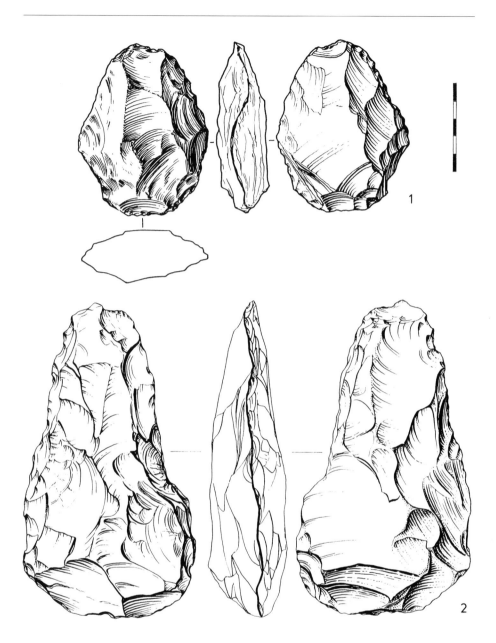

Fig. 18. Kudaro I. Bifaces. Scale in cm.

occur in the fauna Mosbach I, while *Dicerorhinus etruscus* and *Macaca* occur in Le Vallonnet (Ljubin *et al.* 1985a). Bones of *Dicerorhinus etruscus* and *Ursus deningeri* were found at Bammental and Jockrim, Hangenbieten and Mauer as well as Nanterre. The presence of species such as *Mimomys, Homotherium and Eucladoceros* suggests that the fauna from the lower Kudaro levels could correspond to the Tiraspol fauna of the Russian Plain,

which is characterized by *Ursus deningeri, Dicerorhinus etruscus* and arvicolids with rootless molars (Alekseeva 1977) and also the late Galerian fauna of western Europe (Azzaroli 1983). The fauna might also belong to the beginning of the east-european Singil' fauna-complex. Similarities to the Kudaro fauna, but with indications of a dryer climate, also exist within the faunal material of the Acheulean levels V and VI of the Azych cave in Azerbaijan.

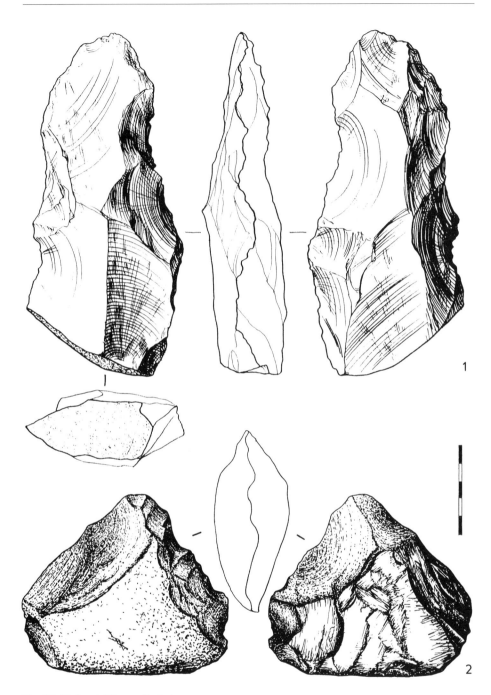

Fig. 19. Kudaro I. Bifaces. Scale in cm.

Palaeontological age assessments should be cautiously used, however, in view of the special conditions of the Colchis refuge. The rather slow rate of evolutionary changes within some species has been stressed several times already (*Ursus deningeri - Ursus spelaeus, Equus stenonis - Equus caballus*) for the Caucasus region, as well as the survival of some relict species (*Proochotona*) and the special evolution of the fauna in this region (Gabunia 1959;

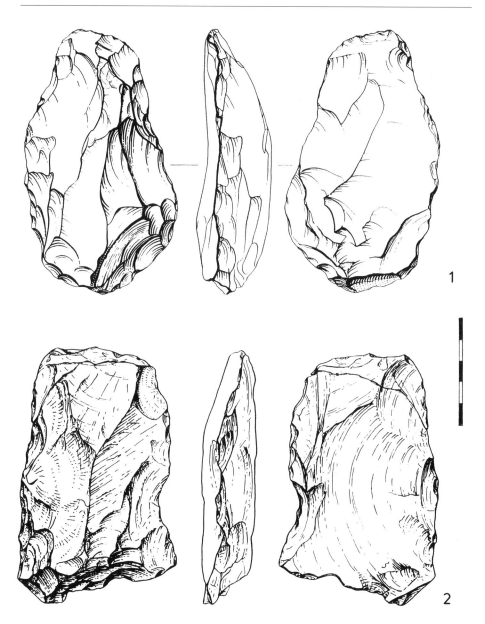

Fig. 20. Kudaro I. Bifaces. Scale in cm.

Baryšnikov 1977; Markova 1982). "The reason of this could be a long isolation of the Caucasus fauna" (Baryšnikov and Dedkova 1978) and also the existence of the Colchis refuge during the cold periods.

The palaeobotanical observations also indicate a longer survival of Pliocene relicts in the Colchis flora, compared to western Europe and other Caucasus regions. The reasons are the special climatic conditions, first of all the humid subtropical climate of the Colchis, which is still a stable

refuge of floral relicts (Čočieva 1982). As mentioned earlier in this paper, the core of the Colchis vegetation consists of tertiary relicts and about 20% of the Colchis flora is endemic (Pavlov 1948; Kolakovskij 1961).

In any case the new results seem to indicate a higher age of the lower Acheulean layers of Kudaro I. The lower part of level 5v formed during a dry-warm, possibly earlier Middle Pleistocene, period. The humid-warm subtropical climate phase (level 5b) might correlate to another Middle

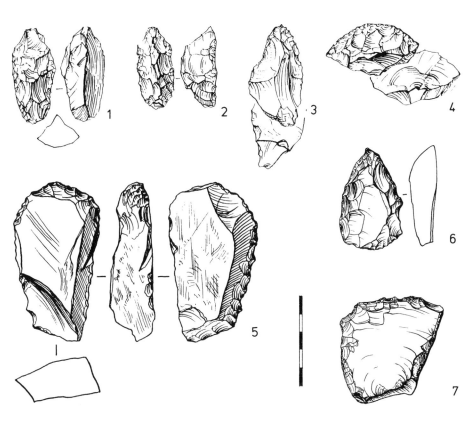

Fig. 21. Kudaro I. Flake-tools. Scale in cm.

Pleistocene interglacial. But these dates are preliminary, as the special evolution of fauna and flora in the Colchis makes the comparison with the European biostratigraphy difficult.

2.3.3. Kudaro III

The Kudaro III cave (Fig. 22) is situated beneath the caves Kudaro I, II and V, in the fourth level (from below) of the cave-system. The entrance is at 1564 m OD and 220-230 m above the Džodžori-river.

Pleistocene and Holocene sediments are 6-7 m thick and fill 80-90% of the cave. In the most important transversal section 10 levels could be identified. Levels 3-4 date to the Middle Palaeolithic, 6-8a are Acheulean levels. The marked humidity in the cave led to sinter formation, fragments of sinter being an important component of the cave's deposits.

Fauna

(after Baryšnikov 1977, 1980, 1987, 1991a; Baryšnikov and Dedkova 1978; Vereščagin and Baryšnikov 1980 b; Baryšnikov and Baranova 1982, 1983; Baryšnikov and

Nikolaev 1982; Baryšnikov and Cerepanov 1985). As yet the main part of the fauna from the Middle Palaeolithic levels 3-4 and the Acheulean level 5 is determined and published. For the other Acheulean layers (6-8a) there are only preliminary lists based on determinations. The still incomplete faunal lists (Acheulean and Middle Palaeolithic levels combined) comprise 40 mammal species, 15 birds, 2 reptilia, 2 amphibia and 1 species of fish. From the Acheulean levels 7-8a there are 2374 determined bones of larger mammals. The small fauna has not yet been analysed yet.

The lower Acheulean levels (8a, 8, 7) are strongly dominated by remains of *Ursus deningeri praekudarensis* (*Spelaeus deningeri praekudarensis*) which represent more than 85% of the determinable larger mammal bones. Bones of adult animals dominate. Very big upper last molars, some of them longer than 48 mm (males?) are present. Many molars especially from level 8 are heavily to very strongly worn. Milk teeth seldom occur – but from level 5v there are more than 500 milk canines. In levels 7 and 8, as in the upper Middle Palaeolithic levels from Kudaro I, bones of old animals are numerous (Baryšnikov and Dedkova 1978). The bears died naturally, without any human interference.

Pollen analysis

The palaeobotanical samples from Kudaro III analysed earlier came only from the upper three levels, from material extracted from the longbones in the laboratory (Ljubin and Levkovskaja 1972). More recently samples were taken directly from the section K-S, which resulted for levels 1-5 in the definition of 11 pollen zones (Levkovskaja 1980). The lower zones (10-5) showed a repeated alternation of warm and cold phases. During the cold phases (cryomeres) there were always less pollen and spores. The occurrence of conifer pollen in all cryomeres indicates a more humid and colder climate during these periods than today. The levels from the warm phases (thermomeres) contain much more pollen and spores. These pollen spectra differ in composition, especially in the presence of exotic species as well as the AP and NAP values.

Lithic artefacts

The only partially excavated Acheulean levels yielded 91 artefacts. In levels 6 and 7 the raw material is mainly bad quality local rock (flint with fissures, silicified limestone), but at the same time there are artefacts of good flint from non-local sources in these layers. In levels 5, 8 and 8a only local raw materials are present. These are often suitable such as sandstone pebbles and in some cases slate.

A majority of the artefacts from all levels are flakes and – especially in level 6 – flake-fragments and debris from local flint. Chips are rare and retouched tools are not numerous (12-13 pieces). Most of the tools – biface, proto-bifaces, side-scrapers, cleaverlike tools – come from level 5. The three "proto-bifaces" were made out of a low-quality sandstone. The artefacts of the middle Acheulean levels include two flint artefacts from non-local flint.

Chronology and palaeoenvironment

An indication of the age of the various assemblages is given by some absolute dates. TL-dating of sediments resulted in three dates: Acheulean horizon 8a: 560 ± 112 Kyr BP, the eroded lower part of the Middle Palaeolithic layers and the transition to Acheulean layer 5: 252 ± 51 Kyr BP and 245 ± 49 Kyr BP (Ljubin and Kulikov 1991; Ljubin 1993a-b). There are also two Uranium-Thorium dates on bone material from the lower part of Middle Palaeolithic layers in the 1957 sondage (Čerdyncev et al. 1959): 110 ± 10 Kyr BP and 80 Kyr BP.

Information on aspects of both the palaeoenvironment and the age of the layers is provided by the changing percentages of deer, mountain goat and cave bear, as worked out by G.F. Baryšnikov. Additional indications are provided by the morphological characteristics of wolf and cave bear. In the lower Acheulean levels (8a-7) differences in species composition are small; the percentages of bones of mountain goat, inhabiting the higher mountain regions, and red deer, living in forested environments, is more or less the same throughout these layers. In level 8a and 7 there are some bones of more forest indicative animals such as beaver, porcupine and lynx, which until now are unknown from level 8. Additional indications are given by the carnivores. From level 7 there are two maxilla fragments of a small wolf. Based on the length of the upper canine (23 mm) this wolf was similar to *Canis lupus lunellensis* of Lunel Viel (Bonifay 1971). As for the cave bear remains, it is only possible to conclude that the teeth are comparable in size and structure to *Ursus deningeri praekudarensis* (*Spelaeus deningeri praekudarensis*) of level 5v of Kudaro I (Baryšnikov, in press).

In the upper Acheulean layers (6-5) cave bear also dominates, but there are some differences in the overall species composition: level 6 is characterized by the occurrence of warmth indicators such as *Emys orbicularis* and *Ursus mediterraneus*, together with alpine species like *Cuon* and Caucasian turkey (*Tetraogallus caucasicus*). Bones of red deer are not numerous. The fauna of level 5 contains beaver, porcupine and *Ursus mediterraneus* as well as many bones of red deer and mountain goat. The molars of cave bear show a combination of archaic and evolved features indicating a transitional form between *Ursus deningeri praekudarensis* from Kudaro I, level 5v and *Ursus deningeri kudarensis* from Kudaro III, level 4v.

In the Acheulean layers the cave bear dominates with 84-87% (levels 7-8) up to 92-98% (levels 5-6), in the Middle Palaeolithic levels this animal attains 77,2% (level 4) and 71,1% (level 3). The Middle Palaeolithic levels are also characterized by different percentages of *Cervus elaphus* and *Capra caucasica*: in level 4 *Cervus elaphus* is represented by 18,3%, while *Capra caucasica* is only represented by some bones, whereas level 3 contains 5,9% of *Cervus elaphus* and 6,9% of *Capra caucasica* (Ljubin and Levkovskaja 1972; Vereščagin and Baryšnikov 1980b). In the Acheulean layers bones of goat and deer are not numerous but red deer is especially in level 5 better represented than goat.

More warmth demanding species like *Macaca*, two species of porcupine and the etruscan rhino occur in the lower Acheulean horizons of Kudaro I (level 5v), but are absent in the Acheulean levels of Kudaro III. This corresponds well to the morphological features of the wolf and the cave bear that indicated a younger age for the Acheulean layer of Kudaro III.

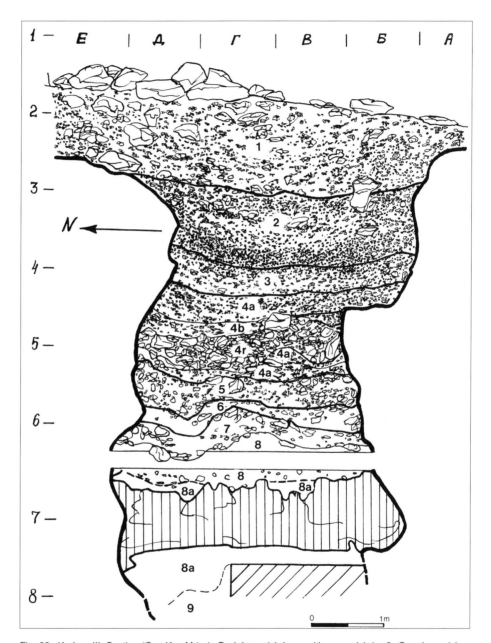

Fig. 22. Kudaro III. Section (O_1 - K_1 - M_1). 1: Dark brownish loam with many debris; 2: Grey brownish loam with unsorted slope-debris and big limestone blocs; 3: Pale loam with medium and coarse debris and some bigger blocs; 4: Dark greyish loam in places greenish, with many debris and limestone fragments; 5: Compact yellowish loam with differently rounded debris; 6: Yellow brownish loam, clayey and crumbly; 7: Less compact, clayey loam, greenish-grey; 8: Dark brown crumbly loam with many debris, coarse in the upper part; 8a: Brown loam with phosphate dissolutions and isolated small debris; 9: Brown compact sticky clay; 10: Light yellow sandy loam with gravels.

The pollen analysis enlarges the possibilities of dating and palaeogeographical reconstruction. The flora of the Acheulean levels of Kudaro III, studied by G.M. Levkovskaja, is different from the extant vegetation by the types of exotic plants present. In almost all the samples there are pollen of many regional exotics, plants which occur to-day in other regions in the Caucasus. During the formation of the Acheulean layers some of these exotic species were even dominant - *Pterocarya* sp. and *Pistacia* sp. in the thermomeres 3 and 4 of the levels 6 and 7. The composition of the transregional exotics is also multifarious: *Adiantum* cf. *pedantum* , cf *Gingko* sp., (level 10), *Tsuga* sp., *Cedrus* sp., *Glyptostrobus* sp., *Parrotia* sp., *Carya* sp., *Osmunda cinnamomea* ssp.

The exotic species vanished in different regions in different periods and it is therefore impossible to date the sediments of the cave by their extinctions. Some of the criteria worked out in western Europe can not be applied to the Caucasus region. *Pterocarya*, for example, was present in Central Europe during the Middle Pleistocene (Zagwijn 1957, 1963), but in the Caucasus it still belongs to the modern vegetation. However, the high number of exotics in the Acheulean layers indicates a high age for these deposits. According to Gričuk (1982 Tab. 39) the percentage of the north-american, east-asian and balkanic-colchidis elements in the palaeovegetation of the previous Soviet Union clearly decreases after the Lichvin Interglacial. During the Mikulin Interglacial these components almost disappear. In our region the plants of the Colchis flora give no age indication because they are still present in the recent vegetation. However, the Acheulean layers of the Kudaro caves contain a number of american/east-asian and southeast-asian plants: *Tsuga* sp., *Carya* sp., Taxodiaceae, *Glyptostrobus* sp., *Eucommia* sp., *Osmunda cinnamomea*.

The composition of the flora is multifarious up to the end of the early climatic optimum in level 5 (pollenzone X) (Ljubin *et al*. 1985a Tab. 1). The antiquity for the Acheulean layers is also indicated by the phytozenoses (the dominance of regional exotics in different periods). Level 8a of Kudaro III displayed six climatic changes (three cryomeres and three thermomeres of different climatic types). For the end of the last thermomere there is a TL-date of 560 ± 112 Kyr BP. Judging from its lithology, level 8 was deposited during a cold period. The levels 6-7 were formed in a period of climatic variability. A warm period (pollen horizon 3), established for levels 6-7, could correspond to the Holsteinian of western Europe. The pollen analytical dates indicate a high age for the Acheulean level 5, which lower part can be correlated to the base of level 5a at Kudaro I.

The palaeontological age assessments of G.F. Baryšnikov and the pollen analysis of G.M. Levkovskaja indicate slightly different ages for the Acheulean horizons of Kudaro III. The different opinion of the palaeontologist may depend on the small size of the excavation in the oldest Acheulean horizon and the resulting small size of the faunal assemblage. In addition the microfauna of these levels has not been studied yet. The differences between the Kudaro I and Kudaro III faunas also reflect the different origins of the faunal remains. At Kudaro I the anthropogenic factor dominated, while Kudaro III was only rarely visited by humans, and is first of all a natural bone accumulation.

2.3.4.   Cona

The Cona cave (Fig. 23) is situated in the Džavski region (South Ossetia, Georgia) on the southern slope of the limestone mountain Bub (Val'-Choch) at an altitude of 2100 - 2150 m OD, 250-300 m above the valley, and 5-6 km south of the Kudaro caves (Fig. 1). The cave entrance is orientated SSW and sheltered to the west and north by narrow rock-spurs. Cona is the biggest cave site of the Caucasus region, with excavations possible over an area of 1.000 m², of which 140 m² have been excavated.

Palaeolithic finds in the Cona cave were discovered in 1958. The first 2×2 m sondage in the entrance area went through the three upper layers (Neolithic, Mesolithic, Middle Palaeolithic), and the success of this work led to a large excavation programm which finished in 1978.

Stratigraphy

The sediments in the cave were eventually subdivided into 10-11 levels (Kalandadze 1960, 1961, 1962, 1965). The description of the transversal section d_1-h_1 observed in 1961 by A.N. Kalandadze seems to characterize the sedimentary sequence fairly well (Kalandadze 1962) (Fig. 23). It is to be noted, however, that later on a more complex subdivision of the sequence has been proposed (Tušabramišvili 1978; 1984).

Between the various levels there are more or less pronounced erosional features. Especially marked were the erosional phenomena in the lower part of the section. Kolbutov (1961) observed that the loam of the lower Acheulean layer contained a gravel horizon 0,60 - 0,80 m thick.

The profile contains some characteristic horizons which can be correlated to layers in the Kudaro caves. First of all this concerns the archaeological sterile light yellow loam with many limestone debris (level 4), which may correspond to the glacial maximum of the last glaciation. Likewise the dark grey loam with small limestone debris and Middle Palaeolithic finds (level 5a) can be observed in the Kudaro caves. The discordantly underlying yellowish sandy loam (level 6) forms the topmost Acheulean layer both at Cona and in the Kudaro caves, while the lower part

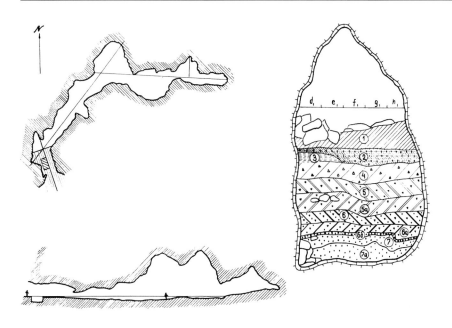

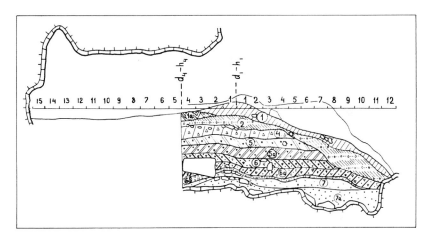

Level		Lithology	Finds
1	0,76 m	Humus, soil formation	
2	0,70 m	Brownish loam with limestone blocs	Mesolithic
3		Yellowish loam	Mesolithic
4	0,75 m	Light yellow loam with many limestone debris	
5	0,59 m	Yellowish loam with limestone debris	Middle Palaeolithic
5a	0,80 m	Dark grey loam with small limestone debris and ochre	Middle Palaeolithic
6	0,55 m	Yellowish sandy loam	Upper Acheulean
6a	0,45 m	Light yellow sandy loam with limestone debris	Upper Acheulean
6b	0,25 m	Dark brown "rusty" loam	Upper Acheulean
7	0,45 m	Greenish grey loamy coarse sand	Lower Acheulean
7a	0,35 m	Yellowish-reddish loamy sand with big limestone blocs	Lower Acheulean

Fig. 23. Cona, transversal section d1-h1, after Kalandadze 1962.

of the Acheulean levels consists both at Cona and in the Kudaro caves of greenish-grey coarse sands with much limestone debris (level 7).

Fauna

The Cona deposits yielded about 15,000 animal bones, including remains of lizards and birds (Vekua *et al.* 1981, 1987; Burčak-Abramovič 1971). Wet screening did not take place, and 99,4% of the bones are from larger animals e.g. *Canis lupus, Vulpes vulpes, Ursus spelaeus, Ursus arctos, Panthera spelaea, Sus scrofa, Cervus elaphus, Capreolus capreolus, Bison priscus, Capra caucasica* and *Ovis* cf. *ammon.*

In their comments on this faunal list Vekua and his colleagues pointed out that the Acheulean levels contained about 7000 bones, virtually all of cave bear (99,1%). In the Middle Palaeolithic layers (5, 5a) the amount of cave bear diminished (62,1 %) with at the same time an increase of artiodactyls (31,7 %). "All the mammals represented in the Acheulean layers occur also in the Middle Palaeolithic levels" (Vekua *et al.* 1987:93). On the other hand, *Cuon* as well as *Sorex* sp., *Meriones* sp., *Lagurus* sp. and *Ellobius* sp. occur only in the Middle Palaeolithic levels. *Hystrix* is only present in the two Acheulean layers (6, 7), and *Allactaga* sp. only in the lower Acheulean horizon (7).

Pollen analysis

Zelikson and Gubonina (1985) conclude that the cave was not far from the upper limit of the forest belt at the time of the formation of the upper Acheulean horizon (6) (to-day it is in the sub-alpine zone). The composition of the upper forest belt was very different from that of the recent forest though: dry slopes had an open forest vegetation with Xerophytes and scattered *Carpinus orientalis*, while on steep slopes and debris-covered slopes *Juniperus* was present. Deciduous trees (oak, maple, ashtree, elm) were rare.

In the deepest part of the Acheulean layers pollen were only seldom preserved (Vekua *et al.* 1987). The middle and upper part contained a high amount of tree pollen, with pine dominating (28-50%) and spruce (3-6%), fir (3-25%) and *Tsuga* (2-8%) less well represented. Deciduous trees were primarily represented by beech (6-19%), alder (6-15%), birch (1-5%) and oak (4%). Hornbeam, lime tree, elm, hazel and rhododendron were present in small numbers only. Especially interesting is the occurrence of exotic genera like *Cyathea* and *Dicksonia*? as well as *Podocarpus, Cedrus, Tsuga* and *Taxodium*. According to Mamacašvili there was a mixed forest with deciduous and coniferous trees in the neighbourhood of the cave during the formation of the Acheulean levels. The Middle Palaeolithic levels did not contain enough pollen, but the archaeologically sterile

level 4 indicates a climatic deterioration. During that time the cave was situated in the subalpine vegetation belt (Vekua *et al.* 1987:98).

Lithic artefacts

The stone artefacts have only been published in a very preliminary and selective way. This review is therefore mainly based on our personal knowledge of the 1959-1961 and 1965 finds and preliminary sketches.

The Lower Acheulean layer (7) yielded only 30 artefacts, found in the eastern part of the entrance area (Kalandadze 1962). Raw material was senonian and turonian flint, sometimes argilit (Kalandadze 1965). Besides 13 flakes there are "simple convex side-scrapers and rough cutting instruments" (Tušabramišvili 1984:12-13).

From the upper Acheulean layer (6) there are 104 artefacts, mostly tools (Figs 24-27). Raw materials are argilit (64), andesit (11), flint (11), silicified limestone (3) and sandstone (5) (Tušabramišvili 1984:13). The tools are dominated by bifaces (29 in the studied series of the 1959-1961 and 1965 excavation; Fig. 24). With the exception of some pieces of sandstone and silificied limestone they were made of locally available slate (argilit). The slate-structure of the raw material influenced the form of the tools. The surface of some bifaces of argilit is heavily weathered and rounded. The bifaces were made out of elongated flat pebbles as well as from flakes, and most of them are long and flat (15). Their edges are straight or only slightly zig-zag-like. The lower end is often sharp, but some pieces display a thicker "butt". Some bifaces are backed. Long-triangular and almost *cordiform* bifaces dominate. Important are the cleavers (10; Figs 25-26), made out of locally occurring rocks: slate (5), quartzite-like sandstone (2), silicified limestone (2) and flint (1). As at other sites, and surely linked with their function, cleavers of glassy homogeneous flint are very rare. Both flake- and bifacial cleavers are present. The cleavers from Cona represent the biggest series from the Caucasian Acheulean. A few flake-tools are also present: points, side-scrapers and denticulated pieces (Fig. 27).

The strong dominance of retouched tools, and the almost complete absence of flakes and cores, underlines the special character of this inventory. We see here the remains of a hunting camp where finished tools were imported. In contrast to base camps, for instance those identified in the Kudaro caves, there was no stone-working on the spot at this site.

Chronology

It is difficult to date the Acheulean levels from the Cona cave. In the literature there is a certain tendency to push its antiquity back in time. Kalandadze (1960, 1961) classified the material as final Acheulean and later as second part of

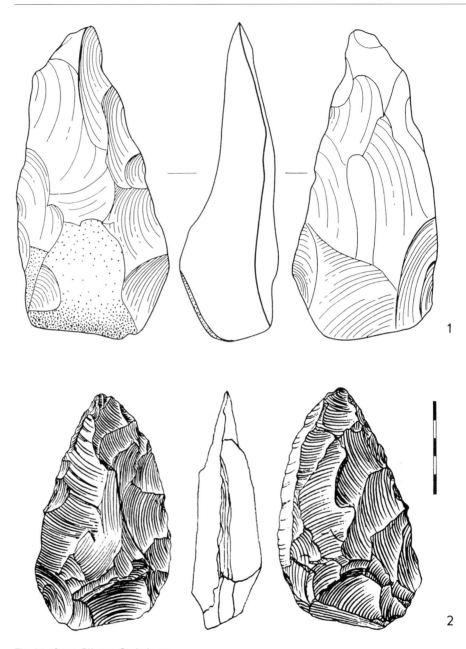

Fig. 24. Cona. Bifaces. Scale in cm.

the Acheulean (Kalandadze 1965), while Tušabramišvili (1978, 1984) spoke of middle Acheulean.

An absolute date is only available for a stalagmite fragment from an "upper horizon": 46 ± 4 Kyr (Uranium/Thorium; Čerdyncev *et al.* 1966).

The chronostratigraphy of cave deposits in the Kudaro-Cona-region depends on the corresponding influences of

climatic oscillations in the mountainous region. This permits a comparison of the sections. The temperate (interglacial) conditions during the formation of the Acheulean layers at Cona and in the Kudaro caves are comparable. The typology of the Cona Acheulean, however, seems to indicate a more evolved, younger Acheulean stage than at Kudaro.

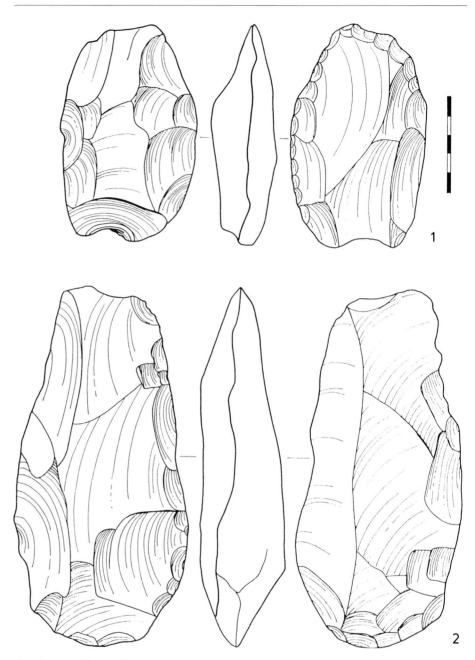

Fig. 25. Cona. Cleavers. Scale in cm.

2.3.5.   *Treugol'naja Cave*

The Treugol'naja cave is located in the western part of the Caucasus on the Baranach plateau, between the Urup river and its small tributary Kuva in the Kuban depression (Fig. 1). The cave is situated at the limit of the present upper forest-belt and the mountain meadows. The cave was discovered in 1986 by L. V. Golovanova. In a test-pit

Pleistocene sediments and Palaeolithic artefacts were found.

The 3-4,5 m thick fill of Treugol'naja cave is complex and disturbed by erosional processes. The eastern part is completely removed and characterized by deep erosional pockets. In the less disturbed western part of the section 14 different lithological units can be identified. The section consists first of loose loamy sands, which are difficult to

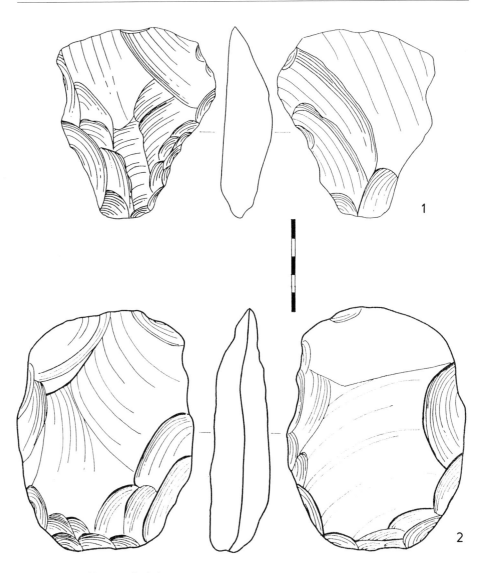

Fig. 26. Cona. Cleavers. Scale in cm.

differentiate. Only the pebble layer (6) in the lower part is a good marker for subdivision. All levels contained pollen (Pospelova and Levkovskaja 1994). Animal bones are recorded from all the Pleistocene layers (Baryšnikov 1990, 1991b). The fauna from the levels 3a-3b with e.g. *Marmota paleocaucasica* and *Saiga* sp. is typical of an open landscape and has been assigned to the last glaciation (Baryšnikov 1991b). The remains of the levels 4-7 represent an interglacial fauna with *Arvicola cantiana* (= *A. terrestris cantiana*), *Ursus deningeri, Stephanorhinus etruscus brachycephalus, Cervus elaphus acoronatus* and *Bison schoetensacki*, a fauna indicative of a wooded environment.

Bones of red deer dominate. Especially in levels 5b and 5v the bones are heavily fragmented. Besides undeterminable pieces there are fragments of long bones, ribs, antler and teeth. Many mollusc studied by L.M. Licharev, have been collected from the lower part of the deposits (levels 5-7): e.g. *Chrondrula tridens, Improvisa pupoides, Menacha caucasicola, Chrondrina clienta caucasica, Pseudochrondrula tuferifera, Quadriplicata aggesta aggesta* and *Sphyradium doliolum*.

During the 1986-1990 excavations 228 lithic artefacts were found. Raw materials are generally locally occurring flat limestone pebbles as well as non-local flint. From level 7b

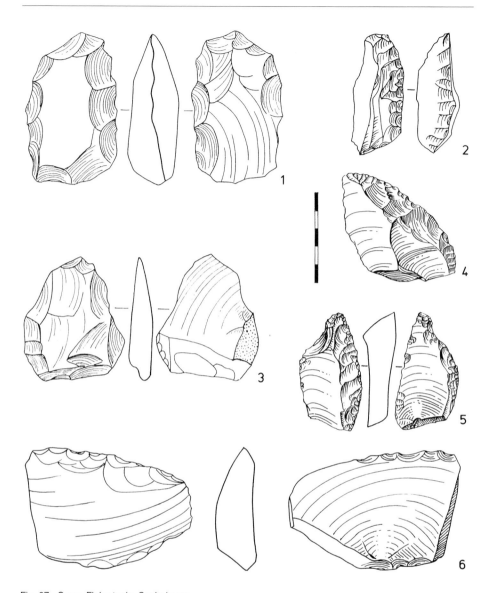

Fig. 27. Cona. Flake-tools. Scale in cm.

comes one flake, from level 7a seven artefacts (small flakes, three retouched flakes). From level 5v there are 8 artefacts (small, sometimes retouched flakes), from level 5b two flakes and from 5a five artefacts (flakes and a side scraper). From the lower part of level 4a as well as from levels 4b and 4v there are altogether about 90 artefacts, mostly flakes. The retouched tools include side-scrapers, 2 *limaces* as well as denticulates and notched pieces. The upper part of level 4a yielded several pebble tools. V.B. Doroničev subdivided the finds, including artefacts from uncertain stratigraphical positions, into two different groups, one being characterized

by pebble-tools (Fig. 28 the other by flakes (Fig. 29). In our opinion he might have overestimated the importance of Lower Palaeolithic stone artefacts by suggesting the former existence of two different cultural traditions.

4.   Conclusion (by V.L. and G.B.)

The oldest site of the Caucasus region, at the same time one of the oldest proofs of human occupation in Eurasia, is Dmanisi in Southern Georgia. Its proposed age of 1.87-1.67 Myr BP (the time of the Olduvai-Event) is based on the results of absolute dating methods, palaeomagnetic

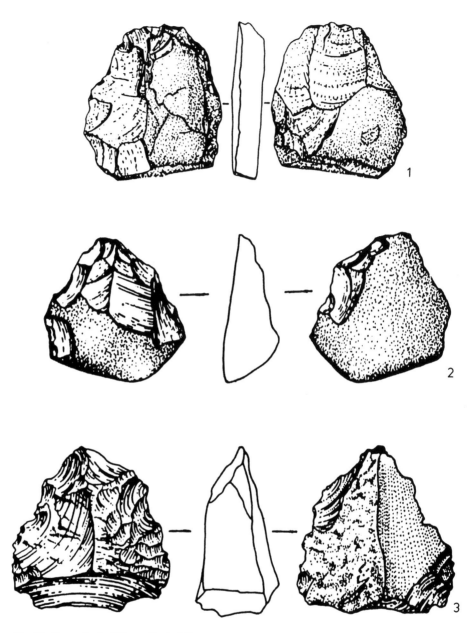

Fig. 28. Treugol'naja. Bifaces. Scale 2:3.

studies and on biostratigraphical evidence. The larger animals including *Archidiskodon meridionalis, Equus stenonis, Gazella* and *Struthio* point to a savannah-like landscape. The ongoing work will give additional information on environment and the way of life of the hominids there.

The finds of Taman and Achalkalaki are dated to the Early - Middle Pleistocene transition. Both sites are first of all characterized by extensive palaeontological material. Especially at Achalkalaki it can be shown that humans participated in the formation of the bone accumulation. Here too, future excavations will yield new results concerning dating, environment and subsistence.

The Lower Palaeolithic cave sites of the Caucasus region date to the Middle Pleistocene. The finds from the lower levels (VII-X) of Azych are not obviously artefacts. The

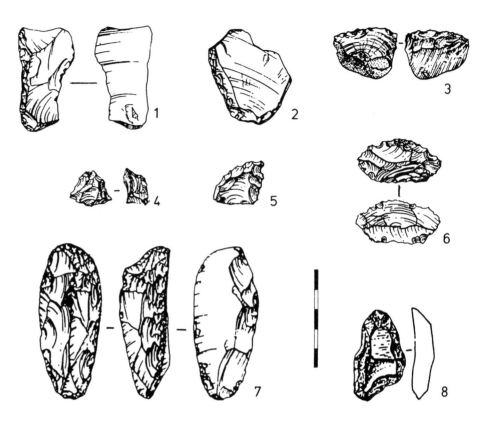

Fig. 29. Treugol'naja. Flake-tools. Scale in cm. After V.B. Doroničev.

oldest archaeological assemblage comes from level 5v at Kudaro, where *Macaca* cf. *sylvana*, *Canis* cf *etruscus*, *Ursus deningeri* and *Dicerorhinus etruscus brachycephalus* point to an older stage of the Middle Pleistocene.

The only preliminary known deeper levels (4-7) of Treugol'naja cave (including *Arvicola cantiana*, *Dicerorhinus etruscus brachycephalus*, *Bison schoetensacki* and *Ursus deningeri*) as well as Azych level VI (with *Dicerorhinus etruscus brachycephalus*, *Dicerorhinus mercki*, *Equus süssenbornensis*, *Bison schoetensacki*) may be

assigned to a middle stage of the Middle Pleistocene.

The upper Acheulean layers of Azych (level V, with the human jaw bone) and Kudaro (levels 5a and 5b) date to a later part of the Middle Pleistocene, as indicated by the fauna, stone knapping-technique (Levallois) and tool-types (flake-cleavers). This is also the case at Kudaro III and Cona.

All Lower Palaeolithic finds of the Caucasus region belong to warmer periods when the neighbouring regions of the sites were forested. This is the case at Kudaro at an altitude of 1600 m OD and even at Cona, at 2100 m OD.

note

1 A. Vekua and L. Gabunia identified the following species at Dmanisi (Vekua and Gabunia 1991, A. Vekua in press): *Testudo* sp., *Lacerta* sp., *Struthio dmanisensis, Hypolagus brachygnathus, Canis etruscus, Ursus etruscus, Ursus* sp., *Martes* sp., *Pachy-* *crocuta perrieri, Pachycrocuta* sp., *Homotherium crenatidens, Megantereon megantereon, Archidiskodon meridionalis, Dicerorhinus etruscus etruscus, Equus* cf. *stenonis, Equus* aff. *altidens, Sus* sp., *Dama* aff. *nestii, Cervus perrieri, Eucladoceros* cf. *senezensis, Cervus* sp. (ex gr. *Arvernoceros ardei), Dmanisibos georgicus, Gazella* sp., *Soergelia* sp., *Ovis* sp.

references

Alekseeva, L.I.   1977   Teriofauna rannego antropogena Vostočnoj Evropy, *Trudy Geologic. Inst. AN SSSR* 300, 29-44.

Aliev, S.F.   1969   *Fauna Azychskoj paleolitičeskoj stojanki. Avtoreferat.* Dissert. kand. biol. nauk. Baku.

Autlev, P.U.   1963   *Abadzechskaja nižnepaleolitičeskaja stojanka.* Majkop.

Avakov, G.S.   1960   *O nachodke karkasa i vorobejnika v nižnečetvertičnych ozernych otlozenijach Juznoj Gruzii.* Doklady AN SSSR 135.

Azzaroli, A.   1983   Quaternary mammals and the "end-Villafranchian" dispersal event - a turning point in the history of Eurasia, *Palaeogeography, Palaeoclimate, Palaeoecology* 44, 117-139.

Baryšnikov, G.F.   1977   Prirodnaja obstanovka i fauna mlekopitajuščich Central'nogo Kavkaza v pozdnem antropogene, *Izvestija Vsesojuznogo Geografičeskogo obščestva,* 246-254.

     1978   Kraznye volki Kavkaza, *Trudy Zoologičeskogo Inst. AN SSSR* 79, 79-90.

     1980   Surok v paleolite Kavkaza. Mlekopitajuščie Vostočnoj Evropy v antropogene, *Trudy Zoologičeskogo Inst. AN SSSR* 93, 50-59.

     1987   Mlekopitajuščie Kavkaza v epochu rannego paleolita, *Trudy Zoologičeskogo Inst. AN SSSR* 168, 3-20.

     1989   Les mammifères du Paléolithique inférieur du Caucase, *L'Anthropologie* 93, 813-830.

     1990   Mammals from the Acheulean Site of Treugol'naya Cave in the North Caucasus (USSR), *Abstracts of the sixth intern. Confer. for Archaeozoology.*

     1991a   *Ursus mediterraneus* v plejstocene Kavkaza i zamečanija po istorii melkich medvedej Evrazii. Paleoteriologiceskie issledovanija fauny SSSR, *Trudy Zoologičeskogo Inst. AN SSSR* 238, 3-60.

     1991b   Fauna ašel'skoj stojanki v peščere "Treugol'naja" na Severnom Kavkaze, *VI. koordinacionnoe soveščanie po izučeniju mamontov i mamontovoj fauny,* 11-12.

     in press   Cave bears from Paleolithic of Great Caucasus.

Baryšnikov, G.F., I.I. Dedkova   1978   Peščernye medvedy Bol'šogo Kavkaza. Sistematika i morfologija mlekopitajuščich, *Trudy Zoologičeskogo Inst. AN SSSR* 75, 69-77.

Baryšnikov, G.F., A.I. Nikolaev — 1982 — Ostatki blagorodnogo olenja iz paleolitičeskich stojanok Kudaro na Kavkaze, *Mamontovaja fauna aziatskoj časti SSSR*, 73-89.

Baryšnikov, G.F., G.I. Baranova — 1982 — O nachodke dikobraza Vinogradova v paleolite Kavkaza. Morfologija i sistematika mlekopitajuščich, *Trudy Zoologičeskogo Inst. AN SSSR* 115, 46-53.

1983 — Gryzuny rannego paleolita Bol'šogo Kavkaza. Fauna, sistematika i biologija mlekopitajuščich, *Trudy Zoologičeskogo Inst. AN SSSR* 119, 100- 138.

Baryšnikov, G.F., G.O. Čerepanov — 1985 — Pticy Bol'šogo Kavkaza epochi paleolita i mezolita, *Ornitologija* 20, 139-160.

Bonifay, M.-F. — 1971 — Carnivores quaternaires du Sud-Est de la France, *Mém. Mus. Hist. Natur. Ser. C* 21/2, 43-377.

Bordes, F. — 1961 — *Typologie du Paléolithique ancien et moyen*. Bordeaux.

Bosinski, G., T. Bugianišvili, N. Mgeladze, M. Nioradze, D. Tušabramišvili — 1991 — Steinartefakte. In: V. Džaparidze, G. Bosinski *et al.* 1991, 93-107.

Bosinski, G., D. Lordkipanidze, G. Majsuradze, M. Tvalčrelidze — 1991 — Die Ablagerungen auf der Basaltlava. In: V. Džaparidze, G. Bosinski *et al.* 1991, 76-83.

Bugianišvili, T.V. — 1979 — Nižnepaleolitičeskie pamjatniki Gare-Kachetskogo ploskogor'ja, *Materialy po archeologii Gruzii i Kavkaza* 8, 60-88.

Burčak-Abramovič, A.I. — 1971 — Materialy k izučeniju plejstocenovych ptic Gruzii (Peščera Cona), *Paleontologičeskij sbornik* 7/2, 37-48.

1980 — Ostatki ptic iz peščery Kudaro I. In: V.P. Ljubin 1980a, 98-110.

Burčak-Abramovič, A.I., V.P. Ljubin — 1972 — Ornitofauna peščery Kudaro I (Zakavkaz'e), *Sovetskaja archeologija* 1972/2, 159-164.

Burčak-Abramovič, A.I., S.D. Aliev — 1989 — Iskopaemaja ornitofauna paleolitičeskoj stojanki Azychskoj peščery na Malom Kakaze v Azerbajdzane *Materialy po ekologii životnych v Azerbajdzane (Baku)*, 72-80.

1990 — Iskopaemaja ornitofauna paleolitičeskoj stojanki Azychskoj peščery na Malom Kavkaze v Azerbajdzane, *Fauna, ekologija i ochrana zivotnych v Azerbajdzane (Baku)*, 44-57.

Cepkin, E.A. — 1980 — Ostatki ryb iz peščery Kudaro I. In: V.P. Ljubin 1980a, 90-97.

Čerdyncev, V.V., N.S. Strašnikov, L.M. Poljakova, T.I. Borisenko, R.S. Enikeev, S.N. Neučesov — 1959 — Opredelenye absoljutnogo vozrasta paleolitičeskich stojanok Kudaro i Kostenki, *Optika, jadernye processy (Izdanie Kazachskogo Universiteta, Alma Ata)*, 59-63.

Čerdyncev, V.V., I.V. Kazačevskij, *et al.* — 1966 — Neravnovesnyj uran v karbonatnych otložzenijach i opredelenye ich vozrasta, *Geochimija* 1966/2, 9-16.

Charitonov, V.M.
1989 Ašel'skie gominidy na territorii SSSR. Doklady Mosk. obščestva ispytatelej prirody, *Obščaja biologija*, 21-24.

Čočieva, K.I.
1982 Relikty pozdnepliocenovych i plejstocenovych flor Kolchidy i ich stratigrafičeskoe značenie, *Četvertičnaja sistema Gruzii*, 107-116.

Doroničev, V.B.
1987 Paleolit Karačaevo-Čerkesii, *Problemy antropologii i archeologii kamennogo veka Evrazii (Irkutsk)*, 48-49.

1992 Ranneašel'skaja stojanka v Treugol'noj peščere, *Voprosy archeologii Adygei (Maikop)*, 102-134.

Džaparidze, V.,
  G. Bosinski,
  T. Bugianišvili,
  L. Gabunia,
  A. Justus,
  N. Klopotovskaja,
  E. Kvavadze,
  D. Lordkipanidze,
  G. Majsuradze,
  N. Mgeladze,
  M. Nioradze,
  E. Pavlenišvili,
  H.-U. Schminke,
  Dz. Sologašvili,
  D. Tušabramišvili,
  M. Tvalčrelidze,
  A. Vekua
1991 Der altpaläolithische Fundplatz Dmanisi in Georgien (Kaukasus), *Jahrbuch des Römisch-Germanischen Zentralmuseums Mainz* 36, 1989 (1991), 67-116.

Fedorov, P.V.
1978 Plejstocen Ponto-Kaspija, *Trudy Geol. Inst.* 310.

Formozov, A.A.
1965 *Kamennyj vek i eneolit Prikuban'ja*. Moskau.

Gabunia, L.K.
1959 O lošadi iz Sagvardžile (Zap.-Gruzija), *Sbornik Geol. Inst. AN GSSR*, 263-271.

1992 Der menschliche Unterkiefer von Dmanisi (Georgien, Kaukasus), *Jahrbuch des Römisch-Germanischen Zentralmus.* 39, 1992 (1995), 185-208.

Gabunia, L.,
  A. Vekua
1981 Terrestrial mammals of the Pliocene and the early Pleistocene and the boundary between Neogene and Quaternary in Georgia, USSR, *Field Conference Neogene/Quaternary boundary, India. IGCP 41 (Calcutta)*, 45-48.

1990 L'évolution du paléoenvironnement au cours de l'Anthropogène en Georgie (Transcaucasie), *L'Anthropologie* 94, 643-650.

1993 *Dmanisskij iskopaemyj čelovek i soputstvujuščaja emu fauna pozvonočnych*. Tbilisi.

Gabunia, L.,
  A. Justus,
  A. Vekua
1991 Der menschliche Unterkiefer. In: V. Džaparidze, G. Bosinski *et al.* 1991, 109-111.

Gabunia, M.,
  A. Vekua,
  M. Tvalčrelidze
1994 Der altpaläolithische Fundplatz Achalkalaki am Amiranis-Berg im Džavacheti-Gebiet (Süd-Georgien), *Arch. Korrespondenzblatt* 24, 237-240.

Gadžiev, D.V.,
  M.M. Gusejnov
1970 Pervaja dlja SSSR nachodka ašel'skogo čeloveka (Azerbajdzan, Azychskaja peščera), *Učenye zapiski Azerb. Gos. Universiteta* 31, 13-21.

Gadžiev, D.V., M.M. Gusejnov, A.V. Mamedov, A.Š. Širinov	1979	Kratkie resul'taty kompleksnych issledovanij Azychskoj drevnepaleolitičeskoj stojanki, *Izv. AN Azerb. SSR, serija nauk o zemle* 1979/3, 10-16.
Golovanova, L.V.	1990	Novje nižnepaleolitičeskie peščernye stojanki severo-zapadnogo Kavkaza. Paleolit Kavkaza i sopredel'nych territorij, *Sbornik, posvjaščennyj 100-letiju so dnja rozdenija člen-korr. AN GSSR Prof. G. K. Nioradze (Tbilisi)*, 35-36.
Golovanova, L.V., V.B. Doroničev	1993	Ašel' severnogo Kavkaza, *Vtoraja kubanskaja archeologičeskaja konferencija (Krasnodar)*, 27-29.
Gričuk, V.P.	1982	Flora i rastitel'nost, *Stratigrafija SSSR, četvertičnaja sistema* 1, 337-374.
Gromov, I.M., V.A. Fokanov	1980	Ob ostatkach pozdnečetvertičnych gryzunov iz peščery Kudaro I. In: V.P. Ljubin 1980a, 79-89.
Grossgejm, A.A.	1942	*Dikie s-edobnye rastenija Kavkaza.* Baku.
	1946	*Rastitel'nye resursy Kavkaza.* Baku.
Guérin, C., G.F. Barychnikov	1987	Le rhinoceros acheuléen de la Grotte Koudaro I (Georgie, URSS) et le problème des espèces relictes du pleistocène du Caucase, *Geobios* 20, 389-396.
Gusejnov, M.M.	1963	Azychskaja peščera - krupnyj karst i drevnejšaja stojanka v Azerbajdzane, *Doklady AN Azerb. SSR* 19, 10-14.
	1965	O rezul'tatach archeologiceskich raskopok v Azychskoj peščere, *Archeologičeskie issledovanija v Azerbaidzane (Baku)*, 6-14.
	1973	O tajnike azychantropov v ašele, *Učenye zapiski Azerb. Gos. Universiteta* 1973/8, 12-16.
	1974	Očagi azychantropov baku-chazarskogo (mindel-riss) vozrasta, *Učenye zapiski Azerb. Gos. Universiteta* 1974/1, 54-63.
	1975	*Archaeology of Azerbaidshan. (Stone Age).* Baku (in Azerbaidshanish).
	1980	Novye archeologičeskie dannye o kuručajskoj kul'ture peščery Azych v Azerdajdzanskoj SSR, *Jzv. AN Azerb. SSR, serija istorii, filosofii i prava* 1980/3, 69-84.
	1981	*Peščera Azych.* Baku.
	1985	*Drevnij paleolit Azerbajdzana.* Baku.
Gvozdeckij, N.A.	1963	*Kavkaz.* Moskva.
Izmajlov, Ja. A.	1990	Geologičeskoe stroenie plejstocenovych otloženij vostočnogo Azovo-Černomor'ja, *Cetvertičnyj period: metody issledovanija, stratigrafija i ekologija (Tallin)*, 36-37.
Kahlke, R.D.	1987	On the Occurrence of *Hippopotamus* (Mammalia, Artiodactyla) in the Pleistocene of Achalkalaki (Gruzinian SSR, Soviet Union) and on the Distribution of the Genus in South-East Europe, *Zeitschr. geol. Wiss.* 15, 407-414.
Kalandadze, A.N.	1960	Basic results of the work of the palaeolithic expedition on the Southern slope of the Central Caucasus in 1959, *Lessons at the scientific session of the historical Institute of the Georgian Academy of Science* 1960, 6-10 (in Georgian language).
	1961	Resul'taty raboty paleolitičeskoj ekspedicii 1960 g. na južnom sklone Srednego Kavkaza, *Itogi polevych archeologičeskich issledovanij na territorii Gruzinskoj SSR v 1960 g*, 3-7.

	1962	Itogi rabot paleolitičeskoj ekspedicii na južnom sklone srednej časti Kavkazkogo chrebta v 1961g, *Itogi polevych archeologičeskich issledovanij na territorii Gruzinskoj SSR v 1961 g*, 3-6.
	1965	Conskaja peščera i ee kul'tura, *Peščery Gruzii* 3, 32-36.
	1969	Conskjaja peščera i ee kul'tura, *Actes du VI e Congres international de Speleologie (Ljubljana)*, 339-353.
Kikodze, Z.K.	1986	Bifas-kolun v ašele Kavkaza, *Vestnik Gos. Muzeja Gruzii* 38, 55-69.
Kikodze, Z.K., I.D. Koridze	1978	Kratkij otčet o rabotach provedennych Paravanskoj razvedyvatel'noj archeologičeskoj ekspedicii za 1977g, *Archeologičeskie ekspedicii Gos. Museja Gruzii* 7, 19-26.
Klopotovskaja, N., E. Kvavadze, D. Lordkipanidze	1991	Vorläufige Mitteilung zur Paläobotanik. In: V. Džaparidze, G. Bosinski *et al.* 1991, 92.
Kolakovskij, A.A.	1961	*Rastitel'nyj mir kolchidy*. Moskva.
Kolbutov, A.D.	1961	Geologičeskie i geomorfologičeskie uslovija mestonachoždenij Jugo-Osetinskich paleolitičeskich stojanok. Voprosy stratigrafii i periodizacii paleolita, *Trudy komissii po izučeniju četvertičnogo perioda* 18, 109-119.
Korobkov, I.I.	1967	Itogi pjatiletnych issledovanij Jaštuchskogo paleolitičeskogo mestonachoždenija, *Sovetskaja archeologija* 1967/4, 194- 206.
	1971	K probleme izučenija nižnepaleolitičeskich poselenij otkrytogo tipa c razružennym kul'turnym sloem, *Materialy i issledovanija po archeologii SSSR* 173, 61-99.
Levkovskaja, G.-M.	1980	Palinologičeskaja charakteristika otloženij v peščerach Kudaro I i Kudaro III. In: V.P. Ljubin 1980a, 128-151.
Ljubin, V.P.	1954	Paleolitičeskie nachodki v Jugo-Osetii, *Kratkie soobščenija Instituta Istorii mater. kul'tury* 54, 49-61.
	1959	Vysokogornaja peščernaja stojanka Kudaro I, *Izvestija Vsesojusn. Geograf. obščestva* 91, 173-183.
	1960	Nižnepaleolitičeskie pamjatniki Jugo-Osetii. Paleolit i Neolit SSSR, *Materialy i issledovanija po archeologii SSSR* 79, 9-78.
	1961	Verchneašel'skaja masterskaja Džraber (Armenija), *Kratkie soobščenija Instituta Archeologii* 82, 59-67.
	1969	Rannij paleolit Kavkaza, *Priroda i razvitie pervobytnogo obščestva*, 154-168.
	1974	Prirodnaja sreda i čelovek v plejstocene Kavkaza, *Pervobytnyj čelovek i prirodnaja sreda*, 169-177.
	1975	Vozobnovlenie raskopok peščery Kudaro III, *Archeologičeskie otkrytija* 1974 g, 457.
	1977	*Must'erskie Kul'tury Kavkaza*. Leningrad.
	1978	Raskopki Kudarskich peščer v Jugo-Osetii, *Archeologičeskie otkrytija 1977 g*, 485-486.
	1980a	*Kudarskie peščernye paleolitičeskie stojanki v Jugo-Osetii. (Voprosy, stratigrafii, ekologii, chronologii)*. Moskva.

	1980b	Nekotorye itogi izučenija litogostratigrafičeskich i biostratigrafičeskich pokazatelej kudarskich peščer. In: V.P. Ljubin 1980a, 153-156.
	1980c	Geografičeskoe položenie peščernych stojanok Jugo-Osetii. In: V.P. Ljubin 1980a, 13-32.
	1981a	Nižnij paleolit Kavkaza (istorija issledovanij, opornye pamjatniki, mestnye osobennosti), *Drevnij Vostok i mirovaja kul'tura*, 12-16.
	1981b	Issledovanie kudarskich peščer, *Archeologičeskie otkrytija 1980 g*, 405-406.
	1981c	L'Acheuléen de la partie européenne de l'URSS et du Caucase (matériaux et quelques problèmes), *Anthropologie (Brno)* 19, 33-46.
	1984	Rannij paleolit Kakaza. In: P.I. Boriskovskij (ed.), Paleolit SSSR, 45-93.
	1989	Paleolit Kavkaza. Paleolit mira, *Paleolit Kavkaza i severnoj Azii*, 9-142.
	1990	Stojanki v skal'nych ubežiščach: specifika i metodika polevych issledovanij, *Kratkie soobščenija Instituta archeologii* 202, 68-77.
	1993a	Chronostratigrafija paleolita Kavkaza, *Rossijskaja archeologija* 2, 5-14.
	1993b	La chronostratigraphie du Paléolithique du Caucase, *L'Anthropologie* 97, 291-298.
Ljubin, V.P., G.M. Levkovskaja	1972	Peščera Kudaro III. (Jugo- Osetija). Paleolit i Neolit SSSR, *Materialy i issledovanija po archeologii SSSR* 185, 25-40.
Ljubin, V.P., V.E. Ščelinskij	1972	Novye dannye o nižnem paleolite Sočunsko-Abchazkogo Pričernomor'ja, *Bjulleten' komissii po izučeniju četvertičnogo perioda* 38, 88-98.
Ljubin, V.P., N.V. Rengarten, A.G. Černjachovskij, G.F. Baryšnikov, G.M. Levtovskaja	1978	Peščera Kudaro I, *Archeologija i paleogeografija rannego paleolita Kryma i Kavkaza*, 76-87.
Ljubin, V.P., G.F. Baryšnikov, G.A. Černjachovskij, N.B. Selivanova	1985a	Peščera Kudaro I (opyt kompleksnogo issledovanija), *Sovetskaja archeologija* 1985/3, 5-24.
(Lubine), V.P., A.G. Tcherniachovski, G.F. Barychnikov, G.M. Levkovskaja, N.B. Selivanova	1985b	La Grotte de Koudaro I (résultats des recherches pluridisciplinaires), *L'Anthropologie* 89, 159-180.
Ljubin, L.P., G.F. Baryšnikov	1985	Ochotnič'ja dejatel'nost' drevnejšich (ašelo-must'erskich) obitatelej Kavkaza, *Kratkie soobščenija Instituta archeologii* 181, 5-9.
Ljubin, V.P., O.A. Kulikov	1991	O vozraste drevnejšich paleolitičeskich pamjatnikov Kavkaza, *Sovetskaja archeologija* 1991/4, 5-8.
Majsuradze, G., E. Pavlenišvili, H.-U. Schmincke, Dz. Sologašvili	1991	Paläomagnetik und Datierung der Basaltlava. In: V. Džaparidze, G. Bosinski *et al.* 1991, 74-76.

Markova, A.K. 1982 Mikroteriofauna iz paleolitičeskoj peščernoj stojanki Azych, *Paleontologičeskij sbornik* 19, 14-28.

Maruašvili, L.N. 1971 *Geomorfologija Gruzii*. Tbilisi.

Morgan, J. de 1909 Les stations préhistoriques d'Alagheuz, *Rev. Ecole Anthropol.* 19.

Muzeibov, M.A., 1961 Azychskaja peščera, *Učenye zapiski Azerb. Gos. Universiteta* 1961/1, 69-73.
M.M. Gusejnov

Nesmejanov, S.A. 1989 Peščernyj genetičeskij kompleks, *Bjulleten' komissii po izučenija četvertičnogo perioda* 58, 86-96.

Nikiforova, K.V. 1982 Stratigrafičeskoe rasčlenenie i korreljacija verchnepliocenovych i četvertičnych otlozenij, *Problemy geologii i istorii četvertičnogo perioda (antropogena)*, 36-89.

Ostrovskij, A.B., 1977 Novye dannye o stratigrafii i geochronologii plejstocenovych morskich terras Černo-
Ja.A. Izmajlov, morskogo poberež'ja Kavkaza u Kerčensko-Tamanskoj oblasti, *Paleogeografija i*
A.P.Ščeglov *et al.* *otloženija plejstocena južnych morej SSSR*, 61-68.

Paničkina, M.Z. 1950 *Paleolit Armenii*. Leningrad.

Pavlov, N.B. 1948 *Botaničeskaja geografija SSSR*. Alma Ata.

Pospelova, G.A., 1994 Otraženie klimatičeskich izmenenij v magnitnoj vospriimčivosti osadocnych porod,
G.M. Levkovskaja *Doklady Rossijskoj AN* 334/2.

Praslov, N.D. 1984 Geologiceskie i paleogeografičeskie ramki paleolita. Razvitie prirodnoj sredy na territorii SSSR i problemy chronologii i periodizacii paleolita. In: P.I. Boriskovskij (ed.), Paleolit SSSR, 17- 40.

Roebroeks, W., this The earliest occupation of Europe: a reappraisal of artefactual and chronological
T. van Kolfschoten volume evidence.

Ščelinskij, V.E. (Shchelinskij) 1993 Outils pour travailler le bois et l'os au Paléolithique inférieur et moyen de la Plaine russe et du Caucase, *Traces et fonction: les gestes retrouvés. ERAUL 50*, 309-315, Liège.

Ščelinskij, V.E., 1970 Ob opyte geologičeskoj stratifikacii novych archeologičeskich pamjatnikov Cernomor-
A.B. Ostrovskij skogo poberež'ja severo-zapadnogo Kavkaza, *Periodizacija i chronologii plejstocena*, 5-8.

Selivanova, N.B. 1980 Materialy issledovanija grubooblomočnoj časti rychlych otloženij Kudaro III. In: V.P. Ljubin 1980a, 39-50.

Širinov, A.Š. 1966 Geomorfologičeskaja datirovka vozrasta Azychskoj peščernoj stojanki paleolitičeskogo čeloveka, *Izvest. AN Azerb. SSR, Ser. nauk o zemle* 1966/5, 12-14.

Sulejmanov, M.B. 1979 Sovremennoe sostojanie kompeksnych issledovanij v paleolitičeskich peščerach Azych i Taglar (Azerb. SSR), *Izvest. AN Azerb. SSR, Ser. nauk o zemle* 1979/6, 43-49.

1982 *Sreda obitanija pervobytnogo čeloveka jugo-vostoka Malogo Kavkaza (po dannym paleolitičeskich peščer Azych i Taglar)*. Avtoref. diss. kanad., Moskva.

Tintilozov, Z.K. 1976 *Karstovye peščery Gruzii*. Tbilisi.

Tintilozov, Z.K., 1969 Speleoelogija izvestnjakovogo massiva Kudaro-Buba, *Tezisy itogov naucn. sessii Instituta*
Š.Ja. Kipiani, *geografii AN GSSR* 169, 15-17.
V.M. Džiškariani,
D.M. Simonišvili

Tušabramišvili, D.M.   1962   Archeologičeskie razvedki v uščele'e r. Kvirila, *Vestnik Gos. Muzeja Gruzii* 23-b, 34-43.

1978   Itogi rabot Cučchvatskoj i Conskoj archeologičeskich ekspedicij za 1976-1977 gg., *Archeologičeskie ekspedicii Gos. Museja Gruzii* 6, 5-18.

1984   Paleolit Gruzii. Vestnik Gos., *Museja Gruzii* 37-B, 5-27.

Vekua, A.K.   1962   *The Lower pleistocene mammalian fauna from Achalkalaki.* Tbilisi (in Georgian language).

1987   The Lower Pleistocene Mammalian Fauna of Achalkalaki (Southern Georgia, USSR), *Paleontographica Italica* 74, 63-96.

1991a   Istorija životnogo mira-pozvonočnye, *Gruzija v anthropogene*, 308-381.

1991b   Vlijanie celoveka na faunu pozvonocnyk i ego rol' v vymiranii vidov, *Gruzija v anthropogene*, 382-392.

in press   Die Wirbeltierfauna von Dmanisi (Georgien, Kaukasus) und ihre biostratigraphische Stellung.

Vekua, A.K.,   1981   Paleolitičeskaja fauna iz peščer Zapadnoj Gruzii, *Peščery Gruzii. Speleologičeskii sbornik* 9, 38-50.
  C.D. Gabelaja,
  A.G. Muščelisvili

Vekua, A.D.,   1985   Novye paleontologičeskie nachodki v okresnostjach Calka, *Soobščenija AN GSSR* 118, 373-376.
  D.G. Džigauri,
  R.I. Torozov

Vekua, A.D.,   1987   K izučeniju paleolitičeskoj fauny pozvonočnych peščery Cona, *Peščery Gruzii. Speleologiščeskij sbornik* 11, 92-100.
  C.C. Gabelaja,
  A.G. Muščelisvili,
  N.S. Mamacašvili

Vekua, A.,   1991   Die Wirbeltiere von Dmanisi und ihre stratigraphische Stellung. In: V. Džaparidze, G. Bosinski *et al.* 1991, 83-91.
  L. Gabunia

Veličko, A.A.,   1969   Geologičeskaja istorija Russkoj ravniny, Kryma i Kavkaza v plejstocene i vozrast paleolithičeskich kul'tur, *Priroda i razvitie pervobytnogo obščestva na territorii Evrop cast SSSR*, 8-41.
  I.K. Ivanova,
  V.M. Muratov

Veličko, A.A.,   1980   Paleogeografija stojanki Azych-drevnejšego poselenija pervobytnogo čeloveka na territorii SSSR, *Izvest. AN SSSR Serija Geogr.* 1980/30, 20-35.
  G.V. Antonova,
  E.M. Zelikson,
  A.K. Markova,
  M.M. Monoszon,
  T.D. Morozova,
  M.A. Pevzner,
  M.B. Sulejmanov,
  T.A. Chalčeva

Vereščagin, N.K.   1957a   Ostatki mlekopitajuščich iz nižnečetvertičnych otloženij Tamanskogo poluostrova, *Trudy zoologičeskogo instituta* 22 (Materialy po istoriii fauny četvertičnogo perioda (antropogenal SSSR)), 9-74.

1957b   Plejstočenovje pozvonočnye iz peščery Kudaro I v Jugo.Osetii i ich značenie dlja razrabotki istorii fauny i landsaftov Kavkaza, *Doklady AN SSSR* 113/6, 1347-1349.

Vereščagin, N.K.,   1980a   Ostatki mlekopitajuščich v vostocnoj galeree peščery Kudaro I (raskopki V. P. Ljubina 1957-1958). In: V.P. Ljubin 1980a, 51-62.
  G.F. Baryšnikov

| | 1980b | Ostatki mlekopitajuscich iz peščery Kudaro III. In: V. P. Ljubin 1980a, 63-78. |

Zagwijn, W.H.   1957   Vegetation, climate and time-correlations in the Early Pleistocene of Europe, *Geologie en Mijnbouw* N.S.19, 233-244.

1963   Pleistocene stratigraphy in the Netherlands, based on changes in vegetation and climate, *Verhandel. Kon. Ned. geologisch mijnbouwkundig genootschap. Geol. Ser.* 21-2, 173-196.

1975   Variations in climate as shown by pollenanalysis, especially in the Early Pleistocene of Europe. In: A.E. Wright and F. Moseley (ed.), *Ice ages: ancient and modern*, 137-152. Geol. J. Spec. Issue 6.

Zamjatnin, S.N.   1937   *Paleolit Abchazii.* Trudy Instituta abchazskoj kul'tury 10. Suchumi.

1949   Nekotorye dannje o ni_nem paleolite Kubani, *Sbornik muzeja antropologii i etnografii* 12, 485-498.

1961   *Očerki po paleolitu.* Moskva/Leningrad.

Zelikson, E.M.,   1985   Smeščenie vysotnoj pojasnosti kak osnova rekonstrukcii klimatičeskich izmenenij v
Z.P. Gubonina   gornych stranach, *Metody rekonstrukcii klimatov*, 37-45.

Zubov, A.A.   1980   O zube archantropa iz peščery Kudaro I. In: V.P. Ljubin 1980a, 152.

Vassilij Ljubin
Institute of Archaeology
Dvorzovaja Nab. 19
St. Petersburg
Russia

Gerhard Bosinski
Forschungsbereich Altsteinzeit
Schloss Monrepos
56567 Neuwied
Germany

Jean-Paul Raynal
Lionel Magoga
Fatima-Zohra Sbihi-Alaoui
Denis Geraads

13   The earliest occupation of Atlantic Morocco: the Casablanca evidence

Recent work in the Casablanca area considerably modified earlier interpretations of its prolific Palaeolithic record. New results reported in this paper stress the absence of traces of a very early human occupation. The main part of the rich Acheulean sequence at Casablanca dates from the second part of the Middle Pleistocene, though palaeomagnetic data suggests that the earliest traces of human activities date from before the Brunhes-Matuyama boundary (Thomas-1 quarry, level L). Throughout the Acheulean sequence the same lithic raw materials were used, which allows comparison of technological characteristics of the various assemblages.

1.   Introduction

The Casablanca region, on the Atlantic coast of the Moroccan Meséta, is rich in Palaeolithic sites preserved in an exceptionally well developed series of littoral deposits (Fig. 1). This series formed the basis for the definition of the majority of the stratotypes of the classical stages of the Maghreb's marine Pleistocene (Neuville and Ruhlman 1941; Biberson 1961; Texier *et al.* 1985). The deposits yielded various fossils of hominids (Biberson 1956; Ennouchi 1969, 1972), which are at the origin of the first anatomically modern humans (Hublin 1991). Recent work has established a new lithostratigraphical (Texier *et al.* 1994; Lefèvre *et al.* 1994), biostratigraphical and archaeological framework (see Table 1), that will be used in this paper to discuss the age of the first occupation of the Casablanca region and to present some aspects of its Acheulean sequence.

2.   From the Pliocene to the Middle Pleistocene

The base of the stratigraphic series of Casablanca is of Pliocene age (Raynal *et al.* 1990), dating from before the Quaternary volcanism of the Middle Atlas (El Graoui 1994).

The oldest fossiliferous site in the Casablanca sequence is the Lissasfa karst complex, developed in the top of littoral deposits that have their base at about 170 m above present sea level[1]. Its microfauna, which contains *Paraethomys* sp., *Ruscinomys* sp., *Mus* sp. and Gerbillidae, suggests a Middle or Early Pliocene age.

Ahl-Al-Oughlam is a younger site, systematically excavated from 1989 onwards, and located in a shoreline cut in beach deposits at 108 m above sea level (Raynal *et al.* 1990). Its vertebrate fauna, by far the richest one of the North African late Cenozoic and only comparable to the rich sites of eastern Africa, suggests an age of around 2.5 Myr BP (Geraads 1993a; 1995). More than 70 species have been identified, belonging to all main groups: fishes, reptiles (giant tortoise, lizards, snakes, crocodiles and the rare Amphisbaenidae), various birds (with a remarkable coexistence of penguin and ostrich, and with pseudodontornithes, giant sea birds with false teeth) and mammals, the most common group. Carnivores are represented by 23 taxa, 13 of which are new (Geraads, in press), e.g. Hyaenidae (*Crocuta*, *Pliocrocuta*), a sabre-toothed felid, Mustelidae, Canidae (*Vulpes*, *Nyctereutes*), the oldest known bear from Africa and a morse. The herbivores comprise elephant, a mastodont, a fossil pig (*Kolpochoerus phacochoeroides*), a bovid-sized giraffe (*Sivatherium maurusium*), antelopes (*Kobus* and *Damaliscus*), a three-toed horse (*Hipparion*), a rhinoceros (*Ceratotherium*), a monkey (*Theropithecus*), as well as a large variety of rodents and insectivores. It is obvious that the large predators played a major role in the formation of this fossiliferous site, of which we have a representative sample now. Traces of hominids, be it as fossils or in the form of artefacts, are completely absent in this large assemblage, and the Ahl-Al-Oughlam site thus seems to date from before their arrival in the Maghreb.

The Early Pleistocene of Casablanca, not well known in detail yet, is currently the object of systematical research, and various stratigraphical units have been identified between 45 and 100 m above sea level. No important fossiliferous site is known yet, and no stone artefacts have been recovered *in situ*. Finds recovered from deposits formerly attributed to the Maarifien, the Moulouyen or the Salétien are either *geofacts* collected from high-energy littoral facies (old collections of Biberson in the Déprez quarry and recent collections by J.P. Raynal and D. Lefèvre in the Bir As Smar pit), or are recent artefacts from superficial colluvial deposits, as in other sites in Morocco (Raynal and Texier 1989): at yet there is no 'Pebble Culture' *in situ* at Casablanca.

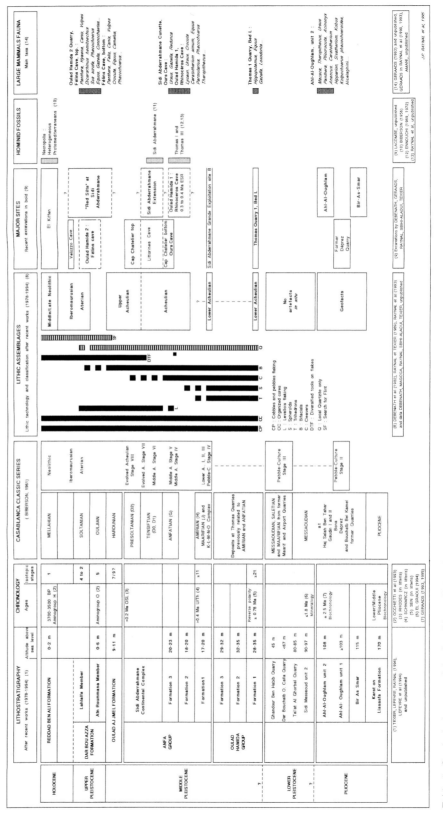

Table 1. Synthetical survey of the Casablanca Palaeolithic record and its geological context.

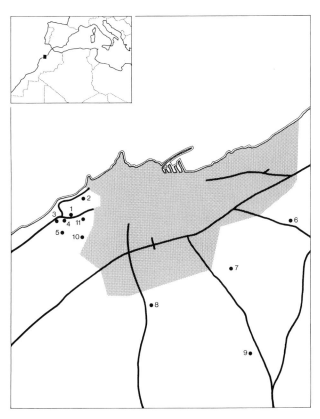

Fig. 1. Location of sites in the Casablanca area: 1. Sidi Abder-rahmane; 2. *Grotte des Ours*; 3 Sidi Abderrah-mane Extension; 4. Thomas 1; 5. *Grotte des Rhinocéros* Oulad-Hamida 1; 6. Ahl-Al-Oughlam; 7. Bir As Smar; 8. Sidi Messaoud; 9. Lissasfa; 10. Ghaudour Ben Habib; 11. Sidi Al Khadir East.

3.   The Middle Pleistocene

The Middle Pleistocene is characterized by abundant human occupation. Deposits of this period are very well developed and display great lithostratigraphical detail: seven marine units are identified, stepped between 9 and 35 m above present sea level and covered by continental fossiliferous deposits (Texier *et al.* 1994). The abundant finds discovered in the quarries of Sidi-Abderrahmane, Thomas-1 and Oulad Hamida-1 allow us to characterize the contemporary 'animal' environment and to establish the main lines of the local Acheulean sequence.

Throughout the sequence arkoses and cambrian feldsparic quartzites – often referred to as El Hank quartzites – form the principal raw materials. They were abundantly present in various sizes on the former beaches and rocky outcrops, and give the assemblages a rather 'archaic' character. Experiments with these rocks have given us a good idea of their flaking characteristics. The raw materials are very though and

massive, and very hard to flake, though knapping is facilitated by making use of plane surfaces, natural or arteficial ones. Fractures are very clear: hard percussion created decorticated surfaces with well marked negative scars and also entailed frequent knapping accidents such as breakage of flakes or pebbles along the axis of percussion (Siret breaks, accidentally broken pebbles, *galets à un enlèvement fendus*).

Flint constitutes only about 5% of the raw materials, up untill the Upper Acheulean, when flint was sought for more systematically. Flint is locally available in the form of small pebbles (1 to 5 cm in diameter) in various coarse grained littoral deposits.

The exploitation of the same raw materials throughout the Acheulean sequence at Casablanca allows a comparison of the technological characteristics of some representative series. They are presented here along the lines of the classification model developed on basis of a study of the assemblages from Unit L of the Thomas quarry, briefly explained below. This model is based on the character of the working surfaces, their disposition and exploitation; it integrates dynamic aspects (sequences of production of flakes and of shaping, reduction of objects, re-use etc.) and functional ones (specific morphology, transformation by usage...). Seven main groups are discerned:

Group 1: flaking carried out by using cortical striking platforms
Group 2: flaking from one non-cortical striking platform, possibly re-adjusted
Group 3: flaking using two non-cortical striking platforms for one and the same working surface
Group 4: flaking using three to five non-cortical striking platforms for one and the same working surface
Group 5: flaking from non-cortical striking platforms belonging to various working surfaces
Group 6: exploitation/shaping of flakes and fragments
Group 7: objects transformed by usage

The group-subdivisions thus repose upon technological and/or secondary morphological criteria (such as re-use of striking platforms, recurrence of flake removals, length of blanks (both arteficial and natural ones), surface size of flake removals and presence/absence of cortex).

Group 4 contains most objects with multiple flake removals. Starting with flaking from cortical striking platforms (group 1) and followed by an increase of flaked surfaces this group contains the majority of complex and/or typical objects. The most complete bifaces as well as the best exploited cores are within this group. Group 6, with cores on flakes and fragments and tools on flakes testifies to the final stages of the knapping process.

Items transformed by usage or re-utilization are at the origin of part of the observed assemblage variability. Table 2 surveys some characteristics of four representative series of the Acheulean sequence at Casablanca, as assembled from 1978 onwards during excavations by the *Mission préhistorique et paléontologique française au Maroc* and the *Institut National des Sciences de l'Archéologie et du Patrimoine* at Rabat: member L of the Thomas-1 quarry (TH L1 and TH L5), the *Grotte des Rhinocéros* of the Oulad Hamida-1 quarry (GDR) and Sidi-Abderrahmane Extension (SAE). Table 1 only considers the effective totals of the various groups with exclusion of (natural) blanks.

Table 2: see text for explanation

Sites: Age:	TH L1 >0.78 Myr BP		TH L5 ?		GDR ±0.4 Myr BP		SAE <0.4 Myr BP	
Groups	n	%	n	%	n	%	n	%
1	18	6	18	4.8	77	15	31	5.4
2	56	18.8	79	21.2	71	13.8	62	10.7
3	38	12.8	11	2.9	23	4.5	96	16.6
4	124	41.6	61	16.4	110	21.5	199	34.5
5	18	6	66	17.7	35	6.8	5	0.9
6	36	12.1	97	26	100	19.5	181	31.4
7	8	2.7	41	11	97	18.9	3	0.5
Total	298	100	373	100	513	100	577	100

The earliest occupation known yet has been discovered in the Thomas-1 quarry, in level L of the Formation 1 of the Oulad-Hamida Group (Raynal and Texier 1989). The assemblage contains flakes struck from discoidal cores and from polyhedrons. Besides chopping-tools, polyhedrons and some cleavers, bifaces form the most characteristic element within the tools. They are often partial only and usually display lateral or lateral-distal concavities, that make up the point of the bifaces.

The fauna from this site is dominated by hippopotamus, like the probably somewhat younger site of Tighenif (Ternifine) in Algeria, and contains furthermore elephant, zebra and gazelles. Palaeomagnetic data suggests an age in excess of 0.78 Myr BP for the main part of this local early Acheulean sequence (Sen, *in litteris*).

Various sites (Sidi Al Khadir, Gandhour Ben Habib, Oulad Hamida 1) have yielded small assemblages dominated by debitage. These assemblages are being studied now, and can be dated in the first part of the Middle Pleistocene (Group of Oulad Hamida). The main part of the Acheulean sites from the Casablanca sequence, including the hominid sites from the Thomas quarries (Geraads *et al.* 1980), however date from the second half of the Middle Pleistocene (Anfa Group). The *Grotte des Rhinocéros* of the Oulad-Hamida-1 quarry (Raynal *et al.* 1993) yielded a rich lithic industry and an abundant fauna with about 50

vertebrate species (Geraads 1993b,1994) that indicate a rather open and dry environment. ESR-dating of tooth enamel of *Ceratotherium simum* (Rhodes *et al.* 1994) gives the assemblage an age of about 400 Kyr BP. The abundant remains of white rhinoceros suggest specialized hunting by hominids. Compared to the local early Acheulean one can observe an increase of discoidal cores and of flake production; cleavers are rare while bifacial pieces are larger, characterized by convex and/or concave edges that constitute a pointed extremity (cf. Fig. 2).

In the Thomas-1 cave the level that yielded the human mandible in 1969 is now under excavation. The recovered assemblage is quite different from the series of the *Grotte des Rhinocéros*, as it is dominated by flaked pebbles, and comparable to the series collected at the time of the discovery of the jaw (Geraads *et al.* 1980). This variability can probably be explained by the small size of the sample recovered from the infill yet.

A more recent stage is well illustrated at Sidi-Abderrahmane-Extension. Here we observe an important use of block-fragments and frequent recycling of rolled artefacts with multiple scars. Flakes are mainly produced from discoidal cores and polyhedric forms are quite rare. So are predetermined flakes, but these coexist with a diverse toolkit on flakes. Bifacial pieces are generally made on flakes and mostly display convex sides and tend towards ovate forms, even to discoidal ones. Cleavers are rare here.

The upper part of the Acheulean sequence is represented at the Cap Chatelier site, with an age in excess of 200 Kyr (optically stimulated luminescence dates by Rhodes 1990): production of predetermined flakes and thin, small bifaces, a diverse set of tools on flakes and very few cleavers (Debenath *et al.* 1982).

The Acheulean series of Casablanca are thus characterized by a large homogeneity, which is to a large extent the result of the use of the same mineral resources over various hundreds of thousands of years. The raw material, abundantly available in all sizes, allowed a production of large flakes or voluminous fragments of pebbles and blocks. The only constraint consisted in the transport of heavy objects, making voluminous flaked items rare in the excavated sites. The various types of blanks introduced to the sites are very well recognizable in the bifaces of the various series.

The industries testify to a certain stability throughout the Middle Pleistocene (lateral dissymmetrie proper to a partial shaping, for example), but they also bear witness of an increasing complexity of elementary modes of reduction and of a continuous technological enrichment in which earlier acquirements resurge (the polyhedric proximal part of some bifaces of the *Grotte des Rhinocéros*, for example). The observed changes in the morphology of the various

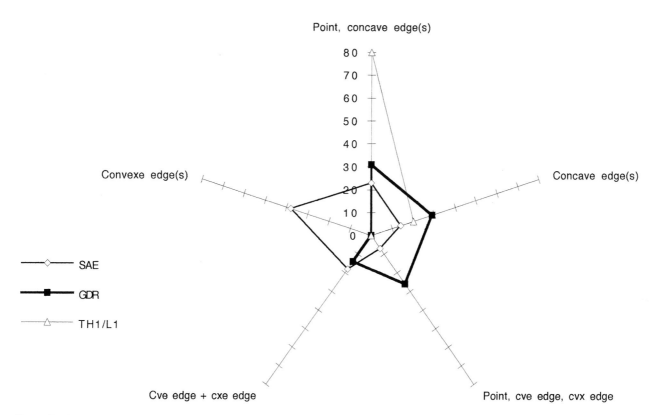

Fig. 2. Distribution (in %) of various biface edge-types of the assemblages – SAE (Sidi Abderrahmane Extension), GDR (Grotte des Rhinocéros), TH1/L1 (Thomas 1 Quarry, Level L1).

objects can be quantified; for instance the remarkably regular change over time of the angle formed by the directions of the two flake removals that delimit a sequence of flake removals on one (or two) working surfaces. The neat correlation between the number of flake removals and the number of striking platforms (cf. Fig. 3) is a technological constant (a succession of x flakes originating from one platform), verified in experiments and determined by the mechanical characteristics of the raw material. Within this 'Acheulean' unity the changes within the bifaces reflect in our view a morpho-functional evolution, relayed in time by a more systematic production of flakes, including predetermined ones.

A comparison of the probable use of the objects identified in our classification with experimental results (Toth 1985) leads to the following conclusions regarding the activities performed at the sites: Thomas-1 L1: some stone working, hide slitting, heavy duty butchery, bone breaking; Thomas-1 L5: stone working dominates, light duty butchery; *Grotte des Rhinocéros*: stone working

important, hide slitting, light and heavy-duty butchery, bone breaking; Sidi-Abderrahmane Extension: stone working important, hide slitting, light duty butchery, bone breaking.

The large scale excavations that are in progress now at Casablanca will allow us to develop these preliminary interpretations in more detail and to propose more specific functional hypotheses for the various sites discussed here.

4.   Conclusions

As a result of the recent and ongoing work in the Casablanca region a few concluding points can be stressed here:

– as yet the Casablanca region has not yielded any evidence of very early human occupation of the Moroccan Atlantic coastal area

– palaeomagnetic data suggests that the earliest traces of human occupation date from (just?) before the Brunhes-Matuyama boundary (0.78 Myr BP)

Mean number of flake removals compared to number of striking platforms

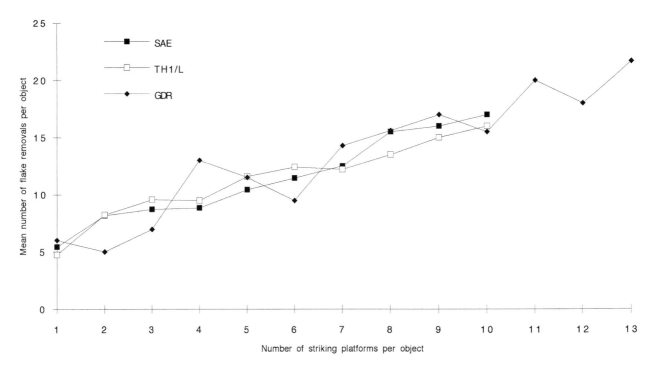

Fig. 3. Mean number of flake removals compared to number of striking platforms, for three assemblages: SAE (Sidi Abderrahmane Extension), GDR (Grotte des Rhinocéros), TH1/L1 (Thomas 1 Quarry, Level L1).

– throughout the variability demonstrated by our recent excavations various morpho-technological stages are discernable. These do not allow a formal subdivision of the Acheulean sequence but the appearance of predetermined flaking techniques, applied to the principal raw material (quartzite), nevertheless characterizes a rather recent phase of this sequence.

Finally, our current state of knowledge is presented here in the form of the synthetical table 1; while significantly modifying earlier data, the current framework reflects only a provisional stage of our ongoing research.

Autorisation de publier no. 462 du 14 juin 1995

note

1 The site was discovered May 17th 1995, by D. Lefèvre and J.P. Raynal.

references

Biberson, P.

1956   Le gisement de l'Atlanthrope de Sidi Abderrahmane, *Bulletin d'Archéologie marocaine* 1, 38-92.

1961   Le cadre paléogéographique de la Préhistoire du Maroc atlantique et Le Paléolithique inférieur du Maroc atlantique, *Publications du Service des Antiquités du Maroc*, Rabat.

Debenath, A., J.P. Raynal, J.P. Texier	1982	Les industries des *Homo erectus* marocains: chronologie, typologie, *Premier Congrès international de Paléontologie humaine, Résumés*, 84-85, Nice.
El Graoui, M.	1994	*Contribution à l'étude des formations littorales quaternaires de la région de Casablanca (Maroc): sédimentologie, microfaciès et minéraux lourds.* Thèse de l'Université de Bordeaux 1.
Ennouchi, E.	1969	Découverte d'un Pithécanthropien au Maroc, *C.R. Acad. Sci. Paris* D, 269, 763-765.
	1972	Nouvelle découverte d'un archanthropien au Maroc, *C.R. Acad. Sci. Paris* D, 274, 3088-3090.
Geraads, D., P. Beriro, H. Roche	1980	La faune et l'industrie des sites à *Homo erectus* des carrières Thomas (Maroc). Précisions sur l'âge de ces hominidés, *C.R. Acad. Sci. Paris* 291(II), 195-198.
Geraads, D.	1980	La faune des sites à *Homo erectus* des carrières Thomas (Casablanca, Maroc), *Quaternaria* 22, 65-94.
	1993a	*Kolpochoerus phacochoeroides* (Thomas, 1884) (Suidae, Mammalia) du Pliocène supérieur de Ahl al Oughlam (Casablanca, Maroc), *Géobios* 26(6), 731-741.
	1993b	Middle Pleistocene *Crocidura* (Mammalia, Insectivora) from Oulad Hamida 1, Morocco, and their phylogenetic relationships, *Proceedings Kon. Ned. Akademie v. Wetenschappen* 96(3), 281-294.
	1994	Rongeurs et Lagomorphes du Pléistocène moyen de la "Grotte des Rhinocéros", Carrière Oulad Hamida 1 à Casablanca, Maroc, *N. Jb. Paläont. Abh.* 191(2), 147-172.
	1995	Rongeurs et insectivores (Mammalia) du Pliocène final de Ahl Al Oughlam (Casablance, Maroc), *Géobios* 28(1), 99-115.
	in press	Carnivores du Pliocène terminal de Ahl Al Oughlam (Casablanca, Maroc), *Géobios*, submitted.
Hublin, J.J.	1991	*L'émergence des Homo sapiens archaïques: Afrique du Nord-Ouest et Europe occidentale.* Thèse d'Etat de l'Université de Bordeaux 1.
Lefèvre, D., J.P. Texier, J.P. Raynal, S. Occietti, J. Evin	1994	Enregistrements-Réponses des variations climatiques du Pleistocène supérieur et de l'Holocène sur le littoral de Casablanca (Maroc), *Quaternaire* 5(3-4), 173-180.
Occhietti, S., J.P. Raynal, P. Pichet, J.P. Texier	1993	Aminostratigraphie du dernier cycles climatique au Maroc atlantique, de Casablanca à Tanger, *C.R. Acad. Sc. Paris* 317(II), 1625-1632.
Raynal, J.P., J.P. Texier	1989	Découverte d'Acheuléen ancien dans la carrière Thomas I à Casablanca et problème de l'ancienneté de la présence humaine au Maroc, *C.R. Acad. Sci. Paris* 308(II), 1743-1749.
Raynal, J.P., J.P. Texier, D. Geraads, F.Z. Sbihi-Alaoui	1990	Un nouveau gisement paléontologique plio-pléistocène en Afrique du Nord: Ahl Al Oughlam (ancienne carrière Déprez) à Casablanca (Maroc), *C.R. Acad. Sci. Paris* 310(II), 315-320.

Raynal, J.P.,
D. Geraads,
L. Magoga,
A. Hajraoui,
J.P. Texier,
D. Lefevre,
F.Z. Sbihi-Alaoui
1993 La Grotte des Rhinocéros (Carrière Oulad Hamida 1 – anciennement Thomas III, Casablanca), nouveau site acheuléen du Maroc atlantique, *C.R. Acad. Sci. Paris* 316(II), 1477-1483.

Rhodes, E.
1990 *Optical Dating of Quartz from Sediments*. Thèse de doctorat. University of Oxford: Oxford.

Rhodes, E.,
J.P. Raynal,
D. Geraads,
F.Z. Sbihi-Alaoui
1994 Premières date RPE pour l'Acheuléen du Maroc atlantique (Grotte des Rhinocéros, Casablanca), *C.R. Acad. Sci. Paris* 319(II), 1109-1115.

Texier, J.P.,
J.P. Raynal,
D. Lefèvre
1985 Nouvelles propositions pour un cadre chronologique raisonné du Quaternaire marocain, *C.R. Acad. Sc. Paris* 301(II), 183-188.

1994 Contribution pour un nouveau cadre stratigraphique des formations littorales quaternaires de la région de Casablanca (Maroc), *C.R. Acad. Sci. Paris* 318(II), 1247-1253.

Toth, N.
1985 The Oldowan Reassessed, a Close Look at Early Stone Artifacts, *Journal of Archaeological Science* 12, 101-120.

Jean-Paul Raynal and Lionel Magoga
Université de Bordeaux 1
Institut du Quaternaire
UMR 9933 CNRS and GDR 1122 CNRS
Avenue des Facultés, F-33405 Talence Cedex
France
and
Mission préhistorique et paléontologique française au Maroc

Fatima-Zohra Sbihi-Alaoui
Institut National des Sciences de l'Archéologie et
du Patrimoine
Avenue John Kennedy, Casier Postal
Rabat-Souissi
Maroc

Denis Geraads
Laboratoire de Paléontologie des vertébrés et
Paléontologie Humaine
Université de Paris VI, case 106
4 place Russieu, 75252 Paris cedex O5
France,
UMR 152 CNRS, Musée de l'Homme
Place du Trocadéro, 75116 Paris
France
and
Mission préhistorique et paléontologie française au Maroc

Gerhard Bosinski

14   Stone artefacts of the European Lower Palaeolithic: a short note[1]

G. de Mortillet regarded lithic artefacts as a measure of human evolution. He saw this progression as unilinear and without regional differences, Acheulean handaxes characterized the Lower Palaeolithic and especially rough handaxes were thought to represent the earliest stage named Chellean (De Mortillet 1883). By introducing several Acheulean substages Breuil not only modified this subdivision but first of all and contrary to the spirit of De Mortillet's unilinear evolution he constructed various cultural traditions: parallel to the "biface culture" (Abbe-villian, Acheulean) existed a "flake culture" (Clactonian, Levalloisian), each with its own geographical and environmental distribution (Breuil 1932).

Today both the idea that Lower Palaeolithic artefacts neatly represent stages of human evolution as well as the assumption that they characterize different cultural traditions are not very popular among archaeologists. Various contributions in this volume underline the notion that Lower Palaeolithic artefacts do not represent clear chronological units or historical traditions. This may be one of the reasons why less attention is paid to lithic artefacts than, for instance, to faunal remains or environmental data. However, stone artefacts form by far the most common category of finds from the Lower Palaeolithic. Their presence testifies to the presence of humans, and stone artefacts are the only truly durable markers of the earliest occupation of Europe. The oldest sites contain lithic artefacts, characterized by flakes with sharp cutting edges that enabled hominids to gain access to meat, an adaptational advantage that allowed a fast population increase and subsequent extension of early hominids into Eurasia.

Artefacts and Non-Artefacts

Since the well-known eolith discussion at the beginning of the twentieth century (Rutot 1902; see also Adrian 1948) it is common knowledge that there is a large grey area where no objective criteria to distinguish artefacts from natural products apply. The products of volcanic activities serve as an example; these include the so called tephrofacts discussed in this volume by Raynal, Magoga and Bindon (see also: Bosinski et al. 1980; Bonifay 1991). Also in river gravels and stone lines (cailloutis) it is not always

possible to separate artefacts from non-artefacts (cf. Schmude 1992). All attempts to clarify the differences between artefacts and natural products (cf. Pattersons 1983; Kule-meyer 1986; Albrecht et al. 1994) are hampered by the fact that Lower Palaeolithic stone working techniques were so simple that they could easily be imitated by natural processes, such as fracture during volcanic eruptions and rock falls and by stones hitting each other in high energy fluvial contexts (cf. Roebroeks 1986; 1994; Roebroeks and Van Kolfschoten, this volume). In such a context the necessarily rigorous selection of artefacts will result in a small series of lithics that might represent only a fraction of those pieces originally made by hominids (cf. Gaudzinski, in press).

Somewhat better conditions exist at sites in fine-grained shore or river bank sediments (Miesenheim I: Turner, in press), travertine sands (Bilzingsleben: Mania and Weber 1986) or loess deposits (Achenheim: Junkmanns 1991; 1995).

Raw Materials

Virtually all Lower Palaeolithic stone artefacts are made out of silicified rocks which occurred at or close to the sites. The term "local", which one often encounters in the scientific literature, should be restricted to sites directly situated on the raw material outcrops, which often have the character of a workshop. In the European Lower Palaeolithic such sites are rare, Cagny-la-Garenne and Boxgrove being two examples of this category. In many cases the siliceous rocks which hominids utilized did not occur at the site itself but at a distance of a few kilometres (Floss 1994). Isolated raw materials from distances of about 20 km (Orgnac), up to 30 km (Terra Amata) or even from "larger distances" (Kudaro I) are exceptions, indicating that it was unusual to transport lithic artefacts from one site to another.

There is a functional relationship between tool-types and types of raw material. The numerous small flakes are predominantly from homogeneous fine-grained siliceous rocks. In contrast, cleavers and pebble tools are mostly made out of tough, coarse materials. In the few cases where "pebble tools" were made of flint, we might be dealing not with tools but with cores for flake production (cf. the "pebble cores" from 'Ubeidiya: Bar-Yosef and Goren-Inbar

1993). The choice of raw material for bifaces is not as clear cut. Many of them are on quartzite and basalt, like the cleavers and pebble tools, while in flint-rich regions there are numerous bifaces made on brittle flint. Bifaces were also made out of bone as is well documented at sites including Fontana Ranuccio, Malagrotta.

The stratigraphic successions of Lower Palaeolithic levels, in Europe for instance Petralona, Orgnac and Tautavel, show that the choice of raw materials developed through time. In the upper layers of these sites the amount of homogeneous siliceous rocks is higher than in the lower layer.

Flaking Techniques

The characteristic small flakes of the Lower Palaeolithic were struck from small to medium-sized cores. The striking platform may have been prepared by one or a few blows, but the reduction face was not prepared and became irregular during flaking. Correspondingly there is no difference between preferential and preparatory flakes. Core reduction was realised by direct "hard" percussion. Low quality rocks like quartz were also worked in a bipolar way, resulting in specific cores and flake types with large straight distal and proximal extremities which may be splintered and look like *pieces esquillées* (Kobayashi 1975).

Hammerstones seem to have been chosen *ad hoc* and subsequently abandoned; hammerstones with clear concentrations of percussion scars testifying to a longer use, are rare. In later phases of the Lower Palaeolithic larger massive flakes with thick striking platforms were produced in the special Clactonian technique described first in England (Clacton-on-Sea, Swanscombe etc.).

At the end of the Lower Palaeolithic elongated flat flakes occasionally are present and were produced from cores with prepared reduction faces. Such prepared cores are known for instance from Cagny-la-Garenne, Lunel Viel and from Kärlich-Seeufer, where they occasionally display a convex prepared reduction face and a prepared-striking platform. Consequently there is a difference between preferential and preparatory flakes. This Levallois technique continues and subsequently develops in the Middle Palaeolithic.

Retouched Flakes

Flakes served as cutting tools, their sharp edges being used without retouching and often displaying signs of use. A characteristic phenomenon of the Lower Palaeolithic are smaller flakes with notched and/or denticulated retouched edges. These small tools are very numerous in every more important inventory; they reflect a kind of activity that was wide-spread and common all over the Lower Palaeolithic, presumably wood working. As a result of their function these small tools are irregular shaped and difficult to classify. They therefore gave the impression of Lower

Palaeolithic tools being "unstandardized". Continuously retouched working edges are rare in these assemblages. The British site High Lodge is an exception to these observations about Lower Palaeolithic knapping techniques, tool types and working edges, and remains an enigmatic phenomenon (Ashton *et al.* 1992).

At High Lodge flakes with slightly convex or almost straight scraper edges are common and may be classified as simple or transversal side-scrapers. There are also *racloirs déjétés* (*Spitzschaber*) with almost straight edges. Thick elongated points with irregularly retouched denticulated and notched edges are usually classified as Quinson points. Small and short end-scrapers with regularly retouched scraper-ends are common.

In bigger inventories (for instance Bilzingsleben and Dmanisi) burins occur, sometimes multiple ones, and some on truncations. The burin bevels sometimes shows signs of use; but in general, intentional burins are an exception though in the European Lower Palaeolithic.

Pebble Tools

A meaningful classification of pebble tools is a difficult enterprise. The traditional subdivision into unifacial choppers and bifacially shaped chopping tools is the most convenient classification. Almost all the chopping tools are alternately worked and surely were not cutting tools. Additional subdivisions focusing on the amount of the worked surface, the amount of cortex, or the shape of the working edge are possible and useful in the description of big series as for instance from surface collections and from terrace bodies (see for example Collina-Girard 1976; Tavoso 1978; Krüger 1994; Fiedler 1994).

Primary context sites with a variety of find material, including bones, in general contain only a limited number of pebble tools. Hence it does not seem urgent to elaborate a more sophisticated subdivision of these simple tools.

Cleavers

Cleavers are subdivided into bifacial cleavers with large cutting edges and flake cleavers made on big flakes. Bifacial cleavers are *sputniks* of Acheulean bifaces as they occur everywhere in the same context. In contrast, flake-cleavers (Tixier 1956; Tavoso 1975) appear at the end of the Lower Palaeolithic and are much more numerous and characteristic in the early Middle Palaeolithic at sites with a dominance of the Levallois technique and only isolated bifaces.

Bifaces

As a result of recent work, first of all in northern France (Tuffreau and Antoine, this volume) and southern England (Roberts, Gamble and Bridgland, this volume) the classification and subdivision of bifaces lost much of its charm, as these studies demonstrate that there are no recognizable typological trends in time. Especially the traditional view concerning the evolution from roughly worked early bifaces to more evolved ovates and elongated bifaces can not be supported by the evidence from the European Lower Palaeolithic.

Typological variability of bifaces could be determined by function; it is, for instance, difficult to imagine that the elongated bifaces with alternately shaped (zig-zag-like) edges served the same purpose as the English "twisted ovates".

Inventory Types

In the European Lower Palaeolithic there are first of all two inventory types: Type A assemblages contain flakes, retouched flakes, and pebble tools, Type B assemblages have comparable artefacts, but in addition they contain bifaces and cleavers.

A first group of Type A-sites is represented by Dmanisi and possibly Orce, older than 1,5 Myr BP and thus older than the first bifaces (cf. Bosinski 1995). The flakes, retouched flakes and pebble tools from these sites show no major differences from the African Oldowan sites and could be classified as "Oldowan". The second, much more important, cluster of Type A-sites (such as Verteszöllös, Petralona, Gajdan, Isernia and Bilzingsleben) dates to the Middle Pleistocene and is contemporary with the Acheulean. These sites are not limited to a specific time-span but date from various Middle Pleistocene periods, including the late Lower Palaeolithic (Bilzingsleben). Their geographical distribution covers the whole of inhabited Europe, including its southern and western parts where Acheulean assemblages also occur. It is a situation comparable to the East African one, with comparable discussions and arguments (cf. Leakey 1975; Stiles 1980).

The Type B-sites contain all the Type A-artefacts as well as bifaces and cleavers, and are traditionally classified as "Acheulean". At these sites the number of bifaces and cleavers varies considerably, but it does not seem very useful to restrict the term "Acheulean" only to sites with a high percentage of bifaces (Tuffreau 1987). Contrary to the Type A-sites the Acheulean displays a specific distribution pattern, that includes the Caucasian region, the southern European peninsula and western Europe, while no Acheulean sites are known from central and eastern Europe.

The Caucasus region is linked to the African "cradle" of bifaces and cleavers by Asia Minor and the Levantine corridor. From the Caucasus region these types could have

extended to southern and western Europe. For the southwest European finds, Alimen (1975) proposed a connection to North Africa over Sicily and the Strait of Gibraltar. The fact that the Middle Pleistocene faunas from both sides of the strait are not related cannot be used as an argument against contact by humans.

The character of the possible relationship between Type A and Type B has been the subject of many discussions. It is important that there are Type B-sites with only isolated bifaces and cleavers (e.g. Soleilhac, Tautavel, Lunel Viel, Aldène and Venosa-Loreto) which in the absence of these isolated pieces would completely correspond to Type A-sites. In addition the Lower Palaeolithic succession of Venosa-Notarchirico contains alternating levels with (a) many pebble tools from limestone, some bifaces of quartzite and flint, and smaller flakes from flint as well as (b) layers (Alpha E, E 1) containing first of all retouched and unretouched flakes of flint, but no bifaces (Mussi, this volume).

The examples referred to above could indicate that there was no fundamental difference between Type A and Type B sites. The presence or absence of bifaces and cleavers might depend on the kind of activities performed at a site. In this context it is striking that Lower Palaeolithic sites with many elephant bones, such as Torralba, Ambrona, Aridos, Fontana Ranuccio, La Polledrara and Kärlich-Seeufer, generally yield high percentages of bifaces and cleavers. The situation at Venosa-Notarchirico is especially indicative of this point: this site yielded a skull of a young elephant lying upside down with a disarticulated, broken mandible. The elephant's bones were surrounded by bifaces, pebble tools, and flakes. Here it seems obvious that bifaces and pebble tools served to dissect an elephant (Piperno 1992; Mussi, this volume); such a function could explain the spatial distribution of bifaces. The Aridos 1 - elephant was at least accompanied by some waste flakes of biface production (Raposo and Santonja, this volume) and only at Aridos 2 and La Polledrara the elephant bones were found without bifaces and cleavers.

note

1 This short note provides some personal comments concerning the Tautavel discussion on European Lower Palaeolithic stone industries, that was chaired by the author. The comment was updated in March 1995 (cf. Bosinski 1995).

references

Adrian, W. 1948 *Die Frage der norddeutschen Eolithen.* Paderborn.

Albrecht, G., 1994 Zur Unterscheidung von Artefakten und Naturbruch an der Fundstelle Sehremuz. In:
H. Engelhard, G. Albrecht and H. Müller-Beck (ed.), 1994, *Das Paläolithikum von Sehremuz bei Samsat*
H. Müller-Beck, *am Euphrat.* (Tübinger Monographien zur Urgeschichte 10), 121-131, Tübingen.
G. Unrath

Alimen, M.H. 1975 Les "isthmes" hispano-marocain et siculo-tunisien aux temps acheuléens, *L'Anthropologie*
79, 399-436.

Ashton, N.M., 1992 *High Lodge. Excavations by G. de G. Sieveking 1962-68 and J. Cook 1988.* London:
J. Cook, British Museum Press.
S.G. Lewis,
G. Rose (ed.)

Bar-Yosef, O., 1993 *The Lithic Assemblages of 'Ubeidija: A Lower Palaeolithic Site in the Jordan Valley.*
N. Goren-Inbar Jerusalem: The Hebrew University of Jerusalem.

Bonifay, E. 1991 Les premières industries des Sud Est de la France et du Massif Central. In: E. Bonifay
and B. Vandermeersch (ed.), *Les premiers européens*, 63-80, Paris: Editions du C.T.H.S.

Bosinski, G. 1995 Die ersten Menschen in Eurasien. Sechste Rudolf Virchow-Vorlesung 1992, *Jahrbuch des*
Römisch-Germanischen Zentralmuseums Mainz 39, 1992 (1995), 131-181.

Bosinski, G., 1980 Altpaläolithische Funde von Kärlich, Kreis Mayen-Koblenz (Neuwieder Becken),
K. Brunnacker, *Archäologisches Korrespondenzblatt* 10, 295-314.
K.P. Lanser,
S. Stephan,
B. Urban,
K. Würges

Breuil, H. 1932 Les industries à éclats du Paléolithique ancien. I. Le Clactonien, *Préhistoire* 1, 125-190.

Collina-Girard, J. 1976 *Les industries archaiques sur galets des terrasses quaternaire de la plaine du Roussillon*
(P.O., France). Travaux du Labor. de Paléontologie humaine et Préhistoire 1, Marseille.

Fiedler, L. 1994 *Alt- und mittelsteinzeitliche Funde in Hessen.* Führer zur hessischen Vor- und Frühgeschichte 2. Stuttgart.

Floss, H. 1994 *Rohmaterialversorgung im Paläolithikum des Mittelrheingebietes.* Monogr. des Römisch-
Germanischen Zentralmus. 21, Mainz: RGZM.

Gaudzinski, S., in press *Kärlich-Seeufer. Untersuchungen zu einer altpaläolithischen Fundstelle im Neuwieder*
Becken (Rheinland, Deutschland). Mainz: RGZM.

Junkmanns, J. 1991 Die Steinartefakte aus Achenheim in der Sammlung Paul Wernert, *Archäologisches*
Korrespondenzblatt 21, 1-16.

1995 Les ensembles lithiques d'Achenheim d'après la collection de Paul Wernert, *Bull. de la*
Soc. préhist. franc. 92, 26-36.

Kobayashi, H. 1975 The experimental study of bipolar flakes. In: E. Swanson (ed.), *Lithic technology: making*
and using stone tools, 115-127, The Hague-Paris.

Krüger, H.   1994   *Die altpaläolithische Geröllgeräte-Industrie der Münzenberger Gruppe in Oberhessen.* Materialien zur Vor- und Frühgeschichte von Hessen 10. Wiesbaden.

Kulemeyer, J.   1986   *Die alt- und mittelpaläolithischen Funde von Kärlich.* Diss. Köln.

Leakey, M.D.   1975   Cultural Patterns in the Olduvai Sequence. In: K.W. Butzer and G.L. Isaac (ed.), *After the Australopithecines*, 477-493, The Hague: Mouton.

Ljubin, V.P.,   this   The earliest occupation of the Caucasus region.
   G. Bosinski,   volume

Mania, D.,   1986   *Bilzingsleben III. Homo erectus – seine Kultur und Umwelt.* Veröffentlichungen des
   Th. Weber   Landesmus. für Vorgeschichte in Halle 39. Berlin.

Mortillet, G. de   1883   *Le Préhistorique. Antiquité de l'homme.* Paris: Reinwald.

Mussi, M.,   this   The earliest occupation of Europe: Italy.
                              volume

Pattersons, L.W.   1983   Criteria for Determining the Attributes of Man-Made Lithics, *Journal of Field Archaeology* 10, 297-307.

Piperno, M.   1992   Il Paleolitico inferiore. In: A. Guidi and M. Piperno (ed.), *Italia preistorica*, 139-169.

Raposo, L.,   this   The earliest occupation of Europe: the Iberian Peninsula.
   M. Santonja   volume

Raynal, J.-P.,   this   Tephrofacts and the first human occupation of the French Massif Central.
   L. Magoga,   volume
   P. Bindon

Roberts, M.B.,   thise   The earliest occupation of Europe: the British Isles.
   C.S. Gamble,   volume
   D.R. Bridgland

Roebroeks, W.   1986   On the "Lower Palaeolithic" site La Belle Roche: An alternative interpretation, *Current Anthropology* 27, 369-370.

                              1994   Updating the Earliest Occupation of Europe, *Current Anthropology* 35, 301-305.

Roebroeks, W.,   this   The earliest occupation of Europe: a reappraisal of artefactual and chronological
   T. van Kolfschoten   volume   evidence.

Rutot, A.   1902   Les industries primitives. Défense des éolithes. Les actions naturelles possibles sont inaptes à produire des effets semblables à la retouche intentionelle, *Mém. de la Soc. d'Anthrop. de Bruxelles* 20, 1-67.

Schmude, K.   1992   Zwei cromerzeitliche Artefakt-Fundplätze in der Jüngeren Hauptterrasse am Niederrhein, *Eiszeitalter und Gegenwart* 42, 1-24.

Stiles, D.   1980   Industrial taxonomy in the Early Stone Age of Africa, *Anthropologie (Brno)* 18, 189-207.

Tavoso, A.   1975   Les hachereaux sur éclats de l'Acheuléen Montabanais, *Quartär* 26, 13-31.

                              1978   *Le Paléolithique inférieur et moyen du Haute Languedoc.* Thése de l'Etat. Marseille.

Tixier, J.   1956   Le hachereau dans l'Acheuléen nord africain. Notes typologiques, *Congr. préhist. de France, 15e session*, Poitiers-Angouleme, 914-923.

Tuffreau, A. 1987 *Le Paléolithique inférieur et moyen du Nord de la France (Nord, Pas-de-Calais, Picardie) dans son cadre stratigraphique*. Thèse Doctorat d'Etat Université de Lille, Lille.

Tuffreau, A., P. Antoine this volume The earliest occupation of Europe: Continental Northwestern Europe.

Turner, E. in press *Miesenheim I. Excavations at a Lower Palaeolithic Site in the Central Rhineland of Germany*. Mainz: RGZM.

Gerhard Bosinski
Forschungsbereich Altsteinzeit
Schloss Monrepos
56567 Neuwied
Germany

Martin J. Aitken

15 Chronometric techniques for the Middle Pleistocene

A brief outline is given of the following dating techniques: potassium-argon, uranium-series, fission track, luminescence (TL and OSL), electron spin resonance (ESR), amino acid racemization (AAR), obsidian hydration, and geomagnetic reversal stratigraphy. Oxygen isotope chronostratigraphy is also mentioned, both in respect of fossil marine microfauna and in respect of ice obtained by means of long cores extracted from the polar ice caps; recent revisions to the astronomically-based dating of oxygen isotope stages beyond Stage 16 are indicated as well as to the potassium-argon dating of reversal stratigraphy, the Brunhes-Matuyama transition now being placed at 0.78 Myr ago.

1. Introduction

The various techniques that are briefly outlined here may be conveniently grouped into those based on radioactive decay or build-up (potassium-argon; uranium-series; calcium-41), on the effects of radioactivity (fission tracks; luminescence; electron spin resonance), and on chemical change (amino acid racemization; obsidian hydration). All these are processes intrinsic to the sample. In addition there are the time scales provided by geomagnetic reversals and by astronomical calibration of the oxygen isotope chronostratigraphy; for convenience of reference some detail of these are given including mention of the recent slight lengthening of both at the beginning of the Middle Pleistocene.

Of the chronometric techniques of interest for the earliest occupation of Europe it is the potassium-argon and fission track techniques that are the most well-developed, followed by uranium-series (to the extent that the occupation was subsequent to that technique's limit of around 500 Kyr). Since these are only applicable in certain geological regions there is strong interest in the use of electron spin resonance (ESR) and luminescence; neither have been much tried archaeologically beyond several 100 Kyr, but ESR should encompass a million years without difficulty and there are indications that, unexpectedly, luminescence may reach beyond half-a-million. Both of the chemical change techniques are handicapped by their strong dependence on environmental conditions and when a number of glacial/

interglacial cycles are encompassed within the burial period the strong temperature-dependence is a particular drawback.

The possibility of using calcium-41 is still highly problematic, and radiocarbon dating, while very powerful in later periods, has too short a limiting range to be relevant; effectively it is *c.* 40 Kyr BP at present and highly unlikely ever to exceed *c.* 70 Kyr BP.

2. Potassium-argon dating

2.1. BASIS

With its enormous range (*c.* 10 Kyr to around 400 Myr) this technique has been, and is, of crucial importance. It is based on the accumulation, in volcanic lava and ash, of argon-40 produced from the slow radioactive decay of any potassium-40 present (potassium-40 is a naturally-occurring isotope of potassium). The event dated is the volcanic eruption; during this, and while lava is molten, previously accumulated argon (a gas) is released thereby setting the radioactive clock to zero. The age is derived from the measured ratio of argon-40 to potassium-40.

Argon-argon dating has the same basis but employs an advantageous technique. One advantage is that potassium and argon are determined on exactly the same sub-sample thereby avoiding possible errors due to inhomogeneity; another advantage is that the argon can be gradually released by stepwise heating of the sample and an age can be determined at each step. Constancy in age (an 'age plateau') is indicative of reliability. Effects causing the age to be erroneously too low are those which give rise to release of accumulated argon during burial such as mineral alteration (due to weathering), or secondary heating; on the other hand incomplete release at time-zero of previously-accumulated argon would give rise to an age that is erroneously too old, as also the presence of absorbed atmospheric argon. Because of differential argon release at different stages of the heating these interfering effects manifest themselves through upset to the age plateau; analysis by the *isochron technique* is also diagnostic.

Use of a laser for heating permits dating of single grains (of the order of 1 milligram or less). This allows potassium-rich grains only to be selected; also older, contaminating grains to be detected and avoided.

2.2. APPLICATION

Obviously the important question is the relationship between the human occupation and the volcanic products that are dated. Where two layers of lava, or ash, bracket the archaeology there is no problem (except, sometimes, a rather wide bracket). A recent example where the question of association is critical is the 1.8-1.6 Myr ages for hominid cranial material from Java (Swisher *et al.*, 1994); whereas the dating of the hornblende crystals is not in doubt, excellent age plateaux and isochrons having been obtained, the association of the crystals with the fossils is indirect.

More relevant to Europe is the date of 0.73 Myr ago obtained for the Italian site of Isernia (Sevink *et al.*, 1981; Coltorti *et al.*, 1982); one should note here that neither of the determinations utilised the advantageous argon-argon technique, though the agreement between two laboratories using different minerals is suggestive of reliability. However without the evidence of an age plateau the possibility cannot be ruled out that in both cases the age obtained was erroneously in excess because of incomplete removal of argon at time-zero.

3. Uranium-series

3.1. BASIS

An eventual decay product (a 'daughter') of naturally-occurring uranium-238 is thorium-230 and when the former is present in newly-formed crystals the gradual build-up of the latter can be used for dating. The most widespread application is to cave speleothems (stalactites, stalagmites and flowstones); newly-formed calcite (calcium carbonate) contains only uranium-238 and its daughter uranium-234; thereafter there is build-up of thorium-230 according to its half-life of 75.4 Kyr and the ratios between these three allow the age to be determined. In some circumstances the ratio between the two uranium isotopes can be used for dating – on a much longer timescale. There is also another naturally-occurring isotope of uranium, uranium-235, and build-up of its daughter protactinium-231 (half-life, 34.3 Kyr) can be used for shorter range dating, usually in combination with thorium-230.

The traditional measurement technique is by *alpha spectrometry*. This requires between a few grams and a few tens of grams of sample; the upper age limit is around 350 Kyr. A much superior approach, very much more expensive and demanding of expertise, is by *thermal ionisation mass spectrometry* (TIMS); sample weights can be lower by a factor of 10 and in good circumstances the age range can be from a few hundred years to about 500 Kyr. *Gamma spectrometry* can also be used, with the advantage of being able to measure a whole specimen (e.g. the Arago cranium), but with the serious disadvantages of increased uncertainty and decreased reliability.

3.2. APPLICATION

There has been widespread application to speleothems but also, with varying degrees of success, to spring-deposits, marl, caliche, calcrete, molluscan shells, ratite egg shells (e.g. ostrich), and teeth (particularly the enamel). Application to bone has long been tried but, with exceptions, the data have been problematic. Coral is an excellent material; although not of direct archaeological interest, with the high accuracy obtainable using the TIMS technique it has a very important role in extending carbon-14 calibration beyond the tree-ring limit.

Sample purity is one important question; particularly with the sample-types just mentioned, but also with speleothems too, there is the possibility that detrital grains (containing thorium-230) were incorporated at crystal formation thereby making the apparent age erroneously too old; various methods, including the isochron technique, are employed to deal with such 'dirty calcite'. Two other interfering effects are recrystallisation and secondary deposition (overgrowth) – both are detectable through microscopic examination of thin sections. Recrystallisation allows mobilisation of uranium and thorium; this is one form of 'open system' in which the age is distorted by loss or gain. In general, an indication that 'closed system' conditions have not existed is given by an unacceptable spread in coeval samples. Because aragonite is intrinsically unstable (converting to calcite) any such samples, unfortunately rather rare, are their own proof of integrity.

4. Calcium-41 and other radioisotopes

The effective *c.* 40 Kyr BP limit of carbon-14 inevitably prompts the question as to whether there is another cosmogenic radioisotope with a half-life more appropriate for the Middle Pleistocene. Some possibilities (with half-lives given in parenthesis) are: aluminium-26 (720 Kyr); beryllium-10 (1500 Kyr); calcium-41 (*c.* 100 Kyr); chlorine-36 (300 Kyr). Although there is some possibility of using aluminium-26 and beryllium-10 for sediment cores, it is only calcium-41 that holds any prospect for archaeological application, on account of its occurrence in bone. However, whereas carbon-14 is formed in the upper atmosphere and is spread, through forming carbon dioxide, more or less uniformly through the biosphere and the oceans, calcium-41 is formed from non-radioactive calcium-40, in the top metre or so of soil and although it enters bones via plant life there is no mechanism for spreading worldwide; hence local variations influenced by soil history are to be expected and so the time-zero level is uncertain. A further problem is the difficulty of measurement, even using accelerator mass spectrometry.

5.   Fission tracks

As with potassium-argon the main involvement is through application to volcanic material with which human remains have been associated. Existing tracks in minerals of such material are erased by the heating inherent in the volcanic eruption. Thereafter spontaneous nuclear fission of uranium-238 in the mineral causes gradual re-accumulation; the tracks can be counted using an optical microscope and hence, after determining the content of uranium and the sensitivity of the mineral for track acquisition, the time that has elapsed since the eruption can be evaluated. Some suitable minerals are zircon, obsidian, mica, sphene and apatite; however, attempts to date the apatite component of bone and teeth have so far met with difficulty.

Application in recent archaeology is usually ruled out by sparsity of tracks; for the Middle Pleistocene the more likely problem to be encountered is *fading*, i.e. some loss of tracks with time. Several techniques have been developed to deal with this, among them the *plateau correction method*. In this, there are successive annealings of increasing stringency and after each a measurement is made of the ratio of the number of 'as found' tracks remaining in one portion to the number of artificially-induced tracks remaining in another portion. Track size is another parameter that is useful.

As with laser dating of single grains by the potassium-argon technique it has the strong advantage of utilising only a few grains, thereby minimising contamination risks. The main application has been to hominid evolution in East Africa.

6.   Luminescence dating

6.1.   BASIS

This comprises thermoluminescence (TL) and optical dating, the latter utilising optically-stimulated luminescence (OSL). These methods are based on the cumulative effect of nuclear radiation on the position of electrons in the crystal structure of certain minerals, mainly quartz and feldspar.

The nuclear radiation is provided by trace amounts of potassium-40, rubidium-87, thorium and uranium that are naturally present in the sample and its surroundings. The dating signal is obtained, in the case of TL, by heating grains extracted from the sample and measuring the light emitted by means of a highly sensitive photomultiplier; in the case of OSL the luminescence is obtained by shining light on the grains; lasers and halogen lamps can be used, and also, except with quartz, infrared-emitting diodes – in which case the luminescence may be termed IRSL.

The TL technique was first used in application to pottery, the event dated being the firing by the ancient potter (thereby setting to zero the previously accumulated TL).

Subsequently it was extended to stalagmitic calcite (which has zero TL at formation) and to burnt flint. The latter application, along with the ESR dating of tooth enamel, has had particularly important impact on hypotheses concerning the relationship between anatomically-modern humans and Neanderthals. The OSL signal from quartz and feldspar, and to a lesser extent the TL signal, can also be set to zero by exposure to daylight; this occurs during transportation and deposition of windblown sediment (such as loess and sand) and similarly, but less effectively, for waterlain sediment. In the latter case use of OSL is particularly advantageous compared to TL.

For either method it is necessary to evaluate the *dose-rate* of nuclear radiation that the sample has been receiving during burial. This is done partly by radioactive analysis in the laboratory and partly by on-site measurement (of the penetrating gamma radiation that reaches the sample from its surrounding soil and rock, up to a distance of about 0.3 m). It is also necessary to estimate the water content of sample and soil/rock – because any water present attenuates the nuclear radiation.

6.2.   APPLICATION

The age range is highly dependent on sample-type, technique, and site; at present several hundred thousand years is a typical upper limit for flint, quartz, calcite, and sediment; however if some types of feldspar are present in the latter there is a tendency for the age to be underestimated, particularly beyond 50 Kyr. This is through signal instability *(fading)* and the so-called '100 Kyr barrier' in European and Chinese loess has been the subject of much discussion and technological research; on the other hand for loess from Alaska and New Zealand TL ages up to 800 Kyr have been reported (Berger 1992).

With flint and quartz the age range limitation arises from saturation rather than fading; hence sites of low radioactivity (i.e., low dose-rate) are advantageous. The Middle Pleistocene potential of quartz has been demonstrated by Huntley *et al.* (1993; 1994) who have obtained consonant TL ages up to 800 Kyr for a succession of high sea level dune sands in Australia. Another approach to long range dating with quartz is use of the 'red TL peak'; this peak does not suffer from saturation and hence can be used irrespective of the level of site radioactivity. On the other hand it is applicable to volcanic products rather than sediment; a consonant age has been reported (Miallier *et al.*, 1994) for pumice dated at 580 Kyr ago by potassium-argon.

It is to be noted that Russian (and some other) workers have long been obtaining million-year ages for sediments and regard the approach of the rest of the luminescence community as being on the wrong track (see, for instance, Slukov *et al.*, 1993); this view is reciprocated.

Except at the limits of the technique the accuracy attainable is usually in the range 5-10% of the age. The ultimate barrier to better accuracy is uncertainty about the average dose-rate during the burial period; because of geochemical leaching the radioactivity may be different from that measured today and likewise the water content because of climatic fluctuation. As mentioned above the water absorbs a proportion of the radiation flux and hence sites which have always been bone-dry are advantageous.

Collection of sediment samples is best done by a laboratory specialist as special precautions need to be taken in order to avoid the slightest exposure to daylight. The usual approach is to drive a short steel tube (about 5 cm diameter by 10 cm long) into the section, the exposed ends being discarded during laboratory processing (in very subdued red light); if the sediment is consolidated then a lump can be taken and the surface scraped off in the laboratory. The hole made for extraction of sample is used for measurement of the gamma-ray dose-rate, either with a portable gamma spectrometer (taking an hour), or, by burial of a small capsule filled with a highly-sensitive thermoluminescence powder (for upwards of several months, preferably a year).

7.   Electron Spin Resonance (ESR)

This is yet another way of measuring the cumulative effect of nuclear radiation. Its principal archaeological applications have been to tooth enamel and to stalagmitic calcite. In time range ESR reaches back to several million years ago; its lower limit is a few thousand years. As with all techniques, careful selection of measurement parameters is necessary for valid results.

The above remarks about dose-rate evaluation are applicable but with additional complexity in the case of tooth enamel, due to uranium migration into the tooth. Because of this two ages are quoted, these being based on the two assumptions about the timing of the uranium ingress: *early uptake* (EU) and *linear uptake* (LU). If the internal radiation flux is dominant the EU age will be substantially lower than the LU age (but never lower than by half) whereas if the flux is predominantly from the burial soil the difference is unimportant. Large teeth (e.g. elephant, mammoth) are preferred; usually separate determinations on about a dozen samples are averaged.

Because the uranium-series technique is also affected by uranium migration, but to a different degree, it is possible to eliminate the uptake uncertainty by applying both techniques to the same sample. Obviously this doubles the work and there is also limitation in accuracy – to about ±10% of the age, whereas the accuracy for a 'straight' ESR date if a particular uptake model is assumed is a little better than for luminescence, though similarly limited by uncertainty about average water content.

8.   Amino Acid Racemization (AAR)

The dating is based on the slow conversion within a protein molecule of an amino acid (such as aspartic) from its **L** form, at formation, to its **D** form, until an equilibrium mixture of the two is reached. Epimerization of isoleucine is another reaction utilised, notably in the dating of ostrich eggshells. These processes are strongly influenced by environmental conditions, temperature in particular. Site-by-site calibration against radiocarbon is usual and for good reliability the samples used for this should be of the same type and same preservation condition as the ones being dated.

In early application the technique acquired a reputation for unreliability, particularly in application to poorly preserved bone. However good reliability is now being obtained by careful selection of sample types (such as ostrich eggshell as mentioned above, well-preserved bone, and tooth enamel), strict attention to the validity of the radiocarbon dates used for calibration, and more stringent laboratory procedures. Using aspartic acid the last 50-100 Kyr can be covered and, using the epimerization of isoleucine, reaching half-a-million years is feasible. Besides extension of age range another advantage over radiocarbon is the comparative ease of measurement and hence lower cost – so that an archaeologist can undertake a much wider sampling of site than could be afforded using radiocarbon only.

In the context of the Middle Pleistocene it is particularly important to keep in mind the strong influence of temperature; it is not only necessary to measure the present-day value at the site but also to estimate the temperature history of the site through whatever glacials and interglacials have occurred during the burial period. Even only as far back as the last interglacial this introduces added uncertainty and it becomes appropriate to calculate ages on the basis of different temperature scenarios (see, for example, Miller *et al.* 1993). An alternative approach to calibration, particularly in the case of shells, is *amino-stratigraphy;* characteristic (**D/L**) ratios are established as being representative of particular climatic phases, it being important to keep in mind that **D** to **L** conversion rates for shell are species-specific as well as environmentally dependent. A recent application to sites extending into the Middle Pleistocene of northwestern France has been reported by Bates (1993).

9.   Obsidian Hydration

This too is a chemical process strongly influenced by environmental conditions, particularly temperature. It is based on the slow formation of hydration rims on freshly-cleaved obsidian. Until the late 1970's the favoured approach was by regional calibration using known-age samples. Since then the emphasis has been on obtaining absolute ages independent of other techniques or archaeological chronology. This approach requires two major evaluations in addition to measurement of the hydration rim itself: (i) the effective burial temperature and (ii) laboratory measurement (at elevated temperature and pressure) of the rim growth-rate for each type of obsidian that is dated.

Dates have been reported in the age range from 200 to l00,000 years ago. Growth-rates vary widely between different parts of the world; the comparatively rapid hydration rates in tropical countries allow more recent dating than in Arctic regions.

10. The Geomagnetic Reversal Time Scale (GRTS)

A fossilised record of the direction of the past geomagnetic field (generated through dynamo action in the earth's molten core) is provided by the weak but permanent magnetisation that is acquired by lava as it cools down, likewise for baked clay and heated stones; sediment may also acquire a fossilised record during deposition (under suitable conditions) or during subsequent consolidation. This latter type of magnetisation is even weaker and it is less robust, being vulnerable both to disturbance and to 'overprinting' during later periods when the field may have a different direction; however various magnetic 'cleaning' techniques can be used to eliminate such overprints and so determine the primary direction. Sediment has the strong advantage of giving a much more continuous record than lava; on the other hand, particularly when the magnetisation is acquired during consolidation, it may be the average direction over several hundred years that is recorded, thereby smoothing-out rapid changes as well as introducing a time lag.

Roughly every million years there is a reversal of the direction of the field on the earth's surface; this follows a dying-down of the earth's dynamo, there being a 50:50 chance of it starting up in the opposite direction to formerly. The sequence of such reversals is the basis of the magnetic time scale (alternatively called the *Geomagnetic Polarity Time Scale* – GPTS). The major reversals are known as *chrons* (e.g. the Matuyama chron; this reversed chron preceded the present 'normal' polarity Brunhes chron); there have also been shorter episodes of changed polarity and these are known as *subchrons* (e.g. the Jaramillo; this normal subchron lasted about 60 Kyr and occurred near the end of the Matuyama).

In earlier terminology classifications such as 'aborted reversals', 'excursions', and 'events' were used. These tended to be used for episodes of directional instability and they were not necessarily worldwide; localised episodes occur when, during a period of weak main dynamo, the field from electrical eddies near the surface of the molten core gain dominance; however such situations usually result in violent changes of direction

which stop short of reversal. The effects of physical disturbance to the sediment may be mistaken for such an episode and such confusion is one of the factors that make it important to interpret the magnetic record conservatively. Such effects may also be misinterpreted for the occurrence of a reversal too and when a reversal is being inferred there should always be full publication of the magnetic data so that assessment of the strength of the evidence, and perhaps later reassessment, can be made. A case in point is the Italian site of Isernia mentioned earlier for which, to this author's knowledge, there has still been no proper publication of the magnetic data more than a decade after it being tentatively reported that the fossil-bearing sediment was deposited during the Matuyama chron. Until the data are presented this assignment should be treated with strong reservation.

At one time it was hoped that weaker variations in direction than the above might be effective in dating Palaeolithic sediments but it is only over the last few thousand years that these secular variations have proved useful and even then, mainly for pottery kilns and hearths rather than sediments. Such dating is usually categorised as archaeomagnetism rather than palaeomagnetism.

The chronology of the various chrons and subchrons is based primarily on potassium-argon dating of the lava in which the magnetic direction was recorded and until recently the accepted ages were those given by Mankinen and Dalrymple (1979); however re-evaluations (e.g., Baksi *et al.* 1992; Baksi 1993; Spell and McDougall 1992) indicate a slight lengthening of the timescale so that the Brunhes-Matuyama boundary is now placed at 0.78 Myr (rather 0.73 Myr), the Jaramillo subchron from 0.99 to 1.05 Myr (rather than 0.90-0.97 Myr), and the Olduvai subchron from 1.78 to 2.02 Myr ago (rather than 1.67-1.87 Myr).

Because the succession of reversals is also recorded in the sediment cores from which oxygen isotope variations are obtained, the chrons and subchrons can also be dated astronomically (see below). In fact the revisions mentioned above were subsequent to, and in agreement with, the astronomically-based indications obtained by Shackleton *et al.* (1990).

Loess (notably in China) also carries both a magnetic record and a climatic record; the latter is manifested as variation in magnetic susceptibility on account of loess having a lower susceptibility than the intervening palaeosols.

11. Oxygen Isotope Chronostratigraphy

This chronostratigraphy is based on the climatic dependence of the isotope ratio (oxygen-18 to oxygen-16) in marine fossil microfauna, studied in long cores taken from the ocean floor. The ratio is primarily influenced by

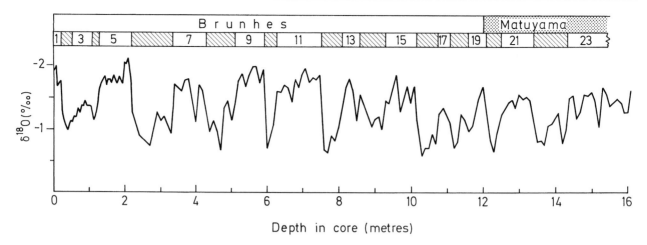

Fig. 1. Oxygen isotope variation in the microfaunal remains of core V28-238 from the Pacific (redrawn from Shackleton and Opdyke 1973; 1976). The vertical scale indicates the deviation (in parts per thousand) of the oxygen-18 content from a standard; the more negative the deviation the warmer the climate. Dates for the stages are given in Table 1. Using longer cores many more stages than shown here have now been identified. Essentially the same pattern of variation is found in cores obtained elsewhere around the world, in agreement with the interpretation of the variations as primarily reflecting the amount of water locked up in the polar ice caps and in glaciers. Magnetic measurements on the sediment in this and other cores indicate that the Brunhes-Matuyama transition occurred during Stage 19.

the amount of water locked up in polar ice caps and glaciers; hence it reflects worldwide climate. Figure 1 is an example of the variations found and it also indicates the succession of cool and warm stages defined on the basis of the ratio; warm stages have odd numbers and cool stages have even. The same pattern of variation has been found in ocean cores from different parts of the world and the correlation with it of continental climate is evidenced in various ways, e.g. magnetic susceptibility variations, pollen frequency variations in peat bogs; pollen indications in ocean cores.

Table 1. Oxygen isotope stage: commencement ages (in Kyr).

Stage	Age	Stage	Age
1	12	11	423
2	24	12	478
3	59	13	524
4	71	14	565
5	128	15	620
6	186	16	659
7	245	17	712 (689)
8	303	18	760 (726)
9	339	19	787 (736)
10	362	20	810 (763)
		21	865 (790)

Note: For Stages 1-16 the ages are as given in the SPECMAP calibration of Imbrie *et al*. (1984); for Stages 17-21 the ages are from Bassinot *et al*. (1994) with the SPECMAP ages given in parenthesis; for Stages 1-16 the revised ages do not differ from SPECMAP ages by more than 5 Kyr.

Isotope variations indicative of climate are also found in long cores drilled into the polar ice caps; these show more detail than the marine cores and there is indication that there is correlation with European interstadials.

As mentioned above the remanent magnetisation of the sediment in the ocean cores allows correlation with the geomagnetic reversal time scale and hence the absolute dating by potassium-argon of the lavas in which the elements of the reversal sequence are observed can be transferred to the cores and hence to the stages. However now that it has been established that there is good correlation between the climatic pattern indicated by the isotope ratio and the Milankovitch astronomical predictions based on changes in the earth's orbital motion (eccentricity of the orbit around the sun; obliquity of the ecliptic; precession of the equinoxes) the succession of stages can be dated astronomically and hence with better accuracy – to the order of around 5 Kyr.

12. Concluding remarks

An important characteristic of the foregoing techniques is that they are absolute, in the sense of giving ages in calendar years that are based essentially only on laboratory measurements; excepting the magnetic time scale and amino acid in its calibrated form, they are independent of any other chronology, archaeological or otherwise.

Certainly some give rather wide error limits and there have been cases of unreliability and adjustment but the importance of their independence should not be undervalued. In the long run the "so-called absolute dating methods" (Roebroeks 1994: 303) will give a firmer foundation to the understanding of human development than biostratigraphy; powerful and important though the latter may be it is the mercy of regional non-synchroneity when used on between-region basis. In particular it should be an urgent priority to confirm by chronometric dating the validity of the 'vole clock' (Gamble 1994: 275) as a half-million year time marker throughout Europe.

Criticisms of the chronometric techniques are often in respect of results obtained in a technique's infancy and/or results not properly published; sometimes also unreliability stems from poor association of the samples used with the archaeology. Such criticisms do less than justice to the present state-of-the-art of potassium-argon dating (in its single grain argon-argon mode) and to mass-spectrometric uranium-series dating (TIMS); the former now has the remarkable achievement of reducing error limits in million-year samples to a few percent and the latter of being a basis for calibrating radiocarbon ages. Although the techniques of luminescence and ESR are not yet fully developed their contribution has already been of critical importance in the understanding of the origin of modern humans (e.g., Aitken and Valladas 1992; Schwarcz and Grün 1992). The further progress of these more widely applicable techniques needs the continued stimulation of application and during that necessary phase there will inevitably be some results later shown to be unreliable. But it is in the long term interests of archaeologists to tolerate these – and to minimise their impact by ignoring results not properly published in a fully-refereed journal, with due assessment of reliability. Ultimately it is only thanks to chronometric techniques that it is possible to make any estimate of the pace of human development and the order of events on a worldwide basis.

This paper has attempted only the briefest outline of the techniques concerned; further details, and more references to original papers, can be found elsewhere (for instance, Aitken 1990; Smart and Frances 1991; Taylor and Aitken 1995).

references

Aitken, M.J.	1990	*Science-based dating in archaeology*. London and New York: Longman.
Aitken, M.J., Valladas, H.	1992	Luminescence dating relevant to human origins. In: M.J. Aitken, C.B. Stringer and P.A. Mellars (eds), *The origin of modern humans and the impact of chronometric dating*, 27-39, Princeton, New Yersey: Princeton University Press.
Baksi, A.K., V. Hsu, M.O. McWilliams, E. Farrer	1992	^{40}Ar/^{39}Ar dating of the Brunhes-Matuyama geomagnetic field reversal, *Science* 256, 356-357.
Baksi, A.K.	1993	A new Geomagnetic Polarity Time Scale for 0-17 Ma. *Geophysical Research Letters* 20 (15), 1607-1610.
Bassino, F.C., L.D. Labeyrie, E. Vincent, X. Quidelleur, N.J. Shackleton, Y. Lancelot	1994	The astronomical theory of climate and the age of the Brunhes-Matuyama magnetic reversal, *Earth and Planetary Science Letters* 126, 91-108.
Bates, M.R.	1993	Quaternary aminostratigraphy in northwestern France, *Quarternary Science Reviews* 12, 791-809.
Berger, G.W.	1992	Dating loess up to 800 ka by thermo-luminescence, *Geology* 20, 403-406.

Coltorti, M.,
M. Cremaschi,
M.C. Delitala,
D. Esu,
M. Fornaseri,
A. McPherron,
M. Nicoletti,
R. van Otterloo,
C. Peretto,
B. Sala,
V. Schmidt,
J. Sevink

1982   Reversed magnetic polarity at an early lower palaeolithic site in Central Italy, *Nature* 300, 173-176.

Gamble, C.   1994   Time for Boxgrove man, *Nature* 369, 275-276.

Huntley, D.J.,
J.T. Hutton,
J.R. Prescott

1993   The stranded beach-dune sequence of south-east Australia: a test of thermoluminescence dating, 0-800 ka, *Quaternary Science Review* 12, 1-20.

1994   Further thermoluminescence dates from the dune sequence in the south-east of Australia, *Quaternary Science Review*, in press.

Imbrie, J.,
J.D. Hays,
D.G. Martinson,
A. McIntyre,
A.C. Mix,
J.J. Morley,
N.G. Pisias,
W.L. Prell,
N.J. Shackleton

1994   The orbital theory of Pleistocene climate: support from a revised chronology of the marine $d^{18}O$ record. In: A. Berger, J. Imbrie, J. Hays, G. Kukla and B. Saltzman (eds), *Milankovitch and Climate, part I*, 269-305, Dordecht, Holland: Plenum Reidel.

Mankinen, E.A.,
G.P. Dalrymple

1979   Revised geomagnetic polarity timescale for the interval 0-5 m.y. B.P., *Journal of Geophysical Research* 84 (B2), 615-626.

Miallier, D.,
J. Fain,
S. Sanzelle,
T.H. Pilleyre,
M. Montret,
S. Soumana,
C. Falguères

1994   Attempts at dating pumice deposits around 580 ka by use of red TL and ESR of xenolithic inclusions, *Radiation Measurements* 23, 399-404.

Miller, G.H.,
P.B. Beaumont,
A.J.T. Jull,
B. Johnson

1993   Pleistocene geochronology and palaeothermometry from protein diagenesis in ostrich eggshells: implications for the evolution of modern humans. In: M.J. Aitken, C.B. Stringer and P.A. Mellars (eds), *The origin of modern humans and the impact of chronometric dating*, 49-68, Princeton, New Jersey: Princeton University Press.

Roebroeks, W.   1994   Updating the earliest occupation of Europe, *Current Anthropology* 35, 301-305.

Schwarcz, H.P.,
R. Grün

1992   Electron spin resonance (ESR) dating of the origin of modern man. In: M.J. Aitken, C.B. Stringer and P.A. Mellars (eds), *The origin of modern humans and the impact of chronometric dating*, 40-48, Princeton, New Jersey: Princeton University Press.

Sevink, J.,
E.H. Hebeda,
H.N.A. Priem,
R.H. Verschure

1981   A note on an approximately 730,000-year-old mammal fauna and associated human activity sites near Isernia, Central Italy, *Journal of Archaeological Science* 8, 105-106.

Shackleton, N.J., A. Berger, W.R. Peltier — 1990 — An alternative astronomical calibration of the lower Pleistocene timescale based on ODP site 677, *Transactions Royal Society Edinburgh, Earth Sciences* 81, 251-261.

Shackleton, N.J., N.D. Opdyke — 1973 — Oxygen isotope and palaeomagnetic stratigraphy of equatorial Pacific core V28-238: temperatures and ice volumes on a 10^3 and 10^6 year scale, *Quaternary Research* 3, 39-55.

1976 — Oxygen-isotope and palaeomagnetic stratigraphy of equatorial Pacific core V28-239: Late Pliocene to latest Pleistocene. In: R.M. Cline and J.D. Hays (eds), *Investigation of Late Quaternary Paleooceanography and Paleoclimatology*, Memoir 145, Geological Society of America, 449-464, Colorado: Boulder.

Slukov, A.L., S.A. Shakhovets, L.T. Voskovskaya, M.G. Lyashenko — 1993 — A criticism of standard TL dating technology, *Nuclear Instruments and Methods in Physics Research* 73, 373-381.

Smart, P.L., P.D. Frances (eds) — 1991 — *Quaternary dating methods: a user's guide*. Technical guide no. 4, Quaternary Research Association, Cambridge.

Spell, T.L., I. McDougall — 1992 — Revisions to the age of the Brunhes-Matuyama boundary and the Pleistocene geomagnetic polarity timescale, *Geophysical Research Letters* 19, 1181-1184.

Swisher, C.C., G.H. Curtis, T. Jacob, A.G. Getty, A. Suprijo, Widiasmoro — 1994 — Age of the earliest known hominids in Java, Indonesia, *Science* 263, 1118-1121.

Tarling, D.H. — 1983 — *Palaeomagnetism*. London and New York: Chapman and Hall.

Taylor, R.E., M.J. Aitken (eds) — 1995 — *Chronometric Dating in Archaeology*. New York: Plenum Press.

Martin J. Aitken
Emeritus Professor of Archaeometry
Oxford University
6 Keble Road
Oxford OX1 3QJ
United Kingdom

Clive S. Gamble

16   The earliest occupation of Europe: the environmental background

The aim of this contribution is to examine some of the environmental issues surrounding the earliest occupation of Europe. The evidence presented both in this volume and at the ESF workshop in Tautavel raised issues about site reconstructions, regional comparisons, the definition of Europe and the impact of different chronological scales for modelling the rate of human evolution and the role of environmental selection. The evidence considered here is oxygen isotope stage 9 and older (>300Kyr), and its archaeology is placed under the Lower Palaeolithic flag of convenience. In this discussion environment is taken to refer to the physical changes to the continent and the effect this had upon plant and animal resources. The social environment of the earliest European hominids is not considered here. However, the colonizing ability of these hominids, which must have involved social factors, is briefly discussed and alternative environmental models are reviewed which explain the timing of colonization.

1.   Introduction

Environmental analysis involves many spatial and temporal scales (e.g. Butzer 1982). I draw the distinction here between *local* (or site based) analysis which can, when preservation is good, provide evidence for the day-to-day activities of early hominids and *regional* studies where time averaging due to geological processes often necessitates a long-term view of behaviour. The former can be said to inform us on an ecological timescale about the various ways that hominids dealt with the immediate conditions of existence – weather, food, water, predators and other hominids. The regional scale can, on occasion, address the same immediate selection pressures although with less chronological precision. However, it is widely accepted in Lower Palaeolithic studies that our data at this scale refer to geological (or evolutionary) timescales.[1] These provide us with the opportunity to observe long-term evolutionary processes. The proper use of environmental data when interpreting the Lower Palaeolithic requires that we keep these analytical concepts firmly in mind.

The aim of this contribution is to examine some of the environmental issues surrounding the earliest occupation of Europe. The evidence presented both in this volume and at

the ESF workshop in Tautavel raised issues about site reconstructions, regional comparisons, the definition of Europe and the impact of different chronological scales for modelling the rate of human evolution and the role of environmental selection. The evidence considered here is oxygen isotope stage (OIS) 9 and older (>300 Kyr), and its archaeology is placed under the Lower Palaeolithic flag of convenience. In this discussion environment is taken to refer to the physical changes to the continent and the effect this had upon plant and animal resources. The social environment of the earliest European hominids is not considered here. However, the colonizing ability of these hominids, which must have involved social factors, is briefly discussed and alternative environmental models are reviewed which explain the timing of colonization.

2.   Local environments and hominid locales

2.1.   INTRODUCTION

The papers in this volume demonstrate that the local environment of Lower Palaeolithic hominids must be considered as a landscape. The archaeological notion of site as applied to anything but caves has little relevance to the business of understanding hominid behaviour from this period. What we are dealing with are locales within landscapes where the density or preservation quality of material is such that excavation has been deemed worthwhile.[2]

The long-term investigations at Bilzingsleben and neighbouring travertine deposits (Mania, this volume), the Venosa basin (Mussi, this volume), Boxgrove and the Sussex coastal plain (Roberts *et al.*, this volume), the East Eifel volcanic field (Bosinski, this volume), the Cagny sites (Tuffreau and Antoine, this volume), the Manzanares and Jarama terraces and the Guadix-Baza basin (Raposo and Santonja, this volume) point to an analytical scale that is much larger than either the size of any individual area excavated within these landscape projects, or even the estimate of potential deposits for future excavation. This landscape approach is also apparent in the work at the Caune de l'Arago (De Lumley, pers. comm.)[3] and Kudaro (Ljubin and Bosinski, this volume) where the cave deposits provide a means to explore changes in the surrounding catchments.

A landscape approach is also evident in the discussion of why areas as separated as Scandinavia (Holm and Larsson, this volume), the Riano basin in central Italy (Mussi, this volume) and the Ebro depression in Iberia (Raposo and Santonja, this volume) have not produced finds of this period, even though in the last two regions Middle Pleistocene sediments are present. Only at the scale of landscapes is it possible to assess whether material would have survived (Scandinavia), and if so where, or that insufficient research has been undertaken (Ebro) or finally that occupation was never possible for such hominids (Riano).

The size of these landscapes is generally defined by the distribution of similar Quaternary geology and the maintainance of comparable contexts for preservation. For example, the Venosa basin measures 50×3 km and is filled to a depth of 30-50 m. The 40 m raised beach of which Boxgrove is a part extends for at least 20 km with sediments preserved in a band of 100-200 m in front of a collapsed chalk cliff. The East Eifel volcanic field covers, albeit intermittently, an area of at least 20×25 km, while the Guadix-Baza basin near Granada which contains deep Early and Middle Pleistocene sediments forms an oval of 100×60 km (Santonja and Villa 1990).

The European evidence concerning the settlement of these varied landscapes points to two well known 'normal' environments. Firstly, open locales are frequently associated with bodies of water ranging from marine lagoons to river banks, braided streams, lakes (of various sizes), travertine springs, swamps and marshes. For example, the Lower Palaeolithic landscape alongside the Via Aurelia was densely settled. Its many coastal lagoons and back country bogs and swamps provide an example of the ecologically highly productive local environments which hominids preferred (Mussi, this volume). Middle Pleistocene faunas with *Hippopotamus* and *Trogontherium* (giant beaver) are common here and in many parts of Europe. Beaver helped form the local environment at Miesenheim I, which consisted of swamps with patches of forest. Along these overgrown banks of the Pleistocene Rhine hominids hunted and scavenged (Bosinski, this volume).

Secondly, closed locales are represented by caves and rockshelters of varied sizes. In many cases the surrounding topography and catchments for the caves are more diverse in terms of vegetation and the animal resources they support than the open locales.

These two normal environments can be interpreted as possessing above average possibilities for preservation as well as providing an obvious focus for what are seen as key aspects in Lower Palaeolithic survival – shelter, water and hunting opportunities at animal watering places. Deciding whether such normal environments are representative of wider (i.e. away from rivers and caves) patterns of past landuse remains problematic.

These locales also supply information on two main types of 'normal' acivities. These involved the butchery and processing of animals at Isernia Sett. I t. 3a elephant, bison and rhino, Venosa-Notarchirico elephant (Mussi, this volume), Cagny l'Epinette young bovids and equids (Tuffreau and Antoine, this volume), Miesenheim roe and red deer, equids (Bosinski, this volume), Bilzingsleben many taxa but notably rhino (Mania, this volume), Kudaro cave bear (Ljubin and Bosinski, this volume), Arago many taxa but notably musk ox, reindeer and mouflon (De Lumley, pers. comm.) and Boxgrove rhino, deer, bison and an equid (Roberts *et al.*, this volume). The second normal acitivity involved the selection and knapping of stone at these locales. Refitting has been undertaken at many of these sites and in most cases the source of the raw materials has been traced to the local catchment. The distances involved are all less than 80-100 km from the locales and generally under 30 km. The local nature of these lithic catchments is well shown in a recent study of Arago (Lebel 1992). Sometimes the distances were immediate as at Boxgrove (Roberts *et al.*, this volume) where four flint blocks were carried 70m from the collapsed sea cliff to a horse carcass.

On closer examination the normal environments do occasionally raise interpretative problems for some of these normal activities. For example, at Hoxne the in-situ archaeological material was abandoned in a few centimeters of permanent water through which people must have waded (Wymer 1985: 169). The environment in the Lower Gravels at Swanscombe is described by Conway (1970: 60) as a 'muddy pool' which contained the Clactonian 'floor'/midden. The artefacts at Kärlich-Seeufer are found right at the waters edge (Bosinski, this volume), while at Isernia Sett. I t. 3a the mud flat on which the animal bones and artefacts were deposited was covered by a debris flow (Mussi, this volume).

Local conditions such as these provide environmental reasons why the normal activities recovered at these locales, where preservation is generally reckoned as good, do not include huts, pits and post holes even though the material is sometimes in-situ. Our prime data may simply come from either the edge of settlement areas or be some distance from them. However, it may be that similar conditions of deposition and preservation are more widespread than we think and consequently we should not abandon the search for formal campsites in the Lower Palaeolithic. The Bilzingsleben II travertine (Mania, this volume) provides the best, possibly the only, current contender for such a settlement type.

However, the lack of hearths, and their associated patterns of debris accumulation in either cave or open locales, does suggest that we will always be dealing with traces of very different types of settlement traces during this period.[4] In this context the details of the stone built hearth at Solana del Zamborino (Raposo and Santonja, this volume) in the Guadix-Baza basin requires further scrutiny.[5]

2.2.   HOMINID ENVIRONMENTAL TOLERANCES

The form of settlement and its regional patterning is important in the context of characterising the environmental tolerances of Lower Palaeolithic hominids. The typical local environments in many parts of Europe show a diverse set of conditions ranging from interglacial to glacial and open to closed forest conditions (Roebroeks et al. 1992: Table 1). At the Bilzingsleben II travertine (Mania, this volume) the pollen indicates a diverse, oak-mixed-forest with southern species. This is interpreted as a light, dry oak woodland interspersed with meadows in the immediate vicinity of the hominid locale. Dense forest was only found in the nearby valley and may well have been avoided by the hominids.[6] The lack of hominid traces in the heavily wooded Riano basin of central Italy is contrasted with their presence at Isernia and other Italian locales where the environment has been reconstructed as open woodland (Mussi, this volume). The evidence for thinning of the interglacial forests of eastern England (C. Turner 1970), presumably by fire-assisted hominids, may possibly be a further expression of a typical preferred vegetational environment, that is open, mosaic woodland. The oncolith deposits at the Carpentier quarry, Abbeville, contain pollen which shows that under a temperate climate a mosaic landscape of forest-steppe existed (Tuffreau and Antoine, this volume).

Evidence also exists to show hominids occupying a range of successive biotopes at a single locale. At the Caune de l'Arago these are related to major changes in environmental conditions and involve occupation during glacial, interstadial and interglacial conditions (De Lumley, pers. comm.). At Boxgrove occupation is found throughout the interglacial OIS 13 and into the subsequent major cold phase (Anglian/Elsterian), the most severe in terms of continental ice advance during the Middle Pleistocene (Roberts et al., this volume). Cagny-la-Garenne and Cagny-Cimetière have occupations during full interglacial stages as well as in subarctic and under more continental climatic conditions (Tuffreau and Antoine, this volume). However, these contrasted climatic conditions were not universal in Middle Pleistocene Europe. The Iberian Lower Palaeolithic still proves difficult to order according to a regional Quaternary stratigraphy. One reason is that the difference between interglacial and glacial conditions in this southerly and oceanic part of Europe are much less pronounced than in more northerly or more continental areas.

2.3.   PROBLEMS OF ENVIRONMENTAL RECONSTRUCTION

Both the synchronic and diachronic evidence points to potentially wide environmental tolerances for Middle Pleistocene hominids. These understandably are very coarse measures relating to vegetation zones, temperature and the presence of ice. It is therefore unsurprising that controversy exists concerning the ability of these, and later hominids, to exploit particular biotopes, for example the dense interglacial forests (Gamble 1986; Tuffreau 1987, 1990; Roebroeks et al. 1992; Conard 1992). One reason for this debate lies in the very qualitative descriptions that exist to describe past vegetation as reconstructed by either pollen or molluscan evidence. Such imprecision reflects the methodological difficulties of palynology where catchment sizes vary from pollen site to pollen site. When this factor is combined with differential pollen rain between taxa it is possible to see why synchronic reconstructions are problematic. In the case of molluscan evidence the patchy nature of modern data on species tolerances, distributions and life histories adds to the problems of environmental reconstruction, particularly at a synchronic scale. Yet it is at the synchronic level that we need precision in order to reconstruct activity in ecological time, since it is at this timescale that selection pressure on hominid behaviour is most pronounced.

2.4.   MOSAIC HABITATS

For methodological reasons we can therefore expect that environmental reconstructions of local environments at a synchronic level will continue to typify Middle Pleistocene hominids as tolerant of a wide range of conditions. This suggests that present techniques and forms of analysis are not telling us very much. Auguste (in press) has argued differently. He points out that in northern France the Lower and Middle Palaeolithic records testify to hominid occupation during interglacial, interstadial and early glacial conditions (Tuffreau and Antoine, this volume; Roberts et al., this volume). The last phase saw a great reduction in the number of Palaeolithic finds. This nearly continuous occupation was possible because at all times, he argues, there existed a mosaic of environments rather than undifferentiated vegetation zones. These mosaics are similar to Guthrie's (1984, 1990) model of the mammoth steppe where its 'fabric' is compared to the weave in a plaid, rather than striped, textile.

Two points about these plaid, mosaic environments deserve elaboration. Firstly, such mosaics contribute to *resiliant* environments. Disruption to the environmental

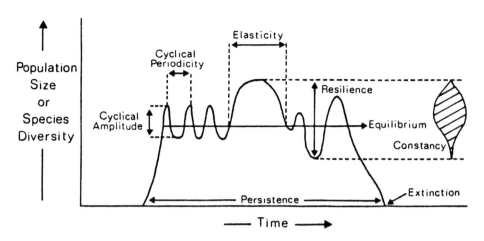

Fig. 1. Properties of ecological stability (from Foley 1984).

fabric in ecological time through fire, storm, overgrazing or volcanic and tectonic activity is quickly patched-up. Recolonization distances are short due to the mosaic structure of a biotope such as Guthrie's mammoth steppe or the open woodlands of some of the interglacials. They do not require climatic change to facilitate conditions for migration in the event that 'repairing' the mosaic is necessary. Therefore resiliant environments tolerate greater amounts of fluctuation (Foley 1984: table 1.2 cf. Fig. 1).

Equally, any local disturbances that might affect hominids could be compensated by short migrations to another part of their range. The alternative, *brittle* environment, has slow recovery times due to many factors such as soil fertility and migration distances for plants and animals.[7] Cyclical disruption in ecological time that may take place on an annual or decade basis will therefore have a potentially greater impact on an omnivore such as a hominid.

Secondly, the mosaic model presents a more *dynamic* view of past environments than is often the case in palaeoecological reconstructions. All too frequently the goal of such reconstructions has been descriptive rather than explanatory. For example, it has been stated on many occasions that early hominids can no more be characterised as red deer hunters than as oak forest foragers. They were not specifically adapted to particular animal or plant communities but rather by the selection pressures that such elements, when combined, exerted on behavioural solutions to environmental problems. It is this interaction which produces the dynamic in human adaptation and which can be explained through the principles of evolutionary ecology (Foley 1984).

However, we are still some way from such analyses. What is now needed is an investigation of those mosaics.

This may require a new approach to such standard techniques as pollen analysis since what we require goes beyond the zonal palaeovegetation map (eg. Zagwijn 1992a: Fig. 1), useful as these are, to an internal breakdown of the mosaic components of such broad vegetation types as steppe and steppe-tundra. However, if the mosaic model is to avoid future over-generalisation as a description of Pleistocene vegetation the structure of the plaid (Guthrie 1984: Fig. 13.1) will need quantitative description. This would be comparable to discussion elsewhere of key concepts in hominid palaeo-ecology of refugia (Vrba 1988), dispersal (Tchernov 1992) and colonization (Gamble 1993a).[8]

3.   Regional environments and long-term evolutionary processes

3.1.   INTRODUCTION

Europe can be shown to be a large enough geographical unit to observe variation in key resources and the impact this had on the structure of regional Palaeolithic records (Gamble 1986). These key resources were vegetation communities and the animals they supported. These varied in predictable ways due to the effect of latitude, longitude and relief on energy capture and its translation into usable food sources for hominids. The regional Palaeolithic records are not expected to vary in terms of artifact types but in terms of the quantity of materials available for study and the degree of continuity in regional occupation through all phases of an interglacial/glacial cycle. The former is a coarse measure of population density while the latter measures changes in behaviour which broadened the hominid niche.

3.2. GEOGRAPHICAL LIMITS

With this model we can begin to see why it is important to have some idea of the limits to Palaeolithic Europe. The debate over the occupation, or not, of non-mosaic interglacial forests may have focused attention on our ability to use static environmental descriptions in a dynamic manner. However, such discussion should not detract from the fact that Middle Pleistocene Europe saw only a partial colonization of the continent. For example, the ESF workshop confirmed (Praslov, this volume) that there are no OIS 9 sites or older on the plains of Russia and the Ukraine.[9] Middle Pleistocene occupation is only found between the Black and Azov seas and not further north. These plains are ringed to the south by evidence for early occupation. The Caucasus provides evidence as at Kudaro I and III, Tsona and Achalkalaki, while recent finds at Dmanisi in Georgia establish a solid Early Pleistocene presence (Ljubin and Bosinski, this volume). Recent research in Turkey and Greece (Darlas, this volume) has also produced Middle Pleistocene evidence. Some of the locales in these southern areas are also at comparatively high altitude, sometimes above 1500 m. Such high altitude sites have not been reported for other parts of Europe. Isernia lies in a landscape where rugged mountains go up to 1400 m but these were much lower, as they would have been in the Caucasus, at the time of occupation (Mussi, this volume).

The eastern unglaciated limits to the European region of Middle Pleistocene occupation therefore seem to be well established. Neither can erosion and the destruction of evidence be suggested as the reason for absence (Praslov, pers. comm.). To the north the limits remain unknown due to glacial scouring of the evidence (Holm and Larsson, this volume). There is no a-priori reason to suppose that the Middle Pleistocene sites of Germany, Belgium, France and England represent the limits of northern occupation (Brinch-Petersen, pers. comm.). The question must be how much further north would population have extended? The only answer will come through a greater understanding of the ecological tolerances of these hominids.

3.3. THE MAMMOTH STEPPE AND MIDDLE PLEISTOCENE HOMINID RANGE

In this respect Guthrie's mammoth steppe (1984, 1990), which links Alaska with western Europe, provides a wider biotope for evaluating the relations between Middle Pleistocene hominids and their environments. Guthrie has correctly characterised Pleistocene biotic communities as 'novel assortments' of elements rather than the common view that coniferous forests or tundras "have a long, complex evolutionary history of fine tuning and are much as they have been since ... time primeval (1984:289)". The

mammoth steppe has a considerable antiquity (see below) as an ecologically complex, medium to high latitude suite of vegetation mosaics that produced a diverse fauna of grazing generalists. This depended primarily upon longer growth seasons which were internally varied. Guthrie shows how these can be most clearly differentiated on a north-south, latitudinal transect (1990: 263ff). However, Middle Pleistocene hominids only used a small part of this huge biotope (*ibid*: Fig. 9.12).[10] Their restricted distribution suggests that the mammoth steppe was differentiated, in terms of suitability for hominid use, on a west-east transect. The degree to which the mammoth steppe varied internally has not been discussed in any detail by Guthrie. However, one factor contributing to any such differentiation would have been the pattern of animal migrations into Europe. During colder phases the main mammoth steppe herd animals came from the east while during interglacials taxa migrated into northern Europe from southern Europe (Van Kolfschoten 1992: Fig. 1).

This circumstance suggests that Europe north of the Alps and Carpathians was generally a comparatively rich mosaic environment. This was the situation during the warmer, forested phases as well as the colder open phases. Under both climatic regimes the richness of that mosaic can be defined *in relative terms* by the conditions in the rest of the mammoth steppe. Obviously for Middle Pleistocene hominids the structure of food resources in these mosaics was very different. Key factors would have been prey density, its mobility and reliability as measured by population fluctuations.

Putting this mosaic model into the wider context of the Eurasian/Beringian mammoth steppe, we can see that, irrespective of interglacial or glacial conditions, the controlling factor on the northern and eastern distribution of Middle Pleistocene hominids was the oceanic effect (Von Koenigswald 1992: 45). Only this ameliorating effect could, combined with the zonal distribution of upland and mountain in Europe, have produced the dual mosaic pattern that had the effect of concentrating animal resources in this western arm of the Eurasian landmass.

The details of exactly how the oceanic effect worked and varied in its impact between different glacial/interglacial cycles is still debated. Those concerned with palaeovegetation reconstructions are still divided over the controlling role of either temperature or moisture as the critical element in major vegetation changes (Tzedakis 1993: 438; Zagwijn 1992b; Suc and Zagwijn 1983; De Jong 1988). However, the essential feature of the European vegetation is that speciation during the Quaternary was low to non-existent (Tzedakis 1993: 440). This was probably also the case for the European large mammals. The reason that Europe possessed a dual mosaic structure, rather than alternating

plaids to stripes[11] (Guthrie 1984), is that both elements of
the biotope repeatedly migrated into Europe rather than
evolved within the region. Variation in amplitude of the
oceanic effect between oxygen isotope stages controlled
these migrations.

3.4.   REFUGIA AND MOSAICS

During glacial phases, plant species became locally
extinct in northern Europe. Vegetation zones were not
depressed south and instead taxa, especially tree species,
survived in localised refugia in southern/ Mediterranean
Europe from where re-colonization took place in succeeding
warmer phases. Animals were also part of these southerly
refuges (Van Kolfschoten 1992). From a European
perspective, local extinctions in warmer periods meant that
the Asian/Beringian mammoth steppe came to form a sort
of huge refugia.

The location and composition of the refugia within
Europe no doubt varied, due to contingent factors, from
glacial period to glacial period. This explains why, although
broadly similar patterns exist for each forest re-generation
in northern Europe, each interglacial also possesses an
individual floral character (De Jong 1988). Moreover, the
timing and mixing of the dual mosaics (steppe:forest)
produced what in modern animal community terms are very
strange associations of animals,[12] but which can be
understood in terms of the generalists such environmental
structures favour (Guthrie 1984; Geist 1978).

This long term pattern of successive colonizations
favoured those areas of northern Europe which were in
close proximity to the topographically diverse refuge areas.
Re-colonization distances would be short and likewise the
timescale for forest regeneration. The reduced effects of
seasonality in the west of the continent would also have the
effect of more tightly packed vegetation mosaics. On the
contrary in the east, outside the distribution of Middle
Pleistocene hominids, distances between the plains and the
sheltered refuge areas were greater. Seasonality, as
measured by intra-annual variation in temperature, would
also be much greater and the cells in the mosaics would be
more widely spaced. Biotopes in the west would therefore
be more ecologically resilient because they were less prone
to crashes in animal numbers and faster migration/recolo-
nization rates. The main factor reducing such seasonality is
the oceanic effect.

3.5.   HOMINID MOBILITY

The discussion has so far suggested that within the
European area settled by Middle Pleistocene hominids we
can recognise two significant regional habitats – plains and
uplands. In her contribution Mussi develops the mosaic
hypothesis in relation to one of these habitats, the Italian

peninsula. She reminds us that due to topography extensive
ecological zonation (stripes rather than plaids) has never
been possible and that the hallmarks of a refugia – spatially
compact high diversity and exponential growth in plant
populations – are commonly found. This would have
favoured the persistence of animal species. At a local scale
the mosaic principle is picked up in the rich, diverse
swamps and lagoons.[13] Mussi elaborates the model to
propose that the richness of the Lower Palaeolithic in Italy
was linked to these environmental circumstances where,
within short distances, foragers were able to take advantage
of such conditions.[14] Therefore, the richness of the elements
in the environmental plaid, and their proximity, served as a
means to reduce risk[15] by moving to alternative, productive
resources.

While less extreme in terms of topography, and mitigated
by the shorter growing seasons of more northerly latitudes,
we can see that locales in Germany (Mania, this volume;
Bosinski, this volume), northern France (Tuffreau and
Antoine, this volume) and England (Roberts *et al.*, this
volume) were also positioned in relation to such mosaic
structures. In particular, the use of riparian woodlands
would have provided the best opportunities for scavenging
and the avoidance of predators (Blumenschine 1986:
Table 5.8) particularly along the overgrown banks of the
Pleistocene Rhine as at Miesenheim I (Bosinski, this
volume). Within reasonable distances there was often
sufficient altitudinal variation to produce the conditions for
mosaic habitats. However, compared to Italy the distances
involved would have been greater and more easily stretched
by climatically forced changes to plant and animal
communities. If mobility was a key tactic of Middle
Pleistocene hominids in combatting risk, then the distance
between feeding patches within the mosaic would become
critical. While we cannot yet specify such distances it
would seem that the absence of these hominids in Scandinavia and the Russian plains would provide case studies to
determine what these distances were by examining the
mosaic structure of the Pleistocene biotopes in these areas.

4.   **Long-term changes**

4.1.   INTRODUCTION

Resilience can be defined ecologically as the amount of
fluctuation that can be tolerated, and after which the system
can return to equilibrium (Foley 1984:10). The main
properties of ecological stability are shown in figure 1
where attention is also paid to cyclical amplitude and
periodicity.

The effects of climatic cycles clearly varied in terms of
amplitude during the Middle Pleistocene. In Iberia the weak
signals have made it difficult to distinguish between
temperate and cold stages on the basis of sediments, pollen

Table 1

Occupation of Europe by	2 Myr	1.5 Myr	1 - 0.9Myr	0.73 Myr	0.5 Myr
Starts at OIS		57	33	19	13
Number of interglacial/ glacial cycles	c. 40	27	15	8	5
Length of cycles mean Kyr range Kyr sd		56 117 - 38 26.45	68.2 117 - 38 30.56	90.5 117 - 47 23.61	102.4 117 - 84 14.22
Number of stages ≥ OIS 5e core 552A	9*	7*	5	2	2
Number of stages ≥ OIS 2 Core V28-239	15*	13*	9	6	4
Site(s) Author	Soleilhac Bonifay 1991 Orce Gibert 1992	Chilhac Guth Kärlich Bosinski Beroun Fridrich 1991	Vallonnet De Lumley 1988 Monte Poggiolo Peretto 1992 Korolevo Ranov 1991	Isernia Peretto 1991 Stránská skála Valoch 1991	Boxgrove Roberts et al. this volume Isernia Roebroeks & van Kolfschoten this volume

* = minimum number estimated from incomplete core data
compiled from Ruddiman et al. 1986; Shackleton and Opdyke 1973; Shackleton et al. 1988

and faunas (Raposo and Santonja, this volume).[16] By contrast, in England the OIS 12 ice sheet (Anglian) re-diverted the Thames and had dramatic effects on the evolution of this region's landscape. As a result it left deposits which are readily distinguishable from the interglacials which preceeded and succeeded it.

The amplitude of climatic cycles also changed during the Quaternary. De Jong (1988) and Zagwijn (1992b) have shown how the Bavel interglacial at 1 Myr BP saw the first succession in the immigration, spread and decline of forest elements in northern Europe. Prior to this date the inter-glacials lack such characteristic successions. They attribute this to changes in the intervening cold periods which for much of the early Pleistocene were less severe. Refuge areas may well have been closer while different soil conditions at the beginning of interglacials prevented the spread of acidiphilous elements like *Abies* and *Picea* (Zagwijn 1992b: 587).

Amplitude in the climatic signal had therefore increased. Within the Middle Pleistocene further variation exists with the correlation between high ocean values (Shackleton 1987) and the appearance of *Abies* in northern Europe (De

Jong 1988). These extreme interglacials were OIS 5e, 9 and 11 when oceanic climate with high precipitation and warm winters predominated. If these correlations between the deep sea and the pollen records are correct then they describe conditions which pertain to only some 8% of the Middle Pleistocene.

4.2.   LONG AND THE SHORT CHRONOLOGY

The importance of long term variation in cyclical amplitude and periodicity for hominid occupation comes to the fore when we consider the environmental consequences of either a long or short chronology for occupying the continent.

In particular there have been attempts (M.-F. Bonifay 1980; Zagwijn 1992b) to link major changes in the European fauna and vegetation to orbital forcing of the Pleistocene climate. This involves both the amplitude of some key cycles (notably OIS 12) as well as changes in the periodicity of these cycles between the Early and Middle Pleistocene.

Adherence to either the long or short chronology for the initial occupation of Europe has fundamental implications for the use of environmental evidence. At one level this means dealing with more, or less, animal taxa (Cordy 1992), a variable number of hominid species, and the different structure of interglacial vegetation cycles the longer the time span for human occupation is extended back beyond the Middle Pleistocene (Zagwijn 1992a: 586).

The climatic cycles recorded in the deep sea record are also the proxy data most commonly used to investigate questions of environmental selection on hominids (Vrba *et al.* 1989; Brain 1981; Prentice and Denton 1988; Gamble 1993a). For example, if a long chronology for the occupation of Europe of 2 Myr, 1.5 Myr, 1 Myr or 900 Kyr is preferred, this will produce different long-term environmental selection as represented by the number, frequency and comparative amplitudes of the oxygen isotope stages. However, if a short chronology of either 730 Kyr or 500 Kyr is adopted then the accumulated effects of the generalised climatic record are very different (see also Foley 1994).

In Table 1 the environmental scale of the interglacial/glacial cycles are examined. If hominids first colonized the continent at 500 Kyr BP then the differences between the length of the cycles was much less, as shown by a lower standard deviation, than would have been the case with an earlier entry. Colonization at 500 Kyr BP was followed by five climatic cycles of very comparable duration and dominated by intermediate environmental conditions (Gamble 1986: table 3.5). Much greater variability would have faced the earliest European hominids if colonization had first occured 730 Kyr BP or earlier (Table 1). But this greater variation in cyclical rhythms has, if a long chronology is favoured, to be seen against a diminution in the frequency of the extreme climatic events. These are the high sea level interglacials (Shackleton 1987) and the large continental glaciations (Zagwijn 1992b) that are so characteristic of the short, 500 Kyr, chronology. If we take this time span as a climatic yardstick for comparing the remaining Pleistocene cycles in relation to either extreme oceanic conditions (stages ≥ OIS 5e) or extreme continentality, as shown by high ice values (all stages ≥ OIS2), we arrive at the following proportions:

Date of first occupation	Number of cycles	*High sea levels & forests* % of cycles ≥ last interglacials (OIS 5e)	*Low sea levels & ice caps* % of cycles ≥ last glacial maximum (OIS 2)
500 Kyr	5	40	80
736 Kyr	8	25	75
900 Kyr	15	33	60
1,5 Myr	27	26	48

The trend revealed by these oxygen isotope data is very clear. The longer cycles of the last 500 Kyr are very different in terms of the frequency of high ocean and high ice conditions than the earlier cycles. Amplitude effects, as measured by environmental extremes, are markedly different. The proportion of extreme conditions decreases significantly the longer the chronology, especially for high sea level interglacials. These are represented by only a quarter of the cycles in the last 1.5 Myr. The higher frequency of continental ice advances is a feature of the shortest chronology presented here for the occupation of Europe.

However, the usual way to analyse these data is not by using the competing claims for the earliest human settlement to mark the divisions, but rather to set the boundaries by studying climatic change in its own right. This is undertaken in Table 2 for the Brunhes and Matuyama Chrons. The latter Chron is only examined back to 1.6 Myr due to the availability of reliable data (Ruddiman *et al.* 1986). The reason for selecting these Chrons as an environmental framework stems from their apparent association with orbital changes which in turn forced climatic change.

Table 2

Brunhes Chron	**0.012-0.787 Myr**
Starts at OIS	19
Number of interglacial/ glacial cycles	
Length of cycles mean Kyr	96.71
range Kyr	117- 47
sd 17.02	
Matuyama Chron	**0.736 - 1.636 Myr***
Starts at OIS	63
Number of interglacial/ glacial cycles	22
Length of cycles mean Kyr	40.91
range Kyr	45 - 38
sd 2.01	

* Matuyama Chron lasted from 2.47 - 0.736 Myr.
Data only available for 'Pleistocene' section (Ruddiman *et al.* 1986: table 3)

The data in Table 2 reveal a well known aspect of Quaternary climatic cycles (Pisias and Moore 1981; Ruddiman and Raymo 1988); namely that during the Matuyama Chron the dominant periodicity for a full cycle is 41 Kyr. This can be matched to the rhythm of orbital obliquity – the tilt in the earth's rotational axis. The Brunhes Chron is more complex with the period between 900 Kyr to 450 Kyr showing a mean of 54 Kyr for a full cycle, while according to Ruddiman and Raymo (1988:6) the 100 Kyr cycles became dominant after 450 Kyr ago. But even among Pleistocene geologists chronological unanimity is lacking. Prentice and Denton (1988:390) see the transition between the ice budgets of the two rhythms occurring between 900 Kyr and 700 Kyr, with the 100 Kyr cycles dominating the entire Middle Pleistocene/ Brunhes Chron. These are important chronological differences for hominid colonization of Europe, especially if an environmental reason involving climatic forcing is being sought.

When examined for the proportion of high and low sea level cycles we find the following pattern:

Chron	Number of cycles	High sea levels & forests % of cycles ≥ last inter-glacials (OIS 5e)	Low sea levels & ice caps % of cycles ≥ last glacial maximum (OIS 2)
Brunhes 0.012-0.73 Myr	8	25	75
Matuyama 0.73-1.63 Myr	22	23	32

From these data we can see that the Chrons are very comparable in the proportion of high sea level interglacial cycles. What distinguishes them are the well known, major continental ice advances of the Brunhes. As Shackleton (*et al.* 1988: 685) asks, where are the traces of the Matuyama ice sheets which appeared with a 41 Kyr periodicity but a very low environmental amplitude? A question that has already been addressed in relation to the Middle Pleistocene sequence in Iberia (Raposo and Santonja, this volume).

4.3. A CRITIQUE OF THE QUATERNARY CASE FOR GRADUALISM

Such low impact, high impact differences have still to be assessed in terms of colonization and behavioural change. This may be difficult as those putting forward climatic forcing as an explanation for hominid speciation (Brain 1981; Vrba 1988; Prentice and Denton 1988) have discovered. The correlations remain tempting, but tenuous. Moreover, the differences in climatic cycles and the scale of their continental ice caps in the last 500 Kyr was not the result of changes in earth's orbit but more probably major tectonic activity affecting climate (Ruddiman and Raymo 1988).

As a result the importance of the contribution of these evolutionary, or geological, timescales to human evolution remains unclear. One good reason for this uncertainty is, as discussed above, that evolution takes place on an immediate or ecological timescale. Converting these processes from the general to the specific remains problematic and is accentuated when colonization and behaviour are the main interest.

However, the implications of a short and long chronology do not stop with demonstrating the role of climate in human evolution. Table 1 also points to the amplitude of changes. The longer the chronology for initial occupation the more possible it is to argue that hominids reached Europe during 'easier' climatic times. Although the Pleistocene begins at 2.5 Myr (Zagwijn 1992b) the first significant ice advances take place almost a million years later at 1.6 Myr, which is still the official Pliocene/ Early Pleistocene boundary. Thus, a long chronology allows a gradual view of behavioural evolution. Humans had plenty of time to adapt to the variable frequencies and persistance of conditions of Pleistocene climates as well as the long term trend toward increasingly extreme conditions. Thus the long chronology supports a gradual view of change.

But there is a problem with such simple gradualism. Namely that the mechanisms for behavioural change are never spelt out but instead are regarded as slowly additive and accretional. As a result no independent check exists on the appropriateness of any of the preferred time scales on-offer (Table 1) to produce by gradual means long term change. This imprecision helps to explain why so many versions of the long chronology exist. It is up to the individual worker to set what she/he believes is an appropriate length of time to achieve the advances in technology and culture which archaeologists have revealed. For this reason individual claims for a variety of chronologies persist in the literature for many years and are rarely critically examined because the underpinning argument of gradualism appears to be irrefutable (Roebroeks and van Kolfschoten, this volume).

The argument against a short chronology is therefore usually founded on the requirements of gradual evolution. The assessment of those favouring a long chronology must be that 500 Kyr or even 730 Kyr is too short a period to account for the changes seen both in Europe and worldwide. Yet these estimates, if examined historically, are also relative. For example, Zeuner, following Milankovitch, estimated the length of the European Pleistocene as 600 Kyr (1959:213). Indeed, in *Dating the Past* (1958: figure 80) this figure accounts for human evolution in all parts of the world. Ten years later Oakley increased human evolution seven-fold to 3.5 Myr (1969) and included the Australopithecines, ignored by Zeuner. Oakley's figure has been confirmed. Furthermore, it is now expected, thanks to the molecular clock, that the human chimp split occured some 5 Myr ago and that one day we may find fossils to fill the 4-5 Myr gap.[17]

4.4.   THE SHORT CHRONOLOGY; CONTINGENCY OR PROCESS?

However, the short chronology also adopts a gradualistic rather than punctuated approach to the process of change. This prompts us to ask how gradual *is* gradual? Therefore in order to avoid accusations of just being a spoiling argument the short chronology must be evaluated in terms of what it tells us about the goals of Palaeolithic studies, accounting for change and stasis in hominid behaviour, which the long chronology does not. This assessment can best be undertaken by asking questions. We want to know why Europe was colonized at c. 500 Kyr as well as the tolerances, in terms of amplitude and frequency which hominids could cope with.

Alan Turner (1992) has argued that the reason for a more substantial occupation of Europe from 500 Kyr BP onwards is to be found in the changing structure of the large carnivore guilds, well shown at Petralona (Darlas, this volume). Between 600-400 Kyr there was a marked faunal turnover during which the large flesh eaters (*Homotherium* and *Megantereon*) and the carcass destroyers (*Pachycrocuta perrieri* and *P. brevirostris*) became extinct. This left only the leopard, lion, spotted hyena and wolf as Europe's major carnivores. According to Turner this change in the carnivore guild would have greatly improved the conditions for hominid scavenging since the giant hyenas were no longer present to consume carcasses. It may also have improved hunting success now that the flesh eaters (the sabre and dirk toothed cats) had also disappeared. Turner concludes by suggesting (*ibid*: 122) that any hominid occupation prior to 500 Kyr BP would have faced intense competition from the carnivores. While population may have reached the continent it would have been for short periods of time and left little archaeological trace. After 500 Kyr the nature of the archaeological record changes dramatically (Roebroeks and van Kolfschoten 1994), a reflection of reduced selection pressure from previously key competitors.

This same change has been documented by Cordy (1992) who has divided the period from OIS 26 - OIS 2 into eight faunal biozones. The 'hinge' in the faunas falls between OIS 13 and OIS 12 at 440 Kyr BP, with four biozones on either side. The two periods these biozones comprise are each 400 Kyr in duration. What is apparent is the general increase in herbivore diversity, especially among the rhinos, large bovids, ovicaprids and antelopes after OIS 12. The only changes in carnivore diversity involve the decline of the hyenas and large cats.

Table 3 compares the faunal composition of Cordy's (1992) four biozones either side of 440 Kyr. The figures shown are the average number of species for each of the major taxa in the four biozones. This shows, for example, that the number of rhino species doubles in the biozones after 440 Kyr.

	Biozones I-IV OIS 26-13	440 Kyr	Biozones V-VIII OIS 12-2
Mammoths	1.25		1.25
Rhinos	1		2
Horses	1.75 - 2		1.5 - 1.75
Bos	1.75 - 2		2.75
Ovibos	1.5 - 2		1
Ovicaprids	1.25		2 - 2.25
Antilope	0		1.25
Cervus	6.25 - 7.75		5.5 - 6.75
Canis	1 - 1.25		1.25
Vulpes/Alopex	1.25		1.5 - 1.75
Cuon	1.75 - 2		1
Ursus	1.5 - 1.75		2
Hyena	2 - 2.75		1.25
Large cats	2.5 - 3		1

From these data it is possible to argue that community diversity generally increased between the Early and Middle Pleistocene and continued to do so during the Middle Pleistocene. The figures strongly indicate a long-term process of community evolution rather than being contingent upon a short timescale event to shape the European fauna. Such a profound event can be detected in the decimation of the European fauna in the Late glacial/ Holocene transition (Guthrie 1984; Von Koenigswald 1992). The greater community diversity can be linked to the changes in cyclical periodicity (Tables 1 and 2) as indicated by the deep sea cores. A strong link is suggested between the longer cycles, dominated by conditions intermediary between the full interglacial and full glacial and which account for *c.* 60% of the last 440 Kyr. This diversity is probably an indication of the evolution of the highly productive mammoth steppe. Van Kolfschoten (1990) and E. Turner (1991) have shown that in western Germany the first truly glacial faunas occur at Ariendorf 1 with *Dicrostonyx* and *Rangifer*.[18] This assemblage dates to an older phase of the Saalian, probably OIS 8 (303 - 245 Kyr BP) and so immediately after the period covered by the ESF workshop (Bosinski, this volume). This is of interest in terms of human occupation because western Germany currently lacks any occupations dated to OIS 10 and 9. A case might possibly be made that occupation was still intermittent on a regional basis prior to the full establishment of the mammoth steppe. It is therefore tempting to revise Turner's chronology and see the period from 500-300 Kyr as one of hesitant, intermittent occupation on a regional basis between northern and southern Europe, while after

300 Kyr BP occupation strengthens due to the maturation of the full mammoth steppe during the long cold phases of the interglacial/glacial cycles (cf. Roebroeks and Van Kolf-schoten, this volume).

5.   When and why was Europe colonized so late? A personal conclusion

At the Tautavel workshop there was considerable discussion over the "gates of Europe" as a barrier to settle-ment. If hominids were present in North Africa (Raynal *et al.*, this volume) at around 800 Kyr BP and in the Middle East and the Caucasus (Bosinski, this volume) by at least 1 Myr BP and probably, in the case of Georgia and Israel, much earlier, why did a further 500-900 Kyr elapse before the uplands and plains of Europe were first colonized?

From a short chronology perspective there seem to be three alternatives. Firstly, that the dates are inflated for the earliest appearance of hominids outside sub-Saharan Africa. A critical review of the claims for ancient findspots throughout the Old World would be clearly welcome, but was beyond the scope of the present workshop. However, our re-assessment of the European data now provides a yardstick against which to measure the various claims from elsewhere for early colonization. One aspect of this scrutiny will involve characterizing the normal environments which preserve evidence of hominid activities in other parts of the Old World. The character of the Palaeolithic record and its critical assessment in terms of chronological and archaeol-ogical integrity is clearly a project for future international collaboration.

Such an investigation would only seem worthwhile, how-ever, if we have a framework expressing the degree of chronological precision we deem necessary to settle the issue of when the colonization of Europe and the other regions of the Old World took place. The likelihood of arriving at a consensus view at the level of the individual cycle, of either 41 or 100 Kyr duration (Table 1) seems currently remote. I would suggest, following Bonifay and Vandermeersch' discussion of the physical anthropological evidence (1991: 317), that we should start with 500 Kyr blocks (Foley 1994). Let us then see which block between 0-2 Myr BP provides consistent and verifiable evidence in terms of agreement over the status of artifacts, hominid remains, and dating methods, as well as the integrity and character of those normal environments which preserve our evidence. Having identified which block we should be searching in we can then become more precise, as this volume shows.

But let us assume that the hominids at Sidi Abderrah-mane and Dmanisi did indeed wait at the gates of Europe for very long periods of time. This suggests a second, environmental reason to explain the delay. A physical barrier seems the best answer and this could be the straits of Gibraltar, an enlarged Caspian/Black Sea, or the topographically undifferentiated plains of the Ukraine. These barriers do however look extremely permeable given the timescales and climatic changes that took place between 1 Myr and 0.5 Myr BP. They are not the permanent ocean barrier that existed between south east Asia and Australia. It is exactly this permeability which is perhaps the strongest card in the hands of those favouring a long chronology. However this is confusing the likelihood of colonization with its actuality. Hence the concentration of early claims in those areas adjacent to the gates of Europe rather than in the north of the continent. Indeed supporters of early colonization in mediterranean and southern Europe (Table 1) would presumably draw their barrier at the margins of the northern plains or argue, as Turner (1992) has done, for multiple entries that did not lead to a permanent foothold in the continent because of the barrier presented by carnivore competition. But what the long-chronology model needs to address are those very thresholds of archaeological visibility which it uses to support the patchy pre 500 Kyr claims. How do we quantify such an ephemeral presence and compare it with the permanent occupation after 500 Kyr? What are the likely parameters, in terms of artifact densities by time horizon and landscape and region, that would adequately test the model ? These archaeological issues are not addressed by any of the long chronology's supporters. They cannot address them because they have no environ-mental framework which allows them to investigate hominids as colonizing animals. This framework is apparent among the proponents of the short chronology who are less inter-ested in pursuing an origins paradigm and more concerned with understanding past hominid behaviour.

The barrier view divides Europe. Moreover, it divides Europe along traditional archaeological fault lines. It makes initial colonization look comparable to the Holocene arrival of the farmers who moved first into the mediterranean and only later onto the plains of the north. I prefer a third model which unites Europe, north and south. The reason for such a unified (suitably Maastricht!) view of the Lower Palaeo-lithic settlement of the continent is based upon the environmental approaches that have been reviewed. I would argue that Middle Pleistocene colonization took place precisely because the complementary environments of plains and uplands existed. The combination of southern plant and animal refugia, faunal migrations from the east, the variable westerly oceanic effect and, at a regional scale, the existence of mosaic landscapes were the necessary conditions for permanent colonization, whether achieved in a single or, as seems most probable, series of colonizing events. We have seen that colonization took place during a long-term trend of increasing faunal diversity. This culminated at the end of OIS 9 with the possible appearance of the mammoth steppe (Guthrie 1990), that was most probably the result of changes in the periodicity and amplitude of the interglacial/glacial cycles. Hominid colonization was therefore part of climatic and biotope changes that took place in evolutionary time and at a continental scale. The limitations on this unified colonization were precisely those which stalled the hominids at the eastern gates of Europe - extreme seasonality in the complementary plains environment. In terms of hominid behaviour this seasonality could only be overcome through greater annual mobility and the fissioning of population. These necessary distances and separation of population in the widely spaced plant and faunal mosaics of the plains could not be supported by the mechanisms available to Middle Pleistocene social systems (Stringer and Gamble 1993; Gamble 1993a,b). As a result populations in the spatially compact regions of the Caucasus, Middle East and North Africa did not expand into Europe. Only with alterations to the seasonality regimes in central and western Europe, which co-incided with changes that were detrimental to the large carnivores, did a match emerge between the scale of the hominids social systems and the spatial structure of resources in the environment which permitted colonization.

One of the urgent tasks which now faces environmental approaches to the Middle Pleistocene is the quantification of the spatial structure of these landscapes, locally,

regionally and for the entire continent. Furthermore, we need to agree from which end of this spatial framework we will begin the investigation of hominids as colonizing animals. Do we start small and work up, or begin with the continent and work down to the local environment. The scale I would advocate starts at the level of the continent itself, poorly defined as it may be on its eastern and northern margins. Only at this scale can we examine the proposition *that any one region of Europe could only be colonized if it was colonized at the same time as most of the others*. Elsewhere (Gamble 1986: Fig. 3.1) I have specified nine regions for the study of the Palaeolithic settlement of Europe. Initial colonization starting at 500 Kyr BP can be demonstrated for eight of them. Only the North East region lay vacant during the Middle Pleistocene. Proceeding down the spatial scale we can see how regions and even landscapes were settled. By increasing our resolution we can begin to examine the relationship between colonizing populations, habitat choice and population dynamics which took place over the long-term and at spatial scales which involved continent wide adaptations and which archaeologists have rarely considered. Examining these issues is one reason why the debate between a long and short chronology is important. However, to be meaningful, such a debate should now be based on the premise that the colonizing capabilities of these hominids was not limited solely by environmental conditions but rather by their own organizational responses to the structure of such environments.

notes

1 See Gamble (1993a) for discussion.

2 See Isaac (1981) for a general discussion of Lower Palaeolithic landscapes in terms of scatters and patches of archaeological material. As he points out the patches are what we commonly call sites. A locale combines both terms.

3 Contributions and comments prepared for and presented at the Tautavel workshop, but which are not included in this volume are indicated as 'pers. comm.' in the reference.

4 Compare the Bilzingsleben 'campsite' with the highly patterned evidence from the Late Glacial open locales such as Verberie, Etiolles and Pincevent (Audouze 1987).

5 This locale is also probably younger than 300 Kyr BP.

6 Mania also mentions the common problem of contradictory environmental evidence which can face such precise reconstructions. At Schöningen 12 the molluscan evidence points to open and the pollen to closed terrain.

7 The classic brittle environment is the tropical rain forest which despite enormous biomass, productivity, species diversity and

hence ecological stability, nonetheless recovers very slowly if disturbed.

8 Disagreement over the so-called wooden curtain (Roebroeks *et al.* 1992) which did, or did not, limit hominid occupation in Middle and Late Pleistocene Europe may well be resolved in a more productive analysis of differential forest mosaics and how these can be identified from the palaeoecological record.

9 see Aitken this volume for discussion of claims for very early Russian Plain sites on the basis of TL dating.

10 The claims for 500 Kyr BP dates for sites in Siberia (Morell 1994) remain implausible for reasons of science based dating and associated archaeology.

11 Until the special circumstances of the Holocene produced stripe zonation (Guthrie 1984: 263ff).

12 For example musk ox and leopard in Mediterranean France (De Lumley, pers. comm.).

13 See Kelly 1983 for details of the massive biological productivity of swamps and water bodies.

14 See Soffer (1989) for a discussion of this short distance, zonal compression, for Middle Palaeolithic occupation in the Crimea.

15 Defined as the failure to meet dietary requirements.

16 This must have been partly due to the depression of the polar front and gulf stream southwards during the colder periods.

17 Since finishing this paper White et al 1994 have now done just that with the discovery of *A. ramidus* in the Awash valley. To put such finds in context; Oakley placed the occupation of Europe at >500Kyr based on a relative age for the Mauer mandible

(1969:300). His careful assessment allowed Europe some 14% of the chronology then alloted to human origins. The various chronologies (Table 1) set against a figure of 5 Myr for human ancestry allow human occupation of Europe 40%, 30%, 20%, 15% and 10% of this time span.

18 This is not however the oldest occurence of *Rangifer* in Europe which extends back at least to OIS12 (Cordy 1992:89).

references

Audouze, F.	1987	The Paris Basin in magdalenian times. In: O. Soffer (ed.), *The Pleistocene Old World: regional perspectives*, 183-200, New York: Plenum.
Auguste, P.	in press	Adaptations biologiques et culturelles des Prénéandertaliens et des Néandertaliens aux modifications paléoécologiques et fauniques en France septentrionale, *Nature et Culture*, Actes Colloque Liège, ERAUL.
Blumenschine, R.	1986	*Early hominid scavenging opportunities: implications of carcass availability in the Serengeti and Ngorongoro ecosystems*. Oxford, British Archaeological Reports International Series 238.
Bonifay, E.	1991	Les premières industries du Sud-est de la France et du Massif Central. In: E. Bonifay and B. Vandermeersch (eds), *Les premiers Européens*, 63-80, Paris: CTHS.
Bonifay, E., P. Vandermeersch	1991	Vue d'ensemble sur le très ancien Paleolithique de l'Europe. In: E. Bonifay and B. Vandermeersch (eds), *Les premiers Européens*, 309-19, Paris: CTHS.
Bonifay, M.-F.	1980	Relations les données isotopiques océaniques et l'histoire des grandes faunes européennes plio-pleistocenes, *Quaternary Research* 14, 251-62.
Bosinski, G.	this volume	The earliest occupation of Europe: Western Central Europe.
Brain, C.K.	1981	Hominid evolution and climatic change, *South African Journal of Science* 77, 104-5.
Butzer, K.W.	1982	*Archaeology as human ecology*. Cambridge: Cambridge University Press.
Conard, N.J.	1992	*Tönchesberg and its position in the Palaeolithic prehistory of northern Europe*. R-GZM Monograph 20, Bonn: Habelt.
Conway, B.W.	1970	Geological investigation of Boyn Hill terrace deposits at Barnfield Pit, Swanscombe, Kent, during 1979, *Proceedings of the Royal Anthropological Institute* (1971), 60-4.
Cordy, J.-M.	1992	Apport de la paléomammologie à la paléoanthropologie en Europe. In: M. Toussaint (ed.), *Cinq millions d'années, l'aventure humaine*, 77-94, Liège: ERAUL.
Darlas, A.,	this volume	The earliest occupation of Europe: The Balkans.

Foley, R.A.	1984	Putting people into perspective: an introduction to community evolution and ecology. In: R.A. Foley (ed.), *Hominid evolution and community ecology*, 1-24, New York: Academic Press.
	1994	Speciation, extinction and climatic change in hominid evolution, *Journal of Human Evolution* 26, 275-289.
Fridrich, J.	1991	Les premiers peuplements humains en Moravie (Tchécoslovaquie). In: E. Bonifay and B. Vandermeersch (eds), *Les premiers Européens*, 195-202, Paris: CTHS.
Gamble, C.S.	1986	*The Palaeolithic settlement of Europe*. Cambridge: Cambridge University Press.
	1993a	*Timewalkers: the prehistory of global colonization*. Far Thrupp: Alan Sutton.
	1993b	Exchange, foraging and local hominid networks. In: C. Scarre and F. Healy (eds), *Trade and exchange in prehistoric Europe*, 35-44, Oxford: Oxbow Monograph 33.
Geist, V.	1978	*Life strategies, human evolution, environmental design*. New York: Springer Verlag.
Gibert, J.	1992	*Proyecto Orce-Cueva Victoria (1988-1992): Presencia humana en el Pleistoceno inferior de Granada y Murcia*. Orce, Museo de Prehistoria.
Guthrie, R.D.	1984	Mosaics, allelochemics and nutrients: an ecological theory of Late Pleistocene megafaunal extinctions. In: P.S. Martin and R.G. Klein (eds), *Quaternary extinctions: a prehistoric revolution*, 259-98, Tucson, Arizona: University of Arizona Press.
	1990	*Frozen fauna of the mammoth steppe*. Chicago: Chicago University Press.
Holm, J., L. Larsson	this volume	The earliest occupation of Europe: Scandinavia.
Isaac, G.	1981	Stone age visiting cards: approaches to the study of early land use patterns. In: I. Hodder *et al.* (eds), *Pattern of the Past: Studies in Honour of David Clarke*, 131-55, Cambridge: Cambridge University Press.
Jong, J. de	1988	Climatic variability during the past three milion years, as indicated by vegetational evolution in northwest Europe and with emphasis on data from The Netherlands, *Philosophical Transactions of the Royal Society of London* B 318, 603-17.
Kelly, R.	1983	Hunter-gatherer mobility strategies, *Journal of Anthropological Research* 39, 277-306.
Koenigswald, W. von	1992	Various aspects of migrations in terrestrial mammals in relation to Pleistocene faunas of central Europe. In: W. von Koenigswald and L. Werdelin (eds), Mammalian migration and dispersal events in the European Quaternary, *Courier Forschungsinstitut Senckenberg* 153, 39-47.
Kolfschoten, T. van	1990	The evolution of the mammal fauna in the Netherlands and the middle Rhine Area (Western Germany) during the late Middle Pleistocene, *Mededelingen Rijks Geologische Dienst* 43(3), 1-69.
	1992	Aspects of the migration of mammals to northwestern Europe during the Pleistocene, in particular the reimmigration of *Arvicola terrestris*. In: W. von Koenigswald and L. Werdelin (eds), Mammalian migration and dispersal events in the European Quaternary, *Courier Forschungsinstitut Senckenberg* 153, 213-20.
Lebel, S.	1992	Mobilité des hominides et systemes d'exploitation des resources lithiques au paléolithique ancien: La Caune de l'Arago (France), *Canadian Journal of Archaeology* 16, 48-69.

Ljubin, V., G. Bosinski	this volume	The earliest occupation of the Caucasus region.
Lumley, H. de	1988	La stratigraphie du remplissage de la grotte du Vallonet. *L'Anthropologie* 92: 407-28.
Mania, D.,	this volume	The earliest occupation of Europe: the Elbe-Saale region (Germany).
Morell, V.	1994	Did early humans reach Siberia 500,000 years ago?, *Science* 263, 611-2.
Mussi, M.,	this volume	The earliest occupation of Europe: Italy.
Oakley, K.P.	1969	*Frameworks for dating fossil man.* London: Weidenfeld and Nicolson.
Peretto, C.	1991	Les gisements d'Isernia la Pineta (Molise, Italie). In: E. Bonifay and B. Vandermeersch (eds), *Les premiers Européens*, 161-168. Paris: CTHS
	1992	*I Primi Abitanti della Valle Padana: Monte Poggiolo Nel Quadro delle Conoscenze Europee.* Milano: Jaca Book.
Pisias, N.G., T.C. Moore	1981	The evolution of Pleistocene climate: a time series approach, *Earth and Planetary Science Letters* 52, 450-8.
Praslov, N.D.,	this volume	The earliest occupation of the Russian Plane: a short note.
Prentice, M.L., G.H. Denton	1988	The deep-sea oxygen record, the global ice sheet system and hominid evolution. In: F.E. Grine (ed.) *Evolutionary history of the "robust" australopithecines*, 383-403, New York: Aldine de Gruyter.
Ranov, V.A.	1991	Les sites très anciens de l'age de la pierre en URSS. In: E. Bonifay and B. Vandermeersch (eds) *Les premiers Européens*, 209-16. Paris, CTHS.
Raposo, L., M. Santonja	this volume	The earliest occupation of Europe: the Iberian Peninsula.
Raynal, J.-P., L. Magoga, F.-Z. Sbihi-Alaoui, D. Geraads	this volume	The earliest occupation of Atlantic Morocco: the Casablanca evidence.
Roberts, M.B., C.S. Gamble, D.R. Bridgland	this volume	The earliest occupation of Europe: the British Isles.
Roebroeks, W., T. van Kolfschoten	1994	The earliest occupation of Europe: a short chronology, *Antiquity* 68, 489-503.
	this volume	The earliest occupation of Europe: a reappraisal of artefactual and chronological evidence.
Roebroeks, W., N.J. Conard, T. van Kolfschoten	1992	Dense forests, cold steppes, and the Palaeolithic settlement of northern Europe, *Current Anthropology* 33, 551-86.
Ruddiman, W.F., M.E. Raymo	1988	Northern hemisphere climate regimes during the past 3Ma: possible tectonic connections, *Philosophical Transactions of the Royal Society of London* B 318, 1-20.

Ruddiman, W.F.,
   M. Raymo,
   A. McIntyre   1986   Mayuyama 41,000-year cycles: North Atlantic Ocean and northern hemisphere ice sheets,
                                        Earth and Planetary Science Letters 80, 117-29.

Santonja, M.,
   P. Villa   1990   The lower palaeolithic of Spain and Portugal, *Journal of World Prehistory* 4, 45-94.

Shackleton, N.J.   1987   Oxygen isotopes, ice volume and sea level, *Quaternary Science Reviews* 6, 183-90.

Shackleton, N.J.,
   N.D. Opdyke   1973   Oxygen isotope and palaeomagnetic stratigraphy of equatorial Pacific core V28-238,
                                        Quaternary Research 3, 39-55.

Shackleton, N.J.,
   J. Imbrie,
   N.G. Pisias   1988   The evolution of oceanic oxygen-isotope variability in the north Atlantic over the past
                                        three million years, *Philosophical Transactions of the Royal Society of London* B 318,
                                        679-88.

Soffer, O.   1989   The Middle to Upper Palaeolithic transition on the Russian Plain. In: P. Mellars and
                                        C. Stringer (eds), *The Human Revolution: behavioural and biological perspectives on the
                                        origins of modern humans*, 714-42, Edinburgh: Edinburgh University Press.

Stringer, C.,
   C. Gamble   1993   *In search of the Neanderthals: solving the puzzle of human origins*. London: Thames and
                                        Hudson.

Suc, J-P.,
   W.H. Zagwijn   1983   Plio-Pleistocene correlations between the northwestern mediterranean region and north-
                                        western Europe according to recent biostratigraphic and palaeoclimatic data, *Boreas* 12,
                                        153-66.

Tchernov, E.   1992   Dispersal, a suggestion for a common usage of this term. In: W. von Koenigswald and
                                        L. Werdelin (eds), Mammalian migration and dispersal events in the European
                                        Quaternary, *Courier Forschungsinstitut Senckenberg* 153, 21-25.

Tuffreau, A.   1987   *Le Paléolithique inférieur et moyen du Nord de la France (Nord, Pas-de-Calais,
                                        Picardie) dans son cadre stratigraphique.* Thèse Doct. État Univ. Sci. Techni. Lille
                                        Flandres Artois.

                                1990   Le Paléolithique moyen récent dans le nord de la France. In: Paléolithique moyen récent
                                        et Paléolithique supérieur ancien en Europe. Colloque international Nemours (mai 1988).
                                        Mémoire Musée Préhistoire Ile-de-France 3, 159-65.

Tuffreau, A.,
   P. Antoine   this   The earliest occupation of Europe: Continental Northwestern Europe.
                                volume

Turner, A.   1992   Large canivores and earliest European hominids: changing determinants of resource
                                        availability during the Lower and Middle Pleistocene, *Journal of Human Evolution* 22,
                                        109-26.

Turner, C.   1970   The Middle Pleistocene deposits at Marks Tey, Essex, *Philosophical Transactions of the
                                        Royal Society of London* B 257, 373-440.

Turner, E.   1991   Pleistocene stratigraphy and vertebrate faunas from the Neuwied basin region of western
                                        Germany, *Cranium* 8, 21-34.

Tzedakis, P.C.   1993   Long-term tree populations in northwest Greece through multiple Quaternary climatic
                                        cycles, *Nature* 364, 437-40.

Valoch, K.   1991   Les premiers peuplements en Moravie (Tchécoslovaquie). In: E. Bonifay and B. Vander-
                                        meersch (eds) *Les premiers Européens*, 189-94, Paris: CTHS.

Vrba, E.S.	1988	Late Pliocene climatic events and hominid evolution. In: F.E. Grine (ed.), *Evolutionary History of the "Robust" Australopithecines*, 405-426, New York: Aldine de Gruyter.
Vrba, E.S., G.H. Denton, M.L. Prentice	1989	Climatic influences on early hominid behavior, *Ossa* 14, 127-156.
White, T.D., G. Suwa, B. Asfaw	1994	Australopithecus ramidus, a new species of early hominid from Aramis, Ethiopia, *Nature* 371, 306- 12.
Wymer, J.J.	1985	*Lower Palaeolithic Sites in East Anglia*. Norwich: Geo Books.
Zagwijn, W.H.	1992a	Migration of Vegetation during the Quaternary in Europe. In: W. von Koenigswald and L. Werdelin (eds), Mammalian migration and dispersal events in the European Quaternary, *Courier Forschungsinstitut Senckenberg* 153, 9-20.
	1992b	The beginning of the ice age in Europe and its major subdivisions, *Quaternary Science Reviews* 11, 583-91.
Zeuner, F.E.	1958	*Dating the Past*. London: Methuen.
	1959	*The Pleistocene period*. London: Hutchinson.

Clive S. Gamble
Department of Archaeology
University of Southampton
SO9 5NH Southampton
United Kingdom

Wil Roebroeks
Thijs van Kolfschoten

17   The earliest occupation of Europe:
a reappraisal of artefactual and chronological evidence

A reappraisal of the artefactual and chronological evidence for the earliest occupation of Europe – with proper attention to its limitations and its reliability – makes for a short chronology. The first solid traces of hominid activities in this part of the world are around 500,000 years old.

1.   Introduction

Establishing the earliest documented evidence for human occupation has always involved controversy, usually centred around the *artefactual character* of assemblages and/or their *chronological position*. Examples of such controversial cases are Brixham cave, the eolith-problem, Calico Hills, the KBS-tuff controversy and, very recently, the age of the earliest hominid remains from Java (Swisher *et al.* 1994). Our science thrives on such disagreements; discussions (ideally) test the strength of data and hypotheses and thus provide us with constant fresh and solid ground to build our archaeological theories.

One of the reasons to plan a workshop on 'The Earliest Occupation of Pleistocene Europe' was the virtual absence of scientific discussions on this subject. Despite the large number of meetings devoted to Europe's first traces of settlement (e.g. Andernach 1988: "Die erste Besiedlung Europas"; Paris 1989: "Les premiers peuplements humains de l'Europe" [Bonifay and Vandermeersch 1991]; Milan 1990:; "The Earliest Inhabitants of Europe") the dates given to the first 'Europeans' vary enormously, depending on the book or the journal one opens. On the 'very old' side, Bonifay and Vandermeersch (1991) present a number of sites allegedly dating from earlier parts of the Early Pleistocene, around two million years ago (*cf.* Ackerman 1989; Delson 1989). An age of about one million years is considered a good estimate for the first occupation of Europe by most workers (*cf.* Rolland 1992), referring to sites such as Le Vallonet in France (De Lumley *et al.* 1988) and Kärlich A in Germany (Würges 1986; 1991; Bosinski, this volume). In contrast to these long chronologies we demonstrate in this paper that Europe's earliest human traces are considerably younger, dating from well into the Middle Pleistocene. We have come to this conclusion while trying to give a synthesis of the evidence presented in pre-circulated papers by attendants of the Tautavel-meeting and data collected in our own research. Our paper begins with a short review of the artefactual character of assemblages and the chronological framework of the Quaternary, focussing on how sites are put in a chronological succession (section 2). In section 3 we survey the biostratigraphical position of important mammalian assemblages (from both archaeological and non-archaeological sites), while section 4 reviews early sites in central and northwestern Europe. We then turn to evidence from other parts of Europe and close with brief discussion of the implications.

2.   The earliest occupation of Europe: artefacts and chronology

2.1.   EVALUATING THE ARTEFACTUAL CHARACTER OF ASSEMBLAGES

One century ago, Palaeolithic archaeologists were involved in a fierce debate over the alleged existence of Tertiary humans in Europe. *Eolithophiles*, both on the continent and in Britain, presented thousands of flints from Tertiary deposits, that in their opinion were humanly worked implements. The long lasting debate over the character of 'eoliths' assemblages produced a vast literature on the subject, summarised in popular handbooks from those days, like Sollas *Ancient hunters and their modern representatives* (1911), Obermaier's *Der Mensch der Vorzeit* (1912) and Boule's *Les Hommes Fossiles* (1921). This debate led to very detailed field observations and experiments and so created a vast body of knowledge concerning the variety of artefact-like forms produced by various natural processes. The crux of the matter is elegantly summarized by Warren (1920:250):

"What is important, however, is the fact that such phenomena as the flaking of flints and occasional bulbs and also edge-knapping are produced by causes entirely apart from direct human effort. The likeness between the flaking produced by Nature and that produced by human agencies is sufficient to shift any burden of proof upon those who maintain the human origin of the stones; and this must not be done by a careful selection of picked specimens, but by a survey of the whole group" (Warren 1920: 250).

The artefactual nature of 'primitive' assemblages has been an omnipresent issue ever since. In 1958 for instance, J. Desmond Clark's study of natural fractures of pebbles showed very convincingly (in the African context of 'Kafuan' industries in river valleys) that nature can make 'pebble tools': they are produced by a sharp 'follow through' blow, very unlikely under water, but possibly the result of a rock falling from above on to a wedged pebble (Clark 1958). These fractures can simulate artificial fracture to such a remarkable degree, that these specimens would not be out of place in any "Pebble Culture" context. His studies once again stress that one cannot build a strong argument for early occupation on the basis of pieces with only a few negatives, selected out of river-laid deposits. In fact, any analysis of early sites must take into account the whole range of natural conditions at the site that could produce artefact-like forms, as well as the geological setting of the find-spot (see Raynal *et al.*, this volume, for a good example of such an approach).

It is for these reasons that for instance Tuffreau (1987) and Tuffreau and Antoine (this volume) do not accept the Ferme de Grâce (Somme) terrace material as evidence for Early Pleistocene occupation of northern France (*contra* Bourdier *et al.* 1974), or that Santonja and Villa (1990) and Raposo and Santonja (this volume) consider isolated pieces collected from Iberian river terraces as too rare and undiagnostic to prove human settlement in the Early Pleistocene, while Mania (this volume) has serious doubts about the German *Schotter-Paläolithikum* (gravel-palaeolithic).

In section 4 we evaluate some important early sites by the issues in the eolith debate. It is of course necessary to have a good knowledge of the assemblages and their context, either by a detailed site-publication or by first-hand knowledge. Unfortunately, only a small number of 'early' sites have been published in such a detail that evaluation of interpretations concerning the artefactual character of 'primitive' assemblages is possible. We start our review therefore with the evidence from central and northwestern Europe, where we have first-hand knowledge of the relevant assemblages. The findings from that area are confronted with those from other areas in section 5.

2.2.   THE CHRONOLOGICAL FRAMEWORK

The classical subdivision of the Pleistocene period is by the glacial-interglacial scheme, based on the extensions of glaciers in the Alpine area and in northern Europe. Four different extensions were recorded in the Alpine area (Günz, Mindel, Riss and Würm), and in northern Europe only three (Elster, Saale and Weichsel). Glacigenic deposits were linked with cold intervals in which ice-sheets formed,

separated from each other by warm-temperate intervals. Detailed investigations of pollen-bearing deposits in northwestern Europe yielded a rather complete record of the complex history of the vegetation in that area. Palaeobotanical data was transformed into palaeoclimatic information, making a terrestrial chronostratigraphical subdivision of the Pleistocene (cf. Fig. 1 and Zagwijn 1985), a scheme that has been the standard for northwestern Europe.

Preliminary results of recent investigations in an open lignite mine at Schöningen near Helmstedt (Germany) and in the Don-Basin (Russia) indicate, however, that the figure 1 subdivision is incomplete. The Pleistocene sediments exposed in the Schöningen quarry date from the Elsterian to the Holocene and are rich in palaeobotanical, malacological and palaeontological information, while Middle Pleistocene artefacts are present too (cf. Thieme *et al.* 1993). Studies of the Middle Pleistocene sequences indicate that there were at least three phases with a distinct, well developed interglacial vegetation between the Elsterian and the Saalian till. It is however not clear yet whether the two older warm-temperate periods there were separated from each other by a distinct cold (glacial) phase. Theoretically they might have been separated by an important but relatively short cooler fluctuation, more or less comparable to the stronger intra-Eemian fluctuations recently reported by the GRIP-members (GRIP 1993), or to the intra-Stage 7 'cold' interval, sub-Stage 7b (cf. Andrews 1983).

Long sequences in the Don Basin show at least five glacial/interglacial cycles in the time span between the Brunhes/Matuyama boundary and the Oka (= Elsterian) glaciation. Two ice-sheet extensions earlier than the Elsterian could be recorded in the sections. The most important ice-sheet there was that of the Don Glaciation, covering the Don Basin much further south than the ice-caps of the Oka-Elster, the Dnjepr-Saale and the Valdai-Weichsel. Two disctinct interglacial intervals and one cold phase separate the Don Glacial from the Oka Glacial phase. Correlation between the Don Basin and northwestern Europe, mainly on the base of mammal fauna-associations, indicates that the northwestern standard subdivision is incomplete for the lower part of the Middle Pleistocene, i.e. in the first half of the "Cromerian Complex". The incompleteness of the standard continental subdivision is also apparent when comparing it with the oxygen isotope record, which counts 9 interglacial and 9 glacial phases within the Brunhes Epoch.

The oxygen isotope record, the most detailed subdivision of the Quaternary sofar, is regarded as *the* timescale one should try to refer to. It is a global record, thought to reflect changes in the total amount of ice the world over, as there is remarkably little variation among cores taken from different areas. It is also a rather continuous record,

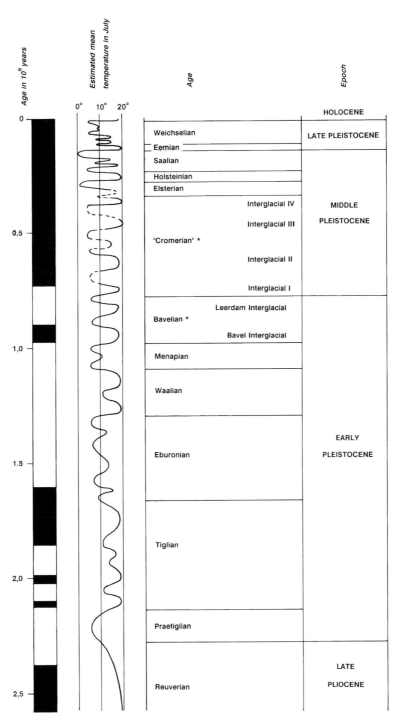

* Several glacials and interglacials within one Age

Fig. 1. Climate curve for the Quaternary in the Netherlands (after Zagwijn 1985). Age in million years. Temperature in degrees C, estimated mean for July. * includes several glacials and interglacials.

providing an arguably complete survey of the entire Quaternary. And it is a kind of 'Esperanto' record, easy to 'understand' for workers from various parts of the world, not bothered by the details and intricacies of the various *regional* subdivisions such as the northwestern European one mentioned above. This 'user-friendliness' is certainly a very important factor in the increased usage of the deep-sea record for correlation-purposes. We must however not forget that correlation to the oxygen isotope stages is often mainly based on very simple 'counting' procedures, on the results of absolute dating methods and on (often implicit) assumptions, for example that the maximum inland-ice extension corresponds to the highest O^{18}-values. Unfortunately, terrestrial sections are dominated by *gaps*. Absolute dates, in many cases contradictory and inaccurate, should not be the only base for a chronological correlation. Using the maximum ice-extension for land-sea correlations poses problems as soon as one exchanges the narrow 'national' perspective for a broader 'European' one: the southernmost extension in Great Britain was the Anglian (= Elsterian), in the Netherlands it was the Saalian ice-cap, and in the Don Basin it was the Don glaciation! These problems can lead to different correlations between the continental subdivision and the oxygen isotope record (see the two options presented in Fig. 2).

Although not denying the enormous advantages of the deep sea record over the terrestrial climatic data we prefer the continental subdivision of the Quaternary (Fig. 1) as the basic framework for correlation over the oxygen isotope record as long as there are no reliable correlation methods (in other words: as long as the absolute dating methods are contradictory and inaccurate). Uncritical use of the deep sea stages creates a pseudo-certainty that hides the basic stratigraphical problems inherent in all kinds of terrestrial correlations.

3.   The chronology of Quaternary mammalian fossil assemblages

The use of palaeobotanical evidence for long distance correlation to the standard terrestrial subdivisions is hampered by the absence of evolutionary trends in plants and by the inter-regional variations in characters of vegetation. Mammalian fossils are alternative important biostratigraphic indicators. Their use in dating and correlating deposits is based on the fact that most of the mammals have an extensive distribution area and that a number show a rapid evolution and/or migratory shifts within the Quaternary (cf. Lister 1992). The composition of the mammalian fauna has changed relatively fast during the Quaternary due to the processes of evolution, extinction and migration of species; a number of mammal biozonations have been established by different authors. Some of these

are based on the smaller mammal fauna, others on the larger or on both. However, most of these zonations have not been defined according to the guide for stratigraphic nomenclature published by Hedberg (1976) and the terminology used by some authors is furthermore extremely confusing (cf. Van Kolfschoten 1990).

Many palaeontologists work with the biostratigraphical subdivision of the Quaternary based on the Arvicolidae succession, as proposed by Fejfar and Heinrich (1981), which is in fact a modification of the Hungarian smaller mammal zonation established by Kretzoi (see e.g. Kretzoi, 1965; Kretzoi and Pécsi, 1979; Van der Meulen, 1973). Fejfar and Heinrich (1981) established three well defined biozones (stages in their terminology) for the Pleistocene: Villányian, Biharian and Toringian. A biozonation on the basis of changes in the larger mammal fauna was constructed by Italian palaeontologists (Azzaroli *et al.* 1988). Their subdivision of Villafranchian and Galerian faunas is used in large parts of Europe and Asia despite the fact that the boundary between both biozones is poorly defined, as will be discussed below.

3.1.   THE SMALLER MAMMALS: BIHARIAN - TORINGIAN

Biharian faunas differ from the preceeding Villányian faunas by the occurrence of *Microtus*. The Villányian faunas can be recognised by the dominance of *Mimomys*, the Biharian faunas by the co-occurrence of *Microtus* and *Mimomys*, and the Toringian "Stage" by *Arvicola - Microtus* assemblages. The Biharian is divided into two "sub-stages": the Early Biharian with *Microtus (Allophaiomys)* and the Late Biharian with *Microtus (Microtus)*.

The transition from the Villányian to the Biharian in the Early Pleistocene corresponds more or less with the Tiglian/Eburonian transition. Faunas such as Tegelen (the Netherlands) belong to the Villányian, while the Early Biharian comprises faunas such as Le Vallonet (France), Monte Peglia (Italy) and Betfia 2 (Romania).

The transition of *Microtus (Allophaiomys)* to *Microtus (Microtus)*, marking the transition from the Early to the Late Biharian, dates to the early part of the Bavelian complex, roughly correlated to the Jaramillo.

Faunas such as West Runton (Great Britain), Stránská Skála, Prezletice (Czechia), Tarkö (Layer 16) (Hungary), Ilynka I-II and Ilynka IV (Russia) belong to the Late Biharian. The genus *Mimomys* is represented by only one species, the large *Mimomys savini*, in most of these faunas. A second *Mimomys*, a smaller form often referred to *Mimomys (Cseria) pusillus*, occurs only in the faunas Kärlich C and E (Germany) and in Ilynka IV and Ilynka I-II. The occurrence or absence of the smaller *Mimomys* is probably a stratigraphical marker, which can be used to subdivide the Late Biharian faunas into an older group with,

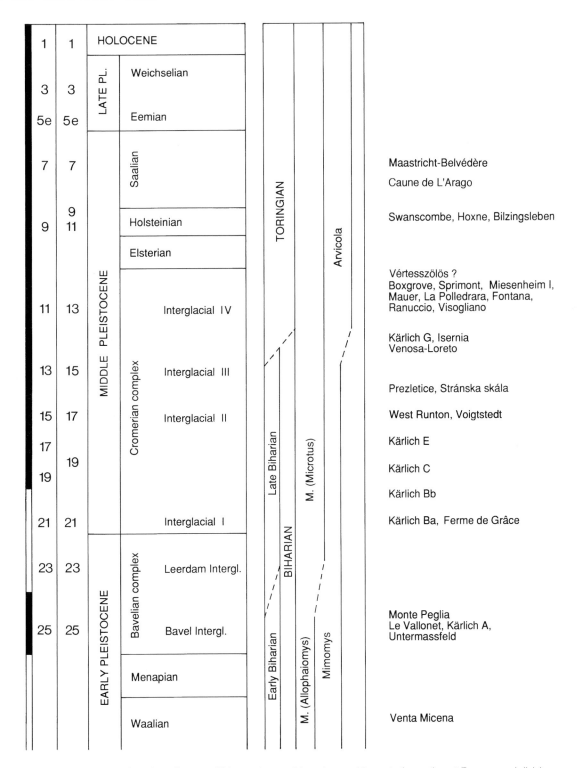

Fig. 2. Tentative correlation of small mammal biozonations and faunal assemblages to the northwest European subdivision of the Quaternary and to various oxygen isotope stages.

and a younger group without the smaller *Mimomys*. The faunas Kärlich C and E date from the Brunhes Epoch which indicates that the the smaller *Mimomys* disappeared later than the Brunhes/Matuyama boundary.

An extensive study of the smaller mammal faunas from the Don Basin resulted in a subdivision of the Late Biharian faunas on the basis of evolutionary trends in the M_1 of lagurines ((*Prolagurus* and *Lagurus*) and the M_1 of *Microtus (Terricola) (= Microtys [Pitymys])* (Kasantseva 1987). A correlation between the western and central European Late Biharian faunas and faunas from the Don Basin is hampered by the mainly easteuropean distribution of lagurines. Furthermore, our knowledge of the different *Microtus*-morphotypes present in the western and central European faunas is insufficient. One can only say that the Late Biharian covers the later part of the Bavelian complex and most of the Cromerian complex, a time span with at least five glacial/interglacial cycles. The faunas with two *Mimomys* species date from the earlier part of that time span, the faunas with only *Mimomys savini* from the later part.

A very important stratigraphical marker is the transition of *Mimomys savini* to *Arvicola terrestris*, which corresponds to the Biharian-Toringian boundary, in the second half of the Cromerian complex (Van Kolfschoten 1990; Von Koenigswald and Van Kolfschoten, in press). Since the most primitive representative of the genus *Arvicola*, *Arvicola t. cantiana* (often cited as e.g. *Arvicola cantiana* or *Arvicola mosbachensis*), is known from Cromerian Interglacial IV deposits (Van Kolfschoten 1990), the transition took place before Interglacial IV of the Cromerian Complex. *Arvicola* appears for the first time in the Kärlich section in the fauna from Kärlich G. The heavy-mineral association of the Kärlich G deposits and the mammal fauna indicate a Cromerian Interglacial III or a (beginning of) Cromerian Interglacial IV age (Van Kolfschoten and Turner, in press; Von Koenigswald and Van Kolfschoten, in press). The *Mimomys-Arvicola* transition has been documented in western (Chaline 1986), central (Fejfar and Heinrich 1981) and eastern Europe (Terzea, in press). In northwestern Europe the transition took place in the second half of the Cromerian-complex. This seems to have been the case in other areas too, as for instance documented by the occurrence of *Arvicola terrestris* before the Elsterian in Central Europe (Terzea, in press) and the occurrence of very advanced *Mimomys savini* in faunas from the Don Basin, dated to second interglacial before the Oka-Elsterian glaciation (Kasantseva 1987). It is to be expected that there was an asynchronicity within the regional transition from *Mimomys* to *Arvicola*, but such transgressions fall outside the chronological resolution of our present dating methods for this time-range.

A problem in this respect is the age of the *Arvicola*-fauna from Isernia (Italy), supposed to be late Early Pleistocene on the basis of radiometric dates for crystals from the site matrix and some palaeomagnetic data (Coltorti *et al.* 1981, McPherron and Schmidt 1983). Isernia has yielded fossil remains of *Arvicola terrestris cantiana* (assigned to the junior synonym *Arvicola mosbachensis* by Sala 1983; Coltorti *et al.* 1982). A study of the material, including that sampled in the period after 1982, allowed the second author to characterize the finds of Isernia as a primitive population of the genus *Arvicola*. Only 80% of the molars (only a few are juvenile) are rootless, whereas 20% show indications for root formation, but are still rootless. The fauna with *Arvicola*, *Elephas (P.) antiquus*, *Stephanorinus hundsheimensis* and without *Mimomys savini*, *Mimomys pusillus* and *Microtus (Allophaiomys)* sp. suggests a Middle Pleistocene age, as it is comparable to central European faunas as Mosbach and Mauer (cf. Sala and Fortelius 1993).

One could accept a late Early Pleistocene age for Isernia only by suggesting an earlier occurrence of *Arvicola* in Italy, in a more or less isolated area of Europe. This is not a plausible argument, however, as there are no indications of a barrier isolating the mammalian faunas in Italy from those of central and western Europe during the Pleistocene. On the contrary, the abundant similarities in the composition of the Early, Middle and Late Pleistocene faunas of Italy and eastern, central and western Europe show a general and almost continuous faunal exchange between these areas during the Quaternary (Von Koenigswald and Van Kolfschoten, in press).

This is a context in which in our opinion the 'absolute' dates for the site cannot be taken at face value, and the site cannot be seen as yielding unambiguous evidence for occupation of Europe at the very end of the Early Pleistocene. A reevaluation of the total dating evidence is necessary, and in the meantime we seriously question the significance of the palaeomagnetic and radiometric dates for the Isernia site.

Toringian faunas can be divided into two groups: an older one with *Arvicola terrestris cantiana* and so-called relict species (such as *Talpa minor*, *Trogontherium cuvieri*) and a younger group with the more evolved *Arvicola terrestris* ssp. A and B, co-occuring with a modern smaller mammal fauna (see Van Kolfschoten, 1990). The first group comprises faunas such as Miesenheim I, Kärlich G, Mauer (Germany), Boxgrove, Westbury-sub-Mendip (Great Britain), Sprimont (Belle Roche) (Belgium), Tarkö (Hungary) with *Arvicola terrestris cantiana* together with *Sorex (Drepanosorex)* sp. and *Pliomys episcopalis* and a number of faunas e.g. Swanscombe (Great Britain), Bilzingsleben (Germany) younger in age and without *Sorex (Drepanosorex)* and *Pliomys episcopalis*.

Late Toringian faunas can be recognized by evolutionary changes in the *Arvicola* molars. Since the early Saalian thinning of the convex sides of the dentine triangles has resulted in changes in the relative thickness of the enamel band of the *Arvicola* molars. This development can be used for stratigraphical correlations of younger, i.e. post-"Holsteinian" faunas, such as those from Caune de l'Arago (Desclaux 1992a; 1992b), Maastricht-Belvédère and Weimar-Ehringsdorf (cf. Van Kolfschoten 1990).

3.2.   THE LARGER MAMMALS: VILLAFRANCHIAN - GALERIAN

The widely used Italian biochronology, with a subdivision in Villafranchian and Galerian faunas, is mainly based on changes in the larger mammal fauna. The Villafranchian, starting about 3 million years ago, covers part of the Pliocene and the Early Pleistocene. It has been subdivided into an early, a middle and a late phase, a subdivison refined by Azzaroli (1977), who divided the Villafranchian faunas into six more or less well-defined faunal units. The beginning of the Villafranchian itself, of some of its units and its end are characterized by pronounced dispersal events (Azzaroli *et al.*, 1988; Sala *et al.* 1992). Azzaroli *et al.* (1988) state that the Villafranchian-Galerian transition (the end-Villafranchian event, 1.0-0.9 Myr BP) saw a complete faunal turnover, with massive extinctions and new, previously unknown adaptations. Late Villafranchian taxa such as *Eucladoceros, Dama nestii, Leptobos etruscus, Sus strozzii* and *Archidiskodon meridionalis* became extinct whereas many taxa (*Megaceros, Soergelia* sp., *Praeovibos priscus, Bison schoetensacki, Equus süssenbornensis, Ursus deningeri*) appear during the Early Galerian.

The transition of the late Villafranchian to the Galerian did not take place at once. According to Azzaroli *et al.* (1988) the transitional phase was of (geologically) short duration because only a few sites have 'naturally mixed' assemblages – an assumption partially based on the inferred Early Pleistocene age of Isernia. They assign a late Matuyama age to the Isernia fauna, and hence infer that faunas from normally magnetized deposits (such as the faunas from West Runton and Voigtstedt) have to be correlated with the Jaramillo event. In such a scenario the Villafranchian/Galerian faunal shift indeed seems both very pronounced and relatively abrupt. In our opinion the faunas from Isernia, West Runton and Voigtstedt are of Middle Pleistocene age, which means that the faunal turnover could have taken place more gradually. For us the 'faunal watershed' is simply the result of a giant temporal collapse, caused by an accumulation of correlation errors.

This interpretation is confirmed by the fauna from Venta Micena, dated at around 1.2 Myr BP, yet already containing several Galerian immigrants (*Megaloceros, Praeovibos, Soergelia* and *Bison*) (Agusti *et al.*, 1987). The end-Villafranchian 'event' in the sense of e.g. Azzaroli *et al.* (1988) therefore probably has a long stratigraphical range, which necessitates a re-definition of the late Villafranchian-Galerian boundary. At the current state of knowledge the terms late Villafranchian or Galerian are of little biostratigraphical value.

4.   The earliest occupation of central and northwestern Europe

4.1.   THE EARLY PLEISTOCENE

The pseudo-artefact problem is especially apparent in some central European Early Pleistocene sites where various (amateur-) archaeologists sampled huge amounts of gravels and came up with primitive looking 'choppers' and 'chopping-tools'. A very good example is the Beroun site, near Prague (Fridrich 1991), where about 80 artefacts were collected from the top of Early Pleistocene river gravels, exposed over an area of about 2000 m^2. Two overlying levels yielded 10 more 'items of industry'. The 80 rolled 'artefacts', mostly 'side-choppers' with only a few negatives, were collected from the gravel surface 'after rain'. According to Fridrich (1991:11), the assemblage "includes choppers, bifaces, proto-bifaces, picks, cleavers, polyhedrons, subspheroids, representing Acheulean s.l., comparable to the African finds ... The age of the set is more than 1.5 million years, serving thus as an evidence that both Europe and Africa were settled approximately in the same time by people with analogous cultures". The finds, both those published and those displayed in the Prague National Museum, are in the range of what can be collected from natural gravel deposits; they are not acceptable evidence of Early Pleistocene occupation (see Kozlowski 1992 for a comparable interpretation).

The same applies in our opinion to the Musov and Ivan assemblages, described by Valoch (1991 and this volume). Both sites, approximately 40 km south of Brno, were visited by an amateur-archaeologist, who collected hundreds of 'choppers' and 'chopping-tools' from reworked Miocene deposits, present on top of Early or early Middle Pleistocene deposits. As in Beroun, we are dealing with a selection from thousands and thousands of non-modified pebbles. The 'artefacts' have in general only a few irregular negatives, and almost all 'chopping-tools' display completely blunted 'working edges'.

Comparable arguments apply to the other Early Pleistocene sites in Moravia (Brno-Cernovice, with one good flake though, not recovered *in situ*, and Brno-Cernovice Kopec). A nice polyeder from Mladec cave, found in a calcite layer covering the Early Pleistocene sediments there, has no chronological context.

Early Pleistocene artefacts from the river deposits exposed in the Kärlich section (Kärlich A) were found and published by Würges (1986) and Bosinski (this volume). Three 'pebble tools' were flaked on one surface only. The 'best' piece is a pebble, broken along a quartz vein, with two negatives. The pieces fall in the range of naturally produced 'artefacts' (cf. Clark 1958) and they were not recovered in a controlled situation; at best they are to be treated as typical examples of *incertofacts*, a category of pieces of which the artificial character can neither be established with certainty nor excluded. Such pieces (*possibiliths* would also be a good term!) can of course never be used as a solid basis for archaeological theories. The same applies to the trachytic tuff core from Kärlich Ba, recovered outside stratigraphical context (Vollbrecht 1992).

4.2.   THE MIDDLE PLEISTOCENE

Most archaeology textbooks mention the Czech site of Prezletice as one of the earliest sites in Europe. Palaeomagnetic and faunal studies (a fauna with *Mimomys*) have placed it in the beginning of the Middle Pleistocene. The find of what was once thought to be a human molar (now a *Ursus* sp. molar, see Fridrich 1989:29) initiated archaeological excavations (1969-1985) that focused on sediments deposited near an ancient lake at the foot of a lydite massif. The excavation yielded 4 horizons bearing "artefacts" produced out of locally occurring lydite debris. Fridrich (1991, passim) himself stressed that it was very difficult to differentiate between

> "flaking and natural fracturing of raw material in lydite débris.... There is complete lack of flakes or, on the contrary, of primitive cores... treatment of raw material, manufacturing of half-products and their waste fracturing occurred along hidden cleavages in raw material. There are not typical traces after working, namely bulbus, therefore the possibility to recognise and differentiate between artificial working and natural fracturing is extremely low" (Fridrich 1989:35).

Nevertheless, the drawings in Fridrich (1989) display many negatives of flaking and retouch on the 'proto-bifaces', 'picks' and other artefacts recognised among the lydite debris. There is a big discrepancy between the drawings and the photos of the objects. Likewise, the pieces on display in the Prague National Museum in our opinion do not show any convincing traces of human interference.[1]

The site of Stránská skála I, near Brno, yielded a Late Biharian fauna comparable to Prezletice. In 1968 Valoch described some "flakes of hornstone suggestive of human workmanship" recovered from early Middle Pleistocene scree-deposits in the 1910-1945 excavations. He thought the

site was problematic because "Weathered nodules, often naturally cracked and broken, occur in the debris in considerable quantity, making it difficult to identify those chips that could have been flaked and utilised by man" (Musil and Valoch 1968:538; also Valoch 1972). Since then new palaeontological fieldwork has yielded more finds, which have led Valoch to give up his doubts about the artificial character of the stone assemblage selected from the slope deposits and from within two small caves in the Stránská skála exposure (see e.g. Valoch 1987). Three dozen artefacts have been identified by him. These hornstone fragments display no clear traces of human workmanship: there are virtually no bulbs (only three observed), no clear negatives and no ripples. While visiting the site with Dr Valoch the first author could pick up hornstone fragments from the scree-section, which is full of hornstone debris; one wonders what the ratio between 'discarded' and 'accepted' pieces within this deposit actually was.

On these grounds, arguments concerning context and attributes of the finds, the site cannot be considered as proof for an early Middle Pleistocene occupation of Moravia. We therefore support Valoch's early doubts concerning the artefactual character of the assemblage[2]. The site certainly needs another season of fieldwork, this time focused on the archaeological agenda.

The first good evidence from this part of central Europe comes from Sedlesovice near Znojmo, where a quartz artefact was discovered in a loess profile, in the fossil soil PK VI ('Holstein'; see Valoch 1984). The first finds from Poland (Trzebnica) are from around this time horizon too (Burdukiewicz and Winnicki 1988; 1989; also Kozlowski 1992).

For the western part of central Europe, Bosinski (this volume) reports Würges (1986) claims for earlier finds from the top of the Kärlich Mosel gravels (Kärlich Bb). Over an area of 40 × 40 m Würges collected a set of 8 quartzite pieces, some from the top of the gravel deposits, some from the base of the gravels, having slid downslope. Some of the pieces are heavily rounded, others less so. It took Würges more than one year to assemble this set (pers. comm. 1993), very clearly a selection of pieces, whose number is infinite-simally small compared to the whole. The 'primitive' morphology of the pieces and their context lead us to doubt the artefactual character of these, and to interpret them in the same way as Tuffreau did with Ferme de Grâce material.

In our opinion western central Europe has its earliest solid evidence for human occupation around the Cromer IV Interglacial (OIS 11 to 13?), in the form of the finds from Kärlich G, the primary-context Miesenheim I site and the Mauer mandible, all associated with *Arvicola terrestris cantiana* faunas (see Bosinski, this volume). From that time period onwards there are more primary context sites in central Europe, both from temperate and from colder, dryer settings (see Bosinski, this volume; Roebroeks *et al.* 1992).

In the northwest region the earliest solid traces of occupation are more or less contemporaneous with the Miesenheim I site, for example the well preserved find scatters at Boxgrove in southern England (Roberts 1986; 1990; Roberts *et al.*, this volume) and the earliest sites in the Somme valley of northern France (Tuffreau 1987; Tuffreau and Antoine, this volume). The Boxgrove site is tentatively correlated to OIS 13 (Roberts *et al.*, this volume).

Independent of their correlations to the deep-sea record the earliest sites from both central and northwest Europe fall in the *Arvicola terrestris cantiana* range. This also applies to the fauna from the La Belle Roche site at Sprimont (Belgium) (Tuffreau and Antoine, this volume). From that period onwards, there is a large number of well documented primary-context sites in the northwest-central region, with conjoining knapping debris preserved in fine-grained fluvial and aeolian deposits (cf. the contributions to this volume by Bosinski, Mania, Roberts *et al.*, Tuffreau and Antoine, and Roebroeks *et al.* 1992).

5.   Other regions, comparable results?

Like those in the northern regions, Iberian river terraces have yielded isolated pieces, whose human manufacture or precise age have been doubted by various researchers (see above, and Raposo 1985; Santonja and Villa 1990; Raposo and Santonja, this volume). Claims for the existence of Early Pleistocene artefacts and human fossils come from localities in the Guadix-Baza basin near Orce-Vente Micena (cf. Gibert 1992; Raposo and Santonja, this volume), but further fieldwork is necessary to turn these claims into compelling evidence.[3]

Raposo and Santonja (this volume) place the earliest unambiguous traces of human occupation of Iberia in the beginning of the Middle Pleistocene, though such traces are very rare. Some of the best sites are in the Guadix-Baza depression (Granada), famous for its rich Early Pleistocene mammalian faunas. The oldest site, Cullar de Baza, has yielded only a few pieces (six flakes and two choppers), in association with a Middle Pleistocene fauna. The faunal list varies from author to author (cf. Santonja 1992:57), but on biostratigraphical grounds the site is very probably contemporaneous with the earliest sites from the northwest-central region.

The handaxes reported from Atapuerca TD6 date from the Middle Pleistocene, on stratigraphical grounds possibly from OIS 13 (Aguirre 1991; Carbonell and Arsuaga 1992). The fauna from the TD6 level resembles the late Cromerian faunas mentioned above, with one notable exception

though: the presence of *Mimomys* (Carbonell and Arsuaga 1992; Gil and Sese 1991). This suggests that we are dealing with an archaeological site somewhat older than the ones reviewed upon till now. A recent study of the material by A.J. van der Meulen (pers. comm. 1994) however shows that some of the Arvicolids display indications of endemism, and furthermore that the stratigraphical range of *Microtus (Allophaiomys)* is longer in Iberia than in other parts of Europe. This might also be the case with the Iberian *Mimomys savini*.

Endemic features, also well-known from the Colchis area in the Caucasus (Ljubin and Bosinski, this volume), hamper a straightforward correlation between sites in Iberia (and for that matter: the Caucasus) and other parts of Europe. It must be stressed that the time-range of *Mimomys savini* in Iberia is not clear, just as the relationship between the Iberian form of *Arvicola, A. sapidus,* and *A. terrestris,* which only occurs in the extreme north of Spain, in the Pyrenees (cf. Van Kolfschoten 1993). Such information is, however, necessary to establish a correlation between the Atapuerca faunas and faunas from non-Iberian parts of Europe. At the current state of affairs the excavators interpretation of the Atapuerca TD6 level as dating from around 500 Kyr BP seems the best option. The five artefacts recently reported from Atapuerca TD4 (Carbonell and Rodriguez 1994) come from a lower level, but their artefactual character is not uncontested (cf. Raposo and Santonja, this volume).

Italy's settlement history shows no unambiguous indications for an Early Pleistocene occupation (Mussi 1992; this volume). A number of the 'old' Italian sites are surface sites, where a 'primitive' morphology of artefacts has led some archaeologists to infer a high age. In view of its correlation problems, the site of Monte Poggiolo does not provide very firm evidence for Early Pleistocene occupation, though preliminary palaeomagnetic studies indicate that it deserves our attention as a possible candidate (Gagnepain *et al.* 1992). Another problematic site is Monte Peglia, where lithic implements were recovered outside of a stratigraphical context, while the artefactual character of the only piece found *in situ* is questionable (Mussi, this volume). All unquestionable archaeological sites with solid dating evidence date from well into the Middle Pleistocene, and those with abundant faunal remains are more or less comparable in age to the Boxgrove and Miesenheim I sites in the north: Fontano Ranuccio (with hominid remains), Visogliano (human fossils too) and probably also Venosa-Loreto. As already explained, in our opinion, Isernia falls into this time range too (see above).

The Villafranchian[4] bone breccia of the Sandalja I cave (Croatia) yielded an incisor, once considered to be a hominid fossil (Malez 1976 vs. Cook *et al.* 1982) and one small and primitive 'chopper', a single find too undiagnostic to provide a firm ground for Early Pleistocene occupation of former Yugoslavia.

The evidence from Greece, reported by Darlas (this volume), tentatively points to the second half of the Middle Pleistocene for the earliest traces of human occupation there.

While the regions discussed as yet have not yielded solid proof of human occupation prior to the Middle Pleistocene, there are some sites in southern France that seem to be older: a group of sites in the Massif Central, and the famous cave-site of Le Vallonet.

The Massif Central has a large number of sites with rich Early Pleistocene faunas, recovered in a good stratigraphical context. The stone assemblages collected from some of these sites (cf. Bonifay 1991) consist in general of small series, selected out of natural pieces occurring in often coarse-grained deposits. The short communications on these assemblages do not deal with the problems of differentiating between natural and humanly modified pieces (cf. Raynal *et al.*, this volume). In many ways an exception is the Chilhac III site, excavated by Chavaillon (1991; see also Guth and Chavaillon 1985) in order to test Guth's earlier assessments of the site. Among the split pebbles and rocks present in the Chilhac III deposits Chavaillon could identify 46 indisputable artefacts. The age of these artefacts is uncertain for the time being, for reasons elaborated by Chavaillon (1991). In his words "Tout est possible pour Chilhac III" (1991:87; but see: Raynal *et al.*, this volume).

Another well-known Massif Central site is Soleilhac. Unfortunately its lithic assemblage has not been published in detail yet. According to Bonifay, we are dealing with a small assemblage of primitive technology. The quartz pebbles have been more 'shattered' ('brisés') than flaked, whereas the majority of the 'objets de grande taille en basalte' have been made out of natural fragments (Bonifay 1987:13). More important is that the Soleilhac fauna (with *Arvicola, Elephas (P.) antiquus* and *Hippopotamus* (Bonifay 1991) could fit very well into the late Cromerian faunas mentioned above, and it has indeed been correlated to the fauna from Isernia (see e.g. Thouveny and Bonifay 1984). Awaiting the results of further study of the chronology of the site, we see no good reason to infer that Soleilhac provides good indications for an Early Pleistocene hominid occupation (see also: Raynal *et al.*, this volume, for a comparable interpretation).

Le Vallonet has been well published, in a way that allows a detailed evaluation of the artefactual character of the assemblage. The cave has yielded a rich fauna (with *Microtus [Allophaiomys] pliocaenicus*) and a small lithic assemblage, recovered from sediments of 'Jaramillo'-age (age assessments by means of biostratigraphy, absolute

dating (ESR) and palaeomagnetic studies (see various contributions in *L'Anthropologie* 92, 1988; also Bonifay 1991:74-75).

The lithic assemblage comes from stratigraphic Unit III (couches B1, B2, C), loamy sands with many angular rocks and pebbles. These sediments are to a large extent reworked from the Roquebrune Miocene conglomerate deposits present above the cave[5]. The sand and rock/pebble fraction flowed into the Vallonet cave through chimneys and fissures. After Unit III was formed, the sediments were subjected to intensive geochemical weathering, leading to all kinds of "déformation" of the rocks and pebbles in the matrix: "Les cailloux et les galets de ces niveaux sont souvent craquelés avec déplacements de fragments" (De Lumley 1988:416). Excavations in the stony deposits yielded in total seventy pieces from a 'fairly underdeveloped stone tool industry'. Fifty nine of these are interpreted as intentionally modified. Virtually all artefacts were made from limestone pebbles from the Roquebrune Miocene conglomerate. The artefacts consist primarily of flaked pebbles, among which 'percussion tools', 'pebbles with a single convex chip' are the most common (n=13). Well represented are pebbles 'with a single concave chip' (primary choppers, n=8), but these are badly fragmented. Pebble tools (choppers, chopping-tools and atypical chopping-tools) are present (n=10), though not standardised and mostly of mediocre quality. The dorsal surface of half of the 26 flakes consists of 100% cortex, only five flakes have no cortex at all. The majority of the flakes have no butt or a 'reduced' one. At first glance, the Le Vallonet flakes share their main features – absence of platform and bulbs, acute angle with pebble surface – with the majority of naturally produced flakes[6].

The Le Vallonet limestone pieces, partially decarbonated, are occasionally extremely fragile. Some of the rocks and pebbles were fractured, 'craquelés' as a result of the chemical weathering mentioned above. The non-modified as well as the flaked pebbles and rocks in the Unit III matrix display several kinds of surface modifications, with ridges and protruding parts smoothed, or displaying a glossy surface polish. This applies to about 60% of the natural stones present in the matrix. It is to be stressed that comparable phenomena are present on the 'flaked' pieces: "Les pièces de l'industrie lithique découvertes dans le remplissage du Pléistocène inférieur de l'ensemble III n'échappent pas à cette règle générale: un important émoussé adoucit parfois les arêtes et oblitère le modelé des enlèvements. La surface de ces pièces présente souvent un lustrage caractéristique" (De Lumley *et al.* 1988:505).

It is clear that the lithic assemblage from Le Vallonet is a *selection* of 'primitive' pieces picked out from a matrix rich in rocks and pebbles derived from Miocene deposits (see

Table 1. *Schematic* differences within the European Palaeolithic record between the period before and after about 500 Kyr.

BEFORE 500 Kyr BP	AFTER 500 Kyr BP
small series consisting of isolated pieces collected from a natural pebble background	large collections from excavated knapping floors with conjoinable material
disturbed context (coarse matrix)	primary context sites (finegrained matrix)
contested 'primitive' assemblages	uncontested 'Acheulean' and non-Acheulean industries
no humain remains at all	human remains common

the photos of the Unit III sediments in De Lumley *et al.* 1988, Figs 1 to 7). Their characteristics suggest that we are dealing with an assemblage that was not modified by human agents, and instead displays all the characteristics of a selection out of a natural deposit.[7]

6.   Implications

By our reading of the evidence, there is a difference between the European 'archaeological' record from before the *Arvicola terrestris cantiana* time range (for convenience sake here: from about 500 Kyr BP) and the later one (cf. Table 1; also Dennell 1983 for a comparable interpretation). *Before* 500 Kyr virtually all finds come from a disturbed, coarse matrix, afterwards we have primary context sites in fine-grained deposits. The assemblages dating from *before* 500 Kyr BP are virtually all the result of selection of isolated pieces from natural deposits; younger ones are often excavated from knapping floors.

There are two basic ways to interpret these differences. The pre-500 Kyr finds could reflect the sparse traces of inter-mittent occupation of Europe by people with 'primitive' Oldowan-type toolkits, substantial colonization of Europe taking place from about 500 Kyr BP onwards (cf. Turner 1992). Nevertheless, the differences in geological context and recovery procedures between pre- and post-500 Kyr BP sites are problems to be explained by those adhering to this long chronology.

In view of the attributes of the 'artefacts' and contexts of the pre-500 Kyr BP sites we instead interpret these differences as indicating that there is *no undisputable proof for human occupation of Europe prior to about 500 Kyr BP*. The first primary context sites with good archaeological evidence date from a later period within the Middle Pleis-tocene, possibly from about OIS 13 onwards.

Our scenario has several advantages. A first one is that it is *very easy to falsify*. The find of only one Early Pleis-tocene primary context site in the area reviewed here would disprove it, and one would have to conclude that before about 500 Kyr BP occupation existed (but was largely intermittent). New studies of some sites mentioned in our short survey could lead to this result.

A further advantage is that our short chronology is supported by a body of data *independent* of arguments concerning stone tools: the chronological distribution of human remains. The discrepancy between the inferred high age of the earliest European artefacts and the relatively recent date for the earliest European hominid fossils, the Mauer lower jaw and the human remains from Fontana Ranuccio and (possibly) Visogliano, has been a conspicuous problem in the search for the earliest Europeans. From the 'Mauer' time period onwards we have Middle Pleistocene human remains all over Europe: Altamura, Arago, Atapuerca, Biache-Saint-Vaast, Bilzingsleben, Cava Pompi, Castel di Guido, La Chaise, Ehringsdorf, Fontana Ranuccio, Fontéchevade, Grotte du Prince, La Rafette, Lazaret, Mauer, Montmaurin, Orgnac III, Petralona, Pontnewydd, Steinheim, Swanscombe, Venosa, Vergranne, Vértesszöllös and Visogliano, to mention them in an alphabetical order (cf. Cook *et al.* 1982). The recently discovered tibia from Box-grove, a site with one of the earliest *Arvicola terrestris cantiana* faunas, of course fits very well into our scenario too (Roberts *et al.* 1994; Roberts *et al.*, this volume; see also Gamble 1994).

From the long period before the *Arvicola terrestris cantiana* range we do not have a single (uncontested!) tooth yet, despite the huge amounts of other mammalian fossils. Absence of evidence of course is no evidence of absence, and negative evidence has rarely proved durable in archaeology. But absence of exposures of older deposits is not a good counter-argument here. At a large number of palaeontological sites, early Middle and/or Early Pleistocene faunas are recovered from fine-grained deposits. Some of these have been under observation for many decades or even centuries, yielding huge amounts of faunal remains: for instance the Tegelen pits in the Netherlands, Untermassfeld, Voigtstedt and Süssenborn in Germany, West Runton (England), Sénèze (France), Deutsch Altenburg in Austria and the Val d'Arno exposures in Italy. Europe is without any doubt the most heavily researched part of the Old World, with a high-quality record to which many hundreds of workers have contributed over a period of one-and-a-half centuries.

In our scenario Europe is extremely 'marginal', late in time as compared to for instance the Asian evidence as that stands now. The human spread out of Africa went eastwards first, via Ubeidiya (Israel) and Dmanisi (Georgia; see Dzaparidze *et al.* 1989), and hominids were present in the eastern parts of Asia at the end of the Early Pleistocene, at around 800 to 1,000 Kyr BP (Schick and Zhuan 1993, or even earlier, if one accepts the Swisher *et al.* [1994] dates). Europe was occupied later. Soon after we see the first undisputable traces, humans are virtually 'everywhere' in Europe (with as notable and interesting exceptions the Russian plains and Scandinavia).

At issue is not only *whether* the first Europeans arrived much earlier than 500 Kyr BP. What, if any, ecological, climatical or social factors were triggering the occupation at about 500 Kyr BP, or, formulated in another way, what kept hominids out of Europe before 500 Kyr? Some avenues worth exploring may be developments in the social domain (such as the emergence of dispersed mating networks), neural developments associated with brain expansion and differences in the character of the Lower as opposed to the Middle Pleistocene glacial-interglacial cycles[8] (cf. Zagwijn 1992; see also Gamble 1993; Gamble, this volume).

In our scenario the 500,000 'wave' represents the first occupation, virtually synchronous throughout Europe south of the ice sheets. In this view Europe does not seem to have presented big problems to the first occupants, be it perhaps in the northern- and easternmost parts. This image of a swift occupation can very well be the result of the *low chronological resolution* of our dating methods for the Middle Pleistocene (as compared to 14C, whose resolution allows our American colleagues to infer that Palaeoindians colonized the entire New World in just a few centuries: Meltzer 1993). These analogues yield fascinating thought-experiments that have the additional advantage of moving our field into the domain of other disciplines studying the migration of mammal species (cf. Gamble 1993).

While those adhering to (various forms of) a long chronology can make the case for a very gradual adaptation by Out of Africans to the wide range of European habitats, our short chronology supports another view, a rather fast (within the time resolution limits) adaptation, once they are in this *cul de sac* of the Eurasian continent that we call Europe. In this respect our interpretation fits very well into a highly punctuated chronology of what Gamble (1993) has recently called "staccato bursts of colonization", as opposed to earlier views of hominids leaving their African homeland in a slow continuous spread. It is for such reasons that we need to discuss the empirical values and implications of the various long and short chronologies. We hope that our paper can contribute to such an 'updating' of the first 'Europeans'.

Acknowledgements

A first version of this paper was written for a European Science Foundation (ESF) Workshop on The Earliest Occupation of Europe, held at Tautavel (France), November 1993 and subsequently published in the September 1994 issue of *Antiquity*. This paper is a slightly modified version of the *Antiquity* one. The ESF meeting was organised by the ESF Network on The Palaeolithic Occupation of Europe: G. Bosinski (chairman – Neuwied, Germany), W. Roebroeks (scientific secretary – Leiden, The Netherlands), C. Farizy (Paris, France), C. Gamble (Southampton, United Kingdom), L. Larsson (Lund, Sweden), M. Mussi (Rome, Italy), N. Praslov (St. Peterburg, Russia), L. Raposo (Lisbon, Portugal), M. Santonja (Salamanca, Spain) and A. Tuffreau (Lille, France). The members of the Network committee made valuable remarks on the content of our paper. We are further very grateful to F.C. Howell (Berkeley) and A. Turner (Liverpool) and R. Dennell (Sheffield) for their detailed comments on an earlier draft of the paper.

notes

1 In her recent taphonomic study of the Prezletice fauna, Stopp (1994) also did not find any indication of human activity at the site.

2 The first author wants to emphasize his gratitude towards Dr Karel Valoch, who showed him the Moravian assemblages while in Brno, and took him to the Stránská skála site. Despite our scientific disagreement about the interpretation of some assemblages I keep a very good memory of that visit.

3 Apart from discussions over the presence of humans in the Early Pleistocene in that region there is a discrepancy between the age given to the faunal assemblage from Venta Micena and other sites by Gibert and his co-workers (1,8 Myr BP) and the estimates of Agusti *et al.* (1987), who think the Venta Micena assemblage is about 1,2 Myr old.

4 The larger mammal fauna referred to as 'Late Villafranchian' mainly consists of so-called Galerian species, with a range into the later part of the Cromerian-complex).

5 "Les poudingues [puddingstone] affleurent partout ailleurs; il s'agit de galets roulés, généralement grossiers, souvent calcaires mais parfois gréseux, pélitiques ou cristallins, durement cimentés par une matrice gréseuse. Généralement compacts et bien stratifiés, ils se présentent en bancs réguliers avec parfois des lentilles de grès, de taille et de granulométrie variées" (Chamagne 1988:403).

6 Among others, Warren published descriptions and photographs of flaked flints found below Eocene beds (at Grays, Essex), with both bulbs and striking platforms. Some of these even were conjoinable (e.g. Warren 1920, Plate XV, 22:"Photograph of two conjoined flakes showing normal pressure-characters", or 23: "Photograph of four conjoined flakes, also showing normal pressure-characters, but 'struck' from an apparently well-prepared platform".

7 After the publication of the *Antiquity* version of this paper (september 1994) we were informed of the results of White's (1995) study of the Le Vallonet assemblage, also stressing the absence of traces of human activities at this site.

8 Such differences could have resulted in an environmental setting more favourable for a migration of hominids into Europe. There are, however, no clear environmental changes observable in the second half of the Cromerian complex, neither in the palaeobotanical, the malacological or the vertebrate record. Late *Mimomys* faunas (West Runton and Voigtstedt) and early *Arvicola* ones (Boxgrove, Miesenheim I, Mauer) show many similarities and no distinct differences in their composition. All these faunas indicate more or less comparable environmental conditions.

The fact that the appearance of *Arvicola terrestris cantiana* coincides more or less with the immigration of *Elephas (Palaeoloxodon) antiquus* and *Hippopotamus* during the late Cromerian (Von Koenigswald and Van Kolfschoten, in press) might suggest that we are dealing with a kind of faunal turnover. However, we have to realize that our chronological resolution for this time range is fairly limited. One of the earliest *Arvicola* faunas is the one from Kärlich G (Neuwied Basin, Germany). The fauna is associated with artefacts (Bosinski, this volume) and most probably dates from the transitional period of Glacial C to Interglacial IV or from the earlier part of Interglacial IV of the Cromerian complex (Van Kolfschoten and Turner, in press). There is good evidence that the fauna predates the Interglacial IV optimum with conditions favourable for the immigration of *Elephas (P.) antiquus* and *Hippopotamus*, which implies that the three species most probably did not appear simultaneously.

Even the Elsterian glaciation (OIS 12?), the first glaciation in which the northern parts of central and northwestern Europe were covered with inland ice, did not cause a dramatic floral and faunal turnover. Many species - including a number of smaller mammals (*Talpa minor, Trogontherium cuvieri, Sorex (Drepanosorex)* sp.) regarded as relicts from the Early Pleistocene – survived the Elsterian Glacial. Only the large carnivores *Homotherium, Megantereon, Pachycrocuta perrieri* and *P. brevirostris* are not known from post-Elsterian deposits in Northwestern and Central Europe (Turner 1992). Recent studies of the faunal remains from the Reinsdorf Interglacial (OIS 9?) deposits at Schöningen (Mania, this volume) indicate that *Trogontherium cuvieri* also survived the "glacial" conditions between the Holsteinian (OIS 11?) and the Reinsdorf Interglacial. These species became extinct during the next cold period, which separates the Reinsdorf Interglacial from the Schöningen/Belvédère Interglacial (OIS 7?). The extinction of *Trogontherium cuvieri* coincides with an acceleration of the evolution in the enamel differentiation in the molars of *Arvicola terrestris,* as indicated by the faunal remains from Ariendorf 1 (Van Kolfschoten 1990). The Ariendorf 1 fauna (OIS 8) includes *Dicrostonyx, Lemmus lemmus, Mammuthus, Coelodonta antiquitatis* and *?Rangifer tarandus* (Van Kolfschoten 1990; Turner 1991; Roebroeks *et al.* 1992), and is one of the earliest cold stage faunas with a composition indicative for a "Mammoth Steppe" environment; the fauna is comparable to late Saalian (OIS 6) cold stage faunas from Schweinskopf and Wannen in the Neuwied Basin (Germany) and to late Weichselian glacial faunas. The Ariendorf I fauna is indicative for the earliest extension of the Mammoth Steppe that far to the west, roughly coinciding with the first appearance of *Mammuthus primigenius*, the immigration of *Coelodonta antiquitatis* in western Europe and some changes in the horses.

references

Ackerman, S.	1989	European prehistory gets even older, *Science* 246, 28-30.
Andrews, J.T.	1983	Short ice age 230.000 years ago? *Nature* 303, 21-22.
Aguirre, E.	1991	Les premiers peuplements humains de la Péninsule Ibérique. In: E. Bonifay and B. Vandermeersch (eds), *Les Premiers Européens*, 143-150, Paris: Editions du C.T.H.S.
Agusti, S. Moyà-Solà, J. Pons-Moyà	1987	La sucesion de Mamiferos en el Pleistoceno inferior de Europa: proposicion de una nueva escala bioestratigrafica, *Paleont. I Evol., Mem. Esp.* 1, 287-295.
Azzaroli, A.	1977	The Villafranchian stage in Italy and the Plio-Pleistocene boundary, *G. Geol.* 41, 61-79.
Azzaroli, A., C. De Giuli, G. Ficcarelli, D. Torre	1988	Late Pliocene to Mid-Pleistocene Mammals in Eurasia: Faunal succession and Dispersal Events, *Palaeogeography, Palaeoclimatology, Palaeoecology* 66, 77-100.
Bonifay, E.	1987	*Soleilhac 1987. Rapport de fouilles.* Marseille: Laboratoire de Géologie du Quaternaire.
	1991	Les premiers industries du Sud-Est de la France et du Massif-Central. In: E. Bonifay and B. Vandermeersch (eds), *Les Premiers Européens*, 63-80, Paris: Editions du C.T.H.S.
Bonifay, E., B. Vandermeersch (eds)	1991	*Les Premiers Européens.* Paris: Editions du C.T.H.S.
Bosinski, G.,	this volume	The earliest occupation of Europe: Western Central Europe.
Boule, M.	1921	*Les Hommes Fossiles. Eléments de paléontologie humaine.* Paris: Masson.
Bourdier, F., J. Chaline, A.V. Munaut, J.J. Puissegur	1974	La très haute nappe alluviale de la Somme, *Bulletin Ass. Franc. Et. Quat.* 11, 137-143.
Burdukiewicz, J.M., J. Winnicki	1988	*Trzebnica - Najstarsze Slady Obecnosci Czlowieka na Ziemiach Polskich.* Towarzystwo Milosników Ziemi Trzebnickiej.
Burdukiewicz	1989	Nowe Materialy Paleolitu Dolnego Z Trzebnicy, *Woj. Wroclaw. "Silesia Antiqua"*, XXXI, 9-17.
Carbonell, E., J.L. Arsuaga	1992	*Excursion a los yacimientos mesopleistocenicos de la Sierra de Atapuerca (Ibeas de Juarros/Atapuerca, Burgos). 1 Julio 1992. Workshop Evolucion Humana en Europe y los yacimientos de la Sierra dè Atapuerca*, Tarragona.
Carbonell, E., X.P. Rodriguez	1994	Early Middle Pleistocene deposits and artefacts in the Gran Dolina site (TD4) of the 'Sierra de Atapuerca' (Burgos, Spain), *Journal of Human Evolution* 26, 291-311.
Chaline, J.	1986	Continental Faunal Units of the Plio-Pleistocene of France, *Mem. Soc. Geol. It.* 31, 175-183.
Chamagne, B.	1988	Environnement géologique de la grotte du Vallonet (Roquebrune-Cap-Martin), *L'Anthropologie* 92, 399-406.

Chavaillon, J.   1991   Les ensembles lithiques de Chilhac III (Haute Loire): typologie, situation stratigraphique et analyse critique et comparative. In: E. Bonifay and B. Vandermeersch (eds), *Les Premiers Européens*, 81-91, Paris: Editions du C.T.H.S.

Clark, J.D.   1958   The natural fracture of pebbles from the Batoka Gorge, Northern Rhodesia, and its bearing on the Kafuan industries of Africa, *Proceedings of the Prehistoric Society* 24, 64-77.

Coltorti, M.,   1981   Reversed magnetic polarity at an early Lower Palaeolithic site in Central Italy, *Nature*
   M. Cremaschi,   300, 173-176.
   M.C. Delitala *et al.*

Cook, J.,   1982   A review of the chronology of the European Middle Pleistocene hominid record, *Yearbook*
   C.B. Stringer,   *of Physical Anthropology* 25, 19-65.
   A.P. Currant,
   H.P. Schwarcz,
   A.G. Wintle

Darlas, A.   this   The earliest occupation of Europe: the Balkans.
                              volume

Delson, E.   1989   Oldest Eurasian stone tools, *Nature* 340, 96.

Dennell, R.   1983   *European Economic Prehistory. A New Approach.* London: Academic Press.

Desclaux, E.   1992a   *Les petits vertèbres à la Caune de l'Arago (Tautavel, Pyrénées Orientales). Paléontologie, paléoécologie, taphonomie.* Thèse de Doctorat. Paris: M.N.H.N.

                              1992b   Les petits vertèbres de la Caune de l'Arago à Tautavel, *Bulletin du Musée d'Anthropologie préhistorique de Monaco* 35, 35-64.

Dzaparidze, V.,   1989   Der altpaläolithische Fundplatz Dmanisi in Georgien (Kaukasus), *Jahrbuch des Römisch-*
   G. Bosinski,   *Germanischen Zentralmuseums Mainz* 36, 67-116.
   T. Bugianisvili *et al.*

Fejfar, O.,   1981   Zur biostratigraphischen Abgrenzung und Gliederung des kontinentalen Quartärs in
   W.D. Heinrich   Europa an Hand von Arvicoliden (Rodentia, Mammalia), *Ocologae geol. Helv.* 74 (3),
                                      997-1006.

Fridrich, J.   1989   *Prezletice: A lower palaeolithic site in Central Bohemia (Excavations 1969-1985).* Pragae: Museum Nationale Pragae.

                              1991   The oldest Palaeolithic stone industry from the Beroun highway complex, *Antropozoikum* 20, 111-128.

Gagnepain, J.,   1992   Etude magnétostratigraphique du site de Ca'Belvedere di Monte Poggiolo (Forli, Italie), et
   I. Hedley,   de son contexte stratigraphique. Premiers résultats. In: C. Peretto (ed.), *I Primi Abitanti*
   J.-J. Bahain,   *della Valle Padana: Monte Poggiolo*, 319-335, Milano: Jaca Book.
   J.-J. Wagner

Gamble, C.S.   1993   *Timewalkers. The Prehistory of Global Colonization.* Phoenix Mill-Stroud-Gloucesthire: Alan.

                              1994   Time for Boxgrove man, *Nature* 369, 275-276.

                              this   The earliest occupation of Europe: the environmental background.
                              volume

Gibert, J. (ed.)   1992   *Presencia humana en el Pleistoceno inferior de Granada y Murcia.* Granada: Museo de Prehistoria.

Gil, E., C. Sese	1991	Middle Pleistocene small mammals from Atapuerca (Burgos, Spain). In: *Datations et Charactérizations des Milieux Pléistocènes. Actes du Symposium 11 et 17 de la 11ème R.S.T. Clermond Ferrand 1986. Cahiers du Quaternaire* 16, 337-347.
GRIP (Greenland Ice-core Project) Members	1993	Climate instability during the last interglacial period recorded in the GRIP ice core, *Nature* 364, 203-207.
Guth, C., J. Chavaillon	1985	Découverte, en 1984, de nouveaux outils paléolithiques à Chilhac III, (Haute Loire), *Bulletin Soc. Préhist. franc.* 82, 56-64.
Hedberg, H.D.	1976	*International stratigraphic guide. A guide to stratigraphic classification, terminology and procedure.* New York: John Wiley and Sons.
Jeannet, M.	1979	Note sur quelques élements de microfaune reçus en 1979, *Nouv. Arch. Museum d'Histoire Naturelle de Lyon* 17, 59-64.
Kasantseva, N.E.	1987	*Paleogeograficeskie uslovija obitanija nizneplejstocenovyx faun melkix mlekopitajuscix bassejna srednego Dona.* Dissertation, University of Moscow, Moscow.
Koenigswald, W. von, T. van Kolfschoten	in press	The *Mimomys-Arvicola* boundary and the enamel thickness quotient (SDQ) of *Arvicola* as stratigraphic markers in the Middle Pleistocene, *Proceedings of the SEQS Cromer symposium 1990.*
Kolfschoten, T. van	1990	The evolution of the mammal fauna in the Netherlands and the middle Rhine Area (Western Germany) during the late Middle Pleistocene, *Meded. Rijks Geol. Dienst* 43 (3), 1-69.
	1993	On the origin of the Middle Pleistocene larger voles, *Quaternary International* 19, 47-50.
Kolfschoten, T. van, E. Turner	in press	Early Middle Pleistocene mammalian faunas from Kärlich and Miesenheim I and their biostratigraphical implications, *Proceedings of the SEQS Cromer Symposium 1990.*
Kozlowski, J.K.	1992	Les premiers habitants de l'Europe centrale et orientale. In: C. Peretto (ed.), *I Primi Abitanti della Valle Padana: Monte Poggiolo Nel Quadro delle Conoscenze Europee,* 69-91, Milano: Jaca Book.
Kretzoi, M.	1965	Die Nager und Lagomorphen von Voigtstedt in Thüringen und ihre chronologische Aussage, *Paläontologische Abhandlungen* 2 (3), 587-660.
Kretzoi, M., M. Pécsi	1979	Pliocene and Pleistocene development and chronology of the Pannonian Basin, *Acta Geol. Acad. Sc. Hung.* 22, 1-4, 3-33.
Leakey, M.	1984	*Disclosing The Past. An Autobiography.* New York: Doubleday & Cie.
Lister, A.	1992	Mammalian fossils and quaternary biostratigraphy, *Quaternary Science Reviews* 11, 329-344.
Ljubin, V., G. Bosinski	this volume	The earliest occupation of the Caucasus region.
Lumley, H. de	1988	La stratigraphie du remplissage de la grotte du Vallonet, *L'Anthropologie* 92, 407-428.
Lumley, H. de, A. Fournier, J. Krzepkowska, A. Echassoux	1988	L'industrie du Pléistocène inférieur de la grotte du Vallonet, Roquebrune-Cap-Martin, Alpes-Maritimes, *L'Anthropologie* 92, 501-614.

Lumley, H. de,
A. Fournier,
Y.C. Park,
Y.Yokoyama,
A. Demouy
1984
Stratigraphie du remplissage pléistocène moyen de la Caune de l'Arago à Tautavel - Étude de huit carottages effectués de 1981 à 1983, *L'Anthropologie* 88, 5-18.

Malez, M.
1976
Excavation of the Villafranchian site Sandalja I near Pula (Yugoslavia). In: K. Valoch (ed.), *Les premières industries de l'Europe*. IXe Congrès UISPP, Collogue VIII, 104-123, Nice.

Mania, D.,
this volume
The earliest occupation of Europe: the Elbe-Saale Region (Germany).

McPherron, A.,
V. Schmidt
1983
Paleomagnetic dating at Isernia la Pineta. In: C. Peretto, C. Terzani and M. Cremaschi (eds), *Isernia la Pineta, un accampamento piu antico di 700.000 anni*, 67-69, Bologna: Calderini.

Meltzer, D.J.
1993
Pleistocene Peopling of the Americas, *Evolutionary Anthropology* 1, 157-169.

Meulen, A.J. van der
1973
Middle Pleistocene Smaller Mammals from the Monte (Orvieto, Italy) with Special Reference to the Phylogeny of *Microtus* (Arvicolidae, Rodentia), *Quaternaria* XVII, 1-144.

Musil, R.,
K. Valoch
1968
Stránská skála. Its meaning for Pleistocene Studies, *Current Anthropology* 9, 534-539.

Mussi, M.
1992
Il Paleolitico e il Mesolitico in Italia. Bologna: Stilus.

this volume
The earliest occupation of Europe: Italy.

Obermaier, H.
1912
Der Mensch der Vorzeit. Berlin: Allgemeine Verlags-Gesellschaft.

Peretto, C. (ed.).
1992
I Primi Abitanti della Valle Padana: Monte Poggiolo Nel Quadro delle Conoscenze Europee. Milano: Jaca Book.

Raposo, L.
1985
Le Paléolithique inférieur archaïque au Portugal. Bilan des connaissances. *Bulletin Soc. Préh. franc.* 82 (6), 173-180.

Raposo, L.,
M. Santonja
this volume
The earliest occupation of Europe: the Iberian Peninsula.

Raynal, J.-P.,
L. Magoga,
P. Bindon
this volume
Tephrofacts and the first human occupation of the French Massif Central.

Roberts, M.B.
1986
Excavation of the Lower Palaeolithic site at Amey's Eartham Pit, Boxgrove, West Sussex: A preliminary report, *Proceedings of the Prehistoric Society* 52, 215-245.

1990
"Amey's Eartham Pit, Boxgrove". In: C. Turner (ed.), *Field Excursion Guide Book*, The Cromer Symposium Norwhich 1990, SEQS, 62-77, Cambridge.

Roberts, M.B.,
C.B. Stringer,
S.A. Parfitt
1994
A hominid tibia from Middle Pleistocene sediments at Boxgrove, UK, *Nature* 369, 311-313.

Roberts, M.B.,
C.S. Gamble,
D.R. Bridgland
this volume
The earliest occupation of Europe: the British Isles.

Roebroeks, W.,   1992   Dense Forests, Cold Steppes and the Palaeolithic Settlement of Northern Europe, *Current*
   N.J. Conard,   *Anthropology* 33, 551-586.
   T. van Kolfschoten

Roebroeks, W.,   this   The Tautavel workshop: an introduction.
   T. van Kolfschoten volume

Rolland, N.   1992   The Palaeolithic Colonization of Europe: An Archaeological and Biogeographic Perspec-
                                      tive, *Trabajos de Prehistoria* 49, 69-111.

Sala, B.   1983   La Fauna del giacimento di Isernia La Pineta. In: C. Peretto, C. Terzani and M. Cremaschi
                                      (eds), *Isernia la Pineta, un accampamento piu antico di 700.000 anni*, 71-79, Bologna:
                                      Calderini.

Sala, B.,   1992   Mammal dispersal events in the Middle and Late Pleistocene of Italy and Western Europe,
   F. Masini,   *Courier forsch.-Inst. Senckenberg* 153, 59-68.
   G. Ficcarelli,
   L. Rook,
   D. Torre

Sala, B.,   1993   The rhinoceroses of Isernia La Pineta (early Middle Pleistocene, Southern Italy), *Palaeon-*
   M. Fortelius   *tographia Italica* 80, 157-174.

Santonja, M.   1992   La adaptacion al medio en el Paleolitico inferior de la Peninsula ibérica. Elementos para
                                      una reflexion. In: A. Moure Romanillo (ed.), *Elefantes, ciervos y ovicaprinos*, 37-75,
                                      Santander: Univ. de Cantabria.

Santonja, M.,   1990   The Lower Palaeolithic of Spain and Portugal, *Journal of World Prehistory* 4, 45-94.
   P. Villa

Schick, K.D.,   1993   Early Paleolithic of China and Eastern Asia, *Evolutionary Anthropology* 2, 22-35.
   D. Zhuan

Sollas, W.J.   1911,   *Ancient Hunters and their Modern Representatives*. London: Macmillan. 2nd edn
                       1924   1924.

Stopp, M.   1994   *Early Human Adaptation in the Northern Hemisphere and the Analytic Implications of
                                      Taphonomy*. PhD Thesis Cambridge (England): University of Cambridge.

Swisher C.C.,   1994   Age of the earliest known hominids in Java, Indonesia, *Science* 263, 1118-1121.
   G.H. Curtis,
   T. Jacob,
   A.G. Getty,
   A. Suprijo,
   Widiasmoro

Terzea, E.,   in press Mammalian events in the Quaternary of Romania and correlations with climatic
                                      chronology of Western Europe, *Acta zool. cracov.*

Thieme, H.,   1993   Schöningen (Nordharzvorland). Eine altpaläolithische Fundstelle aus dem mittleren
   B. Urban,   Eiszeitalter, *Archäologisches Korrespondenzblatt* 23, 147-163.
   D. Mania,
   T. van Kolfschoten

Thouveny, N.,   1984   New chronological data on European Plio-Pleistocene faunas and hominid occupation
   E. Bonifay   sites, *Nature* 308, 355-358.

Tuffreau, A. 1987 *Le Paléolithique inférieur et moyen du Nord de la France (Nord Pas-de-Calais, Picardie) dans son cadre stratigraphique*. Thèse Doctorat d'Etat Université de Lille, Lille.

Tuffreau, A., this volume The earliest occupation of Europe: Continental Northwestern Europe.
 P. Antoine

Turner, A. 1992 Large carnivores and earliest European hominids: changing determinants of resource availability during the Lower and Middle Pleistocene, *Journal of Human Evolution* 22, 109-126.

Turner, E. 1991 Pleistocene stratigraphy and vertebrate faunas from the Neuwied ßasin region of Western Germany, *Cranium* 8, 21-34.

Valoch, K. 1972 Gab es eine altpaläolithische Besiedlung der Stránská skála? In: R. Musil (ed.), *Stránská skála I 1910-1945* (Anthropos 20 [N.S. 12]), 199-204, Brno: Moravské Museum.

 1984 Early Palaeolithic in Moravia, Czechoslovakia, *Proceedings of the Prehistoric Society* 50, 63-69.

 1987 The Early Palaeolithic Site Stránská Skála I near Brno (Czechoslovakia), *Anthropologie* XXV (2), 125-142.

 1991 Les premiers peuplements humains en Moravie (Tchécoslovaquie). In: E. Bonifay and B. Vandermeersch (eds), *Les Premiers Européens*, 189-194, Paris: Editions du C.T.H.S.

 this volume The earliest occupation of Europe: Eastern Central and Southeastern Europe.

Vollbrecht, J. 1992 *Das Altpaläolithikum aus den unteren Schichten in Kärlich*. Magisterarbeit, Universität Köln, Köln.

Warren, S.H. 1920 A Natural 'Eolith' Factory beneath the Thanet Sand, *Quarterly Journal Geol. Soc.* 76, 238-253.

White, C. 1995 La Grotte du Vallonet: Evidence of Early Hominid Activity of Natural Processes? Paper presented at the Palaeolithic-Mesolithic day meeting, British Museum London, March 17th 1995.

Würges, K. 1986 Artefakte aus den ältesten Quartärsedimenten (Schichten A-C) der Tongrube Kärlich, Kreis Mayen-Koblenz/Neuwieder Becken, *Archäologisches Korrespondenzblatt* 16, 1-6.

 1991 Neue altpaläolithische Funde aus der Tongrube Kärlich, Kreis Mayen-Koblenz/Neuwieder Becken, *Archäologisches Korrespondenzblatt* 21, 449-455.

Zagwijn, W.H. 1985 An outline of the Quaternary stratigraphy of the Netherlands, *Geologie en Mijnbouw* 64, 17-24.

 1992 The beginning of the Ice Age in Europe and its major subdivisions, *Quaternary Science Reviews* 11, 583-591.

Wil Roebroeks and Thijs van Kolfschoten
Faculty of Pre- and Protohistory
Leiden University
P.O. Box 9515
2300 RA Leiden
The Netherlands

general index

site index